The Old French Crusade Cycle

GENERAL EDITORS:
Jan A. Nelson
Emanuel J. Mickel

The Old French Crusade Cycle

VOLUME I
La Naissance du Chevalier au Cygne

ELIOXE

EDITED BY EMANUEL J. MICKEL, JR.

BEATRIX

EDITED BY JAN A. NELSON

with an essay on the manuscripts of
the Old French Crusade Cycle by

GEOFFREY M. MYERS

THE UNIVERSITY OF ALABAMA PRESS

Library of Congress Cataloging in Publication Data

Main entry under title:

The Old French Crusade cycle.

Vol. 1 includes an essay on the mss. of the cycle
by G. M. Myers.
1. Epic poetry, French.   2. French poetry--To
1500.   3. Crusades--Poetry.   I. Nelson, Jan.
II. Mickel, Emanuel J., 1937-   III. Myers,
Geoffrey M.
PQ1311.O43.   841'.03   76-30489
ISBN 0-8173-8501-0 (v. 1)

Contents

DEDICATED TO THE MEMORY OF
PROFESSOR
URBAN TIGNER HOLMES, JR.

1900 - 1972

ACKNOWLEDGMENTS

The editors are indebted to The University of Alabama, Indiana University, and the University of Nebraska for their support of this undertaking. The initial purchase of micro-film from the various manuscripts of the Crusade Cycle was made possible by funds provided by the University of Nebraska and Indiana University. In addition the project was supported by Research Grants Committee of The University of Alabama, Indiana University, and the University of Nebraska through summer research grants to the editors. Indiana University also made funds available for duplicating services and for clerical assistance.

The editors are particularly grateful to Professor Stelio Bassi, Director of the Biblioteca Nazionale Universi-taria di Torino for his kind assistance in matters pertain-ing to Turin MS L-III-25, to Professor Larry S. Crist for his interest and advice, to Professor Peter R. Grillo for his advice and assistance in matters concerning the post-*Jérusalem* material, and to Professor Geoffrey M. Myers for his special contribution in the description of the manu-scripts of the Cycle.

Finally, the editors wish to express their deep and loving appreciation for the patience which their wives and children have shown during the long preparation of this volume.

October 1975   Jan A. Nelson
                                       Emanuel J. Mickel, Jr.

INTRODUCTION :

THE OLD FRENCH CRUSADE CYCLE

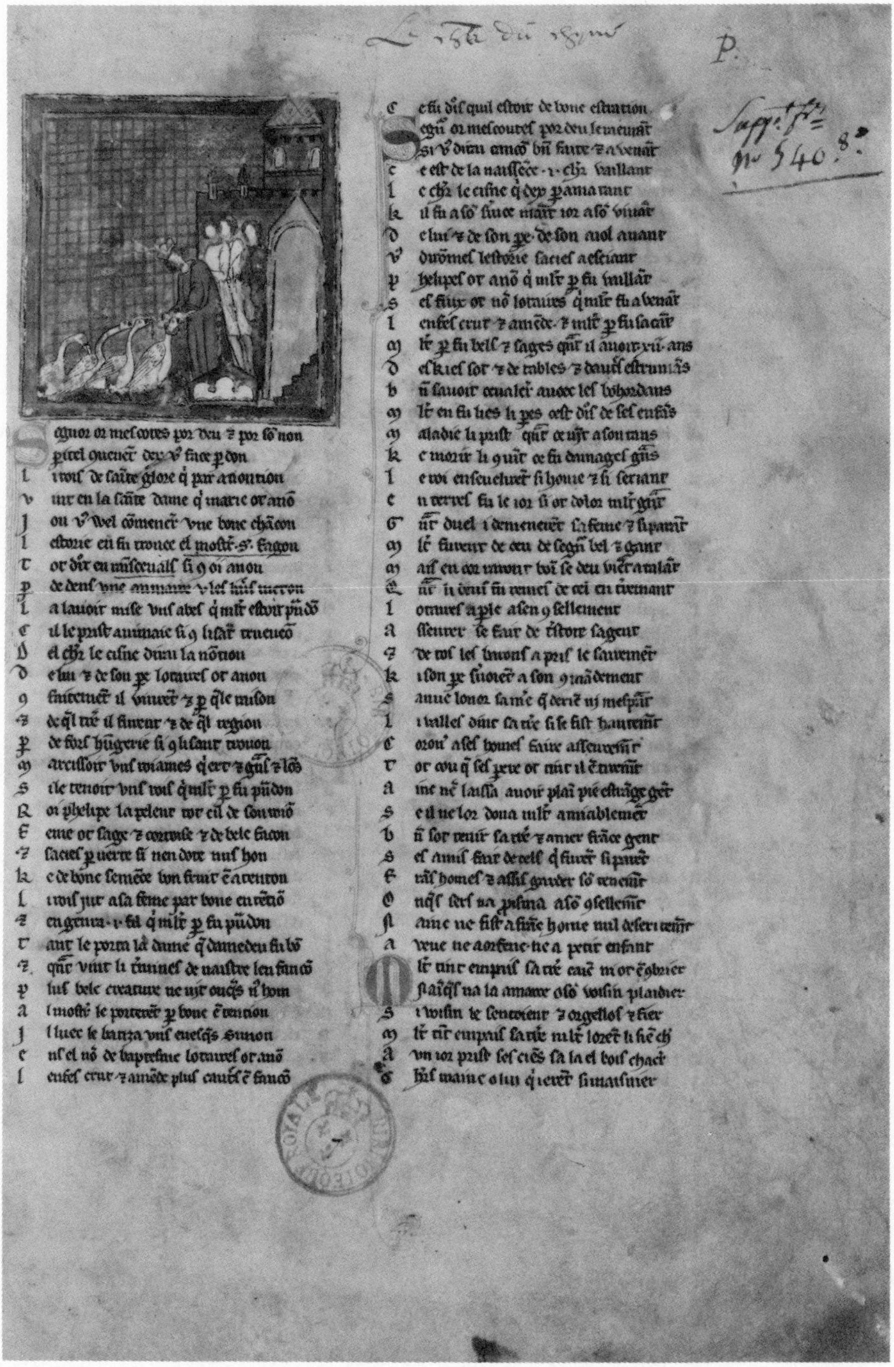

Paris   Bibliothèque Nationale MS
fonds français 12558 fol. 1r

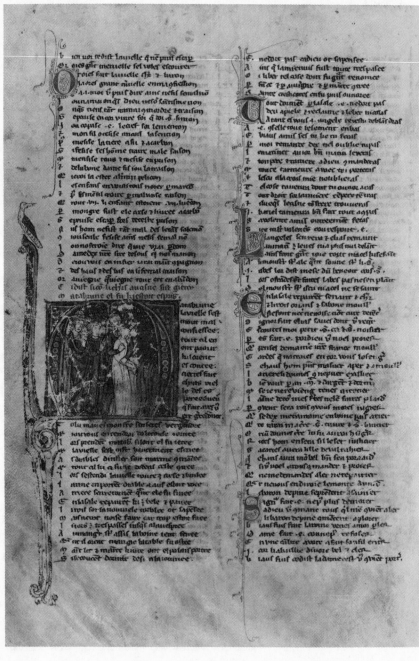

Paris   Bibliothèque Nationale MS fonds français 786 fol. 102^{v}

PLAN OF PUBLICATION

The *Old French Crusade Cycle*, when published in its entire-
ty, will comprise a series of eight volumes:

Vol. I *La Naissance du Chevalier au Cygne*
   Elioxe, ed. Emanuel J. Mickel, Jr.
   Beatrix, ed. Jan A. Nelson

Vol. II *Le Chevalier au Cygne* and *La Fin d'Elias*, ed.
   Jan A. Nelson

Vol. III *Les Enfances Godefroi*, ed. Emanuel J. Mickel,
   Jr.

Vol. IV *La Chanson d'Antioche*, ed. Jan A. Nelson with
   Introduction by Emanuel J. Mickel, Jr.

Vol. V *Les Chétifs*, ed. Geoffrey M. Myers

Vol. VI *La Chanson de Jérusalem*, ed. Nigel R.
   Thorp

Vol. VII The *Jérusalem* Continuations: *La Chrétienté
   Corbaran*, *La Prise d'Acre*, *La Mort Godefroi*,
   and *La Chanson des Rois Baudouin*; ed. Peter R.
   Grillo

Vol. VIII The *Jérusalem* Continuations: The London and
   Turin Redactions, ed. Peter R. Grillo

"The Manuscripts of the Old French Crusade Cycle" by
Geoffrey M. Myers, included in Volume I, is intended, with
some future elaboration, to serve the entire series.

ABBREVIATIONS

The following is a list of the abbreviations of the titles for the various branches or major episodes of the *Old French Crusade Cycle* accepted as standard by all now associated with the series:

NChCy	*Naissance du Chevalier au Cygne*
El	*Elioxe*
Bt	*Beatrix*
ChCy	*Chevalier au Cygne*
FE	*Fin d'Elias*
EG	*Enfances Godefroi*
Ant	*Chanson d'Antioche*
Cht	*Chétifs*
Jér	*Chanson de Jérusalem*
CCor	*Chrétienté Corbaran*
PA	*Prise d'Acre*
MG	*Mort Godefroi*
RB	*Chanson des Rois Baudouin*
Cont	*Jér* Continuations in *E*, *G*, and *I*
Cont[2]	*Jér* Continuations in *I* and *T*
CCGB	*Le Chevalier au Cygne et Godefroi de Bouillon*

THE MANUSCRIPTS
OF THE CYCLE

The vast cycle of epic poems concerning events and person-
ages connected with the First Crusade has received relative-
ly little attention from medievalists since its rediscovery
by historians in the mid 19th century. Their interest cen-
tered naturally around the veracity of the texts and, since
it was apparent that the poems were basically fabulous in
nature, they were little inclined to give them serious con-
sideration. However, Paulin Paris, the first editor of the
Chanson d'Antioche, argued heatedly against the general view
and is largely responsible for having established the his-
torical authenticity of this portion of the cycle, though he
showed little interest in the poems from a literary stand-
point.[1] It was, then, only with the rising interest in
folklore and the Old French epic in the late 19th and early
20th centuries that scholars began the study of various por-
tions of the cycle with a view toward elucidation of the
literary and textual questions they posed. Unfortunately the
initial studies did not lead to the publication of reliable
editions, and the Crusade Cycle remains today essentially
unavailable to students of medieval literature.[2]
    The epic of the First Crusade has survived in three
readily identifiable states: a cyclical form consisting of a
number of recognizably individual epics arranged in chrono-
logical order with respect to their content, a consolidated
form in which a unified whole has been achieved, and a prose
abbreviation of the subject matter.[3]   The following table
provides a list of all the extant manuscripts organized with
reference to the three states together with the *sigles* em-
ployed by the various scholars who have worked with them.
The editors have adopted those proposed by Krüger for use in
this edition inasmuch as his has been the most thorough ac-
counting.
    The forms in which this material has survived imply an
evolutionary process which leads from disconnected early
poems to the unified epic embracing the entire scope of the
First Crusade, a process that involves both accretion and
cohesion.
    Paulin Paris early concluded, and successors have all
agreed, that the cycle had its beginning in the *Chanson*

TABLE I*

	Paris 1848	Stengel 1873	Smith 1912	Krüger 1936	Duparc-Quioc 1955	Sumberg 1968
Cyclical Form:						
1. Paris BN 12558	C	A	A	A	A	C
2. Paris BN 786	A	C	B	B	D	A
3. Paris BN 795	D	D	C	C	B	D
4. Paris BN 1621	B	F	D	D	C	B
5. Paris BN 12569	F	G	E	E	G	F
6. Paris Arsenal 3139	E	B	G	G	F	E
7. Bern 320		H		F	E	H
8. Bern 627			S	S		
9. London BM Royal MS 15 E VI				H		
10. London BM Additional MS 36615				I		
11. Turin BN L-III-25				T		
Consolidated Form:						
1. Brussels BR 10391				R		compilation belge
2. Lyon BM 744				L		
Abbreviated Prose Form:						
1. Paris BN 781 (Cyclical)				P		G
2. Kopenhagen Thott 416 (Consolidated)				K		

*Krüger cites four additional cyclical manuscript fragments, which are discussed below in conjunction with Table II. A further substantial fragment preserved in Oxford, Bodleian Library, Hatton 77, unknown to Krüger, is given the *sigle* O.

d'Antioche. This poem is believed to have been written in the years immediately following the First Crusade by Richard the Pilgrim, an eyewitness to the events described. His original text has not survived, the extant version being a late 12th century redaction by Graindor de Douai. The latter also revised the anonymous *Chanson de Jérusalem* and was perhaps the first to realize even partially their potential by combining them with still a third poem, perhaps his own, *Les Chétifs*. In any case these three poems are generally regarded as the nucleus of the cycle.[4]

The process of growth here is similar to that which contributed to the formation of the other epic cycles. Its center and point of reference is always the principal figure of the nucleus, Godefroy de Bouillon. Taking advantage of Godefroy's popularity, subsequent poems added to the cycle develop the hero's ancestral background, relate post crusade events leading to his death, and provide an ultimate confrontation between the crusading armies and Saladin. This process of accretion began early, for there is evidence of the association of the Swan Knight with Godefroy de Bouillon before the end of the 12th century,[5] not long after the establishment of the more historically oriented nucleus. It is significant that no single epic associated with the cycle has survived in pre-cyclical form, this despite ample internal evidence of independent origin and existence for at least some of them. Nevertheless, the process seems to have been slow and especially subject to the means and whims of numerous redactors. This can be concluded from the fact that every extant manuscript provides a different version of the cycle, a fact which is true not only in terms of the number of cyclical elements or branches but also in terms of the form of the individual branches.

There is a similar individuality with respect to the achievement of a cohesive whole. The manuscripts vary in this respect not only from manuscript to manuscript, but from branch to branch within a given manuscript. It is possible to hypothesize that, in one instance, a redactor had at his disposal individual texts of the various branches, which he then fused with uneven success, while another had a combination of previously fused individual texts with which to work. As a result one must conclude that there were probably as many attempts at a unified poem as there are cyclical manuscripts.

The following table is offered by the editors only as a convenient means of visualizing the various cyclical forms in terms of the traditional branches.[6]

Table II lists the content, however negligible it may be in certain cases, of every known extant verse manuscript

TABLE II[7]

	BN 12558	BN 786	BN 795	BN 1621	BN 12569	ARS. 3139	BM 15EVI	BM 36615	BERN 320	BERN 627	TURIN LIII25	HATTON 77	DOUCE 381	LAON FRAG	JEANROY FRAGS	MONE FRAG	PROSE BN 781
Elioxe	X																
Beatrix		X	X	X	X		X				X						X
Elioxe – Beatrix			X	X				X									
Chevalier au Cygne	X	X	X	X	X	X	X	X	X	X	X						X
Fin d'Elias		X	X	X	X	X		X	X		X						
Enfances Godefroi	X	X	X	X	X	X	X	X	X	X	X				X	X	X
Retour de Cornumarant	X	X	X	X	X	X		X			X						X
Chanson d'Antioche	X	X	X	X	X	X		X	X		X			X	X		X
Chétifs	X	X	X	X	X	X		X	X		X	X					X
Chanson de Jérusalem	X	X	X	X	X	X	X	X	X		X		X				X
Chrétienté Corbaran					X	X		X									
Prise d'Acre					X			X									
Mort Godefroi					X												
Chanson des Rois Baudouin					X			X									
Cont.²											X						

or fragment and of the Prose redaction. There must have
been many more manuscripts which have not survived, and the
little information that can be gleaned about these will be
discussed later.[8]
     The table sets out the maximum number of branches into
which the cycle can be subdivided for modern editorial con-
venience. It should be noted that the present division into
branches, or continuations of branches, does not always co-
incide with that actually conceived by the scribes who wrote
the manuscripts, in those cases where a formal division is
maintained by means of blank spaces, miniatures, or large
ornamental capitals. It seems, as has been suggested above,
that in many cases redactors attempted to smooth over the
joints rather than draw attention to them. As a result, at
certain points, different versions of the cycle contrive
different articulations between the individual branches so
that the link-ups between the component parts of the cycle
are by no means standard. This is especially so of the
legendary branches concerning the ancestry of Godefroy de
Bouillon, in which the complications are best explained by
the irregular order of their composition. The first of
these to be written were the *Chevalier au Cygne* and *Enfances
Godefroi*, to which later a preface was added, the *Naissance
du Chevalier au Cygne*, surviving in the *Elioxe*, *Beatrix*, and
Elioxe-Beatrix versions. At a later date the episode usu-
ally known as the *Fin d'Elias* was appended to the *Chevalier*,
and that of the *Retour de Cornumarant* to the *Enfances*,
though which of these continuations was written first is a
matter of conjecture. For greater clarity tables have been
drawn up to illustrate the more complicated variations in
articulation.
     The different transitions from Branch I to Branch II
have been studied in detail by W. R. J. Barron[9] and by the
present editors in their article on MS BM Royal 15 E VI.[10]
The table below is modelled closely on the table on p. 541
of that article. But whereas that one is based on MS *H*, the
present table takes MS *B* as a base, and the manuscripts are
arranged according to their immediate classification. MSS
F, *I* and *T* are all victims of lacunae at this point and have
not been included. MS *S* has one folio missing at the begin-
ning.
     The original opening of the *Chevalier au Cygne* is al-
most certainly the laisse in "-er" beginning:
        "Segnor, oiez cancon qui molt fait a loer,
         Par itel convenant le vos puis je conter,"
                              (*A* fol. 20ᵛ col. 1)
In both *A* and *B* this laisse is headed by a miniature.[11]
Whatever the different bridge passages may be between the

TABLE III

ARTICULATIONS FROM BRANCH I TO BRANCH II

BRANCH I	Elioxe	Beatrix					Elioxe-Beatrix	
	A	B	E	H	C	D	G	S
-ier	-	105^r	20^r	325^r	25^v	9^v	27^v	-
+ 1 -ant	-	-	-	325^r	-	-	-	-
-ine	-	105^r	20^r	-	25^v	10^r	27^v	-
-or	-	105^r	20^r	325^r	25^v	10^r	27^v	-
-é	-	105^r	20^r	-	25^v	10^r	27^v	-
-on	-	105^r	20^v	325^r	25^v	10^r	27^v	-
-ans	-	105^r	20^v	-	25^v	10^r	28^r	-
-is	-	105^r	20^v	-	-	-	-	-
BRANCH II								
1 -er	20^v	105^v	20^v	325^v	-	-	-	-
2 -on	20^v	105^v	20^v	325^v	-	-	-	-
3 -ĭe	20^v	105^v	21^r	-	-	-	-	1^r
4 -ence	21^r	105^v	21^r	-	-	-	-	1^v
5 -ant	21^r	105^v	21^r	325^v	-	-	-	1^v
6 -el	21^v	106^r	21^v	325^v	26^r	10^r	28^r	2^v

two branches, all versions reunite with the laisse in "-el" beginning:

> "Des or s'en vait li cisnes, s'enmaine son batel,"
>   (*A* fol. 21^V col. 1)
>   (Hippeau I, p. 110)

The *Chevalier* usually ends with a laisse in "-ent" (*A* fol. 45^V col. 1). The original transition from that branch to the *Enfances Godefroi* probably read as found in MSS *ADS*:

> Last laisse of *Chevalier*:   -ent
> Two transitional   -age
>   laisses: -on
> First laisse of *Enfances*:   -ans

However, at a later stage, MSS *BCEFGIT*[12] interpolate between these two branches the *Fin d'Elias*. Some of these manuscripts (*BCT*) retain the laisse in "-age" (together with a short one in "-on," *BC* only) as a transition to the *Fin d'Elias*, and then repeat it, in its general tenor, but suitably adapted to do duty as transition to the *Enfances*. Because of this virtual repetition, the articulation in *BCT* from Branch II-*Fin d'Elias* is rather clumsy, whilst the omission of these laisses the first time round in *GI* and the recasting of the bridge passage in *E* at least represent an effort to solve the problem. These transitions are detailed in Table IV (based on the readings of *B*), which covers the last common laisse in the *Chevalier* to the first in the *Enfances*.[13]

From this table it follows that the first common laisse of the *Fin d'Elias* is that in "-ie" beginning:

> "Signour, oiés cancon de vreté establie,
> Onques miudre ne fu par (ms pas) jougleor oïe."
>   (*B* fol. 124^V col. 2)

and the first common laisse of the *Enfances Godefroi* is that in "-ans" beginning:

> "Quant Ide la cortoise ot passé .XIIII. ans,
> Si fu toute formee et parcreue et grans."
>   (*A* fol. 45^V col. 2)
>   (Hippeau I, p. 259)

This branch ends with a laisse in "-ee" which constitutes a call to order and a preliminary announcement of the *Chanson d'Antioche* which in *AF* follows immediately. It is also after this laisse that *H* ends its version of the "Cygne" cycle material, whereas that of *S* is terminated three laisses previously by a lacuna.

However, seven manuscripts, *BCDEGIT*, continue with the *Retour de Cornumarant*. They all retain the laisse in "-ee" in an abbreviated form, suitably adapted to lead into the new episode, the first laisse proper of which is in "-iés"

TABLE IV

ARTICULATIONS FROM BRANCH II — *FIN D'ELIAS* — BRANCH III

BRANCH II		A	D	H	S	B	C	T	G	I	E	F
Last laisses of *Chevalier*:	-i	45r	35v	332v	78r	124r	49v	23r	55r	19r	48v	-
	-é	45r	35v	332v	78v	124r	50r	23r	-	-	49r	-
	-ent	45v	36r	332v	79v	124r	50r	23r	-	-	-ee	-
Transitional laisses:	-age	45v	36r	-	80r	124v	50r	23v	-	-	-on	-
	-on	45v	36r	-	80r	124v	50v	-	-	-	-ent	-
Continuation of BRANCH II *Fin d'Elias* First laisses:	-is	-	-	-	-	124v	50v	23v	55r	19v	-	-
	-ie	-	-	-	-	124v	50v	23v	55v	19v	49r	-
Last laisse:	-in	-	-	-	-	134v	63v	38v	70r	31r	60r	9v
Transition to *Enfances*:	-age	-	-	-	-	134v	63v	38v	70r	31r	60v	9v
	-on	-	-	-	-	134v	63v	38v	70r	31r	60v	9v
BRANCH III First laisse:	-ans	45v	36r	332v	80v	134v	64r	38v	70r	31v	60v	9v

beginning:
> "Quant Tieris de Louvaig fu el bos embuschiés,
> Ses compaignons apele si les a araisniés."
> > (*C* fol. 88^r col. 2)
> > (Hippeau 2, p. 137)

The *Retour* ends with a repetition of the laisse in "-ee,"
announcing the *Antioche* (which has clearly been split to ad-
mit the interpolation).[14]

The historical nucleus of the Crusade Cycle begins with
the *Chanson d'Antioche* in which most manuscripts (but not
EGI[15]) agree in starting with a call for silence:
> "Segnor, soiés en pais, laisiés la noise ester,
> Se vos volés cancon glorieuse escouter."
> > (*A* fol. 59^r col. 1)

In general the scribes of the manuscripts themselves accord
much more importance to the transition from the legendary
"Godefroy de Bouillon" material to the "Crusade Cycle" prop-
er: two of them, *A* and *C*, leave a blank space at the end
of the preceding branch and start the *Antioche* on a fresh
side (*A* prefacing it with a full page of miniatures also),
while two others, *F* and *T*, which normally do not have any
divisions at all, indicate the new branch by means of a
large flourished initial.[16]

The beginning of *Les Chétifs* is usually clearly desig-
nated in the decorated manuscripts by a miniature or large
capital at the head of the laisse in "-ie" beginning:
> "Or s'en fuit Corbarans tos les plains de Surie,
> N'enmaine que .II. rois ens en sa conpaignie."
> > (*A* fol. 113^v col. 2)

which is also the point at which the Oxford fragment opens.
This implies that the copyists were in general agreement
about the existence of this epic as a separate branch, and
its exact location. The division between the *Chétifs* and
the *Chanson de Jérusalem*, on the other hand, is a modern
convenience and does not correspond to any demarcation in
the manuscripts themselves. It is probable that Graindor de
Douai — who, it is assumed, combined these two branches —
sought to effect a smooth transition from the fabulous
branch to the quasi-historical one. For the scribes of *C*,
G, and *A* the next significant change of material comes at
the place where the Crusaders finally reach Jerusalem and
have the Holy Places pointed out to them from afar by Peter
the Hermit, with *C* and *G* placing a miniature (and a rubric
in *G*) before the laisse in "-a"[17] beginning:
> "Dans Pieres li Ermites sor son asne monta,"
> > (Hippeau, p. 37)

whilst *A* registers the division with a full page of minia-
tures on fol. 143^v and a single one at the head of the first

laisse, in "-ons," on fol. 144ʳ (Hippeau, p. 42). Indeed the
whereabouts of a division for editorial purposes — the indi-
cations in the manuscripts are not being followed on this
occasion — is a disputed point, and it seems that, despite
some opposition,[18] the place chosen by Hippeau in his edi-
tions of fragments of *Les Chétifs* and *Jérusalem* is the most
favorable, this being the first laisse in which attention is
directed away from the "Chétifs" to the movement of the Cru-
sading army, beginning:

"Dedens Jerusalem s'armerent li felon,
.L. mile furent li encrieme gloton."
                        (*A* fol. 136ᵛ col. 2)
                        (Hippeau, p. 3)

The *Jérusalem* ends with an announcement of more mate-
rial to come, usually expressed in these, or like, terms:

"Or commenche canchons, ja millor nen orés
Comment Acre fu prise et les autres cités,
Et Sur et Thabarie u Turc avoient més,
Et si comme li Temples fu des barons peuplés,
Et l'ospitaus assis u Jhesus fu posés;
Al Temple pour servir fu Harpins adonés."
                        (*C* fol. 256ʳ col. 2)

However, this promise of further adventures is not ful-
filled by the majority of manuscripts, which are content to
terminate the cycle at this point. Four manuscripts only
carry additional branches known collectively as the post-
Jérusalem continuations and none of these volumes has any
indication whatsoever of where one episode ends and the next
begins. The various titles which have been provided to
distinguish these episodes — *Chrétienté Corbaran*, *Prise d'A-
cre*, *Mort Godefroi*, *Fin de Baudouin*, *Débuts*, or *Guerres
Saladin* — were all consecrated for material in *E* and *G*,
which until recently were the only known continuation manu-
scripts.[19] The rediscovery of *I* and *T*, both of which con-
tain substantially more post-*Jérusalem* material than either
E or *G*, has rendered the division into branches of these
continuations almost valueless, because although the same
themes remain in *IT*, the texts themselves are generally re-
worked and amplified and no longer correspond to the ramifi-
cations as previously conceived. All that can be said by
way of generalization is that the *Chrétienté Corbaran* is
present in recognizably the same form in *EGI*, the *Prise d'A-
cre* in *EI*; these same poems appear in a totally recast form
in *T*. After that the *Mort Godefroi* and *Chanson des Rois
Baudouin* are found in one form in *E* and in another in *IT*,
sufficiently different to make impossible the collation of
these three manuscripts together. The reworking of these
epics as found in *IT* is being provided with the general
blanket term *Cont.*[2]

The following physical description of the manuscripts of the Old French Crusade Cycle is based on the formula adopted by Miss A. de la Mare in her catalogue of the Lyell Manuscripts in the Bodleian Library.[20]   However, as all the manuscripts, with the exception of *H*, were copied within a period roughly between the middle of the thirteenth and the first quarter of the fourteenth centuries, no reference has been made to the material on which they are written, since they are all on parchment or vellum, or to the type of script.

All these manuscripts have been described before,[21] the Paris ones more than the others, with a greater or lesser degree of accuracy, and no attempt has been made to evaluate all the previous polemics devoted to them. The purpose of this study is to assemble as much factual information about the manuscripts as possible and to deal at greater length with some aspects which have hitherto been neglected.

Where no precise information is available, the provenance of the manuscripts has been judged from the dialect of the scribe(s) and the style of decoration, if any. Except for *H*, *I*, and *O*, all the manuscripts appear to have been copied in northeastern France, in that area otherwise known as Picardy.

The analysis of the flourishing of certain manuscripts is based on the work of Mrs. Sonia Patterson,[22] the only substantial study in the field, and on personal observations.

The manuscripts now have "modern" (post-medieval) bindings of various sorts that have not been described. The only exception is Hatton 77, which has retained its medieval binding. Where possible some account of the history of the manuscript has been given.

The manuscripts are arranged alphabetically according to their *sigles*, except for the Prose version *P*, which has been placed last. There follows an analysis of some manuscripts of the Cycle which are now lost.

A. Hatem has stated that: "Pour être mené à bonne fin l'examen critique des six manuscrits de Paris demanderait de longues années" (p. 87, note 19). Since his day the number of manuscripts taken into consideration has increased and the following section constitutes a physical description of some thirteen volumes. The highly complex problems appertaining to manuscript tradition will be dealt with by the editors of the individual branches.

We would like to take this opportunity of acknowledging our debt of gratitude for the advice and assistance received from M. Francis Avril, in the B.N., Dr. Christian von Steiger in Bern, Signora Carla Beraldi in Turin, and more

especially from Mr. Malcolm B. Parkes, of Keble College,
Oxford, who initiated us into the science of manuscript de-
scription.

Paris Bibliothèque Nationale MS fonds français 12558 (A)

   This manuscript[23] was copied by a single scribe in the
North East of France in the middlé of the second half of the
thirteenth century; the last five folios have been recopied
by a second scribe about a century later.[24] It measures
330 x 240 (230 x 160) mm.   It is composed of IV parchment
endleaves (I pastedown, II canc.) + 192 + II parchment end-
leaves (II pastedown). The folios are numbered 1-94, 96-
193. Collation: i^8-vi^8, vii^{10}, viii^8-ix^8, x^8 (1 missing
after fol. 74), xi^8-xxiii^8, xxiv^8 (8 canc. after fol. 193).
The quire signatures have been preserved. The text is dis-
tributed in two columns of 45 lines.

   Generally held to offer the oldest version of the First
Cycle of the Crusade, MS *A* is the only manuscript to contain
the *Elioxe* version of the *Naissance du Chevalier au Cygne*,
beginning:
         "Segnor, or m'escotés, por Deu et por son non,
          Par itel convenent Dex vos face pardon."
                         (fol. 1^r col. 1)
There follow: *Chevalier au Cygne* (20^v col. 1-45^v col. 2);
Enfances Godefroi (45^v col. 2-58^r col. 1); fol. 58^r col. 2
is blank and fol. 58^v has a full page of miniatures. The
Crusade Cycle proper begins with the *Antioche* (59^r col. 1-
113^v col. 2).   There is a lacuna of one folio between fols.
74 and 75.[25] *Chétifs* (113^v col. 2-136^v col. 2); *Jérusalem*
(136^v col. 2-192^v col. 2),[26] which ends:
         "Ci finerai mon livre ou dit en ay assés,
          Tous ceulz qui l'ont oy et celles de tous lés,
          Soient apres leurs jours es sains cielx couronnés.[27]
Fol. 193^r and 193^v are blank except for some jottings de-
scribed below.

   The initial capitals of each laisse are blue and red
alternately, and flourished.   The finely executed flourish-
ing of this manuscript shows a combination of components of
both French and English design.[28] MS *A* is one of the few to
divide the branches formally with miniatures, and contains
several other illuminations apart from these. The following
is a summary of the content of the miniatures found in *A*.
1) Endleaf IV^v; This is a full page of miniatures cut out
    of the original parchment and glued down onto the end-
    leaf, comprising six scenes from the *Naissance*, reading
    from left to right and top to bottom:
      a. Elioxe finds Lotaire asleep by the fountain.

    b.   Elioxe and Lotaire ride into the castle accompanied by Samonie.

    c.   Elioxe, lying in bed after childbirth, is shown her seven children, in baskets, by her mother-in-law.

    d.   Monicier takes the children to the hermit's chapel.

    e.   The children are turned into swans and fly into the air.

    f.   The swans are fed at the "vivier."

2)   fol. 1^r col. 1; Lotaire fixes collars round the swans' necks.

3)   fol. 20^v col. 2; Elyas is pulled in his boat by the swan towards the castle of Emperor Othon at Nimaie.[29]

4)   fol. 45^v col. 2; The castle of Bouillon burns down and the swan flies in to rescue the magic horn.

5)   fol. 52^r col. 1; Calabre casts her spell in the presence of the Soudan de Perse, Cornumarant, and other pagan worthies.

6)   fol. 58^v; A full page containing six scenes from the *Antioche*, reading from left to right and top to bottom:

    a.   The Pope absolves crusaders at the council of Clermont.

    b.   Crusaders on the march, on foot and on horseback.

    c.   A battle scene between Christians and Turks.

    d.   The Turks make a sally out of Antioch.

    e.   The Christians under the wall of Antioch prior to taking the city.

    f.   Corbaran sitting outside his tent receives a messenger.

7)   fol. 59^r col. 1; Christ and the two thieves on the Cross.

8)   fol. 103^r col. 1; The Christians ride out of Antioch before the battle, with Adhémar du Pui holding the Holy Lance.

9)   fol. 113^v col. 2; Corbaran flees from Antioch with two kings and the body of Brohadas.

10)   fol. 122^v col. 1; Corbaran leads the "Chétifs" home from Sarmasane.

11)   fol. 128^v col. 2; Baudouin de Beauvais exorcises the devil by thrusting his sword into the Satanas's mouth.

12)   fol. 133^r col. 1; Harpin de Bourges looks up into the tree in which the monkey is sitting with Corbaran's nephew.

13)   fol. 143^v; A full page containing five scenes from the *Jerusalem*.

    a.   A crusader grooming, his wife shoeing, horses.

    b.   A crusader holding a large basket and winnowing

corn (?).

c. A large horizontal miniature taking up both squares, depicting various siege operations. In the extreme left and right margins are catapults with their slings being held down, whilst in the centre Jerusalem is subject to both scaling and mining.

d. Turkish worthies playing chess.

e. A knight shoots an arrow to bring down the carrier pigeons sent out by the Turks.

14) fol. 144^r col. 1; The Christians look down on Jerusalem from the hill of Josaphas.

15) fol. 162^r col. 1; The Christians visit the hermit on the Mount of Olives.

16) fol. 167^r col. 1; The coronation of Godefroi de Bouillon.

17) fol. 168^V cols. 1 and 2; A scene from the battle of Ramla with the Christians on the left, holding the Cross.

The miniatures are depicted against backgrounds of solid gold or of plain blue and dull red, speckled with white stars, or of rather thickly drawn grills of the same colours, and sometimes orange, on a coloured *fond*.

On fol. 193^V are two jottings: "Vostre bon maistre Lippe que (?) sonne"[30] and "J'en suis de Luxembourg." It is also possible to make out a faint inscription in very large handwriting, probably done in charcoal, "ladādo pot" (possibly "Cadādo"). The same words are found on the recto of endleaf IV at the beginning of the volume, there in full, "ladando pot." The one in charcoal is the earliest of these writings, as the lower of the ones in ink slightly covers it, and they all appear to have been executed in the early fifteenth century.

With the knowledge that *A* belonged to Philip the Good, Duke of Burgundy, it is possible to infer that the manuscript was once in the possession of the famous Pot family, advisors and ambassadors to the Valois Dukes of Burgundy throughout their existence. Especially prominent in the affairs of state were Regnier Pot (1362-1432)[31] and his grandson Philippe Pot (1428-1494),[32] both Knights of the Golden Fleece, with a less distinguished son, Jacques Pot, in between. It is difficult to interpret "ladando"; it is not the family motto which during Regnier's life was "A la Belle," and later "Tant L Vault."[33] Possibly it is a corruption of "laudando." "Maistre Lippe" appears to be a nickname for Philippe. The note "J'en suis de Luxembourg" is not unexpected considering the relationship between Burgundy and that Duchy, which was finally annexed in 1443.[34]

In 1467 this manuscript belonged to the library of Philip the Good. In Joseph Barrois' edition of the inventory taken in that year after the Duke's death,[35] it appears with the number 1347, described as:

"Ung livre en parchemin couvert de cuir rouge, intitulé au dos: *Le Chevalier au Cysne*, escript à deux coulombes en prose, bien historié au commenchement; commenchant *Seigneur, or m'escoutez pour Dieu et pour son nom*, et le dernier feuillet, *ains ne povres ne riches.*"

It appears again in the 1487 inventory (Barrois no. 1797):

"Ung autre grant volume couvert de cuir rouge, à deux cloans et cincq boutons sur chacun costé, historié et intitulé: *Le livre du Chevalier du Cigne*, comenchant ou second feuillet: *Es cavernes del mont là ot habitement*, et finissant ou dernier: *soyent après leurs jours es sains cyeulx coronez.*"

The fact that it is described as being in prose is misleading, and illustrates the need for great caution when examining medieval catalogue descriptions, but there is no doubt whatever that B.N. fr. 12558 is the volume in question, since all four references concur exactly with those in the manuscript. It remained in the ducal library until at least 1643 when it appears in the catalogue of Sanderus.[36] It does not figure in the next catalogue, of Franquen (1731),[37] and by 1774 it is already in the Royal collection in Paris. (The medieval binding described in the old inventories has been replaced by the usual red morocco found on B.N. manuscripts, with a design characteristic of the work done in Louis XV's reign.) What happened to this manuscript between 1643 and 1774 we have not been able to trace.[38]

Paris Bibliothèque Nationale MS fonds français 786 (B)

BN fr. 786[39] was copied in Tournai by a single scribe in the middle of the second half of the thirteenth century. Its measurements are 310 x 230 (260 x 180) mm. It is composed of II paper endleaves + 273 + II paper endleaves, collating: i^4 (I canc.), ii^8-v^8, vi^6, vii^8-x^8, xi^4, xii^8, xiii^6, xiv^8-xxxv^8, xxxvi^8 (7, 8 canc. after fol. 273). Most quire signatures and some catchwords have been preserved. The First Cycle material is written on quires numbered from i-xxii in the manuscript and the *Roman d'Alexandre* begins on the quire originally numbered xxiii. From this it is clear that the scribe intended the Crusade material to be the first literary item of the volume followed by the *Alexandre*.

The present inversion of this order probably dates from the first binding. The text is distributed in two columns of 60 lines.

Folios 1-3 contain a Calendar of Saints in black, blue, and red, drawn up after the usage of Tournai. Evidence of provenance is provided by the name of the patron saint of that town, "Lehire," (Eleutherius) noted in blue against the 20th of February. Against the 9th of May there is the entry, in red, of "La ducasse Nostre Dame," in other words the dedication of the Cathedral of Tournai. Unfortunately the scribe does not provide any of the keys necessary for dating the calendar. All we have to go on is a definite *terminus a quo*, provided by the entry against the 25th of August of the translation of Saint Lehire, which took place in 1247, and a possible *terminus ad quem*, in the omission against the same date of Saint Louis, canonised in 1298, who usually appears on Tournai calendars.[40] In fact the style of the handwriting and miniatures of this manuscript point to a date roughly between the two.

Beside each month is a small miniature depicting the seasonal activities. P. Paris (*Les Manuscrits*, p. 165) lists some of these but not altogether accurately, so we will enumerate them here. January; an old woman sitting in front of a fire, drinking. February; a man holding a torch, representing Candlemas. March; a man digging. April; a young man holding a flower in his right hand. May; a knight on horseback, with a falcon on his wrist. June; a man carrying a bundle of wood (or a large basket ?) on his shoulders. July; two people haymaking. August; a man cutting the corn. September; a man sowing. October; someone picking grapes. November; a swineherd with a pig, gathering acorns. December; a man baking bread.[41]

From fol. 4r col. 1, MS *B* contains four branches of the *Roman d'Alexandre*,[42] by Alexandre de Paris, beginning:

"Qi viers de rice estore viut entendre et oïr,
    Pour prendre bon exemple de proecce aquellir..."

and continuing on fol. 84v col. 1 with *Le Vengement Alexandre*, by Gui de Cambrai, ending on fol. 91v col. 2:

"Tresc'al jour kes ocist tous Judas Macabés,
    Et conquist lor roiaumes, cou dist l'autorités."
    Explicit d'Alexandre.

This volume contains the complete First Cycle of the Crusade, with all its branches, but without any post-*Jérusalem* continuations, beginning on fol. 92r col. 1 with the *Beatrix* version of the *Naissance*:

"Signour, or ascoutés, ke Dex vous doinst scilenche
    De lui croire et orer en boine providence."

which ends on fol. 105r col. 2. *Le Chevalier au Cygne* fol-

lows, (105ᵛ col. 1-124ᵛ col. 1); *Fin d'Elias*, (124ᵛ col. 1-
134ᵛ col. 2); *Enfances Godefroi*, (134ᵛ col. 2-153ʳ col. 1);
Retour de Cornumarant, (153ʳ col. 1-160ᵛ col. 2); *Antioche*,
(160ᵛ col. 2-209ʳ col. 2); *Chétifs*, (209ʳ col. 2-232ʳ col.
2); *Jérusalem*, (232ʳ col. 2-273ʳ col. 1). The rest of fol.
273 is dotted with illegible scrawls (the parchment is rub-
bed) and the outside edge is torn.

The scribe divides all the material in this volume into
chapters, headed by rubrics in red which do not necessarily
correspond to modern critical divisions.[43]   All these ru-
brics are immediately above a miniature depicting the same
subject in pictorial terms. They are as follow for the
First Cycle of the Crusade:

1) fol. 92ʳ col. 1; Chi coumence li roumans dou cevalier
                       au chisne et de Godefroit de Buil-
                       lon, coument il prist Jherusalem.

2) fol. 98ʳ col. 1; Ci dist si con Elias et Mauquarés se
                       conbatirent ensanle.

3) fol. 102ᵛ col. 1; Ci dist si con li cevaliers au cisne
                       fist gieter Matabrune el fu ki es-
                       toit espris.

4) fol. 105ᵛ col. 1; Ci dist si con no baron en alerent
                       le Sepucre aourer et prisent An-
                       dioce en lor voie.[44]

5) fol. 110ᵛ col. 2; Ci dist si con uns archeveskes es-
                       pousa le chevalier au chisne et le
                       ducoise de Buillon. (The corre-
                       sponding miniature is at the top of
                       111ʳ col. 1.)

6) fol. 114ᵛ col. 1; Ci dist si con li cevaliers au cisne
                       tua Garin de Roce Ague et Segart de
                       Monbrin, et si houme conbatent d'au-
                       trepart.

7) fol. 117ᵛ col. 1; Ci dist si con li cevaliers au cisne
                       enmaine sa gent. Et Mirabiaus en-
                       maine sa fame qui faisoit mout grant
                       duel.

8) fol. 121ᵛ col. 1; Ci dist si con li chevaliers au
                       cisne envoia a Othon l'empereor un
                       brief et li rois Otes le fist lire a
                       .I. clerc.

9) fol. 124ʳ col. 2; Ci dist si con .I. palais ardoit et
                       .I. cisnes vint avolant parmi le fu
                       si prist .I. cor d'ivore ki pendoit
                       a .I. estel.

10) fol. 127ᵛ col. 1; Ci dist si con couca le cevalier au
                        cisne ensanle entre .II. auteus u on
                        cantoit messe, et il (devint) hom.

11) fol. 134^r col. 2; Ci dist si con li ducoise de Buillon
et Yde sa fille et li cevaliers au
cisne et si baron s'en vinrent au
port u il devoient paser.

12) fol. 137^v col. 2; (This rubric very rubbed.)   Ci dist
si con la contesse fist pendre l'en-
fant par les piés et li fist (rendre
le lait) k'il avoit mangié.   (The
miniature, at the head of fol. 138^r
col. 1 depicts Yde making Eustace
disgorge the milk which the nurse
had given him.[45])

13) fol. 142^r col. 1; Ci dist si con on fist Godefroit ce-
valier ki puis fu sires de Buillon.

14) fol. 146^r col. 2; Ci dist si con Godefrois de Buillon
se conbati a .I. cevalier ki avoit a
non Guis.

15) fol. 149^v col. 1; Ci dist si con li rois Cornumarans
et ses conpains estoient devant .I.
abé, si parloient a lui.

16) fol. 153^v col. 1; Ci dist si con Cornumarans se con-
bati rustement a Thieri l'Alemant et
a ses conpagnons.

17) fol. 157^v col. 1; Ci dist si con li Sarrasin asalirent
Corbaran et Solimant et Cornumarant,
et cil .III. tuerent mout de Sarra-
sins.

18) fol. 162^r col. 1; Ci dist si con Pieres li Hermites
monta sor .I. asne et s'en ala a
Roume.

19) fol. 165^v col. 2; Ci dist si con Bauduins et Godefrois
s'en vont vers Jherusalem, et se de-
partirent de lor mere mout tenrement
plorant.

20) fol. 170^v col. 1; Ci dist si con Solimans et sa gens
s'en fuient hors de Nike, mout grant
doel faisant, et lor puins batant.

21) fol. 173^v col. 2; Ci dist si con Bauduins et sa conpa-
gnie se conbatirent as Sarrasins, et
en ocisent mout, et prisent la cité.

22) fol. 178^r col. 1; Ci dist si con no crestien sont de-
vant (Andioce) et l'asalent mout
souvent.

23) fol. 181^v col. 2; Ci dist si con li paien prisent Re-
naut Procet (sic) et le batoient
mout laidement.

24) fol. 186^v col. 1; Ci dist si con li paien ofroient a
Mahoumet, qui en haut estoit assis,

or et argent.

25) fol. 189ᵛ col. 1; Ci dist si con Bauduins envoia par mesages pour souscours au roi Corbarant. (i.e. Bauduin sends to the Emperor Alexis for help against Corbaran, as depicted in the miniature.)

26) fol. 193ᵛ col. 2; Ci dist si con no baron montoient as murs d'Andioce par une esciele, et li esciele ronpi, si tua .II. de nos barons.

27) fol. 197ᵛ col. 1; Ci dist si con li mere Corbarant prent congié a lui si s'en reva en son regne.

28) fol. 202ᵛ col. 1; Ci dist si con Corbarans et Amedelis estoient en .I. castiel et regardoient nos barons qui iscoient d'une cité.

29) fol. 206ʳ col. 1; Ci dist si con Godefrois de Buillon trenca le tieste a Brohadas. (The miniature is at the head of col. 2.)

30) fol. 209ʳ col. 2; Ci dist si con Corbarans s'en fuit, s'enporte Brohadas ki n'a point de tieste.

31) fol. 214ʳ col. 1; Ci dist si con Ricars de Caumont se conbat a Sorgalé et li trenca l'orelle toute jus.

32) fol. 218ʳ col. 1; Ci dist si con Corbarans s'en reva et Bauduins (ms Ricars) a faite le batalle.

33) fol. 223ʳ col. 1; Ci dist si con Bauduins se conbat a .I. serpent en une roce et li ciés sen frere gist encoste lui.

34) fol. 227ʳ col. 2; Ci dist si con une serpente enporte Jehan d'Alis, et Harpins de Beorges en demaine grant doel.

35) fol. 229ᵛ col. 1; Ci dist si con .IIII. lion vinrent vers Harpin ki estoit en une foriest, et le volrent estranler.

36) fol. 234ʳ col. 2; Ci dist si con Jehans d'Alis et si houme se conbatent a lor anemis et en ocient a plenté.

37) fol. 238ʳ col. 2; Ci dist si con li rois de Jherusalem estoit a ses fenestres et il vit l'ost des Francois qui voloient asalir Jherusalem.

38) fol. 242ʳ col. 1; Ci dist si con li rois de Jherusalem et nostre gens se conbatirent ensan-

le, et i ot grant ocision d'une part
et d'autre.

39) fol. 246ʳ col. 2; Ci dist si con li rois Godefrois li-
vra a Raimon de Saint Gille une es-
ciele de gent mout ricement armee.

40) fol. 249ᵛ col. 2; Ci dist si con li rois de Jherusalem
maine mout grant doel, et Cornumaran
ses fius le reconforte.

41) fol. 253ᵛ col. 1; Ci dist si con no baron aloient a
prociession, et trouverent sor le
mont d'Olivet .I. hermite qui lor
dona consel de prendre Jherusalem.

42) fol. 257ᵛ col. 2; Ci dist si con li rois Godefrois fu
corounés et si houme le coronerent.

43) fol. 262ʳ col. 1; Ci dist si con li amiraus seoit sor
.I. faudestuet, et Cornumarans des-
cent de sen ceval et s'en vint par-
ler a lui.

44) fol. 265ᵛ col. 1; Ci dist si con li rois Godefrois et
Marbrins se conbatirent en .I. camp
sans plus de gent.

45) fol. 270ʳ col. 1; Ci dist si con Cornicas et Tumas de
Marle se conbatirent ensanle, et
mout grant bataille avoit entour
aus.

There are 23 similar rubrics and miniatures in the *Roman d'Alexandre*. The miniatures are all drawn against a dark blue or red background, speckled with groups of three white dots. The majority of them are placed in the interior of a large capital letter at the beginning of a laisse, and accompanied by an illuminated border. Other laisses begin with alternate red and blue flourished initials.

This manuscript is entitled, after its first major item, *Le Roman d'Alexandre*, and is not easily identifiable in medieval catalogues due to the vast number of Alexander manuscripts. However, in a handwritten catalogue of the library of Henri III,[46] dated 1589, there is the mention of a "Roman du roy Alexandre," (no. 2540). By the process of eliminating all other manuscripts classified under the heading of "Alexandre" it is likely that this refers to BN fr. 786. Evidence that the manuscript was accessible in court circles at that time is that, as P. Meyer has already pointed out,[47] at the top of the first folio of the *Alexandre* there is the sixteenth century rubric: "Rommant d'Alexandre qui fut sire de tout le monde" written in the hand of Claude Fauchet.[48] This manuscript is not definitely listed as having been in Fauchet's own collection,[49] and he has not claimed possession of it as he often did in his own books by

signing his name, nor are there the characteristic under-
linings found in volumes which he read pen in hand. The
same folio also bears the figure 194, which is the number of
this manuscript in the Second Catalogue of the Royal col-
lection by Pierre and Jacques Dupuy (1645).[50] MS *B* is thus
the first manuscript of the First Cycle to find its way into
the Bibliothèque Nationale. It must have been a mid-six-
teenth century acquisition, because it is not found in the
Catalogue of the Royal collection at Blois, in 1544.[51]

Paris Bibliothèque Nationale MS fonds français 795 (C)

This manuscript[52] was executed by three scribes, work-
ing probably in central Picardy towards the end of the
thirteenth century. It measures 320 x 240 mm. (written
space, fols. 11-70, 220 x 155; fols. 71-256, 220-260 x 165
mm.). It is composed of IV paper endleaves (I pastedown) +
256 + II paper endleaves, collating: i^{12} (1, 5 missing),
ii^{12}-ix^{12}, x^4, xi^{12}, xii^{10}, xiii^8, xiv^{12}-xvii^{12}, xviii^8 (8
cut out after fol. 195), xix^{12}, xx^8, xxi^{12}-xxiii^{12}, xxiv^6
(6 canc. after fol. 256). Catchwords, but no quire signa-
tures, appear on some fols. (140^v, 152^v, 164^v, 188^v, 207^v
(traces), 227^v, 251^v). The text is written on two columns
to the page, with 40 lines a column from fol. 11-70 and 34-
40 lines from fol. 71 to the end.

This volume has the same contents as *B*, namely all the
branches of the Cycle without any later continuations. The
first quire, fol. 1-10, presents problems and will be dis-
cussed in detail later. The First Cycle begins on fol. 11^r
with the *Beatrix* version of the *Naissance*, beginning:
       "Signeur, oiés canchon ki mout fait a loer,
            Par iteil couvenant le vos puis je conter..."
There follow, *Chevalier au Cygne* (26^r col. 1-50^v col. 1);
Fin d'Elias (50^v col. 1-64^r col. 1); *Enfances Godefroi* (64^r
col. 1-88^r col. 2); *Retour de Cornumarant* (88^r col. 2-98^r
col. 1). After the end of the *Retour* is the explicit "Chi
faut li estoire del chevalier au cisne," and the word "Ex-
plicit," followed by the quatrain:
       "A la fin de cest livre ou j'ai pené jour
            Voil prier a la dame ou toute douchours
            Que deprit a son fil doucement que tant⸺⟩maint.
            Que me giet de pechiet et que m'ame el ciel
Fol. 98^r col. 2 is blank, and *Antioche* occupies fol. 98^v
col. 1-165^r col. 1; *Chétifs* (165^r col. 2-192^r col. 2); *Jéru-
salem* (192^r col. 2-256^v col. 1). There is a lacuna of one
fol. after 195, corresponding to the material in Hippeau, p.
20-24. Fol. 256^v col. 2 is blank.

The "Cygne-Godefroi de Bouillon" material was written

by three scribes; scribe A from fols. 11^r-48^v. Scribe B takes over on fol. 49^r, the second folio of the quire, and continues to fol. 70^v. The third scribe C, inferior both in ability to copy correctly and in quality of handwriting, begins on a fresh quire at fol. 71^r and executes the rest of the manuscript.

The first quire as it stands is something of a problem. The first three folios are now given over to various poems in French and Provençal, written by several scribes in the fourteenth century, all of which have been described elsewhere, and none of which concerns us here.[53] What is of concern to us is that originally these folios, together with fols. 4^{r-v}, 5^r, 10r col. 2 and 10^v, were blank.[54] The texts which were originally in this quire now fall between fol. 5^v and 10r col. 1, in other words in the second half of the quire only. On fol. 5^v col. 1 there is, headed by a large miniature, and in the hand of scribe C, the usual proem to the *Beatrix* beginning:

"Or escoutés, signour, que Dieus vous doinst science,
De lui croire et amer en boine providence..."
and containing three laisses, followed by (fol. 6^r col. 1-7^r col. 1) a *Salut d'Amour*,[55] beginning:

"Dieus qui le mont soustient et garde,
Soustiegne m'amie en sa garde."
and ending:

"Ami amés, ami avés,
Quant mius porrai sel troverés."
On fol. 7^r col. 2 is *Le Dit de Blancheflour et de Florence* beginning:

"El mois de mai avint l'autrier,
.II. pucheles en .I. vregier..."
and ending on fol. 10r col. 1:

"Ichi est Florenche enfoie,
Qui au chevalier fu amie."
Explicit.

This is followed on col. 1 by an extract from the *Dits de Droit du Clerc de Voudroi*,[56] beginning:

"Drois dist et jel ferai estable,
Que puis que li hons siet a table..."
and ending:

"Sot debonaire deporter,
Et sage debonaire amer."
Of this material, that on fol. 6^r col. 1 is the work of scribe B, while the rest is that of scribe C. This close collaboration between these two scribes, both in the poetic material in the first quire and (together with scribe A) in the rest of the manuscript, suggests strongly that this particular volume is the product of a scriptorium.

W. R. J. Barron has discussed the problem of the first quire at some length.[57] His main theory is that the *Beatrix* on fol. 11 begins with the proem normally reserved for the *Chevalier*. Because of this someone later might have thought that the "manuscript had lost a leaf containing the three opening laisses found in other *Beatrix* texts and have arranged for them to be copied from such a source" (p. 521) because the first line of the *Chevalier* proem — "Signeur, oiés canchon ki mout fait a loer" — is also the first line of the fourth laisse of the *Beatrix* proem.[58]

Barron states that the "material in the first gatherings is extraneous, disparate in nature and apparently copied at a later date than the body of the manuscript." (p. 521) But the copyists of this material in quire one are in fact the very scribes who *did* write the body of the manuscript. (Possibly Barron, concerned only with the *Naissance*, did not examine the rest of the text.) However, he is right in claiming that the material on fol. 5ᵛ was added expressly to fill the supposed lacuna at the beginning of the *Naissance*, and should, therefore, as such, be "facing the assumed continuation." (p. 521)

The problems can be reduced to three. Why do the added laisses appear on fol. 5 and not facing fol. 11? Why is the rest of the material extraneous and why were the first four fols. and fol. 5ʳ originally blank? We believe that these questions can be answered. The fundamental error which resulted in the present confusion in the first quire lay probably with the initial binder. Originally one bifolium (present 4 + 5 which form the middle bifolium) which contained the *Beatrix* proem *and nothing else* was prepared in such a manner that the text would appear on the verso of the second folio, i.e., facing present fol. 11ʳ. It is possible, if we are dealing with a scriptorium, that several manuscripts were waiting to be bound. At some stage this isolated bifolium was mixed up with some pages of a collection of "chansons" which were waiting to be bound at the same time.[59] In the confusion that ensued, the bifolia containing the "chansons" were inverted, so that the blank folios which were originally at the end of the "chansons" manuscript, and would probably have been cut out, became the opening folios of quire one.[60] This is the only logical way to explain how there is extraneous material beginning half way through the quire, and why the *Beatrix* proem is not in its rightful place. The binder could hardly have been expected to be acquainted with all the contents of the books he was to bind — especially if he was an itinerant craftsman — so he may not have realised his mistake.

BN fr. 795 is decorated with alternate blue and red

flourished capitals at the beginning of each laisse, the work of two artists, the first to fol. 106^V, the second from fol. 107^r to the end. The manuscript is illuminated, but only in the part written by scribe C. It was evidently up to the scribe to decide whether or not there should be miniatures, so that scribes A and B only leave enough space for large flourished initials, of which there are two in the first part of the manuscript, on fol. 11^r col. 1 and fol. 50^V col. 1, the beginning of the *Naissance* and the *Fin d'Elias* respectively. Scribe C favors both the large flourished initial and the miniature and leaves space for both — including a miniature on fol. 5^V. There are fifteen miniatures in all, mostly enclosed in a capital letter and some accompanied by an illuminated border. The following is a summary of the subject of the miniatures:

1) fol. 5^V; Beatrix and Oriant looking down from a tower see below them a woman holding twins.
2) fol. 119^V col. 2; Mounted Christians fight Saracen foot soldiers below the walls of Antioch.
3) fol. 120^r col. 1; The crusaders try to storm over the Pont de Fer.
    fol. 156^V col. 2; Two miniatures, one below the other, showing scenes from the Battle of Antioch.
4) The Turkish army advancing.[61]
5) An encounter between crusaders and Turks.
6) fol. 165^r col. 1; Another skirmish between crusaders and Turks.
7) fol. 165^r col. 2; Corbaran and four other knights flee from the Battle of Antioch.[62]
8) fol. 169^V col. 2; Corbaran takes the "Chétifs" from Oliferne to Sarmasane for the "duel judiciaire."
9) fol. 170^r col. 1; Corbaran presents his champion to the Soudan.
10) fol. 175^V col. 2; Corbaran leads the "Chétifs" away from Sarmasane.
11) fol. 198^r col. 1; The crusaders before Jerusalem, praying to God, whose hand appears in the sky.
12) fol. 204^r col. 1; Mounted crusaders before the walls of Jerusalem.
13) fol. 213^r col. 1; Knights on mobile wooden castles storm Jerusalem.
14) fol. 220^r col. 1; One of the towers of Jerusalem is bombarded by a catapult.
15) fol. 246^r col. 1; A skirmish between Christians and Turks during the Battle of Ramla.

These miniatures are all depicted on a solid gold background and are characterised by the use of vivid red and yellow colors, especially for shields and the protective covering on the horses. On the whole the Christians, symbolically, carry pointed "écus anciens" often with a lion on them, whilst the Turks use the round "targe," emblazoned with a scorpion.

The manuscript was given to the BN by an anonymous donor at some period between 1645 and 1682.[63]

Paris Bibliothèque Nationale MS fonds français 1621 (*D*)

BN fr. 1621 was copied by a single scribe in the middle of the thirteenth century in the North East of France.[64] It measures 285 x 210 mm. (written space; fols. 1-207, 215-245 x 170-180 mm.; fols. 208-225, 210 x 150-160 mm.). It is composed of II paper endleaves + 225 + II paper endleaves (the first of which is numbered 226), collating: i^8 (?) (missing), ii^8-xiv^8, xv^8 (4 cut out after fol. 107), xvi^{12} (2, 6, 7 canc. 11 missing; see below), xvii^6 + I, (The binding is too tight here to allow us to establish the true relationship of this single leaf to its neighbors.); xviii^8-xxvi^8, xxvii^6, xxviii^6 (4, 5, 6 canc. after fol. 207), xxix^8-xxx^8, xxxi^2. The top and bottom of the folios have been cropped so as to remove all trace of the quire signatures and catchwords, except at the bottom of fol. 32^v where the indication .V.[9] and the top half of the word *huimais* (the correct catchword for fol. 33) has been preserved. The text is distributed in two columns of 40 lines.

The manuscript lacks a quire at the beginning. As it stands the text begins in the middle of the *Beatrix* version of the *Naissance* with the lines:

"Si qu'il en a colpé .II. des bendes d'arjant
Le fu en fait voler si qu'il virent la jant."
(Nelson, lines 1487-88)

This branch continues up to fol. 10^r col. 2; there follow *Chevalier au Cygne* (10^r col. 2-36^r col. 2); *Enfances Godefroi* (36^r col. 2-60^r col. 1); *Retour de Cornumarant* (60^r col. 1-69^r col. 2); *Antioche* (69^r col. 2-128^r col. 1). There are lacunae in the text of the *Antioche*. In quire xv the fourth leaf, between fols. 107 and 108 has been cut out, leaving a gap corresponding to the material in P. Paris, *Ant.*, II, Chant Sixième, 777-941.

The outside edge of fol. 108 has been torn off so that the final words on recto col. 2 and the initial words of verso col. 1 are missing. Quire xvi (fols. 112-119) originally had 12 folios, three of which presented a stub. Two of these stubs remain, between fols. 116 and 117, which are the stubs of fols. 115 and 116. However, the folio which should follow fol. 118 has been lost, and with it the corresponding stub, which should appear between fols. 112 and 113. Whereas there is a textual lacuna between fols. 118

and 119, corresponding to the material in P. Paris, *Ant.*,
II, Chant Huitième, p. 218-225, there is no lacuna between
fols. 112 and 113, which is evidence that the missing leaf
in that place originally consisted of a stub.

Finally in the Crusade Cycle come *Les Chétifs* (128r
col. 1-152v col. 2) and *Jérusalem* (152v col. 2-207v col. 1)
which ends in conformity with all the manuscripts terminat-
ing at this point. Fol. 207v col. 2 is blank, and the three
remaining folios of this quire (xxviii) have been cut out.
There are no formal divisions between any of the branches of
the First Cycle. The last eighteen folios of the manuscript
contain the prose *Chronique de Turpin* (208r col. 1-225r col.
1) beginning:

> "Chi commenche l'estoire que Torpins li arche-
> vesques de Rains fist et traita du bon roi
> Charlemagne."

and ending:

> "Et mainte paine avoit fait et enduré por es-
> sauchier saint crestienté a l'onor Deu et mon
> Segnor saint Jaqueme et le bon roi Charlema-
> gne et saint Denise de Franche."

Fols. 218-223 have all had the top outside corner torn
away, so that parts of the text are missing. Fol. 225r col.
2 and verso are blank except for some scrawls in a fifteenth
century hand.[65]

The manuscript is not illuminated but the initial capi-
tals of each laisse are blue and red alternately, and flour-
ished. The *Chronique de Turpin*, although copied by the same
scribe has been decorated by a different flourisher.[66] The
Chronique begins with a large flourished blue and red capi-
tal with red infillings.

Across the top of fol. 1 is a sixteenth century rubric,
in the hand of Claude Fauchet: "C'est la conqueste de Jéru-
salem & origine de Godefroi de Boulongne ou Bouillon. Il a
esté composé après le voiage que Philipe Auguste fit en Su-
rie,"[67] to which a second hand has added in the right hand
margin, "avec l'ystoire de Charlemagne." This manuscript
actually belonged to the celebrated scholar, as illustrated
at the bottom of fol. 1 by the inscription "C'est à moi,
Claude Fauchet, 1596."[68] The volume is filled with the
underlinings and crosses commonly found in Fauchet's manu-
scripts, and on the recto of the first back endleaf he has
drawn up a list of the events to which the crosses refer
(discussed and edited by Espiner-Scott, *Claude Fauchet*, p.
163 and *Documents*, p. 201-202). MS *D* later passed (indi-
rectly) into Cardinal Mazarin's collection, where it bore
the number 194,[69] and then entered the Royal library in 1668
and is found under the number 7628 in the 1682 catalogue.

Paris Bibliothèque Nationale MS fonds français 12569 (*E*)

MS *E*[70] was executed by a single scribe working in the middle of the second half of the thirteenth century, probably in central Picardy. It measures 320 x 240 (225 x 180 mm.). It is composed of IV paper endleaves (I, II pastedown) + 265 + IV paper endleaves (III, IV pastedown), collating: i^8-xxv^8, xxvi^{10}, xxvii^8-xxxii^8, xxxiii^8 (7 canc. after fol. 264). There are quire signatures and catchwords, except on fols. 64 (where one has been added later, see below), 72 and 128. The text is distributed in two columns of 40 lines.

This is the most complete extant manuscript, for it contains all the branches of the First Cycle, together with a set of Continuations, and is not physically damaged like the Turin or BM add. manuscript. MS *E* opens with the *Beatrix* version of the *Naissance*, beginning:

"Or entendés, segnour, que Dius vous doinst sience,
S'oiïés boine canchon de mout grant sapience..."
(1^r col. 1-20^v col. 2); *Chevalier au Cygne* (20^v col. 2-49^r col. 2); *Fin d'Elias* (49^r col. 2-60^v col. 2); *Enfances Godefroi* (60^v col. 2-76^r col. 2); *Retour de Cornumarant* (76^r col. 2-85^r col. 2); *Antioche* (85^r col. 2-133^v col. 2); *Chétifs* (133^v col. 2-158^r col. 1); *Jérusalem* (158^r col. 1-215^v col. 1); *Chrétienté Corbaran* (215^v col. 1-221^v col. 2); *Prise d'Acre* (221^v col. 2-233^v col. 2); *Mort Godefroi* (233^v col. 2-244^r col. 2); *Chanson des Rois Baudouin* (244^r col. 2-264^v col. 2), which ends:

"Pour chou a trives rendus, asi lonc terme mis,
Et no bon crestien se garnissent toudis."
After this the scribe has written an explicit of his own composition:

"C'est de Godefroi de Buillon, de le premiere
(ceval)erie ki onkes fust outre mer, et s'en
i a plus k'en livre c'on truist, car c'est
li prise d'Acre et de Nike et de Cesaire et
de Barut et d'Andioce, de Jerusalem, d'Oli-
ferne, d'Aubefort, d'Ermenie, li crestientés
de Corbaran d'Oliferne et des .II. rois de
Nubie et de tous leur roiames, et du mariage
Godefroi de Buillon ki eut le sereur Corba-
ran, roine d'Alenie; et du patriacle premier
ki fu en Jerusalem ki enpuisouna Godefroi
pour les reliques qu'il envoia a Bouloigne
et a Lens, et tant de roi en roi ki se con-
batirent a Salehadin."
The scribe is quite aware, and even proud, of the novelty of the latter part of his book — "et s'en i a plus k'en livre c'on truist" — an aspect which is singled out in an-

other inscription (fol. 255^v) in which he states: "Je n'ai
tant plus en ce nouviel livre ke Blugasdas feri .I. Francois
en l'escu, biel voisin, et ci fenist li prumiers livers
(sic) de G(odefroi) de Buillon." (This is a commentary on
the action at the bottom of col. 2 of that page.) The true
novelty of the material lies in the continuations after the
Chrétienté, a version of which already existed in 1268, in
MS *G*, usually taken to be an earlier manuscript than *E*.
Certainly of the three extant manuscripts to contain post-
Chrétienté material *E* is markedly older than *I* or *T*.

The folio after 264 has been pulled out and fol. 265^r
contains a fourteenth century catalogue of "romances," form-
ing a collection along with *E*, beginning: "Vecit les nonz
dez rommans qui sont Monseignieur..."[71]   G. Paris wonders
whether any of these manuscripts have come down to us, but
does not attempt to satisfy his curiosity. We have not man-
aged to trace any manuscripts containing these various
"rommans," in an examination of certain BN manuscripts, in
an effort to discover the same hands that have contributed
marginalia in *E*.

Sumberg considers the manuscript to be intended for
reading, and it has every indication of being much read.
J. Porcher qualifies it as "malheureusement très usé, comme
beaucoup de ces romans fort lus." As a matter of fact its
state of preservation is far better than implied in that
statement. Evidence of its wide readership is found in the
large number of annotations and inscriptions. Apart from
that on fol. 255^v and the catalogue we can read on fol. 64^v
the line, in a cursive hand: "Hic fuit Guido dictus Flamin-
gus qui fecit istam cedulam." This has been generally taken
to refer to the scribe. This attribution is, however, un-
justified. The inscription is accompanied, to the left, by
a large black .VIII. in Roman numerals, unique in the manu-
script. The scribe, who normally includes small Roman quire
signatures, has omitted to do so on this occasion and it is
probable that Guido made good the omission by drawing this
large quire signature and signing his effort. The writing
is cursive, whereas when the scribe writes in the margin he
does so in his usual gothic hand. The misleading word is
"cedulam" which is out of place here whatever it is meant to
refer to. A volume of these dimensions is unmistakably a
"liber," as the scribe himself calls it. We believe that
Guido was referring to his large Roman quire signature, but
erroneously described it as a "cedulam" instead of a
"sigillum" (?).

On the blank verso of fol. 210 the name "Guillaume de
la Fonteinne" occurs twice.[72]   Unfortunately neither of
these two characters has been identified. More interesting

than those examples is that of the person who has written
six annotations at the bottom of various folios of the manu-
script. Sumberg (p. 112) draws our attention to only two of
these notes, claiming that "La main qui a écrit ces deux da-
tes semble être la même qui a indiqué le nom du copiste,
c'est-à-dire Guy le Flamand." This is not the case. The
duct of the two hands is completely different.

These six notes relate to some of the high points of
the First Crusade; the fall of Nicaea, the fall of Antioch,
the defeat of Kerbogha (Corbaran of the epic); the encamp-
ment of the Crusaders before Jerusalem, the fall of the Holy
City, and the death of Godefroy de Bouillon. All are pre-
cise dates and all follow, almost verbatim, the French
translation of William of Tyre.[73] Whether or not this his-
torically minded reader was the Monseigneur referred to in
the catalogue it is impossible to tell, since there is no
mention of a copy of this work in the collection; it may
have been a later acquisition.

This manuscript has no formal divisions between the
branches. Initial capitals of each laisse are in gold, en-
closed in a colored framework roughly equivalent to the
shape of the letter, alternately dark red and blue, with one
color for the interior of the capital, and one for the exte-
rior. There are no flourishes. A miniature at the begin-
ning of the text (fol. 1r col. 1) shows Beatrix and Oriant
in the tower looking down on the woman holding twins. The
elaborate architectural framework of trefoiled gothic win-
dows points to its Artesian origin. There are also five
miniatures on fol. 210r. Despite their somewhat stereotyped
nature, it appears that the scenes on this page of illumina-
tion, which is placed before the end of the *Jérusalem*, look
forward to the *Chrétienté*. The top left-hand space is taken
up by some lines of text. In this manuscript the miniatures
read first down the left hand column then down the right
hand column. The scenes depicted on this page are:
1)   Knights outside a town, presumably Oliferne.
2)   A council of war. Corbaran is being advised by the
        Vesque de Forois. (Cf. fol. 219v col. 2)
3, 4) An army riding.
5)   An army riding. Trumpets are being blown by heralds
        in the background.
On fol. 234v is a full page with eight scenes from the *Prise
d'Acre*. The reference to the action which is depicted is
given in brackets.
1)   The Christians encamped before Acre. (222r col. 1)
2)   A battle scene between the Christians and Dodekin de
        Damas. (222v)
3)   A fortified town surrounded by armies on both sides.

This appears to be the point where Tancred is encir-
cled in "Césaire" by the army of Dodekin. (225^r
col. 2)

4)   Baudouin's men prepare to catapult a swarm of bees
into the Tour Maudite at Acre. (233^v col. 1)
5)   The crusaders enter Acre. (233^v)
6)   Godefroi and his queen Matrone bid farewell to those
of the barons returning home. On the right some of
the crusaders have already embarked on a boat. (234^r
col. 2)
7)   The same boat approaches Rome. (234^r col. 2)
8)   The Pope blesses the crusaders. (*ibid.*)
All the miniatures have solid gold backgrounds.

At the bottom of fols. 62^v, 87^r and 132^v is a single
escutcheon consisting of six trefoils arranged three, two,
and one underneath each other, with two bars between the
three at the top and the two in the middle. These are not
colored. The owner of this heraldic design has so far not
been established.

This manuscript probably entered the BN at the end of
the eighteenth or beginning of the nineteenth century, but
no information is available as to its provenance.

Bern Burgerbibliothek MS 320 (F)

The surviving parts of MS F[74] were written by a single
scribe in the northeast of France in the middle of the sec-
ond half of the thirteenth century. Its measurements are
255 x 180 (205 x 150) mm. and the text is distributed in two
columns of 40-41 lines per page. It is composed of VI paper
endleaves (I, II pastedown) + 103 + VI paper endleaves (V,
VI pastedown).

This manuscript was rebound in the early seventeenth
century in such a way that the little that remained of the
original content was bound haphazardly with a great number
of bifolia misplaced and some odd folios stuck in out of
order. The following is an attempted reconstruction of the
original collation, based on data provided by the manuscript
itself in the way of quire signatures and catchwords and for
the rest, by a close comparison with the other manuscripts.
The surviving complete quires are all of twelve folios, and
computation of the missing parts suggests that the whole
manuscript was composed of regular quires of twelve folios.
It is impossible to tell whether this manuscript contained
material after the *Jérusalem*[75] but, excluding that possibil-
ity for the present study, it seems that the original number
of folios was 216.

Collation: i^{12} (missing); ii^{12} (all missing except present fol. 13 which came near the end); iii^{12} (all missing except present fol. 14 which came at or near the beginning — the original distance between fols. 13 and 14 was two folios); iv^{12} (1 = fol. 15 [?]; 2-9 missing, 10 = fol. 16; 11 missing, 12 = fol. 78); v^{12} (complete = fols. 1-12); vi^{12} (complete = fols. 17-28); vii^{12} (1, 2 = fols. 29-30; 3-10 missing; 11, 12 = fols. 31-32); viii^{12} (1-4 missing; 5 = fol. 79; 6, 7 missing; 8 = fol. 80; 9-12 missing); ix^{12} (1-8 = fols. 33-40; 9-12 cut out, stubs visible); x^{12}-xii^{12} (complete = fols. 41-76); xiii^{12} (1-5 missing; 6, 7 = fols. 81-82; 8-12 missing; [?]; xiv^{12} (complete = fols. 92-103); xv^{12} (1-4 = fols. 84-85, 88-89; 5-8 missing; 9-12 = fols. 90-91, 86-87); xvi^{12} (1 = fol. 83; 2-12 missing); xvii^{12} (missing); xviii^{12} (1 = fol. 77 [?]^{76}; 2-12 missing).

The extant quire signatures and catchwords are as follows:

fol.	78^V	.IIII.	le fist en mariage.
fol.	12^V	.V.	del maltalent quele ot.
fol.	28^V	.VI.	corb' fist loier.
fol.	32^V	.VII.	or oies qe dix fist.
fol.	52^V	.X.	et li rouges lions.
fol.	64^V	.XI.	as dens li a lescine.
fol.	76^V	.XII.	richars et li caitif.
fol.	103^V	.XIV.	cascuns des mors coulons.
fol.	87^V	.XV.	luns va en caneloingne.

It is certain that the manuscript commenced with one of the versions of the *Naissance*, probably the *Beatrix*, which is the shortest. Without drastic cuts Bern 320 would not have had room for either of the other two versions. What remains now is three folios of the *Chevalier au Cygne*; fol. 13 (corresponding to material in Hippeau 1, p. 140-146); fol. 14 (Hippeau 1, p. 158-164); fol. 15 (Hippeau 1, p. 230-237). The beginning of the *Fin d'Elias* is lacking. An isolated folio, 16 contains material corresponding to B fol. 126 and 127^r. The first complete section of this episode begins on fol. 78:

"N'ainc ne vot ses voisins guerroier ne grever"
(B fol. 127^V col. 2)

and continues on fol. 1^r col. 1-9^V col. 2; *Enfances Godefroi* (9^V col. 2-25^V col. 2); *Antioche* has lacunae; the extant folios can be grouped: 26^r col. 1-30^V col. 2 (the beginning of the branch); 31-32; 33-40; 41-51^V col. 2; *Chétifs* (51^V col. 2-76^V col. 2; only the last few laisses of this branch are missing); *Jérusalem* has a lacuna at the beginning and others throughout the text; folios can be grouped: 81-82; 92-103; 84-85; 88-89; 90-91; 86-87; 83; 77.

The initial capitals of each laisse are in red only, and not flourished, except for one poorly flourished black and red capital at the beginning of the *Antioche*.

At the top of fol. 1 is the late fifteenth or early sixteenth century rubric "Poemata Rythmica de bello sacro ubi singulos carminum versus eodem rythmo desinunt," which may be in the hand of the former owner of the manuscript, Jacques Bongars, who, it is known, took an active interest in the Crusades.[77]

It is possible that this manuscript at some time belonged to Claude Fauchet, mentioned earlier in conjunction with MSS *B* and *D*, or that he at least had access to it. The rubric is probably not by Fauchet, as the hand is slightly different from his, and furthermore he normally wrote in French on his French manuscripts and would certainly have identified the material more precisely than the Latin title does. Because the manuscript is bound with the same white cardboard that characterizes many of the manuscripts in Bongars' collection, it seems that the rebinding and at the same time the misplacement of the folios and possible loss of some of them occurred at a date after it had passed out of Fauchet's hands.

That Fauchet used the manuscript, together with the other manuscript in Bern, *S*, is illustrated by the great number of underlinings which occur in both of them, of precisely the sort encountered in other Fauchet manuscripts, and treating those subjects which are known to have aroused his curiosity.[78] It is probable that he looked at the two manuscripts together, or one soon after the other, as in many places the words underlined are exactly the same in both volumes.[79]

It is not known how the books passed into Bongars' hands, but it is well attested that he possessed some manuscripts which had formerly belonged to Fauchet.[80]

Paris Bibliothèque de l'Arsenal 3139 (G)

This manuscript[81] was copied by a single scribe, probably in the Northeastern region of Picardy,[82] in the year 1268. It measures 300 x 220 (225 x 170) mm. and is composed of VI paper endleaves (I pastedown) + 243 + IV paper endleaves (III, IV pastedown), collating: i^8-xxx^8, xxxi^4 (2 canc.). There are quire signatures in red, but no catchwords. The text is distributed in two columns of 39-40 lines.

This manuscript together with *I* contains the composite *Elioxe-Beatrix* version of the *Naissance* beginning:
      "Signor, oiés cancon ki mout fait a loer,
          Par itel couvenent le vos puis ce conter."
from fol. 1^v col. 1 (fol. I^r is blank)-fol. 28^r col. 2, fol-

lowed by *Le Chevalier au Cygne* (28^r col. 2-55^r col. 2); *Fin d'Elias* (55^r col. 2-70^r col. 2); *Enfances Godefroi* (70^r col. 2-86^v col. 1); *Retour de Cornumarant* (86^v col. 1-95^r col. 2); *Antioche*[83] (95^r col. 2-145^r col. 1); *Chétifs* (145^r col. 1-170^v col. 2); *Jérusalem* (170^v col. 2-231^r col. 1); *Chrétienté Corbaran* (231^r col. 1-243^v col. 2), ending:

> "Puis l'ot rois Corbarans batisie et levee,
> Et apries le rendi et fist noune velee,
> Ensi com vos orés, baron, s'il vos agree."

followed by the colophon:

> "Cest livres fu fais en l'an de l'Incarnation
> Nostre Seigneur Jhesu Crist .M.CC. et .LXVIII."

Like *B*, this manuscript is divided into chapters, headed by a rubric in red, covering both columns at the head of the page, in most cases accompanied by a large horizontal miniature likewise covering both columns, placed now at the top, now in the middle of the page, which expresses the same subject as the rubric in pictorial terms. Sometimes there are also isolated "drolerie" figures in the lower margin. The miniatures, eighteen in all, are usually narrative, in other words, the beginning of the scene is depicted on the left, the ending on the right, for example, the rubric (no. 5) which reads "C'est ensi coument li chevaliers au cisne esposa Beatrix se feme, et coument il jut le premiere nuit avueckes li...." has underneath a miniature showing on the left the wedding ceremony and on the right a large four-poster bed containing the newlyweds with the angel descending. The following is a list of these divisions. Comment is only made when the pattern of having a large miniature underneath is not adhered to. Some of the top margins have been cropped resulting in the mutilation of some of the rubrics, which have been reconstructed when the base of the letters is still showing.

1) fol. 1^v; C'est si coument li rois Orians ki fu taions le chevalier au cisne ala cachier en le foriest et coument il s'endormi sor le riu d'une fontaine, et coument .I. demisele le trova dormant ki li mist se main devant sen viaire, por le solel, et puis l'eut il a feme, si comme li livres le devisera.

2) fol. 9^v; C'est ensi con li mere le chevalier au cisne se delivra des .VII. enfans et coument Matabrune li taie les enfans les envoia por noier par Marcon en le foriest.
(This is supported only by a small miniature in col. 2.)

3) fol. 18^v; C'est ensi con Elyas se conbat a Mauquaret por delivrer se mere c'on voloit ardoir, et

                coument il l'ocist en bataille.

4) fol. 27^v;   C'est ensi con li chevaliers le cisne entra ou batiel et que li cisnes l'amena a Nimaie, et qu'il enprist le batail por le veve dame ducoise de Bullon enviers Renier le Sesne de Saissoigne.

5) fol. 35^v;   C'est ensi coument li chevaliers au cisne esposa Beatrix se feme, et coument il jut le premiere nuit avueckes li, et coument Deus i envoia l'angle ki desfendi a la dame k'ille ne li demandast mie sen non. Et puis li demanda ille, dont elle fu mout corcié, si con li livres devisera.

6) fol. 45^v;   C'est ci coument li chevaliers au cisne pierdi se feme et coument li Sesne li tolirent, et coument il le rescoust puis, si coume li livres devisera apries.
(There is no miniature under this rubric.)

7) fol. 55^r;   C'est chi coument li fenme le chevalier au cisne le demanda sen non, par coi ele le pierdi; et puis le revit ele, si con li livres le devisera chi apries.

8) fol. 69^r;   (Top cropped) .../ le revit, puis k'ele l'eut pierdut, si con li livres devisera ci apries.
(The miniature shows the final meeting between Beatrix, Yde and Elyas.)

9) fol. 95^r;   (Top cropped) C'est ci coument Pierres.... .... baron et coument il en alerent, si con li livres devisera.
(The miniature shows Peter the Hermit preaching the "People's Crusade.")

10) fol. 104^v;   C'est ci coument no baron prisent le cité de Nike a force, si con li livres devisera.

11) fol. 113^r;   (Top cropped) C'est /............./ Andioce, si con li livres devisera.
(There is no miniature under this rubric.)

12) fol. 124^v;   (The whole rubric has been cropped. A miniature half way down the page depicts, on the left, the crusaders outside Antioch, and, on the right, one crusader climbing up the ladder into the city, guided by "Dasien" who is holding a lantern.)

13) fol. 133^v;   (Top cropped) .../ (en)tr'aus por issir et aler conbatre a Corberan, si con li livres devisera.
(There is no miniature under this rubric.)

14) fol. 145^r;   (Top cropped) C'est chi coument Corberans

(s'en va... et coument il portoit [Broha-
das] mort que Godefrois ot) ocis en le ba-
taille, si con li livres devisera.

15) fol. 151r; (Top cropped) (C'est ci coument Richars de
Chaumont se conbati as deus Turs pour le
.../ Courbaran, si con li livres devisera
ci apries.

16) fol. 161v; (Top cropped) (C'est ci coument Bauduins
de Biauvais se conbati au serpent ki avoit
son frere mengiet) si con li livres devise-
ra.
(In the bottom margin there is an isolated
figure carrying a sword and shield con-
fronting a dragon monster, now erased.)

17) fol. 167r; C'est chi coument Harpins de Borges res-
caust l'enfant (ms. le senfant) que li sin-
ges enportoit.
(In the bottom margin is the figure of an
archer who has just sent an arrow into a
monster, in the shape of the back of a
horse.)

18) fol. 176v; C'est ci coument Pieres li Iermites sier-
mouna nos crestiens devant Jherusalem, ensi
con li livres devisera.
(In the bottom margin is a monkey riding on
the back of a dragon, thrusting a sword
into its mouth.)[84]

19) fol. 198v; C'est chi li prise de Jherusalem, et cou-
ment Tumas de Marle se fist lever as fiers
des glaves, si con li livres le devisera.
(The corresponding miniature is at the top
of fol. 199r.)

20) fol. 202v; C'est chi coument li rois des Ribaus (ms.
ribibaus) courouna Godefroi de Buillon a
estre roi de Jherusalem, si con li livres
devisera.

21) fol. 235r; C'est ci coument Corbarans se crestiena, et
li doi roi awecques li, ensi con li livres
devisera.

The miniatures, many of which are now very rubbed, are
all executed against a solid gold background. The manu-
script is also decorated with alternate red and blue flour-
ished capitals at the beginning of each laisse and often at
regular intervals in the middle of long laisses, so that an
exceptionally long laisse may contain up to seven flour-
ished initials.

This volume was in the possession of Armand-Gaston,
cardinal de Rohan, in 1749,[85] and the arms of the Rohan-

Soubise family figure on the back of the binding. It was acquired for the Arsenal on the sale of the Soubise library in 1789.

London British Museum MS Royal 15 E VI (H)

This large manuscript, which was copied in England, is composed of several epics and other works, and was presented by John Talbot, first Earl of Shrewsbury, to Margaret of Anjou, probably on her marriage to Henry VI in 1445. The manuscript itself and all its contents have been exhaustively described before, and readers are referred to the following works: *Catalogue of Western Manuscripts in the Old Royal and King's Collections*, by Sir George F. Warner and Julius P. Gilson, 4 vols., Oxford, 1921; vol. II, p. 177-179. *Catalogue of Romances in the Department of Manuscripts in the British Museum*, by H. L. D. Ward, 3 vols., London; vol. I (1883,) p. 487 ff., 496 ff., 598 ff., 604 ff., 615 ff., 622 ff. *The Chevalier au Cygne* is described on pp. 708-710. For a full account of the section containing the *Chevalier*, see the article by Mickel and Nelson in *Romania*, 1971, *loc. cit.*

There are two systems of foliation in this manuscript, whereby the Crusade Cycle material falls between fols. 273 and 292, as in the Catalogue descriptions, or between fols. 320 and 339,[86] which the editors are adopting in this edition.

The manuscript contains three full branches of the cycle; the *Beatrix* version of the *Naissance* (320r col. 1-325r col. 2,) *Chevalier au Cygne* (325v col. 1-332v col. 2,) *Enfances Godefroi* (332v col. 2-336r col. 1,) followed by some fragments of the *Jérusalem* (336r col. 1-339r col. 2).

London British Museum Additional MS 36615 (I)

This manuscript[87] was executed by several scribes working at the end of the thirteenth or beginning of the fourteenth century, possibly in South Normandy.[88] The scribal divisions of the volume are; scribe A, fols. 1-24; scribe B, fols. 25-91, 97-136; scribe C, fols. 137-164; scribe D, fols. 92-96 (this is a separate quire written by D and added in later,) fols. 165-281. Its measurements are 260 x 185 mm. (written space; scribe A, 200 x 145; B, 200-225 x 145-150; C, 225 x 150; D, 225-230 x 140-160 mm.). The manuscript is composed of I modern parchment endleaf + 281 + I modern parchment endleaf, collating: i[8] (the fols. are out of order and should read 1, 2, 5-8, 3, 4,) ii[8]-iii[8] (both missing), iiii[8]-vi[8], vii[10], viii[8]-xii[8], xiii[8] (missing except for 8

which is fol. 83),[89] xiv[8], xv[6] (6 canc. after fol. 96),
xvi[8]-xxiii[8], xxiv[4], xxv[8]-xxvii[8], xxviii[6] (6 canc. after fol.
193), xxix[8]-xxxv[8], xxxvi[10] (1 canc. after fol. 249), xxxvii[8]
(missing), xxxviii[8]-xxxix[8], xxxx[8] (8 missing after fol.
281). This manuscript has a lot missing, but reconstruction
is usually possible thanks to the contemporary foliation,
which is wanting however in the last part because of the
severe cropping of the top edges. Originally the volume
consisted of 313 fols. of text. The majority of quire sig-
natures and catchwords have been preserved. The text is
distributed in two columns of 48-51 lines.

When complete, this was the longest of all the extant
manuscripts, containing some 62,500 lines, nearly 20,000
lines more than *E*,[90] most of it post-*Jérusalem* continua-
tions. What remains is the *Elioxe-Beatrix* composite version
of the *Naissance* (1r col. 1-8v col. 2). It is this branch
which has suffered the severest mutilation. To start with,
fol. 1r is badly stained and totally illegible.[91] It seems
that there was a miniature across the top of both columns,
below which a red capital "S" can be discerned faintly. The
top of 1v col. 1 is also damaged and the first lines at all
visible are:

> "Tient l'emperere cort a Nimaie establie,
>   La furent assanlé...."
>
> > (*Elioxe-Beatrix* Proem, Barron,
> > p. 512, *1*. 55 and Nelson, *Le
> > Chevalier au Cygne*, *1*. 55 and
> > note.)

After fol. 8 (fol. 4 in the present, incorrect, order) there
is a lacuna of two quires which means that the end of the
Naissance and a substantial part of the *Chevalier au Cygne*
are missing. The quire of the former ends with lines pre-
served only in Arsenal 3139 (fol. 11r col. 2) and at this
point in British Museum Additional MS 36615. They are lo-
cated in the text just after *1*. 395 of the present edition.
The catchwords "Les ongles ont agus..." are also visible.
The remains of the *Chevalier au Cygne* run from fol. 9r col.
1-19v col. 1, beginning with the lines,

> "Quant li roys ot mangié aprés li a lavé,
>   On a es coupes d'or novel vin aporté."
>
> > (Nelson, *Chevalier au Cygne*,
> > *1*. 1493.)

There follow, *Fin d'Elias* (19v col. 1-31v col. 1); *Enfances
Godefroi* (31v col. 1-40v col. 2); *Retour de Cornumarant* (40v
col. 2-47r col. 1); *Antioche* (47r col. 1-81r col. 1); *Ché-
tifs* (81r col. 1-101v col. 1). After fol. 82 is a lacuna of
7 fols. (Myers, *Les Chétifs*, *11*. 209-1366)[92] and fol. 83,
which is an isolated leaf and was probably the last of quire

xiii, contains text on recto col. 1 and part of col. 2 which then leads straight into the text on 84r col. 1.   This mysterious procedure of covering part of the last folio of a quire, leaving the rest blank, and then continuing on a fresh quire is found on two other occasions in the manuscript. On fol. 164v scribe C writes only 26 lines of text, which is then continued by scribe D on fol. 165r. This is understandable with a change of scribe, but later, scribe D copies only a few lines on to fol. 193v, leaves the rest blank, and continues on 194r. In the case of a change of scribe this suggests a miscalculation in the allotment of material to be copied. But why scribes should leave blank spaces in the middle of sections they copied themselves seems inexplainable.   The remainder of fol. 83r is filled with a few jottings including the name Jehan Fagot (or Sagot,) and a square of words reading:

s	a	t	o	r
a	r	e	p	o
t	e	n	e	t
o	p	e	r	a
r	o	t	a	s

Fol. 83v contains a "charm against illness, in French prose, beginning: "axci verrament come Dieux fust et serra," and consisting mainly of a paraphrase of the Apostles' Creed."[93] The interesting fact about this is that it is written in a characteristic English hand of the end of the first quarter of the fourteenth century.

The text of *Les Chétifs* ran originally from fol. 91v-97r, as found in all other versions except that of MS *B*; however, scribe D has copied out the "Satanas mere" episode as found in *B*, and arranged for this extra quire to be inserted at this point, making the note at the foot of fol. 91v "quant vous avez commencié a cest seaume (.... the words at the end of the lines of his note are now all covered with parchment,) sy tournez a une crois jusques a une (.....) Et est en la paige mesurés et (quaré ? ....; with the rest of the text cropped), and indeed he has drawn a large cross on fol. 97r, to indicate the spot where this additional episode falls.

The *Jérusalem* runs from fol. 101v col. 1-146r col. 1, followed by the *Chrétienté Corbaran* (146r col. 2-153v col. 1), *Prise d'Acre* (153v col. 1-165r col. 1).   After that *I* ceases to align itself with the version in *E* and continues with the text found in *T* under the name *Cont.*[2] (165r col. 1-281v col. 2).[94] MS *I* is damaged at the end. The last pages are very rubbed, with some parts of the text torn away, and the final folio missing altogether.   The last lines are illegible but *I* and *T* both end at the point where Saladin has made his preparations for the murder of the *mulane*.[95]

On the blank part of fol. 164^v is some advice on a herbal stimulant, written possibly in the same hand as the text on fol. 83^v, beginning: "que home ne se lasse en cheminant prenez (.......?) l'erbe qui est apellé mere dez hardiz (?) ceste a savoir arceneke, et celle herbe mengue....," followed by a nonsense poem of 28 lines, written by a different hand beginning:

"Je chevaucaie mon chemin de Blais a Corpie
Si ancontre li rois et toute sa meingnie...."

As stated above, fol. 1^r was originally decorated with a large miniature, the only one in the manuscript. Initial capitals of each laisse are red and blue alternately, but not flourished, except for two large capitals, one at the beginning of the second part of *Les Chétifs* (84^v col. 2) and one in the middle of *Cont.*[2] (214^r, col. 1).

It was Robert Cook who first drew attention to the composite nature of this volume; ".... il s'agit, selon toute apparence, d'un manuscrit factice, constitué par un bibliophile ou un jongleur dans l'intention de présenter une suite complète de tous les récits épiques de la croisade...." (*Le Deuxième Cycle*, p. 33) Cook's argument implies that the three series of quires (the first, fols. 1-164; second, 165-193; third, 194-281) are assembled somewhat gratuitously, if we have construed correctly the phrase "d'une origine différente," referring to the second group of quires. This volume is certainly the work of several people, but it seems that they were working together with a purpose in mind, and with a fair degree of cohesion, despite certain places where, as illustrated above, the continuity has been unaccountably interrupted. It should be noted that the format of all the component parts is roughly the same, similarly the formula of writing 50 lines to the column. Furthermore the albeit bare decoration of red and blue initials appears to have been carried out by the same artist. What is certain is that the scribes were copying from (at least) two different manuscripts, which would partly explain the highly complex tradition of transmission found in I, which begins close to G, is close to B in the middle of the old nucleus of the First Cycle (eg. *Chétifs*,) follows E in the first two post-*Jérusalem* continuations and ends up reading with T for the rest. This would also possibly explain why the "Satanas mere" episode has been added into *Les Chétifs*; scribe B was using a manuscript which did not have it; scribe D, using one which did, copied it out from his own model.

The margins of this manuscript have been liberally dotted with jottings, some insignificant like "Ego sum bonus puer" (30^v) others of a more interesting nature, consisting

of references throughout the volume to the following
people. "A mon bon ami Colin de Meause de Marconville"
(1^v); "A mon bon ami Jehan de Meause est (... cropped) (2^r);
"Jehan de Meauce," (58^v); "A mon tres chier ami Jehan de
Marcouville" (61^v) and again on 71^v and 76^v; "Marcouville"
(145^r); "Jehan de Meauce" (170^v) and finally "A mon tres
chier amy Guillaume de (muy ?) (267^v).

It is possible that this is a reference to members of
the Meaucé family[96] of Eure-et-Loir. Meaucé itself is situ-
ated 2 kms. N.W. of La Loupe whilst Marcouville lies 5 kms.
E. of Brezolles, the two only 25 kms. apart.[97] This family
appears to have been founded by Guillaume de Meaucé in
1250,[98] and there are traces in 1432 of another Guillaume,
who was supposedly father of a Jehan de Meaucé (traces in
1455). All are noted as being "Ecuyer."[99]

The elaborate modern binding of this manuscript, inlaid
with ivory panels, is described in the catalogue. This vol-
ume was in the collection formed (in a somewhat infamous
manner) by Joseph Barrois, and sold to the Earl of Ashburn-
ham in 1849, (ms. 14 in the Fonds Barrois).[100] It entered
the BM in 1901, being lot 238 in the sale at Sotheby's of
the Earl's library. So far no information is available as
to how Barrois acquired this manuscript.

Oxford Bodleian Library MS Hatton 77 (O)
(Summary Catalogue 4093)

MS Hatton 77[101] was copied in England by a single
scribe in the middle of the thirteenth century, in a hand
which has been described as "typical of the 'professional'
romance scribes of the time."[102] It measures 275 x 155
(205-215 x 85-95) mm. It is composed of I parchment endleaf
+ 197 + II parchment endleaves, collating: i^8-viii^8, ix^8 (7
missing after fol. 140), x^8-xxiii^8, xxiv^4-xxv^8, xxvi^8 (mis-
sing), xxvii^2. This manuscript is paginated 1-393, but
there are three pages numbered 337 in error. Page 393 is
the first of the back endleaves. There are some quire sig-
natures. The text is written on 40 long lines per page.

Pages 1-371 contain a crusade epic of some 15,000 lines
beginning:
    "Seignurs, bien est seü, et n'est pas lungement,
     Estoient cil proisié et servi largement...."
which P. Meyer has named the *Poème de la Première Croisade
imité de Baudri de Bourgueil*. Between pages 14 and 15 two
leaves have been inserted, a fragment of part of the same
poem, which were found forming the endpaper of a printed
book.[103] There is a lacuna of one folio between pages 140
and 141. The epic ends on page 371 with the lines:

"Ore dites tuit amen, qui l'avez escutee,
  Que ja mes par nul home ne sera tels chantee."
Page 372 is blank. From pages 373-392, beginning on a fresh
quire, is a fragment of *Les Chétifs*, opening with the lines:
"Ore s'en fuit Corberans tuz les plains de Surie,
  Sei tierce s'en vait fuiant del regne de Nubie."
Only one quire of eight folios is complete, corresponding to
lines 1-672 and Appendix IV lines 1-13 of our forthcoming
edition,[104] ending on page 388 with the line:
"Tut issi comm en croiz le penerent tirant."
The next quire, xxvi, is missing and the first line of the
last quire (page 389) is:
"Chascon fiert son per sur la targe listee,"
(line 1398 of our edition).[105] The remaining four pages are
very rubbed and difficult to read, and the fragment termi-
nates on page 392 after laisse 51 with a concluding laisse
(which constitutes our Appendix IX) ending:
"Jhesus soit gracié, qui nus ad hors geté
  De la prison as Turcs, et de grant chaitiveté.
  Amen, amen, amen, par sainte charité."
On page 1, at the beginning of the text of the *Poème de
la Première Croisade*, there is a drawing colored in green,
red, and gold, depicting the siege of a tower. Alongside
the text in the left-hand margin is an archer, whilst in the
right-hand margin there is another archer, and two men using
a mechanical sling. The initial capitals of each laisse are
flourished and, with a few omissions, arranged in a sequence
of alternate red and blue within each quire. The manuscript
has been flourished by different hands, the first from page
1-286, with a second, inferior artist taking over from page
287 to the end.[106]
Page 393 is blank, but sewn at the top is a leaf which
contains a fragment of a French description of the 14 cap-
tures of Jerusalem up to 1244 on one side,[107] and a roll of
accounts on the other. On the verso of this endleaf is a
"letter of instruction," which we will print in full, as it
is not without a certain interest.

Soveignez qe mons. Thomas en seillera le feit
qe jeo lui manda par lor ch(artre). Et s'il
n'a point porté le escrits ou lui, et il as-
sent d'en seller le c(artre), pernez la char-
tre et si allez a Johan Amyce, et il vous fra
un austre apres la chartre. Estre ceo vous
poiez dire au dit Thomas qe vous avez despen-
du entour la defence Symond de Swanlond .XII.
souz et plus, pur treis assoignes vous avez
paié .XII. d. pur cest bref q'est venu sur
lui et moy. Ausi vous paiates .XL. deners a

un amy pur le transcrits de la chartre qe
(Hugh) Andreu le Blont avoit, qe parle qe
cest chose est fee taille. Et si le dit
Thomas le vous demande, ne l'en baillez
point, s'il ne vous alouwe .XL. d. Et qe ceo
le remembrez de touz les taillages qe nous
avoms paié, et demandez alouance de lui.
Ausi vous ne voillez paier plus for que
.XXIIII. mars par an pur ces mesons, ausi
come vous lui garnites a la Chandelour, et il
vous promi ces leaument qe nous ne perdroms
point sur lui. Et vous lui poez monstrer
touz les choses qe nous avoms fait et amen-
dez. Et lui monstrez touz les defautes de
ses mesons de covertures, et coment il nous
promyt q'il les voudra tut apparailler de no-
velle a nostre entre. Et come ils costera
(*sic*) grant chatel avant qu'ils seient amen-
dez. Et remembrez vous qe vous em parlez a
Hugh de Waltham et a Roger de Depham et a
Johan de la Chambre et a Johan de Aschefford,
et lur priez q'il voil estre entour cest bu-
soigne pur lur profist.[108]

The provenance of this letter is unquestionably London
and it was written not later than 1327. It would appear to
have been placed in this volume towards the end of the fif-
teenth century when it was rebound. The blind-stamped bind-
ing is English work of about 1480, with a tool showing a
dragon with its tail in its mouth. The layout points to
provincial origin.

Bern Burgerbibliothek MS 627 (*S*)

This manuscript[109] was copied by a single scribe in
northern France towards the middle of the thirteenth centu-
ry. Its dimensions are 185 x 120 (140 x 90) mm. It is com-
posed of IV paper endleaves, (I,II pastedown) + 117 + IV
paper endleaves (III, IV pastedown) and collates: i^8 (1
missing), ii^8-xiv^8, xv^6; a further quire, xvi, announced by
the catchwords "et franchise et" on fol. 117^v, is missing.
This small volume is written on 26 long lines (25 on fols.
88^r-^{v} and 89^r), and at the end of each line, arranged in a
straight line down the page, is a large punctuation mark.
All quire signatures and catchwords have been preserved.

MS *S* contains only two branches of the cycle, starting
with the *Chevalier au Cygne* (1^r-80^r). The opening folio is
missing, and with it the usual introductory laisses with
which it probably began, and it now commences with the

lines:

> "Tint l'empereres cort a Nimaie establie,
> La furent assemblé gens de mainte partie."
>
> Nelson, *Le Chevalier au Cygne*, *l* 55.

The *Enfances Godefroi* runs from fol. 80^v-117^v ending with the lines:

> "Quant Cornemarans oit qu'il ert aseüré,
> Il est venus au duc si l'a araisoné,
> "Sire dux," dit li rois, "or oiés mon pensé;
> Tant ai veü en vous cortoisie et bonté . . . ."
>
> (Hippeau II, p. 130)

How much of the end of the *Enfances* is lost is a matter for conjecture.[110] It is certain that the manuscript never carried any more than these two branches, due to its small format and the very thick parchment on which it is written, because any extension would have made it far too bulky for its size. It probably had one further short quire containing the final laisses of this branch as found in *A*, *F* and *H*.

The initial capitals of each laisse are in red only, and unflourished.

Over the first folio is a sixteenth century rubric, "Roman est Poeme en françois fort vieux" and the shelf-number of a previous owner's collection, "C 7," in black letters.[111] This manuscript was one of several which Claude Fauchet read during the course of his studies, pen in hand; the various characteristic underlinings found in it have been discussed in conjunction with Bern 320 on p. xliv.[112]

This manuscript is the only one apart from Hatton 77 in which isolated branches are found independent of the rest of the cycle. Whether the two branches in *S* are an example of the independent existence of component parts of the cycle prior to their amalgamation, or whether they have been extracted from a manuscript already possessing the combined cycle is a question which can be more readily answered by a study of the manuscript tradition of the version contained here. However, the very handy size of the volume suggests that it falls into that class known as jongleur's manuscripts. In fact the Laon fragment, which contains extracts from the *Antioche* and is written on 32 long lines per page, has also been described as a jongleur's manuscript.[113] Perhaps for the purpose of public declamation jongleurs used manageable small format manuscripts comprising only one or two branches of a given epic cycle at a time. In its entirety *S* would have contained about 6240 lines, while the Laon fragment, if it only contained the *Antioche*, averaging some 8000 lines, would have run to about 120 folios, the same length as *S*.

Turin Biblioteca Nazionale Universitaria MS L-III-25 (*T*)
(*ex G-II-16*)

This manuscript was badly damaged in the fire in the Turin library in 1904. It was not consultable until after 1953, "date à laquelle une restauration partielle a réussi à séparer les pages jusque-là collées ensemble. Mais en 1968, Peter Grillo a vu ce manuscrit et en a remarqué l'importance. Au cours de l'été de 1969, Grillo et Robert Cook ont rétabli la séquence des feuillets du manuscrit."[114]

It is a manuscript copied by a single scribe in the northeast of France towards the end of the thirteenth century, in two columns of 40 lines per page. It is difficult to assess the original size of the manuscript since the folios have shrunk considerably, as well as having some of the borders burnt away, especially the inside one, because the fire attacked from the spine of the binding. The largest extant folio (117) measures 220 x 165 (190 x 135) mm. and from an analysis of those parts of various folios which appear to have remained intact it is possible that the original dimensions were something in the region of 300 x 230 (220 x 170) mm. at least.

We have it on the authority of Pasini's catalogue[115] that the volume had 368 folios. Up till now only 330 have been accounted for.[116] The losses occur throughout the manuscript, but especially at the beginning. It is impossible to reconstruct the original collation as the manuscript is now composed solely of loose leaves tied up in bundles of 50 folios, and placed in two boxes.[117] Any catchwords and quire signatures were burnt away.

Pasini indicates that the manuscript began with the lines:

"Signeurs, or m'entendés, pour Dieu l'esperitable,
Que Jhesus vous garisse de la main au diable."

This is the *Beatrix* version of the *Naissance*,[118] of which only three folios remain, now numbered 1-3.[119] After come the *Chevalier au Cygne* (4-14, 14a, 15-23ᵛ; lacunae at the beginning); *Fin d'Elyas* (23ᵛ-38ᵛ); *Enfances Godefroi* (38ᵛ-47ʳ col. 1; lacunae at the beginning); *Retour de Cornumarant* (47ʳ col. 1-56ʳ col. 2); *Antioche* (56ᵛ col. 1-91ᵛ col. 2; lacunae in the middle); *Chétifs* (91ᵛ col. 2-116ᵛ col. 2); *Jérusalem* (116ᵛ col. 2-175ᵛ col. 2; lacunae at the end [?]). There follows a long continuation, accounting for half of the content of the manuscript, to which the title *Cont.*[2] has been given (176ʳ-329ᵛ).

The manuscript is decorated with alternate red and blue flourished capitals. There are no formal divisions except between the *Retour* and *Antioche*, where space has been left for a large initial which was never executed.

This volume was in the collection of the Dukes of Savoy.[120] It is not certain when it was acquired, but it is possible that this and other manuscripts of northeastern French origin passed into the Dukes' library on the marriage in 1403 between Mary, daughter of Philip the Bold, Duke of Burgundy, with Amadeus VIII of Savoy.[121] The first mention of it is in a handwritten inventory of the (then) Royal Library of Turin by a certain Abbé Maché, dated 1713 (p. 656, no. 23).[122]

Paris Bibliothèque Nationale MS fonds français 781 (P)

This manuscript[123] was copied by a single scribe working in Picardy at the end of the thirteenth or beginning of the fourteenth century. It measures 320 x 230 (255 x 165) mm. and is composed of II modern parchment endleaves (the first a pastedown) + 150 + VI endleaves (I, II modern parchment; III, IV paper (these four leaves numbered 151-154); V, VI modern parchment, VI pastedown); collating: i^8-vii^8, viii^8 (5 and 7 canc. after fols. 60 and 61 respectively), ix^8-xix^8, xx? (missing). Quire signatures and catchwords are clear in i-viii, but have mostly been cropped in ix-xix. The remaining indications show that the First Cycle material was numbered i-viii and that for the rest the scribe began the quiring again from i-ix, as if the latter was considered as a separate item and not as a mere continuation. The text is distributed in two columns of 40 lines.

This manuscript contains a prose redaction of the First Cycle of the Crusade on fols. 1^r-60^v, which can be subdivided into the *Beatrix* version of the *Naissance*,[124] beginning:

> "Seignour, oiés et escoutés, si porrés entendre et
> savoir comment li chevaliers le chisne vint en
> avant, et le grant lignie qui de lui issi . . . ."
>   (fol. 1^r col. 1; Todd, p. 95)

At this point the author of this version explains why he has taken the trouble to turn the cycle into prose:

> "Et l'ai commenchié sans rime pour l'estore avoir
> plus abregié (ms. abregier,) et si me sanle que
> le rime est mout plaisans et mout bele, mais
> mout est longue."
>   (*ibid.*)

The transition from Branch I to Branch II is summarised in one paragraph ending:

> "Atant ist hors du batel et li chisnes s'en va"
>   (fol. 4^r col. 2; Todd, p. 102)

which corresponds to the line quoted above (p. xix):

"Des or s'en va li cisnes s'enmaine son batel."
Le Chevalier au Cygne opens with a new paragraph:
"Che fu a Pentecouste que li roys tint a Nimaie mout
grande court."
(fol. 4^r col. 2)

There is no *Fin d'Elias* and the transition from Branch II-
III and the first laisse of the *Enfances Godefroi* (9^r col.
1-14^r col. 1) are all summarised in the first paragraph of
fol. 9^r col. 1, ending:
"Se fille fist mout bien aprendre et norir tant que
ele eut .XIII. ans. Assés li requist on de mari-
age; ne a nului ne le vaut otrier."

The *Retour de Cornumarant* begins in the first fresh para-
graph on fol. 14^r col. 1:
"Ensi comme Cornumarans et ses compains s'en aloient,
uns chevaliers le sivoit li tierch, que Godefroys
avoit bani de se tere."

This is a reference to Thierri de Louvain, whose treachery
marks the beginning of that episode.

The *Antioche* (16^r col. 1-34^r col. 2) begins with a
summary of the tradition which places the taking of the
Cross by the crusaders at Bouillon:[125]
"Seignour, a le grant feste qui fu a Buillon afie-
rent li baron qu'il prenderoient les crois et qu'il
iront outre mer. Et par cheste maniere furent les
crois prises"

and then, omitting the details on the Crucifixion, like
FEGI, leads straight into Peter the Hermit's pilgrimage to
Jerusalem. *Les Chétifs* (34^v col. 1-43^r col. 2) begins with
the words,
"Chi vous lairai un poi de nos crestiens. Quant
tamps et liex sera, bien y repaierrons. Se vous
dirons de Corbaran d'Oliferne qui s'en fuit des-
confis . . . ."[126]

The *Jérusalem* leads off from *Les Chétifs* in the middle of a
paragraph, with the words,
"Atant se partent no crestien de le Mahommerie.
Et Godefrois se part de l'ost . . . ."
(fol. 43^r col. 2)

and ends on fol. 60^v col. 1 with a summary of the usual
final laisse:
"Chi apres orrés comment Acre et Sur et Tabarie fu
prise et comment li Temples fu estorés et li Hospi-
taus, et comment Harpins de Boorges se donna au
Temple pour nostre Seigneur servir."
Explicit de Godefroi de Buillon.

Fol. 60^v col. 2, fols. 61 and 62 are blank.
Fol. 63^r col. 1-fol. 147^r col. 2 contains the *Chronique*

d'Ernoul (MS *E* of Mas-Latrie's edition) beginning:
>"Oiés et entendés, seigneur, comment le tere de
>Jherusalem et le sainte Crois fu conquise de
>sarrasins sur crestiens"

and ending:
>"Et apres si amassa grant ost et ala encontre le
>roy Jehan et manda sen fil en Alemaigne. Chi fine
>chis estoires, et fait savoir l'incarnation quele
>ele estoit quant Godefroys de Buillon morut."
>(fol. 147ʳ col. 2)

From fol. 147ᵛ col. 1 to fol. 148ʳ col. 1 is the addi-
tion of Bernard le Tresorier (see Mas-Latrie, *loc. cit.*).
From fol. 148ʳ col. 1 to fol. 150ᵛ col. 2 are a number of
anecdotes concerning the Holy Land and Saladin. The first
begins:[127]
>"Atant vous lairai a parler de ces roys et de cheste
>matiere, si vous dirai de le prophesie de le tere
>de Jherusalem et d'Egypte, ensi comme li fix Acap
>le fist en sen livre."
>(fol. 148ʳ col. 1)

Another, concerning Saladin at the Hospital in Acre, begins:
>"Quant je parlai de Salehadin, si vous oubliai a
>dire comment et en quel maniere il vint a Acre et
>jut a l'Ospital."
>(fol. 149ᵛ col. 1)

Finally is the prose *Ordene de Chevalerie* (fol. 150ʳ col.
1-150ᵛ col. 2, which is incomplete in *P* due to the absence
of the last quire) ending:
>"Tout autressi nete devés vous au jour del juise
>rendre l'ame de vous des pechiés que li cors a
>fais et des meffais qu'il a fais envers nostre
>Seigneur, pour avoir le glore de Paradis qui tant
>est deliteuse que langue ne le porroit"

with below, the catchwords "dire ne oreille."

The manuscript contains five single miniatures, all en-
closed in capital letters and with historiated borders run-
ning round three margins, decorated with birds, animals, and
occasional figures (fols. 1ʳ, 34ᵛ, 63ʳ, 147ᵛ, and 150ʳ).
The miniature at the beginning of the *Beatrix* shows the
young mother still lying in childbed with Matabrune behind
her tendering a basket with the seven puppies for Oriant to
see. That at the head of *Les Chétifs* depicts Corbaran and
the kings coming before the Soudan carrying a bier. Each
paragraph begins with alternate red and blue flourished ini-
tials.

The manuscript was rebound at the end of the seven-
teenth or beginning of the eighteenth century while in the
possession of the bibliophile Châtre de Cangé (MS no. 9 in

his collection),[128] who inserted into the endleaves a tran-
scription on paper of the verse *Ordene de Chevalerie* copied
from present MS BN fr. 837. This volume passed from his
collection into the Royal library in 1733.[129]

Some Lost Manuscripts of the First Cycle of the Crusade.

The foregoing verse manuscripts, together with the four
fragments making, all told, a total of sixteen items, albeit
of varying importance, is an impressive record of survival
for a twelfth century *chanson de geste*. However, as Mme
Duparc has pointed out, "les manuscrits du cycle ont été
beaucoup plus nombreux que ceux que nous possédons" (*Le Cy-
cle*, p. 17), and indeed an examination of medieval cata-
logues and inventories bears witness to the great popularity
of the "Roman de Godefroy de Bouillon," or as it is more
rarely named in them, "*Le Chevalier au Cygne.*"[130]

In the catalogue of the library of Charles V,[131] drawn
up by Giles Malet, the royal librarian, in 1373 and in later
revisions there are no fewer than fourteen items which pur-
port to be "Romans," "Livres," "Histoires," or "Chroniques
de Godefroy de Bouillon, de la terre d'oultre mer," or simi-
lar indications.[132] Of these, two verse manuscripts call
for particular attention. One is described as "Godefroi de
Buillon, de la conqueste d'oultre mer, rimé, bien vieil en
papier,"[133] which begins on the second folio: *Et quant li
roys,* and whose first words on the final folio are: *La en
fist son deduit* (1032). We have not been able positively to
identify this manuscript as a version of either the First or
the Second Cycle. The second folio words could be a variant
of lines in the *Beatrix* or *Elioxe*, or of their corresponding
remaniement in the Second Cycle — the exact hemistich does
not occur. The fact that it is written on paper, and the
tone of the phrase *La en fist son deduit* (which we have not
been able to find in the texts), suggest that this is an
early manuscript of the *CCGB*.

About the other item there is no doubt whatsoever. "Un
livre du chevalier au cisgne et de Godefroi de Buillon, de
la terre d'outre mer, en rime," beginning on the second fo-
lio: *Elle a fait contre Dieu,* with first words on the last
folio: *Car moult estoit le jour* (1030). Here, for once, we
have the precious information that it was about "Le Cheva-
lier au Cygne." The second folio words determine this as a
manuscript of the First Cycle and, more precisely, one con-
taining the *Beatrix* version of the *Naissance*, as the hemi-
stich in question is line 220 of the present edition:

"Ele a fait contre Dieu et contre toute jent;
      Ele n'est pas loiaus, pour voir le vous creant."

The fact that the first line of the second folio is as advanced as this, in other words with some 219 lines on the first folio,[134] implies either that the material was greatly abbreviated, or that the manuscript was of a large format, with two columns of 60 lines per side, as found in MS *B*. Allowance can then be made for a first page title and miniature.

We have not been able to identify the words on the last folio. This is always a more difficult task, given that many of the extant manuscripts end at different points of the cycle. The words have not been found as a variant of any of the more regular places chosen to terminate a manuscript, and it may possibly belong to one of the post-*Chrétienté* continuations.

If it has been shown that Charles V had at least one manuscript, now lost, which contained the First Cycle, it can be illustrated also, fortunately with greater precision, that Philip the Good, Duke of Burgundy, possessed two manuscripts of the First Cycle and a fragment of the *CCGB*. One of these is the present MS *A*, and its history has already been described above. The fragment is item 1386 in Barrois' *Bibliothèque Protypographique*, and is clearly concerned with the Second Cycle.[135]

The other manuscript of which there is any trace is the most interesting and the most frequently attested. It first appears in an inventory of 1420, edited by G. Doutrepont,[136] no. 177:

> "Item, ung autre livre nommé GODEFFROY DE BUILLON commençant ou IIe fueillet *Femme ne povoit*, et ou derrenier fueillet *Pour combatre au serpent*, couvert de cuir blanc."

If the identity of this manuscript is obscured in the catalogue of 1467 of the Duke's library in Bruges and of the books in his chapel there (Barrois nos. 706 and 1152 respectively),[137] by being described as *parlant de Lancelot du Lac*, it nevertheless reads on the second folio: *Que feme ne povoit*, and on the last: *Pour combatre au serpent*, and is "un vielz livre en rime, en parchemin, clos d'ais a cuir blanc." This same manuscript, this time correctly identified, reappears in the catalogue of 1487 (Barrois 2088) where we are given the full line *Que feme ne puet a nul enganrement*, and the last line of the manuscript *Que ly Empereurs est mort que le regne a gasté*.

Previous scholars have taken this to be a Second Cycle manuscript, agreeing with A. Bayot's contention that the first line of the second folio is a variant of the *CCGB* line 216. However, in this passage at the beginning of the *Naissance*, in which Beatrix states categorically that any woman

who has more than one child at the same time has certainly
had more than one man, the same sentiment is expressed.
Furthermore, in the *CCGB* the word "engenrement" is not used,
whereas the First Cycle *Beatrix* uses it twice in the same
laisse, *ll*. 68 and 78. We recall that the passage runs as
follows, with Beatrix saying:

> "Ne creroie pas houme en cest siecle vivant
> Que fame puist avoir ensemble c'un enfant,
> S'a .II. houmes n'estoit livree carnelement.
> .I. en puet ele avoir, pour voir le vous creant,
> Ne ja plus n'en ara a .I. engenrement."
>
> (*ll*. 64-68 of the present
> edition)

Yet the line in the lost manuscript is probably not identi-
fiable as a variant of that, because, as will become appar-
ent later, only some 67 lines is too few for the first fo-
lio.[138] Rather it is to be seen as an expansion of the pas-
sage where, later, when Beatrix herself has given birth to
seven children at once, Matabrune throws her words back at
her:

> "Ne vous souvient or pas del fol devisement
> Que vous jurastes Dieu, le Pere tout poisant,
> C'une fenme ne puet avoir c'un seul enfant,
> S'a .II. houmes n'estoit livree carnelement."
>
> (*ll*. 131-134 of the present
> edition)

This would allow for about 132 lines on the first folio.

We are fortunate in being able to identify the end of
this manuscript accurately due to the two indications given
by various cataloguers. The first words of the last folio
Pour combatre au serpent immediately recall *Les Chétifs*,[139]
the only place in the Crusade Cycles where there is any such
fantasy. In fact this hemistich is found twice in the poem,
and the one referred to here (the second time) occurs in
line 3100 of our forthcoming edition.[140] We remember that
Bauduin de Beauvais is up in the Mont de Tigris fighting the
Sathanas. Corbaran goes up after him leading his Turks and
a good force of "Chétifs," but leaving behind the wounded,
in the charge of Richard de Chaumont, to guard the camp.
Meanwhile the Soudan de Perse arrives on the scene with a
vast contingent with the intention of ridding the country of
the beast. The Soudan, seeing that an army is already en-
camped below the mountain, sends scouts on ahead to see if
they are friend or foe. When their respective identities
have been established, Richard informs the Soudan's messen-
gers that Carbaran has gone up into the mountain:

> "Sor le mont de Tigris en est li rois alés,
> .IIII. cens Sarrasins en a o lui menés,

> *Por conbatre al serpent* qui tant est redoutés."
>   (lines 3098-3100.)

At first glance the very last line of the manuscript: *Que ly Empereurs est mort que le regne a gasté* appears wholly out of place here. There is no Emperor in the Crusade Cycle who indulges in such bellicose activities. Apart from that the word "Empereurs" is suspect because it contains too many syllables for the hemistich. What should replace it, surprising as the difference may seem, is the word "serpent," for which it is clearly a misreading. In the manuscript these words must have been abbreviated as they usually are, and a too hasty cataloguer took "s'pēt" for "ēp'eur" or a similar formula. For not only does the Sathanas lay waste the country, but the actual line is attested:

> "La novele est alee par trestot le regné
> *Que li serpens est mors qui le regne a gasté.*"
>   (lines 3268-69)[141]

It is to be noticed that the distance between the two lines in question is 169 lines in *A*, 159 in *C*, 162 in *F* and 161 in *T*. The other manuscripts[142] have a slightly different reading at line 3100 and want lines 3268-69 due to a long omission, whilst *B* interpolates the long "Sathanas mere" episode at this point.[143] The proximity of the distances given above suggests strongly that the lost manuscript itself had the usual number of 160 lines per folio. The fact that the manuscript includes the information that the news of the Sathanas' death spread far and wide places it with the manuscripts containing the oldest version of *Les Chétifs*.[144]

It is probable that at the head of the first folio stood a large miniature covering the top of both columns, like that in *G*, which would account for the figure of 132 lines deduced above.

In conclusion we appear to be dealing with a volume written in two columns of forty lines each per page, which contained a *Beatrix* version of the *Naissance* and which, as early as 1420, ended abruptly three quarters of the way through *Les Chétifs*, of which it contained an "old" version.

It is sad to relate that both of these manuscripts in the Duke of Burgundy's library still appear as late as 1797 in Gérard's catalogue[145] (the Second Cycle fragment is no. 775; the First Cycle manuscript, no. 1005) but that they have both disappeared by 1839, the date of Marchal's inventory, from which they are absent.[146]

We come finally to the library of that ardent sixteenth century bibliophile and pioneer of medieval French scholarship, Claude Fauchet, who has already been mentioned in connection with several of the First Cycle manuscripts. He himself left no details of the vast collection he possessed

and most of what we know about his library has been gleaned
from external evidence. Happily for us he read most of his
books pen in hand and it is usually not difficult to identi-
fy his handwriting or his underlinings, or his special habit
of placing a cross against an item that aroused his curiosi-
ty. We have concluded in previous sections that Fauchet
used, or had access to, MSS *B*, *D*, *F* and *S*. In his works,
Fauchet quotes five times from the First Cycle, three in the
*Recueil de l'origine de la langue et poésie françoise, ryme
et romans*,[147] and two in his treaties on officers of the
royal household. These citations run as follow, arranged in
their order in the Cycle:[148]

(1)   "Li forestier s'en tourne qui ot nom Malaqurrez
                              (read Malquarrez)
        A l'hermitage vint hideux & hurepez."
This is from the beginning of the *Beatrix* and corresponds to
lines 478-479 of this edition.
(2)   "Velus estoit com Leus u Ours enkaiënez,
        Les ongles grans & lons, les cevals meelez,
        La teste hurepee n'ert pas souvent lavez."
which describes Elyas, a little further on, lines 798-800.
The next extract is taken from the end of the *Beatrix*:
(3)   "Les tables ont ostées Sergent et Escuyer."
line 3105. After that comes a couplet from the *Enfances Go-
defroy*:
(4)   "Al départir commande son chambellan Geoffroy
        Qu'il lor donnast cinq sols par le souverain Roy."
which is lines 2600-1 in vol. II of Hippeau. Finally, from
the *Antioche*:
(5)   "La peussiez voir tant viez draps depanez,
        Et tante grande barbe & tant ciez hurepez."
which is lines 445-6 of Chant VIII of P. Paris' edition.

      The manuscript from which these five quotations were
taken was certainly not BN fr. 1621. If the date — 1596 —
on the first folio is the date of acquisition, then Fauchet
only possessed it fifteen years after the *Recueil* was writ-
ten. Added to which, the first two examples are lacking
there because the first quire of this manuscript is missing,
and was when Fauchet owned it. For example (3) *D* reads
"serjant et boteiillier." Given that the purpose of the ex-
ample for Fauchet was the use of the word "escuyer," he must
have had before him a version with that reading. BN fr.
1621 is therefore excluded. Bern 627 is excluded also,
since it contains none of the examples. Nor is Bern 320 a
valid candidate as the model from which Fauchet took his
quotations, because that, too, was mutilated at that time
and anyway does not contain the episode concerning (4) in
the *Enfances*. Nor, finally, are the examples from BN fr.

786, in which the number of variant readings is too great; and since we know that Fauchet did not take any examples from this manuscript for his studies on the *Roman d'Alexandre*,[149] it seems unlikely that he would have used it for the Crusade Cycle.

The only possible conclusion is that Fauchet used another manuscript, which is now lost, as none of the examples correspond exactly to any of the extant manuscripts. Mme Espiner-Scott judges from comparisons of surviving manuscripts and Fauchet's transcriptions of them, that he usually modernised the spelling but remained faithful to the text.[150] However, we think that on this occasion, at least in the case of examples (1), (2) and (5), which are all grouped together in the *Recueil* for the purpose of explaining the word "Hurepez," Fauchet recorded the orthography of his model fairly accurately. In (3) and (4) it is likely that it has been changed, e.g. "chambellan" replacing the medieval "canberlenc" or suchlike, and that the phrase "Que il lor doinst," which is found in the extant manuscripts, has been altered to the more comprehensible "Qu'il lor donnast." If all these lines are from the same manuscript, we can deduce that it contained the *Beatrix* version of the *Naissance*, and that it can be roughly grouped with MSS *BCDEG* as far as the example from the *Enfances* is concerned, the only manuscripts which include this additional material. In fact the manuscript with which the readings concur most, though by no means completely, is BN fr. 12569. The manuscript contained the *Antioche*, from which it can fairly safely be assumed that it continued with *Les Chétifs* and the *Jérusalem*, and, if it is indeed close to *E*, probably some post-*Jérusalem* continuations as well.

We hope that we have, in this brief survey — which does not claim to be a complete review of all medieval and renaissance inventories, far from it! — brought to light and correctly construed some information about three lost manuscripts of the First Cycle of the Crusade. Without a doubt there were many more still.[151]

Geoffrey M. Myers

1. Paulin Paris considered various aspects of the Crusade Cycle in several studies: 1) *Histoire Littéraire de la France*, vols. xxii and xxv; especially pp. 350-402, vol. xxii, 1895. 2) *Les Manuscrits français de la Bibliothèque du Roy*, vol. 6, pp. 168 ff. 3) Introduction to his edition of *La Chanson d'Antioche* (Paris: Techener, 1868). 4) "Nouvelles études sur la Chanson d'Antioche," *Bulletin du Bibliophile et du Bibliothécaire*, 1877, pp. 433-59 and 1878, pp. 97-121.

2. See bibliography for contributions by E. Stengel, P. Paris, H. Pigeonneau, G. Paris, H. A. Smith, M. Einstein, H. A. Todd, A.-G. Krüger, and S. Duparc-Quioc.

3. This discussion applies to the entire cycle and should not be confused with W. R. J. Barron's somewhat similar terminology in his discussion of the *Naissance*. It should be noted that of the Prose MSS Paris, BN 781 provides an abbreviated version of the cyclical form and Kopenhagen, Thott 416, an abbreviated version of the consolidated form. There also exists a full length Latin prose redaction of the *Beatrix*, Oxford, Bodleian Library: Rawlinson Misc. 358. It has been edited by Baron de Reiffenberg, *Le Chevalier au Cygne et Godefroid de Bouillon*, vol. I (Brussels, 1846), pp. 181-205. The Spanish *Gran Conquista*, which is derived from a lost cyclical redaction, is mentioned below in the discussion of the various versions of the *Naissance*.

4. See note 1, above. An excellent recent summary of the *Ur-Antioche* question is provided by R. F. Cook and L. S. Crist in *Le Deuxième Cycle de la Croisade*, p. 79 and note 12 of the same page.

5. William of Tyre, *Historia Rerum in Partibus Transmarinis Gestarum*, Book IX, Chapter 6. The author refers to the supposed relationship of Godefroy to the Swan Knight: Praeterimus denique, cygni fabulam, unde vulgo dicitur sementivam eis fuisse originem eo quod a vero videatur deficere talis assertio. . . . It has been suggested that this book was written not later than 1173. Gui de

Bazoches also makes reference to the relationship of the House of Bouillon to the Swan Knight in a letter probably written between 1175-1180. See Robert Jaffray, *The Two Knights of the Swan* (New York, 1910), pp. 3-5.

6. Only manuscripts associated with the cyclical form are taken into account by Table II. Thus, BN 781 is included and Kopenhagen, Thott 416 is excluded.

7. The four fragments mentioned by Krüger are: a fragment found by F. J. Mone, published in *Anzeiger für Kunde der deutschen Vorzeit*, 4 (1835), 80 f., reprinted by W. Foerster, *Der Karrenritter und das Wilhelmsleben*, (Halle, 1899); p. clxxii, note 1, and identified as part of the *Enfances Godefroi* by G. Paris in *Romania*, 29 (1900), 106; a fragment of 319 lines of the *Jérusalem* in the Bodleian Library, Douce 381, edited by S. Duparc-Quioc at the end of her article "Les Manuscrits de la *Conquête de Jérusalem*," *Romania*, 65 (1939), 183-203. Two fragments, probably from the same manuscript, one containing 112 lines of the *Enfances*, the other 135 lines of *Antioche* were described and edited by A. Jeanroy, *Revue des Langues Romanes*, 42 (1899), 489-99, and the "Laon Fragment" which contains an extract from the *Antioche*, was identified and printed by R. Bossuat, *Neuphilologische Mitteilungen*, 32 (1931), 110-118. All these fragments will be evaluated in the relevant editions.

8. See below, p. lx.

9. "Versions and Texts of the *Naissance du Chevalier au Cygne*," *Romania*, 89 (1968), 481-538.

10. "BM Royal 15 E VI and the Epic Cycle of the First Crusade," *Romania*, 92 (1971), 532-556.

11. MS *G* marks its abbreviated transition by a rubric and a miniature on fol. 27^v.

12. The beginning of the *Fin d'Elias* is missing in *F*.

13. It is not possible to discuss all the problems related to this particular articulation at this juncture. A detailed description has already been given by the editors in the study of MS. BM Royal 15 E VI, p. 546 ff., where there is a similar table; it is a subject to which they will return in forthcoming volumes of the Cycle.

14. Except for *T* which omits the laisse in "-ee" the second time round.

15. MSS *EGI* omit the first 14 laisses of the *Antioche*, effectively using the previous laisse in "-ee" to introduce this branch. MS *T* omits the first laisse in "-er" and begins with the second, in "-ier."

16. Strictly speaking, the scribe of *T* has left a space for a large capital which was never executed.

17. MS *C* fol. 198r col. 1; *G* fol. 176v.

18. Mme Duparc suggests that the *Jérusalem* should begin at the point where the "Chétifs" leave Oliferne (*Le Cycle*, p. 18). We prefer to retain the section describing their journey to Jerusalem, in which they are the sole Christian protagonists as part of *Les Chétifs*. Paul Meyer's criticism of Hippeau's choice of beginning for the *Jérusalem* (*compte-rendu* of Hippeau's edition in *Bibl. de l'Ec. des Chartes*, 31(1870), 227-231) is invalid on the grounds that he never appreciated the distinctions created by P. Paris of *Antioche-Chétifs-Jérusalem* and prefers to call this nucleus the *Chanson de Jérusalem*, as is clear when he describes the *Chétifs* fragment in *O* as part of the *Jérusalem*. Ideally these three branches should be edited together *d'un seul trait*.

19. These continuations were the last parts of the cycle to be named and to attract scholars' attention. Originally they were just catalogued as part of the *Jérusalem*. The gradual breaking down of the continuations into branches was started by H. Pigeonneau, *Le Cycle de la Croisade et la famille de Bouillon* (Saint-Cloud, 1877), p. 196 ff., continued by E. Roy in "Les Poèmes français relatifs à la première croisade: Le Poème de 1356 et ses sources," *Romania*, 55 (1929), 411-468, and completed by A. Hatem, *Les Poèmes épiques des croisades: genèse, historicité, localisation* (Paris, 1932), p. 116. Cf. also R. F. Cook et L. S. Crist, *Le Deuxième Cycle de la Croisade* (Geneva, 1972), pp. 80-81. As stated, these titles only hold good for *EG*. The amended titles and the term *Cont.*[2] for much of the material in *IT* are those suggested by Professor Peter F. Grillo, their present editor, who has kindly communicated to us the results of his most recent evaluation. He himself will be elucidating the complexities of the problem in his own editions (volumes VII and VIII of the Cycle). In the meantime we have taken the liberty to adapt some of his phraseology for use in the above paragraph.

20. Albinia de la Mare, *Catalogue of the Collection of Medieval Manuscripts Bequeathed to the Bodleian Library,*

Oxford, by James P. R. Lyell (Oxford, 1971); form of Catalogue Entry, pp. xxx-xxxiii. We have preferred the use of Roman numerals in describing the collation. Endleaves have not been included in the collation.

21. The following works are the principal descriptions of the ensemble of manuscripts. References to articles on individual manuscripts will be found in the relevant section. Le Roux de Lincy, "Analyse du Roman de *Gode-froi de Bouillon*," *Bibliothèque de l'Ecole des Chartes*, 2(1840), 441-444. He considers five manuscripts. P. Paris describes three manuscripts of the Royal collection at length in *Les Manuscrits françois de la Bibliothèque du Roi*, 7 vols. (Paris, 1836-1848); vol. VI. In his edition of the *Chanson d'Antioche*, he describes the six Paris verse manuscripts in a section entitled "Indication des Manuscrits," vol. 1, p. lxvii-lxx. Up to this time the MSS are found under their old catalogue number; BN fr. 781 (ex 7188[5]); 786 (ex 7190); 795 (ex 7192); 1621 (ex 7628); 12558 (ex Ancien Supplément 540[8] [1]); 12569 (ex Anc. Suppl. 105); Arsenal 3139 (ex Belles-Lettres 165). H. Omont, *Catalogue des manuscrits français*, 5 vols. (Paris, 1868-1902); vol. I. H. Omont, *Catalogue de l'ancien supplément français*, 3 vols. (Paris, 1895-1896); vol. II. A. Hatem includes a description of the six Paris verse MSS, pp. 87-116. S. Duparc-Quioc studies the MSS relating to the *Jérusalem*, *Romania*, 65(1939), 183-203. This article reappears in substantially the same form in her *Le Cycle de la Croisade* (Paris, 1955), pp. 9-17. References to the later work only are given. L. A. M. Sumberg describes eight manuscripts in *La Chanson d'Antioche* (Paris, 1968), pp. 32-138. (Unfortunately this is a work which has to be treated with considerable caution.) Other scholars, H. Pigeonneau (p. 9) and M. Einstein ("Beiträge zur Ueberlieferung des *Chevalier au Cygne* und der *Enfances Godefroy*," *Romanische Forschungen*, 30(1911), 725-727,) have also mentioned the manuscripts, but since these works are largely based on that of their predecessors and do not contribute anything original to the study of the MSS, references to them will not normally be given.

22. *Paris and Oxford University Manuscripts of the Thirteenth Century*, unpublished B. Litt. thesis deposited in the Bodleian Library (1970). (MS B. Litt. d. 1457) See also the same author's "Comparison of Minor Initial Decoration: a Possible Method of Showing the Place of Origin of Thirteenth-century Manuscripts," *The Library*,

27(1972), 23-30. Unfortunately Mrs. Patterson's the-
sis appears to be as yet the sole work in the field of
flourishing in the thirteenth century, and because she
restricts herself to Oxford and Paris University MSS it
can only be taken as a rough guide to the type of
flourishing in other MSS. Most useful is the "Cata-
logue of Components of Decoration" drawn up in the sec-
ond part of the thesis, and the comparison between
English and French flourishing on p. 127, plate XLIII.
It is to be hoped that more work can be done in this
hitherto neglected field of manuscript decoration and
that the results will be published.

23. For previous descriptions see: L. de Lincy, p. 443; P.
Paris, *Ant.*, vol. I, p. lxviii; Omont, *Anc. Suppl.* vol.
II, p. 558; Hatem, p. 87-97; Duparc-Quioc, *Le Cycle*,
pp. 10-11; Sumberg, pp. 61-85.

24. This MS has been dated variously from the beginning of
the thirteenth century to the middle of the fourteenth.
The latter date, given in Omont's *Anc. Suppl.*, has per-
sisted unchallenged until now. Mme Duparc, who origi-
nally supported the late date, has told us that she has
since changed her opinion on the dating of *A* and now
places it in the second half of the thirteenth century.
Certainly, the writing, the somewhat primitive minia-
tures, more especially the style of the faces and hair,
together with the very neatly executed flourishes,
point to the middle of the second half of that century.
On the other hand, the last five folios, written in a
slightly forward-sloping hand, with loosely, hastily
drawn flourishes in red and brown are characteristic of
the mid-fourteenth century. The variant in the name of
the *remanieur* of the *Antioche*, Graindor de *Dijon* for
Douai (fol. 59r col. 1), has been usually taken as a
sign that *A* is a "Burgundian version" of the Cycle.
However, *A* contains all the features common to Picard
although diluted to a great extent with francien forms.
But because it does not exhibit regularly the features
characteristic of the N.E. Picard region, as found in *B*
and *G* (q.v.) it should probably be placed in the S.W.
area, as defined by C. T. Gossen, *Grammaire de l'ancien
picard* (Paris, 1970), p. 147.

25. Corresponding to the first XIV laisses of Chant Qua-
trième of P. Paris, *Ant.*, vol. I.

26. The first scribe ends on fol. 187v col. 2. Fols. 188-
193 are a different parchment from the rest of the MS,
whiter and thinner. It seems certain that the second

scribe has transcribed the end of the poem from a dam-
aged original, probably embellishing it a little, and
inserted his six folios into the remains of the extant
24th quire, of which fol. 187 and the corresponding
stub, which is still visible after fol. 193, consti-
tuted the outside bifolium.

27. The claim that the second scribe, if he was copying the
original, made embellishments is based on the fact that
the final laisse, although the same in essence, is not
the same in detail as that of *A*'s closest neighbours in
the *Jérusalem*, *C* and *D*, or, indeed all the other MSS
which include this laisse. For example there is no
reference to the "moniage" traditionally attributed to
Harpin de Bourges found elsewhere — "Al Temple pour
servir fu Harpins adonés" — and the three last lines
quoted above are unique to *A*. This seems the only ex-
planation of why *A*, so reliable a base for the majority
of the Cycle, differs so widely in this laisse, where
most other MSS concur.

28. Although the characteristic French components, the
Hair-pin and Hair-pin Prolonged (Mrs. Patterson's "H"
and "HP") feature at the top of the design, the cor-
responding English one, the Open loop "A," especially
surmounting a Long-stalked bulb "B" is predominant.
The same goes for the flourish at the bottom, where the
components "B" and "A" are far more common than the
corresponding French Long flourish "E." On the other
hand the predominantly French component, the Cat's paw
"D," is found in abundance.

29. For a fuller description of this miniature, see Mickel
and Nelson *op. cit.* p. 540.

30. Sumberg (p. 62) hints at a relationship between this
"maistre" and one mentioned in the *Antioche*, but fails
to take into account that the jotting was written by a
different scribe, in the fifteenth century.

31. See J. Pot, *Histoire de Regnier Pot* (Paris, 1929).

32. The life of this statesman is found in H. A. Simpson,
Simpson and Allied Families, 2 vols.; vol. II, *Philippe
Pot Grand Seneschal of Burgundy* (Somerville, N.J., 1935).
Both of these Pots had the spirit of the Crusade at
heart. Regnier accompanied John the Fearless (then
John of Nevers) on the ill-fated Crusade of 1396, and
was held prisoner by Bajazet (J. Pot, p. 43 ff.). Phi-
lippe, if he never actually participated in a Crusade,
at least pledged his support, with a display of some-

what rash enthusiasm, for the one Philip the Good proposed at the Banquet of the Pheasant in 1454, described by R. Vaughan, *Philip the Good* (London, 1970), p. 298.

33. The origin of the motto "Tant L Vault" is discussed by J. Pot, p. 53. For "A la Belle," see the same page, note 1.

34. R. Vaughan, p. 278 ff.

35. Joseph Barrois, *Bibliothèque Protypographique* (Paris, 1830). Cf. R. F. Cook in *Le Deuxième Cycle*, p. 40, note 91.

36. Antonius Sanderus, *Bibliotheca Belgica Manuscripta*, Insulis (Lille), 2 vols. 1641; vol. II no. 222. The manuscript is also mentioned in the handwritten catalogue drawn up by the librarian Viglius in 1577. A concordance of all these catalogues, together with that of Barrois, is found in Fr. J. Marchal, *Catalogue des manuscrits de la Bibliothèque Royale des Ducs de Bourgogne*, 3 vols. (Brussels, 1842); vol. I, p. ccliv.

37. Ed. in Marchal, *loc. cit.*

38. Presumably it entered the BN after the early 1740's, the time of the formation of the "Ancien Supplément Français," in which this MS bore the number 540^8 (1).

39. For previous descriptions see: P. Paris, *Les Manuscrits*, vol. VI, pp. 165-200; Omont, *Catalogue*, vol. I, p. 81; P. Meyer, *Romania*, 11(1882), 264; Hatem, pp. 102-106; Duparc-Quioc, *Le Cycle*, p. 12; Sumberg, pp. 33-48.

40. Tournai calendars are described by Abbé V. Leroquais, *Les Bréviaires manuscrits des bibliothèques publiques de France*, 6 vols. (Paris, 1934), vol. I, p. 199; vol. II, pp. 66, 158, 162; vol. IV, p. 281, and the same scholar's *Les Psautiers manuscrits latins des bibliothèques publiques de France*, 3 vols. (Macon, 1940), vol. I, pp. 189, 220, 230.

41. P. Paris expresses some surprise at seeing someone digging in a miniature for March. However, numerous examples are attested in Leroquais' *Les Livres d'heures manuscrits de la Bibliothèque Nationale*, 3 vols. (Paris, 1927). (See the references for March in the index.) The picture for June poses more of a problem. We have not found any examples of anyone carrying anything, except hay, in June. It seems as if this illustration is out of season. If the man is carrying

"échalas pour vignes," as Paris suggests, then March is the month traditionally reserved for this activity. If it is meant to be a large bundle of faggots, then an autumn month would be more timely. The miniature for November is a combination of two scenes usually given independent treatment, namely the "élevage des porcs" and "la glandée." The activity for December is clearly the popular "enfournement du pain." The round objects in the foreground are loaves of bread, not horseshoes, as Paris conjectures. There are no examples in Leroquais of the shoeing of horses depicted as a seasonal occupation.

42. A more detailed account of the *Roman d'Alexandre* contained in this MS is found in P. Meyer, *op. cit.*, pp. 214-19 and 264, and also in D. J. A. Ross, *Alexander Historiatus*, The Warburg Institute Surveys 1, (London, 1963), pp. 10-14. The text of *B* has been edited by H. Michelant, *Le Roman d'Alexandre* (Stuttgart, 1846).

43. P. Paris gives a summary list of all the rubrics in the manuscript, relating to the *Alexandre*, pp. 166-68, and in the Crusade Cycle, pp. 196-200. Sumberg gives those concerning the *Antioche*, pp. 34-35.

44. This rubric and miniature at the beginning of the *Chevalier* is really out of place. It depends on the first few lines of the branch which look forward to the Crusade.

45. H. A. Smith has examined this episode in detail in "Studies in the Epic Poem *Godefroi de Bouillon*," *PMLA*, 27(1912), 142 ff.

46. MS BN fr. 5585; ed. in H. Omont, *Anciens Inventaires de la Bibliothèque Nationale*, 5 vols. (Paris, 1908-1921); vol. I, p. 386.

47. *op. cit.*, p. 264.

48. For other references to Claude Fauchet, see also the descriptions of *D*, *F*, *S*, and the section on lost manuscripts, pp. lxiii-lxv.

49. There is a list in J. G. Espiner-Scott, "La Bibliothèque de Claude Fauchet," *Documents concernant la vie et les oeuvres de Claude Fauchet* (Paris, 1938), pp. 205-13. Although Fauchet had access to this MS, he did not use it for quotations in his works concerning his studies of the *Roman d'Alexandre*. See Mme Espiner-Scott, *Claude Fauchet, sa vie, son oeuvre* (Paris, 1938), p. 165, note 4.

50. Omont, *Inventaires*, vol. III, p. 13.

51. *ibid.*, vol. I.

52. See also de Lincy, p. 443; P. Paris, *Les Manuscrits*, vol. VI, pp. 221-28; Omont, *Catalogue*, vol. I, p. 83; Hatem, pp. 106-08; Duparc-Quioc, *Le Cycle*, p. 11; Sumberg, pp. 85-95.

53. For a description of these additions, see P. Paris, *op. cit.*, p. 221 ff., and P. Meyer in "Les Saluts d'Amour," *Bibliothèque de l'Ecole des Chartes*, 6e série, 3 (1867), 139.

54. Note that this quire originally had 12 folios, of which the first and the fifth, presumably blank, were cut out.

55. P. Meyer gives the full text of this piece in the article mentioned above, pp. 139-45.

56. Ed. P. Ruelle, *Les Dits de Droit du Clerc de Voudroi* (Brussels, 1969). See esp. p. 15.

57. *op. cit.*, pp. 520-21.

58. It follows from our argument that the person who thought that the manuscript was deficient and arranged to make good the lacuna was none other than the third scribe, C; witness the fact that the addition is in his hand.

59. Possibly the three short pieces noted above were intended to form part of a "recueil" similar to that found in BN fr. 25566 — the sole MS of the *Jeu de Saint Nicholas*.

60. A simple experiment with pieces of paper is sufficient to demonstrate that this claim is perfectly possible.

61. Presumably it is the Turkish army, since the knights are carrying round "targes," which usually distinguishes them from the Christians. Many of these stereotyped battle scenes do not really reflect one particular event, but are merely expressions of military operations generally.

62. Despite the fact that at the beginning of *Les Chétifs* it clearly states that he fled with only two others!

63. It is not in Dupuy's 1645 catalogue, but is in the inventory of Nicholas Clément in 1682, ed. in Omont, *Inventaires*, vol. VI (ancien, 7192).

64. Cf. de Lincy, pp. 441-42; P. Paris, *Ant.*, I, lxviii; Hatem, pp. 97-102; Duparc-Quioc, *Le Cycle*, p. 9; Sumberg, pp. 49-60. All scholars agree with Leroux de Lincy's statement that this manuscript was "exécuté vers l'année 1250." It is certainly one of the earliest manuscripts of the cycle, together with Hatton 77 and Bern 627.

65. It is possible to decipher the cryptic note: "de normendie .xix. 1. .ix. s. ix. d." at the bottom of the text in col. 1, and the inscription: "tiengz tes filles trop mielx (...?) que jou abreames ne (penes ?) say leur apenre byau (manieres ?) Et pour oyseuze ne les tieng." It seems from this that the manuscript was still circulating in Picardy, to judge by the language, in the fifteenth century.

66. The repertoire of components of the second flourisher is less varied than that of his predecessor, and his lines are much thicker. His designs are characterised by frequent use of serrated components, totally absent from the work of the first flourisher, of the sort found, for example, in the Infilling Components 2, 2h, in Mrs. Patterson's "Components of Decoration," p. iii.

67. The mention of Philippe Auguste's crusade in the title is traditionally interpreted as a reflection of the passage from the *Enfances Godefroi*, unique to this manuscript, in which Calabre predicts the Third Crusade under the French king. (This whole episode of Calabre's prophecy has been studied by L. S. Crist in *Le Deuxième Cycle*, pp. 114-19. The laisse in question is edited in an appendix, p. 176, laisse VI.) However, since this reference to Philippe Auguste is not found in any other MS, there is no reason to suppose that the cycle was written after 1191, as implied by the rubric. It shows rather that a well informed jongleur or scribe associated with the tradition of *D* is not the scribe of the MS himself, and has taken Calabre's prophecy as an opportunity to display his erudition and to bring his version "up to date." On the contrary, lack of any mention of Philippe Auguste in the other MSS implies that the cycle was composed before his crusade.

68. We are inclined to take this as the date of acquisition. At all events he did not use this MS for quotations concerning the First Cycle in his works. (For references and argument, see p. lxiv.) But it is possible that the MS was one of the few that remained after the pillaging of his substantial library by the forces of

the Duke of Mayenne in 1591 (cf. J. G. Espiner-Scott, *Claude Fauchet*, p. 86; *Documents*, p. 87) on which he then put his name and the date as a sure means of identification lest a similar catastrophe should overtake him again, given the instability of the times; for it seems that despite his appeals very few of his MSS were ever returned to him.

69. Omont, *Inventaires*, vol. IV, p. 288.

70. Previous descriptions: P. Paris, *Ant.*, I, p. lxx; Omont, *Anc. Suppl.*, II, p. 562; Hatem, pp. 112-16, Duparc-Quioc, *Le Cycle*, p. 13; J. Porcher, *Les Manuscrits à peintures en France* (The catalogue of an exhibition of illustrated MSS held in the BN in 1955). Part II "*du XIIIe au XVIe*" (Paris, 1955), p. 32 (no. 59); Sumberg, pp. 103-14. Porcher dates MS *E* "vers 1270," whilst Sumberg suggests "vers 1275" as a rough date on the strength of a mention of "Julien Cesaire," pp. 103, 109.

71. Ed. G. Paris, *Romania*, 17 (1888), 104-05. He identified these "rommans" as the history of "*Orose*," *Marques de Rome*, *Anseïs de Carthage*, *Auberi le Bourguignon*, *Lancelot du Lac*, *Garin le Loherain*, *Partonopeus de Blois*, *Le Somme le Roi*, and "Le Chevalier qui ala en Enfer," which Paris takes as "le chevalier "Owen" qui descendit . . . dans le "puits saint Patrice". . . (p. 105.)

72. Sumberg claims that this may be the jongleur. In view of the fact that he states that the manuscript was intended for reading — and in addition the fact that the hand is fourteenth century — this seems improbable.

73. Ed. in *Recueil des historiens des Croisades* (Occidentaux), vol. I. The texts of the notes are as follows. We have considered it worth while printing the version of William of Tyre alongside no. 5 to illustrate the similarity.
    1) (fol. 94v) La cites de Nique fut prise par les barons dessus dis en l'ancarnacion (*sic*) nostre Seigneur Jhesu Crist mil et quatre vins et .XVII. ans, el mois de juign, le .XX.e jour del mois. (William of Tyre, p. 128)
    2) (fol. 115r) La cites d'Antioche fut prise l'an mil .IIII.XX. et .XVIII., el mois de juign, le tiers jour du dit mois. (William of Tyre, p. 233)
    3) (fol. 133r) La desconfiture que firent ly crestien dessus dis de Corbaran, roy d'Oliferne, devant Antioche fut faite l'an mil .IIII.XX. et .XVIII. el mois

de juign, le .XVIIIe jour du dit mois. (William of Tyre, p. 273)

4) (fol. 157^v) En l'an de l'Incarnation Jhesu Crist mil et quatre vins et .XIX., el mois de juign, le .VIIe jour del mois fut logiés ly os de la crestienté devant la cité de Jerusalem. (William of Tyre, p. 329)

5) (fol. 185^r) La seinte cites de Jerusalem fu prise en l'an de l'Incarnation Jhesu Crist mil et quatre vins et dis et neuf el mois de juingnet le quinsieme jour del dit mois a ung samedy entour eure de nonne, le tierc an puisque ly pelerin avoient enprise cele voie. Lors estoit de Rome apostoiles Urbains li secons, et empereres des Romans Henris, rois de France (ms. et) Phelippes, empereres de Constantinoble Alexis.

. . . . . . fu prise la seinte citez de Jerusalem en l'an de l'Incarnacion Jesucrist .M. et .IIII.XX. et .XIX. el mois de juingnet, le .XV.iesme jor del mois a un vendredi a eure de none, le tierz an puisque li pelerin avoient emprise cele voie. Lors estoit apostoiles de Rome Urbainz li segonz, empereres des Romeins Henris, rois de France Felipes, empereres de Constantinoble Alexis . . . . (William of Tyre, p. 361)

6) (fol. 239^r) Godefroy de Buillon, roy de Jerusalem trespaca le dis et huitieme jour de juing l'an .M. et .C. Enterrés fu en l'eglise del Sepulcre (puis ?) le lieu de monte Calvaire u notres Sires fu mis en la crois. Dieux ait l'ame de luy. (The month should read "juingnet," July. William of Tyre, p. 399.) As far as no. 5 is concerned, the day on which Jerusalem fell was Friday, not Saturday. There are two traditions concerning the exact time. Some MSS read "*entour* eure de nonne" as in the annotation, others "*a* eure de none" as in the printed edition.

74. Previous descriptions: H. Hagen, *Catalogus Codicum Bernensium* (Bern, 1875); M. Einstein, p. 72; Duparc-Quioc, *Le Cycle*, pp. 14-15; Sumberg, pp. 120-31; P. Grillo, quoted in Cook et Crist, *Le Deuxième Cycle*, p. 80, note 14.

75. Mme Duparc believes that it did; *Le Cycle*, p. 15. We are inclined against this view on the grounds that an "annonce" in a text is no guarantee of the existence of the material announced. The most developed "annonce" of the *Chrétienté Corbaran* is in *A* fol. 129^r col. 2 and fol. 135^v col. 2 (this one unique to *A*). Since *A* is the oldest version of the cycle, it is the least likely to have continuations, and indeed does not. All the MSS contain the first "annonce" whether they have the *Chrétienté* or not.

76. A comparison with the other MSS shows that this odd folio 77 must have come very near the end of quire xvii or beginning of quire xviii. There are no quire signature or catchwords on it, so it is probably the first of quire xviii.

77. He was the editor of many of the Latin chronicles of the Crusades, some of which, e.g. Jacques de Vitry, are still only available in this early edition: *Gesta Dei per Francos sive Orientalium Expeditionum et Regni Francorum Hierosolimitani Historia* (Hannover, 1611).

78. Fauchet's interest lies particularly in customs, the structure of medieval society, the names of characters and places, armor and weaponry. See Espiner-Scott, *Claude Fauchet*, p. 323 ff.

79. The line *Pain beneoit lor donne et vin sacré pour boire* is in *F* 13^r col. 1, *S* 19^v; the names of characters, *Aynors d'Espine, Joserans li fiers, Mirabaus de Taburs, Foucars de Riniers, Segars de Monbrin*, *F* 14^r col. 1, *S* 28r/v; medieval offices, "le *chastellain* Guion," *S* 93^v, *F* 17^v col. 2; the celebrated line from the *Enfances*: "Que j'ai sous *mon mantel un duc, un conte, un roi*," in *S* 91^r, *F* 17^r col. 1. Further common underlinings: "*Ses elmes fu perciés*," *S* 98^r, *F* 19^r col. 1; "*et l'onor de Boilon*," *S* 100r, *F* 19^v col. 2; *et passim*. On *F* 13^r col. 1, we also find "*cambrelains*," (cf. quotation [4] p. cxiv.)

80. MSS Bern 163, 309, 340, 451.

81. Previous descriptions: L. de Lincy, p. 444; P. Paris, *Ant.*, I, p. lxix; H. Martin, *Catalogue des manuscrits de la Bibliothèque de l'Arsenal*, 9 vols.; vol. III

(Paris, 1887), 254. Hatem, pp. 108-112; Duparc-Quioc, *Le Cycle*, p. 13; Sumberg, pp. 95-103.

82. The provenance of MS *G* has been determined by the prevalence of the very strong north-eastern Picard/Walloon feature of the diphthongisation of blocked tonic open "e," e.g. "apries" (cf. Gossen, p. 59). He claims that this is characteristic of the Lille, Tournai, Mons, Douai area. MS *B*, from Tournai, also exhibits this feature, but to a lesser extent.

83. The transitional laisse in "-ee" between the *Retour* and the *Antioche* has been taken as marking the beginning of the latter branch. See p. xxi above.

84. This miniature has been described in detail in H. Martin et Ph. Lauer, *Les Principaux Manuscrits à peintures de la Bibliothèque de l'Arsenal* (Paris, 1929); p. 16, and reproduced, Pl. X.

85. See BN, MS Nouvelles Acquisitions françaises, 3203 (t. XX), fol. 145. We are indebted to Peter Grillo for this reference.

86. This latter system is the original medieval one. It has been used by Duparc-Quioc, *Le Cycle*, p. 16; Barron, and Mickel and Nelson.

87. See H. L. D. Ward, *Catalogue of Additions to the Manuscripts in the British Museum in the years 1900-1905* (London, 1907), pp. 157-159. Also Cook et Crist, *Le Deuxième Cycle*, p. 32 f.; 89 f.

88. The marked Picard forms and orthography found in the majority of MSS are absent from *I*. The French is standard, but scribe B, and occasionally C, constantly interchanges the graphies "s" and "c," and employs the form "a" for "au/al"; e.g.: "chevachier," "saver," (cf. Gossen, p. 115) found rarely in Picard but often in Norman texts. See also the discussion of "Jehan de Meauce," p. lii.

89. See below for explanation of this isolated leaf.

90. Cf. Cook et Crist, p. 81.

91. Barron has examined the beginning of *I* in detail, pp. 494-95.

92. MS *A*, fol. 115^V col. 1-121^V col. 1.

93. *Catalogue of Additions*, p. 158.

94. See Cook et Crist, p. 89.

95. Cook et Crist, p. 90.

96. We are indebted to Peter Grillo for this suggestion.

97. See L. Merlet, ed. *Dictionnaire Topographique du Département d'Eure-et-Loir* (Paris, 1861).

98. De la Chenaye-Desbois et Badier, *Dictionnaire de la Noblesse*, vol. XIII (Paris, 1868), p. 564.

99. H. J. de Morenas, *Grand Armorial de France*, vol. V (Paris, 1948), p. 30.

100. See L. Delisle, *Manuscrits du Cte. d'Ashburnham* (....) *observations sur les plus anciens manuscrits du fonds Libri et sur plusieurs manuscrits du fonds Barrois* (Paris, 1883).

101. This MS was described by P. Meyer in *Romania*, 5 (1876), 1-63.

102. Mr. M. B. Parkes (personal communication).

103. P. Meyer described these leaves and their provenance, and printed a facsimile in *Romania*, 6(1877), 489-94. This crusade epic is also found complete, with a continuation, in BM Add. MS 34114, which Meyer described with Hatton 77, and in a fragment of 1,184 lines, also formerly the endpapers of a printed book, from the Brasenose College Library, Oxford, now MS B.N.C. d. 56. This fragment has never been described. Meyer took it to be part of the continuation in the BM MS, but in fact it is part of the crusade epic proper, corresponding to the material in Hatton 77, p. 169, 1. 17 – p. 176, 1. 32; p. 198, 1. 38 – p. 213, 1. 26; p. 235, 1. 13 – p. 242, 1. 19. For the relationship between the *Poème de la Première Croisade* and the First Cycle *Antioche* see Duparc-Quioc, *Le Cycle*, pp. 77-80.

104. MS *A*, fol. 113^v col. 2-117^v col. 1, and MS *D*, fol. 132^r col. 2.

105. MS *A*, vol. 121^v col. 1.

106. These flourishes are of the sort described by Mrs. Patterson as falling within the period 1240-1260.

107. Ed. by P. Meyer, *Romania*, 5(1876), 59.

108. The names contained in this letter are easily identifiable as sometime Aldermen of the City of London (except for John of Aschefford and John Amyce, who is always qualified as "clerk" in contemporary documents). Apart from that, two elements link up these names; they owned property and they were implicated in some way or other in the great Eyre of 1321. John de la

Chambre, Hugh de Waltham, Roger de Depham and Simon de Swanlond were all accused of conspiracy, and the first two accused especially of perpetrating a tax fraud, in which "every taxation and tallage in London should be assessed by their ordering, and whoever they wished to elevate or to oppress might be tallaged by them accordingly, keeping the third penny of every collection for themselves..." (H. M. Cam, *The Eyre of London, 14 Edward II, A.D. 1321*, edited for the Selden Society, 2 vols. [London, 1968], Vol. I, p. 49) John was found guilty and fined £20, but the others were acquitted, due mainly to the sympathetic interests of the jury, one infers! However, the above letter would appear to provide evidence that these men were indeed involved in some tallage fraud or other "pur lur profist." If it does concern these particular misappropriations, then it must be dated about 1312, the time at which they were alleged to have taken place. At all events, a *terminus ad quem* is provided by the death of John de la Chambre in 1327. We have not been able to identify the writer or addressee, or the Thomas in question; there were several people of that name involved in the Eyre. Further information can be obtained from M. Weinbaum, "London unter Eduard I und II" in *Vierteljahrschrift für Sozial- und Wirtschaftsgeschichte*, Beiheft 27-30 (Stuttgart, 1933); and Gwyn A. Williams, *Medieval London from Commune to Capital* (London, 1963).

109. Previous descriptions: H. Hagen, *loc. cit.*; A. G. Krüger, *Romania*, 23(1894), 445-49; M. Einstein, p. 725.

110. Krüger (p. 448) computed that some 104 lines were missing, whilst M. Einstein put the number at 60.

111. Dr. Christian von Steiger, director of the Burgerbibliothek, has studied the previous shelf marks found in Bongars' manuscripts but is not able to identify the library from which this one originally came. A similar mark, "C 8" is found in Bern 634, a MS of the same format as *S*, and with an inscription describing it as "fort vieux" in the same hand as that in *S*.

112. In *S* we note further typical underlinings by Fauchet. "D'un *bliaut* ert vestue *de l'ueure de Cartage*," 71ᵛ; the names "*Bologne*, mere fu *Godefroi*, *Eustace*," 72ʳ; words associated with medieval social structure, "*vavassor*," "*cortois et vilain*," "*fil de palasine*," "*orine*," 74ʳ; "*borjois et vavassor*," 77ʳ; the expression "*a la chiere grifaigne*" several times.

113.   R. Bossuat, p. 110. The fragment bound in between pa-
       ges 14 and 15 of Hatton 77 (cf. p. lii, note 103)
       also answers the supposed requirements of a jongleur's
       manuscript. It is of very small format and written on
       30 long lines per page.

114.   Cook et Crist, *Le Deuxième Cycle*, p. 88. Since that
       time we have visited Turin and verified the order, in-
       serting another folio between fols. 14 and 15 and mak-
       ing a few minor alterations. It should be stressed
       that this description of MS *T* is only provisional. At
       the time of going to press, the final foliation has
       not been established, and any changes in numbering
       will be communicated in a later volume in the series.

115.   Josephus Pasinus, *Codices Manuscripti Bibliothecae Re-
       gii Taurinensis Athenaei*, 2 vols. (Turin, 1749); vol.
       II, p. 474; Codex XXXVIII; G.-II-16.

116.   Further searches have still to be carried out for
       missing folios which may have been placed erroneously
       in other boxes.

117.   Placed in the second box were also fragments of other
       MSS. These have been identified as two frags. from
       the *Roman de la Rose*, the one being several folios
       from the beginning of the poem, from MS L-III-28, and
       a small frag. from the end of another, unidentified
       MS, which was otherwise destroyed. There were also
       eight fols. from the beginning of the *Roman de Flori-
       mont*, L-II-16, corresponding to lines 173-1384 in A.
       Hilka's edition (Göttingen, 1933). These have been
       restored to their rightful place where possible. Fi-
       nally there was a small frag. in Latin, identified, by
       Dr. Alessandro Vitale-Brovarone of the University of
       Turin, as part of a commentary on the Song of Songs.

118.   Cf. Barron, p. 484.

119.   These fragments have been edited in an appendix to
       this edition.

120.   This ducal, later royal, library forms the basis of
       the present Biblioteca Nazionale Universitaria. A
       recent article by Sheila Edmunds, "The Medieval Li-
       brary of Savoy," *Scriptorium*, 24, ii (1970), 318-27 and
       25, ii (1971), 253-84, studies the ducal collection
       but does not mention L-III-25.

121.   See R. Vaughan, *Philip the Bold* (London and Harvard,
       1962), p. 89. Strictly speaking, the marriage between
       these two took place in 1393, for political reasons,
       and the consummation did not take place until ten

years later.

122. This inventory is now deposited in the BNU in Turin.

123. Previous descriptions; P. Paris, *Les Manuscrits*, vol. VI, pp. 157-160; Omont, *Catalogue*, vol. I, p. 80; Le comte de Mas-Latrie, ed., *Le Chronique d'Ernoul et de Bernard le Trésorier* (Paris, 1871), p. xxxix; P. Riant, "Inventaire sommaire des manuscrits de l'*Eracles*," *Archives de l'Orient latin*, vol. 1(1881), p. 249; Duparc-Quioc, *Le Cycle*, p. 17; Sumberg, pp. 114-20.

124. Ed. H. A. Todd, *PMLA*, 4(1889), pp. 95-102.

125. For a discussion of this tradition see Sumberg, p. 117.

126. The first two sentences are a resumé of the last laisse, in "-ee," of the *Antioche*.

127. The content of these final items is established by L. S. Crist in *Le Deuxième Cycle*, p. 113. We have followed his divisions. For the prose *Ordene de Chevalerie* see "Les Rédactions en prose de l'Ordre de Chevalerie," by Hilding Kjellman, in *Studier i modern språkvetenskap*, 7(1920), pp. 139-77.

128. See BN MS Nouvelles Acquisitions françaises 5682.

129. See M. Châtre de Cangé, *Catalogue des livres du Cabinet de M.**** (Paris, 1733); and L. Delisle, *Le Cabinet des Manuscrits de la Bibliothèque Impériale*, 4 vols. (Paris, 1868-1881); vol. I, p. 411.

130. It is well known that the terms "Roman" or "Histoire" or "Livre" or "Chronique de Godefroy de Bouillon" cover all the material dealing with the First Crusade, including the French translation of William of Tyre, the so-called *Livre d'Eracle*, and its various continuations, and both the First and Second Cycles of the Crusade. For the latter we are adopting the abbreviation *CCGB* proposed in Cook et Crist, *Le Deuxième Cycle*, p. 9, note 1. The greatest help given by the medieval cataloguer is in the provision of the first words of the second folio and the last folio of the manuscript, which was standard practice and the easiest way of identifying a volume in a collection. As one of the examples below shows, these indications are often imprecise. For the rest of the description, these early catalogues are notoriously inaccurate, as witness *A* being described as *en prose*, and one of the lost MSS noted as *parlant de Lancelot du Lac*. It is only when a combination of data concurs that it be-

comes possible to identify the contents of a given volume.

131. Ed. by Léopold Delisle in *Recherches sur la Librairie de Charles V*, 2 vols. (Paris, 1907); vol. II. He also included an edition of this inventory in his *Cabinet des Manuscrits de la Bibliothèque Impériale*, 4 vols. (Paris, 1868-1881), vol. III. All examples above are taken from the *Recherches*, which gives a fuller description.

132. These are items 985 and 1022-1034 in Delisle. Most of these are identifiable by the indications given as versions of *Eracle*. Also described is another verse MS but which has no details as to its exact content and so cannot be identified. "Godeffroy de Billon, de la conqueste d'oultre mer, qui fu de la contesse de Pennebrok, couvert de soie a queue et rimé. Baillé par le Roy au Dauphin le 29 de decembre 1398." (1026) Of all these manuscripts, not one appears to have survived.

133. What exactly does Giles Malet mean by "bien vieil"? The fact that the manuscript is on paper proves that it could not have been very old. Perhaps it is, indeed, the version of the poem which is old, i.e., the First Cycle. We are inclined to believe that "bien vieil" is just an example of the casual use of this somewhat meaningless expression often encountered in medieval catalogues. It is more likely that by the time manuscripts came to be made of paper the popularity of the First Cycle had already been eclipsed by its mid-fourteenth century *remaniement*. Of course, it is possible that the term "en papier" is incorrect.

134. Note that this line is l. 197 in *C*, l. 214 in *E* and l. 144 in *H*.

135. This is described as "Ung livret en papier couvert de parchemin, contenant deux quayers, escript en rime, et parle du *Chevalier au Chisne*, quemanchant ou second feuillet, *Plaisance entra en lui*, et le dernier feuillet, *et dient li enffant*" and has already been correctly identified by Alphonse Bayot ("Fragments des manuscrits trouvés aux Archives générales du Royaume, deuxième notice; F, Le Roman en vers de Baudouin de Flandre," *Revue des Bibliothèques et Archives de Belgique*, 4(1906), 429-38.) as a MS of the *CCGB*. The first indication is line 89 of the Brussels MS (10391) edited by Reiffenberg. Bayot declares, however, that "c'est un livret de deux cahiers, *dont l'objet n'est*

pas clair" (p. 432), our italics. This is evidently
only a fragment as the description shows, but what is
its exact scope? In this case the end is not diffi-
cult to postulate, since there is only one place in
the *CCGB* where children say anything, namely at the
point when the young Godefroi and his two brothers
swear to Yde that they will uphold the fight against
the Saracens:

"*Et dient ly enfant*: "Nous sommes dézierant
De faire tout le bien c'on nous va conseillant."
                    (*CCGB* 3503-4.)

The existence at this place of the hemistich in ques-
tion stands in favor as the correct location, although
the description "deux quayers" does not. For this
line would come very nearly at the beginning of the
last folio of *five* regular quires of eight folios.
The fact that the first line on the second folio of
the lost MS is line 89 of the Brussels MS suggests
that this is a typical fifteenth century paper *chanson
de geste* manuscript, written on 45 long lines. At 90
lines a folio, the first line of the last folio of
five quires would be line 3510 — remarkably close to
the number of the line in the Reiffenberg edition!
This means that either the "livret" concerned had five
quires, or if it really did have only two, then, by
1467, the date of the inventory, the first and fifth
quires alone were extant and bound together. The
presence of this fragment gainsays Emile Roy's state-
ment that "aucun exemplaire du poème (i.e. *CCGB*) ne
figure dans les anciens inventaires actuellement con-
nus de la librairie des ducs de Bourgogne" in *Romania*,
55(1929), p. 419.

136. Georges Doutrepont, *Inventaire de la 'Librairie' de
      Philippe le Bon (1420)* (Brussels, 1906).

137. The same MS was described twice in error. Presumably
      it must have been moved from the library to the chapel
      after the catalogue of the former, and before that of
      the latter, were drawn up.

138. Unless, of course, the MS began on the verso of fol. 1
      like MS *G*, in which case a total of 40 lines per col-
      umn as suggested below would still be acceptable, al-
      lowing for a miniature.

139. Readers will search in vain for this episode in the
      fragments of *Les Chétifs* published in the Appendix of
      vol. II of Hippeau's *Chevalier au Cygne*, because he
      omits it. Anyway the MS he uses, *D*, has a different

reading for the first line in question, and omits the second.

140. MS *A*, fol. 131^r col. 2.

141. MS *A*, fol. 132^r col. 1.

142. MSS *D*, *E*, *G* and *I*.

143. MS *B*, fol. 224^v col. 2. MS *I* also includes this epi-sode, but added in at a later date than the original redaction. See p. 1.

144. The problem of the grouping of manuscripts is far from solved. Mme Duparc thinks that the oldest version of the *Jérusalem* is represented by *ACD* (her *ABC* in *Le Cycle*, pp. 10-11) and has communicated to us that she considers this grouping to be valid for the *Antioche* as well (despite Sumberg, p. 135 ff.). For *Les Chétifs* we read *ACF*, with *T* usually representing a version just slightly more recent than that of those three, but not as recent as the others. MS *D* reproduces now an old, now a recent version. This classification certainly holds good for the variants of the two pas-sages in question.

145. Ed. in Marchal, *loc. cit.*

146. In fact a large number of manuscripts, representing about 10% of those catalogued by Gérard in 1797, have disappeared by the time of Marchal's inventory, and yet there are no further depredations by the French — all of which have been fairly well documented any-way — and no natural disasters recorded. This strikes us as a suspicious situation which would well bear further investigation.

147. Published in Paris in 1581 by Mamert Patisson.

148.ʹ Quotations (1), (2) and (5) are taken from the *Re-cueil*, pp. 36-37, and (3) and (4) from the *Origines des Dignitez et Magistrats de France, recueillies par Claude Fauchet*, printed in the complete *Oeuvres de feu M. Claude Fauchet* (Paris, 1610), from chapters X ("Des Maires du Palais, Seneschal, Grand Maistre, Grand Es-cuyer de France"), fol. 482^r, and XI ("Du Chambrier & Chamberlain"), fol. 486^v. Fauchet incorrectly quali-fies example (4) as 'parlant de l'Evesque du Pui.' Examples (3) and (4) are printed in Espiner-Scott, p. 163.

149. See *B*, note **49**.

150. Espiner-Scott, p. 178, note 3, *et passim*.

151. Peter Grillo has just brought to our notice reference
      to a further manuscript of the "Roman du Chevalier au
      Cygne et de Godefroi de Bouillon," formerly in Tournai
      (MS 103). See P. Faider and P. van Sint Jan, *Ca-*
      talogue des manuscrits conservés à Tournai, Gembloux,
      1950, p. 111. A letter from the librarian confirmed
      that this manuscript was destroyed during the war.
      Fortunately an early catalogue (A. M. Wilbaux, *Catalo-*
      gue des Manuscrits de Tournai, Tournai, 1860, pp. 43-
      44) establishes that this was a MS of the Second Cy-
      cle.

La Naissance du Chevalier au Cygne

TEXTS AND AFFILIATIONS

The first branch of the cyclical form has been called variously *Naissance du Chevalier au Cygne* and *Enfants-Cygnes*. The titles are significant, for they indicate problems related to the text. The former, chosen by Todd,[1] emphasizes the importance of the first branch to the cycle as a whole and focuses attention on the birth of the Swan Knight, the legendary grandfather of Godefroy de Bouillon, as the important feature of the story. Contrarily, the latter title, given by Gaston Paris,[2] suggests the independence of the swan-children story, only later attached to the legend of the Swan Knight.

That the story of the swan-children is an independent tale totally disassociated from the Swan Knight legend is well attested by its appearance in Germanic folk tradition. Several versions of the story and analogous mutations can be found in stories collected by Grimm and Andersen. Most scholars[3] have asserted the probable Germanic and specifically Lotharingian origin of the tale.[4] Its later attachment to the Swan Knight legend is the result of the presence of swans in the tale. They undoubtedly suggested to the poet its possible use as an explanation of the origin of the Swan Knight.

The earliest known written version of the story is found in Johannes de Alta Silva's *Dolopathos, sive de Rege et Septem Sapientibus* composed around 1190.[5] This Latin collection is a loose imitation of the oriental *Sintipas*, but very different from the Latin version, *Historia Septem Sapientum*, and the French *Roman des Sept Sages*. Among the eight stories included within the frame, only three are from the *Sintipas*. The remaining five are from other sources, perhaps oral, since Johannes claims to have used such material.[6] The story of the swan-children is the seventh story in the group. Since the various versions of the legend used in the Swan Knight cycle are closely related to the narrative found in the *Dolopathos*, a summary of this form of the tale will be helpful.

As the story opens a young man, who, like other characters in the tale, remains nameless, is hunting and

becomes lost in pursuit of a white stag. In his wan-
derings he comes upon a fay who is holding a golden
necklace and is bathing in a fountain. Struck with
love, the youth and the fay consummate their union
that night. Versed in astrology, the fay reads her
destiny in the stars and discloses that she will give
birth to six sons and one daughter. In the morning
the young man returns with the girl to his castle.
Annoyed by the union, the youth's mother seeks unsuc-
cessfully to persuade her son to break with the girl.
As predicted, seven children are born, each with a
golden chain about the neck. The mother substitutes
seven puppies for the children and orders a servant to
take the infants into the forest to destroy them. Un-
able to bring himself to kill them, the servant leaves
them under a tree, where they are found and cared for
by an old hermit. When the mother relates to her son
that his wife has given birth to seven dogs, he has
the girl buried up to her breasts in the courtyard and
there she remains for seven years. Some time later,
again while hunting, the young man encounters the
children in the forest. He tries unsuccessfully to
catch them and returns to relate the strange encounter
to his mother. Suspicious, his mother learns from the
servant that the children had not been put to death
and dispatches him in search of them. When the ser-
vant finds the children, the six sons are bathing in
the form of swans. The daughter is sitting on the
bank of the pond guarding the golden chains. These
the servant manages to steal and returns to the cas-
tle. The necklaces are given to a goldsmith to be
made into a goblet. However, he is unable to melt
them and succeeds only in damaging one of the chains.
The goldsmith makes the goblet with other gold and re-
tains the necklaces himself. The six swan-children,
unable to return to human form, fly away with their
sister, who is able to change from human to swan form
at will through the power of her necklace. They set
down in a pond near their father's castle. He sees
the swans and, as if by premonition, orders that they
not be harmed. Each day the daughter goes to the cas-
tle to obtain bread for her brothers. On her return
she feeds the buried woman, whose identity remains un-
known to her. Observing these events, the young man
calls the girl to him, notices the golden necklace,
which resembles that owned by his wife, and persuades
the girl to relate her story. The grandmother over-
hears the story and plans to have her servant kill the

girl. Her father, however, interrupts the attempt and
the grandmother subsequently confesses her crime. The
goldsmith is brought forth and all of the children are
restored to human form except the one whose necklace
had been damaged. The swan then joins one of his
brothers. This association announces the Swan Knight
legend and the text specifically notes in reference to
the swan that it is the one "quod cathena aurea mili-
tem in navicula trahat armatum." The story closes
with the release of the mother, whose place is taken
by the wicked grandmother.

This is the basic story, then, which was used to explain the
origins of the Swan Knight. In all there are four versions
of the tale altered to varying degrees in an effort to make
a closer connection with the Swan Knight branch: 1. *Elioxe*,
2. *Beatrix*, 3. a composite form, comprised of the first
1361 lines of *Elioxe* spliced to all but the first 200 lines
of Beatrix, and 4. *Isomberte*, known only in the Spanish *Gran
Conquista de Ultra-mar*.[7]

Elioxe

The version of the epic entitled *Elioxe* is found in its
entirety only in BN 12558 (fol. 1*a*-20*c*). The composite ver-
sion, however, provides two fragments: Arsenal 3139 (fol.
1*a*-27*b*) and British Museum Additional MS 36615 (fol. 1*a*-8*d*).
The latter provide a text corresponding to *ll*. 1-1345 of BN
12558. Although the author changes the tale somewhat in
adapting it to the epic cycle, it remains, nevertheless, the
closest to the independent story found in *Dolopathos*.

The story opens during a hunt. King Lothair, ruler of
a country beyond Hungary, loses his way and stops to
rest beside a beautiful fountain. Elioxe emerges from
within the mountain, ministers to the sleeping King
and awaits his waking. Meeting then, and after some
mutual explanation, it is agreed that King Lothair
take her for his wife. After agreeing to become his
wife, Elioxe announces to the King that she will give
birth to seven children. From the descendants of these
children, whose birth will cost her life, there will
emerge one who will be a king in the Orient. Upon the
return of the couple to the castle, the King's mother,
Matrosilie, tries in vain to thwart the marriage. A
short time later a pagan king, Gordoce de Palie, in-
vades Lothair's realm and forces the young King to de-
part in defense of his rights. While he is away,

Elioxe gives birth to the children and, in doing so,
dies. Matrosilie places the seven children in two
baskets and orders her servant, Monicier, to take them
into the forest. The servant takes the children, but
leaves them outside the window of a hermit's hut,
where they are found and raised by the hermit and his
sister. Meanwhile, Matrosilie informs the King that
Elioxe had given birth to seven serpents and had per-
ished from wounds inflicted by them. Seven years
later one of the King's servants, Rudemart, seeks
shelter at the hermitage and comes upon the children.
Motivated by greed for the gold necklaces, Rudemart
relates to Matrosilie what he has seen and she immedi-
ately sends him to obtain the necklaces. Rudemart re-
turns and removes the chains from the six sleeping
boys, but, unaware of the number of children, does not
obtain the necklace from the girl, who remains unno-
ticed. The six boys, changed into swans, fly to a
pond near the castle of their father, who orders that
they not be harmed. Unaware of the order, the King's
nephew, Plantoul, tries in vain to kill one of them
for his uncle. When he tells of his failure, Lothair
becomes violently angry and throws a gold basin at
him. The basin is broken and Matrosilie gives one of
the gold chains to a goldsmith for repair. Meanwhile,
the hermit sends the girl away to the city to find
protection. On her way, she is directed to the King's
monastery, erected in honor of the children's mother.
There she is given bread, which she takes to the pond
to moisten. She sees the swans, recognizes them as
her brothers, and feeds them. The seneschal, who has
observed the strange friendliness of the swans, re-
ports to the King, who goes to observe their behavior
for himself. The girl tells her story to the King and
he recognizes the queen-mother's treachery implicit in
it. She in turn confesses and returns the five neck-
laces still in her possession. Five of the swans are
restored and armed as knights. The sixth, whose neck-
lace had been melted down, must remain a swan. Four
of the knights go to seek their fortunes, while the
fifth, known henceforth as the Swan Knight, is unwill-
ing to leave his swan-brother. Together they set out,
the swan pulling his brother's boat, and arrive in
Nimwegen after a voyage of some two months.

The similarity of the *Dolopathos* and the *Elioxe* texts has
caused considerable speculation concerning their relation-
ship. Pigeonneau argued that Johannes had drawn from the

Elioxe.[8] In his review article of Todd's edition, Gaston Paris refuted this contention and asserted that the differences between the two indicate a common source used by both authors. Paris points out that the *Dolopathos* has traits manifestly more primitive in nature and obviously derived from an older source.[9] He adds further that the *Elioxe* has chivalric and feudal elements totally lacking in the *Dolopathos*. He also rejects the possibility that the *Elioxe* draws on the *Dolopathos*, in that the "transformation facultative" of the children, missing in the *Elioxe*, would otherwise be present. In rejecting a source relationship between the two, Paris hypothesizes that the texts derive from a common source and that the differences can be explained by the inevitable transformation which takes place in oral transmission.[10]

As for the date of composition, Paris concludes that the *Elioxe* can not have been written later than the early 13th century nor earlier than the late 12th century. He considered BN 12558 to be of the early 13th century and his suggested *terminus ad quem* derives from this opinion. Textual references to the popularity of the romances of the Round Table, on the other hand, provide the *terminus a quo*.[11]

The question concerning the relationship among the various versions was reconsidered by Jeanne Lods, who sought to establish in what way the author of *Elioxe* changed the story as found in *Dolopathos*.[12] The first point noted concerns the initial episode of the hunt. Although its elements remain similar to those found in the *Dolopathos*, there is a marked change in tone. The lady met by the young king is no longer a "fée."[13] Mlle Lods feels that the *Elioxe* poet found the details of the meeting in *Dolopathos* "un peu trop paienne" (p. 810) and hence changed them to suit his taste. Having removed the supernatural, the poet was left with elements, such as the fountain, which were no longer pertinent:

> ...il est visible que l'auteur suit son modèle sans se demander si l'épisode conserve sa raison d'être dans la perspective nouvelle qu'il entend donner au récit, perspective historique, non mythologique. (pp. 810-11)

This attitude also explains the fact that the children no longer change form at will, the chains having become only a device by which they can regain their human form once they have been changed by Matrosilie's machinations. Another difference cited by Mlle Lods is the generally more realistic description in *Elioxe*, a reflection of the nearly bourgeois approach in the treatment of the king's mother and her surroundings.

In conclusion, Mlle Lods argues that the author of *Elioxe* used and modified the *Dolopathos* to suit the new, "historical" context of the tale. There is, though, one element in *Elioxe* which indicates the use of oral tradition. The dream which Elioxe has concerning the seven apples and flowers reflects an element found in one of the Germanic tales studied by Müller, where the girl, in quest of her brothers, stops to pick seven "lis" and thereby delays their return to human form. Since the episode is not found in *Dolopathos*, it was probably drawn from oral sources.[14]

Beatrix

A second version is the *Beatrix*. Unlike the *Elioxe*, this version is considerably altered with regard to the oral tale represented in the *Dolopathos*. It is complete in four manuscripts: BN 786 (fol. 92*a*-105*b*), BN 795 (fol. 5*c*-5*d* and 11*a*-26*b*), BN 12569 (fol. 1*a*-20*c*), and British Museum Royal MS 15 E VI (fol. 320*a*-325*c*). Four other manuscripts preserve fragments: BN 1621 (fol. 1*a*-10*b*), which lacks the first 1488 lines with reference to BN 786; Arsenal 3139 (fol. 10*b*-28*a*), which lacks the first 200 lines with reference to BN 786, British Museum Additional MS 36615 (fol. 4*a*-4*d*), which provides a text corresponding to *ll.* 201-396 of BN 786; and Turin L-III-25, see Appendix. Finally, the *Beatrix* also provided the general base for the opening episodes in both the consolidated poem and the prose abbreviation.

The story opens long after the marriage of King Oriant[15] and Queen Beatrix, with the childless couple looking down from their tower at a woman with twins. Maliciously jealous, Beatrix replies to her husband's favorable observations with the opinion that multiple birth is proof of adultery. That very night the unfortunate queen conceives seven children and subsequently gives birth to six boys and one girl. Each is born with a silver chain about the neck. The mother-in-law, Matabrune, is a woman devoted to evil. She removes the infants and orders her servant, Marcon, to take them into the forest and to kill them. Marcon is unable to do this and simply abandons them. They are discovered by a hermit, who undertakes their care and protection. Meanwhile, Matabrune tells her son that his wife has given birth to seven dogs and that she deserves death. Oriant refuses to render such a judg-

ment, but permits his mother to cast Beatrix into
prison. Some years later one of Matabrune's servants,
Malquarēs, sees the children at the hermitage and in-
forms Matabrune, who sends him to remove the silver
chains. He succeeds in taking six of them while the
hermit and his favorite, one of the boys, are away.
The six immediately turn into swans and fly to a pond
outside their father's castle. Matabrune decides to
have the chains made into a cup. When the goldsmith
attempts to carry out her wishes, he finds that one of
the chains provides enough silver for two cups. These
he fashions, giving one to Matabrune and keeping the
other, together with the five unaltered chains, for
himself. Some fifteen years pass and Matabrune is fi-
nally able to persuade Oriant to permit the execution.
Beatrix will be burned alive unless a champion be
found who can defend her successfully. In this moment
of need, an angel appears to the hermit, explains the
circumstances, and orders that the remaining brother
be sent the next day to defend his mother. Raised
like the young Perceval, the boy knows nothing of civ-
ilized life or knightly combat,[16] thus emphasizing
that victory is obtained through faith in God.[17] The
youth arrives in the city, is baptized with the name
Elias, defeats Matabrune's champion, frees his mother,
and provides for the restoration of his sister and
four of his brothers to human form. The brother whose
chain was used in making the cups must remain a swan.
Upon the defeat of her champion, Matabrune flees to
her castle where she is besieged by Elias. Again vic-
torious, he has the evil old woman burned at the stake
prepared for his mother. Following the orders of an
angel, he then departs in a boat drawn by his swan-
brother and, after a combat at sea and a final encoun-
ter with Matabrune's vengeful brother, arrives at Nim-
wegen.

Aware that the story's primary purpose was to disclose the
origin of the Swan Knight, the author altered the central
focus of the narrative from the single daughter to one of
the sons.[18] He also revised many of the episodes and the ba-
sic nature of some of the characters. Instead of the open-
ing scene relating the hunt, the episode of the fountain,
and the wooing of the lady, the story begins after the mar-
riage of Oriant and Beatrix. When the seven children are
born, Matabrune claims that Beatrix gave birth to seven pup-
pies, insinuating that such a birth could only be the result
of repeated sexual relations with a dog. From this point

forward, the story resembles the oral tale only in a very general way. It is true that the children are abandoned and found by a hermit, who then raises them until they are discovered by Matabrune's henchman; but the central element of the story becomes the emergence of the Swan Knight, his divine mission, and the ultimate redemption of Beatrix.

Apparently basing his opinion on the opening lines of the poem, Gaston Paris held that the *Beatrix* version was written during the second half of the 12th century and that it was not a mere redaction of earlier work:

> L'auteur ne suivait pas une chanson plus an-
> cienne, et croyait être le premier à donner
> au récit qu'il mettait en vers la forme de
> chanson de geste. (*Romania*, 2[1873], 323.)

Contrarily, Mlle Lods proposes that the *Beatrix* author knew the *Elioxe* and the *Dolopathos* as well as oral tales. Although it is clear that the poet has reoriented the text toward the Swan Knight legend, there are details which indicate an awareness of the other versions. Knowledge of the *Elioxe*, for instance, is suggested by their mutual use of the melted chain episode. Similarly, knowledge of the *Dolopathos* may be seen in Matabrune's slanderous implication of a bestial relationship with dogs. The treatment of the forest in which Elias is raised, on the other hand, suggests to her a connection with the oral forms of the tale. Mlle Lods concludes, therefore, that one cannot determine the age of the text, inasmuch as each work draws from the entire tradition. Each version, then, should be studied as an independent work elaborated and developed by the author, who employed elements from the tradition as well as personal modifications designed to adapt the story to the purpose he intended.

Composite Version

Elements of both the *Elioxe* and the *Beatrix* contributed to a composite version which has been preserved in two manuscripts: Arsenal 3139 and British Museum Additional MS 36615. Reference to these has been made above. Essentially the first 1345 lines follow the *Elioxe*. The only changes are those made in anticipation of the *Beatrix*: the suppression of passages relating to the death of the king's wife and the adoption of proper names from the latter text.[19] The rest follows the *Beatrix* without modification. Significantly, both elements readily collate with the corresponding cyclical manuscripts and, indeed, contribute to knowledge of the textual tradition. It is difficult, then, to consider the text preserved in these manuscripts as constituting a distinct version of the *Naissance* branch. The editors have chosen, therefore, to collate these with the *Elioxe* and the *Beatrix* versions rather than to provide a third text.

Prior Editions of the Naissance Branch

To date there have been three editions of the *Naissance du Chevalier au Cygne*.

1) Frédéric A. F. T. Baron de Reiffenberg. *Le Chevalier au Cygne et Godefroid de Bouillon.* Vol. I. Bruxelles, 1846. This edition formed a part of the massive collection entitled *Monuments pour servir à l'Histoire des Provinces de Namur, de Hainaut et de Luxembourg.* It is based on Bruxelles MS 10391 and so provides a text of the 15th century redaction, which forms a part of the consolidated epic. The editor's introduction and extensive notes are impressive and invaluable. The same, unfortunately, cannot be said of the text. Comparison with the manuscript immediately reveals frequent unidentified emendations and an insistence on regular alexandrine rhythm, which is completely at variance with the scribe. Furthermore, the editor was unaware of the variant Lyon 744.

2) Célestin Hippeau. *La Chanson du Chevalier au Cygne et de Godefroid de Bouillon.* Vol. I. Paris, 1874. This edition provides a text of the *Beatrix* version. It is, however, an unreliable one. The editor chose to use BN 1621 as his base, but felt no obligation to respect it. There are numerous changes introduced without indication and the first 1488 lines, taken from BN 12569, are unidentified.

3) Henry Alfred Todd. *La Naissance du Chevalier au Cygne ou Les Enfants Changés en Cygnes. PMLA* 4(1889). This excellent edition has provided the only available text of the *Elioxe* version to date. The base manuscript is of necessity BN 12558. Variant readings are given from Arsenal 3139, but British Museum Additional MS 36615 was unknown to the editor.

The editors' purpose is to provide reliable texts of both versions of the *Naissance* branch and to facilitate access to the entire textual tradition by means of an accurate and complete critical apparatus.

The base manuscript for each version represents, in the editors' opinion, the most satisfactory of the extant cyclical texts in terms of completeness and general agreement with the textual tradition. In other words, the base for each version is the one text which, after comparison with all other pertinent manuscripts, is seen to preserve all episodes of the narrative and to contain the fewest unique readings.

Elioxe

Of the three manuscripts which preserve this version, only BN 12558 (*A*) is complete. It is, therefore, the single possible base.

Only a very general idea can be had concerning the relationship between the three manuscripts. W. J. Barron, the first to take up this question, decided that both *G* and *I* follow *A* rather closely, but that they differ significantly enough to indicate that they are not directly descended through it. The results of collation confirm this opinion while providing a somewhat more precise statement:

1) *AGI* agree without variation in 171 of 1345 lines.
2) *AG* agree without variation against *I* in 195 lines, *GI* against *A* in 249 lines and *AI* against *G* in 49 lines.
3) *AG* agree in preserving 21 lines not found in *I*, *GI* against *A* in 41 lines and *AI* against *G* in 7 lines.
4) Disregarding the lines deleted in *GI* to facilitate the splice with *Beatrix*; *AG* agree against *I* in wanting 33 lines, *GI* against *A* in 35 lines and *AI* against *G* in 5 lines.
5) Considering the first 500 lines of collation; *AG* agree against *I* in 152 individual readings, *GI* against *A* in 94 readings and *AI* against *G* in 104 readings.

The pattern of agreement between the three manuscripts out-
lined here suggests the following conclusions:
1) *AGI* are, indeed, closely related texts.
2) A direct relationship does not exist between any
    two of the texts.
3) *GI* form a group within the tradition.
4) *I* shows the greatest tendency to vary from the tra-
    dition.
Thus, although *A* is the only possible base for an edition of
Elioxe, it can be accepted with considerable confidence.
This is especially true when there is agreement with *G*. On
the other hand, its authority is open to question in the
presence of a demonstrably superior agreement between the
variant texts.

Beatrix

Eight manuscripts preserve the text of this version:
four in fragmentary or otherwise incomplete form, four with-
out extensive lacunae. BN 1621 (*D*) has suffered the loss of
its initial quire and the text of *Beatrix* survives only from
laisse sixty-nine. Collation begins with *1.* 1487 of *B*. Ar-
senal 3139 (*G*), one of the two manuscripts which contain the
spliced *Elioxe-Beatrix*, provides the latter text only from
laisse nine. British Museum Additional MS 36615 (*I*), the
other to preserve the spliced version, likewise provides the
Beatrix beginning with laisse nine but the text is inter-
rupted by a lacuna of sixteen folios. Collation begins with
1. 201 of *B* and continues through six lines added at *1.* 396.
Turin MS L-III-25 (*T*) was badly damaged by fire in 1904.
The *Beatrix* text is found on the fragments of the first
three folios of the surviving manuscript and is legible only
with the aid of ultra-violet light. Collation begins with
1. 2500 of *B* and continues with lacunae through *1.* 3029.
The four remaining manuscripts provide texts which are com-
plete inasmuch as they are without extensive lacunae. A
comparison of each of these with the entire textual tradi-
tion, however, reveals that BN 795 (*C*) and British Museum
Royal MS 15 E VI (*H*) lack material authenticated by a con-
sensus of the other available texts. Both of these also
manifest an evident effort at abbreviation. The effect of
this effort is readily apparent from a comparison of the
number of lines collated from each manuscript: *B* 3196, *E*
3149, *G* (*Beatrix* material only) 2846; but *C* 2442 and *H* 1681.
The two remaining manuscripts, BN 786 (*B*) and BN 12569 (*E*)
are closely related in every respect and represent the com-
mon form of the *Beatrix* narrative as attested by the textual
tradition as a whole. There are no gross features to dis-

tinguish the two, though *B* shows itself to be somewhat more consistent with the consensus than *E*. The latter varies from that by adding one laisse, 43 *bis* with respect to this edition, which is not attested elsewhere and by lacking one laisse, 105 of this edition, which is preserved in *BDG*. No such addition or deletion of laisses occurs in *B*. Of the two, *E* also exhibits unique variation much more frequently: 1138 times in 3149 lines as opposed to an extraordinarily conservative 153 times in 3196 lines in *B*. This superior agreement with the textual tradition as a whole suggests the choice of *B* as the most appropriate base for the present edition.

The present editor is in complete agreement with W. R. J. Barron's conclusion that "it would be futile to construct a stemma on the basis of a handful of manuscripts where the narrative variants suggest that the textual tradition was complex and the redactive process generally quite conservative." (Barron, p. 527) Nevertheless, an analysis of variation in wording, as opposed to Barron's analysis of variation in narrative structure, has brought to light some rather persuasive evidence of relationships among the manuscripts which have preserved the *Beatrix* in French verse and which have, therefore, contributed to this edition. This evidence does not contradict Barron's conclusions; on the contrary, it tends to confirm them. This is particularly so with respect to *BE* (cf. Barron, pp. 527-528) and *CG* (cf. Barron, p. 502) and as concerns the general relationship of what he terms the primary redaction (i.e. *BE C DH*) to the spliced *Elioxe-Beatrix* (cf. Barron, pp. 501-502).

The diagram presented below is not offered as a stemma purporting to illustrate the entire textual tradition of the *Beatrix*, rather it is offered as a convenient means of visualizing the relationships which have come to light during the process of detailed collation.

B   E   C   G I T   D   H

It should be noted that the fragmentary condition of *D*, *I*, and *T* together with the abbreviated state of *C* and *H* limits the scope of collation from which evidence based on the witness of all manuscripts is available.

BE

Convincing evidence that *BE* form a group within the

tradition is available at any point in the text. The fol-
lowing has been selected as representative:

1) *1*. 190   *BE*: Se Jhesu Cris n'en pense par sa
                      sainte (p. le soie b. *E*) bonté; *C H*:
                      Se Dieus n'em pense li rois de ma-
                      jestet.

2) *11*. 1696-1698   *BE*: Descendi une nue ki fist mal al
                      gloton/ La veüe li torble par tel
                      devisīon/ Ne veīst une goute por le
                      tresor Othon; *CG DH*: Fait de la
                      crois salir sans plus (nule *C*; point
                      G H) d'arestoison/ .I. serpent a
                      .II. testes ja (onques *C H*) tel ne
                      vera (vit *C H*) on/ A une ague coe
                      longue et graisle en (u. longue
                      queue qui fu ague e. *G*) son (*C H*
                      want).

3) *1*. 1736   *BE*: Del relever se paine Malquarés
                      durement; *CG DH*: Et Malquarrés se
                      paine de relever forment.

4) *1*. 1858   *BE*: Li cisnes s'en retorne arriere
                      tous dolans; *CG DH*: Li cisnes s'en
                      repaire el (au *G*; ou *H*) vivier tous
                      (moult *H*) dolans.

5) *11*. 2739-2743   *BE*: *CGT DH* See text and variants.

6) *1*. 2768   *BE*: Li sire qui ens maint est el
                      grignor (e. plus haut e. *E*) estaje;
                      CGT DH: Li sire qui en ot (a *DH G*)
                      l'onour (l'avoir *G*) et l'eritaige
                      (e. tot l'usage *DH G*).

7) *11*. 2927-2931   *BE*: *CGT DH* See text and variants.

8) *BE* alone preserve laisse 145 of the present edition
    and further agree in their articulation with the
    second branch of the cycle.

DH

    The evidence pointing to a *DH* relationship is admitted-
ly tenuous. The incomplete state of the text in *D* reduces
the collation from which such evidence is available by
roughly half as compared with that for *BE*. But the possibi-
lity of evidence is even more dramatically reduced by the
nature of *H*. This text, a 15th century redaction, lacks
seven laisses (82, 93, 96, 100, 101, 104, and 136 of the
present edition) which are authenticated in *BE D* and *G*.
And, as noted above, it tends generally to abbreviate by the
omission of individual lines. Furthermore, it is marked by
a higher incidence of unique variation than that observed in

any other text of the *Beatrix* tradition: 1052 times in 1681
lines. Much, if not most, of this can be explained as the
result of the modernization of its language. Despite this
there remains significant evidence of a kinship between *D*
and *H* which excludes the other texts of the tradition. The
following are most convincing:

1) *l.* 1912   *BE CGT*: Que li fera jehir coument esploitié a; *DH*: c. ele esploita.

2) *l.* 2161   *BE G*: Oiant tous les barons a haute vois s'escrie (*C wants*); *DH*: O. tot le barnage a.

3) *l.* 2519   *BE CGT*: Tout cil en ont (c. orent p. *G*) paour ki l'orent escoutee; *DH*: p. qui oent le desvee.

4) *l.* 2681   *BE CG*: En la mer le jeta ne viut que l'aient mie; *DH*: m. l'a jeté n. (v. qu'en a. *H*).

5) *l.* 3136   *DH* agree in alone preserving one line at this point in *B*.

CG

Although *C* is also characterized by a general tendency
to abbreviation and to unique variation (1385 times in 2442
lines), the existence of this relationship is attested fre-
quently. The following is offered as the most persuasive
evidence:

1) *l.* 653   *CG* alone preserve a passage at this point announcing the exploits of Godefroi, Bauduin, and Ustasse.

2) *l.* 1307   *BE H*: Le destrier ont saisi .II. vallet de Bretagne (*D unavailable*); *CG*: d. Grifaigne.

3) *l.* 1412   *BE H*: Isnelement et tos en piés vous relevés (*D unavailable*); *CG*: En piés resalés sus onques (que ja *G*) n'i ariestés.

4) *l.* 1499   *BE DH*: Ainc n'oïstes tant fiere en cest siecle vivant; *CG*: f. par le mien ensiant.

5) *l.* 1502   *BE D*: Si que demi l'a tout et colpé et fendu (*H wants*); *CG*: Que les flours et les pieres en a jus abatut.

6) *l.* 1617   *BE DH*: La dame fait grant dol pour Elias l'enfant; *CG*: La royne a g.

7) *l.* 1694   *BE DH*: Sor la crois de l'escu va ferir a bandon; *CG*: Sor l'escut va fe-

rir en (a *G*) la crois a b.

8) *1.* 2490   *BE DH*: Counissiés vostre mordre, trop poēs demorer (Tant c., m. ca ne p. *H*); *CG*: Se tos n'iestes confiessé tart venrés au parler.

9) *11.* 2520-2532   *BE DH*: *CGT* See text and variants.

10) *11.* 2566-2567 *BE DH*: *CGT* See text and variants.

The foregoing evidence strongly suggests a basic organization of the *Beatrix* tradition along three lines as represented in *BE*, *CG*, and *DH*. This is confirmed by the variation observed in the two following lines:

1) *1.* 1659   *BE*: La dame se dolouse, pour Elias s'esmaie.

                     CG: La royne a gran duel pour Elias s'esmaie.

                     DH: La dame fait grant dol pour Elias s'esmaie.

2) *1.* 1815   *BE*: Cil ki perdent les lor cisne sunt lor vivant.

                     CG: Et cil qui les perdirent furent cisne volant.

                     DH: Et chil qui le perdoit (perdroit *H*) chisnes ert son vivant (c. seroit voyant *H*).

A similar organization of variation is attested in numerous other lines, although obscured somewhat by unique variation or by the absence of a witness. For example: *11.* 1523, 1855, and 2359.

There remains the question of the two severely fragmented texts of *I* and *T*. Patterns of agreement revealed during collation definitely indicate that each of these is closely related to *G* to the exclusion of *C*. This points to the existence of a subgroup associated with the line identified in *CG*. Unfortunately, a precise determination of the relationships within this subgroup is impossible inasmuch as the *GI* and *GT* collations do not correspond. One hypothesis does, however, suggest itself. *G* and *I* agree in preserving the spliced *Elioxe-Beatrix* redaction. They would, therefore, be related through its archetype to the exclusion of *T* which, judging from Pasini's description, preserved the *Beatrix*.

GI

The following agreements indicate a close relationship between *G* and *I*:

1) *1.* 231   *BE H C*: Qu'il l'ardra en .I. fu voiant toute sa jent (i. ardra sa feme v. *C*; *D unavailable*); *GI*: Qu'il

		le fera ardoir sans nul respitement.
2)	*1.* 233	*GI* alone add a line at this point in *B*.
3)	*1.* 303	*GI* alone add a line at this point in *B*.
4)	*1.* 362	*BE H C*: E Dex fait li hermites par ton coumandement (*D unavailable*); *GI*: p. ton disne coumant.
5)	*1.* 367	*GI* agree in a goat as the animal sent by God to provide milk for the swan-children against a doe in *BE C H*.
6)	*1.* 367	*GI* alone add a line at this point in *B*.
7)	*1.* 396	*GI* agree in a major modification of laisse 22 beginning at this point in *B*. See text and variants.

This relationship is further suggested by the following variants in which *GI* agree against multiple variation or wanting evidence: *11.* 239, 268, 271, 273, 274, 277, 303, 313, 353, 358, 368, 369, and 374.

GT

As in the case of *GI*, it can be observed that *T* regularly agrees with *G* and, furthermore, that they frequently agree against *C*. Unfortunately, the marked tendency of *C* to vary independently reduces positive evidence to a minimum. Only three instances occur in which *C* agrees with *BE DH*, or with representatives of *BE* or *DH* against *GT*:

1)	*1.* 2549	*B C*: Par moi te mande Dex ne l'oublie (oublier *C*) tu pas (*E DH want*); *GT*: D. si ne l'oublie p.
2)	*1.* 2733	*BE*: Or ont assés alé li cuvert mescreant; *D C*: a. a boire l. (*H wants*); *GT*: a. beüt l.
3)	*1.* 2784	*BE DH C*: Elias les salue cui en estoit mestiers; *GT*: e. droituriers.

This minimal positive evidence is, however, strengthened by the agreement of *GT* in the following:

1)	*1.* 2810	*GT* agree in preserving a line at this point in *B* which is not found in *BE*, *DH*, or *C*. Although the evidence of *T* is limited to the first three letters of the first word of this line, it is clear that it was common to *GT*.
2)	*1.* 2985	*GT* agree in wanting this line which

is authenticated in *BE*, *DH*, and *C*.

3) *11.* 2986-2992   *GT* agree in wanting this entire passage which is authenticated in *BE*, *D*, and *C*. The agreement of *GT* with *H* in wanting this passage is almost certainly due to extreme abbreviation in the latter text which has dropped 22 of the 28 lines of this laisse.

Finally, *GT* agree against an independently varying *C* in the following: *11.* 2559, 2564, 2566, 2566 *Add*, 2569, 2720 *Add*, 2729, 2734, 2744 *Add*, 2781, 2783, 2923, 2924, 2976, 3008, 3018, 3021, 3023, and 3024.

There remains to be considered the evidence of variation which contradicts the relationships proposed in the foregoing discussion. Such evidence is to be found throughout the collation. Upon examination, however, much of it can be rejected as banal or accepted as coincidental when weighted against the preponderance of other evidence. One apparent relationship is, on the other hand, particularly persistent. *C* agrees with *H* in wanting laisses 27-31, 82, 93, 96, 100, 101, 104, and 136 of this edition all of which are authenticated in *BE*, *D*, and *G*. *CH* also agree with *E* in wanting laisse 105 and with *G* in wanting laisse 110. The passage narrated in laisses 27-31 relates Elias' frequent presence at his father's castle over a period of some three years. Since this episode is obviously inconsistent with the subsequent emphasis placed on his total ignorance of civilization when he arrives to defend his mother, its suppression is almost surely the result of an effort to improve the logical structure of the narrative. Coincidence of purpose in the face of such patent inconsistency is not difficult to accept. This could, then, account for the absence of the same passage in both texts. None of the other individual laisses wanting in both *C* and *H* is essential to the narrative and their common intent to abbreviate could again explain their agreement as coincidence. This seems to be confirmed by the fact that *C* and *H* do not agree rigorously in the many individual lines which they have omitted nor in particular variation. This is especially convincing in the light of the positive evidence indicating *BE*, *CG*, and *DH* as belonging to separate branches of the tradition.

In conclusion it is possible to say that, although the text of *B* was chosen as the base for the present edition largely by a process of elimination, its authority is in no way jeopardized by the detailed evidence of collation.

Essentially the editors have endeavored to reproduce the base manuscript as closely as possible. All emendations which appear in the text are clearly indicated by their enclosure within brackets. Rejected readings are always given in full in the notes together with whatever clarification may be necessary. As a matter of policy, emendation has been kept to a minimum and has been introduced only where the base is physically defective or where there is objective textual evidence of error. Furthermore, the suggested emendation will be, wherever possible, the reading of the most closely related variant; that is, *G* in the case of *Elioxe* and *E* in the case of *Beatrix*. In this way the reader will always be informed as to the actual reading of the base and the editors' reasons for an emendation as well as its source and authority.

The recommendations of the 1925 Convention as published in *Romania*, 52(1926), pp. 243-249, have served as a general guide for the other standard modifications of or additions to the manuscript text:

1. Identification of the text has been facilitated by numbering the laisses in the left margin and every fifth verse in the right margin.

2. Placement of the edited text with respect to the manuscript text has been facilitated by the indication of folio and column in the right margin. The four columns of each folio are designated by the letters *a* through *d*.

3. The text has been punctuated.

4. Proper nouns have been capitalized.

5. A distinction has been made between *i* and *j*.

6. A distinction has been made between *u* and *v*.

7. An acute accent has been used to mark a final accented *e* or *es* when confusion might otherwise be possible.

8. A diaeresis has been employed to indicate hiatus.

9. Roman numerals have been maintained, although superscript elements have been transcribed on line with and following the base element. The single points which regularly enclose Roman numerals in the manuscripts have been maintained.

10. Abbreviations have been resolved in accordance with

the scribal norms observed in the individual base manu-
scripts. Thus, while no unusual usage occurs, the norms ob-
served in the two texts of this edition differ slightly.

TABLE OF ABBREVIATIONS

Abbreviation	BN 12558 Elioxe	BN 786 Beatrix
1) Nasal Bar	The nasal bar in BN 12558 will be re-solved as *n* within a word and as *n* when final except in *hom*.	The nasal bar in BN 786 will be resolved as *n* within a word except when followed by *b* in which case it will be resolved as *m* and when placed over *o* followed by a nasal consonant in which case õ will be resolved as *ou*. When final it will be resolved as *n* except in *hom* and *preudom*.
2) 9	con	con/ cou/ com in keeping with the norms observed for the nasal bar.
9venir	convenir	couvenir
9vent	convent	couvent
3) ⌒		
-m͡t		-ment
b͡n	bien	bien
n͡re	nostre	nostre
sar͡r		sarrasin
v͡re	vostre	vostre
4) ∂ superscript		
bia∂		biaus
escu∂	escus	
ma∂		maus
n∂	nos	nous
pl∂	plus	plus
tag∂	agus	
v∂	vos	vous
but:		
d∂	duscal	
n∂	nus (nullus)	nus (nullus)
p∂	puis	puis

5) superscript vowel (except over q)

b^{a}nc		branc
g^{a}maire		gramaire
g^{a}nt		grant
rec^{e}ant		recreant
c^{i}e		crie
c^{i}st	crist	
mesp^{i}son		mesprison
p^{i}ent		prient
p^{i}nces		princes
c^{o}istre	croistre	
d^{o}it	droit	droit
p^{o}vost		provost
t^{o}eve	troeve	

6) superscript vowel over q

Mauq^{a}re(s)		Mauquare(s)
esq^{a}rteles		esquarteles
jusq^a		jusqu'a
q^{a}nq̄		quanque
q^{a}nt		quant
q^{a}res		quares
q^{a}rt		quart
q^{a}rtier		quartier
q^i	qui	qui

7)

q̄	que	que
q̄l		quel
q̄le	quele	quele

8) ω superscript

p$^\omega$		pour
sign$^\omega$	segnor	signour
t$^\omega$ner		tourner

9) $\mathcal{v}$ superscript

p$^{\mathcal{v}}$	por
segn$^{\mathcal{v}}$ie	segnorie

10) $\mathcal{ω}$ superscript

p$^{\mathcal{ω}}$udo		preudom

11) $\emptyset$ superscript

g$^{\emptyset}$ns	grans
olt$^{\emptyset}$ge	oltrage
q$^{\emptyset}$nt	quant
q$^{\emptyset}$ance	quarance
Rudem$^{\emptyset}$s	Rudemars
t$^{\emptyset}$vellies	travellies

12)

ch'r(s)	cevalier(s)	cevalier(s)

13) đ   denier(s)

14) dest'   destrier

15) .E.   Elias

16) Ih'u(s)   Jhesu(s)   Jhesu(s)

17) Matabᴶ   Matabrune

18) ᵱ   par/per   par
     ᵱe   pere

19) S.   saint / sainte / sains
     ş'   saint
     c̨tes   saintes (1. 812)

20) ∫t'   sont   sunt

21) ŝ   sans

22)   ⱴ   vers
     ⱴdoiant   verdoiant
     ⱴroit   verroit
     ⱴtuos   vertuos

23) ⸜ϛ   est   est

24) ꝛ   et   et

25) An apostrophe serves in both manuscripts as the abbre-
     viation for either *re* or *er*. This extremely common
     sign serves in numerous combinations.

26) ˢ serves in both manuscripts as the equivalent of *ier*.

27) ml't   molt   mout

The Record of Variants

Variation is defined for the purposes of this edition as a difference in meaning or in the expression of meaning. Thus synonyms are included among the variants. Only minor alterations of word order and purely orthographic or dialectal differences are left unrecorded.

The record of variants is organized by reference to laisse and line as they appear in the edited text. At the head of each laisse the *sigles* are given for the manuscripts being collated. In this way a quick appraisal of the textual tradition is possible without reference to the information contained in the introduction and notes.

Variant readings are given in full and are located by means of the preceding and the following words as they appear in the edited texts. Initials are used for words of more than one letter. A capital indicates that the word represented is capitalized in the edited text.

The variant manuscript is identified by its *sigle*. When more than one manuscript preserve the same variant reading, the identifying *sigles* are organized so as to reflect the relationships of the manuscripts within the tradition.

All variation is given for each line of text and is recorded as it occurs from left to right. A comma is used to separate two or more variant readings within one line of the same manuscript. A semicolon is used to separate the variant readings of different manuscripts or groups of manuscripts. It is possible, therefore, that a semicolon separate either differing variation with reference to a single given reading in the base text or variants located with reference to different points in the base text. This procedure has the disadvantage of breaking up the text of a given variant manuscript, but the advantage of providing immediate recognition of manuscript grouping at each point of variation. Suspension points indicate illegible text. Variation within variation is shown in parentheses. Conjectural readings among the variants are shown within square brackets. Lines not preserved by the base manuscript are indicated by the term *add(s)* and are separated by a slash when more than one. Lines not preserved in a variant text are indicated by the term *want(s)*. Diacritical marks and signs of punctuation are not provided for the variants themselves. Abbreviations are resolved. All explanatory material in the record of variants is printed in italics in order that it be immediately distinguished from textual material.

NOTES

1. From *ll.* 34-35 of the text. *PMLA*, 4(1889).
2. G. Paris, *Romania*, 19(1890), pp. 314-40.
3. Le Roux de Lincy proposed that the tale's origin was in Oriental tradition. There is little to substantiate this view and it has found little support.
4. As was fashionable among 19th century researchers into the origins of the world's religions, Wilhelm Müller saw a relationship between the swan-children tale and the legend of the Swan Knight in that each represents a nature or solar myth. Like the myth of Demeter and Persephone, they symbolized the life cycle, the recurring seasons, growth and decay, life and death. Wilhelm Müller, "Die Sage vom Schwanritter," *Germania*, 1(1856), pp. 418-40.
5. Shortly after, a rather faithful French translation into octosyllabic verse was made by a certain Herbert. The text has been edited by C. Brunet and A. de Montaiglon, *Li romans de Dolopathos* (Paris, 1856).
6. In his article "Sur quelques formes de la légende du Chevalier au Cygne," *Romania* (1905), Huet cautions accepting Johannes' statement. Huet argues that the *fée*'s prediction concerning the seven children to which she will give birth is evidence against an oral source, since reading in the stars and astrology are not "des idées vraiement populaires." (p. 207) Furthermore, he claims that the passage is too poetic to have been added by a writer of Johannes' capability. Thus, he argues that he was drawing from a *conte*. He suggests that the story used was originally composed from elements of two tales: "Frères métamorphosés en oiseaux" and "Deux soeurs jalouses de leur cadette." To explain the author's claim of an oral source, Huet proposes that Johannes heard it related by a jongleur who did not wish to release his manuscripts and simply noted down the major elements of the story. He further suggests that the "lost poem" was already attached to the Swan Knight cycle, thus explaining the reference made by Johannes at the end of the text.
7. The names *Elioxe*, *Beatrix*, and *Isomberte* were adopted by Gaston Paris to distinguish readily among the three

texts. The names are those given the mother of the seven children in the three versions.

8. H. Pigeonneau, *Le Cycle de la Croisade et de la Famille de Bouillon* (Saint Cloud, 1877).

9. G. Paris stresses two principal differences: (1) In *Dolopathos* the children are able to change into swans at will, a trait also found in the oral versions. In *Elioxe* the children are unaware of this possibility and are only transformed once. (2) The survival of the mother in *Dolopathos* and the cruel punishment to which she is subjected, an element totally lacking in *Elioxe*, is considered a "...description évidemment très primitive et qui ne peut avoir qu'une explication mythologique..." (p. 319).

10. The arguments of Gaston Paris do not allow for the possibility that the *Elioxe* poet, while perhaps deliberately using the *Dolopathos*, deleted the aspect of the "transformation facultative" and the survival and punishment of the mother. Since his purpose is to relate the origin of the Swan Knight, these elements are no longer of primary importance. From all indications, the folk tale involved a continuing cycle in which the single daughter, through her loyalty and diligence, saved her six brothers, was herself married, and had seven children, who repeated the same fate. However, it is almost certain that Johannes did not use the *Elioxe*, not because there is not a chivalric and feudal element, but because the features of the *Dolopathos*, changed in the *Elioxe*, agree with the independent legend in the form unassociated with the Swan Knight epic.

11. The phrase "late 12th century" is vague. Our knowledge concerning the period of popularity of the romances of the Round Table is not so definite that such a reference could not have been made at least as early as the third quarter of the 12th century. Too much depends on extant materials, the assumption that Chrétien essentially popularized Arthurian material, and the dubious theory that the 11th and early 12th centuries belong to the cruder, warlike epic. It seems prudent to give more importance to the statement of William of Tyre which, although not referring to a written text, indicates that the legendary association of Godefroy with the Swan Knight tale, also from oral tradition, was well known by 1170-1180. It is difficult to see why the swan-children could not also have been part of the *Godefroy* by this date.

12. J. Lods, *Mélanges Crozet*. Mlle Lods asserts from the beginning that the author of *Dolopathos* probably used a

well known Belgian or Lotharingian conte.

13. While it is true that the supernatural element is not so prevalent or openly developed in *Elioxe*, the entire episode takes place in a strange atmosphere which suggests the "other world." The young king becomes totally lost in an unknown area which can not be too far from his own kingdom. The lavish and unusual description of the fountain scarcely suggests ordinary reality and the girl's sudden appearance from "la montaigne" lend an aura of fantasy to the encounter. This, coupled with the reference to the girl as a *fée* in line 1635, may indicate that the author, although reducing the supernatural element, still intended to place the encounter outside the plane of ordinary reality. Mlle Lods considers the reference to this girl as a *fée* to be the result of negligence, the poet having forgotten that he had made the girl human.

14. Additional literary evidence is cited: the sleeve with which the girl covers the sleeping king, reminiscent of King Marc's glove in the Tristan story, and the king's recreant attitude which reminds one of the Arthurian manner.

15. It has been speculated that the name Oriant derives from the fact that the couple's descendants will produce "un roi d'orient." It should also be noted that this may be further evidence of the attempt to unite the tale with the literature of the First Crusade.

16. The incongruity of the boy's uncivilized upbringing and complete ignorance of civilization, even though he frequently visited the château, has been noted by several scholars.

17. This is yet another instance where the author makes a closer relationship with the cycle of the crusade, emphasizing the divine mission of the youth and the foundation of the lineage providentially ordained to undertake the holy mission of the First Crusade.

18. It should be noted that the *Isomberte* version found in the Spanish translation further changes the tale by suppressing the daughter altogether.

19. See Barron, pp. 500-11, for a detailed discussion.

BIBLIOGRAPHY

Barrois, Joseph. *Bibliothèque protypographique, ou librairies des fils du roi Jean, Charles V, Jean de Berri, Philippe de Bourgogne, et les siens.* Paris, 1830. See also Marchal, Fr. J.

Barron, W. R. J. "Versions and Texts of the *Naissance du Chevalier au Cygne.*" *Romania*, 89(1968), 481-538.

Bayot, Alphonse. "Fragments des manuscrits trouvés aux Archives générales du Royaume, deuxième notice, F; Le Roman en vers de Baudouin de Flandre." *Revue des Bibliothèques et Archives de Belgique*, 4(1906), 429-38.

Blondeaux, F. "La Légende du Chevalier au Cygne." *Revue de Belgique*, 2ᵉ série, 35(1903), 176; 38(1906), 158-76, 230-42; 39(1907), 40-49, 371-80.

Bongars, Jacques. *Gesta Dei per Francos sive Orientalium expeditionum et regni Francorum Hierosolimitani Historia.* Ed. Jacques de Vitry. Hannover, 1611.

Bossuat, Robert. "Sur un fragment de la *Chanson d'Antioche.*" *Neuphilologische Mitteilungen*, 32(1931), 110-18.

Cam, Helen Maud. *The Eyre of London, 14 Edward II, A.D. 1321*, edited for the Seldon Society. 2 vols. London, 1968.

Catalogue des Bibliothèques du Roy à Paris. See H. Omont, *Les Anciens Inventaires.*

Catalogue des Manuscrits du Cardinal Mazarin. See H. Omont, *Les Anciens Inventaires.*

Catalogue of Additions to the Manuscripts in the British Museum for the years MDCCCC-MDCCCCV. London, 1907.

Châtre de Cangé, Jean P. *Catalogue des Livres du Cabinet de M***.* Paris, 1733.

Chenaye-Desbois et de la Badier. *Dictionnaire de la Noblesse.* Vol. XIII. Paris, 1868.

Clément, Nicholas. See H. Omont, *Les Anciens Inventaires.*

Cook, Robert Francis et Larry Stuart Crist. *Le Deuxième Cycle de la Croisade: Deux études sur son développement.* Geneva, 1972.

Craster, H. H. E. and Falconer Madan. *A Summary Catalogue of Western Manuscripts in the Bodleian Library at Oxford.* Vol. II, part II. Oxford, 1922.

Crist, Larry Stuart. See Cook.

Delisle, Léopold Victor. *Le Cabinet des manuscrits de la Bibliothèque impériale (nationale): Etude sur la formation de ce dépôt, comprenant les éléments d'une histoire de la calligraphie, de la miniature, de la reliure, et du commerce des livres à Paris avant l'invention de l'imprimerie.* 3 vols. Paris, 1868-81.

Delisle, Léopold Victor. *Les Manuscrits du Compte d'Ashburnham: Rapport au Ministre de l'instruction publique et des beaux arts, suivi d'observations sur les plus anciens manuscrits du fonds Libri et sur plusieurs manuscrits du fonds Barrois.* Paris, 1883.

Delisle, Léopold Victor. *Recherches sur la librairie de Charles V.* 2 parts. Paris, 1907.

Dinaux, A. *Trouvères, jongleurs et ménestrels du nord de la France et du midi de la Belgique.* 3 vols. Paris, 1836-63.

Doutrepont, Georges. *Inventaire de la "Librairie" de Philippe le Bon (1420).* Bruxelles, 1906.

Doutrepont, Georges. *Mises en prose des épopées et des romans chevaleresques du XIVe au XVIe siècle.* Bruxelles, 1939.

Duparc-Quioc, Suzanne. *Le Cycle de la Croisade.* Paris, 1955.

Duparc-Quioc, Suzanne. "Les Manuscrits de la *Conquête de Jérusalem.*" *Romania*, 65(1939), 183-203.

Dupuy, Jacques, et Pierre. See H. Omont, *Les Anciens Inventaires.*

Edmunds, Sheila. "The Medieval Library of Savoy." *Scriptorium*, 24(1970)2, 318-27; 25(1972)2, 253-84.

Einstein, M. "Beiträge zur Ueberlieferung des *Chevalier au Cygne* und der *Enfances Godefroy.*" *Romanische Forschungen*, 29(1911), 721-63.

Espiner-Scott, Janet Girvan. *Claude Fauchet, sa vie, son oeuvre.* Paris, 1938.

Espiner-Scott, Janet Girvan. *Documents concernant la vie et les oeuvres de Claude Fauchet.* Paris, 1938.

Faider, P. et P. van Sint Jan. *Catalogue des Manuscrits Conservés à Tournai.* Gembloux, 1950.

Fauchet, Claude. *Origines des Dignitez et Magistrats de France, recueillies par Claude Fauchet,* in *Oeuvres de feu M. Claude Fauchet.* Paris, 1610.

Fauchet, Claude. *Recueil de l'origine de la langue et poésie françoise, ryme et romans.* Paris, 1581.

Foerster, Wendelin. *Der Karrenritter und das Wilhelmsleben.* Halle, 1899.

Franquen. See Marchal, Fr. J.

Frey, A. L. *The Swan Knight Legend.* Nashville, 1931.

Gautier, Leon. *Les Epopées françaises.* 4 vols. Paris,

1878-92.

Gayangos, Pascual de. *La Gran Conquista de Ultramar.* Madrid, 1858. Vol. 44 of the *Biblioteca de Autores Españoles.*

Gesta Dei per Francos sive Orientalium expeditionum et regni Francorum Hierosolimitani Historia. See Bongars.

Gossen, Charles Théodore. *Grammaire de l'ancien picard.* Paris, 1970.

Hagen, Hermann. *Catalogus Codicum Bernensium.* Bern, 1874.

Hatem, Anwar. *Les Poèmes épiques des croisades: Genèse, historicité, localisation. Essai sur l'activité littéraire dans les colonies franques de Syrie au Moyen Age.* Paris, 1932.

Hilka, Alphons. *Le Roman de Florimont.* Göttingen, 1933.

Hippeau, Célestin. *La Chanson du Chevalier au Cygne et de Godefroid de Bouillon.* 2 vols. Paris; 1874, 1877.

Hippeau, Célestin. *La Conquête de Jérusalem, faisant suite à la Chanson d'Antioche......et renouvelée par Graindor de Douai au XIIIe siècle.* Paris, 1868.

Huet, G. "Sur quelques formes de la légende du Chevalier au Cygne." *Romania*, 34(1905), 206-14.

Inventaire de la Librairie de Blois (1544). See H. Omont, *Les Anciens Inventaires.*

Jaffray, Robert. *The Two Knights of the Swan, Lohengrin and Helyas: A study of the legend of the Swan-Knight, with special reference to its two most important developments.* London and New York, 1910.

Jeanroy, A. "Deux fragments des Chansons d'Antioche et du Chevalier au Cygne." *Revue des Langues Romanes*, 42 (1899), 489-99.

Kjellman, Hilding. "Les Rédactions en prose de l'Ordre de Chevalierie." *Studier i modern språkvetenskap*, 7 (1920), 139-77.

Krogmann, W. "Die Schwanenrittersage." *Archiv*, 171(1937), 1-16.

Krüger, A. G. *Die Quellen der Schwanritterdichtungen.* Hannover, 1936.

Krüger, A. G. "Les Manuscrits de la Chanson du Chevalier au Cygne et de Godefroy de Bouillon." *Romania*, 28(1899), 421-26.

Leroquais, Victor. *Les Bréviaires manuscrits des bibliothèques publiques de France.* 6 vols. Paris, 1934.

Leroquais, Victor. *Les Livres d'heures manuscrits de la Bibliothèque Nationale.* 3 vols. Paris, 1927.

Leroquais, Victor. *Les Psautiers manuscrits latins des bibliothèques publiques de France.* 3 vols. Macon, 1940.

Lincy, Le Roux de. "Analyse du *Roman de Godefroi de Bouillon.*" *Bibliothèque de l'Ecole des Chartes*, 2(1840-41),

437-60.

Lods, Jeanne.   "L'Utilisation des thèmes mythiques dans
    trois versions écrites de la légende des enfants-cy-
    gnes." *Mélanges offerts à René Crozet*.   Poitiers,
    1966, pp. 809-20.

Lot, F. "Le Mythe des enfants cygnes." *Romania*, 21(1892),
    62-67.

Maché, Abbé. *Index Alphabétique des livres qui se trouvent
    en la Bibliothèque Royale de Turin en cette année 1713*,
    (....)&.   Catalogue handwritten in Turin, 1713. Depo-
    sited in the Biblioteca Nazionale.

Marchal, François Joseph Ferdinand. *Catalogue des manus-
    crits de la Bibliothèque royale des Ducs de Bourgogne*.
    Bruxelles, 1842.

Mare, Albinia de la. *Catalogue of the Collection of Medie-
    val Manuscripts Bequeathed to the Bodleian Library,
    Oxford, by James P. R. Lyell*. Oxford, 1971.

Martin, Henry Marie Radegonde. *Catalogue des manuscrits de
    la Bibliothèque de l'Arsenal*. 9 vols. Paris, 1885-94.

Martin, Henry Marie Radegonde. *Les Principaux manuscrits à
    peintures de la Bibliothèque de l'Arsenal à Paris*. Pa-
    ris, 1929.

Mas-Latrie, Jacques Marie Joseph Louis le Compte de. *Chro-
    nique d'Ernoul et de Bernard le Trésorier*. Paris,
    1871.

Maury, A. *Croyances et légendes du moyen age*. Paris, 1896.

Merlet, Lucien, éd. *Dictionnaire topographique du Départe-
    ment d'Eure-et-Loir, comprenant les noms de lieu an-
    ciens et modernes*. Paris, 1861.

Meyer, Paul. *Compte-rendu* of C. Hippeau's *Conquête de Jéru-
    salem*. *Bibliothèque de l'Ecole des Chartes*, 31(1870),
    227-31.

Meyer, Paul. "Etudes sur les manuscrits du *Roman d'Alexan-
    dre*." *Romania*, 11(1882), 213-32.

Meyer, Paul. "Le Poème de la Croisade imité de Baudri de
    Bourgueil. Fragment nouvellement découvert." *Romania*,
    6(1877), 489-94.

Meyer, Paul. "Le Salut d'amour dans les littératures pro-
    vençale et française." *Bibliothèque de l'Ecole des
    Chartes*, 6e série, 3(1867), 124 et suiv.

Meyer, Paul. "Un récit en vers français de la première
    Croisade fondé sur Baudri de Bourgueil." *Romania*, 5
    (1876), 1-63.

Michelant, Heinrich Viktor. *Li Romans d'Alexandre par Lam-
    bert li Tors et Alexandre de Bernay*. Stuttgart, 1846.

Mickel, Emanuel J., Jr. and Jan A. Nelson. "BM Royal 15 E
    VI and the Epic Cycle of the First Crusade." *Romania*,
    92(1971), 532-56.

Mone, Franz Joseph. "Literatur und Sprache: XVIII Aus dem Wilhelm von England." *Anzeiger für Kunde der deutschen Vorzeit*, 4(1835), 80-81.

Morenas, Henri Jougla de. *Grand Armorial de France*. Vol. V. Paris, 1848.

Müller, Wilhelm. "Die Sage vom Schwanritter." *Germania*, 1 (1858), 418-40.

Omont, Henri Auguste. *Catalogue des manuscrits français, Ancien fonds*. 5 vols. Paris, 1868-1902.

Omont, Henri Auguste. *Catalogue général des manuscrits français, Ancien supplément français*. 3 vols. Paris, 1895-1896.

Omont, Henri Auguste. *Les Anciens Inventaires et catalogues de la Bibliothèque nationale*. 5 vols. Paris, 1908-1921. This work contains the following inventories used in the present study:

Répertoire alphabétique de la Librairie de Blois (1518). Vol. I, 2-154.

Inventaire de la Librairie de Blois lors de son transfert à Fontainebleau (1544). Vol. I, 155-264.

Catalogue des Bibliothèques du Roy à Paris (1589). Vol. I, 265-475.

Dupuy, Jacques et Pierre. *Catalogus Librorum Manuscriptorum Latinorum Recentiorum, Gallicorum, Italicorum et Hispanicorum Bibliothecae Regiae, Pars Secunda (1645)*. Vol. III, 3-164.

Clement, Nicholas. *Catalogus Librorum Manuscriptorum (...) Bibliothecae Regiae (1682)*. Vol. III, 165-514; IV, 1-186.

Catalogue des manuscrits du Cardinal Mazarin (1668). Vol. IV, 280-361.

Paris, Gaston. Review article of Oesterley's edition, *Johannis de Alta Silva Dolopathos*. *Romania*, 2(1873), 481-503.

Paris, Gaston. Review article of Todd's edition, *Naissance du Chevalier au Cygne*. *Romania*, 19(1890), 314-40.

Paris, Gaston. "Un ancien catalogue de manuscrits français." *Romania*, 17(1888), 104-05.

Paris, Gaston. "Un fragment épique." *Romania*, 29(1900), 106.

Paris, Paulin. "Etude sur les poèmes épiques des Croisades." *Histoire littéraire de la France*, 22(1895), 350-402; 25(1888), 507-618.

Paris, Paulin. *La Chanson d'Antioche*. 2 vols. Paris, 1848.

Paris, Paulin. "Nouvelles études sur la *Chanson d'Antioche*." *Bulletin du Bibliophile et du Bibliothécaire*, 1877, pp. 433-59; 1878, pp. 97-121.

Paris, Paulin. *Les Manuscrits françois de la Bibliothèque du Roy*. 7 vols. Paris, 1836-48.

Pasinus, Josephus. *Codices Manuscripti Bibliothecae Regii Taurinensis Athenaei*. 2 vols. Turin, 1749.

Patterson, Sonia. "Comparison of Minor Initial Decoration: a Possible Method of Showing the Place of Origin of Thirteenth-century Manuscripts." *The Library*, 27 (1972), 23-30.

Patterson, Sonia. "Paris and Oxford University Manuscripts of the Thirteenth Century." Unpublished Baccalaureus Litterarum thesis deposited in the Bodleian Library, 1970. MS. B. Litt. d. 1457.

Pigeonneau, H. *Le Cycle de la Croisade et de la famille de Bouillon*. Saint-Cloud, 1877.

Poisson, G. "L'Origine celtique de la légende de Lohengrin." *Revue Celtique*, 34(1913), 182-202.

Porcher, Jean. *Les Manuscrits à peintures en France*. Part II *Du XIIIe au XVIe*. Paris, 1955. (A catalogue of the exhibition held in the BN in 1955).

Pot, J. *Histoire de Regnier Pot, conseiller des Ducs de Bourgogne*. Paris, 1929.

Reiffenberg, Frédéric A. F. T. Baron de. *Romans du Chevalier au Cygne et de Godefroid de Bouillon*. 3 vols. Bruxelles, 1846-48.

Répertoire alphabétique de la Librairie de Blois. See H. Omont, *Les Anciens Inventaires*.

Riant, Paul. "Inventaire sommaire des manuscrits de l'*Eracles*." *Archives de l'Orient latin*, 1(1881), 247-56.

Ross, David John Athole. *Alexander Historiatus: A guide to medieval illustrated Alexander literature*. The Warburg Institute Surveys, No. 1. London, 1963.

Roy, Emile. "Les Poèmes français relatifs à la première croisade: Le Poème de 1356 et ses sources." *Romania*, 55 (1929), 411-68.

Ruelle, P. *Les Dits de Droit du Clerc de Voudroi*. Bruxelles, 1969.

Sanderus, Antonius. *Bibliotheca Belgica Manuscripta*. 2 vols. Insulis (Lille), 1641-44. See also Marchal, Fr. J.

Schurfranz, Robert L. "The French Swan-Knight Legend." *Dissertation Abstracts*, 20(1960), 2808-09.

Simpson, H. A. *Simpson and Allied Families*. 2 vols. Somerville, New Jersey, 1935.

Smith, H. A. "Studies in the Epic Poem of *Godefroi de Bouillon*." *Publications of the Modern Language Association*, 27(1912), 142-67; 28(1913), 56-78.

Stengel, E. "Die Chansondegeste-Handschriften der Oxforder Bibliotheken." *Romanische Studien*, 3(1873), 380-408.

Sumberg, L. A. M. *La Chanson d'Antioche*. Paris, 1968.

Todd, H. A. *La Naissance du Chevalier au Cygne ou les Enfants changés en cygnes*. Publications of the Modern Language Association, 4(1889).

Vaughan, R. *Philip the Bold*. London and Harvard, 1962.

Vaughan, R. *Philip the Bold*. London, 1970.

Verlet-Réaubourg, N. "L'oeuvre de Richard le Pèlerin et de Graindor de Douai connue sous le nom de *Chanson d'Antioche*." *Position des thèses de l'Ecole des Chartes*, 1932, pp. 153-58.

Viglius. See Marchal, Fr. J.

Ward, Harry Leigh Douglas. *Catalogue of Additions to the Manuscripts in the British Museum in the years 1900-1905*. London, 1907.

Ward, Harry Leigh Douglas. *Catalogue of Romances in the Department of Manuscripts in the British Museum*. 3 vols. London, 1883.

Warner, George F. and Julius P. Gilson. *Catalogue of Western Manuscripts in the Old Royal and King's Collections*. 4 vols. Oxford, 1921.

Weinbaum, Martin. "London unter Eduard I und II." *Vierteljahrschrift für Sozial- und Wirtschaftsgesthichte*. Beiheft 27-30. Stuttgart, 1933.

Wilbaux, A. M. *Catalogue des Manuscrits de Tournai*. Tournai, 1860.

William of Tyre. Ed. in *Recueil des Historiens des Croisades: Historiens Occidentaux*. Vol. I. Paris, 1844.

Williams, Gwyn A. *Medieval London, from Commune to Capital*. London, 1963.

ELIOXE

Edited by Emanuel J. Mickel, Jr.

For Kathleen

1   Segnor, or m'escotés, por Deu et por son non,   1*a*
    Par itel convenent Dex vos face pardon,
    Li rois de sainte glore, qui par anontïon
    Vint en la sainte dame qui Marie ot a non.
    Jou vos wel conmencier une bone chancon,   5
    L'estorie en fu trovee el mostier saint Fagon,
    Tot droit en Rainscevals si con oï avon,
    Par dedens une aumaire u les livres met on;
    La l'avoit mise uns abes qui molt estoit preudon;
    Cil le prist a Nimaie si con lisant trueve on.   10
    Del Cevalier le Cisne dirai la nontïon,
    De lui et de son pere, Lotaires ot a non,
    Confaitement il vinrent et par quele raison,
    Et de quel terre il furent et de quel regïon.
    Par defors Hungerie, si con lisant trovon,   15
    Marcissoit uns roiames qui ert et grans et lons,
    Si le tenoit uns rois qui molt par fu preudon;
    Roi Phelipe l'apelent tot cil de son roion.
    Feme ot sage et cortoise et de bele facon;
    Et saciés par verté, si n'en dote nus hon,   20
    Ke de bone semence bon fruit en atent on.
    Li rois jut a sa feme par bone ententïon
    Et engenra .I. fil qui molt par fu preudon.
    Tant le porta la dame que Damedeu fu bon,
    Et quant vint li termines de naistre l'enfancon,   25
    Plus bele creature ne vit onques nus hom.
    Al mostier le porterent par bone ententïon,
    Illuec le batiza uns evesques Simon,
    Ens el non de baptesme Lotaires ot a non.
    L'enfes crut et amende plus c'autres enfancon;   30
    Ce fu drois, qu'il estoit de bone estratïon.   1*b*

2   Segnor, or m'escoutés, por Deu le raemant,
    Si vos dirai cancon bien faite et avenant,
    Ce est de la naissence .I. cevalier vaillant,
    Le Cevalier le Cisne, qui Dex par ama tant   35
    K'il fu a son service maint jor a son vivant.
    De lui et de son pere, de son aiol avant,
    Vos dironmes l'estorie, saciés a esciant.
    Phelipes ot a non, qui molt par fu vaillant;
    Ses fiux ot non Lotaires, qui molt fu avenant.   40
    L'enfes crut et amende, et molt par fu sacant.
    Molt par fu bels et sages; quant il avoit .XII. ans
    D'eskiés sot et de tables et d'autres estrumans;
    Bien savoit cevalcier avoec les bohordans.
    Molt en fu liés li peres, c'est drois, de ses enfans. 45
    Maladie li prist: quant ce vint a son tans
    Ke morir li convint, ce fu damages grans.

Le roi ensevelirent si home et si serjant,
Enterrés fu le jor, si ot dolor molt grant.
Grant duel i demenerent sa feme et si parant,   50
Molt furent deceü de segnor bel et gant;
Mais encor raront boin, se Deu vient a talant.
Quant li deus fu remés de cel enterremant,
Lotaires a parlé a sen consellement;
Asseürer se fait de trestote sa gent,   55
Et de tos les barons a pris le sairement
Ki son pere servoient a son conmandement.
Sauve l'onor sa mere que de rien n'i mesprent
Li vallés duit sa terre, si se fist hautement
Coroner, a ses homes faire asseürement.   60
Tot cou que ses pere ot, tint il entirement,
Ainc n'en laissa avoir plain pié estrange gent,
Se il ne lor dona molt amiablement.
Bien sot tenir sa terre et amer france gent.
Ses amis fait de cels qui furent si parent,   65
Frans homes [a] assis garder son tenement.[1]
Onques sers n'aproisma a son consellement,
N'ainc ne fist a franc home nul deseritement,
A veve ne a orfene ne a petit enfant.

3   Molt tint em pais sa terre, c'ainc n'i ot enconbrier, 70
Molt tint em pais sa terre, c'ainc n'i ot enconbrier, 70
N'ainques n'ala a marce o son voisin plaidier.
Si voisin le sentoient et orgellos et fier,
Molt tint em pais sa terre, molt l'orent li sien chier.
A un jor prist ses ciens, s'ala el bois chacier;
Cevaliers maine o lui qui ierent si maisnier,   75
Et en haute forest fait il ses rois chachier.   1c
Aprés les rois s'en vont li chien et li bernier,
Et al renc d'autre part ierent li liemier.
Tant ont alé cerkant fort voie et for[t] sentier[2]
K'il ont levé .I. cerf si grant conme aversier;   80
.XIIII. brances ot en son son cervelier;
Il le chacent a force par abai de levrier.
De chiens i ot .II. muetes, nel porent detrïer;
Ne pueent tant haper ne mordre ne pincier
Ne li arcier tant traire as ars de cor manier   85
Ne tot li veneor de lor espius lanchier,
K'il onques le peüscent verser ne trebucier.
As rois en est venus, outre saut de legier;
Ne crient mais veneor, for est de lor dangier.
Fuit s'ent si lonc qu'il n'ot mais nul cien abaier. . 90
Qui caut? Quant perdus est n'i a nul recovrier.
Rois Lotaires seoit sor .I. ceval corsier,
Ki le cerf porsivoit, en sa main .I. espier.
Tant le porsiut a force que vint a l'anuitier.

Tost se fu oubliés por la bisse chacier   95
Ne ne sot u il fu ne ne sot repairier,
Ne maison ne voit nule u il puist herbergier.
El bois se met ariere d[e]sos .I. fou plenier;[3]
La prist herbergerie quant il dut anuitier.
Le frain oste au ceval, laist li paistre l'erbier,   100
Et il le paist molt bien, car il en ot mestier.
Ne dormi ainc Lotaires, ains se prist a vellier.
Son espiel et son cor et s'espee d'acier,
Tot a mis dalés lui car il en ot mestier
Por leu u por ferain u por autre aversier,   105
Ke il le truise prest se il en a mestier.

4   Assés pensa li rois con hom qui seus estoit;
Son ceval garde pres qui volentiers paisoit,
S'espee et son espiel u il molt se fioit.
Li nuis passa issi desci que le jor voit,   110
Adont ne li caut plus en quel païs il soit.
Met la sele et son frain si cevalce a esploit,
Retorner quide ariere, venir a son destroit.
Trespasse bos et landes, ne troeve qui l'avoit;
Il n'ot cien ne abai, borc ne castel ne voit.   115
La caure leva grans qui forment l'agrevoit.
Devers .I. mont s'en va dont il tres bien verroit
.X. liues tot entor, se sor le mont pooit;
Ses cevals lase molt, car travelliés estoit.
Il estoit miedis et la caure anuioit   120
Et lui et son ceval; li rois nient n'en pooit.   1*d*
Au pié de la montaigne uns bels caisnes seoit;
Grans estoit et foillus et grant ombre faisoit.
Bien peüssent .LX. cevalier sans destroit
Seoir desous en l'ombre faire lor esbanoit,   125
Et si ot .I. praiel ki tostans florisoit.
Il voit et l'arbre et l'ombre, l'ore soëf ventoit.
Cil descent del ceval qui repos desiroit,
Le frain oste et la sele au ceval ki suoit
Et li cevals se witre, car sa nature estoit,   130
Dont saut sus et paist l'erbe qui soëf li flairoit.
Rois Lotaires s'en va a la fontaine droit
Qui devers Oriant son sorgon enveoit.

5   La fontaine estoit bele et clere et delitouse;
Al fons avoit gravele qui n'ert pas anuiouse,   135
Onques Tagus n'en ot nule tant presciouse.
Cil fluns Tagus coroit sor terre gravillouse,
La gravele estoit d'or sel quierent gens wisose;
Mais iceste fontaine si est tant gravillouse,
Il n'a gravele al fons ne soit tant vertuouse;   140

Diamans ne metistes qui force ont mervellouse,
Topaces, electories qui tant est jentius couse.
Toutes sont teles pieres qui cele aige ot enclose,
N'i a nule entaillie ne nule imaginouse.
Por cou furent la mises, que nus qui boire en ouse,   145
Ja tant n'ert travelliés que sa cars ne repose;
De giste ne de fievre n'ert ja acoisonouse.
S'est hom qui eüe ait la male erite couse,
Sen front let de cele aigue qui est tant bone couse,
Sempres sera garis, ja n'ert tant angoissouse.   150

6   La s'en vait rois Lotaires qui'st de bon esc̃ient.
Al riu leve ses mains et son vis ensement;
Grant mestier en avoit car tot l'avoit sullent.
Adont lava sa bouce qui de halle li fent,
Et despoilla sa cote et vint sor l'erbe al vent.   155
La s'est couciés a terre sor l'erbe verdoiant,
Et son cor et s'espee et son espiel devant.
La s'endort si con hom qui le laste avoit grant;
La nuit qui passee ert n'avoit dormi niant.
Ez vos une pucele cortoise et avenant,   160
De la grande montaigne vint illuec descendant.
Ne sai que sa biauté vos alaisse contant;
Bele estoit et bien faite et de parage grant,
Et son manoir avoit ens el mont la devant,
Et puceles laiens por faire son conmant;   165
Es cavernes del mont la ot abitement.   2a
Venue en est aval el pré esbanoiant;
Voit le roi la gesir s'esgarde son sanblant,
Si a coisi l'espee et le cor d'olifant
Et l'espiel ki bons ert, noëlés a argant: 170
Bien li sanble qu'il fust del parage vaillant.
Souavet marce l'erbe, ne va mie noisant;
Voit le rai del soleil sor le vis descendant,
Poise li que le halles li va son vis ardant.
Neporquant hom hallé, jel tieng a avenant.   175
Sa mance qu'il avoit a s'espaulle pendant
Li estent sor le vis por le soleil raiant,
Puis se retrait ariere vers le ruisel corant.
Ne vaut pas quivriier le cevalier vaillant;
Tant atent qu'a dormi, puis li vint de devant.   180

7   Lotaires s'esperi, si rejeta la mance.
"Dex," dist il, "rois del ciés, donés moi hui quaance,
Longement ai esté en cest bos en esrance;
Encor sui jo assez, ce me senble, en balance."
Saine soi de la crois u il a grant fiance,   185
Et puis reclainme Deu u il a sa creance.

Regarde la pucele, n'avoit si bele en France.
"Pucele, si con Dex vous fist a sa sanblance,
Si garde il vo cors et vo grant honerance;
Ce vos vient de grant cuer et de grant sapiance   190
Que vos m'avés ci faite et aise et aombrance."
"Sire," dist la pucele, "bien sanblés de vaillance,
Mais co wel jo savoir, par quele mesprisance
Entrastes en mon bos? Ene cou enfance?
J'en porrai, se jo woel, molt tost avoir venjance;   195
Mi centisme arai tost a escu et a lance,
Se je trovoie en vos ranprosne ne beubance.
[Ma] terre est bien gardee, si a grant porveance;[4]
Jo ai homes assez qui sont de grant vaillance."
Lotaires li respont par grant humeliance: 200
"Dame, con il aroit en vos plus d'onerance
Et valor et bonté, et tant plus de soufrance
Troverai jo en vos, jo i ai grant fiance.
Ier porsivi .I. cerf tote jor par enfance,
Grant et fort et ramu de .XIIII.ime brance.   205
Jel sivi jusc'al vespre si que par anuiance,
Ne m'en seuc retorner, ains fui en grant balance,
Ke ors, leu u lion n'en presiscent venjance
De moi et de ma beste; ce fust grans destorbance.
Tote nuit fui el bois, l'espiel tinc par le mance,   210
Et mes cevals paisoit herbe et foille en la brance.2*b*
Quant Dex dona le jor et je vi l'aube blance,
Si restrains mon ceval si fui mains en dotance;
Montai por cevalcier, aler a connissance.
Ne sai quel part je sui, ne ne quier pas beubance;   215
Metés moi al chemin, pucele de vaillance,
Si porterai de vos bone novele en France."

8   "Damoisials, al respondre vos tieng auques a sage,
Moi sanble que ne dites ne orguel ne oltrage;
Et nonporquant, amis, només moi vo parage.   220
Li miens pere fu rois et de grant vasselage,
.IX. cités m'a laisié quites en iretage.
De .L. castels ai jo le segnorage,
Et quanqu'il i apent vient tot a mon servage,
Et voiier et maieur tot rendent treüage."   225
Li danzels li respont qui fu de bon corage:
"Damoisele, je sui d'un molt lontain manage.
En cest bois ving chacier, si me torne a folage
Quant ersoir me perdirent mi home en cest boscage."
"Amis," dist la pucele, "bien sanble a vo corage   230
Que vos estes frans hom et de vaillant linage.
Avés encore prise feme par mariage
U amie esgardee d'aucun roial parage,

Que vos welliés avoir a oissor vostre eage,
Dont vos aiés enfans noris par segnorage?" 235
"Naie, voir, damoisele, onques n'en oc corage.
Jo nen euc onques feme, n'entendi a tel rage.
En ciens et en oisiaus ai usé mon eage,
Et quant mestiers me fu, si refis vaselage,
Et s'ai gardé ma terre c'on ne m'en fist damage. 240

9 Puis qu'avons conmencié ci de feme a parler,
Se vos n'aviés ami, vaurié[s] me vos amer?[5]
Por vo valor qui'st grans vos vaurai honerer
Et tenir loiaument a moillier et a per,
Et de toute ma terre ferai dame clamer, 245
Et les enfans qu'avrons vaurai bien ireter."
Et respont li pucele: "Bien le voel creanter,
Cou que vos avés dit ne fait a refuser;
Mais or vos plaise .I. poi de mes dis escoter.
Se me prendés a feme, por voir vos puis conter, 250
Vostre linages ert espandus outre mer
Et jusqu'en Oriant le verra on r[egn]er."[6]
"C'est cou," ce dist li rois, "que tant puis desirer."
"Escoute encore, rois, si m'oras d'el parler.
En la premiere nuit aprés nostre espouser, 255
Que vauras vraiement a ma car deliter,   *2c*
Jo te di par verté loiaument sans fauser
Que tu de .VII. enfans me feras encarger:
Li .VI. en ierent malle, et pucele al vis cler
Iert li sietismes enfes, co ne puet trespasser. 260
Lasse! Moi, j'en morrai de ces enfans porter.[7]
Et quels talens me prent que jo m'en doie aler
La u il m'estavra de tele mort pener,
Mais que teux destinee doit par mi moi passer?
Et m'estuet travellier et tel mort endurer 265
Por le linage acroistre qui ira outre mer,
Et qui la se fera segnor et roi clamer.
Encor te vaurai jo autre cose conter:
Cascuns de ces enfans aura sisne d'or cler[8]
El col d'une caaine que bien porra mostrer; 270
A tot co naistront il jel vos di sans doter.
Conmandés les enfans par grant cure a garder,
Quel part que vos soiés, u en terre u en mer
Ou en pais ou en guerre, vos en estuet pener."

10 Or se teut la pucele quant ot dit son talent. 275
Rois Lotaires oï molt bien tot son convent,
Mais mervelle li sanble de cel anoncement,
Conment tot co poroit venir entierement.
Il esgarde celi qui tot son cuer esprent,

Promet li et otroie a amer loialment.   280
Le menra avoec lui en sa terre a sa gent,
Aprés l'espousera con rois segnerilment.
De l'esrer s'aparellent tost et isnelement.
La pucele Elioxe apela .I. sergent,
Samonie, sa pucele, qui'st de bon escïent: 285
"Jo woel a vos parler, ca venés erranment."
Cele ist de la montaigne tost et isnelement:
"Je sui ci, damoisele, dites vostre talent."
"Samonie, enselés moi de rice afeutrement
Ma blance mule isnele, et met le frain d'argent,   290
Le poitral qui est d'or et fais molt ricement
Li laciés a la sele qui est d'ivoire blanc;
Gardés que soit ferree et deriere et devant,
Et soient tot li fer ou d'or fin ou d'argent.
Mes escrins, mes forgiés, por porter ensement;   295
Et metés i des reubes .VII. paire [seulement],[9]
Et mes aornemens que vos tenés sovent;
Si faites .I. soumier del palefroi ferrent.
Vos meïsme en prendés tot a vostre talent."
Samonie, la pucele, ot molt bien et entent   300
Tot le voloir sa dame et son conmandement;   . 2d
Revint a la montaigne, fist aparellement
Molt rice a oës sa dame, a son oës ensement.
Prent .I. frain el tresor ovré d'or et d'argent,
Li poitrals est d'or fin alumés d'or luisent,   305
La siele est si vaillans que .IIII. Venissent
Ne l'esligascent mie de quanqu'il ont vaillant.
Li arcon et les alves sont d'un os d'olifant;
La sorsiele en estoit d'un paile escarimant,
Dusqu'a la terre en vont quatre langes batant.   310
Ele prent .II. escrins, met ens son garniment,
Dras de soie a vestir en grant cointoiement,
Une rice coroie a pieres qui resplent,
.XII. pieres i a, cascune ki resprent,
C'Adans avoit coillies en .I. ruisel corant   315
En paradis u Dex l'avoit fait ja manant.
Afices et aniaus, ce n'oblia noient,
Boistes et ongemens qui sont souef flairant,
Et abosnes assés et ciers atornement.[10]
Tot cou mist es escrins et carga sor Ferrent   320
A l'aiue qu'ele ot d'un vertuos sergent;
Ele ot ausi meïsme .I. ceval avenant.
Quant ot aparellié, vint a sa dame errant.

11   Lioxe fist monter li rois par cortoisie,
Et il cevalce en coste a senestre partie.   325
Lioxe a aregné, par le resne le guie,

Et Sa[m]onie cevalce avoec par conpaignie.[11]
Lés le bos cevalcierent par une praerie,
Por adrecier lor voie dont li rois ne set mie.
Tant ont alé le sente lés le voie enhermie   330
Ke li rois voit les tors de sa grant manandie,
S'en i avoit ne mais c'une liue et demie.
Or a tant cevalcié, pres est d'une hucie,
Met le cor a sa bouce dont douce estoit l'oïe;
Si a soné le cor que tote est estormie   335
La cités et la tors, si saut sus sa maisnie.
"Oés la mon segnor," cascuns d'els tos s'escrie,
"Montés, alons encontre, si le faisons joïe."
Si font il con il dïent, poignant a une hie,
Salüent lor segnor et il les en merchie.   340
Sa mere vient encontre et il si l'a baisie,
Et tot li cevalier a molt grant conpaignie.
Rois Lotaires lor dist: "Segnor, ne faites mie
Joie ne feste a moi, mais a ma doce amie.
Jo l'ainc tant que cou est et ma cose et ma vie;   345
Jou l'ainc sor tote rien, nel vos celerai mie."   3*a*
Adont fu la pucele hautement recoillie,
De tos les cevaliers jentement conjoïe.
Des palefrois descendent, vont en la tor antie;
Sonent gigles, viïeles et font grant melodie.   350
Rois Lotaires sor tos les enforce et aïe,
Bien tient .C. cevaliers avoec lui de maisnie.
Il mande dus et princes qu'a lui par compaignie
Viegnent tot a sa cort et si verront s'amie
Qu'il vaudra prendre a feme, ne dem[ö]era mie.[12]   355

12 Sa mere voit l'afaire et l'aparellement,
Bien demostre en son fait tot son proposement;
Des noces s'aparelle et en mostre sanblant.
D'une part l'en a trait si li dist son talent:
"Bels fiux, que penses tu? Nel fai sifaitement!   360
Tu ne prenderas feme ensi soudainement.
Jo te querai oisor tot al los de no gent.
Ci pres maint Anotars qui a grant tenement,
Rois est de grant puissance s'a maint rice parent;
Et Michaël le duc et Rodain l'amirent: 365
Andoi sont si cosin germain, mien escïent.
Icil a une fille, damoisele vaillent,
Jel te ferai avoir; maintien toi sagement."
"Ke dites vos, ma dame? Tot cou n'i a noient!
Jo nel lairoie mie por plain .I. val d'argent   370
Ke n'espeuse Elioxe, la pucele al cors gent;
Puis que Dex le me done, jo nel refus noient.
Jo sui rices assez, car j'ai grant tenement;

Jo ne crien mes voisins por guerre qu'il movent.[13]
Il n'ont parente nule qui me viegne a talent.   375
Ceste est et bele et sage et de bon esciẽt;
Jo l'aim, jel voel avoir, jo l'avrai loialment."
"Bels fils," co dist la mere, "tu ne prises nĩent
Cou que jo te di ci de mon consellement."
Quant assez ont parlé, atant se departent.   380
Lotaires aparelle ses noces festeument;
Il mande ses fievés de tot son tenement
K'il soient a ses noces devant li en present,
Et mande .I. arcevesque qu'il tenoit a parent:
Gerars avoit a non. Cil i vient gentement   385
Et .C. cevalceeurs; molt maine bele gent.
A cort vient al perron, del palefroi descent.
Vient al roi sel salue; li rois salus li rent.
Main a main s'entretienent et vont el pavement
Seoir sor une coute d'un vermel bougerent;   390
La li dist son afaire, ne li cela nĩent.   *3b*
L'arcevesques li loe, puis qu'il en a talent
De feme avoir o lui sel prenge loialment.
Et li rois li respont: "Par Deu omnipotent,
De lonc l'ai amenee si li ai en covent   395
Loiauté a tenir par non d'espousement."

13   La feste est plenteĩve et grans et segnoris;
     La assamblent li prince de par tot le païs,
     Si vienent a la feste le roi qui'st lor amis;
     Molt ot gent el palais qui fu de marbre bis.   400
     La sont li jogleor, cantent lais, notent dis,
     La lor donent li prince cotes et mantels gris;
     Ki set dire u canter bonement est oïs.
     En la place as vallés et as escus vautis
     Desregnent l'uns vers l'autre lor valor et lor pris. 405
     Hurtent, luitent as bras; s'uns en ciet s'a haus cris.
     Si ne puet eschaper sans molt grant hueïs.
     D'autre part sont li ors et li cien, .VIII. u .X.,
     Ki la refont grant joie et grant pesteleïs;
     D'autre part sont li singe qui lor font les faus ris.410
     Tout issi a la feste s'est cascuns entremis
     Des plus bels gius a faire qui lor furent apris.
     El demain quant li jors fu auques esclarcis
     Et rois Lotaires est et parés et vestis
     Et li grans pules est en la sale acoisis,   415
     L'arcevesques s'en va au mostier saint Felis
     Et s'est segnerilment a l'autel revestis.
     Li rois i est venus, bien a .LX. et dis
     De cevaliers, haus homes, princes, dus et marcis,
     Ki tot ierent vaillant, si les tient a amis.   420

La pucele adestra li princes Anseïs,
Et uns dus qui ot non Antelmes li Petis.
Au mostier le menerent devant saint crucefis,
La font lor orisons, puis si sainent lor vis.
L'arcevesques demande qu'il estoient la quis.   425
Rois Lotaires respont: "Bels sire, ciers amis,
Je woel que me donés Elioxe al cler vis
Et si le m'espousés tot al vostre devis;
Voiant vos li donrai, en non Deu, douëlis,
La tierce part del regne dont jo sui poëstis."   430
Et respont l'arcevesques: "Tot co est bien assis."
Dont a prise Elioxe par les dois c'ot vautis,
Si le dona Lotaire, et li Saint Esperis
Lor doinst joie et honor a lor vie tosdis.
Aprés prent .I. anel qui estoit d'or masis,   435
Si li a mis el doit *in nomine patris*   3c
Et el non del Saint Fil et del Saint Esperis.
Puis a chanté la messe, et il fu bien oïs.
Cil jors fu solenels partot et festeïs.
Aprés messe conmence feste et bohordeïs: 440
On lieve les quintaines la u on fiert tosdis,
Et jogleor i cantent et lais et sons et dis.
Les viandes i sont en tos lius plenteïs.
Li rois done mervelles, siglatons et samis,
Escarlates et vers, pelicons vairs et gris;   445
N'i remaint a doner palefrois ne roncis,
Nés d'or, coupes d'argent: c'est poi, ce li est vis.
Il done fiés et terres a ses mellors amis,
N'i a nul qui li ruist en voist escondis.

14 Siet jors dura la feste qui bien fu conmencie,   450
Mais a l'uitisme jor fu auques departie;
En lor liu s'en reva li grans cevalerie.
Rois Lotaires remaint ensanble sa maisnie,
.LX. cevaliers de molt grant segnorie.
Donc vint a Elioxe, sa douce ciere amie: 455
"Bele suer," dist li rois, "la feste est departie
Des sorvegnans qui vinrent, qui nous ont fait joie.
Or conmence la nostre, Dex nos soit en aïe;
Des ore mais ensanble deliterons no vie."
Il se coucent ensanble quant nuis fu enserie,   460
L'une cars conut l'autre, Nature nes oublie;
L'uns rent l'autre son droit et font lor cortoisie,
Qu'amors a estoré entre ami et amie;
Quant ont lor volenté et lor joie aconplie,
Si n'est mais damoisele, ains est dame joie,   465
Elioxe la bele, que Dex doins segnorie.
Andoi gisent en bras, ele s'est endormie;

Dont a songié .I. songe dont molt est esmarie,
Qu'ele gisoit coverte d'unes pials de Rousie
En .I. lit bien ovré a ouevre triforie.   470
Li lis estoit covers de roses en partie,
Des le moitié aval tos li lis enrougie,
L'autre moitiés amont est de lis le florie.
Es roses vers les piés ot .VII. pumes mucies,
Pumes de paradis que Dex a en baillie;   475
Ains hom ne vit si beles qui fust en mortel vie.
Cele cose a sa mere ens es roses coisie,
Toutes .VII. li toloit et enbloit par envie;
As .VI. colpoit les keues et la setisme oblie;
Nes giete mie puer molt s'en est bien gaitie,   480
Mais les pumes jeta en une desertie.   *3d*
A cest mot s'esvella Elioxe, s'escrie:
"Lieve sus, rois Lotaires, por Deu, aïe! aïe!"
Rois Lotaires se lieve, celi a enbracie:
"Sainiés vos, bele suer, que Dex vos beneïe,   485
Et vostre ame metés tos cels en conmandie
Ki baillent le cors Deu en la messe serie.
Porqu'estes vos, ma douce, issi espaorie?"
Cele a mal en sa teste, tote l'a estordie,
El ne desist .I. mot, ki li donast Pavie.   490
Cil le tint en ses bras conme feme espasmie,
Il l'acole et si l'a en la bouce baisie.
Cele revint en sens, s'a memoire coillie.
"Douce suer," dist li rois, "jo vos ai enbracie.
Que vos est avenu? Nel me celés vos mie.   495
Ne soiés pas honteuse envers moi, doce amie."
"Songe, sire, et fantosme m'ont ma teste espartie,
Mais a Deu conmanc jou et mon cors et ma vie.
Jel di a Damedeu et a sainte Marie
Et a trestos les sains qu'el ciel ont segnorie: 500
Tornés le moi a bien, si ferés cortoisie.
Mes lis est tos espars de flors en colorie,
Et jo euc en ces roses .VII. cosetes mucies;
C'estoient .VII. pumetes dont l'abre fu florie
La u Adans mest ja la premiere partie;   505
Et il en fu jetés par sa grant felonie.
Se mes ot on tolu par molt grant estoutie,
Et cil quis en porta retint en sa baillie
Les keues, et les pumes jeta en terre ermie,
Que mais n'en fust parole veüe ne oïe;   510
Les .VI. en jeta puer, et le sieme i oublie.
E! Dex, que puet ce estre et ce que senefie?"
"Dame," ce dist li rois, "ne vos esmaiés mie,
Dex vous confortera, qui tot a en baillie.
.VII. pumes sont .VII. fil, dont Dex vos en delivre;   515

S'il est aucuns malvais qui de vos ait envie,
N'oubliés pas por co a mener bone vie.
Soiés bone aumosniere et tostans bien garnie,
S'onerés sainte eglise et le sainte clergie;
Se veés de povre home la car mesaaisie,   520
Tant li faites por Deu qu'ele soit raemplie;
Et se vos veés povre qui li fains enaigrie,
Viande li donés tant que soit rasasie;
Cels qui por Deu vos prïent por Deu faciés aïe,
Si arés gracie en terre et en ciel glorie et vie."   525

15 Doucement apaia Lotaires sa moillier,   4*a*
    Qui molt ert effr[a]ée de le ente songier.[14]
    Il le baise et acole et fait tot son dangier
    Por la freor del songe del tot entr'obliier.
    Quant tant orent jeü jors prist a esclairier,   530
    Les jentius dames vindrent au lit esbanoier.
    Les autres font les bains por la dame aaisier,
    Del tot li font ses aises tant con ele a mestier;
    Et li rois est levés, dont vindrent cevalier.
    En la chapele au roi fist on aparellier   535
    Et revestir .I. prestre por le devin mestier.
    Li rois i est venus por Damedeu proier,
    Et tot si conpaignon o lui por festoier.
    Li prestre est revestu u il n'ot qu'ensegnier,
    Messe del Saint Espir qui tot puet consellier   540
    A conmencié en haut, sa voi[s] fait sohaucier;[15]
    De canter et de lire fait ofise plenier.
    Li cambrelens le roi qui avoit le mestier
    Aporta son segnor .III. ofrandes d'or mier,
    Ce furent .III. bezant, c'est ofrande a princier.   545
    Et a cascuns qui est la venus al mostier
    A doné autresi .I. estrelin denier.
    Et li rois est alés l'ofrande conmencier,
    Et li autre s'en vont a lui aconpaignier.

16 Dont a on aporté .II. bacins d'argent cler,   550
    U li capelains va por ses dois respaumer;
    Puis a fait el calise pain et vin manister;
    Et aigue, con drois est, avoec le vin meller.
    Il entre en son service le cors Jhesu sacrer.
    Rois Lotaires qui la ert venus por orer;   555
    Il est agenoilliés por mius humelier,
    Et ses mains lieve en haut si conmence a penser
    Et dire de bon cuer por Damedeu löer:
    "Dex, qui plus iés poissans c'on ne puist deviser,
    Qui nostre premier pere por ton non aorer   560
    Mesis en paradis, si li donas a per

Et a moillier Evain por ensanble abiter.
Diables i ala por aus desireter,
Mangier lor fist le fruit dont ne durent goster;
Adont s'entreconnurent et virent nu ester,   565
D'un figier prisent foilles por lor cars esconser;
Et tu i alas, Sire, a eus vausis parler:
'Adan, u iés alés? Vien ca, ne te celer.'
Dist Adans: 'Je sui ci, si m'a fait meserrer
Eve, que me donas a moillier et a per.'   4*b* 570
'Por cou que mon conmant m'a si fait trespasser,
Or t'en iras,' dist Dex, 'en autre terre ester;
De tes mains t'estavra desor mais laborer,
Et Evain ta moillier en dolor enfanter.'
Mort furent ambedoi, si les estut aler   575
En infer u nus hom ne pot ainc reposser.
Après lui en convint tos ses enfans aler,
Kaïn, Abel et autres que jo ne sai nomer;
Noë et Abrehan, Moÿset al vis cler,
Tous les fils Ysraël, que on ne puet nonbrer;   580
Et Jessé et David et Salemon le ber.
Dex, il t'en prist pitiés del danne restorer,
La tiue gent vausis de torment ramener,
Sagement le fesis por Deable enganer;
Dex, tu fesis ton fil en une feme entrer   585
Par l'angle Gabriël, qui li vint aporter
Ton message en l'orelle, et el le valt graer.
La parole qu'il dist tu li fesis entrer
Par l'orelle ens el cuer et del cuer encarner:
Cele cars devint hom, ainc ne s'en pot vanter   590
Hom qui a li peüst carnelment deliter.
Cou fu contre nature, n'ainc ne s'en valt clamer
Nature, dont fesis tot le siecle estorer.
Ele seut tant de bien, bien le valt creanter.
Cele cars devint hom, que la fesis entrer   595
Sens car[nel] assamblee, se t'i vausis celer[16]
En envers le diable por lui a dominer;
Car se il te seüst, ja ne t'osast tempter
Ne ne t'osast traïr ne faire en crois pener;
S'il nel te fesist faire, hom ne l'osast penser,   600
Ne nus ne nos venist de la mort racater.
Dex, tu te covris si qu'il ne te pot viser,
Ne Juïf ne diable ne porent tant tanter
C'onques en toi eüst s'onme non al parler.
Sire, en infer alas por les portes quasser,   605
Tu en entras laiens por tes amis jeter,
Et Adam et Abel, cel legier baceler,
Noë et Abrehan qui tant pot desirer
Que tu venisces la por els descaaner,

Et .C. mile milliers que jo ne sai nomer. 610
Sire, cou fesis tu, bien le sai sans douter;
D'illuec dedens tierc jor fesis apert et cler
Ke tu estoies Dex et fesis susciter
La car de mort a vie que tu laisas pener.
De ta surrexïon puet on assez parler, 615
Ki les tesmoins en out oï sovent soner: 4c
Marien Madelaine, Pieron le claceler
Et les .II. pelerins qui mal vaurent aler,[17]
Et cels que tu rovas a destre part jeter
La roit; por ses poisons pris fu del depaner. 620
De ta surrexïon ne doit nus hom douter.
Tu alas et venis tes amis conforter,
Ki ne s'osoient pas as Juüs demostrer.
Al jor d'Asentïon vausis el ciel monter,
Tes amis n'oblias, ains les vausis tenser. 625
La u ierent ensamble qu'il n'osoient parler,
Trestos li plus coars devint hardis et ber.
Sains Pieres por l'ancele n'osa .I. mot soner,
Devint li plus hardis, ainc puis ne valt cesser.
Il vint al cief del mont par le non Deu crier; 630
Prisons ne cartre oscure ne li pot estoper,
La bouce ne desist co que cuers puet penser.
Dex, si con co fu voirs c'on te puet reprover
Toutes ces grans mervelles que m'as oï conter,
Et jo le croi sans faille de bon cuer et de cler, 635
Si me doinses tu, Dex, Elioxe ma per
En cest siecle mortel tel vie demener
Que tu daignes nos ames en ton conduit mener,
Et sustance en cest siecle por nos honors salver;
Et le fruit de son ventre li laises tel garder 640
Que ele en soit delivre por sa vie salver,
Que on en puist le fruit en fons rengenerer;
Et le songe qu'a fait done en bien deviner.
Dex, tu le nos otroies, qui nos as a garder."

17 Li rois Lotaires a finee s'orison; 645
Il a levé sa main, si a sainié son fron,
Si fait crois desor lui a Deu beneïcon.
A cel point dona pais et asolutïon
Li clers qui a l'autel fist ministratïon.
On parcanta la messe, ne targa s'un poi non, 650
Li chapelains a fait del beneïr son don
De son calise d'or entor et environ,
Et li rois se saina des le pié jusqu'en son,
Desci c'al bas ortel qu'il tenoit sor le jon,
Et del senestre espaulle dusc'al destre mohon. 655
Dont s'en vont cevalier en la sale a bandon,

Si conmence la joie entor et environ;
Cevalier et sergant, jogleor et garcon,
Tant maintienent la feste, cascuns en a son don.

18 Un jor sist en la canbre li rois, s'est porpensés;   660
Ses giestes et ses fais a trestos recordés: 4d
N'i remaint uns afaires qui ne soit ramenbrés,
Conment ses mariages avoit esté trovés,
Et conment ele dist quant il estoit privés
De li premierement, qu'il avoit engendrés   665
.VII. enfans tos ensanble; ses cors seroit finés
Al terme de .IX. mois, quant seroit delivrés.
De tos icés afaires s'est li rois recordés.
Encore en i ot .I. qui n'est mie obliés,
Que cascuns des enfans estroit encaanés   670
El col d'une caaine, a tot co seroit nés.
Il ne set s'il a nul des enfans engendrés,
Por icou vaura il li termes soit contés
En mois et en semaines et en jors tos només,
Que ne soit uns sels jors qui en soit trespassés   675
Des le jor que il primes prist de li delités;
Por cou est plus sovent en mason demorés,
Ne cevalce pas tant con il a fait d'asés;
Si quident si voisin que il soit asotés
Et que sa terre prenge qui vaura, de tos lés.   680
Mais de co que il pensent est il assez remés.

19 Uns rois paiens, Gordoces, a sa terre envaïe
Et degasté sa marce par feu et par bruïe.
Tot maine a son destroit, aignels et bergerie,
Vilains met en prison, il nes espargne mie;   685
Fors des castels a tote la terre mal baillie.
Li clains s'en vient al roi et il molt s'en gramie.
Il a juré son cief que ensi n'ira mie
De cou qu'il li a fait et sa terre bruïe
Et ses homes menés par sa grant estoutie,   690
Et les avoirs tolus; n'en perderont demie,
Trestot l'estavra rendre desi qu'a une alie.
Mais il ne set qu'il face, que molt est aprocie
Li gesine Elioxe qui est sa ciere amie.
Li termes estoit pres, nel pot alongier mie;   695
.III. semaines i ot, en doute ert de sa vie;
En balance ert ses cors de faire une aramie
Envers le roi Gordoce qui'st plains de felonie,
U il atende l'ore sa feme qui l'en prie.
Il le met a raison, car grant destrois l'aigrie: 700
"Conselliés moi, ma douce, grant mestier ai d'aie.
Jo ai esté caiens por vos en grant partie,

Que jo ne cevalcai ne ma cevalerie;
Ici voloie atendre veoir la segnorie
Del fruit que vos portés, que Dex a en baillie.   705
Or m'angoisse deca Gordoces de Palie,   5a
Si me destruist ma terre et met en desceplie
Mes homes et mes gens dont li cuers m'asoplie.
G'irai vers lui a force et ma grans os banie,
Et se jo li puis faire conperer s'estoutie,   710
De sa gent ferai plaine ma grans cartre en ermie,
Prisons et raencons. Tot en vo conmandie
Jo vos lairai ma mere, dame Matrosilie,
Qu'ele penst, del tot soit vo volentés conplie.
Jo li pri con ma mere, rien ne vos entr'oblie,   715
Et s'ele vos corouce, mal feroit, et ma vie
Seroit mais a tos jors a son oés defenie.
"Mere, je vos en pri." Joint ses mains s'umelie,
Baise les mains sa mere, molt doucement larmie:
"Por Deu, ma doce dame, or pensés de m'amie.   720
Quant jo venrai de l'ost et ma jente maisnie,
Si ferons grant baudor et grant feste joïe,
Et on m'aportera .I. fil par segnorie
Que j'avrai ausi cier con mon cors et ma vie."

20 Elioxe a oï, qui le cuer ot dolent,   725
    Et le plaint et le plor et le dolousement
    Que fait li rois Lotaires, et ele li consent.
    Ele l'en apela, si li dist belement:
    "Sire, grant duel avés de no departement,
    Volentiers demoriés, bien voi, a vo talent;   730
    Vos irés en la marce si conduirés vo gent,
    Car se vos lor falés n'ont nul secorement.
    Por Deu, proiés vo mere qu'ele n'oblit noient,
    Et pór la vraie crois que quierent peneent,
    Cou que de moi naistra qu'ele gart bonement;   735
    Mestier avra encore, se Deu vient a talent,
    Et els et autre gent, s'il vivent longement."
    La mere vint atant, ne s'atarga noient,
    Si a dit a son fil molt amiablement:
    "Fiux, jo t'ainc autretant con moi, mien escïent,   740
    Et qui tu ameras, amerai le ensement;
    Se j'ai de toi neveu, joie et devinement
    Avra tos jors de moi, et esbanoiement."
    "Dame," dist Elioxe, "cil qui fist Moÿsent
    Vos rende le bienfait que vos ferés l'enfant;   745
    Mes cors vos est livrez, al Deu conmandement;
    Sovent est avenu, si nel mescroi nïent
    Que de vie trespassent a lor enfantement."
    Lotaires voit le duel, nel pot plus longement

Soufrir ne endurer, va s'ent el mandement,   5*b* 750
Si mande .I. escrivent [c]il i vint erranment;[18]
Et li rois li endite et mostre son talent,
K'il face partot letres tant con sa terre estent
A trestos ses fievés, qu'il viegnent erranment
Lui aidier et secorre, car mestier en a grant,   755
Et qui demöerra sel conperra forment.

21 Lotaires fait escrire letres enseelees,
    S'en envoie garcons par puis et par valees;
    Mande tos ses fievés par totes ses contrees,
    Sor quanque de lui tienent en terres grans et lees, 760
    Qu'a lui viegnent a armes cleres enluminees.
    Il en a grant mestier car on li a gastees
    Et arses ses grans viles, destruites et preees;
    S'amainent cevaliers, s'aront bones soldees.
    Tot soient assemblé dedens .XV. jornees   765
    Al Castel de Nisot as montaignes quarrees;
    Ki de cou li faura, se il n'a bien mostrees
    Ses essoines loiaus, s'ierent abandonees
    Ses terres, ses maisons en .I. feu enbrasees;
    Et il sera encontre a bones gens armees,   770
    A .V.C. cevaliers a grans targes roees,
    Et atot .M. sergans, trestos testes ferrees,
    Sans les arbalestier, qui feront places lees.

22 Les letres sont escrites et les corlius envoient
    Semonre ses fievés, que o lui en s'ost soient;   775
    Vienent as cevaliers qui volentiers les voient;
    Il mostrent les seiaus et les letres desploient;
    Lisent et le besoigne le roi a lor iex voient,
    Al besoing s'aparellent et d'armes se conroient.
    Li viel home d'eage de grant pitié larmoient,   780
    Li jovene sont tot liet, qui d'armes se desroient.
    Li jovene cevalier qui gaaignier voloient
    Enarment ces escus et ces haubers desploient;
    Ces coifes et ces cauces, trestot ensanble froient,
    Quierent lances d'osiers, fers de glave i enploient; 785
    Garcon et escuier ces bels cevals conroient.
    Li ovrier qui d'alesne et de poncon servoient
    Rekeusent et recloent les seles qu'il avoient;
    Liment ces esperons, ces torsoires manoient.
    Gambisons, genellieres as fenestres pendoient.   790
    Tot portent cevalier, acontent et acroient;
    Montent, vont s'ent al roi qui les letres disoient.
    Vers les prés descendirent qui durement verdoient;
    Li un lievent ensegnes qui vers le ciel balloient,
    Li autre vont es prés, as cevals herbe soient;   5*c* 795

La atendent l'uns l'autre jusc'al jor qu'atendoient
Que lor sire venist que il molt desiroient.
.II. liues et demie de terre porprandoient,
Si con lés la riviere de longes s'estendoient;
La atendent le roi, que point ne s'en gramoient.   800

23 Li rois Lotaires vient, ne demeure nïent.
    Li carins en duroit tot arouteement
    .II. liues grans plenieres, si aloit ricement;
    Si portent fer et armes et cevals ensement.
    Quant cil qui es prés ierent le virent, erranment   805
    Vont encontre le roi, sel salüent molt gent.
    Lor service presentent al roi molt ricement,
    Et li rois les mercie et lor salus lor rent.
    A ses castels s'en va ses garnist sagement,
    S'i laisse cevaliers, ca .IIII.XX., ca cent,   810
    Et serjans et viandes et armes a talent;
    Le marce a bien garnie, ne dote mais nïent.
    Dont a mandé ses os que viegnent erranment,
    Car sor Gordoce ira vengier son maltalent.
    En sa terre est entrés, a lui congié ne prent;   815
    Il art et bors et viles et castels et raient,
    S'est nus qui contredie, ne borc ne casement.
    Il met siege erranment et fait son sairement,
    Se il dedens .III. jors nel rendent quitement
    Et il les puet tenir, il les pendra al vent;   820
    Ja nen aront proiere ne nul racatement.
    La paors qu'il ont grant les en fait laidement
    Fuïr fors des castels sans or et sans argent.
    Li rois prent les avoirs, ne troeve quil desfent,
    Et conmande a ses geudes c'on les tors acravent   825
    Et tors et for> et forteces et fosses ensement.
    Bien est .XV. jornees en la terre a la gent
    Qui Deu n'aiment ne croient, ains sont paiene gent;
    Et truevent bien garnie la terre ricement,
    Si les siut li carins qui aporte tostent   830
    Viande et fer et clau que tot ont en present.
    S'i sont li cevalier qui le cemin gardent.
    Paien s'en sont fuï en Artage le grant;
    Ce est une cités que on tient a vaillant,
    Fremee est de bon mur et d'une aigue corant;   835
    Remise ot a non l'aigue qui les va acaignant.
    En mer cort de ravine et si va molt bruient;
    Ele porte navie, par la vont li calant
    Ki portent les mesages en Perse al roi soudant.
    .IIII. bras par deriere et .IIII. par devant,   5d   840
    Vait l'aigue en la cité, ensi le vait fermant;
    A cascune a bon pont et carniere tornant,

Et une tor molt haute de marbre tot luisant.
Loges i a entor qui sont joint a ciment,
Si a .C. arbalestes a puelie tendant,   845
Et .C. arbalestiers molt rices fief tenant;
La ne puet nus passer qui de mort ait garent,
S'il n'a en la tornele ami et conniscent;
Ce sont les avangardes de la cité devant.
Entor la cité ot aigue douce corant,   850
.III.C. piés a de lé de[se]ure ens el naiscant,[19]
Et li mur i sont lé aprés en acaignant,
Et de .C. piés a altre a une tor levant,
Masice, de hautece, une lance tenant,
Teus .V.C. en i a par la vile esforcant.   855
Cascune a .V. [ton]els de .C. haubers tenant;[20]
Tot entor a gisarmes et grans haces pendant,
Et ars et arbalestres, et quarials i a tant
Que de la grant plenté ne trovrés voir disant.
Borgois a en la vile qui sont d'avoir manant,   860
Bacons et pois et feves, et bon vin, et forment
Ont; dusques a .VII. ans ne lor fauroit nïent,
S'il n'en croisoit en terre .I. boistel ne plain gant;
Si en avroient il a oés tote lor gent
Qui laiens esteroient lor cité desfendant,   865
Dont i a .XXX. mile trestos armes portant.
La sont venue trestot li paien afuiant
De .XV. grans jornees querre de mort garant.

24 Rois Lotaires porsiut paiens a grant effroi,
    Il les chace si fort qu'il les met a desroi;   870
    Il a Deu en aïe, de qui il tient sa loi.
    Il monte une montaigne s'esgarde desos soi,
    Voit le cité d'Artage, le fierce, le bufoi,
    Et vit qu'ele iert molt fors, s'apiele un suen secroi
    Les bons engigneors Nicolas et Joifroi: 875
    "Apelés vos ai ci, segnor, par bone foi.
    Baron, ceste cités (si lor mostra al doi),
    Pensés conment jo l'aie, jo voel grever le roi.
    De l'avoir qui ens est, si con je pens et croi,
    Aront no soldoier soldees et conroi.   880
    Faites moi ma besoigne, si vous metés en moi;
    Jo ferai a vo gré par verté et par loi."
    "Sire," dist Nicolas, "se Deus garist Joifroi,
    Nos ferons tel engien laval en cel jonqoi   6a
    De coi nos abatrons d'Artage le boufoi."   885

25 Li rois ne valt avant nule maniere aler,
    Ains fait par tote l'ost et banir et crier
    K'i se logent aval, dont oïssiés corner

Plus de .C. mile cors et buisines soner.
Cascuns fice son tref quil sace u asener;   890
L'autres fice une lance, sel [l]aise venteler[21]
Et balloier l'ensegne; li autres va forer,
Et li autre se painent des cevals conreer,
Et li autre as quisines font le feu alumer,
Et font les fus saillir des f[u]si[a]us ahurter.[22]   895
Li cevalier de pris alaiscent cembeler
Volentiers a la porte, s'il peüscent mener
Cevals ne traire en destre por sor els conquester;
Mais li marès est grans, n'osent por affondrer.
Neporquant si i vont .XX. legier baceler   900
Tant que il porent si dure terre trover
Que lor ceval les puisent sans enfangier porter;
Et si font une esciele de cevaliers armer
Qu'il font en .I. saucoi mucier et aombrer,
Que se mestiers lor est, qu'il s'i poront fier.   905
Cil s'en vont dusc'as pons, il les ont fais lever;
N'i a mestier cenbels, nes en porent jeter.

26 Assez ont cembelé, mais n'i porent rien faire,
Ne de cels de laiens nes .I. sol ca fors traire;
Car s'il veniscent fors ce lor peüst molt plaire,   910
Ne ja tant n'en veniscent en place ne en aire
Que il nes ocesiscent sans crier et sans braire.
Por mius estre fremé ont il fait lor pons traire,
N'ainc a mur n'a fenestre ne troverent viaire.
El retor se sont mis li cevalier Lotaire.   915
Por co ne remanra ne lor face contraire,
Car s'il ne puet par force, l'avra par engin faire.[23]
Il mande Nicolas, et Joifroi qui ert maire,
Que onques mais ne finent de lor engiens portraire,
Si aient abatu de lor gent de put aire   920
L'orguel et le boufois qui si lor puet desplaire;
Et il mandent ariere, par une nef font faire,
Feront il ens entrer par desos la tor maire,
S'il velt et boin li est mon segnor roi Lotaire.

27 Par desous la cité bien a liue et demie   925
Avoit par mi .I. mont une molt grant trencie.
Toute l'aigue qui cort par la cité garnie
Et devant et deriere, qui iert en .V. partie,[24]
Trestote rasambloit par mi la praerie   6*b*
Et par mi .I. boscet de sapin qui verdie.   930
Toute s'en passe la, sous la roce naïe,
Si que la avoit rente de treü establie
De tous avoirs passans qui i vient a navie.
La s'en ala Joifrois, il et sa conpaignie,

Bien ot .C. carpentiers, cascun hace entesie;   935
Le boschet abatirent trestout a une hie,
Tos les arbres esmondent, ostent la ramellie
Et loient par faisiaus, ainc n'i remest bracie.
Les gros ciés aguisierent trestot en esquarie,
Et puis s'i font le feu, s'ont la pointe bruïe.   940
Dont le laisent floter ausi conme navie,
Et l'aigue les en porte dessi qu'a la trencie
Ki iert entre .II. mons, la l'ont sus resacie.
Dont s'en vont bien .LX. et quatre a une hie,
Ki hïent les mairiens en la terre et enguie,²⁵   945
Por faire bone escluse, que l'aigue ne past mie.
.II. renges font de pels et en mi ramellie,
Et si l'ont bien de terre et caucie et foucie,
Nes l'erbe ont aportee d'aval la praerie,
Et si ont de la roce colpee et detrencie   950
La piere issi tres grande c'une ne trairoit mie
Uns cars a .X. cevals, por tot l'or de Pavie.
Or est l'escluse faite et tres bien sospoïe;
L'aigue ne pot issir, s'ert la valee enplie.
Li rois i met .M. homes, par terre et par navie,   955
Boins bacelers et jovenes plains de grant aatie,
Qui garderont l'escluse, que ne soit desgarnie.

28 Or s'en reva Joifrois ariere al roi parler:
    "Sire rois, nos estuet cest altre bois colper,
    Et faire une autre escluse por la cité grever."   960
    "Or va," ce dist Lotaires, "fai tost, ne demorer."
    Cil vait a grant conpaigne por le bos carpenter.
    Caisnes abat et faus font a terre verser,
    Et a faites les ais et lignier et doler,
    A poi[s] et a estoupe les fait joindre et cloer.²⁶   965
    .XX. piés a li planciés qu'il a fait estorer,
    Et a .III. piés de haut le fait entor bender;
    De tels planciés fait .XX. qu'il fera tos floter,
    Es .X. a fait desfenses por lor cors aombrer
    De cevaliers qu'iront la bataille endurer;   970
    A cels dedens iront, se mestiers est, capler.
    Et baus fait aguisier, por faire as murs hurter,
    Encontre coi li mur ne poroient durer
    Ne les tors desfensables u on les puist mener.   6c
    Aprés fait une escluse sel fait bien enterrer,   975
    De gros mairien entor ficier et passoner,
    De pieres et de rains bien kaukier et presser,²⁷
    Que nule fuisons d'aigue ne puet oltre passer.
    Dont fait totes les nés del païs ariver
    Et joindre l'une a l'autre bien forment et serrer.   980
    L'eve croist et le val veïssiés araser.

Joifrois en est venus devant le roi ester.
"Sire rois," dist li il, "faites vo gent armer,
Cevaliers et serjans lor cors bien conreer."
"Bien as dit," dist li rois; dont fait .I. cor soner;985
Après le cor a fait par tot son ban crier,
Que tost voisent as armes mescin et baceler;
De cors et de buisines font tot le val tranbler.
Joiant s'en vont et lié, pour l'avoir conquester
Ki est en la cité que on ne puet nonbrer.   990

29 Armé sont cevalier et bien et noblement
    Por aler en bataille contre paiene gent.
    Arbalestier sont mis as baotes devant,
    Et li cevalier sont rengié siereement;
    Serjant et escuier aficierent forment   995
    Qu'il lor feront assez de mal et de torment.
    .V. escieles ont fait, en l'aigue vont najant;
    Al harnas sont remés bien cevalier .V. cent,
    Qui gardent les cevals et maint bon garniment.
    Joifrois vint a l'escluse et si serjant aranpent,   1000
    Et conduisent les baus aguisés par devant
    Ki as fors murs d'Artaje ferront premierement;
    Et l'aigue les en porte tant ravinousement,
    Ja n'i eüst il baus ne altre engignement,
    Que fors seulement l'aigue qui cort a grant torment 1005
    N'aresteroient il, ne [duroient] noient.[28]
    Quant l'aigue vient as murs ne laise n'escrevent
    Trestot le premier mur qu'il vait consivent;
    En la cité s'espart et noie tant de gent,
    Nes poroit on nonbrer par nul enbrievement   1010
    Nus escrivens qui soit par nesun escïent.
    Cil qui ierent as tors et el haut mandement
    Quidoient par desfense avoir boin tensement;
    Mais cil qui les grans baus aloient conduisent
    Hurtent si fort as tors, toutes les estroent,   1015
    Et l'aigue qui ens entre noie avaine et forment.
    Les garnimens qui flotent recoit on voirement,
    Mais de la gent qui sont noié a tel torment
    Ne vos puet clers conter, ne jogleres qui cant, 6d
    Les cens et les milliers qui sont mu et taisant,   1020
    Dont l'arme en est partie ne mais ne sont vivant;
    Et femes et enfant et la menue gent,
    Car il en ont premiers le martiriement.
    Maint quident eschaper et fuir en noant;
    La u la gens le roi, qui tos jors vont najant,   1025
    Les voient, si les traient et fierent maintenant
    U del arc u de glavie, ja n'en aront garant.
    Auquant se rendent pris et vont merci criant,

Mais n'en eschape nus, se co n'est amirant
U princes u casés de rices fiés tenant,   1030
S'il en laient nul vif, u rice home granment.

30 Toutes les .V. eschieles sont en la vile entrees.
De bones gens i ot tos jovenes .X. navees,
Et voient cele gent piesmement tormentees.
Les unes flotent sus, l'autres sont affondrees,   1035
L'unes traites par mi, les autres espee[e]s[29]
D'une glavie par mi; i sont molt malmenees.
Bien ont aval la vile de tors .C. effondrees;
Venu sont al dongnon et as fenestres lees,
Quierent de cevaliers armes bien a[p]restees;[30]   1040
La sont li cevalier, les testes bien armees,
Si sont prest d'endurer grans estors et mellees.
Cil desous traient la saietes empenees,
Assez les ont la sus soufert et endurees.
Pels a[s]sés lor lancierent s'ont lor nés
                                        effondrees,[31] 1045
Et fait molt grans damages de bones gens loees.
Une navee en muerent qui d'armes sont penees,
Il et tote lor nés en est a terre alees;
Li fers les trait aval, la sont acouvetees.
Or se restent les gens roi Lotaire grevees.   1050

31 Li assaus est remés, si se traient arriere,
Consel prendent qu'il voelent en plus forte maniere
Assaillir le donjon; il n'ont poi[n]t de perriere,[32]
Mais il feront hurter et devant et deriere
Des baus qu'il ont agus a la grant tor pleniere;   1055
Et s'il est hom la sus qui mece fors sa ciere,
Arbalestier trairont de lor arbalestriere.
Or viegnent hurteor plus isnel de levriere,
Si hurtent a la tor que ce lor est a viere,
A cels qui sont la sus, qu'il soient en crolliere   1060
De pret u de marois. Atant mostra sa ciere
Li niés le roi d'Artage par une baotiere,
Bien a la teste armee et d'elme et de coifiere;
Et uns arciers l'avise qui tres par mi l'uelliere 7*a*
Le fiert ens el cervel qu'el haterel deriere   1065
Li parut li quarriaus, et il ciet sor le piere.
On li sace le flece qui fu de fort osiere,
Li fers est remasus ens en la cerveliere.
On li a osté l'elme et la coife doubliere,
Et aprés le hauberc dont la maille est d'or miere.   1070
Puis le coucent tot mort de lonc sor une biere.

32 Lors est li niés le roi molt a grant destorbier:[33]

Car il n'avoit laiens nul mellor cevalier;
Se il fust crestiiens molt se peüst proisier.
Li rois fait molt grant duel, n'i ot que corecier.   1075
"Segnor baron," fait il,"[s]avés moi consellier?[34]
Nos serons caiens pris encore ains l'anuitier;
Ne gart l'eure que voie ceste tor trebucier.
Rendons nos a cel roi, soions si prisonier;
S'il velt de nos avoir ne argent ne or mier,   1080
Nos l'en donrons assez, tot plain son desirier;
Nos cors et nos avoirs metons en son dangier."
"Sire," ce dïent il, "bien fait a otroier;
Dites qui vos volés faire au roi envoier."
"S'il n'est autres quil die, faites moi messagier," 1085
Dist uns clers qui iert la, qui se fait latimier;
Clers estoit de lor loi, molt set bien fabloier.
"Alés," cou dist li rois, "dites le roi Lotier
Que jo desir a lui par trive plaidoier
Et par non d'acordance; alés sans atargier,   1090
Prendés la une targe sel faites cloficier
Une crois d'un blanc drap por plus tost apaier."

33 Cil s'en monte en la tor, es haus quertials en son,
Si ot la crois pendue et traite en son b[l]azon.[35]
Il ot la teste armee, si cria a haut ton: 1095
"Oiés! Oiés, segnor, une fiere raison;
Ciesés, ne traiés mais, ne hurtés al donjon.
Trives mande mesire al roi de grant renon
Par non de fine acorde, s'atorner l'i puet on."
Li rois vient cele part, qui'n a oï le son;   1100
Le retrait fait soner, que bien l'entendi on.
Onques puis ne hurterent a quarrel n'a perron,
Ne ne traist d'arbaleste par nesune ocoison.
Co dist li latimiers, qui estoit el donjon:
"Oiés! Oiéz, segnor, une fiere raison: 1105
Li rois qui caiens est a Lotaire par non
Et si conpaignon tot se renderont prison,
Que il salves lor vies viegnent a raencon.
Del lor pöés avoir maint marc et maint mangon,   7b
Si en laisiés aler lor cors a garison;   1110
De tot l'or que prendrés ne donroit .I. boton,
Car plus vos en donra que ne conteroit hom.
Or responde li rois, si die et nos l'oron."
Avant se traist li rois sos l'escu au lion,
Ja parlera en haut, qui qu'en poist ne qui non.   1115
"Latimier," dist li rois, "ja n'en conselleron,
Di ton segnor avant, qu'il guerpisce Mahon,
Et tot si conpaignon si croient en Jhesum
Et demandent batesme, et nos lor otrïon

Trestot conmunalment et vie et raencon;   1120
Et se faire nel voelent ja nes deporteron
Que ne raient l'asaut a force et a bandon,
Et vo tor abatue, et eux pendu en son."

34 Dist li latimiers, "Sire, ariere voel aler
De vostre mandement a mon segnor parler;   1125
Mais tant que jo irai, faites trives doner."
Cil vient a son segnor les noveles conter:
"Sire, se vos volés ariere dos jeter
Mahon et Apollin, et Jhesu aorer,
Si vos faites en fons batisier et lever   1130
Et tot cil qui ci sont, vo demaine et vo per,
Sauve vo raencon vos en laira aler;
Et se vos ne volés cest afaire graer,
Il fera vostre tor trestote defroer
Et a .I. haut pegnon vos trestos encroer."   1135
"Par Mahon!" dist li rois, "molt velt cis hom derver,
Qui ne velt espargnier rois ne prince ne per.
Qu'en löés vos, segnor, des vies rachater?
Volés laisier Mahon et Jhesu aorer?
U tot faire, u laisier, n'avons que demorer."   1140
On a mis le respons sor Faburon l'Escler.
Dist Faburons: "Segnor, ne nos fesist fauser
Nos deus por nule rien, s'il nos vausist amer.
Il nos a fait caiens laidement enconbrer,
Et nos donrons sa teste qui'st de fin or et cler,   1145
As crestiiens la fors por vie rachater,
Et qu'il nos facent tos a lor Deu racorder.
Alons, rendons nos armes, n'avons que detrïer."
Il deslacent lor elmes d'acier poitevin cler,
Et les coiffes de fer font ariere jeter,   1150
Et les espees nues devant lor pis porter.
.I. puestic ont overt par u voelent passer;
La prent li rois d'Artage Lotaire a apeler:
"Rois, jo vieng ci a vos, mi demaine et mi per, *7c*
Nïent por autre cose mais por merci crier,   1155
Se toi plaist et bon t'est por nos vies salver;
Se tu raencon vels, assés en pués conter."
Rois Lotaires respont: "Batisier et lever
Et enoindre de cresme et tos crestiener,
Et quanque vos porés a batesme amener   1160
Vos convient, se volés vos vies rachater;
Et qui cou ne fera, de la teste a couper
Sera trestos seürs, ne s'en pora douter;
Ca vo main, sel volés plevir et creanter."
"Oïe, sire, tenés m'espee d'acier cler,   1165
Et ma foi dont je doi Jhesu Crist aorer."

Autretel font li autre, ne l'o[s]ent refuser.[36]
"Or rendés," dist li rois, "les tresors qu'amasser
Avés fait es escrins, et l'argent et l'or cler,
Car j'en vaurai assez mes soldoiers doner;　　　　　1170
Et jo vos en vaurai en ma terre mener,
Desci que nos porons .I. evesque trover
Ki vos pora uns fons beneïr et sacrer,
U on vos puist trestos en fons rengenerer."
Et respont li paiens: "Bien le voel creanter　　　　1175
Trestot de bone foi, de verté sans fauser.
Li tresor sont noiié: faites l'eve avaler,
Que nos puisons ariere ens es canbres entrer."
Li rois mande Joifroi qu'il viegne a lui parler,
Et il i vient molt tost sans plus de demorer.　　　1180
"Joifroi," ce dist li rois, "faites nos atierer."

35　Joifrois vait a l'escluse, si ne demore mie,
　　Les pels en esraca et l'aigue en est widie;[37]
　　La terre se mostra qui tote fu noïe.
　　Il n'avoit en Artage de la gent païenie　　　　　1185
　　Plus que .C. homes vis; tote ert la gens perie.
　　Cil vont por querre l'or dont la vile est garnie,
　　Assez en aporterent et a grant segnorie.
　　Por cou qu'en la cité ot tant de gent noïe,
　　Ki gisent par ces places en brai et en fangie,　　1190
　　En fait li rois Lotaires en .I. canp verdie
　　Porter tot le tresor c'on li met en baillie.
　　Le roi paien en maine et tote sa maisnie.
　　Li rois fait assanbler se grant cevalerie,
　　Soldoiers et serjans qui ierent en s'aïe,　　　　1195
　　Et il conmence a faire sa rice departie;
　　Plus donne au plus vaillant et mains a la maisnie.
　　Cil qui il done mains hautement l'en mercie;　　　*7d*
　　Ki la valt demorer s'ot rice manandie.
　　Aprés soldees a li rois sa gent banie,　　　　　1200
　　K'il en velt repairier, s'a se conestablie
　　Mis en l'ariere garde et si a establie
　　L'avangarde de gens qui sera fervestie;
　　Mais la paiene gent, icels n'oblie mie.

36　Il va par ces castels que il avoit conquis,　　　1205
　　U il ot ses provos et ses cevaliers mis;
　　Tels i a qu'il abat, auquans en a garnis,
　　Et des prisons ausi tels i a sont ocis
　　Et les testes colpees et enfouïs tos vis
　　U pendus a haus caisnes, onques n'en ot mercis,　1210
　　Tant qu'il vint en sa marce al cief de .XV. dis.
　　La manda .I. evesque et abés dusqu'a dis,

Et li vesques a fais uns sains fons beneïs[38]
En une haute eglise mon segnor saint Patris.
Aprés le benicon a oile et cresme mis,   1215
Ploncié i a le roi del cief outre le vis;
Parins en fu li rois et abé dusqu'a dis,
Patrices ot a non, del non al saint fu pris.
Et les autres paiens a tos issi baillis;
Tot sont fait crestiien, Mahons est relenquis.   1220
A Jhesu font fiance, deables soit honis.
Li rois en fillolage lor dona Monbregis,
Un castel molt vaillant, et tos les apendis,
Et bien .LX. viles qui la sont el païs;
Se li a tot rendu ce qu'il avoit conquis,   1225
Fors les tresors qu'il ot as soldoiers partis.
Li paiens li a foi et ligeé promis
Et si remaint ses hom de quanqu'est poëstis.

37 Molt fu li rois Lotaires el cuer esleeciés
    De co que Dex l'a si, et les siens, avanciés,   1230
    Que ses anemis a desos ses piés plaisiés;
    Deu et ses sains en a hautement grasiiés;
    Sen filluel et ses homes en a tos renvoiés.
    Tels est al main joians, al vespre est coureciés.
    Li rois vait par sa marce con cil qui ert haitiés.   1235
    Entrués que li rois a les paiens si brisiés,
    Et il est durement demorés et targiés,
    Elioxe sa feme, dont Deu prenge pitiés,
    A atendu son terme qui li est apro[c]iés[39]
    Si con del melaler dont li fais est molt griés.   1240
    Ele va par ses canbres, se li deut molt li ciés,
    Ses dens estraint ensanle, ses mals est enfor[ciés.][40]
    Les dames qui soufroient des enfans les mesciés   8a
    Sevent bien le malage, qu'il est bien angoissiés;
    Bien set que de cest mal n'ert ja siens [s]ire
                                      liés.[41] 1245

38 Les dames sont en paine de cele dame aidier,
    Et molt ont de dolor, quil voient travellier
    A si grande hascie et son cors escillier;
    Mais por nïent se paine qui Dex ne velt aidier,
    Et cil qui Dex aiüe, söef puet somellier.   1250
    Une mervelle avint que je vos voel noncier:
    Quant Deu plot que la dame peut son fais descargier,
    .VII. en a on trovés, as enfans manoier.
    Une jentil pucele ont trovee al premier;
    Li autre sont vallet, Dex les gart d'enconbrier.   1255
    Une caaine d'or avoit cascuns, d'or mier;
    La laisent les enfans a terre formoier,

A la dame entendirent, qui en ot grant mestier.[42]
Bien le demaine mals et devant et derier,
Bien set qu'a terre mere li estuet repairier;   1260
L'eure de mort li est sor main sans detriier.
De batre sa poitrine, de Damedeu hucier,
Cou est tote s'entente, que n'i a que targier.
Saint Esperit del ciel ne ciese de prier
Que li sains Abrahans s'arme puist avoier.   1265
"Ahi! Lotaires, sire, con pöés detriier?
Jamais ne me verrés con vos avoie cier."
Lors a levé sa main et por son vis sainier
Al ciel lieve ses iex, lors li convint clugnier.
"Dex, tot est fait de moi! Fai moi aconpaignier   1270
As sains angeles del ciel, se vos en puis proier."

39 Morte est bele Elioxe, l'espris s'en est alés,[43]
    Et par tote la sale en est li cris levés.
    Li cors gist estendus d'un paile acovetés,
    Li luminaires est del clergiet alumés;   1275
    Li clergiés est venus dont Dex est aorés
    Et li devins mestiers est al cors celebrés
    A crois, a filatires, a encensiers brasés.
    El demain fu li cors a l'eglise portés,
    Mais dedens les parois nen est il pas entrés.   1280
    Li messe est conmencie et haute et solenés
    Et serjans et borgois ot a l'ofrande assés,
    Mais de cevaliers est en l'ost tos li barnés.
    Aprés messe est li cors jentement enterrés,
    A le maisiere gist del mostier tos serrés,   1285
    Et li pules en est en maison retornés.
    Assez fu li cors plains et criés et plorés.

40 Puis que la roïne est, Elioxe, entieree,   8b
    La mere al roi en est en maison retornee,
    Tot erranment en est en ses canbres entree;   1290
    La sont les .IIII. dames cascune escavelee,
    Encor mainent lor duel por la dame honoree.
    Cou dist la mere au roi: "Mostrés ca la portee[44]
    De coi ma bele fille est morte et enterree."
    Les dames respondirent: "C'est mervelle provee;   1295
    Dame, .VII. en i a tot a une litee."
    ".VII.! Por la bele crois, mervelle avés contee,
    Jo ne vauroie mie qu'ele me fust mostree;
    Plevissiés ca vos fois que c'ert cose celee,
    N'a home ne a feme qui de mere soit nee   1300
    Ne sera ceste cose ja par vos relevee."
    Ensi li ont les dames [par foi] acreantee.[45]
    La dame en apela Monicier de Valee;

Cerkié a et corut par lui mainte contree.
Il est venus a li: "Dame, que vos agree?"   1305
"Tu iés mes hom, et foi m'as tu aseüree;
Jo t'ai bien fait, encor n'en sui mie lasee.
Une rien [a] a faire, co soit cose celee;[46]
Ne le te dirai pas sel m'avras afiee
Ta foi que nel diras, ne par toi n'ert contee."   1310
"Tenés, dame, ma foi con l'avés devisee."
"Fai moi deus cofinials en la selve ramee,
Si mes aporte ca anuit a la vespree."
Cele dist, et il fait; n'i a el demoree.
Fait sont, a li revient aprés none sonee.   1315
El les prant s'a mis ens assez herbe fenee;
Si conmanda as dames c'on mece ens la portee
Dont la feme son fil ert morte et enterree.

41 Mainte fois en proverbe selt li vilains retraire
    Que taie norist sot; ceste fait le contraire: 1320
    Ne nourist sot ne sage, car ele est de put aire;
    Ains ocit et destruit, nen velt norecon faire.
    Double mere est la taie quant ele est de bon aire,
    Mais des enfans son fil set molt bien mordre faire;
    Tant con ses fils est fors est ele et dame et maire,1325
    Mais s'il fust en maison, n'osast por son viaire
    Mostrer son felon cuer, qui est de mal afaire.
    "Monicier," dist la dame, "anuit a la brunaire
    Des estoiles del ciel me querrés .I. repaire
    En la forest qui est de ces bestes corsaire.   1330
    Porte ces cofinials dont en ai une paire
    La u je mais n'en oie rien nule qui desplaire
    Me puist ci ne aillors. Sés que jo te voel faire? 8c
    Provosté te donrai aprés, si seras maire
    D'un castel que jo ai, que jo tieng en douaire: 1335
    Cou ne te porra mie mes fils li rois retraire."
    "Dame," dist Moniciers, "de vostre bien atraire,
    Ki me vauroit doner tos les poisons de [m]aire,[47]
    Ne les prendroie jo, por qu'il vos dust desplaire."[48]

42 Moniciers atent tant que nuis soit enserie;   1340
    Ne velt pas que on face de lor liu baerie,
    Car il velt sagement faire [l]a conmandie[49]
    Sa dame la roïne qui molt en lui se fie.
    Son ceval ensiela, ses cofinials n'oblie;
    Il s'est mis a la voie en la selve en hermie,   1345
    Et cevalce as estoiles; s'a l'espee sacie.
    Crois a fait en son front, que malfés nel quivrie.
    Il ira bone voie, car Damedex le guie.
    Il avoit ja erré .VII. liues et demie,

Et li cos ont canté, il a la vois oïe;   1350
Del chief aore Deu, de langue le gracie:
"Dex!" fait il, "que puet estre que j'ai ci en baillie,
Ke ma dame mist ci et onques n'en vi mie?
Aparmain le sent jo, que por le fain formie;
Par foi, que que ce soit, je sai bien qu'il a vie." 1355
Il jete la sa main si sent car qui molie:
"Dex, jo quit que c'est enfes, se Dex me face aïe;
Ja par moi n'ert donés a beste en sauvecie,
Se jo puis trover liu que de mort soit garie.
Li peciés soit ma dame de ceste felonie."   1360

43 Tant a erré li sers, molt li puet anuier,
    Mais por pité le laise, qu'il nes velt descargier,
    Son fais; ains ira tant, se il puet avoier,
    K'il trovera foillie u maison u mostier
    U il pora son fais aombrer et mucier,   1365
    Que leu ne autre beste nes veniscent mangier.
    Tant ala totes voies qu'il oï abaier
    Un cien, et dist que la vaura il repairier,
    Se il puet et il troeve en aucun liu sentier.
    Totes voies cevalce et fait le bos froisier,   1370
    Por cou, se li ciens l'ot, que plus doie noisier,
    Et il sivra l'abai, por sa voie abregier.
    Il cevalce a l'a[b]ai, pense de l'esploitier[50]
    C'ainc ne fina si vint tot droit a .I. mostier.
    Petis ert et devant ot .I. peneanchier   1375
    U li bons hom seoit le jor por ombroier,
    Ki laiens ert ermites et Deu avoit molt cier.
    Il estoit ja levés s'ert alés saumoier   8d
    De devant son autel por Deu esloengier;
    Et li ciens si sivoit .I. leu qui el buscier   1380
    Ert venus en la haie por les bestes mangier
    Que l'ermites faisoit la au vespre entoitier.
    Moniciers descendi, s'a pendu .I. panier
    A la loge devant tot serré le mostier,
    Et l'autre a la fenestre la u soloit mucier   1385
    Li ermites son cief por lui esbanoier,
    Por esgarder le tans, quant il devoit cangier,
    U li airs estoit mius, u devoit esclairier.
    Moniciers se retorne, n'i velt plus detriier,
    Tot issi con il vint est retornés arrier.   1390
    Il n'avoit alé d'une liue .I. quartier
    Quant li aube creva, quil prant a ravoier,
    Et il a tant erré k'a eure de mangier
    Refu la dont il vint, n'i fait autre dangier;
    Asiet soi a la table dalés .I. escuier.   1395
    Sa dame quant le voit prant soi a leecier,

Mais ne le vaut illuec devant gent araisnier.
Quant il orent mangié, si vont napes sacier
Senescaus qui cou ert en cief et en mestier,
La dame entre en sa canbre sor .I. lit apoier,   1400
Et par une pucele a mandé Monicier.
Cil vint, qui cou atent, sans point de detriier,
Et quant il sont ensamble la canbre font widier,
Dont se prendent ensanble andoi a fabloier.
"Dame," co dist li sers, "pené m'ai d'esploitier   1405
Le besoigne que vos me conmandastes ier.
Fait est si que jamais n'en orés jor plaidier;
J'ai bien alé .X. liues par le bos en ramier,
Por querre u jou peüsce jus mon fais descargier;
N'est pas la u le mis, s'il i ot que mangier."   1410
"Tu as bien fait, amis, tu aras bon loier,
De quan que t'ai promis ne te vaurai boisier."

44 Ci le lairons ensi, si dirons des enfans
    Qui sont es cofinials que porta li serjans.
    En la chapele estoit li ermites laians   1415
    La nuit devant l'autel tos seus et tos dolans
    Des peciés qu'avoit fais, dont estoit repentans.
    Matines ot cantees, si n'ert pas aparans
    Li jors, ains atendoit que il fust auques grans,
    Por canter prime et messe, et puis s'alast as cans, 1420
    Et fouïr et hauer a paine et a ahans,
    Por semer .I. poi d'orge, dont il aroit al tans
    Por lui et por sa suer qui o lui ert manans;   9a
    Car il avoit paor durement del cier tans.
    Il vint a la fenestre sel desfrema laians;   1425
    Il l'ovri, mais n'avoit ciel n'estoiles luisans.
    Li paniers ert encontre qui li vait aombrans;
    Il ne set que cou est, molt s'en va mervellant.

45 Li ermites ne puet veoir ne esgarder
    Le jor par la fenestre que il soloit mirer;   1430
    Li vaisel sont encontre si nel pot remuer.
    "Dex," fait il, "que co est qui me puet estouper
    La fenestre par u li jors me seut entrer?"
    Il est alés entor, si a fait enbraser
    Une foille de sap por cele cose oster;   1435
    Le vaissel a overt, le fain prent a oster,
    Quatre enfans a trové au fain desvoleper.
    "Ce m'a Dex envoié," fait il, "al ajorner."
    Il a remis le fain por le caure garder;
    Lieve les iex en haut, si vaut Deu graciers,   1440
    L'autre cofinel voit si le cort remuer,
    S'a trové .III. enfans; or en puet .VII. conter;

Ki tot li sont remés por nourir et garder.
"Dex," cou dist li ermites, "jo t'en doi aorer,
Que leus ne autre beste nes vint ci devourer;   1445
Molt sont bel, Dex les vaut a s'ymage former."
Il en va sa seror Ermogene apeler.
"Suer," co dist li sains hom, "molt devons Deu amer,
Qui mervelle nos velt sifaitement mostrer;
Il nos a envoié .VII. enfans a garder,   1450
Jou parins, vos marine en soions al lever.
Faites une cuviele la devant cel autel
De la clere fontaine et emplir et raser;
Et aubes porveés as enfans affubler.
G'irai jusqu'a .VI. liues prestre Vincan rover,   1455
Qu'il me prest oile et cresme por els lor droit doner."
Cele respont: "Por Deu servir en bien ovrer
Ne me verrés vos ja, se Deu plaist, reculer."
Cil s'en va si con cil qui n'a que demorer,
Vint al prestre Vincan sel prent a saluer.   1460
Cil li rent son salu, si le cort acoler:
"Conment est? Que vos faut? Venés vos reposer."
"Sire," fait li ermites, "faites nos delivrer
Oile et cresme a enfans en fons rengenerer;
Dex m'en a doné .VII., jo nes doi refuser."   1465
"Volentiers, bels dous sire, foi que doi saint Omer,
Car a si fait besoing le doit on aprester.
Enne vos plaist ancois .I. petit a disner?"   9*b*
"Nenil," dist li ermites, "car jo me voel haster;
Ne sai se li enfant pueent tant demorer."   1470
Il a pris son afaire, si s'en prent a raler;
En maison est venus tos las a l'avesprer.
"Que font nostre enfant, suer, pueent mais endurer?"
"Oïl," dist ele, "sire, vos poés bien souper."
"Non, suer," dist li ermites, "il nos estuet pener   1475
De ces enfans ancois; alés les aporter."
Cele est corue pruec et il va por le sel.
Les enfans presegna, non lor fist deviser,
Crois el front et el vis et sel asavourer,
Le nés et les orelles de salive limer,   1480
Et les beneïcons que il set bien canter.
Puis les met el mostier et ses fait regarder,
Que netement peüssent es benois fons entrer.
Tot sont net, et mis sont en fons rengenerer.
Es pis et es espaulles sont enoint d'oile cler,   1485
Et cresme lor a mis en son le cerveler,
Non le Pere et le Fil, que Dex puet tant amer,
Et le Saint Esperit, que il les puist garder.
Dont lor fait ciés et piés en dras envoleper
Et candoiles es mains, et donques repposser,   1490

Et del lait de ses chievres a grant plenté doner
Et de ferine d'orge papines conreer.
Mais une cose i a qui ne fait a celer,
Dont li sains hom se prent sovent a porpenser
Que quant il les leva, a cascun .I. coler   1495
Trova loié el col, de bon fin or tot cler.
D'ensi que les trova n'en vaut nul remüer,
Et conmanda tres bien c'on lor face salver.
"En foi," dist li ermites, "or est tans de souper;
Dex otroit nos enfans tehir et amender."   1500

46 L'estoire nos a dit la devant et conté
Que rois Lotaires ot mené tot son barné
Encontre .I. roi paien, et si l'avoit maté
Tant qu'il tenoit la loi de la crestïenté;
Et ses parins estoit si l'ot de fons levé,   1505
Se li avoit assez de sa terre doné
Et les soldoiers ot lor soldees livré:
Il aloit par sa marce gardant sa salveté.
Entrués avoit sa feme cest siecle trespassé,
Et on avoit le cors festelment enterré.   1510
Co ne set nient li rois au corage aduré,
Nequedent si a il a ce sovent pensé;
Car il avoit son cors laisié molt agrevé   9c
De la grande hascie del fais qu'avoit porté.
Sa mere a pris en li de faintise .I. pensé.   1515
Ele en apele a li .I. sage clerc letré;
Ses canceliers estoit, s'en faisoit son privé.
"Canceliers, je vos quit home de grant bonté;
Je vos voel regehir .I. mien parfont secré,
Mais gardés que par vos ne soit nului mostré."   1520
"Ne place a Deu, ma dame; saciés par verité,
Ja vo consel n'orés de moi escandelé."
"Escris dont," dist la dame, "salus et amisté
A Lotaire mon fil, que je l'ai molt amé;
De sa feme Elioxe o le gent cors mollé,   1525
Morte est, et si avons ja le cors entieré.
Grosse fu voirement, et si s'a delivré
De .VII. serpens qui ont tot son cors desciré,
Et de mors et de trait trestot envenimé,
Et aprés se sont mis en l'air, s'en sont volé;   1530
Et de cou sonmes nos molt forment adolé,
Ne jamais ne serons por rien reconforté,
Si iert a nos venus s'ara a nos parlé.
Escrisiés co, bels sire, que vos ai endité."
Cil escrist erranment, que tot ot apresté,   1535
Et quant il l'ot escrit, si l'a enquarelé;
Et la dame le prist, si l'a enseelé,

S'apela son corliu: "Ca venés, Malmené,
Va tost al roi sel quier tant que l'aiés trové
De ma part le salue, et lui et son barné,   1540
Et les letres li done, si aras fait mon gré."
"Fait iert, dame," dist il, "tot a vo volenté."

47 Li corlius fu tos pres, va s'ent sans atargier,
Trois jornees corut, car le pié ot legier.
A le quarte fist tant qu'a eure de mangier   1545
Vint al roi, sel trova; tos iert las de plaidier.
Il li baille le brief, li rois le fist froissier
Son capelain qui la estoit sos .I. lorier.
Le brief desploie et list, si a pris a noncier
Al roi cou que les letres sevent senefiier.   1550
Ensus se traient tot, et prince et cevalier.
"Vo mere vos salue, car ele vos a cier;
Vo feme si est morte, s'en a grant destorbier.
Grosse fu; quant co vint a son fais descargier,
Sire, se je l'os dire, ne vos doit anuier."   1555
"Di tost," co dist li rois, "quan c'on m'a fait
                                        nonchier."
".VII. serpens aporta, qui son cors entoscier
Eurent fait et desrompre; onques hom maniier   *9d*
Nes peut, qui lués n'eüst tot le cors hireciet;
Saciés que tant estoient li serpent lait et fier."   1560
"E! Las," ce dist Lotaires, "de grant dolor plenier
A fait mon cors avoir qui co m'a fait nonchier;
Or avoie grant joie, or ai grant destorbier.
Ne se puet nus el monde longement leecier,
Qu'en la fin de se joie ne l'estuece estancier   1565
Aucune a[ver]sités qui fait son cuer ploier.[51]

48 Bele Elioxe, k'est nobletés devenue?
Molt m'estes ore tost et emblee et tolue,
Poise moi que je n'ai encor novele eüe.
Je quit que Dex ait fait de vostre arme sa drue,   1570
Se vos a fait el ciel porter en une nue.
Onques de toutes femes ne vi si bele nue;
Dex et Nature i misent tote leur entendue,
La biautés que aviés m'estoit el cuer ceüe.
Sansue trait le sanc quant se tient a car nue,   1575
Ausi vostre biautés m'a sucie et tolue
La joie de mon cuer u grans dolors m'argue.
Mar fu vostre biautés, dont m'arme est irascue,
Et vo vertus ausi qui mon cuer me partue;
Tant con vos vesquisiés ne me fust ja tolue   1580
Honors, ne segnorie ja ne me fust teüe,
Moi et tote ma gens, la grans et la menue.

Par vos primes m'estoit ceste gracie venus,
Que j'avoie victore de la gent mescreüe;
De la joie del ciel soit vostre ame peüe."   1585

49   Li baron s'esmervellent, qu'est le roi avenu.
Orains estoit joians, or a le giu perdu.
Il sont venu avant, mais ne sont pas meü.
"Sire rois, qu'avés vos? De qu'as consel creü?
Entre toi et ton clerc as tu damage eü?   1590
Quel besoing t'a tes clers ore ramenteü?
Puisque sonmes ici d'ostoier esmeü
Tu nos as de soldees trestos si bien peü
Et nos sonmes si bien de t'amor enbeü.
Quan qu'il en a ici li grant et li menu,   1595
Isi bien nos iés ore trestos el cuer keü,
Que se vels guerroier Mahomet et Kahu,
Prenderons nos avuec, ja n'ert contretenu."
"Segnor," co dist li rois, "et grant joie et salu
Vos doinst tos Damedex, bien m'avés maintenu,   1600
Et vos estes trestot mi ami et mi dru
Mais bien saciés, por voir, que molt m'est mesceü.
La roïne Elioxe m'a tot mon cuer tolu;   10*a*
C'ert la plus sage dame qu'encore aie veü,
Molt m'a la soie mors durement confondu,   1605
Quant s'aïe et son sens m'a si tost retolu."
"Sire," dïent li prince, "Dex a molt grant vertu,
Mellor arés encore c'onques ele ne fu.
Nus ne doit desperer, mais avoir bon argu;
Mellor arés encore, Dex doinst s'arme salu."   1610

50   "Segnor," co dist li rois, "bone gens honoree,
Beneoite soit l'eure que fustes assanblee.
Ralés en vo païs, cascuns en sa contree.
G'irai veïr ma mere qui'st molt desconfortee,
Sel reconforterai car molt est adolee."   1615
Or cevalce li rois a maisnie privee,
Puis qu'il est en sa terre, n'a cure de posnee.
Or cevalce a grant force, si haste sa jornee:
Au tierc jor descendi en sa sale pavee.
Quant sa mere le vit, a terre ciet pasmee,   1620
Et il a d'autre part sa chiere envolepee
Del cor de son bliaut qui'st de porpre roee.
Cevalier qui la sont la dame ont relevee;
Sous piece, quant se fu .I. pot reporpensee,
Ses crins trait, bat ses palmes, sa face a desciree;1625
Dont s'est a hautes vois conme feme escriee:
"Ma fille, u estes vos? Qui vos a emportee?
Jo vos amoie tant, ma fille douce nee,

Con se jo vos eüsce en mon ventre portee.
La mors, u iestes vos, qui le m'avés emblée?"   1630
Cou est fause dolors, por toute la crïee;
Mais li rois qui son cuer ot torble et sa pensee,
Ne se pot acieser, car il l'ot molt amee.
Assés i a de cels qui dolor ont menee,
Por la dame li un, li autre por la fee   1635
Qui piec'a estoit morte, est en terre posee,
Por lor segnor li autre, a qui nïent n'agree.
Cil se demaine si conme feme adolee.

51   Plantols, uns cevaliers qui ert de sa maisnie,
Molt l'ama; ses niés ert, de sa seror joïe.   1640
Il saut sus, ja dira parole bien oïe:
"Oncles, tu iés tenans de molt grant segnorie,
Grant terre as desos toi en garde et en baillie,
Se vient a ton besoing molt grans cevalerie,
Et tot vienent a toi en force et en aïe.   1645
Se il savoient ore que menasces tel vie,
Il ne te priseroient le vaillant d'une alie.
Femes doivent plorer quant cuers lor atenrie,   10*b*
On les doit conforter qui les tient de maisnie.
Tu amas molt la dame et ele fu t'amie,   1650
Dex mete la soie arme en pardurable vie.
Fai faire sor le cors mostier u abeïe,
Et s'i met de tes rentes et s'i asiet clergie
Qui par nuit et par jor por Elioxe prie.
Soiés de bel confort, faites ciere haitie,   1655
Reconforte ta mere qui tote est esbahie;
Se tes cuers est dolans, tostans fai ciere lie."
"Bien dist Plantols li preus," co respont la maisnie,
"Plus en fera li rois qu'a ses homes ne die;
Cascun jor face aumosne, et par rente establie   1660
Qui onques en demant, qu'il n'i faille mie."

52   Li rois par bon consel devint bons almosniers,
Il done pain et blé, livres, marcs et deniers.
Il a clers assanblés s'a fait novials mostiers,
Done livres, calises, vestimens, pailes ciers,   1665
Textes et candeliers et crois et encensiers,
Et rentes lor dona tant con lor fu mestiers.

53   Or sont assis li clerc, ne finent de proier
Tos les sains Damedeu, qu'il puisse consellier
Roi Lotaire et sa mere et l'arme sa moillier.   1670
Auques se prant li rois de son duel a coisier,
Si conpaignon le font auques esleecier.
Li cevalier le mainent sovent esbanoier,

As eskiés et as tables et prendre et gaaignier;
Mais en nule maniere nel pueent solacier.   1675
Une ore a pris li rois sa mere a araisnier:
"Mere," dist il, "por Deu, molt me puis mervellier,
Onques ne peuc oïr le verté aficier,
Conment fist Elioxe a le mort travellier.
D'unes letres que g'euc me ramenbra l'autrier,   1680
Que en l'ost m'envoastes par .I. garcon corsier;
Jo en fis lués le cire mon capelain froisier,
Il me conmenca lués mervelles a noncier.
Or me deveriés vos mot a mot acointier:
Bien sai qu'ele fu grosse. Qui fu au travellier?" 1685
"Bels fils," co dist la mere, "vels tu reconmenchier
Ton duel et ta tristrece et ton grant destorbier?
Grosse fu, voirement, d'un hisdeus adversier
Ki tot son bel cors fist de venin entoscier;
Cou fu uns lais serpens, jo le vi hirecier.   1690
Ele s'en delivra; quant on le dut baillier,
Si esbati ses eles sans plus de detriier,
Si essora en l'air, n'ot soing de repairier.   10*c*
Le cors de li fist si durement martriier,
Ne mires ne carnins ne li pot ainc aidier.   1695
Morte fu, s'enfouimes le cors pres del mostier."
"E! Dex," co dist li rois, "con jo euc son cors chier."
Dont conmence a penser et son cief a broncier:
"Ha! Dex, ele me dist c'al premerain couchier
Que seriiens ensanble, por nos cors delitier,   1700
Ke il li convenroit .VII. enfans encargier;
Al mostre aroit cascuns caaine el col d'or mier.
Or parole ma dame d'un si fait aversier.
Jo ne sai mais le quele je tiegne a mencoignier;
Jo le lairai atant, n'en voel plus fabloier."   1705
Or est li rois tos seus, veves et sans moillier,
Fierement tient sa terre, n'est en nului dangier;
N'a si hardi voisin qui ja l'ost guerroier.
On le tient por bon home et por bon justichier;
De nul jugement dire ne velt il detriier,   1710
Mais tost après le clain jugier et afaitier.
Issi tint il sa terre .VII. ans sans enconbrier;
Dont li est pris talens de lire et d'encerkier
Quans travers, quans treüs tenoient si voier,
Et si viegnent molt bien conter a l'eskekier.   1715
Li clers list les escris, si troeve tel rentier,
Bien a passé .VII. ans qu'il ne vint paier,
Tel i a .III., tel deus; le roi prent anuier,
Ja lor vaura par letres de son talent nonchier.

54 Li rois garde le clerc, si li sanble sacant: 1720

"Escrisiés as rentiers que jo par brief lor mant,
Dedens .XL. jors viegnent faire creant
De quan que il a moi doivent estre rendant;
Et si viegnent garni si con por droit faisant."
Li clers a fait les letres trestot al roi conmant,   1725
Et le saiel de cire et le brief fors pendant.
Li rois a regardé et ariere et avant:
"Qui portera ces letres? U iés tu, Malquidant?"
Entrués qu'il regardoit, estes vos .I. serjant,
Je quit c'on l'apeloit Rudemart le vaillant;   1730
A son pere ot esté, se li ot doné tant
Dont il avoit assez a trestot son vivant.
Ses pere l'ot molt cier, qu'il le savoit sacant,
Ses terres et ses fiés et ses rentes contant;
Li rois l'a apielé et il i vint errant.   1735
"Rudemart," dist li rois, "n'i voi plus aparant
De la besoigne faire mais el muler amblant.
Montés tost si portés ces letres a garant.   10*d*
Quel part que vos venés c'on vos port honor grant,
Car c'a escrit es letres que veés ci pendant.   1740
Si dites mes rentiers, si con il sont coillant
Mes rentes, mais treüs ausi soit rendant
De cou qu'il ont reciut de droit conte faisant
Dedens .XL. jors devant moi en present;
Et se il co ne font, mal m'ierent atendant."   1745
Rudemars li respont: "Bien ferons vo conmant."
Les letres prent, si va a la roïne errant.
"Dame," dist il, "j'en vois le preu le roi querrant."

55 Rudemars s'aparelle si con de bien errer.
    Il fait des .IIII. piés son mulet refierer,   1750
    Sa siele renaier, son penel rabourer,
    Esperons et estriers, caingles pour recaingler;
    [Ne] mes ses torselieres ne vaut il oblïer,[52]
    Hueses, cape et capel, por son cors aonbrer,
    Et boiste por ses letres, que mius les puist garder.1755
    Quant Dex done el demain que dut l'aube crever,
    Il prent se cose preste si s'en prent a aler.
    Or s'en va Rudemars, ne velt plus demorer,
    Par [l]es baillius le roi qu'il set molt bien trover.[53]
    Molt set bien u il mainent, n'en puet nus escaper; 1760
    Il les semont trestos devant le roi aler,
    Por conter devant lui u por gage livrer;
    U sans gage u sans plege n'en poront retorner.
    Tostans mostre ses letres, por lui asseürer.
    Bien a .VII. jors erré, ainc ne vaut sejorner;   1765
    La u prist le disner, la ne vaut ainc souper.
    Les baillius de la marce a il fait tos tranbler,

S'al .XL. isme jor ne sont la por conter,
Li rois a lor mesaise les en fera mener.
Cil li otroient tot, ne l'osent refuser,   1770
Car il mostre ses letres qu'il pueet molt doter.
Cil a fait son message, met soi el retorner,
Mais c'est par autre voie, car il s'en velt raler,
A grans jornees velt le païs trespasser.
A Lesbon, .I. castel, la va prendre .I. disner,   1775
Et puis se met a voie pour son oire haster.
Passe .I. grant brueroi, puis li estuet entrer
En une grant forest, mais ne s'i sot garder.
Il ne trueve maison u il puist osteler,
Et li jors se tornoit del tot al avesprer.   1780
Il se crient de sa beste, des leus del devourer,
Car se il fust a pié, garandir et tenser
Se peüst et deseure .I. grant arbre monter;   11a
Or li estuet a terre lui et son mul garder.
La forés si est grans, maint ors et maint sengler,   1785
Qui le cerkast a ciens, i peüst on trover.
La nuis n'ert mie torble, la lune luisoit cler.
Il se trait sos .I. arbre por son cors reposer,
Et il va a sa mule le frain del cief oster
Et l'arcon de sa sele li va outre jeter;   1790
Le cavestre li lace el pié por eschaper.
La mule paist de l'erbe tant con en pot trover.
De l'avaine nel pot nïent aprovender.
Il s'asiet desos l'arbre, car ne set u aler,
Saine soi del deable, que nel puist enganer,   1795
Et si a trait le brant dont li cotel sont cler,
Del dormir n'a talent, ains est en mal penser.
Issi li convint la tote nuit demorer;
Et tantost con il vit l'aube aparant crever,
Si met le frain sa mule si le vait recaingler.   1800
Il monte et quiert cemin por jornee haster,
Mais ancois sona prime qu'il puist cemin trover,
Et quant entrés i est ne set u veut mener.
Carité a assés de longement juner;
Il n'a ne tant ne quant dont il puisse disner.   1805
Vers none oï .I. cien et glatir et uller,
Assés l'a escouté, cele part velt torner;
Quant plus aproce pres, si a oï canter
Un choc que uns ermites fait en son més garder.
Il pense la a gent, la vaura osteler,   1810
Se Dex li consentoit que la peüst aler.

56 Rudemars tos lassez cele part vint traiant,
Il estoit molt aflis, travail ot eü grant;
Encore estoit en juns des le jor de devant.

Il a trové l'ermite son cortil encloant,   1815
Dont les bestes li erent forment adamagant.
Li lievre et porc et cerf et li cevroel salant
Toute jor li mangüent ses coles en brostant,
Dusqu'a dont que li cien i vienent abaiant.
Rudemars a parlé hautement en oiant: 1820
"Bels preudom, cil vos saut qui maint en Oriant,
Et de la sainte Virgene nasqui en Belliant.
Por cel segnor vos pri dont vos vois reclamant,
Que vos faites anuit une aumosne molt grant.
Laisiés moi o vos estre hui mais a remanant,   1825
A mangier me donés por Deu le raemant.
Certes jo ne mangai tres ier none sonant,
Toute jor ai erré par bos, par desrubant."   11*b*
Cil a levé son chief, si li vait regardant,
Avis li est qu'il soit preudom, a son sanblant.   1830
"Dont estes vos, bels sire, et qu'alés vos querant?"
"Sire, jo vois le preu mon segnor porchacant;
Jo semoing ses voiers qu'a lui viegnent errant,
Et si porc ci ses letres a cest saiel pendant."

57 "Amis," dist li ermites, qui fu de bone vie   1835
Et de grant carité, "hui mais n'en irés mie;
De la moie viande arés une partie,
Et si prendés hui mais o moi herbregerie;
Ostés vo mul le frain; en cel pré qui verdie
Le loiés par le pié, qu'il ne s'eslonge mie.   1840
Et s'en soiés assés por gesir anuitie,
Car vos n'averés keute fors de l'erbe delie,
Ne de linceus noient; plus n'i arés aïe."
Rudemars fu molt liés et de Diu le mercie;
Il a pris sa faucille, s'a de l'erbe soïe,   1845
Tant en porte en maison qu'il ne s'en repent mie;
Sa mule maine o lui, aprés l'erbe le lie.
L'ore atent de mangier, mais que molt li detrie;
Ne vaut mangier ses ostes, si fu tens de conplie.
Il a tant atendu que l'ore est avesprie.   1850
L'ermites garde en haut, si a s'[oev]re laisie[54]
Il trait a sa chapele, si ore tant et prie
Qu'il dist vespres del jor et de sainte Marie,
Et vegile des mors, par bon loisir fenie.
Dont vient a sa seror qui avoit en baillie   1855
Son pain et sa despense: "Suer, enmiudrons no vie;
Nos avons ci .I. oste, faites plus grant boulie."
"Sire, au boin eür, ne m'atargerai mie."
Ele prent sa ferine qui'st d'orge bien delie,
Et del lait de ses cievres, honte en ai que jel die,1860
S'a fait le grant paiele .I. doit plus que mie.[55]

Quant la viande est quite et la table est drecie,
On a devant cascun mis la soie partie.
Dont samble Rudemart qu'il ait Puille saisie,
Tos les daintiés le roi ne prise il une alie;   1865
Molt manga volentiers, car famine l'aigrie,
De cel bon pain d'avaine et del mangier d'orgie,
Et but de la fontaine qui bien est refroidie.

58 Rudemars fu saous, et Deu en rent mercis
Et a saint Juliien, qu'a bon ostel l'a mis.   1870
Il garda entor lui, si a veü laïs
Enfans mangier ensanble, bien en i avoit .VI..
Tuit mengierent ensanble en pais et en seris,   11*c*
Ne font un point de noise, molt fu l'uns l'autre amis,
Et cascuns ot el col .I. loien d'or faitis.   1875
C'esgarda Rudemars, s'en a jeté .I. ris:
"Dex! Con je m'esmervel de ces enfans petis;
C'est la, co quit, lor mere qui tos les a norris;
D'un grant et d'un eage sont molt bien, ce m'est vis.
Ostes," dist Rudemars, "por les sains esperis,[56]   1880
Sont tot cist enfant vo que je voi ci assis?"
"Ostes," dist li ermites, "j'en sui pere adoptis;
Jes ai gardés caiens .VII. ans tos acomplis,
Que jes trovai ensanble en fain muciés et mis,
Et de saint cresme et d'oile tos crestiiens les fis,1885
Et ma suer les a tos en si grant cure mis
Qu'ele ausi conme mere les apele tosdis.
Cel loien que cascun a entor le col mis
Aporta il a lui, ja ne iere entredis
Que por moi soit ostés jusc'al jor del juïs;   1890
Il est d'or et si croist a mesure tosdis."
Et Rudemars respont: "Dex les garde, li pis."
Li preudom rent ses graces a Deu et ses mercis,
Et Rudemars respont: "De Deu soit beneïs,
Et cil par qui il est de bien si raemplis."   1895
Quant ont assés parlé, si se traient as lis,
Et Rudemars fait tant, ses mus est esternis;
Litiere li a faite trestote a son devis,
Mais d'avaine doner n'est il ne fais ne dis.
Et Rudemars selonc s'est cociés tos vestis,   1900
Car il fu las d'errer, si fu tos endormis.
La dort desci adont que jors est esclarcis;
Et quant il voit le jor errant est sus salis
Et monte en son mulet qui est d'esrer ademis.
A l'oste prent congié si s'est d'illuec partis,   1905
Si a tant cevalcié par bois et par lairis
K'el demain endroit tierce al palais qui'st valtis
En est venus au roi; ja estoit mïedis

Quant il parla a lui, si li nonca ses dis
Que si rentier mandoient par bouce et par escris: 1910
Li rois les a molt bien et volentiers oïs.
Al roi a pris congié, d'illuec s'est departis,
A sa dame est venus qui l'ot molt cier tosdis.

59 La roïne le voit, si li dist: "Bien vegniés!
    Que faites, Rudemart? Estes vos tos haitiés?   1915
    Avés vos ore bien vos travals enploiés?"
    "Oïe, certes, ma dame, Dex en soit graciiés.
    Dame, jo ai bien fait son conmant, co saciés;   11*d*
    Mais jo ai esté puis durement esmaiés.
    Quant me mis el repaire el bos fui forvoiés,   1920
    Une nuit juc el bos sos le rain tos cociés;
    L'endemain errai tant que jo fui herbregiés
    El bos ciés .I. saint home, ja fui bien pastoiés;
    La vi jou grans mervelles, dame, ja nel querriés."
    "Di, por Deu, Rudemart." "Al bon eür, oiés: 1925
    Je vi la .VI. enfans trestos bien arengiés
    Entor une escuiele, et si bien afaitiés
    C'un seul mot ne disoient, et s'ert cascuns loiés
    El col d'une caaine dont li ors ert proisiés,
    Bons rouges ors d'Arrabe qui si est covoitiés.   1930
    Li bons hom les norist, Dex li ot envoiés,
    S'ierent tot d'un eage et d'un grant, co saciés."
    "Rudemart," dist la dame, "jamais mes amistiés
    N'arés en vo vivant, se vos ne porchaciés
    De ces caaines d'or que vos le mes doigniés."   1935
    "Dame," dist Rudemars, "por nïent travelliés;
    Jo nel lairoie mie por estre a mort jugiés."
    "Rudemart, paine t'ent, bien seras soldoiés;
    Tu averas m'amor et des moies daintiés."

60 Rudemars fu pensis, ne sot quel part torner;   1940
    En aucune maniere l'estuet atapiner
    Qu'il revoist as enfans les caaines oster.
    Unes cisoires quiert dont il les puist colper,
    Et une viés eskerpe u il les puist bouter;
    Viés housials decrevés et solliers por aler,   1945
    Cemise et braies noires, esclavine afubler
    Et bordon que il fait tot de novel fierer,
    Et .I. capel feutrin por son cief l'ombrer;
    Son vis a taint d'un fiel d'un grant pisson de mer
    Qu'il avoit piec'a fait al keu le roi server.   1950
    Or est atapinés, or pense del errer,
    .III. jornees a piet a fait por la aler.
    A l'ermite est venus, sel prent a sermoner:
    "Sire preudom, por Deu qui le mont doit salver,

Que Dex en paradis face vostre arme aler!   1955
Laisiés moi anuit mais avoec vos osteler;
Enfers sui et enflés; ce quit, m'estuet crever.
Sire, par Deu carnés me, se vos savés carner,
Tante mecine ai bute, nel puis mais endurer;
As puisons saint Rumacle m'en alai meciner.   1960
Une fois sui alis et l'autre voel crever,
Lieve, por Deu, ta main, fai ma dolor cieser;
Se tu saines mon ventre bien porai esmiudrer."   12a
Li ermites le voit si forment dolouser,
Ne li puet son ostel de pitié refuser;   1965
Fait li crois sor son ventre que il vit si enfler,
Et dist .III. pater nostres por le mius ajuer,
Que deables nel puist mal baillir ne grever.
Aprés dist qu'il fera une erbe destemprer
Quant il vaura coucier, sel vaura abevrer,   1970
Que il puis ne le voie tant con jors puet durer.
"Alés seïr, bels sire, alés vos reposer,
U jesir sor cele herbe, car las vos voi d'esrer."

61   Li pelerins malades fist molt feble sanblant,
Ausi se dolousoit con s'eüst grant ahant,   1975
Et l'ermites en a pité et doucor grant.
Des öes li a fait quire trestot a son talant,
Mais de pain ne pot il gouster ne tant ne quant;
Del lait se fist doner con enfant alaitant.
L'ermites prent sanicle, .I. erbe verdoiant,   1980
Et osmonde et fregon, qui molt ot vertu grant,
Se l'estampe et destempre, vient a celui puirant.
Cil le prent en sa bouce, de boire fait sanblant,
Mais onques n'en passa le col ne poi ne grant,
Ains le va entor lui en l'erbe dejetant,   1985
L'ermites le saina, si s'en ala corant,
Que plus ne le veïst en cel jor en avant;
Non fist il onques puis en trestot son vivant.
L'ermites se couca et clost son huis devant,
Et cil remest ca fors desor l'erbe gisant,   1990
Si a levé la teste, entor lui va gardant
Por veïr de l'ostel trestot le convenant.
La litiere a veüe u gisent li enfant;
Assés sont pres de lui, mais si secreemans
Velt faire son malise, si bien, si coiement,   1995
Que nus de la maison nel voist apercevant.
Il dort si con li autre, s'atent tant convenant;
La se gist et repose jusqu'a l'aube aparant.
Li ermites se lieve, ses saumes vait runant
Et entre en sa capele, si a leü son cant;   2000
Et sa suer lieve sus, ses cievres maine en camp.

La pucele se gist coverte d'un drap blanc,
Li .VI. enfant remainent en lor lit tot dormant.
L'ostes, qui son colp gaite, se lieve en son seant
Si regarde entor lui, s'esquerpe vait querant   2005
U les cisoieres sont qui molt ont bon trencant.
As enfans est venus souavet en ta[i]sant,[57]
Les caaines lor coupe cascune o le pendant.   12*b*
Tot remet en l'escerpe, le fer et l'or luisant;
Dont revient a son lit, va soi aparellant,   2010
C'al cemin se velt metre tot sans congié prendant.

62 Li tapins s'acemine, onques n'i prist congié,
Con cil qui coiement a fait sa malvaistié;
Les caaines enporte qu'a conquis par pecié.
Es le vos ens el bos tapi et enbuscié;   2015
Il ne tient nul cemin, mais par .I. marescié,
Sans cauce et sans housel, sans caucer, tot nu pié.
Quant vint a miedi bien s'en est eslongié,
Dont a pris son housel, si a caucié son pié.
Or s'acemine fort, bien a fait son marcié,   2020
Sans calenge a conquis tot co qu'a covoitié.
En .II. jors et demi a il tant travellié
Que il est la venus u li rois tint son sié,
Mais par defors la vile a son estre cangié;
Ainc de quan qu'il porta ne en main ne en pié   2025
Ne retint fors l'esquerpe u il avoit mucié
Icou dont la roïne li avoit molt proié.
Il a repris ses dras que il avoit cangié,
A la roïne vient, si s'asiet a son pié.
"Dame," dist il, "cil sire, qui par sa grant pitié 2030
Vint racater le mont, que Malfés ot loié,
Vos saut et quan qu'avés mis en vostre amistié."
"Tu dis bien, Rudemart, conment as esploitié?"
"Dame, jo ai tant fait, ves me ci repairié,
Et si ai tant alé et quis et porchacié   2035
Que je vos aporc ci bon or, fin et proisié;
Faites ent vo plaisir." Et cil li a puirié.
La roïne les prent, si l'en a merciié
Et de bon gueredon l'a molt bien soldoié.

63 Rudemars ot laisiés les .VI. enfans en lor lis,   2040
Tot ierent d'un eage, tot .VI. assez petis.
Lor coses en porta con malvais et fuitis,
Il n'i avoit celui ne fust si endormis,
S'on le vausist ocire, ne s'en fust il fuïs;
Tant dorment li enfant que jors fu esclarcis.   2045
Quant li premiers se fu de son songe esperis,
Il dejete ses bras ausi con par delis.

Il senti par ses menbres, les grans et les petis,
Que nature cangoit et en cors et en vis;
Et en bras et en janbes par tot a pan[n]es mis,[58]   2050
S'est devenus oisiaus si blans con flors de lis,
De parole former n'estoit pas poëstis.
Ausi fist il as autres, tant qu'il sont trestot .VI. 12c
Blanc oisel devenu, si se sont en l'air mis;
Mius resambloient cisne c'autre oisel a devis,   2055
Il sont blanc, s'ont lons cols, et si ont les piés bis.
Tot c'esgarda lor suer qui avoit son cief mis
Desos son covertor, mais c'un poi pert ses vis;
Longement ot baé et esgardé tosdis
Conment li pelerins qui estoit langeïs,   2060
Quant il ne vit nului, si est alés as lis;
Mais ne seut qu'il i fist; aprés s'en est fuïs.

64 Li oisel sont en l'air, s'aprendent a voler.
    Nature les aprent, qui les ot fait muer
    Estre d'ome en oisel, mais la ne pot ovrer   2065
    Que sens d'ome cangast, mais la ne puet ovrer.[59]
    Celui ont porsivi quis ert venus embler
    Lor ensegnes qu'il durent lor eages porter;
    Perdues sont, se Dex ne les velt regarder.
    Porsivi ont celui qui nes pot eskiver   2070
    Qu'il ne l'aient veü la u il velt aler.
    El castel sont entré u Lotaires li ber,
    Qui rois ert de la terre, se faisoit dangerer.
    Il amoit le castel, ne s'en vaut remuer;
    Ses pere i tint son sié, il le vaut restorer,   2075
    Car la fu il norris, et la prist il a per
    Elioxe la bele, qui tant fist a loer.
    La fu morte la dame, la le fist enterrer
    Et la seent les rentes dont fait messes canter
    As eglises qu'il a fait del sien estorer.   2080
    Li castials siet molt bien por home dangerer.
    D'une part est li bos u puet aler vener,
    Et d'autre part riviere sos le maistre piler
    De la tor u il puet cascun jor, al lever,
    Par .I. petit guicet ses mains al flos laver,   2085
    Et poissons assez prendre, por avoir al disner.
    Outre l'eve sont pré c'on puet .II. fois fener,
    Et fontaines i a dont li riu sont molt cler;
    Aprés ot .I. vivier u li rois fait server
    Poissons grant de manieres, quant il se velt haster,2090
    Que pesciere qui pesce les puist tost aprester.
    Les vignes et l'arbroie n'i doit on oblier,
    Dont li vin et li fruit font forment a amer.
    Les coutures i sont por forment pur et cler,

Portent dont on poroit .III. castels conreer; 2095
Por ce se velt li rois adiés la reposer.
La sont alé li cisne, la les fist trespasser
Nature qui lor fist les eles por voler, 12*d*
Et sens d'ome qui chace le laron qui embler
Ert venus cou que Dex lor vaut toudis server, 2100
Et la Deu porveance qui s'i vaut amostrer.
El vivier se descendent, s'i prendent a voler;
Poissons i troevent gros, la fist bon pasturer.

65 Novele vint al roi que .VI. cisne novel
Mainent en son vivier, mais il font grant maisel 2105
Des poissons qui la sont, prendent a tel reviel
Qu'a paines i remaint poissons ne pissoncel;
Mais il n'atendent home ne vienent a apel.
"Conbien a," dist li rois, "que la sont cil oisel?"
"Sire, il a bien .X. jors que g'iere en cel praiel, 2110
Ses vi sor la fontaine ester ens el gravel,
Et puis ses ai veüs pelukier al solel."
"Par Deu," ce dist li rois, "ce me est or molt bel.
Or conmant qu'il n'i ait ne viel ne jovencel[60]
Qui de rien les quivrie, car en malvaise pel 2115
Meteroie sa car, et en malvais flaiel
Jo le ferroie si que boulir le cervel
Li feroie a mes mains d'espee u de coutel.

66 Plantols n'ot mie oï ceste manace faire;
Niés ert le roi Lotaire, et frans et de bon aire. 2120
En riviere ert alés, oisials porte .II. paire,
C'ert ostoirs et faucons; et arc porte por traire.
Dont li vient uns hairons par devers son viaire;
Le faucon laisse aler qui de voler le maire,
Tant le maire et demaine qu'il l'abat ens el aire, 2125
Et en l'aigue u li cisne qui'stoient tot Lotaire[61]
Ot conmandé que nus ne lor face contraire.
Et Plantols a grant paine fait son oisel fors traire;
Encor ne se velt pas vers son ostel retraire,
Car il voloit encore faire cose qui paire. 2130
Il a son arc tendu, si entoise por traire,
Volentiers porteroit le roi bon quisinaire;
La saiete entesa desci al fer por traire,
Mais la corde li fent desci que el tenaire,
Et li cisne s'en volent tres par mi le vivaire, 2135
Qu'il n'ont point de paor de l'arcier de put aire.
Se Plantols fu dolans, si pert a son viaire:
Qui tot le depecast, n'en peüst il sanc traire.
Il a rüé tot puer, si se met el repaire.

67   Il ot tant demoré, li rois sist al mangier;   2140
     Plantols descent sos l'arbre, il et si cevalier,
     Lor cevals enmenerent garcon et escuier.
     Plantols s'en vait puiant sus el palais plenier, 13*a*
     Li rois se sist au dois, et Plantols qui l'ot cier
     Li presente .I. hairon por lui esleecier.   2145
     "Bels niés, u fustes vos alés por rivoier?"
     "Bels sire," dist Plantols, "a cel forcor vivier
     Sos le bois fis aler un mien faucon muier;
     Cest hairon eslevai, nel finai de cacier
     Dusqu'adont que il fu en .I. est[an]c plonciés;[62]   2150
     A paines peuc avoir mon faucon montenier,
     Et jo euc grant paor qu'il ne deüst noier;
     La avoit .VI. oisials, qui sont grant et plenier,
     Et blanc con flors de lis; jo pris mon arc manier,
     Si en vauc traire a l'un, ne m'i seuc afaitier: 2155
     La saiete fendi par dalés le tenier,
     Li oisel s'en volerent, ne peuc nul arcoier."
     Quant li rois ot cel mot, si prent a courecier:
     "Comment!" dist il, "Plantoul, g'euc fait mon ban
                                     criier,
     Que nus ne destorbast les oisiaus del vivier;   2160
     Par les plaies mortels, vos le conperrés cier."
     Li rois saut sus em piés, u il n'ot qu'aïrier,
     Tient .I. coutel trencant qui tos estoit d'acier;
     Ja alast son neveu ens el cuer estechier,
     Quant salent contre lui doi jentil cevalier   2165
     Qui recivrent a force sel prendent a coisier.
     Por cou ne remaint mie, il prent la nef d'or mier
     Sel rue aprés Plantoul qu'il le voloit quaisier.
     Mais cil en est guencis joste .I. piler arier,
     La nef hurte al piler, si fait le pié froisier.   2170
     Sa mere est sus salie sel corut redrecier,
     Et Plantols descendi contreval le plancier.

68   Li rois est coureciés, grant piece se coisa,
     Et toute la vespree son maltalent runga.
     Plantols est main levés, en la capele entra,   2175
     La se sist joste l'uis tant que li rois venra.
     Li capelains i vint, de canter s'atorna,
     Rois Lotaires i vint, grant conpaigne mena.
     Il entre en sa capele, et cil qui covoita
     As piés li est ceüs, et merci li proia   2180
     Et trestot l'en proierent, et li rois l'en leva
     Et por tante proiere trestot li pardona,
     Par si que a ses cisnes nul jor mais ne traira;
     Sor les sains de l'autel, de cou l'aseüra.

69 Or est Plantols a cort niés le roi et amis,   2185
   Des oisials del rivier est il eskius tosdis,
   Car li rois les a ciers et en cuer li sont mis,
   Et li oisel ont pais de tos ceus dou païs.   13*b*
   Or pueent asseür noer par l'egueïs
   Et mangier des poissons, des grans et des petis,   2190
   Ja par home vivant n'en ert fais contredis.
   Et li piés de la nef qui estoit soldeïs,
   Qui par maltalent fu jetee au piler bis,
   Estoit tos defroés et la nés autresis;
   La mere au roi le garde, si l'a en son sauf mis.   2195
   Ele mande .I. orfevre qui estoit ses amis;
   Cil i vient volentiers qui molt ert liveïs.
   "Amis," dist la roïne, "conment sera remis
   Uns piés en ceste nef et fors et bien assis,
   Et la nef rebatue?" Cil respont a ses dis: 2200
   "Le pié estuet refaire de nuef, trop est malmis.
   Voire," dist li orfevres, "j'en ferai .I. fondis;
   Se vos or me bailliés, icis ert avoec mis."
   La roïne aporta .IIII. anels d'or masis.
   "Dame," dist li orfevrez, "poi i a, ce m'est vis,   2205
   A ce que vos volés qu'il soit bels et jentis."
   La roïne s'en va, n'a angle n'i ait quis,
   Des caaines li menbre que Rudemars ot pris;
   Une en a aportee, mais co fu a envis.
   Ce li dist li orfevrez: "C'est ci bons ors jentis, 2210
   Rouges, et par cestui ert l'autres colouris."
   Dont li dist la roïne: "As ent assez, amis?
   Je quit, bien puet soufire, se l'as en oevre mis."

70 Cil font et forge et oevre le pié si con devant,
   Si que la nés sist bien sor table fermemant.   2215
   Miudre est ore assez et s'a le pois plus grant;
   Molt plaist a la roïne l'uevre que voit parant.
   L'ovrier a soldoié de bon loier vaillant,
   Car il a faite l'uevre trestot a son talant.
   Tant a fait la roïne par son loier donant,   2220
   Qu'ele a les caaines de bon fin or luisant
   C'orent entor lor cols loié li .VI. enfant;
   Mais l'une en est desfaite, fondue en fu ardant,
   Et li enfant devinrent oisel en l'air volant.
   Et tant sont aprocié le cuvert souduiant   2225
   Qu'il ierent el vivier sos le castel vaillant
   U lor ensegnes ierent qu'il vont porsivant.

71 Or nos estuet ariere a l'estoire raler.
   Li ermites del bos qui si soloit garder
   Les .VI. freres germains qu'il ne pot endurer   2230

Qu'il eüscent mesaise, s'il lor peüst oster,
Fu par matin alés a son mostier orer.
La fu bien tant que tans fu de prime soner;   13c
Pense soi que tans est qu'en labor doit aler,
Mais ains ira del pain a ses enfans doner.   2235
D'un grant pain torte d'orge vait .VII. pieces colper,
Dont est venus au lit por eux desvoleper;
Ne troeve se dras non. "Qu'est co, por saint Omer?
Sont nostre enfant si main la fors alé juer?"
Il va la u il suelent plus sovent converser,   2240
A tot le pain taillié les ala porgarder;
Quist amont et aval, ses prist a apeler,
Mais nus ne li respont, tant sace esfrois mener.
Revient s'ent en maison, prist soi a regarder
La u lor suer couca al vespre aprés souper.   2245
"Fille," dist il, "vos freres, quis fist si main lever?
Jo lor iere venus ca del pain aporter,
Por mengier dusqu'adont que nos devrons disner,
Car jo voloie aler .I. petit labourer;
Or criem molt qu'il ne puisent tant lor fain
                                   endurer." 2250
"Sire," dist la pucele, "jo les en vi voler;
Li pelerins salvages qui donastes souper,
Il ala cascun d'els entor le col limer,
Dont si s'aparella, si se prist a l'esrer.
Mi frere s'esvellierent, tos les vi tresmuer   2255
Et par cele fenestre la fors as cans voler."
"Fille," dist li hermites, "tu ne fais fors gaber!"
"Ne vos sai autre cose," fait ele, "raconter."
Dist li sains hom: "A Deu s'en puisent il aler,
El ciel avoec les angeles s'en puiscent il voler;   2260
Tien, fille, prent cest pain, pense del desjuner,
Et g'irai en l'ortel aucune cose ovrer."

72 Molt fu dolans l'ermites de ses enfans petis,
    Car al norir avoit et coust et travail mis.
    Il n'en a autre duel en son cuer entrepris,   2265
    Mais il prie por els, que li Sains Esperis
    Les avoit en tel liu qu'il ne soient malmis;
    Nequedent s'atent il maintes nuis et mains dis,
    S'il en oroit noveles u en fais u en dis.
    Il a bien atendu semaines plus de .X.,   2270
    Nus ne vient de procain ne de lontain païs
    Qui li die ques ait veüs ne mors ne vis.
    Vient s'ent a la pucele qui li cuers est pensis
    Et dolans de ses freres qu'ele ot perdus tos .VI..
    Dist li: "Ma douce amie, conment vos est avis   2275
    De vos freres qu'avés ensi desmanevis?"

"Sire," ce respont ele, "n'en ai ne giu ne ris,
Ains en est en mon ventre mes cuers forment maris." 13*d*
"Pucele, co est drois, perdu as .VI. amis,
Jo les ai longement et amés et cieris, 2280
Et de cou que j'avoie et gardés et norris;
Et jel fis volentiers, certes non a envis.
Alet en sont a Deu, ne sai quis a ravis;
Or en soit Jhesus garde et li Sains Esperis
Et tot li sains que Dex a avoec lui eslis 2285
Por manoir avoec lui en son saint paradis.
Mien voel eüssent il al aler congié pris."

73 "Amie, fille douce, molt me venist a gré
Qu'il eüscent encore avoec moi demoré;
Porveü lor eüsce pain et dras, et doné, 2290
Tant conme il peüssent sofrir ma poverté.
Mais puis que issi est, jo les conmant a Dé;
De lor vie soit garde la sainte Trinité.
Douce suer, je vos ai pres de .VII. ans gardé,
Bien quit que tot li .VII. sont compli et passé; 2295
Et vos meïsme avoec, tot par ma volenté
En irés aprés eux u Deu venra a gré.
Ne vous voel mais guarder, n'en voel estre emcombré.
Bel enfant a en vos, assez avés belté
Et gent cors segnoril bien fait et bien mollé. 2300
S'un robeor avoit en cest bos aresté,
Tost vos aroit fait lait et vos mesaasmé,
Nient por le vostre preu, mais por sa volenté;
N'en voel estre en cremor ne en malvais pensé.
Alés a une vile u il ait pain et blé, 2305
Servés a une dame tant qu'ele de son gré
Vos doinse por service et loier et bonté.
Gardés vos de folor, gardés vo caasté,
Cremés Deu et amés, de bien arés plenté."
Et la pucele a tot oï et escouté, 2310
Ne s'en pot pas tenir, durement a ploré:
"Sire, que dites vos, por Deu de majesté?
Qui m'avra si le pain sans dangier apresté
Conme vos le m'aviés, et sans besoing, doné?
Nului ne conistrai quant tant arai erré. 2315
S'uns hom m'a une nuit en son toit ostelé,
El demain par matin m'ara tost congeé.
Sire, retenés moi, por sainte carité."
"Non ferai, voir, pucele, ne me vient pas a gré."
Dont prent .I. mantelet gros tisu, tot usé, 2320
Ce li a sor le cief et contreval jeté,
Et un de ses pains d'orge li a desos bouté. 14*a*
"Biele suer," dist l'ermites, "n'arés gaires alé,

Quant qui que soit verrés d'errer aceminé,
Qui vos avoiera tant que arés trové   2325
Recet u borc u vile, castel u fremeté
La u vos vaurés traire senpres a l'avespré."

74   L'ermites lait sa fille ens el cemin plorant,
Si en revient ariere. Cele va regardant;
Quant nel puet mais veïr, si va ses poins tordant. 2330
Assise s'est .I. poi, atant es vos errant
.I. boskellon qui maine sa laigne a .I. jumant.
"Damoisele," dist il, "vos menés dol molt grant,
Qu'avés vos a plorer? qui vos va destraignant?"
"Sire," dist la pucele, "ja mais en mon vivant   2335
N'arai jo si boin pere con je vois hui perdant;
Ci el bos m'a laisie, ens s'en reva mucant."
"Taisiés vos, bele nee, j'ai .I. petit enfant,
Vos manrés avoec moi sel m'irés conportant;
Venés ent avoec moi." Ele lieve en estant   2340
Si porsiut le bon home qui le va cariant;
En maison est venus a soleil esconsant.
Evroïne, sa feme, li vient ester devant,
En son brac li aporte son enfancon riant.
Cil rue le cavestre sor le col del jumant,   2345
L'enfant prent en ses mains sel baise en acolant.
"Evroïne," dist il, "je vos amaint sergant
Qui no fil nos ira au mains ci delitant."
"Sire," dist Evroïne, "n'alés pas co disans;
Il n'a en tot cest siecle arme nule vivant   2350
Qui je creïsse mie a garder mon enfant.
Mais une nuit u deus li soferrons; atant
Voist querre sen esduit al Damedeu conmant."

75   Il s'en vient en maison, sa laigne a descargie
Et sa beste traiant a le grebe loïe,   2355
Et la dame Evroïne s'ostesse a herbregie,
De sa viande l'a une nuit pastoïe;
El demaine l'a au mius qu'ele pot consellie.
"A .X. liues ci pres siet molt bien aaisie
Une vile u li rois Lotaires tient maisnie,   2360
Et li fait cascun jor molt grande departie;
Arme qui i venra n'en ira ja faillie,
Qu'ele n'ait tant de pain qu'en sostenra sa vie.
Por l'arme sa moillier qui del siecle est partie,
Bien a .VII. ans passés que si fu establie   2365
L'ausmosne a la roi cort, ne encor ne falt mie.
La irés vos manoir, bele suer, doce amie;   14*b*
En .II. jors i venrés souavet ains conplie."
La pucele respont et forment l'en mercie:

"Damedex le vos mire, bien m'avés consellie." 2370
Or s'en va la pucele, Dex li soit en aïe;
Bien a le jor alé .III. liues et demie,
En une vile en entre, d'ostel ne rova mie;
En mi le vile estut conme feme esbahie,
Garde amont et aval et nule rien ne prie. 2375
La avoit une dame a son huis apoïe,
La pucele vit simple et de biauté garnie,
Et a li herbregier ses cuers li asouplie.
A li parole et dist: "Dont estes vos, amie?
Que porgardés vos ci? Avés vos conpaignie?" 2380
Cele li respondi conme feme asouplie:
"Dame, je sui del bos, si m'en sui departie;
Mes pere ne me velt mais avoir en baillie,
Si m'en sui ca venue, Dex me soit en aïe;
Jo n'ai nïent d'ostel, ne de pain une mie." 2385
"Bele suer," dist la dame, "ne vos esmaiés mie,
Hui mais remanrés ci, en ma herbregerie;
Vos arés bon consel, se jo puis, et m'aïe,
Que ne remanrés pas o moi desconsellie."
En maison sont alees, s'a celi aaisie 2390
Desci qu'a l'endemain, que li jors esclarcie;
Del soleil qui leva est li caure raïe.
Les povres gens assanblent a la cort segnorie;
La seent et atendent tant c'aient recoillie
L'aumosne qui sera a cascun departie 2395
Por l'arme la roïne, que Dex ait en baillie.
"Bele suer," dist l'ostese,"bien est drois que vos die:
Vos irés a la cort a la grant departie,
Si averés del pain por sostenir vo vie
.I. jor trestot entier desci que a conplie. 2400
S'irés a la fontaine qui laval cort serie
(N'est mie lonc de ci, n'i a c'une hucie),
Se vos en aportés une boine buirie;
La voie est ca desos, ne puet estre cangie."

76 Lors respont la pucele: "Dame, molt volentiers; 2405
Mais por ce que n'i faille, g'irai al pain premiers."
Son mantel affubla qui molt estoit legiers,
Qui de drap ert sans pel et si n'estoit pas ciers;
Vait s'ent laiens as autres si estut sor ses piés,
Se main trait et del pain li done l'aumosniers. 2410
Dont s'en va as fontaines, droit al cor des riviers
Ki la sorgent et corent desous les oliviers, 14c
Por le bonté de l'eve dont bels est li graviers.
S'asist la la pucele en qui n'est nus dangiers,
De mangier la son pain li est pris desiriers. 2415
Ele le brise en l'eve, bons li est li moilliers;

Seciés ert en son sain, s'en ert grans li mestiers.

77 Li cisne ont aperciut celi son pain mangant;
    Li un vienent al no et li autre avolant,
    La pucele qui'st la revont reconnoissant.   2420
    Ele n'en connoist nul fors tant oisel volant
    Li samble que co sont, et paor en a grant.
    Il vienent entor li, ele lor va soufrant,
    Le pain en la fontaine prendent premieremant;
    Ele n'ose vers eux contrester de niant,   2425
    Por co qu'il ont noirs bés, lons cols et grant carpant.
    Quant cius de la fontaine lor falt, tot erranmant
    Si vont querre de l'autre en son geron devant.
    Cele est tote esbahie qui son pain va perdant;
    Quant ele n'en a mie, arriere va plorant,   2430
    A paines ot sa buire enplie al riu corant;
    Li oisel li venoient lor bés a li frotant.
    En maison vient ariere, ne vait mie targant.

78 L'ostes vit la pucele durement esploree.
    "Comment est," dist a li, "pucele bele nee?   2435
    Ki vos fist nule rien? Dites moi vo pensee."
    Ce respont la pucele: "Molt m'ont espoentee
    Li oisel del vivier, qui a une volee
    Me corurent tot sus quant jo fui avalee
    Aval vers la fontaine por prendre une potee;   2440
    Moi sambloit que deüsce tote estre devoree;
    Mon pain que j'euc jeté aval en la ramee
    M'eurent il ains mangié que fuisce regardee,
    Et quant il lor fali, ainc n'i ot demoree,
    Le piece que jo tinc es mains m'ont il hapee,   2445
    Et puis en mon escorc trestote la mïee;
    Hui mais morrai de fain n'en ai mie servee.

79 "Fille," ce dist li ostes, "molt me puis mervellier
    Que li cisne le roi vos vaurent aprochier;
    Feristes ent vos nul? On n'en ose .I. toucier;   2450
    Li rois en vaut ocire son neveu avantier,
    Por cou que il i traist une fois d'arc manier."
    "Onques n'en toucai nul, dame, par saint Ricier."
    "Vos fesistes bien, fille, car a grant destorbier
    Vos tornast, que li rois vos fesist escillier.   2455
    De mon pain vos donrai hui mais assez mangier,
    Demain en irés querre de l'autre al aumosnier. 14*d*
    Et se je le voi ci aler ne cevalchier,
    Je vos ferai le plait que mellor recovrier
    En arés vos par moi, car en bien l'ai molt cier.   2460
    Atant cil passe la, si va esbanoier.

L'ostesse l'apela: "Ca venés, Herquegier;
Vés ci une pucele dont je vos voel proier
Que vos bien li faciés, car ele en a mestier;
Grant aumosne feroit quel poroit consellier."   2465
"Dont estes vos, pucele, nel me devés noier?"
"Sire," dist la pucele, "je vinc del bos l'autrier.
Ca m'envoia mes pere, ne me vaut plus aidier,
Jo m'en sui ca venue a le cort roi Lotier
Por avoir de l'aumosne, jo en ai grant mestier."   2470
"Bele," dist li vallés, "se vos m'aviiés chier,
A le fois vos donroie de pain plus grant quartier;
Levés haut vo visage, on ne doit pas bronchier."
Prist le par le menton, se li a fait haucier:
"Qu'est cou, ma douce amie, que voi la roujoier?   2475
Moi sanble que co soit de laiton u d'or mier."
"Sire, ce est m'ensegne. Qu'en avés a plaidier?
Jo l'aportai al naistre, del ventre a la moillier
Qui .IX. mois me porta; quant vi[n]t al travellier,⁶³
Si fumes .VII. enfant, d'un ventre parconier,   2480
Dont cascuns ot ensegne ausi faite d'or mier.
Morte en fu nostre mere, Dex qui nos puet aidier
Et en arme et en cors puist s'ame consellier;
Jo qui sui sans consel ne me voelle obliier."
"Bele," dist li vallés, "n'aiés soing d'esmaier,   2485
Se vos volés bien faire et soufrir mon dangier,
Je me vaurai pener de vo bien avancier."

80 Li senescals s'en va, ne velt plus demorer,
    Tot le jor et la nuit ne fina de penser
    Qu'il velt a la pucele priveement parler.   2490
    Engien li estuet faire. Conment porra errer?
    Il les laira trestos en la cort aüner:
    Al cor u la pucele estoit alee ester,
    Ne velt pas cele part conmencier a doner,
    Car il vaura a li sa donee finer.   2495
    Il cerke tos les rens, haste soi del doner;
    Quant vint a la pucele, son don li fait doubler,
    Del pain li done assez plus qu'ele n'ost rover.
    D'illuec s'en est tornee la pucele al vis cler;
    As fontaines s'en va por de l'eve aporter,   2500
    Et si desire molt les oisiaus esgarder.
    Al riu siet et son pain conmence ens a jeter;   15a
    Li oisel qui pres ierent ne vaurent demorer,
    Li un vienent a no et li autre a voler.
    La pucele nes vaut de rien espaventer;   2505
    Il mangüent le pain la u voient floter,
    Cele lor suefre tot ne nes velt destorber.
    Li senescals le roi, qui nel velt oblier

Et grant desirier a qu'il voelle a li parler,
Sa despense conmande .I. serjant a garder.   2510
De lonc vient, car il velt son afaire mirer;
Voit entor la pucele les oisials pasturer.
Ki li desist ancois, nel vausist creanter
Que si priveement osascent abiter
Li oisel entor li, qui s'en soelent voler   2515
Quant nus hom les soloit veïr ne esgarder.
Li senescals conmence le petit pas aler,
Ains cele n'en sot mot, sel vit lés li ester
Et li cisne conmencent tot vers lui a sifler.
Aprés celi s'asist, si le vaut acoler,   2520
Et cele l'aparole com ja oïr porés:
"Ahi! bels sire, en vos a si bel baceler,
Quel desirier avés de povre cose amer,
Quant vos en tant maint liu pöés trover vo per?"
Uns des cisnes s'eslieve, del giu le va haster,   2525
Que par mi le visage li fait l'ele cingler.
Cil jete aprés la main, por ariere bouter;
Li autres par deseure l'est venus assener,
Si le fiert en la teste, le capel fist voler.
Li tiers le vait gaitant, por bien son colp jeter;   2530
Tot .VI. li vont assez grant entente livrer.
Tart li est qu'il se puist d'illueques desevrer;
Son cief de son mantel prent a enveloper,
Si s'en fuit quan que pié l'en porent ains porter.
Li oisel se sont mis ariere a retorner;   2535
A la pucele vont et joïr et froter,
Por cou qu'il l'ont tensee del cointe baceler
Qui la estoit venus a li por desreer.
De la fontaine prant plain pot por aporter
A l'ostesse qui l'a fait .II. nuis osteler.   2540

81   Li senescals s'en est a cort venus fuiant,
Encor quidoit il bien que li oisel volant
Jusques a sa despense le veniscent cacant;
Assis s'est et li sans li revint en seant.
"Por les sains Deu!" dist il, "con me vois esmaiant 2545
Por .III. oisels u .IIII., se jes vi la volant;
Et por cou si me vient a mervelle si grant,   15*b*
C'onques tel oisel eurent sens et memore tant.
Jo quit que mal espir vinrent en els entrant."
Sus lieve, si s'en va ens el palais plus grant   2550
A son segnor parler, sel troeve la seant
Sor une keute painte de paile escarimant.
Dormi avoit .I. poi, ses dois aloit frotant.
"Que cou est, senescal? Quel co[s]e alés querant?"[64]
"Sire, par les sains Deu, molt me vois mervellant 2555

D'une cose qui est hui cest jor avenant.
En cest vostre castel a .I. molt bel enfant,
Molt bele mescinete, jovenete et croissant;
A vostre aumosne vient, son pain querre et rovant.
.I. mantelet afuble, son cief en va covrant; 2560
Une caaine d'or a entor le col grant
Et si fu nee atot, co me va racontant;
Al pain vient, ele en ot .I. bel don avenant;
Un pot prist s'en ala al fontenel corant
U vostre .VI. oisel sont el vivier noant. 2565
Jo le sivi aprés por veïr son sanblant,
Car j'[eu]c a li parlé ancois le jor devant.[65]
Al fontenel seoit, la le trovai brisant
Son pain en la fontaine, et li .VI. oisel blanc
Venoient entor li tot .VI. son pain mangant. 2570
En ses mains le prendoient, en son escorc devant,
Ausi con les eüst norris priveemant.
Jo m'asis la aprés tot porpenseemant
Por acointier a li, por veoir son talant.
L'uns des oisials me vint de l'ele el front
                                    cinglant, 2575
Que tot li oel me furent d'angoisse estincelant;
Et li autre s'eslievent sor moi en l'air volant,
Si me feri de l'ele que il en mi le camp
M'abati mon capel que j'euc el cief seant;
Et li autre s'eslievent par ausi fait talant. 2580
Jo sali sus tos liés qu'en peuc venir fuiant;
Jo cremi que aucuns esperis malfaisant
I eüst li deables envoiet la batant;
Encor criem que n'i soient mis par encantement."
"Senescals," dist li rois, "mervelles vas contant; 2585
Mes cisnes lai tos cois, ne les va quivriant;
Mais a la mescinete me feras connissant
Le matinet a l'ore de l'aumosne donant.
Por cou que de son pain ait aucun remanant,
Jo woel quant tel verras, que tu l'en dones tant 2590
Que ele en puist doner auques a son talant
As cisnes, s'ele vait demain al riu corant.   15c
Por cou vaurai savoir se me vas voir disant."
Dist li senescals: "Sire, tot au vostre conmant
Vos me verés demain al doner esgardant; 2595
Et tant vos di jo bien, por estre apercevant:
La u vos me verrés del doner arestant,
Que jo metrai .III. pains en son escorc devant,
C'ert cele que jo di, celi alés sivant."
"Bien as dit, senescal, et jo plus ne demant." 2600

82 Li jors vient, la nuis passe, l'endemain est venus.

D'une corte reube est rois Lotaires vestus;
Alés est oïr messe, et o lui de ses drus;
Aprés messe si est des mostier descendus.
"Senescal," dist li rois, "que iés tu devenus?   2605
Ces povres gens t'atendent, enn'en feras tu plus?"
"Sire," dist li vallés, "se mes païns ert fendus
Et j'estoie en la place ques eüsce veüs,
Ja avroient del pain, que ja n'i fauroit nus;
Et s'atendoie aïe .I. vallet qui'st la jus."   2610
"Vels tu que jo t'aïe? Je sui fors et menbrus."
"Oïe, sire, enon Deu, que bien soiés venus,
Car que plus i ferés, tant i perderés plus.
"Gardés dont," dist li rois, "ne soit hui mais fendus
N'esquartelés nos pains, tos entirs soit rendus.   2615
Tant ara la soie ame, ce quit, mellor salus
Devant Deu et ses sains en paradis la sus,
Por qui li pains sera donés et espandus.

83   Li senescals a fait pain aporter assez,
      Car li rois est venus del doner aprestés;   2620
      Il n'est del departir nïent acostumés:
      Por co que venus est, de tant est enmiudrés
      Li dons, quant pains entirs est a cascun donés.
      Neporquant je vos di, bien a .VII. ans passés
      Qu'il conmence a doner, encor ne fu lassez.   2625
      Tant a doné li rois que avant est alés;
      Ausi con a une autre li est uns pains donés.
      Et li senescals dist: "Damoisele, tenés;"
      Si l'en done encor .I.; li rois s'est regardés,
      Si s'est aperceüs et si s'est porpensés   2630
      Que ce est cele dont il queroit les vertés.
      Or vausist il ja estre del doner escapés,
      Et cele vausist estre a l'eve vers les prés,
      Por veoir les oisials que tant a enamés.
      La est atot .I. pot ses oires aprestés,   2635
      Por aporter de l'eve dont sa dame ait assés.
      Assise s'est au riu, es les vos avolés,   15*d*
      Tos les cisnes ensanble, qui li vont de tos lés
      Por avoir de cel pain qui la ert aportés.
      Ele en fraint et si brise, si lor en done assés.   2640
      Ez vos le roi quïl siut de lonc, tos aprestés,
      Tos seus et sans conpaigne, d'une cape afublés,
      Ausi con se il fust serjans a cort mandés.
      Vint la, s'i s'est assis desore al destre lés,
      Et cele s'esmervelle, et dist: "Ci que querés?   2645
      Sire, frans damoisials, quels est or vos pensés?
      Ier en i vint uns autres, mais il fu si menés
      N'i venra mais, co quit, si ert li mois passés,

Car li oisel le roi que vos ici veés
Le hurterent si fort des ciés de lor eles, 2650
Qu'il en fu tos liés quant il fu escapés.
Ausi feront il vos, se auques i seés."
"Bele suer," dist li rois, "avés vos encantés
Les oisials qu'a vo mai[n] avés fait si privés?[66]
Vos lor brisiés le pain, il le prendent de grés; 2655
Or m'en donés .I. poi, esprover m'i verrés
S'il vers moi esteroient ausi de volentés.
Donés m'ent, bele suer, le foi que moi devés;
Quant jo iere a l'aumosne, assés en averés."

84 Li rois a pris le pain, les oisiaus en puira, 2660
Bien les a conreés tant que mie en dura;
Nequedent en son cuer de co s'esmervella
Que il sont si privé; ainc mais nes asaia.
Poise li que sovent n'i estoit venus la.
Li sens que il avoient si les aprevisa 2665
La u truevent amor que nul barat n'i a.
Aprés tot cou li rois vers li se retorna:
"Pucele," dist li rois, "qui vos envoia ca?
De quel païs venistes et qui vos amena?
Et qu'est cou a vo col que voi roujoier la? 2670
La pucele l'esgarde et respondu li a:
"Mes pere qui el bos a més molt grant piec'a
Nos .VII. enfans garda tant que .VII. ans passa.
La nuit .I. pelerin qui la vint herbrega,
Vit mes freres ensanble et molt les esgarda, 2675
Et les caaines d'or molt longement visa
Que cascuns ot el col, qu'al naistre aporta.
Malade se fist molt, ainc la nuit ne manga,
Esgarda que ma dame les .VI. enfans couca,
En .I. lit et d'un drap tos les acouveta. 2680
On me couca aillors: garde ne s'en dona.
El demain par matin quant .I. poi esclaira   16*a*
Et mi frere dormirent, onques nus n'en vella,
Coiement leva sus, les loiens d'or enbla.
Ne sai par quel engien, mais molt tos les colpa. 2685
Puis se mist a la voie, moi sanble qu'en ala;
Ala s'ent ne sai u, ne sai quel part torna.
Mi frere s'esvellierent et jetent ca et la
Lor bras, que blance plume tos les acoveta.
Il se leverent sus, li premiers s'en vola, 2690
Et tot li autre aprés, nesun remés n'en a.
Adonques vint mes pere, que del pain m'aporta
Por els doner mangier, mais nul n'en i trova;
Puis les quist sus et jus assez et ca et la.
'Fille, u sont li enfans?' mes pere demanda; 2695

Et jo li respondi que cascuns enpluma
Trestos de blances plumes et puis si s'en vola.
Quant cascuns fu la fors, ne sai u il ala,
Et bien .I. an aprés, petit plus demora,
Si me prist par le main, et del pain me querka;   2700
A .I. quarré sentier me mist, si me laissa.
Tant fis puis que jo vinc a cel bel castel la,
S'ai vescu de l'aumosne le roi c'on me dona."
"Pucele," dist li rois, "el col qui vos loia
La caaine de l'or que rogoier voi la?"   2705
"Del ventre la portai u Nature l'ovra
Et Damedex avant, qui tot puet et pora;
Cou me dist que c'ert voirs cil qui ci m'envoia."

85 "Pucele," dist li rois, "mervelle m'as conté;
Poroit co estre voirs? Dis me tu verité?"   2710
"Oïl, voir," respont cele, "ensi m'est aconté."
"Pucele," dist li rois, "venés a seürté
A l'aumosne le roi; volentiers et de gré
En averois vos tant qu'il seront rasasé,
Li cisne del vivier, ja n'en aiez durté;   2715
Et vos meïsme avoec jusc'al jor apresté."
"Sire, Dex le vos mire, li rois de majesté,
Et le roi autresi que par sa grant bonté
A establi l'aumosne de son droit ireté,
Por l'ame sa moillier, dont il a salveté   2720
Mete l'arme en son ciel, en paradis regné.

86 Rois Lotaires s'en part et si va molt pensant
De cou que la pucele li ala gehissant,
Qu'en la maison l'ermite estoient .VII. enfant,
Et cascuns ot el col caaine d'or luisant   2725
Qui del ventre aporterent la lor mere al naisant,
Et les .VI. en perdirent par laron souduiant.   16*b*
"Quels sisnes puet co estre? Molt m'en vois mervellant;
Aucun sisne roial va li ors demostrant.
Mainte fois ai eü molt mon cuer mervellant   2730
Des dis que j'oï dire Eliox le sacant,
Que la premiere nuit en nostre lit gisant
Que me deliteroie avoec li carnelmant,
De nostre engenrement istroient .VII. enfant
Dont cascuns aroit sisne d'or a son col pendant;   2735
Et tot d'une litiere seroient li enfant
Et lignie en iroit desci en Oriant.
De tot icest afaire ne voï ne tant ne quant,
Et ma mere me dist et si me fist sacant
Que ele avoit eü jo ne sai quel serpant   2740
Qui l'ot envenimee, laisa le mort gîsant;

Li serpens s'en ala lasus en l'air volant.
U ma mere u ma feme, li quels que soit, me mant;
J'en sarai la verté, que qu'ele voist targant."
Tot issi con il ert, ardans de maltalant,   2745
Est montés el palais, n'en dist n'en fait sanblant
Que il soit irascus de rien ne tant ne quant.
Puis entre en une canbre, s'i a veü pendant
Une espee dont sont li cotel bien trencant.
Il l'en porte avoec lui sos son mantel covrant,   2750
Venus est a sa mere, si le trova seant
En sa canbre en .I. lit tote sole coucant.
Ele le voit venir, si li dist en riant:
"Bels fils, dont venés vos, et qu'alés vos querant?"
"Mere," co dist li rois, "molt ai le cuer dolant, 2755
Quant de ma ciere amie me va resovenant
Que j'ai sans nul confort perdu sifaitemant;
Ne jo ne puis savoir s'ele porta enfant
(Le ventre vi jo gros, si le vi soslevant),
Ne de sa mort ne sai con li fu convenant.   2760
Dites m'ent la verté, si con jel vos conmant,
Car jo le voel savoir, ne m'en celés niant."
"Bels fils," co dist la mere, "el porta .I. serpant
Qui toute l'entosca d'un envenimemant.
Morir estut la bele dont ai le cuer pensant."   2765
"Non, mere," dist li rois, "vos dirés autremant;
Molt m'avés or mené par lonc fabloiemant,
Mais par le foi que doi a Damedeu le grant
Le cief vos couperai de m'espee trencant.
(Si l'a sacie fors forbie et flanboiant)   2770
S'autre cose ne dites, ja n'en arés garant."
La dame est esfreé, si jeta .I. cri grant: 16*c*
"Bels fiux, jo te portai et norri alaitant,
Garde toi que deables ne te voist engignant;
Honerer dois ta mere, ce troeve l'en lisant;   2775
S'autres li faisoit cose qui li alast nuisant,
Se li devroies tu aidier tot erranmant."
"Mere," ce dist li rois, "la verté vos demant,
De la mort Elioxe me soiés voir disant;
Se nel dites molt tost, ja sarés con trencant   2780
Sont li cotel de fer que tieng ci en presant."
Dont aesme son coup por li bouter avant.

87 "Bels fiux," co dist la mere, "vels me tu vergonder,
Qui ta mere vels ci ne sacier ne bouter?
Mon pecié te dirai, sel me dois pardoner."   2785
"Dites, mere, del tot vos voel quite clamer,
Par si que ne doiés ne mentir ne fauser;
La mencoigne porés durement conperer,

Et se vos dites voir, ce vos puet delivrer,
Ne ja en nule rien ne m'orés reprover."   2790
"Fiux, entent, puis que jo m'os si asseürer,
Tu oras ma confiese, por Deu or del celer:
Te feme ot .VII. enfans ce me vinrent conter
Les dames qui la furent; quant el dut delivrer
On laisca les enfans a la terre witrer,   2795
S'entendi on a li quant el dut delivrer.
L'endemain quant oï des .VII. enfans parler,
Ses rovai coiement en la forest porter
U les truist salvegine por els tos devourer.
La les envoiai tos, plus ne vos sai conter,   2800
Car nes osoie mie ici pres essorber;
Et de cou vos voel jo, bels fils, pardon rover."
"Mere, encor vos voel jo autre rien demander."

88   "Mere," ce dist li rois, "jo vos ai pardoné,
Mais encore i remaint assez de la verté,   2805
Que tot li .VII. enfant furent encaainé
Al naistre entor lor col de fin or esmeré:
Ces caaines demant, si en faites mon gré."
"Bels fils," co dist la mere, "por sainte carité,
Jo nes vi ne nes tinc, ainques ni fu gardé   2810
De moi ne de ma part, voir t'en ai dit, par Dé."
Et li rois li respont: "U ja ert conperé,
U ja le mes rendrés!" "Fiux, or m'est ramenbré⁶⁷
Que tu envoias querre l'a[u]tre an par ton regné⁶⁸
A tes provos ta rente, que il, a jor nomé,   2815
Le t'eüscent trestot devant toi aporté.
Si trova mes serjans par qui co fut mandé   16*d*
.VII. enfans en l'ostel u on l'ot ostelé,
S'avoient .VII. caaines entor lor col nöé,
D'un sanblant, d'un afaire, et tot .VII. d'un aé;   2820
En un vaisel mangoient cou c'on lor ot doné.
Quant il vint, sel me dist cou qu'il avoit trové,
Jou li priai, si cier qu'il avoit m'amisté,
K'il ne finast ja mais sel m'eüst aporté
Trestot l'or des caaines que il avoit miré.   2825
Il s'en rala ariere, tant a quis et pené
Que cou que li rovai m'a porquis et doné:
.VI. en euc des loiens, .I. en ai jo osté.
Menbre vos que vos vi si fort maltalenté,
Quant pres vostre neveu, par male volenté,   2830
Jetastes vo nef d'or a .I. piler mollé
Par issi grant aïr qu'ele ot le pié quassé?
De l'or qui devant fu et d'autre c'ai sevré
Et d'un des .VI. loiens ai le pié restoré.
Or en remainent .V., la sont tot apresté,   2835

Et vos les arés ja volentiers et de gré,
Par si que maltalent m'aiés tot pardoné."
La dame lieve sus, si li a aporté;
Et il les a reciut, ses a molt regardé
Et en sa cambre mis et repus et salvé.   2840

89 Or set auques li rois de cou qu'il a enquis,
    Car sa mere meïsme l'en a assés apris;
    S'une autre eüst cou fait, ses cors en fust honis,
    Mais por cou qu'est sa mere, ne l'en sera ja pis.
    De cou que il a dit molt en remaint pensis;   2845
    Dusc'al demain atent, que jors fu esclarcis,
    Et tant que l'aumosne est, et li pains, departis,
    Un mantel cort affuble, s'est a la voie mis;
    Ses caaines en porte, et si a .II. pains pris
    Por doner as oisiaus qui des gens sont eskis.   2850
    Il vi si contr'atent la pucele au cler vis,
    Par li les quide plus avoir amanevis;
    Mais ne sens ne memoire n'est mie en els faillis,
    Ains ont bien retenu le sens d'ome et apris
    Que c'est lor suer que la avoit venu tans dis.   2855
    Nature et Destinee i ont lor contredis;
    Nature velt que hom si soit de sens garnis,
    Et Destinee dist le merc qu'ele i a mis,
    Et dist que de son droit sera a li sougis;
    Ne velt por nule rien soit fausé ne faillis.   2860
    Nature dist partot doit bien estre hom servis;
    S'en aporta l'ensegne dont fu par le col pris.   17a
    A cou s'embat Fortune, si escoute ces dis;
    Dist que .II. adversaires fera molt tost amis.
    Ele amaine celui qui de l'or ert baillis   2865
    Que lor ot Destinee tot entor le col mis.
    La pucele vient la, si siet as fontenis;
    Li oisel s'apercoivent si sont venu tot sis.
    Cele froisse le pain, si fu bien recoillis
    Des oisiaus, car cascuns fu ja de pain noris.   2870
    Es vos le roi qui vient, tot soëf s'est assis
    Lés la pucele a destre, et dist li, co m'est vis:
    "Damoisele," fait il, "il m'ert molt bien avis,
    Que les oisiaus avés en mainburnie mis,
    De vostre pain avront, quels que soit, blans u bis."2875
    "Sire," dist la pucele, et si leva le vis,
    "Cascuns va volentiers la u il a apris,
    Et la meïsmement u ses pains li est quis.
    Puis la premiere fois n'i fu fais contredis,
    Car jo ai cascun jor de mon pain que j'ai quis   2880
    A ces oisiaus doner brisiés es fontenis,
    Et cascuns a esté del prendre volentis."

90 "Pucele," dist li rois, "et se jo lor puiroie,
    Venroient il a moi? Volentiers lor donroie;
    Se vos le me loiés, ja droit l'asaieroie,   2885
    Un pain que jo tieng ci devant els froieroie."
    Atant trait fors le pain et devant els le froie.
    Quant il virent le pain, cascuns aprés coloie,
    Vienent et si le prendent, nus d'els ne s'en effroie.
    Entrués qu'il gardent jus il met main a coroie,   2890
    Sace une des caaines et .I. des oisiaus loie;
    Adont le sace a lui, si le tire et avoie
    Tant que fors des fontaines l'a mis a droite voie.
    Cil ne s'eslonge mie ne ne fuit ne desroie.
    Il s'esqeut, et sa plume qui plus que nois blancoie 2895
    Est devenus blans dras, que onques n'i ot roie,
    Dont il remaint vestus. Et puis, que vos diroie?
    Il est devenus hom et li rois s'en effroie;
    Vers sa seror regarde, dont li cuers li tenroie,
    Et dist: "Damoisials sire, certes encor vauroie   2900
    Que fesissiés ausi celui qui la coloie."
    Li rois li jete el col le loien si le loie,
    Sel sace fors de l'eve, et cil point ne desroie,
    Ains s'en vient volentiers et s'en a molt grant joie;
    Et Nature li cange erranment sa monoie.   2905
    D'un oisel fait .I. home, et le roi point n'anoie. 17*b*
    Sa plume est vesteüre qui cuevre et aombroie
    Sa car, qui del grant halle et de l'aige noircoie.

91 Li rois se pot forment de tel rien mervellier,
    Quant li oisel se laisce en tant aprivoier   2910
    C'on li puet la caaine en tor le col lacier,
    Et on le maine a terre sans tirer et sacier,
    Et Nature li vaut sifaitement aidier
    Qu'il reprent forme d'ome; en lui a bon ovrier,
    Ki par miracle fait la cose ensi cangier.   2915
    Li rois a pris la tierce caaine de l'or mier,
    Li tiers oisiaus se laise molt bien aplanoier,
    Et il li gete el col sans plus de l'atargier;
    Ausi avint cestui con il fust au premier.
    Que vos tenroie jo ici par fabloier?   2920
    .II. caaines avoit, celes velt enploier,
    Et cil li vinrent pres por eus aparellier.
    Li doi en vinrent fors, vont s'ent aconpaignier
    As trois qui la estoient; puis prendent a plaidier,
    Et dïent c'ont esté longes peneancier;   2925
    Dex lor a fait merci sel doivent graciier.
    Encore en remaint uns noant par le rivier
    Qui volentiers venist ester al camp plenier.
    Il n'est qui li aiut, ne li a que puirier

Li rois; ce poise lui, ci a grant destorbier,   2930
Quant li .V. en iront par terre esbanoier
Et il remanra seus en l'aigue del vivier.

92 Or sont tot .V. ensanble si sont entr'els parlant,
L'uns en parla premiers qui se tint a sacant:
"Longes avons esté, bels frere, peneant,   2935
Et Damedex nos a faite merci si grant
Par le main cest preudome que veés ci seant;
Mercïons Damedeu, le pere tot puissant
Et cel preudome la, molt me sanble vaillant;
Mais nos ne lairons mie aprés nos remanant   2940
No seror, ains li ermes ci et aillors aidant.
Avoec nos le menrons aventure querant,
Bien sai que c'est no suer et bien est aparant,
Bone ensegne en a ele, veable et conniscant;
Ensamble nos norri l'ermite al poil ferrant.   2945
No frere que laisons en l'eve remanant,
Nos ne li poons nient de rien estre aidant."
Es vos a ces paroles vint li rois maintenant:
"Que c'est, segnor?" dist il. "Qu'alés vos dementant?
Encore i a tel cose dont ne savés niant.   2950
Entre vos savés bien et estes connissant   17c
Ke vos fustes .VI. frere, norri en .I. herbant;
S'avés une seror, pucele et avenant:
En'est ele cou la que vos veés seant?"
"Oïl," respondent il, "par Deu omnipotant."   2955
"Enfant," co dist li rois, "jo dirai mon sanblant:
Ancois que jo eüsce espousé loiaumant
Elioxe la bele, a qui Dex soit garant,
Me devina la bele qu'estroient .VII. enfant
De li, et lor linages iroit en Oriant.   2960
Al naistre aroit cascuns .I. loien d'or luisant
Entor le col laciet, c'est une ensegne grant.
Li enfant furent né, ele remest morant,
Et Dex en mete l'arme en l'ort saint Abrahant.
C'a esté une cose dont j'ai esté dolant.   2965
Porté furent el bos, ne sai u; forvoiant
Ont grant termine esté, .VII. an furent pasant,
C'uns serjans lor embla a cisoire trancant
Lor ensegnes qu'il orent entor le col pendant;
A .VI. en aporta ma mere a sauf faisant.   2970
Jel seuc, ses demandai, des .V. me fist creant,
La siste ot aloee a une nef d'or grant;
Vos .V. en avés vos, n'en a plus aparant.
Por cou wel jo prover, vos estes mi enfant,
Vos manrés avoec moi, des rices fiés tenant,   2975
Car jo tieng cest roiame, si l'ai en mon conmant:

.VII. cités et .L. castels segnerilmant.
Si serés cevalier et mi ami aidant,
Et jou marierai ma fille hautemant,
Soit a roi u a prince u duc u amirant;   2980
Si arai des nevels, s'ierent mi bien aidant.
Cel oisel que la voi en cel rivier noant
Ferai jo bien garder; dusqu'a .XXX. serjant
Le garderont la nuit et le jor autretant."

93   Li rois prent le vallet qui premeraine parla,   2985
     En la face le baise, et puis si l'acola,
     Et lui et tos les autres tos uns a uns baisa;
     Puis vint a la pucele et conjoïe l'a.
     "Fille," [co] dist [li rois], "benois soit qui vos a[69]
     Nourie jusqu'a hui; co qu'il ot vos dona;   2990
     Il vos norri por Deu."   Adont li rois plora.
     "Mais desore en avant saverés que pora
     Faire qui carnelment tos .VII. vos engenra.
     Dex ait merci de li qui es flans vos porta;
     Ele songa .I. songe qui voir senefia,   2995
     Qu'ele avoit .VII. pumetes que en son lit muca; 17*d*
     Les .VI. en embla on et les keues coupa,
     Les pumes rua puer et les keues salva;
     Vos caines sont les keues que on si bien garda,
     Mais de vostre seror li lere forvoia: 3000
     Repuse fu, espoir, u icil l'oublia.
     Assez conois celui qui si les vos coupa
     Et qui couper les fist, mais vos nel sarés ja.
     Venés ent avoec moi, car assez vos donra
     Damedex qui nos tos a s'ymage forma.   3005

94   Li rois s'en va ariere a gente conpaignie,
     Et li cisnes de l'aigue forment aprés colie.
     Li rois vient el palais u sa conpaignie guie;
     Li cevalier l'esgardent et tote sa maisnie.
     Plantols parole a lui, car il de lui se fie: 3010
     "Sire oncles, qui est ore cele bacelerie?
     Bien sanblent trestot frere, qui c'autre cose en die."[70]
     "Par Deu," cou dist li rois, "il sont de ma lignie,
     Si lor portés honor, si ferés cortoisie;
     Car il aront o moi, caiens tel segnorie   3015
     Con ses eüst portés Elioxe m'amie,
     Dont l'arme ait Damedex qui tot bien saintefie.
     Ceste puciele ci, ele sera m'amie,
     Ele ara mon consel et ma force et m'aïe.
     Je le marierai a prince de baillie,   3020
     S'en arai des parens, s'en forcera m'aïe.
     Dont s'en entre en la canbre de marbre labastrie;
     La a trové sa mere seant, si s'esbanie

A une soie niece de biauté raplenie.
"Dame," ce dist li rois, "en cure et en baillie 3025
Vos bail ceste pucele, que jo tieng a amie,
Et jo woel qu'ele soit ausi de vos cierie."

95 Li vallet sont a cort a molt grant segnorage,
Molt i a bels vallés, tot sanblent d'un eage;
Il porsivent le roi quel part qu'il onques aille, 3030
Il se pruevent molt bien cascuns en vaselage.
S'il parolent a gent, bien sanblent estre sage,
Et s'il vont bohordant, il ne sont pas onbrage
De ferir en quintaine ne de porter lor targe;
Et se il esquermiscent par lor esbanoiage, 3035
Por bien covrir d'escu n'aront il ja damage,
Ne por autrui grever ne feront il outrage;
De doner co qu'il tienent, de co sont il molt large,
Par tot le païs va lor cris et lor barnage.
La vienent damoisel qui sont de grant parage, 3040
Il les retienent tos par lor demiselage, 18a
Quan c'onques en i vient et par terre et par nage;
Et si sont avoec eus tot le tans en estage,
Et passent le guaïn et le tans ivernage,
Desci qu'il sont venu a cel tans quaresmage 3045
K'erbe point par ces prés et florisent boscage
Por la doucor ki vient del printans al rivage.
Rois Lotaires qui velt faire grant vaselage
Cascun a conmandé selonc le sien eage
Qu'il soit esvertüés et prenge bon corage. 3050
Il lor donra tos armes le semaine pasquage
Et fera cevaliers por essaucier barnage,
Ses tenra a sa cort tot .I. an de maisnage
Et donra fer et clau et avaine et fourage,
Dras et haubers et elmes, qu'il ne soient onbrage 3055
Quant tans ert qu'il devront mener lor vaselage.

96 Semedi devant pasques a li rois conmandé
Que li .V. vallet aient lor conpaignons mandé;
Si conme por prendre armes il lor a apresté.
Cascuns en est molt liés, grant joie en ont mené; 3060
La roïne fait metre .XXX. cuves el pré
Et si serjant i sont qui l'aigue ont aporté.
Desor cascune cuve avoit tendu .I. tré
Por cou que li bains fust a cascun plus privé.
Et qui onques si baigne la roïne a doné 3065
Cascun cemise et braies qui sont a or broudé,
Et fremail a son col de fin or noielé.
Li braiel sont de soie enlaciet et jeté,
Cascun coroie blance, pendant sorargenté

Et aumosniere ausi de paile et de cendé;   3070
Et en cascune avoit .VI. bezans d'or letré
Dont il feront aumosne, et Dex le prenge en gré;
Et avoec tot icou n'i sont pas oublié
Les coifes et les gans; atant si a cessé.

97 La dame a fait ses dons, li vallet sont joiant,   3075
De Deu et de ses sains le vont tot merciant.
Atant es vos le roi, o lui maint bel serjant
Ki aportent ces dras tant a lor cols pendant;
Miux valoient li drap de saint Quentin le grant.
Il i a maint samit, maint paile escarimant   3080
Et maint drap de Halape, tissu a or luisant,
Baudequins, siglatons, et maint drap aufriquant,
Brunetes, escarlates, et rice vert de Gant;
Et les penes sont vaires et li sable sont grant,
Les ataces de soie valurent maint bezant.   3085
Tant a doné li rois que tot sont revestant,   18*b*
Bien i sont revestu damoisel dusqu'a cent.
Or vienent li lormier esperons aportant;
Li rois en prent .V. paire, cels orent si enfant.
Li enfant ont les autres, cascuns en done avant.   3090
Cascuns ot .XX. vallés a son non atendant
Que li rois revest tos, et il sont molt vaillant.
Dont amainent cevals, li lorain vont sonant;
Il n'i a cevalier n'ait palefroi amblant.
Après done a cascun ceval norois corant   3095
Et .II. roncis cascun, et .I. soumier portant
Qui portera le fer qu'il donra maintenant.
Il a doné .V. brans de le forge Galant;
Li doi furent jadis le roi Octeviant,
La les orent piec'a aportés Troïant,   3100
Quant Miles espousa Florence le vaillant.
Se li dona Florence qui bien le vit aidant
Et encontre Garsile fierement conbatant;
Et Miles dona l'autre a .I. sien conniscant.
Puis furent il emblé par Gautier le truant,   3105
Et cil en est fuïs de la fortpaïsant,
S'en est venus au pere le roi Lotaire errant;
A celui le dona, et il en fist presant.
Li rois les esgarda, bien les a a talant,
S'a Gautier doné fief et fait rice et manant.   3110
Les autres trois avoit en son tresor gisant;
Il ot conquis .I. roi en Aufrique le grant
Quant ala outre mer le Sepucre querant,
Que treü demandoit as pelerins errant.
Il li coupa la teste, onques n'en ot garant,   3115
Et l'espee aporta et .I. elme luisant.

Illuec aprés conquist Caucase l'amirant
Dont l'espee aporta et l'auberc jaserant.
Et l'autre espee fu trovee el flun Jordant,
Ainc ne pot estre blance, tant l'alast forbisant.　3120
Ces .V. espees a li rois cascun enfant
Cainte au senestre lés u bien seent li brant.
Puis lor done colees dont tot sont formoiant,
C'onques mais de perece n'ait en els tant ne quant.
Ausi font il as autres qu'a els sont atendant,　3125
Dont cascuns en a .XX. qui tot sont bien aidant.
Dont les maine li rois en son ostel puiant;
La sont tot el prael desos l'arbre onbroiant.
La atraient le roi .V. tonials .XX. serjant,
Qui tot estoient plain de bon fe[r] flanboiant;⁷¹　3130
Li rois en eslist .V. qui le maille ont plaisant, 18c
Cels dona ses .V. fius el non Jhesu le grant,
Et cauces ploieïces, coifes qui ont pendant:
Turcoises les apelent cele gent venisant.
Puis lor done .V. elmes, qui tant son flanboiant　3135
Tos li prés en flanboie contre solel luisant;
Li candelabre en sont d'or fin arrabiant,
En cascun des nasials ot une gemme grant.
Or ont li .V. lor armes, or donront il avant
Tant que cascuns ara son fer par avenant;　3140
.C. haubers ont donés .C. vallés .V. enfant,
Et toute l'armeüre de fer apertenant
A cevalier qui doit d'armes avoir garant.
On lor aporte escus de painture aparant
Et tains et vermelliés, et sont bien connissant.　3145
Li vint ont .XX. escus qui tot sont a argant,
Mais c'un lioncel noir avoit paint en .I. cant;
Cou sont les conniscances le vallet al noir brant.
Et li autre .XX. ont les aigles d'or luisant,
Dont les canpaignes sont d'azur estincelant.　3150
Li autre avoient paint pucele carolant,
Et la canpaigne estoit de sinople luisant.
Li autre orent pisons de longes en pendant,
Ki poi prisent l'escu; et deriere et devant
A une liste vert entor lui acaignant.　3155
Li autre orent .I. cisne bien fait et conniscant,
La canpaigne fu d'or entor le cisne blanc
Et si ot une liste de vigne verdoiant.
Issi ont .V. devises li .V. frere aparant,
Escus et connissances, et trestot lor sivant.　3160
La roïne lor done par sa noblece grant
.V. ensegnes batues a or arrabiant,
Dont les langes batirent a la sele devant.
Quant li .V. cevalier s'en vont es prés poignant

On lor aporte lances de sap soëf planant.   3165
Il montent es cevals, escus as cols pendant,
Bohorder l'uns vers l'autre vont ces lances brisant;
Les esclices des lances vont contremont volant,
Petit i a d'escus u il n'ait maint trou grant.
Tant a duré la feste que il se vont lasant,   3170
Tot s'en revont ensanble li cevalier vaillant.

98   Quant furent descendu, al mostier vont orer,
      Devant l'image Deu vont lor coupes clamer;
      Uns capelains vint la por els vespres canter,
      Volentiers les oïrent car il cantent molt cler.   3175
      Aprés vespres alerent .I. petitet souper,   18d
      Mais lués sont revenu al mostier saint Wimer;
      La vaurent toute nuit et vellier et ester,
      En estant ierent la desci qu'a l'ajorner;
      Et quant la nuis se prist .I. poi a esconser   3180
      Cascuns fait devant lui .I. grant cierge alumer.
      Le vie saint Morise lor conta uns jogler,
      Qui uns emperere ot conmandé a guier
      Une ost de cevaliers ses anemis grever.
      Le nonbre vos sai bien et dire et deviser: 3185
      C'ert une legïons en coi on doit nonbrer
      .VI. milliers et .VI.C.LXVI., tous ber;
      Tant en ot li preudom desos lui a garder.
      Icil qui mal velt faire plus ne velt demorer,
      Traist a l'empereor, sel prist a encuser   3190
      Qu'il ierent crestiien, tant i savoit blasmer.
      L'emperere les a trestos fais decoler,
      Et les cors fait trestos ens el Rosne ruer;
      Tant i jetent de cors qu'il l'estuet soronder,
      Par prés et par canpaignes et par viles floter.   3195
      Cil furent tot martir por Damedeu amer,
      Et Dex lor puet molt bien el ciel gueredoner.
      Ceste cancons dura desi qu'a l'ajorner,
      Et il furent molt prest d'oïr et escouter;
      Au jor s'en sont alé .I. petit reposer.   3200

99   A tierce se leva li rois par son dangier,
      Issus est de sa cambre, vint el palais plenier;
      La estoient venu si .V. fil tot premier,
      Bien ierent en lor siute pres de .C. cevalier.
      Lués qu'il virent le roi, ses veïssiés drecier!   3205
      Li rois de plaine voïe s'adreca al mostier;
      La vinrent avoec lui cil baceler legier.
      La fist on revestir le bon abé Renier;
      El non del Saint Espir, qui les puist consellier,
      A conmencié la messe et le devin mestier.   3210

Cou c'on offri l'abé valut maint bon denier,
Onques n'i ot celui n'ofrist bezant d'or mier,
Que la mere le roi lor ot doné tres ier.
Après messe s'en vont sus el palais plenier;
On a cornee l'eve, assis sont au mangier.   3215
Les mês ne les savors ne vos puis acointier,
Car il en i ot tant qui molt font a prisier,
Li rois qui tant en fist si bien aparellier.
Forês li rendent bestes por sa cort essaucier,
Li airs li rent oisials c'on manga par dangier,   3220
Si li rendent poisons li aigue et li vivier.   19*a*
Or pöés bien savoir, maint mês i ot plenier
Et boires autresi, bien le puis fiancier;
Bon vin, bones puisons lor orent grant mestier;
Il en i ot assés, ce vos voel acointier.   3225
Li jogleor i font grant noise et grant tenpier;
L'un cante de Martin et l'autres d'Olivier,
Li autres de Guion et li autre d'Ogier.
De la color n'estuet des estrumens plaidier,
Tot sans nule cancon s'i puet on delitier.   3230
On ne demoure plus, errant après mangier
Monterent es cevals por la feste avancier;
Les escus ont as cols, es mains lances d'osier.
La veïst on ensegnes a cel vent balloier,
De totes pars s'amostrent et vienent cevalier.   3235
Cel al noir lioncel, es le vos tot premier,
Plains estoit de deduit por gens esbanoier;
.XX. conpaignon le sivent; tranbler et formoier
Font la terre sous eux, si font il grant tenpier.
Li autres as puceles ne se vaut atargier,   3240
Cil ne velt demorer plus longement arrier;
Il et si conpaignon ne vaurent detriier,
Sor ces escus novials font lances pecoier.
Cil as poissons revint qui si vaura aidier,
Sel veïssiés venir, lui vintisme, coitier!   3245
Cil i vient si bruiant que il fait tos ploier
Les rens de cevaliers u il se velt fichier.
Il n'espargne nului de son escu percier
Et de faire voler, a terre trebucier.
Or vient cil as aigliaus, nes pot on mesprisier,   3250
Bien se pueent mostrer conme bon cevalier;
Que que cil as poisons facent por eux proisier,
Cist maintienent molt mius le camp por festoier.
Il n'ont cure de querre ombre por onbroier,
Ains se fierent es autres, les rens font claroier.   3255
Il li convint fuïr u caïr del destrier
Qui il vont consivant, u l'arcon pecoier.
Cil au cisne revient bruiant con aversier,

Ausi con li ostoirs en anes de rivier
Quant il velt prendre proie et es oisials plongier; 3260
Que que li autre facent, cist font tot esmaier
Cels qu'il voient venir a lor estor cargier.
Cist voelent pris avoir de tot le tornoier
E il l'eüscent tot, quant la vint rois Lotier
Ki lor a conmandé de tot en tot laisier.   3265
Entrués que gius est bels le doit on acoisier.   19*b*

100 Li rois jura ton cief, mar i sera brisie
Hui mais a bohorder ne lance ne demie;
Par un garcon fu la la parole noncie.
Il ciesent et descendent sor l'erbe qui verdie,   3270
Et li pluisor cevalcent vers lor herbregerie.
Jogleor cantent sons et mainent lie vie;
Rices ostels tenoient tot li fil Eloxie,
Car or primes conmence venir lor segnorie,
Li los et la proece et la grans cortoisie.   3275
La novele est par tout et alee et oïe,
Que rois Lotaires tient si grant cevalerie,
Ne redoute voisin qui tant ait felonie,
Que molt tost nel manace a molt poi d'aatie.
Li renons est si grans de bien, de boine vie,   3280
La novele est alee desci qu'en Aumarie,
Tres les pors de Wisant, desci qu'en Romenie,
Et par toute Engleterre u a grant segnorie,
Et par toutes les terres leu on aore et prie
Le glorious Segnor, le fil sainte Marie,   3285
Que par eux .V. est toute proëce resbaudie
Et larghece autresi qui estoit endormie,
Il soustienent tos cels qui lor ruevent aïe,
Qui od els porsivir voelent cevalerie.
Tot cel esté dura la feste plentoïe   3290
Et cascun jor croissoit de cevaliers maisnie.
Maintes foies avés mainte novele oïe
De la cort roi Artu et de sa baronie,
De Gavain son neveu et de sa conpaignie,
Et des autres barons dont la fable est bastie.   3295
Ce fu fable d'Artu u co fu faerie,
Mais ce fu verités, nel mescreés vos mie,
De ces .V. cevaliers et de lor conpaignie,
De Lotaire lor pere qui tant ot segnorie.
Li livre le nos content qui sont d'anciserie,   3300
Qu'a Nimaie est l'estoire en une glise antie
Qui fu fondee el non cele sainte Marie
Ki tel home porta que celui qui tot crie
Et tot fist de nïent par sa grant segnorie.
Rois Lotaires s'esforce, et son cuer pas n'oblie   3305

D'Elioxe la bele la haute prophesie
Ki dist que ses linages iroit vers paienie;
Illueques regneroit par molt grant segnorie
Et li pooirs de Deu li seroit en aïe.
Mais il ne set del quel isteroit la lignie   3310
Ki si s'espanderoit en Oriant partie,   19c
Car tot .V. sont molt preu et de grant segnorie.

101 Un jor ert rois Lotaires alés a sa capele,
A orisons se mist por proier la pucele,
La gloriose Dame qui tant est piue et bele,   3315
Qu'ele son fil proiast de fin cuer, la pucele,
Que il li envoiast a savoir la novele
Au quel de ses enfans queroit cele meriele,
Ki iroit outre mer sor le gent qui favele.
Molt en a Deu proiet et la Virgene pucele.   3320
Entruès qu'il li prioit et de bon cuer l'apele,
Li vint une avisons qui molt fu bone et bele,
C'uns angeles li aporte et li dist la novele
Que c'esteroit icil, seüst le sans favele,
Qui li cisnes menroit traiant en sa nacele,   3325
Et si avra el col d'or fin la caainele.

102 Or trespasse d'esté li saisons et li tans
Et d'iver autresi, est tos passez li ans;
Al tor de l'an revient et avriels et prinstans
Et li tans de Pascor, qui les gens fait joians;   3330
Nes icil qui sont tristre font de joie sanblans.
Li .V. fil roi Lotaire, des autres ne sai quans,
Sont assanblé ensanble, s'ont fait uns parlemans
Que cascuns ira querre, sans conpaigne de gans,
Aventure qui soit a cascun convenans.   3335
Dist cil al noir lion: "G'irai es desrubans
De la noire montaigne, i verai ne sai quans
Et tygres et lupars, dont Dex me soit garans.
A .V. ans revenrai, se jo remaing vivans
Et prisons ne me tient, a mon pere joians."   3340

103 Dist li vallés a l'aigle: "G'irai aventurer
Es forés u on seut les cerubins colper,
Et cedres et ciprés en seut on amener;
La trovera tostans, que ce ne puet fauser,
Tele aventure u jou me porai esprover;   3345
Et Dex par son plaisir, qui tot puet governer,
Me laist par sa pitié en tel liu asener
Dont jo puise le los et conquest raporter.
A .VII. ans, se Deu plaist, m'en vaurai retrover,
Se prisons ne me tient dont [ne] puise escaper,[72]   3350

U mors ne me soprent que ne puise eskiver."
Et dist cil as puceles: "Jo ai oï parler,
La terre d'Aminois molt l'ai oï loer;
La roïne est molt preus, bien set armes porter,
Covrir de son escu et d'espee capler;   3355
Ausi font ses puceles, bien l'ai oï conter: 19*d*
Jes voel aler conquerre, por .X. ans demorer,
Dusque j'aie esté la u jes puise trover;
La roïne amerai qui tant fait a amer."
Cou dist cius as poissons: "Jo voel aler par mer,   3360
Car m'ensegne le doit, jo nel voel remuer.
As aïmans trairai, tant me vaurai grever,
Ja cou ne remanra por .VII. ans demorer;
Savoir voel quel fin fait qui ne puet retorner:
De l'aimande arai tant con porra porter[73]   3365
La nés que jo menrai por moi a gouverner;
Sor la roce u Judas seut venir reposer,[74]
En celi vaurai jo par mon esfors monter."
"Certes," dist cil au cisne, "ne sai le liu trover
U g'irai, mais ne puis aprés vos demorer.   3370
Nos en irons tot .V., Dex nos laist encontrer
Tel cose u nos puisons los et pris conquester;
Mais cil que nos laisons el vivier tant noer,
Qui nostre germains est, il me fait molt penser;
Je l'ainc molt, ne le puis laisier seul demorer;   3375
Se j'en vois jel menrai, se puis engien trover;
Et no suer, la pucele, la gente o le vis cler,
Remanra, nostre pere bien le porra garder;
Et il li porvera a segnor et a per
Home qui bien le doive segnerilment garder."   3380
"Bien ait," dïent il tot, "qui t'aprist a parler."

104 Li parlemens est fais et li consaus fenis,
    D'illueques s'est cascuns a la cort revertis;
    Al roi vienent tot .V., ains n'en fu uns eskis.
    "Rois," co dist cil au cisne, "or nos soiés aidis;   3385
    Nos en volons aler, li consaus en est pris,
    Et par terre et par mer querre aventure et pris;
    Cevals et fer nos done, escus et vers et bis,
    Selonc cou que cascuns a le fais entrepris;
    Trois cevals en ta terre nos porvoi et eslis,   3390
    Et .II. nés dont avrai l'une a mon devis."
    "Voire, sire," respont cil au lioncel bis,
    "Jou voel ceval et fer, que soie amanevis."
    "Et jou," dist cil a l'aigle, "escut a or burnis;
    Mes fers et mes cevals, ce est tos mes delis."   3395
    Cil as puceles dist qu'il en ira envis
    Sans fer et sans ceval: "J'en woel estre garnis."

Et dist cil as poisons: "D'espiel qui soit burnis
Et bien fort enanstés voel jo estre garnis;
Ne elmes ne haubers, cil ne m'ert pas degis,   3400
Ne l'escus as poisons, dont moi menbre tosdis, 20a
Et une nef o moi, la estera mes lis."
Dist cil au blanc oisel: "Autretels ert mes dis!
Jo voel avoir calant, et escu blanc et bis,
U li blans oisiaus soit painturés et escris,   3405
Un espiel qui blans est painturés et forbis,
Si voel une caïne qui soit d'or bien eslis;
De lonc ait une toise, dont ert a mon devis."

105 Il ont fait lor demande lor pere a lor talent,
Ne li pere n'otroie n'il n'escondist noient,   3410
Mais de cou que il ot a le cuer molt dolant;
S'il o lui remansiscent, grant aseürement
Eüst en eus tostans envers tant mainte gent.
Dont a levé son cief, si parla hautement:
"Enfant," dist il, "par Deu qui maint en Orïent,   3415
Jo vos ai molt amés et ain molt voirement;
Remanés avoec moi, et fiés et tenement
Donrai cascun de vos, ensi le vos creent,
Et vos avrois assez proëce et hardement."
Et il li respondirent sans nul delaiement: 3420
"Cou que nos demandons nos donés bonement."
Cou respont roi[s] Lotaire[s]: "Tot al vostre talent[75]
Arés fer et cevals trestot seürement;
Mais durement me poise de vo departement,
Mius vos amaise o moi ens en mon tenement.   3425
Ens la garde al Segnor qui vos fist de noient
Soiés vos conmandé tot parmenablement."
Armes, cevals et nef a cort terminement
Lor a li rois porquis, si lor ment en present,
Et la caïne d'or que cil au cisne atent.   3430
A cel present doner ot molt grant plorement;
Li rois plore ses fils qu'il ama bonement,
Li fil plorent le pere qui remaint seulement,
Et li cevalier sont del desevrer dolent;
Ne quident mais trover qui lor doinst garniment   3435
Ne ceval ne hauberc ne nul affublement:
.C. en caient pasmé el maistre mandement.
Al relever qu'il font i ot dolousement,
Regretent lor segnor qu'il ainment durement.
Cil as cevals s'en vont, mais c'est devinement: 3440
L'uns ne verra mais l'autre a plus procainement,
S'ierent passé .VII. an trestot plenierement.
Cil as poissons a fait son aparellement,
Son escu et son fer met, si nage erranment

Et a voile drecie sigle la mer et fent.   3445

106 Cil as poissons se nage trestot a son talant,   20*b*
    Or le conduise Dex qui jo trai a garant.
    Cil au blanc oisel a porveü son calant,
    Sel fist traire el vivier u il ot esté tant.
    Lués qu'il vint el vivier, es le vos avolant   3450
    Le cisne qu'il aloit a conpaignon querant;
    Des eles le conjot et del bec en frotant.
    Il li jeta el col le loien d'or luisant,
    Puis l'ataca au bort de la nef de devant.
    Li batials par desous avoit le fons trencant;   3455
    Trait li cisnes, la nés va de legier sivant,
    Sifaitement andui vont l'uns l'autre aprendant.
    Il a mis en sa nef l'escut al oisel blanc,
    Et l'espee et l'espiel forbi, roit et trencant;
    D'autre fer n'a il cure, n'en porte tant ne quant.   3460
    Li cisnes va la nef a caïne traiant,
    Tant conme li viviers avoit le fil corant;
    S'entrent en l'Aliose, ce trovons nos lisant.
    C'est une molt grans eve, por .V. jors demorant,
    K'il aloient par rive le ravor eskivant,   3465
    Tant qu'en mer s'enbatirent, al grant flos retraiant.
    Or s'en vont il tot .VI. aventure querant,
    Troi par terre et par bos les cevals cevalcant,
    Li doi en .II. batials, et li sistes traiant.
    Dex! con laisent lor pere coreciet et dolant,   3470
    Et meïsme lor suer en a .I. duel si grant,
    Quatre fois se pasma trestot en .I. tenant.
    Li pere l'en relieve, sel va reconfortant:
    "Taisiés vos, bele fille, ja jor de mon vivant,
    Certes, ne vos faurai, icou vos acreant."   3475
    A itant retornerent ens el palais errant,
    .III. jors demainent duel, al quart vont confortant.
    Et li cevalier oïrent qui s'en vont cevalcant,
    Et cil nagent et siglent qui en mer vont nagant.
    De cascun est estoire et matere molt grant;   3480
    Des .IIII. ne dirons or ne tant ne quant,
    Mais des .II. vos irons un poi amentevant,
    Del cisne qui la nef vait a son col traiant,
    Et del jentil vallet dedens sa nef gisant.
    Tant ont ja esploitié que par mer vont flotant,   3485
    Bien pres .LX. jors sont en mer demorant;
    Dont se traient el Rin, c'est une eve molt grant,
    De coi la mers recoit le flot et le corant.
    La s'en vont encontre eve le rive costoiant,
    Venu sont vers Nimaie, une cité vaillant;   3490
    Voient les tors reluire qui sont fait a ciment, 20*c*

Cele part s'adrecierent par le Jhesu conmant.
Ce fu a Pentecoste, une feste joiant,
Que l'emperere estoit a Nimaie le grant,
Et ierent avoec lui cevalier et serjant.   3495
Ci fine li naisence des .VI. freres atant.
Cil Damedex de glore qui forma Moïsant,
Il gart et beneïe et doinst amendemant
Celui qui ceste estoire a mis si en avant.

NOTES

1. (*1*. 66) h. et a. *A.* Emended on the authority of *G*.
2. (*1*. 79) e. for s. *A.* The reading of the base is al-
   most certainly a scribal error since there is no other
   evidence of the assimilation of final *t* with the ini-
   tial consonant of an immediately following word. There
   is some evidence of the partial assimilation of final *n*
   with a following consonant in the expressions *em pais*
   (*11.* 70, 73) and *em piés* (*1*. 2162). These appear to be
   set expressions which, when they occur, are exceptional
   with respect to the usual scribal practice in BN 12558.
   Cf. note 5 below.
3. (*1*. 98) a. dosos .I. *A*. Emended on the authority of *I*.
4. (*1*. 198) A t. *A.* Emended on the authority of *GI*.
5. (*1*. 242) a. vaurieme v. *A.* The reading of the base is
   again almost certainly a scribal error as there is no
   corroborating evidence for the assimilation of final *s*
   with the initial consonant of an immediately following
   word. Cf. note 2 above.
6. (*1*. 252) o. rauner *A.* G. Paris (*Romania*, 19 [1890],
   328) suggested emending *rauner*, which he believed makes
   no sense here, to *rainner* in keeping with *regner* of the
   Arsenal MS., the only variant text known to him. Al-
   though the base MS appears to distinguish clearly bet-
   ween *u* and *n* in this word, it may well intend *ranner*
   for *rainner/regner*. Or it may be an erroneous tran-
   scription of a similar form. In any case Todd's *raüner*
   renders the second hemistich too long by one syllable.
   The emendation suggested in the present edition is
   based on the authority of *GI*, both of which read
   regner. Cf. *1*. 2721 *regné* for orthography.
7. (*1*. 261) The next five lines (*11*. 261-65) do not ap-
   pear in *GI*. This is undoubtedly deliberate in that the
   deleted passage announces the death of Elioxe in child-
   birth and would therefore be inconsistent with the
   Beatrix version.
8. (*1*. 269) This spelling for "signe," also used for
   "cygne," is an interesting example of word play.
9. (*1*. 296) p. et ensement *A.* The reading of the base
   appears to be a scribal error repeating the immediately

preceding rhyme word. This may be a significant common error linking *A* with *I* which reads *p. ensement*. The reading in *A* is also illogical and for that reason is emended on the authority of *G*.

10. (*1.* 319) Todd emended *abosnes* to read *linaloés* on the authority of *G*. The editor has maintained the reading of the base and suggests the etymon *balsamos*.

11. (*1.* 327) E. Sadonie c. *A*. Doubtless a scribal error for *Samonie*, the servant.

12. (*1.* 355) n. dem era m. *A*. The reading of the base is problematical. There is a well defined space separating *m* and *e* in *dem era* which appears to be bridged by a curved line not entirely unlike a nasal bar. Todd's edition reads *ne demoera mie* with a note concerning only the meaning of the phrase. This is given as "shortly." Todd may have based his reading on *G*: *Qu'il vora prendre fenme ne demoera mie*. The form suggested in the emendation is confirmed by its occurrence in *1.* 756: *Et qui demoerra sel conperra forment*. In both *1.* 355 and *1.* 756 *demoera* clearly functions as a word of four syllables. In contrast, the variant of *1.* 355 in *I* reads: *Qu'il vorra prendre a fame si ne demoura mie*. Similarly *demoriés* occurs in *1.* 730.

13. (*1.* 374) Note that the accent falls on the third person plural ending in *movent*. The other examples of this phenomenon in this text occur in *11.* 380, 832, and 1015.

14. (*1.* 527) e. effree d. *A*. The first hemistich is short by one syllable in the base. Emended on the authority of *GI*. The second hemistich has been the subject of conjecture. The present editor believes that it can be read with *ente* functioning either as an adjective or as an adverb.

15. (*1.* 541) s. voit f. *A*. Emended on the authority of *GI*. First proposed by G. Paris in *Romania*, 19(1890), 329.

16. (*1.* 596) S. car a. *A*. The first hemistich is short by one syllable. The emendation suggested in the edited text was first proposed by G. Paris in *Romania*, 19 (1890), 329. *GI* agree against the base and provide no authority.

17. (*1.* 618) This is a reference to the journey to Emmaus (Saint Luke XXIV, 13-35). The two companions did not wish to continue (*mal vaurent aler*), but Jesus "acted as though he were going on."

18. (*1.* 751) escrivent va s'ent e il i *A*. The scribe erroneously copied *va s'ent* which occurs properly in the same position at the beginning of the second hemistich

in the preceding line. The repeated phrase has been expunctuated by means of a dotted line beneath it, although it is impossible to say who was responsible for this. The second hemistich is long by one syllable. The reading in the base is possibly an erroneous transcription of *cil* as first suggested by G. Paris in *Romania*, 19(1890), 329. The variants differ and offer no authority. The *e* of the base is, however, suspect because the conjunction *et* does not occur in the text in that form.

19. (*1.* 851) l. deure e. *A.* Emended on the authority of *GI*. Todd interpreted this rather obscure passage to mean that the river was "three hundred feet broad (all the way) up to the source." The present editor prefers to interpret it as meaning that the river is three hundred feet wide up to the base of the wall.

20. (*1.* 856) .V. notels d. *A.* Emended on the authority of *GI*. The reading of the base is almost certainly a scribal error as there is no corroborating evidence of similar metathesis.

21. (*1.* 891) s. saise v. *A.* Emended on the authority of *GI*.

22. (*1.* 895) d. faisius a. *A.* Emended on the authority of *GI*. First proposed by G. Paris in *Romania*, 19(1890), 329.

23. (*1.* 917) n. puent p. *A.* Emended on the authority of *GI*. The nasal bar is occasionally omitted or inserted incorrectly. Cf. *11.* 977, 1183, and 1258.

24. (*1.* 928) Todd emended .V. to read .VIII. in order to be consistent with *1.* 840. The present editor has chosen not to emend in view of the agreement *AGI*.

25. (*1.* 945) Todd notes that *enguie* is a singular form where one might expect a third person plural and suggests that *en guie*, separated in the manuscript, may have the sense of *guise* and hence read *en guise...que l'aigue ne past mie.*

26. (*1.* 965) A. poi e. *A.* The emendation suggested in the edited text was proposed by G. Paris in *Romania*, 19 (1890), 329. The variants do not lend support, although *poit* in *G* may well be a scribal error for *pois*, since final *t* is easily confused with the final elongated *s*. The same may be true of *poil* in *I*.

27. (*1.* 977) D. pierens e. *A.* Emended on the authority of *GI*. Cf. *11.* 917, 1183, and 1258.

28. (*1.* 1006) n. duerroit n. *A.* Emended on the authority of *GI*.

29. (*1.* 1036) a. espees *A.* The second hemistich in the base is short by one syllable. The variants differ so

as to offer no authority.
30. (*1*. 1040) b. arestees *A*. The reading of the base is
illogical. Emended on the authority of *GI*.
31. (*1*. 1045) P. arses 1. *A*. Emended on the authority of
G. I varies.
32. (*1*. 1053) o. poit d. *A*. Emended on the authority of
GI. The scribe probably omitted the nasal bar by over-
sight. Cf. *1*. 2479 and 2654.
33. (*1*. 1072) This line appears to be inconsistent with
the context established by the closing lines of the
preceding laisse. G. Paris, in fact, suggested emenda-
tion to *Mors est* in *Romania*, 19(1890), 329. There is,
however, no contextual inconsistency if the nephew's
difficulty is understood as due to his lack of Chris-
tian baptism and the consequent state of his soul after
death. On the other hand, it may simply be a case of
the understatement so frequent in medieval literature.
34. (*1*. 1076) i. faves m. *A*. Emended on the authority of
I.
35. (*1*. 1094) s. bazon *A*. Emended on the authority of *GI*.
36. (*1*. 1167) n. lorent r. *A*. Emended on the authority of
GI.
37. (*1*. 1183) e. laiguen en e. *A*. Emended on the authori-
ty of *GI*. Cf. *11*. 917, 977, and 1258.
38. (*1*. 1213) At this point *G* inserts the following rubric
written across the entire page of fol. 9ᵛ: *C'est ensi*
con li mere le chevalier au cisne se delivra des .VII.
enfans et coument Matabrune li taie les envoia por
noier par Marcon en le foriest. There is an illumina-
tion after the first four lines in column 9*d* which
shows Elioxe in bed with the children. Matabrune is at
the foot of the bed receiving one of the children from
a servant. The illumination is rather small and diffi-
cult to see in terms of detail. See p. xlv.
39. (*1*. 1239) e. aproies *A*. Emended on the authority of
GI. First proposed by G. Paris in *Romania*, 19(1890),
329.
40. (*1*. 1242) e. enforie *A*. Emended on the authority of
G. I varies.
41. (*1*. 1245) s. lire 1. *A*. *GI* want this line. The *l* of
lire is probably a defective elongated *s*.
42. (*1*. 1258) 1. damen e. *A*. Emended on the authority of
GI. Cf. *11*. 917, 977, and 1183.
43. (*1*. 1272) E. lesperis s. *A*. The second hemistich in
the base is long by one syllable. There are no avail-
able variants.
44. (*1*. 1293) *GI* delete the preceding 34 lines which nar-
rate the death of Elioxe in order to be consistent with

the *Beatrix* version which follows.

45. (*1.* 1302) d. por soi a. *A.* The rejected reading appears to be an erroneous transcription of *par foi*, the reading of *GI*.

46. (*1.* 1308) r. a faire c. *A.* The editor has emended independently of the variants in order to retain the text of the base.

47. (*1.* 1338) p. denaire *A.* Emended on the authority of *GI*.

48. (*1.* 1339) At this point *I* adds a laisse (fol. 3*c*) which is found in no other manuscript:

    Maucon se porpensa, qui mout ot le cuer frans,
    Si regarde la vielle, qui le cors Dieu cravant,
    Qui les iex raoeille, les dens est estreignant
    Et la barbe ot longue conme chanus terrant
    Et c'est toute moucue de viellesse devant.
    Bien set ce sont enfant le roy dont est dolant
    Que la vielle tenoit en son escort devant.
    Onquez si dolens hom ne fu mien esciant,
    Du pechié qu'i redoute se va mout dolosant;
    Et s'il ne le fesoit il iroit malemant
    Que la vielle maudite l'occirroit esranmant.
    Pour ce qu'i n'ose passer son conmandemant,
    Por li le fist au plus tres coiement
    A la vespree en va sanz plus delaiement.

49. (*1.* 1342) f. sa c. *A.* *GI* agree with the base, but lack the following line. The reading of the base may be a scribal error caused by the similarity between *l* and the elongated *s*. Although the definite article would seem to be a more satisfactory reading and the present editor suggests this as an emendation in agreement with Todd, there is an identical situation in *1.* 1759. Cf. notes 53 and 64 below.

50. (*1.* 1373) a la pai p. *A.* The reading of the base is clear, but does not make sense. The emendation suggested in the edited text is consistent with the context as established by *1.* 1372. There are no variants available beyond *1.* 1345.

51. (*1.* 1566) A. anons ites q. *A.* Todd maintained the reading of the base and regarded *anons* as a form of *annonce* (See note on p. 112).

52. (*1.* 1753) Qu'on m. *A.* Emended to clarify the text.

53. (*1.* 1759) P. ses b. *A.* Cf. note 49 above.

54. (*1.* 1851) a sore l. *A.* The emendation was first proposed by Todd (p. 113) "... I am now inclined to consider *sore* to be a blunder of the scribe for *s'evre*, 'son oeuvre' (which he took to be *s'eure*, 'son heure' and changed to his own orthography, cf. 1848),..." The

emendation suggested in the present edition is in ac-
cord with the orthographic practice observed in the
manuscript as represented by *oevre* (*11*. 2213 and 2214)
and *uevre* (*11*. 2217 and 2219).

55. (*1*. 1861) The second hemistich is short by one sylla-
ble. G. Paris (*Romania*, 19[1890], 329) suggested
emending to *demie*.

56. (*11*. 1880-1883) These lines are out of proper sequence
in the manuscript where they occur in the order: 1880,
1883, 1881, 1882, and 1884. The more logical sequence
has been indicated in the margin of the manuscript by
the letters *a*, *d*, *b*, and *c*. The latter order has been
followed in the edited text.

57. (*1*. 2007) e. tasant *A*. The present participle of *tai-*
re seems most appropriate in context with *souavet*.
Todd (p. 113) suggested *tastant*.

58. (*1*. 2050) a panmes m. *A*. The manuscript does not
clearly distinguish between *n* and *u* here. Todd read
paumes. In either case it is obvious that the intended
reading is a form of *pinnas* and Todd emended as the
present editor does. It is possible that the frequent
occurrence of *nm* in *A* caused the error.

59. (*1*. 2066) The second hemistich is clearly an inadver-
tent repetition from the preceding line. Unfortunately
there are no variants available.

60. (*1*. 2114) n. jovenencel *A*.

61. (*1*. 2126) Read: ... u tot li cisne estoient qui Lotai-
res ot conmandé que nus ...

62. (*1*. 2150) .I. estoc p. *A*. The reading in the manu-
script is clear. Todd emended to *estanc*, but without
notation. The context does suggest a form of *stagnum*
and the present editor emends in agreement with his
predecessor.

63. (*1*. 2479) q. vit a. *A*. The reading of the manuscript
appears to be an erroneous transcription of *vint* pro-
duced by failure to copy the nasal bar. Cf. *11*. 1053
and 2654.

64. (*1*. 2554) q. cole a. *A*. The elongated *s* is frequently
difficult to distinguish from *l*. That such is the case
here is evident from Todd's reading *cose*. Cf. note 49.

65. (*1*. 2567) c. iuec a. *A*. The reading of the manuscript
appears to be an erroneous transcription of *j'euc*, a
form which is attested in *11*. 2579 and 2828. Cf. Todd
(p. 116).

66. (*1*. 2654) v. mai a. *A*. Cf. *11*. 1053, 2479.

67. (*1*. 2813) Cf. *Beatrix*, note 16. Also *Elioxe 1*. 1935.

68. (*1*. 2814) q. latre a. *A*. The reading of the manu-
script appears to be a scribal error as there is no

corroborating evidence for such a form.

69. (*1.* 2989) F. dist la pucele b. *A.* The rejected reading is obviously incorrect since it is King Oriant who is speaking. The emendation was first proposed by G. Paris in *Romania*, 19(1890), 329.

70. (*1.* 3012) The scribe first wrote *sanglent*. This was then corrected by superimposing *b* on *g*.

71. (*1.* 3130) b. fel f. *A.* Todd maintained the reading of the manuscript and glossed it as the equivalent of *fer*. The latter occurs in *11.* 3140, 3388, 3393, 3395, 3397, 3423, 3444, and 3460. In each of these lines, as in *1.* 3130, *fer* refers to weaponry or armor. The word also occurs in *1.* 3142 with the more basic meaning "iron" or "steel." It is difficult to regard the unique occurrence of *fel* as a legitimate variant form in the face of the numerous examples of the expected *fer*. Given the lack of corroborating evidence, the present editor has chosen to emend.

72. (*1.* 3350) d. jo p. *A.* Todd (pp. 118-19) noted that in this line and the following one there are affirmative and negative clauses, each with virtually the same meaning. Context clearly demands that both clauses have the same meaning. The present editor, however, does not believe that they do in their actual state of preservation and that the emendation suggested in the edited text is necessary.

73. (*1.* 3365) c. porrai p. *A.* Emended to clarify the text.

74. (*1.* 3367) In *Romania*, 19(1890), 335, G. Paris identified *Huon de Bordeaux* as a precedent for associating the *montagne d'aimant* and the *roche de Judas*.

75. (*1.* 3422) r. roit Lotairet t. *A.* The reading in the manuscript is clearly a scribal error. It is perhaps due to confusion of *t* with the elongated *s*.

VARIANTS

64. s. tiere tenir si fist droit jugement *G*.
65. a. fist d. *G*.
68. N'ainc n'ama losengier felon ne sousduiant *G*.
3. *AGI*
70. A grant pais tint s. t. ainc n. *G*.
71. a. a voissin en marce pour p. *G*.
72. Car s., l. sentoient e. *G*.
73. En pais tenoit s. *G*.
76. f. con rois cariier *G*.
77. A. le conroi vont l., l. biesier *G*.
78. i. li lormier *G*.
79. a. tracant fors v. *G*.
81. s. le c. *G*.
82. a. par hucier *G*.
84. N. porent t., n. poindre n. *G*.
86. N. tant l., e. d'acier *I*.
87. Qu'onques l. *I*.
88. A. conrois e. *GI*; v. si s. sus d. *G*.
90. l. que n'ot c. *G*; o. nesun c. *I*.
92. R. Orians s. *GI*; L. coroit sus .I. corant destrier *I*.
93. e. son puing .I. *GI*.
96. n. savoit u *GI*; n. s'en s. *G*.
98. a. desor .I. *G*.
99. h. puisque vit a. *G*; h. puisqu'l vit a. *I*.
100. c. laille pestre en l. *GI*.
101. i. i p. *G*.
102. d. pas li rois a. *GI*.
104. c. s'il e. a m. *G*; l. se il e. *I*.
105. p. vermine u *I*.
106. p. pour lui com hom aidier *G*; *I not clear*.
4. *AGI*
109. *I wants*.
110. p. ensi tant qu'il l. *G*.
111. c. puis e. *GI*.
112. Mist son frain et sa siele s. *GI*.
114. e. haies n. *GI*; q. le voit *G*.
116. f. li grevoit *GI*.
117. Droit vers le m. *GI*.

118. 1. environ se sus monter p. *G*; 1. environ se mon-
      ter y p. *I*.
119. m. ki t. *GI*.
120. Ja e. *GI*; c. montoit *G*; c. levoit *I*.
121. *GI want*.
122. u. grant orme estoit *I*.
123. e. biel o. *G*; e. grant fez y avoit *I*.
124. B. i p. sir c. *G*.
125. Et i estre desous o., 1. estavoir *G*; S. deseure
      o., 1. asavoit *I*.
126. t. frois estoit *G*.
127. o. li vens s. *G*; o. ou il si bel fesoit *I*.
128. r. demandoit *I*.
130. *I wants*.
131. Et li chevax p. *I*; q. molt s. *G*.
132. R. Orians s. *GI*.
133. Q. droit viers O. *G*; *I wants*.
5. *AGI*
136. O. Tigris e. *GI*; n. si p. *G*.
137. f. Tigris c. *GI*; t. merveillouse *I*.
138. g. en iert o. *G*; g. en est o. *I*.
139. f. par est si grasiouse *G*; Mez i., f. estoit la
      graciouse *I*.
140. s. molt v. *G*; s. molt preciouse *I*.
141. D. et meture q. *G*; D. et rubis q. *I*; *G adds*: Ru-
      bins et esmeraudes et jaspes kist goutose; *I adds*:
      Metistes esmeraudes et la pais quist goutouse.
142. T. et letores q. *I*.
143. Trestout sont gentil p. *G*; a. a e. *GI*; Trestout
      sont gentil chose q. *I*.
144. a nesune e. *G*; *I wants*.
145. q. se nos boire y ose *I*.
147. j. ocuisenosse *G*; D. goute n., j. si queminouse *I*.
      This last word is not clear.
148. Ne ja n'avra nos hom sa car si de goutosse *GI*.
149. S'il vient a la fontaine ki si est gloriosse *G*; Si
      vient a la fontaine qui si est seignorouse *I*.
150. S. ne soit g. *GI*.
6. *AGI*
151. v. Oriens q. *GI*.
153. a. le cors a. *GI*; a. grant *I*.
154. d. chaleur l. *I*.
155. v. sous l'arbre a. *G*; c. mist sor illec .... *I*.
      The last word is not clear.
156. t. sous e. *GI*.
157. S'espee et son cor et son espie trenchant *I*.
158. ... jus s., q. las estoit forment *I*.
159. *I wants*.

160. p. qui avoit le cors gent *I.*
161. l. haute m. *GI*; m. vient i. *I.*
164. s. manage a. *I.*
165. p. ales p. *I.*
166. m. avoit a. *G*; m. orent a. *I.*
169. Voit le ceval corsu e. *GI.*
171. B. y pert q. *I*; i. ert d. *G.*
173. s. son v. *GI.*
177. s. son v. *GI.*
178. P. si se traist a. *G.*
179. N. violt p. *G*; *I wants.*
180. p. si l. vient au d. *GI.*

7. *AGI*
181. Oriens e. *GI*; e. puis si senti l. *G*; e. puis qui senti l. *I.*
184. a. cou m'est vis e. *GI.*
186. u toute est s'esperance *GI.*
189. Sire g. *G*; c. vous doinst h. *GI*; S. garisse v. *I.*
190. d. hautece e. *G*; *I wants.*
191. *I wants.*
193. M. or w., q. mesestance *I.*
194. *I adds:* Mout en poez se veuil mout tost avoir ga...ance. *This last word not clear.*
195. e. puis bien s. *G*; Co si en puis avoir mout bien tost l. *I.*
196. a. bien a *G.*
197. v. reproce n. *G*; v. ne orgueil n. *I.*
198. b. garnie s. *G*; s. ai mout grant poissance *I.*
199. s. en ma poisance *G*; *I not clear.*
200. Oriiens l. *GI.*
201. D. si c. *GI*; i. a plus en vous o. *G*; i. a e. *I.*
202. e. noblaice e. *GI*; d. vaillance *I.*
203. v. et j. *G*; *I has a different line, but it is not clear.*
204. Jou p. *G*; Je ai suivi *I.*
205. e. ....beste d. *I. Word not clear.*
206. j. algues par presque forvoiance *G*; j. tant que par ... mescheance *I. Word not clear.*
207. r. si en sui e. *I.*
209. m. u d. *GI*; g. mesestance *G*; g. mescance *I.*
211. f. a l. *G*; h. verde et blanche *I.*
213. f. mis e. *I.*
214. a. par c. *I. GI add*: Mais encor sui entres en grenor forvoiance.
215. p. aler tant ai de maiskeance *G*; p. aler tant ai de mescreance *I.*
216. c. si ferez grant v. *I.*

8. *AGI*

218. La danselle respont ce vous t. je a. *I.*
219. n. desroi ne nul oltrage *G*; *I not clear.*
220. a. dites m. *I which adds*: Oriant li respont que plus il ne .... *Text is not clear.*
225. E. jugeur e. *GI which add*: Ases ai signorie pucielle france et sage.
226. *GI want.*
227. *GI want.*
228. *GI want.*
229. Mais ki e. *G*; *I not clear.*
231. v. soiies f. *G*; v. soiies haus h. *I.*
234. a. feme v. *I.*
235. v. eussies e. *GI which add*: Ki tenist apres vous vostre grant iretage.
236. d. ni ai pas mon usage *G*; d. encore pas ne targe. *I which adds*: Ne encor douce dame ne tard il a outrage.
237. N'euc encore o. *G*; *I wants.*
238. Aus c., e. aus o. *I*; a. eu m. usage *GI.*
239. m. en f. *GI.*
240. Si ai g. *GI.* *G adds*: En dist roys Orians le gentil aus vis fier.

9. *AGI*

242. a. mei vouriez a. *I.* *Text obscure.*
246. v. jou i. *G*; e. voudrai je i. *I.*
248. n. vel jou deveer *G.*
249. p. a m. *I.*
250. f. je vous di sanz fausser *I.*
251. Nostres l., e. estendus o. *GI.*
252. o. regner *GI.*
253. C'est cosse d. *GI*; q. je molt puis amer *G.* *I not clear.*
254. Ce a dit la pucelle escoutez....parler *I.* *Text not clear.*
255. n. souper *G.*
256. v. gire a moi a *G*; ce v. comme espous a *I.*
257. d. loiaument par ureter s. *G*; t. veuil loiaument par....deviser *I.* *Text not clear.*
258. f. enfanter *GI.*
259. i. fil e. *GI.*
260. p. trestorner *G*; n. peuent fausser *I.*
261-265. *GI want.*
268. t. verai j. *G*; E. voudrai j. *I.*
270. c. .I. c. *GI.*
271. n. je v., s. fausser *GI.*
272. e. par g. *G*; *I not clear.*
274. e. convient p. *I*; *G adds*: Et se vous con ne faites a duel veres tourner; *I adds*: Et...vous ce ne ....

..je vous di.... ..../ Et moi et les enfans verrez
a mal torner. *Text not clear.*

10. *AGI*

275. p. ki o. *GI*.
276. Li r. *GI*; r. Oriiens l'ot oi molt boinement *G*; r.
      Oriiens l'ot oi mout doucement. *I which adds*: ...
      ..elle contoit tout ce certainement. *Text not
      clear.*
277. d. tel a. *G*.
278. v. certainement *G*; *I wants*.
279. q. grant bonte e. *I*.
280. o. s'amor et l. *G*; o. tout son cuer bonement *I*.
281. L'enmenra a. *GI*.
282. A. l'espousse c. *G*; Et puis e. *I*.
283. Del aler s'aparaut face hastivement *G*; Face hasti-
      vement mi face morement *I*. *Text not clear.* *GI*
      add: Car pour moi sont mi home ce dist li rois do-
      lent.
284. E. apielle . i . *GI*.
285. *G adds*: Samaine ca venes ne demores noient.
286. a. lui parler sachez a escient *I*.
287. m. sans nul delaiement *GI*.
288. v. coumant *G*; d. je sui ca vraiement. *I which
      adds*: Va tost ce dist Beatrix sanz nul delaiement.
289. S. afeutres m. *G*; S. afeutree d. *I*.
290. M. boune b. *GI*; b. de riche assentement *I*; m. me-
      tes l. *G*.
291. Li pendant q. *I*; p. i sont (soit *G*) mis as cloque-
      tes pendant *GI*.
292. s. d'ivore resplendant *GI*.
294. Li fier en soient d'or li clau soient a. *G*; Li
      clous en soient d'or et li fers soit a. *I*.
295. e. aportes a faities e. *G*; e. m'oportes a faire
      mes commant *I*.
296. r. .VI. p. *I*; p. seulement *G*.
298. p. y baucent *I*.
299. p. .I. t. *G*; p. .I. a *I*.
300. Le commant la royne o. *I*.
301. d. sot elle tout errant *I*.
302. Revient a. *G*; m. fait a. *GI*; Et vient a. *I*.
303. r. avec sa d. *G*; r. a sa d. *I*; d. et al sien e.
      GI.
304. t. a pieres ki resprent *GI*.
306. s. estoit si rice que .IIII. isme piersant *G*; s.
      estoit si rice que roy ne amirant *I*.
307. Pas ne lesgeroient d. *GI*; q. enz apent *I*.
308. l. ars s., u. or luisant *I*.
309. L. soussiele e. *G*; L. sousel estoit *I*.

310. e. ot q. *GI.*
311. p. ses e., e. ses g. *G*; p. les e., e. les g. *I.*
312. g. cort ricement *G*; g. cor dorquement *I.*
313. r. courone a *GI*; q. resprent *G.*
314. p. i ot c. grant vertu rent *I*; c. a vertu grant
     G.
317. a. n'obles aournemens *I.*
318. B. a o. *GI.*
319. Linaloes ases et cermuske liant *G*; *I wants.*
321. o. est vertuenz s. *I.* *GI add*: Hanas i ot d'or fin
     et rices coupes tant (*Text of I not clear*)/ Cuel-
     liers et escuieles rice vasselemant/ Que tous en
     fust cargies li boins soumiers amblans.
322. E. meisme avoit .I. *GI*; .I. destrier a. *I.*
323. Q. l'ot appareille v., a. vient a *I.*

11. *AGI*
324. A dont la fait m. *GI.*
325. *GI add*: Il a pris son espiel et le cor aloie.
326. L. apiela p. *G*; Beatrix l'aregna p. *I*; r. l'enguie
     G.
327. Et la dame cevauce o lui par cortoissie *G*; Et la
     dame chevauche lez li par cortoisie *I.*
328. c. toute u. *GI.*
329. a. le v. *GI*; n. sot m. *G*; v. que l. *I.*
330. l. bos e. *GI.*
332. Et si i. *I.*
333. c. apries u. *G*; c. quar prez u. *I.*
334. d. d'or e. *G*; Mist l., d. est o. *I.*
336. c. por le cor s. *I.*
337. e. lor e. *G*; e. li e. *I.*
338. Montons a. *G*; Montons s'alons e. *I.*
341. m. vint e. *G.*
342. g. seignorie *I.*
343. R. Oriens l. *GI.*
344. n. faitez a *I.*
345. m. joie e. *G*; *I wants.*
346. r. par Deu le fil Marie *GI.*
350. g. et harpes e. *GI*; e. si font m. *I.* *GI add*: Et
     vielles et rotes et mainte cifonie.
351. R. Oriens s. *GI.*
352. a. caus d. *G*; c. avoit il d. *I.*
353. e. contes o l. *GI.*
354. K'il v. a *GI*
355. Qui v., f. si n. *I.*

12. *AGI*
356. La m. *GI.*
357. f. trestout p. *G*; d. a s. *I.*
358. Les n. *GI*; a. tost et isnielement *G*; a. trestout

apertement *I*.
359. s. a d. *I*.
360. t. ne f. *G*; q. faitez vous ne sai s. *I*.
361. p. pas f. isi s. *G*; p. la f. *I*.
362. d. ta g. *GI*; t. donrai ailleurs t. *I*.
363. Ici p. m. Lothaire q. *I*.
364. p. c'est riches ensement *I*.
365. Tu marcisses o lui et Soudant l'amirans *G*; Touz marchissent a li rodos et l'amirant *I*.
367. d. au cors gent. *I which adds*: Respont roys or je nen ....ment (*Text not clear*)/ Yceste que j'ai ci prendrai certainement.
368-371. *I wants*.
372. d. n'i a resfusement *GI*.
374. n. douc m. *G*; v. de gueroier noient *GI*.
376. Iceste e. *GI*; d. biel e. *G*.
377. a. voirement *GI*.
378. m. g'en ai mon cuer dolent *G*; l. vielle s'en ai le cuer dolent *I*.
379. Ne tu ne feras rien d. *GI*.
380. Atant sont departi andoi del parlement *GI*.
381. Oriens a., n. ricement *GI*.
382. m. les f. *GI*.
383. n. sanz nul delaiement *I*.
384. *I wants*.
385. Segars a. *G*; v. noblement *GI*; .I. duc Segars ot n. *I*.
386. A. .C. c. si m. *G*; .C. de chevaliers et mai. *I*.
388. Vint a., sal. il son s. *G*; sal. et son s. *I*.
389. e. si v. *G*; m. sont venu tantost e. *I*.
390. Sieeut s., c. desor .I. b. *I*.
391. a. et tout son erement *GI*. *G adds*: Trestout li a conte ne li cela noient. *I adds*: Trestout li a conte ne li lessa nient.
394. *GI want*.
395. l. l'en a a., l. a e. *I*; *G wants*.
396. t. en n. *I*.
13. *AGI*
401. lais content d. *G*; lais chantent d. *I*.
402. d. li roys c. *I*.
403. K. sot d., b. fu o. *GI*; K. sot lire u *I*.
404. l. sale ot v. *G*; v. ki a. *GI*.
406. L'autre l. *GI*; s'a grans c. *G*; s. en est grant li c. *I*.
407. Et n. *I*.
408. Et a. *I*; s. li cien u des ors .VIII. *GI*.
409. K. laiens font grant noisse e. *G*; K. laiens font grant j. *I*.

411.   Trestout si a *G*; i. font lor f. li baron a devis *I*.
412.   *GI want.*
414.   r. Oriens s'est et caucies et v. *G*; E. li roys Oriens est chaucies et v. *I*.
415.   en el palais reviertis *GI*.
417.   s. al mostier r. *G*; *I wants.*
418.   a .XL. dis *G*; a .LXX. dis *I*.
419.   h. de princes de marcis *GI*.
420.   *GI want.*
421.   a. uns p. *GI*.
423.   m. l'en menerent d. le c. *GI*.
424.   s. ont seigne l. *I*.
425.   d. que e. *I*.
426.   R. Oriens r. *G*; R. Oriens lors dist b., s. comme a. *I*.
427.   q. m'espouses E. *GI*; d. Beatrix a. *I*.
428.   l. me dounes t. *GI*.
429.   V. touz l. *I*; d. el non de Jesu Crist *G*; e. doerai d. *I*.
430.   L. tiere pres d. *I*.
431.   E. dist a. en joie e. *I*; a. icou e. *G*.
432.   Puis a *GI*; p. Beatrix p. *I*.
433.   l. doune le roi e. *GI*; e. dist S. *I*.
434.   L. soit j. *I*; h. en l. *GI*.
435.   *I adds*: Les pierres en valoient tout l'avoir saint Marcis/ Onques ne fu si bons tres le temps Anseis.
437.   d. son F. *I*.
438.   P. a fait le siervice e.   *GI which add*: Rice fu li ofrande k'il ont sor l'autel mis.
439.   f. renoume par trestout le pais *GI*.
441.   Il l. *G*.
442.   Li j. *GI*; e. sons et les et d. *G*; e. font et lais e. *I*.
443.   *GI add*: Li mangiers fu tous prais et il i (e. a tables s. *I*) sont asis/ N'i ot povre ne rice ne fust molt bien servis/ Et quant fu li mangiers et passes (espris *I*) et finis.
444.   d. a merveille s. *I*.
445.   v. mantiaus p. gris *G*; v. et p. ermins *I*.
446.   Ne r. *G*; i. remest a *I*.
447.   Et grans c. *G*; Ne grant c., a. ne mantiau de samis *I*.
449.   q. l'en r. qui s'en voit e. *I*; r. ki li soit e. *G*.

14.   *AGI*
450.   f. que b. *GI*.
451.   f. illec d. *I*.
452.   l. tieres s'en va l. *GI*.

453. R. Oriens remaint (remest *I*) a mesnie escarie *GI*
 which add: Nonporquant si (il *I*) avoit o lui grant
 conpagnie.
455. D. vient a Beatrix la bele leschenie *I which adds*:
 A moi en entendez bele fres douce amie/ Bien de-
 vons gracier le Fil sainte Marie/ Quant je et vous
 avons ytele compagnie.
456. *GI want.*
457. *I wants.*
458. c. vo joie D. *I.*
459. m. assamblons et d. *I.*
460. q. la n. *I.*
461. N. ne s'oublie *GI.*
462. u. embrasce a. par molt grant c. *I*; d. trestout
 par c. *G.*
466. Beatrix l. *I.*
467. g. ensemble e. est e. *I.*
468. Si a *GI*; m. fu e. *G.*
473. m. aval de flor de lys florie *I.*
476. A. nus n. *I.*
477. e. ces r. cueillie *I.*
478. Toutes .VII. li enbloit par envie *G.*
479. c. les testes e. *I.*
480. N. gieta pas envoies m. *G*; N. jeta pas en yaue m.,
 b. agaitie *I.*
482. e. en (et *I*) doute si e. *GI.*
483. s. Orient p. *GI.*
484. R. Oriens s. *GI*; l. si l'a fort e. *G*; l. s'a cele
 e. *I.*
485. C'aves vous b. (avez b. *I*) *GI.*
486. Vostre afaire en c. *G*; Vostre afaire m. en c. *I.*
487. K. lievent l., D. el non sainte Marie *I.*
488. *GI place verse* 488 *after l.* 485.
489. Elle ot m. *G*; C. ot m. *I*; t. l'ot estormie *GI.*
490. Que n. *GI.*
491. f. esmaie *G*; Ele chiet e., f. esbahie *I.*
492. Si l'acolle sel baisse et puis si l'a saissie *G*;
 Cil l'acole et baise et puis si l'a saisie *I.*
493. C. reprent son cuer a. *GI.*
494. a. en baillie *G*; r. Diex vous ait en baillie *I.*
495. n. le me celez m. *I.*
496. *I wants.*
497. t. esperie *G*; m'a m. t. endormie *I.*
498. e. ma teste e. *I.*
502. l. estoit e. de rose e. *G*; l. estoit pares de rose
 c. *I.*
503. .VII. pumetes m. *GI*; j. ai eu e. *I.*
504. p. de la tiere essaucie *I*; a. estoit fuelie *G.*

505. p. feie *G*; p. baillie *I*.
506. g. folie *I*.
507. Ses mes a o. *G*; Si les m'a en t. *I*.
508. c. ki les p. *GI*; p. les tient e. *I*.
511. l. sietisme o. *GI*; j. hors e. *I*.
512. c. i e. *G*.
514. q. nous a *G*.
515. .VII. don d. D. vous face aie *GI*.
516. d. cou a. *GI*.
518. a. com t. *G*; a. que t. *I*; b. en die *GI*.
519. Ounores s., e. trestoute c. *GI*.
520. v. la char d'omme qu'il ait m. *I*.
521. s. aessie *GI*.
522. q. famine (q. de la fain *I*) aigrie *GI*.
523. s. aessie *G*; d. pour aesier sa vie *I*.
524. D. le font a ceuz f. *I*.
525. ciel et en v. *GI*.

15. *AGI*
526. D. apiela Oriens s. *GI*.
527. e. kil ot ente songie *G*; e. de tel chose s. *I*.
529. P. le paor d. *GI*; s. kil violt entrelaisier *G*; s. que veut entrelessier *I*.
530. j. kil p. *G*; Que t. entent au j. qui p. *I*.
531. l. estaminer *I*.
533. f. les a., ele en a m. *G*; t. qu'en a *I*.
534. d. vienent c. *GI*.
535. Et l. *I*.
536. r. le p. *GI*; p. tout pour le Dieu m. *I*.
537. v. quant fu appareiller *I*.
538. c. com pour li f. *I*.
541. v. a essaucier *G*; h. pour sa vois essaucier *I*.
542. c. fait ofisse et del lire mestier *G*; c. fet servise et de lire mestier *I*.
543. r. qu'en a. *G*; r. qui s'avoit l. *I*.
544. s. une o. *I*.
545. f. .VII. b. *I*.
547. d. pour ofrir .I. *GI*; e. d'or mier *G*.
549. v. o l. *G*.

16. *AGI*
551. d. espaumier *GI*.
552. v. aporter *GI*.
553. v. jeter *I*.
555. R. Oriens q. *GI*.
556. p. s'orison crier *G*; p. Dieu merci crier *I*.
557. h. pour Dameldeu loer (orer *I*) *GI*.
560. por toi bien a. *I*.
561. p. et l. *I*.
563. Et d. i vint p. *GI*.

564. f. du f. *I*.
565. A. se counurent e. *GI*.
566. f. prent f. *I*.
567. Tu venis a eus s. *GI*; e. venis p. *I*.
568. ales garde ne me celer *GI*.
570. *I adds*: Lors li respondi Diex sanz plus de l'atarger.
571. a tout f. *G*; c. osastes t. *I*.
572. d. il e., t. arier *I*; t. errer *G*.
573. m. t'esteut il orendroit laborer *I*.
574. m. a d. *GI*.
575. Puis morurent a. *G*; Puis morurent emsemble si les convint a. *I*.
576. p. ains retorner *GI*; i. dont n. *I*.
577. A. euz e. *I*; t. les e. *GI*.
578. e. les a. *G*.
580. Y. qu'il n. *G*; Y. que je ne sai nommer *I*.
581. E. Joseph e. *I*; *GI add*: Daniel le profete ki molt fist a loer.
582. i. te p., d. domage r. *I*; d. racater *G*.
583. t. delivrer *GI*.
584. S. pour deable qui ni porent grever *I*.
585. u. vergene e. *GI*.
586. q. te v. *G*.
587. Son m., o. que ne l. *I*.
588. p. que d. t. la f. *I*.
590. h. ains ne se pot v. *I*.
591. c. habiter *I*.
592. Ne f. *I*; v. blasmer *GI*.
593. s. destiner *GI*.
594. E. i s. *G*; b. qu'ele v. *I*.
595. c. fu si digne en qui tu vos e. *I*; h. en cui tu vos e. *G*.
596. Seus et toi afubler s. *G*; Seust toi afubler si t. *I*.
597. Que contre l. *G*; Encontre l. *I*; l. adotriner *GI*.
600. Si ne t. *I*; *G wants*.
601. m. respiter *I*.
602. c. ains n. *I*.
603. n. te p. viser *I*; p. devisser *G*.
604. e. deite aviser *I*; a. finer *G*; *GI add*: Ne que de mort a vie peus rexusiter.
606. T. i e. *GI*.
607. c. gentil b. *GI*.
608. A. molt peurent d. *GI*.
609. e. reconforter *I*.
610. .C. milliers des autres q. *GI*.
611. t. ce savons s. *I*; l. croi s. *G*; s. fauser *GI*.

612. D'illueques au t. *GI*.
613. D. te fiz rexussiter *I*.
614. Ten cors d. *G*; Et ton cors a martire q. te l. *I*.
615. o. souvent p. *I*.
616-621. *GI want*.
624. A. qu'el ciel vosis m. *GI*.
626. La vinrent tou e. *GI*; e. que vosistes p. *I*.
630. p. le monde crier *I*.
631. n. parteure n. *G*; P. ne bateure n. *I*.
632. d. quant que c. *I*; c. pot p. *G*.
633. c. c'est voirs que m'oes ramembrer *GI*.
634. T. yces m. *I*; q. m'oes raconter *GI*.
635. f. et de fin c. et cler. *GI*.
636. d. biaus Sire E. *G*; d. biaz Sire et Beatrix m. *I*.
638. e. Paradys m. *I*.
639. s. vraie p. *I*; h. garder *GI*.
640. v. s'il vous plaist si g. *G*; v. si vous plaist si sauver *I*.
641. Qu'ele se puist encore a honor delivrer *GI*.
642. Et cou e. *G*; Et qu'en p. *I*.
643. b. definer *GI*.
644. q. tout a. a sauver *GI*.
17. *AGI*
645. r. Oriens a define s'orisson *GI*.
646. m. si se fist benicon *G*; m. si fist beneicon *I*.
647. *GI want*.
648. Apries li d. *GI*.
649. a. se fu mis a bandon *I*.
650. Or part cante l., t. se p. *G*; m. ne dura se p. *I*.
651. *I wants*.
653. Le roi saina par grant devossion *G*; Roys Oriens se seigne sanz nule arestoison *I*.
654. Del ortail de son piet deseure le (son *I*) menton *GI*.
655. *GI want*.
657. Et la joie coumence lasus ens el (cel *I*) doignon *GI*.
658. s. escuier e. *I*.
659. Tout m. *GI*.
18. *AGI*
661. S. iestres e., t. ramembres *GI*.
662. i. remest nus (nul *I*) a. *GI*; n. fust r. *G*; s. recordes *GI*.
663. C. cest m. *I*.
664. *GI want*.
665. La nuit p. *GI*.
666. e. se cou iert verites *G*; e. en Beatrix sa per *I*.
667. m. que (qu'el *I*) s'en doit delivrer *GI*.

668. r. pourpenses *GI*.
669. E. ot i afaire q. n'e. pas o. *I*; *G wants*.
670. e. seroit e. *GI*.
671. c. .I. c. *GI*.
673. P. tout cou v. *GI*.
674. s. e. soit e. j. *I*; j. denomes *G*.
675. Si que uns tous s. j. n'i s. *GI*; s. ja t. *G*.
676. p. s'est a li abites *GI*.
678. i. soloit a. *I*.
679. Cou (Dont *I*) dient s. *GI*; v. qu'il est a. *I*.
680. Qui s. *I*; t. vora prenge ent d. *GI*.
681. p. en est a. *G*; *I wants*.
19. *AGI*
683. s. tiere p., p. envie *GI*.
684. Et m. en s. *GI*; a sa compaigne a. *I*.
685. V. maine e. p. si n. *G*; p. et n. *I*.
686. t. mesballie *G*; *GI add*: As vilains a tolu molt de (grande *I*) gaegnerie.
687. Li plains en v. *I*; e. vint a. *G*.
688. Si a., i. il m. *GI*.
689. Que de ce que sa tiere a ensi malbaillie *I*; f. que se t. a b. *G*.
690. m. a si g. *GI*.
691. *GI want*.
692. T. li esteut r. *I*.
693. s. que f. *GI*.
694. La gentiz Beatrix q. *I*.
695. *GI want*.
696. d. est d. *I*.
697. b. est son cuer d. *I*; s. cuers d. *G*.
699. o. que s. f.. li p. *GI*.
700. r. que g. besoins l'aigrie *GI*.
701. m. dame que m. *I*; d. que mestier a. *G*.
702. v. molt g. *GI*.
703. j. cevaucai n. fis c. *G*; n. liue ne demie *I*.
706. G. de Pavie *I*.
707. Et m. *I*; met a d. *GI*.
708. e. ma g. *G*; *I wants*.
709. i. a l. *I*; e. a g. *GI*.
710. c. sa follie *GI*.
711. g. carcre hermie *G*; c. naie *I*.
712. T. a v. *GI*; e. no c. *G*.
713. d. Matabrulie *G*; d. Matabrunie *I*.
714. p. de vous v. *G*; p. de vous pour Dieu le Fiex Marie *I*.
715. c. a m. r. *G*; p. et commant r. *I*; v. contredie *GI*.
716. E. se v. courecoit m. seroit en sa v. *GI*.
717. j. de m'amor departie *GI*.

718. p. jointes m. *G*; p. pour Dieu le Fiex Marie *I*.
719. m. sa mere et durement l. *I*; mere et sor ses mains
      l. *G*.
720. *GI want.*
721. o. o m. *GI*.
723. a. mon fiex par druerie *I*.
724. cier que m. *G*.
20.   *AGI*
725. Beatrix a *I*; c. a d. *GI*.
727. r. a liquele l. *GI*.
728. *GI want.*
729. d. mon d. *G*; d. mon dolosement *I*.
730. d. jel v. *GI*.
731. s. aideres v. *GI*.
732. Que s. *I*; v. les f. *G*; n. radosement *GI*.
733. D. dites v. *G*; m. que ne m'oblie n. *I*.
734. *GI want.*
735. m. istront gart bien et loïalment *I*; n. mes garle
      b. *G*.
736. e. ce vient a sauvement *I*.
737. *GI want.*
738. m. vient a. *I*; v. avant sans nul atargement *GI*.
739. *GI want.*
740. a. coume meismement *G*; a. com moi meismont *I*.
741. a. loïalment *I*.
742. a. en t. veu j. *G*; j. de d. *I*; e. devissement *GI*.
743. S'en aurai a t. *G*; Avrai je a t. *I*; *GI add*: Cou
      com m'aportera mousterai a la (ma *I*) gent.
744. d. Beatrix c. *I*; f. fiermament *GI*.
745. b. et l'ounor hautement *GI*.
746. M. or sera l. *I*; c. sera l. *G*.
747. a. meres ont (fame en *I*) tel torment *GI*.
748. Qu'a paines respassent de l. *GI*.
749. Oriens v. *GI*; v. la gent n. *I*; d. ne puet p. *GI*.
750. e. vait il e. *I*.
751. e. tost et isnielement *GI*.
753. l. si com s. *G*; *I wants.*
754. i. facent e. *I*; v. errant *G*.
755. s. sans nul atargement *GI*.
756. q. y d. *I*.
21.   *AGI*
757. Oriens f. *GI*; e. et l. *I*.
758. S'envoie .C. g. *GI*.
759. t. lor c. *G*; t. les c. *I*.
760. t. tieres et g. *GI*; g. valees *I*.
761. v. en a. *I*.
764. a. sodoiers a. *GI*; b. jornees *I*.
765. a. bien d. *I*; d. .VII. j. *GI*; .XV. ajornees *G*.

767. Qui a ce l. *I*.
768. S. ensongnes loiaus ierent a. *G*; S. ensaignes icos
i. *I*.
769. Se tiere et s. *G*; m. et en f. *GI*.
771. A .DCC. c. *G*.
772. t. armees *GI*.
773. Fors l. *G*; Et l. *I*.

22. *AGI*
774. e. li coriu (coreur *I*) i couroient *GI which add*:
Et portent les saiaus (ensaignes *I*) u les letres
estoient (pendoient *I*)/ Isnielement s'en vont gai-
res ne demoroient (*I wants*).
775. *GI want*.
777. s. ou l. *I*.
778. Il lissent l. *G*; L. a l. b. que li roys leur en-
voie *I*.
780. d. pitie en l. *I*.
781. Et li jeune en s. lie q. d'armes d. *I*; j. home s.
lie ki armes d. *G*.
782. L. nouviel c. q. au gaang coroient *G*; L. jeune c.
q. besoign coloient *I*.
783. Enarmerent escus e. *G*; Et armes et escus et ses h.
I.
784. C. cauces et ces coifes t. e. frotoient *I*; cau.
tout e. *G*.
785. o. et ces fiers i metoient *G*; o. et ces fers y em-
ploient *I*.
786. ces chevauz y c. *I*; c. frotoient *GI*.
787. Lorains font q., p. ouvroient *GI*.
788. Racesment e. r. ces s. *GI*.
789. c. gorgieres coloient *I*; t. torsoient *G*.
790. f. portoient *GI which add*: Haubregier escuier hau-
bers escus vendoient (Haubergons escutiaux hauberc
escu verdoient *I*).
791. T. prendent c. acatent et cacroient (acroient *I*)
GI.
792. Monte sont vont a *I*; l. nomoient *G*; l. y envoient
I.
793. Ens es p. *GI*.
794. q. contremont b. *GI*; c. voloient *I*.
795. c. li h. *GI*.
797. Q. li s. *GI*; s. venroit que forment d. *I*.
799. con la r. ert d. *G*; c. lonc l. r. de lonc la e. *I*.

23. *AGI*
800. r. ki (et *I*) point ne se desroient (doutoient *I*)
GI.
801. r. Oriens v. *GI which add*: Molt a bielle conpagne
car il (et si *I*) maine grant (mout *I*) gent.

802. Le charoi si endure t. *I*.
803. l. bien p. *GI*; s. va rois r. *G*; p. par le mien es-
cient *I*.
804. e. viande e. *G*; a. mout acesmeement *I*.
805. c. des pres les ont veus apiertement *GI which add*:
Montent en lor cevaus (Lors montent es c. *I*) tost
et isnielement.
806. Le roi ont salue biel et cortoissement *GI*.
807. p. molt deboinerement *GI*.
808. Li r. l. enmercie e. *GI*.
810. Si i met c. *GI*; c. .XI. vins c. *G*; c. .VII.XX. c.
I.
811. a. ensement *GI*.
812. d. plus n. *I*.
813. o. k'il v. *G*; o. qui v. *I*.
814. C'or ira sor Gradoce v. *GI*.
815. e. entres sans congiet folement *GI*. *I adds*: Adonc-
quez chevaucha sanz plus d'atargement.
816. Et villes et castiaus prent tout a son talent *G*;
Ait villes et chastiaus proie raient et prent *I*.
817. N'est nus ki contretiegne n. *GI*; *I adds*: .I. en
ont asegie tost et delivrement.
818. I. li met tost (I. y metent *I*) le siege jure s.
GI.
821. n. achatement *I*.
822. i. en ont l. *GI*; e. font l. *G*.
824. t. ki d. *GI*.
825. a sa gent qu'on l. *GI*; g. que l. *I*; t. cravent *G*.
826. Dognons e. *I*; E. murs e. *G*; for. brissent isniele-
ment *GI*.
827. B. a .XV. j. n'i a tiere ne prent *I*.
828. p. pullent *G*.
829. E. il trueve la tiere garnie r. *GI*.
830. Et li carins le siut trestout seurement *G*; Li cha-
roi les siu trestout serreement *I*.
831. Et portent fer et glaves q. *GI*; c. ki t. *G*; c. de-
si ne sureement *I*.
832. l. baceler q. c. gaitent *GI which add*: Que paien
nes sousprenent ne mainent malement (laidement *I*)/
Rois Oriens cevauce les paiens va cacant.
833. P. en s. *GI*.
834. t. mout v. *I*.
836. R. a a *G*; R. a n. *I*; v. atagnant *GI*.
837. m. dormant *I*.
839. m. au riche roy s. *I*; Perse roi *G*.
841. laige a la c. *GI*; c. qui si l. *I*.
842. e. caïne t. *GI*.
843. m. rice d. m. escarimant *GI*.

844. L. a et tourieles tout entor a canmant *G*; Longe a estore le tout entor ataignant *I*.
846. a. de rices f. *GI*.
848. Si a. *I*; a. u c. *GI*.
850. c. a a. parfonde et grant *G*; a. fort et corant *I*.
851. a deseure l'yaue en n. *I*; e. laissant *GI*.
852. m. en s. haut a. *GI*; h. en a. ataignant *I*.
853. a. a toriele l. *GI*; p. autre a. *I*.
854. Masieres d. *GI*; l. d'estant *G*.
855. v. forcant *I*.
857. g. maces p. *G*.
858. q. jetant *I*.
859. Qui d. *I*; p. me t. *G*; n. treuve v. *I*.
860. s. riche et m. *I*.
861. *I wants.*
862. Ont il d. *G*; Vivre d. .V. a. *I*; l. faura n. *GI*.
863. Si n. *I*; t. plain .I. bouciel tenant *GI*.
864. i. assez a remanant *I*.
865. Avec ceuz qui seroient la c. *I*; e. la c. *G*.
866. .XXX. trestous a. *G*.
868. j. ierent d. *I*.
24. *AGI*
869. R. Oriens p., g. desroi *GI*.
870. s. pries q. *GI*; m. en esfrois *G*; m. a belloy *I*.
871. Et Dieu a (li *I*) e. *GI*.
872. Li roys la grant montaigne esgarde devant s. *I*; montaigne esgarde *G*.
873. Le grant c., l. fierte l. *G*; *I wants.*
874. Il voit q., a. en son recoi *GI*.
875. .II. b. *GI*.
877. Vees ci la c. *G*; Vez ici la c. qui l. *I*.
878. c. l'aions j. *I*; g. lor r. *G*.
879. e. arons j. *I*.
880. s. et armes e. *I*.
881. m. sor m. *GI*.
882. p. le foi que vous doi *GI*.
883. D. sauve J. *I*.
884. Roys f., c. boscoi *I*.
885. Parcoi n. *GI*.
25. *AGI*
886. r. ni v. *I*.
887. t. s'ost e. *GI*.
888. Que se l. *GI*.
889. d. .XXX. m. *GI*; .C. cors *G*.
890. Il n'i a cel ki sace a son tret a (*rest of line not visible*) *G*; quil y sace asener *I*.
891. l. k'il l. *G*; l. qui l. *I*; s. laise v. *GI*.
892. *I wants.*

893. E. li auquent s. *I*.
894. a. escuiers f. *GI*; q. vont l. *G*; *I places verses 893 and 894 after* 1. 895.
895. Si f. le fu s. d. fusiaus a. *GI*; f. au hurter *I*.
896. a. celebrer *GI*.
897. p. aler *I*.
898. Se c. y peussent ou prendre ou c. *I*; p. conrois c. *G*.
899. p. les fondrer *G*; p. l'affonder *I*.
900. v. li l. *GI*.
901. T. com i. porent dure t. *GI*.
902. c. lor p. *GI*.
903. c. amer *I*.
904. Qui f., e. esconser *I*.
905. e. qui se p. *I*; i puisent f. *GI*.
906. C. lors v. *I*; p. si l. *GI*.
907. c. ne les pevent j. *I*; e. puent j. *G*.
26. *AGI*
908. o. il cenbiel ains n. *G*; o. celebre ains i. *I*.
909. c. la l. *G*; c. dedens .I. *GI*; c. dehors t. *I*; f. traire *G*.
910. Que si v. f. y c., peust plaire *I*.
911. Car j. *G*; Que j. t. n'i v. *I*; v. ne e. *G*.
912. *GI want*.
913. o. si f., p. faire *I*.
914. Que n'a huis a *I*; n. mostrerent v. *GI*; t. leur v. *I*.
915. Cil retornent ariere ki el nen puent faire *GI*.
917. Que si n. *I*; f. il violt p. *G*; f. il veut engin traire *I*.
918. *GI add*: Prie lor par amor que s'il puent rien faire.
919. Qu'il ne f. mais d. *G*.
920. d. la g. *GI*.
921. l. doit d. *I*.
922. m. au roi que u. n. corsaire *GI*.
923. i. aler p. desor l. *GI*.
924. e. jou ferai (il fera *I*) cest afaire *GI*.
27. *AGI*
926. u. grande t. *I*.
931. T. l'e. *I*; e. passoit l. *GI*.
932. q. il a. *I*; r. al passage e. *GI*.
933. a. venans qui vienent (venoit *I*) a *GI*.
935. h. tesie *I*.
937. e. et ostent ramie *I*.
939. t. est e. *G*; t. a une hie *I*.
940. l. porte b. *I*.
941. D. les l. *I*.

942.   d. a le marcie *G*; d. a la marine *I*.
943.   m. puis o. *GI*.
944.   D. cent v. b. et .III. *G*; b. .L. et .III. a *I*.
945.   Pour cercher le mares que l'iaue n'i pasmie *I*;   e. aguie *G*.
946.   a. de bruie *I*.
947.   p. ens en mi la marine *I*.
948.   b. tiere e. *GI*; e. fouie *G*; e. herbie *I*.
949.   De li erbe i o. porte devant l. *GI*.
950.   e. trenchie *I*.
951.   Les pieres isi g. *G*; p. ausi g. *I*; u. n'en t. *G*.
953.   e. bien est s. *G*; e. mout b. asoplie *I*.
954.   a. nen puet i. *G*; i. s'est drue la navie *I*.
956.   B. chevaliers e. j. et de *I*.
957.   Q. gaitierent e. *G*; e. qu'ele n. s. gastie *I*.

28.   *AGI*
958.   Ore s'en va J. *I*.
959.   r. encor vel c. *GI*; e. cel a. *I*.
960.   c. garder *I*.
961.   d. li rois f. *GI*; r. or va sanz demorer *I*.
963.   C. et fouz fet il a la tiere v. *I*; f. a tiere fait v. *G*.
964.   Fen les et s'en fait ais et si les fait d. *GI*.
965.   A poit e. *G*; A poil e. *I*; a estoupes l. *G*; a estoupel l. *I*; e. fierer *G*; e. serrer *I*.
966.   l. planchier q., f. ferrer *I*.
967.   Et .IIII. p. *I*.
968.   D. ces p. f. .X. qu'il f. sus f. *I*; t. plantes f., f. jus f. *G*.
969.   p. les c. *GI*.
970.   q. sevent l. *GI*.
971.   Et a c. de laiens s. *GI*.
972.   *GI want*.
973.   E. cou l. *G*.
974.   d. envers aus ariestrer *G*; d. ne poroient endurer *I*.
976.   De grant m. e. ferir e.   *I*.
979.   p. auner *GI*.
980.   b. fermement s. *GI*; e. fermer *I*.
981.   v. tout rasser *G*; *I wants*.
982.   *I wants*.
983.   d. Jofrois f. *GI*.
985.   r. s'a .I. cor fet s. *I*.
986.   t. le b. *I*.
987.   Q. tout v. *GI*.
988.   f. le v. *I*; v. crosler *GI*.
989.   J. en sont e. *GI*.
990.   q. nus n. *GI*.

29.   *AGI*
   992.   *GI add*: Mescin ne baceler ne dormoient nient.
   993.   As baotes s. *G*; Au basset se s. *I*; m. li arcier coiement *GI which add*: Et li abalaistrier ki traient durement.
   994.   r. tous esraument *I*.
   995.   e. sera ficent f. *G*; e. se rafichent f. *I*.
   996.   Ki l. *GI*; a. d'ennuis e. *I*.
   997.   Sis e. *G*; a. de lor gent *GI*.
   998.   As tentes s. *GI*.
   999.   e. les b. *I*.
   1000.   e. il et toute sa gent *GI*.
   1001.   Si c. *GI*; c. l'engin a. *I*; b. vers les murs sagement *GI*.
   1003.   p. si r. *I*.
   1004.   i. droit n. *I*.
   1005.   Q. fort s. *G*; c. si roidement *GI*.
   1007.   a. vint a. *G*; m. que consuit ne crevent *I*; l. ne atent *G*.
   1008.   Tout le premerain balle abat delivrement *GI*.
   1009.   c. s'espant e. *I*.
   1010.   Nus nel p. *GI*; poroit nonbrer *G*; p. conter par nesun nonbrement *I*.
   1011.   *GI want*.
   1012.   e. ou grant m. *I*.
   1013.   Voient par la cite le grant destruisement *GI*.
   1014.   g. bas acordes c. *G*; g. piex aus cordes c. *I*.
   1015.   a. murs que tous l. *GI*.
   1016.   Li a. ki entre ens n. *GI*; e. naie a. *I*.
   1017.   *GI want*.
   1019.   p. nus conter le nonbre vraiement *G*; p. ...bien conter le nonbre vraiement *I*.
   1020.   *GI want*.
   1021.   *GI want*.
   1022.   De f. et d'enfans et de m. *GI*.
   1023.   Cil ont primes recut l. *GI*; p. ytel m. *I*.
   1024.   Mais teus q., f. a garant *GI*.
   1025.   Que la gent Orient ki par tout va n. *GI*.
   1026.   L. noient s. *GI*; v. u les fierent et livrent a torment *G*; f. hardement *I*.
   1027.   Et li plusor escrient mierci molt hautement *GI*.
   1028.   A. sont pris a (par *I*) force et loi durement *GI*.
   1029.   s. ne sont a. *G*.
   1030.   U haus princes cases de rice (d. mout haut *I*) tenement *GI*.
   1031.   *GI want*.
30.   *AGI*
   1033.   *GI want*.

1034. Et v. cele gent justement tormentees *I*; p. conrees
      G.
1035. f. amont autres s. *GI*.
1036. Li un sont t. *GI*; a. d'espees *G*; a. as espees *I*.
1037. De glaves et de lances (lance *I*) i *GI*; m. isi s.
      G; s. mal demenees *I*.
1038. B. ot a. *G*; B. en ont par l. *I*; d. .VII.C. (.VI.C.
      I) e. *GI*.
1039. d. ki bien fu fenestres *G*; d. sanz autres demorees
      I.
1040. Si sont (que *I*) li c. d'a. b. apprestee *GI*.
1041. L. vont l. *GI*.
1042. Apris sont d'e. g. et estors e. *G*; Et prez sont de
      .II. mile g. *I*.
1043. t. saietees e.*I*.
1045. P. passe ont et lanciez s. *I*.
1046. Et vous m. *G*; Et Diex com g. *I*; g. armees *GI*.
1047. n. en muert q. *G*; a. est comblees *I*.
1048. I a t. *I*; e. sont a. *G*; e. ariere a. *I*.
1049. L. sers l. t. ses ont a. *I*; t. ens l. *G*.
1050. O. se (s'en *I*) sentent l. g. Orient molt (a *I*) g.
      GI.

31. *AGI*
1052. C. veulent que prengnent e. *I*.
1053. A. au d. si n'ont point d. *GI*.
1055. D. piex q. *I*; t. de piere *GI*.
1056. e. laiens q. m. hors la c. *I*; h. laiens q. *G*.
1057. A. trairoient d. l. abalestrie *G*.
1058. i que l. *GI which add*: Ne (Qui *I*) ceurt apries le
      lievre (leu *I*) en la lande pleniere.
1059. q. ce semble a *I*.
1060. l. qui s. *I*.
1061. D. pour ondes m. *I*.
1062. p. mi la baetiere *I*.
1063. B. ot sa t. a. d'auberc e. *GI*; d. corsiere *I*.
1064. a. tres p. le lumiere *G*; a. si que p. *I*.
1065. f. el haterel que le cervel d. *I*.
1066. e. tres en mi sa cière *G*; *I wants*.
1067. l. oste l. *I*; q. ert d. *G*; q. est d. *I*.
1068. *GI want*.
1069. *GI want*.
1070. e. dobliere *GI*.
1071. l. en u. *GI which add*: Et font grant duel (dolor
      I) entor ele (cele *I*) gent aversiere.

32. *AGI*
1072. Mors e. *GI*.
1073. i. n'orent l. *GI*.
1074. c. trop s. *I*; m. fesist a p. *GI*.

1075.   r. si en fet d. *I*; d. u n'a q. *G*.
1076.   b. dist i. laissies m. *G*.
1077.   s. encor pris caiens ains a. *G*.
1081.   N. li e. d. touz p. *I*.
1082.   *GI want.*
1083.   d. cil b. *GI*.
1084.   D. que v. vores a cel r. *GI*.
1085.   Si n'est a. kel d. *GI*.
1086.   q. la est q. *GI*. *I adds:* Cousin estoit le roy et
        si....trop chier. *Text not clear.*
1087.   m. sot b. *G*. *I not clear.*
1088.   d. lui sans dangier *GI*.
1089.   l. parler et acointier *GI*.
1091.   l. votre t. *G which leaves rime word blank.*
1092.   c. de blanc d. par son cuer a. *GI*.

33.   *AGI*
1093.   Il s. *G*; Il montent e., t. ou h. chastel e. *I*.
1094.   S. a pendu (tendu *I*) le crois portraite e. un bla-
        son *GI*.
1096.   Avois segnor vous nous feres r. *G*; Ahi sire ami-
        rant or nous faites r. *I*.
1097.   Qu'ases as estruie encontre ce d. *I*.
1098.   mes. li roys qui est d. *I*.
1099.   a. a lui nous renderons *GI*.
1100.   p. quant a oï le ton *I*.
1101-1105.   *GI want.*
1106.   Vien a moi dist li rois si li crie a haut ton *G*; *I*
        wants.
1107.   s. rendent p. *G*; r. en p. *GI*.
1108.   Car pour sauver l. *G*; v. en prison se rendront *I*.
1109.   l. porrez avoir .C. mile et .C. m. *I*.
1110.   a. les c. *GI*.
1112.   Que p. *I*.
1113.   r. et d. *GI*.
1114.   r. a e. *GI*.
1115.   p. li rois q. *GI*.
1118.   c. k'il c. *G*; c. qui touz sont environ *I*.
1119.   E. de ma gent b., n. l'otrierons *G*; n. le te don-
        ron *I*.
1120.   Tout ton commandement e. *I*.
1121.   n. viut j. *G*; ja nel d. *I*.
1123.   e. vous p. *I*. *GI add:* U en aige courant trestous
        les noierons.

34.   *AGI*
1124.   a. en vel a. *GI*.
1125.   v. parlement a *I*.
1127.   Et c. v. au seigneur le message c. *I*.
1128.   a. delessier *I*.

1132. Saveie sa r. *G*; Et sauve'r. *I*; e. fera raler *GI*.
1133. v. ceste cosse ne voles creanter *GI*.
1134. f. ceste t. t. effondrer *I*.
1135. Et si vous fera tous au gibet en cuer *G*; Et a .I. grant gibet vous trestout encroer *I*.
1136. Pour M., r. viut se cil h. *G*; r. mout est.... d. *I*. *Text not clear*.
1137. n. viut e. *G*; r. ne conte n. *I*.
1138. Se (Que *I*) les os no signor volies (voloie *I*) r. *GI*.
1140. *I wants*.
1141. m. a r. Faburon E. *I*.
1142. n. vous f. *I*.
1143. Mahon por n. *GI*; i. vous v. *I*.
1144. f. laiens la dedens e. *I*; l. demorer *GI*.
1145. d. la t. *I*; t. ki de fin or est c. *GI*.
1146. f. nos v. *I*; *GI add*: Et si ferons por eus quan que porons finer (trouver *I*)/ Et si lor prierons de boin cuer sans fauser (*I wants*).
1147. Qu'il n. *GI*; D. acorder *G*.
1148. q. demorer *GI which add*: Paor ai que ne facent ceste tour craventer.
1149. e. lor coifes font oster *G*; e. sanz point de l'arester *I*.
1150. Et les aubers des dos f. apries fors j. *GI*.
1151. *I wants*.
1152. o. la u v. *G*; o. par coi seulent p. *I*.
1153. A. Orient a. *GI*.
1154. j. m'en viegn a *I*; v. ca a *G*; a toi m. baron e. *GI*.
1155. Non p. *GI*; c. fors p. *I*.
1156. S. tu viols e. *GI*.
1158. R. Oriens r. *GI*; L. a dit b. *I*.
1159. e. toi c. *GI*.
1160. p. en b. *I*; a batalle a. *GI*; b. mener *I*.
1163. n. l'en estuet d. *GI*.
1164. Ca venes se v. *GI*.
1166. Si en cierent (Fiancierent *I*) lor fois (foi *I*) a Jhesu a. *GI*.
1167. Ausi fissent l. *GI*; *I adds*: Lors a dit Oriens sanz plus de delaier.
1168. ren. le tresor dist li rois q. *G*; Quar r. le tresor qu'avez fet enserrer *I*.
1169. Par dedens les e. si le faitez donner *I*; e. sel me faites livrer *G*.
1170. s. loer *I*.
1171. *I places this verse after l.* 1172.
1173. v. vourai u. *I*; p. en f. batisier et lever *GI*.

1174.   t. beneir et sacrer *GI*.
1175.   Cou dist li rois p. *GI*; r. Tafur b. *I*.
1176.   *GI want*.
1178.   e. nos c. *GI*.
1179.   J. que v. *G*.
1180.   v. errant s. point d. *GI*; d. l'arester *I*.
1181.   *GI add*: Et l'eve des esclusses faites aval aler/ Si c'a pie peussons par mi la vile aler/ Et Jofrois li otrie sans point de demorer.

35.   *AGI*
1182.   J. vient a *I*; v. as escluses s. *G*; e. que n'i (ne *I*) arieste m. *GI*.
1183.   *GI add*: Aval cort la riviere par si grant aramie/ Cou le puet bien oir d'une liue et demie.
1184.   t. ses seva q. t. estoit n. *GI*.
1185.   A. gent qui n'est noie *I*.
1187.   v. ert g. *G*.
1189.   Portent e., c. ou t. *I*; P. quant e., c. ont t. *G*.
1190.   g. en ses p. et en tant est f. *I*; p. et en tai e. *G*.
1191.   Puis f. rois Orians e., c. ki v. *GI*.
1196.   Sil leur commande a f. si r. *I*.
1197.   d. as p. *G*.
1198.   q. doune le m. *GI*.
1199.   Et ki violt d. en la grant m. *GI which add*: Bien pora demorer sans paor de sa vie.
1200.   A. ses dounes a *G*; A. ses dons si fist de sa gent departie *I*.
1201.   Qui se veut r. en s. *I*; i. s'en violt r. a sa c. *G*.
1202.   Misent l'ariere g. *G*; Mistrent la reregarde e. *I*.
1203.   q. bien est f. *GI*.
1204.   Et paiene g. *G*; g. maine (a *I*) ens en sa conpagnie *GI*.

36.   *AGI*
1207.   a. teus i a k'il garnist *GI*.
1208.   E. li prison a. *G*; Et a li plusor d'euz ne s'en sont asentis *I*.
1209.   U l. *G*; Ont l. *I*; c. u e. *GI which add*: Tant cevauce li rois par plains et par lairis.
1210.   *GI want*.
1211.   Qu'il v. *GI*; i. vient en ses m. *I*; a. jor d. *G*.
1212.   e. d'abes trosc'a d. *G*; a. jusqu'a .VI. *I*.
1213.   *GI want*.
1214.   A u. *I*.
1215.   b. a on le c. *GI*.
1216.   i ont l. r. desi o. *GI*.
1217.   a. trosqu'a d. *G*; a. jusqu'a .VI. *I*.

1218. Partacles o., n. el non le Saint Esperis *I*; n. le
s. *G*.
1219. p. ot t. en si b. *GI*.
1220. c. si ont Mahon guerpis *I*.
1221. En J. ont f. *GI*; f. creance d. *G*.
1222. f. li doune Monbrunis *GI*.
1223. c. merveilleuz e. *I*.
1224. b. .XXV. v. *GI*.
1225. i. a c. *I*; r. quan k'il a. *G*.
1227. p. a sa foit (li a fet *I*) et juret et plevi *GI*.
1228. Qu'il r. *GI*; s. remest s. *I*.

37. *AGI*
1229. f. rois Oriens e. *GI*.
1230. D. si l'a ainsi bien a. *I*.
1233. h. il en a r. *GI*.
1234. j. k'i a., e. iries *GI*.
1235. q. est h. *GI*.
1237. e. longement d. *GI*.
1238. Beatrix s. *I*.
1239. t. que il e. *I*.
1240. c. de .VII. enfans d. *GI*; f. estoit g. *G*; e. trop
g. *I*.
1241. p. la c. *G*.
1242. Les d. *GI*; e. li cris est enforcies *G*; e. par ver-
tu le sachez *I*.
1243. d. ont (qu'ont *I*) soufiert d. *GI*.
1244. b. son m. *G*; m. ki (que *I*) molt est aprocies *GI*.
1245. *GI want*.

38. *AGI*
1246. p. por c. *G*; p. pour leur d. *I*.
1247. Que m. ont grant d. *G*; Qui m. ot de d. que v. *I*.
1248. Et s. *GI*; h. et souffrir et changier *I*.
1249. D. ne vient a. *G*.
1250. Et celi qui D. aune s. *I*; p. consellier *GI*.
1251. Oies u. *GI*.
1252. d. pot s. *GI*; s. cors d. *I*.
1253. troves enfans *G*; a trouve nes enfans m. *I*; e. de
la mollier *GI*.
1255. v. que D. gart d'e. *I*.
1256. c. avoit au col c. *GI*.
1258. e. a g. *G*; e. avoit m. *I*.
1259-1292. *GI want*.

40. *AGI*
1293. r. aportes la portee *GI*.
1294. *GI want*.
1297. l. vraie c. *GI which add*: Cou ne sont pas enfant
c'est diable asanblee.
1298. v. mais q. *GI*.

1299.   f. ce e. *I*.
1300.   q. soit de mere n. *GI*.
1301.   N'esterara c. *G*; v. racontee *GI*.
1302.   Isi l. *G*; d. par foi a. *GI*.
1303.   a. Marke de la V. *GI*.
1304.   *GI want*.
1305.   Cil e. *GI*.
1306.   m. liges hon fois m'as a. *GI*.
1307.   s. ge pas l. *GI*.
1308.   U. cosse ai a f. *G*;   U afaire   veuil f. *I*;   f. que
      (si *I*) vel que soit c. *GI*.
1309.   p. si l'aras a. *GI*.
1310.   e. mostree *GI*.
1311.   *I wants*.
1312.   l. seule r. *G*.
1313.   S. m'en a. *I*.
1314.   Cil li d. fait seront sans nule d. *GI*.
1315.   F. la et si r. *GI*; l. revint a. *G*.
1316.   E. prent s. *I*.
1317.   S'a commande a. d. c'aportes l. *GI*.
1318.   *GI want*.
41.   *AGI*
1319.   Ceste parole   (novele *I*)   siut   (sot *I*) li vilains
      molt r. *GI*.
1320.   t. norir s. *G*; t. norri s. c. a fet l. *I*.
1321.   N'en violt norecon faire c. *GI*; f. qu'elle d. *I*.
1322.   A. l'ocist e. *GI*.
1323.   m. siut (dut *I*) estre t. ki'st d. *GI*.
1324.   b. son vi f. *G*; e. le roy sot ele son gieu f. *I*.
1325.   T. que si e. *GI*.
1326.   o. mie ce faire *GI*.
1327.   N'osast s., c. mostrer ne (en *I*) son a. *GI*.
1328.   Marke cou d. *G*;   Mez ce que d. *I*;   a. al   luminere
      GI.
1330.   d. cest b. *I*.
1331.   Portes ce mantiel ci et trestout cest afaire *GI*.
1332.   e. voie r. *GI*.
1333.   Ne p. *I*; a. cou q. *GI*.
1334.   d. et puis s. *I*; a. te ferai m. *GI*.
1336.   n. me p. *I*.
1337.   D. cou a dit Markes d. *G*;   D. ce dist Malcon d. *I*;
      b. afaire *GI*.
1339.   Ne feroie jou cosse ki vous d. *GI*; v. peust d. *I*.
42.   *AGI*
1340.   Markes (Marcon *I*) atendi t. que nuis   (q. la n. *I*)
      fu s. *GI*.
1341.   f. desor l. *GI*; d. li gaberie *I*.
1343.   *GI want*.

1344. e. son afaire o. *GI*.
1345. I. est m., v. n'en set mot la mesnie *G*; I. se mist
       a, v. que ne se targe mie *I*.

INDEX OF PROPER NAMES

Gordoces, 682, 698, 814; Gordoces de Palie, 706.
Guion, 3228.
Halape, 3081.
Herquegier, 2462.
Hungerie, 15.
Jessé, 581.
Jhesu, 554, 1118, 1129, 1139, 1166, 1221, 2284, 3132, 3492.
Joifroi, 875, 883, 918, 934, 958, 982, 1000, 1179, 1181,
        1182.
Jordant, 3119.
Juliien, s., 1870.
Kahu, 1597.
Kaïn, 578.
Lesbon, 1775.
Lioxe, 324, 326. (See Elioxe).
Lotaires, 12, 29, 40, 54, 92, 102, 132, 181, 200, 276, 343,
          351, 381, 414, 426, 433, 483, 484, 526, 555, 645,
          727, 749, 757, 801, 869, 915, 924, 1050, 1088,
          1106, 1153, 1158, 1191, 1266, 1502, 1524, 1670,
          2126, 2178, 2360, 2469, 2602, 2722, 3048, 3107,
          3277, 3299, 3305, 3313, 3332, 3422.
Mahon, 1117, 1129, 1136, 1139, 1220; Mahomet, 1597.
Malmené, 1538.
Malquidant, 1728.
Marie, s., 4, 499, 1853, 3285, 3302; Virgene, s., 1822,
        3320.
Marien Madelaine, 617.
Martin, 3227.
Matrosilie, 713.
Michaël, 365.
Miles, 3101, 3104.
Moÿsent, 744, 3497; Moÿset, 579.
Monbregis, 1222.
Monicier (de Valee), 1303, 1328, 1337, 1340, 1383, 1389,
                     1401.
Morise, s., 3182.
Nicolas, 875, 883, 918.
Nisot (Castel de), 766.
Nimaie, 10, 3301, 3490, 3494.
Noë, 579, 608.
Octeviant, 3099.
Ogier, 3228.
Olivier, 3227.
Omer, s., 1466, 2238.
Oriant, 133, 252, 1821, 2737, 2960, 3311, 3415.
Palie, 706. (See Gordoces).
Patrices, 1218.
Patris, s., 1214.

GLOSSARY

This glossary is selective. The English equivalents which it provides pertain to the indicated context.

The following abbreviations are used: *adj.*, adjective; *adv.*, adverb; *f.*, feminine; *imp.*, imperative; *imperf.*, imperfect; *impers.*, impersonal; *ind.*, indicative; *infin.*, infinitive; *intr.*, intransitive; *m.*, masculine; *n.*, noun; *pl.*, plural; *part.*, participle; *pers.*, person; *pr.*, present; *prep.*, preposition; *refl.*, reflexive; *s.*, singular; *subj.*, subjunctive; *tr.*, transitive; *v.*, verb.

aaisier, *infin.* of *tr. v.* to comfort; 532.
aatie, *n. f. s.* animosity, 956; provocation, 3279.
abaier, *infin.* of *intr. v.* to bark; 90.
abitement, *n. m. s.* dwelling; 166.
acaindre, *infin.* of *tr. v.* to surround; 836.
acieser, *infin.* of *refl. v.* to cease; 1633.
acoisier, *infin.* of *tr. v.* to calm; 3266.
acoisis, *past part.* of *tr. v.* acoisir to silence; 415.
acoisonouse, *adj.* concerned about; 147.
acontent, *3rd pers. pl. pr. ind.* of *tr. v.* aconter to pay; 791.
acouveta, *3rd pers. s. preterit* of *tr. v.* acouveter to cover; 2680.
acroient, *3rd pers. pl. pr. ind.* of *tr. v.* acroire to purchase on credit; 791.
ademis, *adj.* quick, prompt; 1904.
adestra, *3rd pers. s. preterit* of *tr. v.* adestrer to accompany, to lead; 421.
adolé, *past part.* of *tr. v.* adoler to afflict, to cause grief; 1531.
aesme, *3rd pers. s. pr. ind.* of *tr. v.* aesmer to aim; 2782.
afaire, *n. m. s.* condition; 2820.
afeutrement, *n. m. s.* padding; 289.
afices, *n. f. pl.* clasps; 317.
aflis, *past part.* of *tr. v.* aflire to afflict; 1813.
aigliaus, *n. m. pl.* eaglets; 3250.
aigrie, *3rd pers. s. pr. ind.* of *tr. v.* agrïer to torment; 1866.
aïmans, *n. m. pl.* loadstones; 3362.

aînc, *1st pers. s. pr. ind.* of *tr. v.* amer to love; 345.

alesne, *n. f. s.* awl; 787.

alie, *n. f. s.* sorb-apple; 692.

amaint, *1st pers. s. pr. ind.* of *tr. v.* amener to bring; 2347.

amirant, *n. m. s.* emîr; 2980.

ancele, *n. f. s.* servant; 628.

anciserie, *n. f. s.* antiquity; 3300.

anes, *n. m. pl.* ducks; 3259.

anstes, *n. f. pl.* shafts; 3399.

antie, *adj.* ancient; 349.

apaia, *3rd pers. s. preterit* of *tr. v.* apaier to calm; 526.

aparmaîn, *adv.* immediately; 1354.

apercevant, *adj.* clear; 2596.

aplanoier, *infin.* of *tr. v.* to caress, to smooth; 2917.

apoïe, *past part.* of *tr. v.* apoier to support, to lean against; 2376.

aporc, *1st pers. s. pr. ind.* of *tr. v.* aporter to bring; 2036.

aprendant, *pr. part.* of *tr. v.* aprendre to take, to lead; 3457.

aprés, *prep.* beside, near; 1847.

aprevisa, *3rd pers. s. preterit* of *tr. v.* aprivoiser to tame; 2665.

aramie, *n. f. s.* struggle, battle; 697.

araser, *infin.* of *tr. v.* to fill to the brim; 981.

arcoier, *infin.* of *tr. v.* to shoot (with bow and arrow); 2157.

argu, *n. m. s.* thought, argument; 1609.

argue, *3rd pers. s. pr. ind.* of *tr. v.* argüer to torment; 1577.

arouteement, *adv.* without ceasing; 802.

arrabiant, *adj.* Arabian; 3137.

ataces, *n. f. pl.* ornamental ribbons; 3085.

atapiner, *infin.* of *tr. v.* to hide, to distuise; 1941.

atornement, *n. m. s.* preparation; 319.

aubes, *n. f. pl.* white garments, albs; 1454.

aufriquant, *adj.* African; 3082.

avoit, *3rd pers. s. pr. subj.* of *tr. v.* avoier to guide; 114, 2267.

baé, *past part.* of *tr. v.* baer to stare, to look with astonishment; 2059.

baillius, *n. m. pl.* bails, baileys; 1759.

balloient, *3rd pers. pl. imperf.* of *intr. v.* balloier to float; 794.

baotes, *n. f. pl.* openings, ports; 993.

barat, *n. m. s.* deception; 2666.

baudequins, *n. m. pl.* silken cloth; 3082.

baus, *n. m. pl.* beams; 1001.
bernier, *n. m. pl.* huntsmen; 77.
beubance, *n. f. s.* arrogance; 197.
bisse, *n. f. s.* hind; 95.
bohordeïs, *n. f. s.* jousting; 440.
boisier, *infin.* of *tr. v.* to deceive; 1412.
boistel, *n. m. s.* bushel; 863.
bordon, *n. m. s.* pilgrim's staff; 1947.
bos, *n. m. pl.* woods; 114.
bracie, *n. f. s.* armful; 938.
brai, *n. m. s.* mud; 1190.
bronchier, *infin.* of *tr. v.* to bend, to lower; 2473.
brueroi, *n. m. s.* heath; 1777.
bruïe, *n. f. s.* fire; 683.
bruïe, *past part.* of *tr. v.* bruïr to burn; 689.
bufoi, *adj.* arrogant; 873.
buire, *n. f. s.* jug; 2431.
buirie, *n. f. s.* jugful; 2403.
burnis, *past part.* of *tr. v.* burnir to burnish; 3394.
buscier, *n. m. s.* wood, thicket; 1380.
bute, *past part.* of *tr. v.* boire to drink; 1959.
caingles, *n. f. pl.* girths; 1752.
caïr, *infin.* of *intr. v.* ceïr to fall; 3256.
caisnes, *n. m. pl.* oaks; 122.
calant, *n. m. pl.* boats; 838.
calenge, *n. f. s.* dispute; 2021.
cangie, *past part.* of *tr. v.* cangier to change, to lose; 2404.
cans, *n. m. pl.* fields; 2256.
cant, *n. m. s.* corner; 3147.
capel, *n. m. s.* hat; 2529.
capler, *infin.* of *tr. v.* to hack; 971.
cars, *n. f. s.* flesh; 146.
cariant, *pr. part.* of *tr. v.* carier to carry, to lead; 2341.
carins, *n. m. s.* train, cortege, retinue; 802.
carnins, *n. m. s.* enchantment; 1695.
carpant, *n. m. s.* talon; 2426.
casement, *n. m. s.* fief; 817.
casés, *n. m. s.* vassal; 1030.
caure, *n. f. s.* heat; 116.
cavestre, *n. m. s.* halter; 1791.
cembeler, *infin.* of *intr. v.* to fight; 896.
cembels, *n. m. s.* combat; 907.
cendé, *n. m. s.* silk; 3070.
cervelier, *n. m. s.* head, 81; cerveler, 1486.
chacier, *infin.* of *tr. v.* to hunt, 74; chachier to hide, 76.
choc, *n. m. s.* cock; 1809.
ciés, *n. m. pl.* ends; 939.

ciés, *prep.* at the place of; 1923.

claceler, *n. m. s.* keeper of keys; 617.

clains, *n. m. s.* lament, outcry; 687.

claroier, *infin.* of *tr. v.* to clear; 3255.

clau, *n. m. s.* nail; 831.

cloficier, *infin.* of *tr. v.* to attach, to affix; 1091.

clugnier, *infin.* of *tr. v.* to blink; 1269.

cofinials, *n. m. pl.* small baskets; 1312.

cointoiement, *n. m. s.* adornment; 312.

coïsa, *3rd pers. s. preterit* of *refl. v.* se soisier to be calm, to be quiet; 2173.

coitier, *infin.* of *tr. v.* to spur; 3245.

coles, *n. m. pl.* cabbages; 1818.

coloie, *3rd pers. s. pr. ind.* of *intr. v.* colier/ coloier to lower the head, to bend the neck, 2888; colie, 3007.

conniscances, *n. f. pl.* emblems; 3148.

conportant, *pr. part.* of *tr. v.* conporter to care for; 2339.

conroi, *n. m. s.* supplies; 880.

contrester, *infin.* of *tr. v.* to resist; 2425.

contretenu, *past part.* of *tr. v.* contretenir to refuse; 1598.

convenent, *n. m. s.* agreement; 2.

cor, *n. m. s.* corner, edge; 1622.

cor, *n. m. s.* horn, strength; 85.

corlius, *n. m. pl.* couriers; 774.

corsaire, *n. m. s.* lair, habitat; 1330.

cotel, *n. m. pl.* edges; 1796.

cortil, *n. m. s.* garden; 1815.

coute, *n. f. s.* mattress; 390.

coutures, *n. f. pl.* cultivated fields; 2094.

creant, *n. m. s.* promise; 1722.

crie, *3rd pers. s. pr. ind.* of *tr. v.* crier to create; 3303.

crolliere, *n. f. s.* low ground, hollow; 1060.

cuvert, *n. m. s.* wretch; 2225.

daintiés, *n. m. pl.* delicacies; 1865.

dangerer, *infin.* of *tr. v.* to care for, to control; 2073.

dangier, *n. m. s.* power, 89; difficulty, 1394; wrong, 2414; authority, 2486; will, 3201.

deceü, *adj.* deprived of; 51.

defroer, *infin.* of *tr. v.* to break down; 1134.

degis, *adj.* rejected, scorned; 3400.

delie, *adj.* fine, delicate; 1842.

delités, *n. m. pl.* pleasure; 676.

demiselage, *n. m. s.* maidenhood; 3041.

departie, *n. f. s.* distribution; 1196.

departie, *past part.* of *tr. v.* departir to dispense, to disperse; 451.

deporteron, *1st pers. pl. future* of *tr. v.* deporter to

spare; 1121.

derver, *infin.* of *intr. v.* to go mad; 1136.

descaaner, *infin.* of *tr. v.* to free, to unchain; 609.

desceplie, *n. f. s.* discipline; 707.

desci que, *conjunction* until; 110.

desertie, *n. f. s.* waste land; 481.

desevrer, *infin.* of *intr. v.* to depart; 2532.

desmanevis, *past part.* of *tr. v.* desmaneoir to lose; 2276.

despense, *n. f. s.* distribution, place of distribution; 2510.

desperer, *infin.* of *intr. v.* to despair; 1609.

desreer, *infin.* *tr. v.* to trouble, 2538; cf. desroie.

desregnent, *3rd pers. pl. pr. ind.* of *tr. v.* desregner to defend; 405.

desroie, *3rd pers. s. pr. ind.* of *intr. v.* desreer to go astray; 2894.

desrubant, *n. m. s.* steep slope, precipice; 1828.

destemprer, *infin.* of *tr. v.* to brew; 1969.

destroit, *n. m. s.* district, domaine, 113; difficulty, 124; distress, 700.

desvoleper, *infin.* of *tr. v.* to undo, to uncover; 1437.

detrïer, *infin.* of *tr. v.* to stop, 83; *intr. v.* to be slow, 1848.

deut, *3rd pers. pr. ind.* of *intr. v.* to hurt; 1241.

deviner, *infin.* of *tr. v.* to interpret, 643; to foretell, 2959.

devis, *n. m. s.* wish; 3391.

dois, *n. m. s.* table; 2144.

dolouser, *infin.* of *intr. v.* to suffer, to be in pain; 1964.

douëlis, *n. m. s.* dowry; 429.

duit, *3rd pers. s. pr. ind.* of *tr. v.* duire to govern; 59.

egueïs, *n. m. s.* dike; 2189.

el, *adv.* otherwise; 1314.

enbrievement, *n. m. s.* documentation, listing; 1010.

encargier, *infin.* of *tr. v.* to conceive; 1701.

encroer, *infin.* of *tr. v.* to hook, to hang; 1135.

endite, *3rd pers. s. pr. ind.* of *tr. v.* enditer to indicate; 752.

endroit, *prep.* around, about; 1907.

ene, *adv.* not so (with questions); 194, 2606, 2954.

enfance, *n. f. s.* foolishness, folly; 194.

enfangier, *infin.* of *tr. v.* to mire; 902.

enfers, *adj.* ill; 1957.

enon, *contraction*: in the name of; 2612.

enquarelé, *past part.* of *tr. v.* enquareler to fold into a square; 1536.

ensement, *adv.* also; 303.

enserie, *past part.* of *intr. v.* enserir to become evening;

460.

ensus, *prep.* near; 1551.

ente, *adj.* sad; 527.

entendue, *n. f. s.* intelligence, ability, attention; 1573.

entente, *n. f. s.* attack; 2531.

entesa, *3rd pers. s. preterit* of *tr. v.* enteser to draw (a bow), 2133; entoise, 2131.

entoitier, *infin.* of *tr. v.* to enclose, to shelter; 1382.

entoscier, *infin.* of *tr. v.* to poison; 1557.

entruēs, *adv.* meanwhile; 1509.

erbier, *n. m. s.* grass; 100.

erite, *adj.* vile, heretical; 148.

ermie, *n. f. s.* desert; en ermie, empty; 711.

errant, *pr. part.* of *intr. v.* errer to travel, to go; 323; *adv.* immediately, 1735.

esbanoïage, *n. m. s.* amusement, pleasure; 3035.

esbanoïement, *n. m. s.* amusement, pleasure; 743.

esbanoïer, *infin.* of *tr. v.* to amuse, to please; 3237.

escarimant, *n. m. s.* a type of cloth; 309.

escavelee, *adj.* disheveled; 1291.

escerpe, *n. f. s.* sling, scarf; 2009.

escillier, *infin.* of *tr. v.* to torment; 1248.

esclavine, *n. f. s.* pilgrim's garment; 1946.

esconser, *infin.* of *tr. v.* to hide; 566.

escorc, *n. m. s.* lap, apron; 2446.

escrivent, *n. m. s.* writer; 751.

esduit, *n. m. s.* refuge; 2353.

esfrois, *n. m. s.* noise, commotion; 2243.

eskekier, *n. m. s.* royal treasurer; 1715.

eskius, *adj.* disposed to avoid; 2186.

eskiver, *infin.* of *tr. v.* to avoid; 3351.

esligascent, *3rd pers. pl. imperf. subj.* of *tr. v.* esleecier to pay for; 307.

esloengier, *infin.* of *tr. v.* to praise; 1379.

esmerē, *past part.* of *tr. v.* esmerer to refine, to purify; 2807.

esmiudrer, *infin.* of *intr. v.* to improve; 1963.

espaorie, *past part.* of *tr. v.* espaorir to frighten; 488.

espart, *3rd pers. s. pr. ind.* of *refl. v.* s'espartir to spread, 1009; espartie, *past part. tr. v.* to shatter, to break; 497.

espeees, *past part.* of *tr. v.* espeer to pierce, to spear; 1036.

esperi, *3rd pers. s. preterit* of *refl. v.* s'esperir to awaken; 181.

esqeut, *3rd pers. s. pr. ind.* of *refl. v.* s'escorre to be rescued, to recover; 2895.

esrance, *n. f. s.*; en esrance wandering, lost; 183.

esrer, 283; see errant.
essoines, *n. m. pl.* duties, cares; preoccupations; 768.
essorber, *infin.* of *tr. v.* to destroy; 2801.
estage, *n. m. s.*; en estage in residence; 3043.
estampe, *3rd pers. s. pr. ind.* of *tr. v.* estamper to tram-
       ple; 1982.
estechier, *infin.* of *tr. v.* to strike, to pierce; 2164.
esternis, *past part.* of *tr. v.* esternir to strew; 1897.
estoper, *infin.* of *tr. v.* to prevent, to stop, 631; estou-
       per, to block, 1432.
estoré, *past part.* of *tr. v.* estorer to create, to set up;
       463.
estormie, *past part.* of *tr. v.* estormir to throw into confu-
       sion; 335.
estrelin, *adj.* sterling; 547.
esvertüés, *past part.* of *tr. v.* esvertüer to fortify; 3050.
fabloiement, *n. m. s.* speech, discussion; 2767.
fabloier, *infin.* of *intr. v.* to chat; 2920.
faerie, *n. f. s.* fairy tale; 3296.
faintise, *n. f. s.* dissimulation, deception; 1515.
faitis, *adj.* well made; 1875.
fangie, *n. f. s.* mud; 1190.
favele, *3rd pers. s. pr. ind.* of *intr. v.* faveler to lie;
       3319.
fenee, *past part.* of *tr. v.* fener to mow; 1316.
ferain, *n. m. s.* wild beast; 105.
ferrent, *adj.* iron grey; 298.
fervestie, *past part.* of *tr. v.* fervestir to outfit with
       protective armor; 1203.
feutrin, *adj.* of felt; 1948.
fierce, *adj.* proud; 873.
fierer, *infin.* of *tr. v.* to tip with metal, to shoe (an ani-
       mal); 1947.
fievés, *n. m. pl.* vassals; 382.
filatires, *n. m. pl.* phylacteries; 1278.
fillolage, *n. m. s.* the condition of a godfather with re-
       spect to a godchild; 1222.
foillie, *n. f. s.* hut; 1364.
fondis, *adj.* cast; 2202.
forcor, *adj.* larger; 2147.
forgiés, *n. m. pl.* boxes; 295.
forment, *n. m. s.* wheat; 861.
formoier, *infin.* of *intr. v.* to move about, 1257; formie,
       1354; formoiant, 3123.
fortpaïsant, *pr. part.* of *intr. v.* fortpaïsier to leave
       one's country; 3106.
forvoiés, *past part.* of *intr. v.* forvoier to lose one's way;
       1920.

fou, *n. m. s.* beech; 98.

foucie, *past part.* of *tr. v.* foucir to support; 948.

fregon, *n. m. s.* holly-tree; 1981.

fremeté, *n. f. s.* fortification; 2326.

fusiaus, *n. m. pl.* flints; 895.

gambisons, *n. m. pl.* pourpoint, doublet; 790.

gehissant, *pr. part.* of *tr. v.* gehir to admit, to state; 2723.

geudes, *n. f. pl.* foot soldiers; 825.

gisarmes, *n. f. pl.* a shafted weapon; 857.

giste, *n. f. s.* a place to lie; 147.

gius, *n. m. pl.* games; 412.

glatir, *infin.* of *intr. v.* to bark; 1806.

glise, *n. f. s.* church; 3301.

graer, *infin.* of *tr. v.* to agree, to accept; 587.

gramoient, *3rd pers. pl. imperf.* of *refl. v.* se gramoier to be saddened; 800.

grebe, *n. f. s.* manger; 2355.

guaïn, *n. m. s.* autumn; 3044.

guie, *3rd pers. s. pr. ind.* of *tr. v.* guiier to guide; 3008.

hairons, *n. m. s.* heron; 2123.

halle, *n. f. s.* heat, sun; 154.

hallé, *adj.* tanned by the sun; 175.

hascie, *n. f. s.* torment; 1248.

haterel, *n. m. s.* nape; 1065.

hauer, *infin.* of *tr. v.* to dig; 1421.

herbant, *n. m. s.* prairie; 2952.

hie, *n. f. s.* effort; a une hie, together; 936, 944.

hïent, *3rd pers. pl. pr. ind.* of *tr. v.* hïer to ram; 945.

hirecier, *infin.* of *tr. v.* to bristle; 1690.

housials, *n. m. pl.* boots; 1945.

hueïs, *n. m. s.* noise; 407.

imaginouse, *adj.* sculpted; 144.

irascue, *past part.* of *tr. v.* iraistre to anger; 1578.

jaserant, *adj.* of mail; 3118.

joïr, *infin.* of *tr. v.* to welcome, to caress, 2536; seror joïe favorite sister, 1640.

jon, *n. m. s.* reed; 654.

jonqoi, *n. m. s.* canefield, area overgrown with reeds; 884.

juns, *n. m. s.* fast; 1814.

keu, *n. m. s.* cook; 1950.

keues, *n. f. pl.* tails, stems; 479.

keute, *n. f. s.* mattress, 1842; keute painte, counterpane, 2552.

labastrie, *adj.* alabaster; 3022.

lairis, *n. m. s.* fallow ground; 1906.

langeïs, *adj.* ill (?); 2060.

langes, *n. f. pl.* decorative pendants, tongues, panels; 310.

laste, *n. m. s.* fatigue; 158.
latimier, *n. m. s.* interpreter; 1086.
leecier, *infin.* of *refl. v.* to be cheered, to be happy; 1396.
leu, *adv.* there where; 3284.
liemier, *n. m. pl.* hounds; 78.
ligeé, *n. f. s.* liege homage; 1227.
limer, *infin.* of *tr. v.* to anoint; 1480.
liste, *n. f. s.* border, edge; 3158.
litee, *n. f. s.* pregnancy; 1296.
liveïs, *adj.* venal; 2197.
lorain, *n. m. pl.* reins; 3093.
lormier, *n. m. pl.* saddlers; 3088.
luitent, *3rd pers. pl. pr. ind.* of *tr. v.* luiter to fight; 406.
luminaires, *n. m. s.* light; 1275.
main, *adv.* early; 2175.
mainburnie, *n. f. s.* guard, control; 2874.
maire, *n. f. s.* sea; 1338.
maire, *3rd pers. s. pr. ind.* of mairier to master; 2124.
mairiens, *n. m. pl.* beams, logs; 945.
maisel, *n. m. s.* carnage; 2105.
maisiere, *n. f. s.* wall; 1285.
maisnage, *n. m. s.* residence; 3053.
malage, *n. m. s.* pain, suffering; 1244.
manage, *n. m. s.* manor; 227.
manandie, *n. f. s.* domain; 331.
manant, *adj.* wealthy; 860.
mandement, *n. m. s.* residence; 750.
mangon, *n. m. s.* a type of gold coin; 1109.
manier, *adj.* of or pertaining to the hand; 85.
manieres, *n. f. pl.* manners; grant de manieres, of many kinds; 2090.
manister, *infin.* of *tr. v.* administer; 552.
marce, *n. f. s.* frontier; 71.
marcissoit, *3rd pers. s. imperf.* of *intr. v.* marcir to border, to be located; 16.
maresciê, *n. m. s.* swamp; 2016.
marine, *n. f. s.* godmother; 1451.
melaler, *n. m. s.* travail, labor; 1240.
membre, *3rd pers. s.* of *impers. v.* membrer to remember; 2208.
merc, *n. m. s.* mark; 2858.
meriele, *n. f. s.* chance, luck; 3318.
més, *n. m. s.* house; 1809.
mesaasmé, *past part.* of *tr. v.* mesaasmer to scorn; 2302.
mesciés, *n. m. pl.* misfortunes, pains; 1243.
mescreés, *2nd pers. pl. imp.* of *tr. v.* mescroire to disbe-

lieve; 3297.

mescreüe, *adj.* infidel; 1584.

meserrer, *infin.* of *intr. v.* to fail in one's duty; 569.

mesprent, *3rd pers. s. pr. ind.* of *intr. v.* mesprendre to commit a fault; 58.

mīee, *n. f. s.* crumbs; 2446.

mier, *adj.* pure, refined; 1080.

mire, *3rd pers. s. pr. subj.* of *tr. v.* merir to recompense; 2370.

mohon, *n. m. s.* stump, shoulder; 655.

moi, *n. m. s.* mesure, proper state; 881.

molie, *3rd pers. s. pr. ind.* of *intr. v.* moliier to move; 1356.

mont, *n. m. s.* world; 1954.

montenier; faucon montenier, Elenora falcon; 2151.

mors, *n. m. s.* bite; 1529.

mostre, *n. m. s.* inspection; 1702.

mucies, *past part.* of *tr. v.* mucier to hide; 474.

muetes, *n. f. pl.* packs; 83.

muier; faucon muier, intermewed falcon; 2148.

mus, *n. m. s.* mule; 1897.

nage, *n. m. s.* navigation; 3042.

naïe, *adj.* native, natural, living; 931.

najant, *pr. part.* of *tr. v.* nager to navigate; 1025.

navees, *n. f. pl.* ship loads; 1033.

nef, *n. f. s.* drinking vessel; 2167.

nequedent, *adv.* nevertheless; 1512.

nes, *adv.* even; 909.

noant, *pr. part.* of *intr. v.* noer to swim; 1024.

nöé, *past part.* of *tr. v.* noer to tie, to bind; 2819.

noëlés, noielé, *past part.* of *tr. v.* noëller to inlay; 170.

noier, *infin.* of *intr. v.* to drown; 2152.

noier, *infin.* of *tr. v.* to deny; 2466.

noircoie, *3rd pers. pr. ind.* of *intr. v.* noircoier to be black; 2908.

nontīon, *n. f. s.* announcement; 11.

norecon, *n. f. s.* act of feeding; 1322.

norois, *adj.* northern, norse; 3095.

oēs, *n. m. s.* profit, use; 303.

öes, *n. m. pl.* eggs; 1977.

oïe, *n. f. s.* sound; 334.

oire, *n. m. s.* journey, trip; 1776.

oïssor, *n. f. s.* wife; 234.

olifant, *n. m. s.* ivory; 169.

onbrage, *adj.* somber, hesitant ?; 3033.

onor, *n. m. s.* possession, position; 58.

orains, *adv.* a moment ago, just recently; 1587.

ore, *n. f. s.* breeze; 127.

orgie, *n. f. s.* barley products; 1867.
ors, *n. m. s.* gold; 1930.
ors, *n. m. s.* bear; 208.
ort, *n. m. s.* garden; 2964.
osteler, *infin.* of *tr. v.* to lodge; 1810.
ostoier, *infin.* of *intr. v.* to wage war; 1592.
ouse, *3rd pers. s. pr. ind.* of *tr. v.* oser to dare; 145.
paielle, *n. f. s.* pan; 1861.
painturés, *past part.* of *tr. v.* painturer to depict, to
            paint; 3405.
paire, *3rd pers. s. pr. subj.* of *intr. v.* paroir to appear,
        2130; parant, 2217; pert, 2058.
papines, *n. f. pl.* pap, porridge; 1492.
parage, *n. m. s.* nobility; 163.
parcanta, *3rd pers. s. preterit* of *tr. v.* parcanter to sing
            completely; 650.
parconier, *n. m. pl.* partners; 2480.
pardurable, *adj.* eternal; 1651.
parmenablement, *adv.* perpetually; 3427.
partie, *n. f. s.* difficulty, difficult situation; 702.
partue, *3rd pers. s. pr. ind.* of *tr. v.* partuer to kill;
        1579.
pasquage, *adj.* of or pertaining to Easter; 3051.
passoner, *infin.* of *tr. v.* to support by means of piles;
        976.
pastoiés, *past part.* of *tr. v.* pastoier to feed; 1923.
pavement, *n. m. s.* paved room; 389.
pelukier, *infin.* of *intr. v.* to spread feathers to dry;
        2112.
peneanchier, *n. m. s.* confessional, retreat; 1375.
peneancier, *n. m. pl.* penitants; 2925.
perece, *n. f. s.* indolence, laziness; 3124.
perriere, *n. f. s.* catapult; 1053.
pesteleīs, *n. f. s.* stamping; 409.
pials, *n. f. pl.* expensive cloth; 469.
piece, *n. f. s.*; sous piece, after a time; 1624.
piesmement, *adv.* badly, awfully; 1034.
pis, *adj.* pious; 1892.
pisons, *n. f. pl.* fish; 3153.
plaisiés, *past part.* of *tr. v.* plaisier to pleat, to fold;
        1231.
planant, *pr. part.* of *tr. v.* planer to smooth; 3165.
plentoïe, *adj.* rich, abundant; 3290.
pois, *n. f. s.* pitch; 965.
pois, *n. m. s.* weight; 2216.
porc, *1st pers. s. pr. ind.* of *tr. v.* porter to carry; 1834.
porchacant, *pr. part.* of *tr. v.* porchacier to seek; 1832.
porgarder, *infin.* of *tr. v.* to care for; 2241.

porprandoient, *3rd pers. pl. imperf.* of *tr. v.* porprendre to occupy; 798.

porquis, *3rd pers. s. preterit* of *tr. v.* porquerre to procure; 2827.

porsivir, *infin.* of *tr. v.* to pursue, to follow; 3289.

portraire, *infin.* of *tr. v.* to continue operating (war machines); 919.

porveance, *n. f. s.* provisions; 198.

posnee, *n. f. s.* boasting; 1617.

presegna, *3rd pers. s. preterit* of *tr. v.* presegnier to mark with the sign of the cross; 1478.

proisier, *infin.* of *refl. v.* to gain a worthy reputation; 3252.

pruec, *prep.* out, outside; 1477.

puer, *prep.* outside; 480.

puestic, *n. m. s.* postern; 1152.

puiant, *pr. part.* of *intr. v.* puier to climb, to go up; 2143.

puirant, *pr. part.* of *tr. v.* puirier to present, to proffer; 1982.

puisons, *n. f. pl.* potions; 1960.

pules, *n. m. s.* people; 415.

quaance, *n. f. s.* chance, luck; 182.

quaisier, *infin.* of *tr. v.* to break, to mutilate; 2168.

quans, *adv.* how many; 3332.

quaresmage, *adj.* of or pertaining to Lent; 3045.

quarials, *n. m. pl.* bolts; 858.

quarrel, *n. m. s.* block (of stone); 1102.

quartier, *n. m. s.* portion; 2472.

querka, *3rd pers. s. preterit* of *tr. v.* querker to seek; 2700.

quertials, *n. m. pl.* crenels; 1093.

quintaine, *n. f. s.* target dummy; 441.

quire, *infin.* of *tr. v.* to cook; 1977.

quis; qu'il estoient la quis, what they were seeking there; 425.

quisinaire, *n. m. s.* food; 2132.

quisines, *n. f. pl.* kitchens; 894.

quivriier, *infin.* of *tr. v.* to annoy, to disturb; 179.

rabourer, *infin.* of *tr. v.* to stuff, to pad; 1751.

racater, *infin.* of *tr. v.* to ransom; 601.

raemant, *n. m. s.* redeemer; 32.

raencons, *n. m. pl.* prisoners held for ransom; 712.

raient, *3rd pers. s. pr. ind.* of *tr. v.* raembre to ransom, to hold for ransom, pillage; 816.

ramellie, *n. f. s.* branches; 937.

ramier, *n. m. s.* woods; 1408.

ramu, *adj.* branched; 205.

ranprosne, *n. f. s.* mockery; 197.

raplenie, *past part.* of *tr. v.* raplenir to fill; 3024.

raser, *infin.* of *tr. v.* to fill to the brim; 1453.

ravoier, *infin.* of *intr. v.* to set out on one's way; 1392.

ravor, *n. f. s.* ravine; 3465.

refierer, *infin.* of *tr. v.* to reshoe; 1750.

regehir, *infin.* of *tr. v.* to admit, to state; 1519.

rekeusent, *3rd pers. pl. pr. ind.* of *tr. v.* rekeudre to sew up; 788.

relenquis, *past part.* of *tr. v.* relenquir to abandon; 1220.

renaier, *infin.* of *tr. v.* to repair; 1751.

renc, *n. m. s.* rank; 78.

renges, *n. f. pl.* rows; 947.

repaire, *n. m. s.* return; 1920.

reporpensee, *past part.* of *refl. v.* se reporpenser to reflect, to gather one's thoughts; 1624.

reprover, *infin.* of *tr. v.* to reproach, to reprove; 2790.

repus, *past part.* of *tr. v.* reponre to hide; 2840.

resbaudie, *past part.* of *tr. v.* resbaudir to awaken, to encourage, to cheer; 3286.

respaumer, *infin.* of *tr. v.* to clean, to wash; 551.

resprent, *3rd pers. s. pr. ind.* of *intr. v.* resprendre to gleam; 314.

retolu, *past part.* of *tr. v.* retolre to take back; 1606.

retraiant, *pr. part.* of *intr. v.* to return, to rise (of the tide); 3466.

reviel, *n. m. s.* pleasure, delight; 2106.

rivoier, *infin.* of *intr. v.* to go hawking (for waterfowl); 2146.

robeor, *n. m. s.* thief; 2301.

roie, *n. f. s.* stripe; 2896.

roion, *n. m. s.* kingdom; 18.

rois, *n. f. pl.* nets; 76; roit *n. f. s.*; 620.

runant, *pr. part.* of *tr. v.* runer to mumble, to intone in a low voice; 1999.

runga, *3rd pers. s. preterit* of *tr. v.* runger to ruminate; 2174.

sable, *n. m. s.* sable; 3084.

sacier, *infin.* of *tr. v.* to seize; 2784.

sain, *n. m. s.* breast; 2417.

salvegine, *n. f. s.* wild animal; 2799.

sanicle, *n. f. s.* a medicinal herb, sanicle; 1980.

sap, *n. m. s.* fir; 1435.

saucoi, *n. f. s.* willow-grove; 904.

sauf, *n. m. s.* safekeeping; 2195.

saumes, *n. f. pl.* psalms; 1999.

saumoier, *infin.* of *intr. v.* to recite (psalms); 1378.

saut, *3rd pers. s. pr. subj.* of *tr. v.* salver to save; 1821.

sauvecie, *n. f. s.* wilderness; 1358.

seciés, *past part.* of *tr. v.* secier to dry up; 2417.

secroi, *n. m. s.* secret; 874.

seent, *3rd pers. pl. pr. ind.* of *intr. v.* seïr to sit, 2079; inf., 1972; seés, 2652.

seiaus, *n. m. pl.* seals; 777.

sels, *adj.* single; 675.

selt, *3rd pers. s. pr. ind.* of *intr. v.* soloir to be accustomed to; 1319.

semonre, *infin.* of *tr. v.* to summon, to call together; 775.

sente, *n. m. s.* path; 330.

serie, *adj.* calm, serene, 487; en seris, *adv.* quietly, 1873.

servee, *past part.* of *tr. v.* server to save, to conserve; 2447.

seuc, *1st pers. s. preterit* of *tr. v.* savoir to know, to be able; 207.

sevré, *past part.* of *tr. v.* sevrer to separate, to set aside; 2833.

sié, *n. m. s.* siege; 2023.

sieme, *adj.* seventh; 511.

siet, *adv.* seven; 450.

siglatons, *n. m. s.* silk cloth; 444.

sistes, *adj.* sixth; 3469.

siute, *n. f. s.* retinue; 3204.

sohaucier, *infin.* of *tr. v.* to raise; 541.

soient, *3rd pers. pl. pr. ind.* of *tr. v.* soier to cut, to mow; 795.

soldeïs, *adj.* soldered, welded; 2192.

soner, *infin.* of *tr. v.* to report; 616.

soprent, *3rd pers. s. pr. ind.* of *tr. v.* soprendre to surprise; 3351.

sorgent, *3rd pers. pl. pr. ind.* of *intr. v.* sorgir to surge, to rush; 2412.

sorgon, *n. m. s.* source; 133.

soronder, *infin.* of *intr. v.* to overflow; 3194.

sougis, *adj.* subject; 2859.

sullent, *pr. part.* of *intr. v.* suer to sweat; 153.

surrexïon, *n. f. s.* resurrection; 615.

taie, *n. f. s.* grand mother; 1320.

tapins, *n. m. s.* cunning person; 2012.

tehir, *infin.* of *intr. v.* to grow; 1500.

tenaire, *n. m. s.* grip (?); 2134.

tenant, *pr. part.* of *tr. v.* tenir to hold; en .I. tenant, at once, 3472.

tenier, *n. m. s.* grip (?); 2156.

tenpier, *n. m. s.* storm, tempest; 3226.

tensement, *n. m. s.* protection; 1013.

tenser, *infin.*   *tr. v.* to defend; 625.

termines, *n. m. s.* terme; 25.
tierc, *adj.* third, 612; tierce, 1907.
torble, *adj.* troubled, disturbed; 1632.
tornoier, *n. m. s.* tournament; 3263.
torte, *n. f. s.* loaf; 2236.
travers, *n. m. pl.* toll; 1714.
trĕ, *n. m. s.* tent; 3063.
tres, *prep.* since; 3213.
tresmuer, *infin.* of *intr. v.* to be transformed; 2255.
trespasser, *infin.* of *tr. v.* to pass, 114; to pass over, to
            overlook, 260.
treü, *n. m. s.* tribute; 932.
triforie, *n. f. s.* border of gold engraved in a small arcade
            pattern and set with precious stones; 470. Rf. C.
            Bullock-Davies, *Medium Aevum*, 29(1960), 179.
trive, *n. f. s.* truce; 1089.
uelliere, *n. f. s.* eye socket; 1064.
uller, *infin.* of *intr. v.* to howl; 1806.
vauc, *1st pers. s. preterit* of *tr. v.* voloir to want; 2155.
vautis, *adj.* convex, vaulted; 404.
veïr, *infin.* of *tr. v.* to see; 1614.
vella, *3rd pers. s. preterit* of *intr. v.* vellier to be
            awake; 2683.
veneor, *n. m. pl.* huntsmen; 86.
vener, *infin.* of *intr. v.* to go hunting, to hunt; 2082.
venisant, *adj.* Venetian; 3134.
venteler, *infin.* of *tr. v.* to wave, to flutter; 891.
vertĕ, *n. f. s.* truth; 20.
veves, *n. m. s.* widower; 1706.
viere; ce lor est a viere, it is their opinion/ plan, 1059.
vis, *n. m. s.* opinion; 447.
vivaire, *n. m. s.* pond, fish pond; 2135.
voiier, *n. m. pl.* vicars, lieutenants; 225.
volentis, *adj.* desirous; 2882.
wel, woel, *1st pers. s. pr. ind.* of *tr. v.* voloir to want,
            5; welliés, 234.
widie, *past part.* of *tr. v.* widier to empty; 1183.
wisose, *adj.* idle, lazy; 138.
witrer, *infin.* of *refl. v.* to roll about; 130.

BEATRIX

Edited by Jan A. Nelson

For Carol

Chi coumence li roumans dou Cevalier au Chisne   92*a*
et de Godefroit de Buillon
coument il prist Jherusalem.[1]

1 Signour, or ascoutés. Ke Dex vous doinst [sïence][2]
De lui croire et orer en boine providence.
S'oiés boine cancon ki mout est de scilenche,
Ains n'oïstes si vraie en tout vostre jovence.
Ceste cancons ne viut noise ne bruit ne tence,   5
Mais doucour et ascout et grant pais et scïence.
Del Cevalier au Cisne avés oï consenche,
De ses freres ausi, de grande sapïenche;
Mais onques bien n'oïstes la premiere naiscence
Et con furent tourné a grant exillemence.   10
Ancui l'orés par moi trestout en audïence.

2 Signour, or ascoutés por Dieu l'esperitable,
Que Jhesus vous garise de l'engien au diable.
Teus i a ki vous cantent de la reonde table,
Des mantiaus engoulés de samis et de sable;   15
Mais jou ne vous voel dire ne mencogne ne fable,
Ains vous dirai cancon qui n'est mie corsable,
Quar ele est en l'estore, c'est cose veritable.
En escrit le fist mettre la bone dame Orable
Qui mout fu preus et sage, cortoise et amiable,   20
Dedens les murs d'Orenges la fort cité mirable.[3]

3 Signour, or ascoutés boine gent asolue,
S'oiés boine cancon ki n'est gaires seüe.
L'estore en a estet lonjement repounue,
Ensi con li solaus ki cuevre sous la nue,   25
Dedens une abeïe, mais or est fors issue.[4]
Des or viut nostre Sire qu'ele soit espandue
Et que par les preudoumes soit oïe et seüe.
Del Cevalier au Cisne avés cancon oüe.
Il n'a ci si viel houme ne fame si cenue   30
Qui onques en oïst la premiere venue,
De quel tiere il fu nés, mais ore est entendue.
Jel vous dirai très bien se Dex me prest aïüe.[5]

4 Signour, oiés cancon ki mout fait a löer,
Mout est bone oïr, bien fait a escouter.   35
L'estore en fu trovee en une ille de mer,
Par son droit non l'oï l'Illefort apieler.
En cele ille ot .I. roi ki fu gentius et ber.
Il ot non Orians, [cités ot a garder:][6]
Castiaus et bors et viles pour son cors ounorer;   40
Bien pot en son besoing .CM. houmes mander.

Li rois ot encor mere et s'ot moullier a per;
Sa mere ert .I. diables pour le mont encanter.
Ele ot non Matabrune, ensi l'oï noumer.   92*b*
Ja de plus male vielle n'ora nus hom parler.   45
La moulliers le signor, ki le viaire ot cler,
Ot a non Beatris, si l'oï apieler.
Mout par fu boine dame, nus ne le dut blasmer.
Matabrune la vielle ne le pot ains amer,
Ancois le vot tous jors hounir et vergonder.   50
.I. jour estoit li sire et la dame au vis cler
Monté en une tor por lor cors deporter;
Il ont gardé aval, si ont veü aler
Une povre mescine et .II. enfans porter.
Quant li sires le vit, si coumence a penser;   55
Des biaus ious de son cief coumenca a plorer.
"Ciertes," fait il; "ma dame, poi nos poons amer!
Onques Dex ne nos volt fil ne fille douner.
Je voi une mescine ki la quiert son souper
Qui en porte .II. biaus. Dieu en puet aorer!   60
Il sunt andoi jumiel ce poons nous prouver,
C'andoi sunt d'un samblant, mout sunt ingal et per."

5   "Ciertes," cou dist la dame, "vous parlés de nïent!
Ne creroie pas houme en cest siecle vivant
Que fame puist avoir ensamble c'un enfant,   65
S'a .II. houmes n'estoit livree carnelmant.
.I. en puet ele avoir, pour voir le vous creant,
Ne ja plus n'en ara a .I. engenrement."
Li sires l'entendi, si ot grant mautalant.
"Ciertes," fait il, "ma dame, vous parlés folement!   70
Dex a partout pooir, fos est ki cou n'entent."
Par sorparler a on mout grant anui sovent;
Ansi ot puis la dame, ainc n'oïstes si grant
Si con vous orés dire ains le solel coucant.
Li vespres lor aproce, li jors vait declinant.   75
La nuit se jut li sire lés la dame vaillant;
Par le plaisir de Dieu, le Pere omnipotent,
Engenra .VII. enfans a .I. engenrement.
Pour cou ne doit on dire folie a entïent.
Or revenra la dame ses fols parlers devant.   80
Mout demainent grant joie dusqu'a l'ajornement,
Li sires se leva k'est de bon entïent.
"Ciertes," dist il; "ma dame, jou sai certainement
Que vous estes encainte, Dex vous doinst tel enfant
Dont nous soiens encore honoret et joiant!"   85
La dame s'esmervelle quant son signor entent.
"Dex vous en face, sire," fait ele, "voir disant!"
Mais ne set pas la dame que prés de l'uel li pent,

Quar n'eüst si pensive tant con cuevrent li vent.
[Et la dame et li autre trestout comunalment][7]   90
Au moustier s'en alerent sans nul delaiement.
On lor fait le servise au moustier saint Vincant,
Cascuns d'aus i ofri aniel d'or u d'arjent;
Aprés messe s'en tornent Dameldieu reclamant.
Des or mais vous dirai de la dame sacant   95
Qui porta .VII. enfans jusque al delivrement.

6   La dame a ses enfans portés si con on doit
Tant que ce vint au terme que delivrer devoit.
Au delivrer la dame point de fame n'avoit
Fors la mere au signor ki nïent ne l'amoit,   100
La vielle Matabrune ki en Jhesu ne croit.
La dame se delivre a duel et a destroit
L'un enfant aprés l'autre, si con Dex le voloit.
Al nestre des enfans .VII. fees i avoit   92*c*
Qui les enfans faerent que cascun avenroit,   105
Ensi que li .I. enfes aprés l'autre naiscoit,[8]
Au col une caïne de boin argent avoit.
La vielle s'esmervelle quant les caïnes voit,
Ne set que ce puist estre n'a coi cou s'atornoit.
Li enfant furent né bel et gent et adroit,   110
Li une en estoit fille et .VI. fius i avoit.
Li vielle se pourpense c'un grant mordre feroit,
Diables le soumont cui oevre ele faisoit.
Tel cose a porpensee dont mout bien li devroit
Venir honte et anuis, se devisé estoit.   115
Dameldex l'en rendra sa deserte et son droit
Qu'ele sera hounie ancois que morte soit.

7   Li enfant furent né ensi con je vous cant,
Tout .VII. l'uns aprés l'autre a Dieu coumandement,
Ains plus bel ne nasquirent par le mien entïent.   120
Li une en estoit fille, ce trovons nous lisant,
Et li .VI. furent fil, d'un estre et d'un sanlant;
Cescuns ot a son col une caine d'arjent.
Al nestre nen ot feme ne petite ne grant
Fors la maloite vielle cui li cors Deu cravent,   125
Mere estoit au signor mais Deu n'amoit nïent,
Mout estoit couvoitouse d'avoir or et argent.
La dame a aresnié cui erent li enfant.
"Dame," ce dist la vielle, "par le cors saint Climant,
Je vous ferai ardoir a mon fil le vallant!   130
Ne vous souvient or pas del fol devisemant
Que vous jurastes Dieu, le Pere tout poisant,
C'une fenme ne puet avoir c'un seul enfant
S'a .II. houmes n'estoit livree carnelment?

Or puet dire mes fius par vostre jugement   135
Qu'a .VII. en avés jut par le vo los greant."
Quant la dame l'oï mout se va esmaiant
Quar ele apercoit bien le mauvais couvenant
Que la vielle a el cors l'anemi souduiant
Et que porcacera son anui mout pesant.   140
"Dame sainte Marie," dist la dame en plorant,
"Roïne courounee, Mere au Sauveor grant,
Ne consentés mon cors a mener laidement."
"N'a mestier," fait la vielle, "par le cors saint
                                        Vincant,
Ne vous vaut preiere .I. denier vallisant!"   145
En la sale s'en torne, s'apele .I. sien serjant.
Icil ot a non Markes, se l'estore ne ment;
Preudom ert et loiaus, avoir avoit mout grant.
Hom ert la male vielle qui le va semounant
Qu'il li face une cose dont li va depriant.   150

8   "Amis," ce dist la vielle, "je vous ai mout amé,
Rice houme vous ferai et d'avoir asasé.
Onques ne vous toli .I. denier mouneé,
Encor vous ferai bien, se je vif par aé!
Bien devés pour moi faire toute ma volenté."   155
"Dame," dist li preudom, "ja nen ert demoré
Que jou pour vous ne face quan que vous ert a gré."
"Ja ne vous en crerai," fait la vielle, "par Dé,
Tant que vous le m'aiés fianciet et juré!"
Li preudom li fiance volentiers et de gré,   160
Mais se il seüst cou qu'ele avoit en pensé
Ne li fiancast pas por l'or d'une cité.
Et la vielle li a son afaire conté.
"Amis," ce dist la vielle, "pour Sainte Trinité,   92*d*
De la fame men fil me sunt .VII. enfant né.   165
Portés les tos noier ja nem soit trestorné.
Ne m'en caut en riviere, en marois u en gué;
S'il estoient noié bien averoie ouvré.
Hastés vous, biaus amis, trop avés demoré,
Si gardés sor vos ious que bien soient celé;   170
Que se par vous estoient anonciet ne parlé,
Je vous feroie pendre a .I. arbre ramé,
Ne vous raemberroit tous l'ors d'une cité."
Quant li preudom l'entent tout a le sanc müé,
Ne l'ose contredire tant doute le maufé,   175
Se li a otroié toute sa volenté.
"Amis," ce dist la vielle, "buer fustes onques né!
Or et argent et reubes vous donrai a plenté
Et si vous francirai ains que soit l'ans passés.
Je vois pour les enfans et vous ci m'atendés."   180

"Dame," dist li preudom k'ele a espoënté,
"Vostre plaisir ferai et vostre volenté."
Puis dist entre ses dens: "Caitis! Maleürés!
Coument ferai tel mordre et tele aversité!
Ce sunt enfant le roi, ke tant a desiré."   185
La dame s'en torna, s'a les enfans trovés
Que la dame avoit mis dejouste ses costés.
Ele s'ert endormie car son cors a lasé
Et de son grant malaje travillié et pené.
Tous .VII. les prent la vielle, si les a enportés   190
La u Markes l'atent dolans et abosmés.
"Tenés or," fait la vielle, "ces .VII. desiretés.
Portés les tos noier, si ferés a mon gré.
Puis demenrons grant joie quant revenus serés,
Li mangier et li boire vous seront apresté."   195
"Dame," fait li preudom, "tout sera a vo gré."
Les enfans prent tous .VII., ses a envolepés,
Si les porte noier ja nen iert trestorné,
Se Jhesu Cris n'en pense par sa sainte bonté.

9   Or s'en va li ber Macres isi faitierement.   200
La vielle s'en retorne qui a nul bien n'entent,
Par devant .I. celier s'en pasa tout pensant,
S'a veü une ciene ki ot nouvielement
Faoné .VII. caiaus en .I. destornement.
Ele les prent tous .VII. en son gieron devant   205
Et la lisce a tuee a .I. coutiel trencant,
En .I. pus l'a gietee tost et isnelement.
A son fil est venue qui faisoit joie grant,
Qui atent la nouvele que sa [feme] ait enfant.[9]
Quant il le voit venir, si li vait au devant;   210
Bel et cortoisement le vait araisonant.
"Bien vigniés, bele mere!" dist li rois Oriant.
Et la vielle respont qui rage va pensant,
Se li a dit: "Biaus fius; trop ai mon cuer dolant!"
"De coi?" ce dist li sire, "pour le cors saint
                                 Vincant."   215
"Je le vous dirai ja sans nul delaiement.
Vostre fame a eü mout lait delivrement:
Ces .VII. ciens a eüt, n'i a nul autre enfant!
Vés les ci trestous .VII. u sunt en mon devant.
Ele a fait contre Dieu et contre toute jent,   220
Ele n'est pas loiaus, pour voir le vous creant.
Biaus fius, faite le ardoir et livrer a torment,
Il n'a plus desloial tant con cuevrent li vent."
Li sire a tel paour quant l'avresier entent   93*a*
Que il ne set que dire tant a le cuer dolent.   225
"Dame sainte Marie," fait li rois en plorant,

"Je ne quidoie pas qu'en cest siecle vivant
Euist plus loial fenme, mais or nen croi nïent,
Ne ki plus amast Dieu ne son coumandement."
Tant li a dit la vielle k'il li a en couvent   230
Qu'il l'ardra en .I. fu voiant toute sa jent.
"Biaus fius," ce dist la vielle, "trop targiés
                                        lonjement,
Justice ne doit on respiter tant ne quant."

10 "Biaus fius," ce dist la vielle qui Matabrune ot non,
   "Justice qui tant targe ne pris jou .I. bouton,   235
   Faites le tos ardoir en fu et en carbon.
   Vés ci le provement de sa dampnatïon:
   Les .VII. caiaus que j'ai ici en mon gieron.
   Biaus fius, faite le ardoir que n'i ait raencon
   Et gardés que ja n'ait por riens confiessïon."   240
   "Merci!" ce dist li sire que mout estoit preudom,
   "Quar je le pris a fenme, si nos espousa on;
   La li promis jou foi voiant maint haut baron.
   Ja par moi nen ert arse, mais je vous doins .I. don,
   Que je le gieterai en ma cartre en prison.   245
   Ja n'en istera mais, ciertes, se morte non."

11 "Biaus fius," ce dist la vielle, "qu'avés a delaier
   Que vous n'osés ardoir vostre male moullier?
   Ja n'a plus desloial tant con Dex puet jugier.
   Puis que vous ne volés ne Dieu ne vous vengier,   250
   Je le ferai saisir et a .II. sers loier
   Et jeter en vo cartre, je n'i ai que targier."
   "Mere," ce dist li sire ki redoute a pecier,
   "Faites ent vo plaisir quant nel volés laisier."
   Et la vielle s'en torne, si coumence a hucier   255
   .II. sers de pute orine, Malfaisant et Ricier.
   Ce sunt doi traïtor, si l'oï tiemognier.
   A Matabrune vienent quant l'oïrent hucier.

12 "Dame," ce dist Riciers, "vés ici Malfaisant.
   A vous soumes venu, dites vostre talent,   260
   Car nous ferons pour vous tout a vostre coumant."
   "Venés ent!" fait la vielle. Lors se met au devant,
   Jusques au lit la dame ne se vont arestant.
   Lors l'a faite saisir al put serf Malfaisant,
   Riciers les mains li lie d'une coroie grant.   265
   La vielle de ses puis le va au dos batant[10]
   Et la dame s'escrie qui le cuer ot dolant:
   "Ahi! lasse! caitive! con dur delivrement!
   Dame sainte Marie, con dolerous torment!
   Gloriouse Pucele, secor me isnelement!"   270

Ahi! lase! dolante! u sunt or mi enfant!
Trop tos les ai perdu. Li cuers de doel me fent.
A! Dex! sot onques nus icest martirement!
Jou ne forfis ainc tant, Deu en trai a garant,
C'on me deüst mener issi vilainement."   275
"Taisiés!" fait Matabrune. "C'alés vous sermonant?
Ne vous a pas mestier .I. seul denier vaillant:
Ne Dex ne hom ne fame ne vous sera garant.
Or tos," fait ele as siers, "prendés le isnelement
Et si le me gietés en la cartre plus grant."   280
Li gloton l'ont saisie et deriere et devant,
Vers la cartre l'en mainent li serf mout laidement.

13 Li serf en ont menee la dame toute nue
    Fors que d'une pelice dont ele estoit vestue.   93*b*
    En la cartre l'en mainent sans nule retenue;   285
    Drap ne cousin ne kiute n'a avoec li eüe,
    .I. poi d'estrain li jetent con une beste mue.
    Et li serf s'en retornent cui dolors est creüe:
    Par le plaisir de Deu la veüe ont perdue
    Qui ne lor iert jamais en cest siecle rendue.   290
    Mais cele ki toute a la folie meüe
    N'en a nul mal eü, diable l'ont tenue.
    Et la dame est remese dolante et israscue;
    .XV. ans fu en la cartre, poi boit et poi manjue.
    Or lairons de la dame qu'est a tort mescreüe;   295
    Si dirons des enfans qui grans paine est creüe,
    Se Jhesu Cris n'en pense ki peceors aiüe.

14 Or lairons de la dame, si dirons des enfans.
    Li peres n'en set mot, qu'est només Orians;
    Et Marques les en porte anuious et dolans.   300
    En une forest entre tous tristres et pesans
    Et va par la forest bien .II. liue[e]s grans.[11]
    A une fosse vient dont li aighe est corant
    Et Markes les a pris, del noier est hastans.
    Il oste son mantel, k'il les vot gieter ens.   305
    Dex! A cele mesnie con dolerous tormens,
    Se or ne lor aïe li Pere tous poissans!

15 Markes les a saisis por livrer a martire
    Et li enfant coumencent vers le preudoume a rire.
    Quant li preudom le voit de pitié en sospire.   310
    "E! las! caitis!" fait il. "Et que porai jou dire?
    Se ocis ces enfans m'arme en sera mout pire,
    Il sunt gentil enfant et lor pere est mes sire.
    Ciertes nes ociroie pour tout l'or d'un enpire,
    Or les coumanc a Dieu qui en soit pere et sire."   315

Les pans de son mantel tout erranment descire
Les .VII. enfans i met l'un dalés l'autre a tire,
Puis les coumande a Dieu et au baron saint Gire.

16 Markes a les enfans desor la rive mis,
    Puis les coumande a Dieu, le Roi de paradis,   320
    K'il lor soit bons aidiere, bons pere, bons amis.
    Maintenant s'en retorne courecous et maris;
    Souvent regarde arriere, Deu prie ki est pis,
    Qu'il garde les enfans de leus et d'anemis.
    A Matabrune vient ki li gieta .I. ris.   325
    "Bien vigniés," fait ele, "sunt li enfant ocis?"
    "Dame," fait li preudom, "noié sunt et malmis."
    "Ciertes," fait Matabrune, "mout estes mes amis."
    Atant demandent l'aighe, au mangier sunt assis;
    A grant plenté i orent et mallars et pietris.   330
    Li enfant sunt remés dolant et entrepris.
    Li .I. vait par son l'autre, se li cuevre le vis.
    Ne fu mais teus mervelle des le tans Anseïs.

17 Li enfant sunt remés, li .I. brait, l'autres crie.
    De pere ne de mere n'i ont il nule aïe,   335
    Li .I. vait par son l'autre coume beste esbahie.
    Cescuns a a son col sa cainette saisie.
    Des or mais vous dirai, nel vous celerai mie,
    Que la caïne au col de cascun senefie.
    Tant con aront lor caines ne poront morir mie,   340
    Mais se il les pierdoient, ce raconte lor vie,
    Cisne seroient tout, tous les jors de lor vie.
    S'il perdoient les caines, n'est nus qui m'en desdie,
    Cisne les couvient estre, l'estore le nous crie. 93*c*

18 Mout sunt grans les vertus ke les caïnes ont.   345
    N'ont garde de morir tant con il les aront,
    Mais bien soient seür, se perdues les ont,
    Cisne seront volant par les aighes del mont.
    Li .I. tume sor l'autre grant brait et grant cri font,
    Roëlant et tumant vers le fosset s'en vont.   350
    Este vous .I. hermite ki ot tout blanc le front
    Tant ot esté repus el bos desous .I. mont,
    .XXXVII. ans tous plains dedens .I. crues parfont.
    As enfans vint tout droit qui en grant peril sunt
    Dejouste le fosé dont li gué sunt parfont.   355

19 La u li enfant erent en dol et en torment
    Este vous .I. hermite ki ot mout lonjement
    Esté repus el bos, k'il n'ot veüe jent.
    De reube n'avoit il .I. seul denier vaillant:

De fuelle estoit vestus, n'ot autre vestement.   360
Quant il voit les enfans, si pleure tenrement.
"E! Dex!" fait li hermites, "par ton coumandement,
Qui moi et ces enfans as formés de nïent,
Se vostre plaisirs est k'il vivent lonjement
Envoiés lor soucours, Sire, procainement."   365
Aprés ceste parole ne tarja pas nïent
Quant une cirge vint par mi le bos courant.

20 Et quant li sains hermites ot sa proiere faite,
Este vous une cirge ki les enfans alaite
Que Dex i envoia ki tous les biens enhaite   370
Tout maugré l'anemi ki tous les maus agaite.
Quant li enfant sentirent le beste kes alaite,
Cascuns a sa mamiele sacie et a lui traite.
Bien s'en sunt li .VI. fil et la fille refaite.

21 Quant li hermites voit cou que Dex li envoie   375
En son cuer s'esmervelle et si en ot grant joie.
Les enfans prent tous .VII., en la pane les ploie.
A son ostel s'en va toute la droite voie
Et la bieste de prés tout adés le convoie
Desi a l'ermitage, la u Dex les avoie.   380
La beste les alaite et li hermites proie
Dameldieu cescun jor kes mette a boune voie.
Les enfans ont noris, ne soit nus ki nel croie,
Entre lui et la beste dedens la grant arbroie;
Mais onques n'i mangierent gastiel ne pain a broie   385
Ne autre creature, se fruit non ki rougoie
Et petites racines et mentes de ronscoie
Ancois orent .X. ans, raisons est c'on m'en croie.
On le trueve en l'estore, pour rien n'en mentiroie.

22 Les enfans ont noris de gré et volentiers   390
La beste et li hermites plus de .X. ans entiers.
Quant il furent bien grant, si vont par les rociers
Et querent lor viande par bos et par praiers.
La beste s'en retorne en la forest arier,
O l'ermite remainent qui les avoit mout ciers.   395
Racinettes manjuent et pumes de pumiers,
A mervelles [amendent] et croissent volentiers.[12]
L'ermites lor fait cotes des fuelles de loriers.
L'estore nous raconte, en l'aumaire a Poitiers,
[C'or] lor croist grans anuis et mout fors
                        encombriers,[13]   400
Quar par la forest va .I. maus hom forestiers.
Hom estoit Matabrune et si ert ses rentiers.
Al ermitage vint, li cuviers pautouniers.

Cil bastira tel plait lor signors droituriers   93*d*
Dont il aront grant paine et mout fors encombriers.   405

23 Or m'entendés, signor, Dex vous face merci.
    Cou que Dex viut sauver ne puet estre peri.
    .I. forestier ot on en cel bos establi,
    Matabrune l'avoit alevé et nouri.
    A l'iermitage vint, ensi con je vous di.   410
    Li hermites preudom estoit alés d'enki;
    Quant li enfant le virent, tout furent esbahi.
    Et li maus forestiers s'esmervilla ausi:
    "Ains mais," fait li glotons, "par les plaies de mi
    .VI[I.] si tres biaus enfans tous ensamble ne vi.[14] 415
    Les caïnes qu'il ont valent maint paresis,
    Jel dirai Matabrune ains que j'aie dormi.
    Se ma dame m'en croit, par le cors saint Remi,
    Les chaïnes d'arjent ne lor lairons ensi."

24 Li forestiers s'en torne, ne s'est pas arestés;   420
    De la maison l'ermite s'est maintenant tornés.
    L'estore nos raconte qu'il ot non Mauquarés
    Pour cou k'il ert trop fel et trop desmesurés.
    Desi a Matabrune ne s'est aseürés.
    Quant la vielle le voit, s'a les sorcius levés.   425
    "Bien vigniés," fait la viele, "quels novele[s]
                                dirés?"[15]
    "Dame," dist Malquarés, "jamais teles n'orés.
    J'ai en cel bos laiens .VII. biaus enfans trovés.
    Il sunt tout d'un samblant, d'un tans et d'un aés.
    Je ne vic ainc si biaus puis l'eure ke fui nés."   430
    Quant la vielle l'entent, li sans li est müés.
    "Amis," dist ele a lui, "foi que vous moi devés,
    Ont il nule caïne as cols? Ne me celés!"
    "Dame," fait li maus hom, "se Dex me doinst santé,
    N'i a cel n'en ait une, ja mar en douterés.   435
    Et saciés une cose, et si est verités,
    Que les caïnes valent .VII. mars d'arjent pesés.
    Ne lor remanront mie, se croire me volés."
    "Amis," ce dist la vielle, "alés, ses aportés.
    Cevalier vous ferai quant vous en revenrés."   440
    "Dame," fait li maus hom, "sempres les averés."
    "Or tos," dist Matabrune, "amis, si vous hastés.
    Se il le contredïent, si le mes ociés."[16]
    "Dame, foi que jou doi a tous caus dont sui nés,
    Se il le contredïent au branc que j'ai au lés   445
    Aront il tous les testes des hateriaus ostés."
    "Dont ert li miens voloirs," dist ele, "asoumés."

25 Quant la vielle ot la foi que cil a afïee
    Durement l'en merci et forment li agree.
    "Or tos," fait ele, "amis, n'i ait fait demoree.   450
    Gardés que la caïne soit a cascun ostee
    Et ki le contredist la tieste ait lués colpee.
    Se il estoient mort buer seroie dont nee."
    "Dame," fait li maus hom, "si ert con vous agree."
    Maintenant a li glous sa voie retornee,   455
    Matabrune est remese qui tote est forsenee.
    Marcon fist apieler sans nule demoree
    Et ele li demande la verité provee:
    Li die des enfans, ja ne li soit celee.
    Et Markes li a toute la verité contee   460
    Con li enfant l'arisent en la selve ramee.
    "Et jou en ot pitié, si soit m'arme sauvee;
    Seur .I. vivier les mis, puis fis la retornee."
    Quant la vielle l'entent mout en fu aïree.   94a
    Les ious li fist crever la vielle desfaee.   465
    "E! las!" fait li preudom. "Con male destinee!
    Jou n'ai pas deservi qu'en aie tel saudee."
    A la noise k'il font est la gens asamblee.
    Arriere l'en remaine, dolante et esgaree,
    Sa fame k'il avoit loiaument espousee.   470
    Si enfant font grant dol et ele s'est pasmee.
    Et li cuvers a tant la forest trespassee
    Qu'il vint a l'iermitage sans nule demoree
    Et a cierkiet les angles, si a traite l'espee.
    Trueve .VI. des enfans el bos sor la ramee.   475
    Or les gart nostre Sire et sa vertus nomee
    Que lor joie sera jusqu'a mout poi finee.

26 Li forestiers s'en torne ki ot non Malquarés,
    A l'ermitaje vint, le cief ot hulepés.
    Orés quel destinee, jamais tele n'orés.   480
    Li hermites preudom en ert el bos alés,
    Si avoit avoec lui .I. des enfans menés
    Quar vous savés trés bien, et si est verités,
    Quant on a .VII. enfans de sa car engenrés,
    Si en a on plus cier l'un c'on n'ait l'autre asés.   485
    Si faisoit li hermites celui dont vous oés.
    N'en i a li maus sers fors que les .VI. trouvés.
    Il a traite l'espee dont li puns fu dorés,
    Les .VI. enfans en a si fort espoëntés,
    Qu'il n'en osent mot dire. Si les a escrïés.   490
    Les caïnes lor tolt li traïtres provés
    Et cil batent lor eles, s'en est cascuns volés.
    Or sunt cil .VI. oisiel si con dire m'oés,
    Quar ensi les avoit nostre Sire faés.

Jusqu'al vivier lor pere s'en est cascuns volés.   495
Les caïnes en porte li cuvers desfaés,
Matabrune les rent qui l'en sot mout bons grés.
L'ermites est del bos arriere retornés
Avoec lui l'enfancon qui li estoit remés.
Et quant il n'a les autres en sa maison trovés   500
Mervillous dol demaine, pour poi n'est forsenés.
"E! las!" ce dist li enfes ki ert o lui alés.
"Que ferai de mes freres? Caitis! con mar fui nés!
Dame sainte Marie coument soufiert l'avés
Que on m'a ma seror et mes freres enblés?"   505

27 Li enfes est venus en la maison tout droit
A son signor l'ermite qui mout dolans estoit
Et li enfes ausi grant dolour demenoit
Pour sa suer, pour ses freres, que retrovés n'avoit.
Il les quiert ca et la, la u il les cuidoit,   510
Par le bos, par la rame, ensi con il soloit;
Mais quant par aventure trouver ne les pooit
Une eure aloit dela, autre ca revenoit,
Une eure s'aseoit et autre relevoit.
Ensi menoit sen dol et ensi les querroit,   515
Mais li preudom hermites mout le reconfortoit.
Signor, bien le savés: cou que Dex destinoit
Ne pooit demorer, mais toudis avenoit.
Or oiés grant mervelle, n'est ki le mescroit.
Bien savés que li enfes nule riens ne manjoit   520
Fors que tant li hermites por mangier li donoit:
De son pain, de ses herbes qu'en son cortel trouvoit,
Ausi coume son cors, car mout cier le tenoit.

28 Li enfes fu mout biaus et par creüs et grans,   94*b*
De membres ert bien fais et de cors couvenans,   525
Les ceviaus avoit lons jusque as piés trainans;
Sa cote n'estoit mie .II. deniers valliscans.[17]
Ses pere li bons rois qui ot non Orians
Aprés liue et demie tenoit ses casemens.
De viande avoit mout en son païs, c'ert tans;   530
De grans aumosnes faire est li rois mout pensans
Et que grant departie feroit as povres jens.
L'iermites est el bos de vivre soufraitans,
L'enfancon i envoie avoec les païsans,
De l'aumosne recoivre n'est mie escondisans.   535

29 A l'aumosne en aloit li enfes cascun jor.
Li senescaus le roi le departoit entour,
L'enfant dounoit .II. pieces pour bien et pour amor,
Quar li cuers li disoit k'il ert de franc atour.

Cascuns manjoit la soie ains k'il fust el retor,   540
Mais cil gardoit la soie, puis n'i faisoit son jor
Et retornoit arriere a l'ostel son signor.
Mais ancois k'il pasast le caingle ne la tor
Li couvenoit paser la rive en .I. destor
U el vivier sen pere estoient li contor.   545
Quant venoit a la rive, si demenoit grant plor;
Li cuers li aportoit que il fesist dolour.

30 Ilueques s'arestoit li enfes de boin aire,
Nule cose ne voit qui a lui peuist plaire.
Il pleure tenrement et si ne se puet taire,   550
Les larmes li deceurent tout aval le viaire.
Voit les cisnes nöer par mi le grant rivaire
Ki furent ja si frere et sa suer de boin aire.
Il lor giete del pain, a soi les viut atraire.
Cil counoisent lor frere, si est drois k'il i paire, 555
A lui en sunt venu et prisent a retraire.
Li cisne en sunt venu sor la rive a lor fraire[18]
Del vivier ki estoit roi Oriant lor paire,
Lonjement a tenu en sa cartre lor maire,
Qui ert laide et parfonde, hisdeuse qui mout flaire. 560
Dex l'en acat venjance, li glorïous Salvaire.

31 Tel vie demena li enfes lonjement,
.III. ans trestous pleniers k'il ne tarja nïent
K'il ne fesist adiés isi faitierement.
Puis revenoit arriere prés del avesprement   565
Tout droit a l'ermitaje u l'ermites l'atent.
Or le lairons ici, si dirons en avant.
Si volrons revenir a no coumencement.
Si dirai de la viele cui li cors Dieu cravent,
Que ele a porpensé des caïnes d'argent.   570

32 Quant Matabrune ot fait cel mortel encombrier
Isnelement et tos manda .I. loremier
Et cil i est venus, ne si vot atargier.
Quant la vielle le voit, sel prent a araisnier.
"Amis," dist ele a lui, "je te voel ci cargier   575
.VI. caïnes d'arjent qu'il vous couvient forgier.
Une coupe m'en faites, je vous en voel proier,
Et je vous en donrai mout bien vostre loiier."
"Dame," fait li orfevres, "par le cors saint Ricier,
La coupe vous ferai et le pumiel mout cier;   580
Ja n'en avrai del vostre vallisant .I. denier."
"Ciertes," fait Matabrune, "ce fait a mercier."
Maintenant s'en torna de la li loremier,
Les caïnes en porte que il volra forgier.   94*c*

Quant vint a son ostel ne si vot atargier,   585
Une en prent, la plus bele, que il vorra saier
Quel molle en pora faire et quel coupe forgier.
Cele fondi si bien, si oï tiesmognier,
Qu'il en fist .II. grans coupes sans point de delaier.
"Ains mais, si m'aït Dex," fait il a sa moullier,   590
"Ne vic tel fuison rendre ne argent ne or mier.
Eles sunt de par Dieu, ja nel vous quier noier."
"Sire," ce dist la dame, "jes irai estoier;
Encor nos en puet Dex no bien montepliier."
"Jel lo," fait li preudom, "ce fait a otroier."   595

33 Les caines estoia la dame maintenant,
    En .I. escrin les met mout bien et belement
    Et li boins loremiers d'arjent la coupe prent,
    L'une en prent avoec lui, l'autre sa fame rent.
    A Matabrune en vient ki le voit lïement,   600
    Li loremiers li fait de la coupe present.
    "Ciertes," fait Matabrune, "ci a vasciel mout jent.
    Bien ont refuisoné les caïnes d'arjent."
    Puis dist entre ses dens la vielle coiement:
    "Bien [sui] de cou delivre, alé sunt li enfant;[19]   605
    S'ore estoit la mere arse ne me fauroit nïent.
    Je le ferai ardoir tos et isnielement,
    Puis iert moie la tiere, a mon coumandement,
    Ne m'en fera mais tort nule fenme vivant."
    Atant en est venue a son fil Oriant;   610
    Par son mantiel le tire, se li dist en oiant,
    Qui estoit en la sale ouvree a pavement.
    Li rois avoit au cuer ire et dolor mout grant
    Pour sa fame jentil qui gist en tel torment.
    Atant es vous la vielle ki li vient de devant.   615
    "Biaus fius," dist Matabrune, "c'alés vous atendant?
    Tous li mondes vous tient a mauvais recreant.
    De celi ki si a esploitié malement,
    Quant vous ne volés prendre de nului venjement,
    Tous li mons te hounist et aville forment.   620
    Biaus fius, faite le ardoir et livrer a torment
    Puis prendés vostre fame au los de vostre jent."
    Tant li a dit la vielle qu'il li a en couvent
    Qu'il l'ardra en .I. fu, toute la jent voiant.
    Maintenant fait escrire li rois et garcons prent, 625
    Si mande ses barons tost et isnelement
    Viegnent veoir a cort angouscous jugement
    Qu'il fera de sa fame sans nul arestement.
    La cors fu asamblee ains le quart jor pasant;
    Or sera la dame arse, se Dex ne le desfent.   630

34 La cors est asamblee, si a grant estormie,
     Li .I. pleure et gaimente, l'autres de dolor crie
     Pour la dame vallant qui ert arse et bruie,
     Se Dameldex li rois ne li preste s'aïe.
     .I. poi lairons ici de la dame esmarie,   635
     Si dirons del hermite qui'st en sa manandie
     Et li enfes o lui ki forment se dolie
     De sa suer, de ses freres, pour cou qu'il nes a mie.
     Quant vint vers mïenuit que gens sunt endormie,
     Atant es vous .I. angele a bele conpagnie,   640
     De la clarté de lui tous li lius reflambie.
     Venus est a l'iermite et hautement li crie:
     "Bons hermites, dors tu, sains hom de bone vie?"
     "Naie," fait li hermites, "par ma barbe florie.   94*d*
     Qui est cou ki m'apele? Biaus Sire, Dex aïe!   645
     Se tu iés de par Dieu, ne me celer tu mie
     Et se n'iés boine cose ne t'arester ci mie."
     L'angeles li respondi: "Je sui de la partie
     Dameldieu le tien Pere ki tout a en baillie.
     Par moi te mande Dex, nel celerai toi mie,   650
     Que tu as .I. enfant de mout grant signorie.
     Tu ne sés ki il est, raisons est k'il te die.
     C'iert .I. hom de grant pris et de grant signorie."
     Quant li hermites l'ot vers l'angele s'umelie
     Et li angeles li conte des .VII. enfans la vie.   655

35 "Iermites," fait li angeles, "entent a ma raison.
     Li peres as enfans rois Orians a non
     Et Beatris la mere, ensi l'apiele on,
     Preudefame est et sainte de grant [relegïon].[20]
     Ele a esté .XV. ans en mout male prison.   660
     Tout cou fist Matabrune, qui ait maleïcon.
     Ele ot ces .VII. enfans d'une conjunctïon,
     Mais la mere au signor, qui le cuer ot felon,
     Les envoia noier par .I. houme a bandon.
     La u tu les trovas, la les mist li preudom.   665
     Pour cou ques laisa vivre, la vielle au cuer felon
     Les ious li fist crever a .I. mauvais garcon.
     Jhesu Cris l'en regart, ki soufri passïon,
     Ele en aura encore .I. mauvais guerredon.
     Mauquaré envoia caiens en ta maison   670
     Puis toli les caïnes a cascun enfancon.
     Or sunt cisne noant par les aighes del mont
     Et le roi fist entendre par mauvaise ocoison
     Que tout .VII. li enfant estoient caellon.
     La roïne fist ele metre en la grant prison.   675
     Or sera la dame arse, n'en ara raencon,
     Se Jhesu Cris n'en pense par son saintisme non."

36   "Or t'ai dit des enfans, coument il sunt venu.
     Demain ert la mere arse, pour voir ce saces tu,
     Se Jhesu Cris n'en pense par la soie vertu.   680
     Par moi te mande Dex, si con tu iés ses drus,
     Que l'enfant que tu as avoec toi retenu
     Voist de matin desfendre [sa mere] au branc tot nu,²¹
     A l'escu et as armes, o le ceval crenu."
     "E! Dex!" fait li hermites. "Que est cou? Ke dis tu?685
     Il ne vit onques arme ne lance ne escu,
     Ne ne quide k'il ait el siecle home vestu.
     Ciertes s'il se combat bien l'averai perdu,
     Quant il ne set del siecle vallisant .I. festu."
     "N'a mestier," fait li angeles, "trop ai ci arestu.   690
     Combatre l'estevra el non le Roi Jhesu."

37   "Iermites," fait li angeles, "ne puis plus arester.
     Fait l'enfant de matin a la cité aler,
     Garde que tu le faces asés matin lever.
     Ancois k'il soit midis le couvenra armer.   695
     Pour sa mere desfendre l'estevra adouber,
     C'on li met sus tel cose c'onques nel vot penser.
     Et puis ke Dex le viut ne pora demorer,
     Nel couviegne combatre qui qu'en doie peser.
     Se Dex li viut aidier, nus ne li puet grever."   700
     "Ciertes," fait li hermites, "mervelles t'oi conter;
     Mais puis que Dex le viut, ne l'os pas refuser.
     Sa volenté ferai cui qu'il doie grever."
     "Or dont," ce dist li angeles, "il est prés
                                   d'ajorner.   95a
     A Jhesu te coumanc, k'il m'en couvient aler."   705
     Lors s'en torne li angeles, si coumence a canter.
     Li hermites remaint ki est en grant penser
     Onques toute la nuit ne fina de penser
     Coument si jovenes enfes se sara demener
     Ne se sara aidier, se ce vient al meller.   710
     "E! Dex," dist li hermites, "ki tout as a sauver,
     Qui en la sainte Vergene te laisas aombrer
     Et en la sainte crois t'umillier et pener,
     Cis hom est fius au roi, coument pora aler
     Entre si grant barnage con j'ai oï conter?   715
     Que pora il vestir, ne en son dos jeter?
     Onques n'ot drap vestut, n'a soir ne a vesprer.
     Ferai .I. vestiment, k'il en pora porter,
     De fuelles et de rains, bien en sarai ouvrer
     Tant que Dex nostre Sire li volra el douner."   720
     Venus est a l'enfant, sel prent a apieler.
     "Or sus!" fait il. "Biaus fius, il vous couvient
                                   lever."

"Biaus peres," dist li enfes, "prés sui del creanter.
U irons [nous], biaus peres? Nel me devés celer,[22]
Biaus pere, dites moi u nous devons aler.   725
Irons en la forest pour nos cors deporter?
Je sai des boines poires sauvajes au disner,
C'est li miudres mangiers que on puist recouvrer."
Quant li hermites l'ot, si prent a souspirer.

38 Li hermites remaint et li angeles s'en va,   730
Onques puis li hermites de penser ne fina
Et mout se desconforte, forment s'esmervilla
Coument si jovenes hom la bataille fera.
Dolans est de l'enfant, quide que perdu l'a,
Mout fu en grant pensé desi k'il ajourna.   735
Et quant li jors parut l'enfant en apiela.
"Or sus!" fait il, "biaus fius!" Li enfes se leva
Et quant il fu levés l'iermite en apiela:
"Peres, ke dites vous?" Et cil respondu a:
"Par ma foi, biaus amis, je le te dirai ja.   740
Par moi te mande Dex, ja celé ne sera,
Hui cest jor pour ta mere combatre t'estevra,
On li met sus tel cose que onques nel pensa.
Li enfes s'esmervelle de cou qu'entendu a,
Quar il ne set qu'est mere, ne el mont k'il i a;   745
N'il ne set nule cose, car veües nes a.
"Sire," fait il, "qu'est mere? Et s'on le mangera?
Samble oisiel u beste? Nel me celés vous ja."
"Fius, ains est une fame qu'en ses flans te porta.
Tes peres est li rois ki ancui l'ardera.   750
Va t'ent isnelement, car ja l'eure sera.
D'unes armes de fier armer te couvenra.
La cités est mout prés, biaus fius, or i para
Coument le ferés bien, car Dex vous aidera."
"Je ne sai," fait li enfes, "coument cou avenra;   755
Mais puis ke Dex le viut, nel refuserai ja.
A Dieu, le mien cier Pere, ki tout le mont cria
Coumanc mon cors et m'arme, si soit con lui plaira."

39 "Sire," ce dist li enfes, "car me dites coument
Je me combaterai. Savés vous ent nïent?"   760
"Ciertes," fait li hermites, "j'en sai poi voirement.
Armer te couvenra, de cou sai je bien tant,
Et seras a ceval par le mien entïent."
"Quels beste est cou cevaus?" fait li enfes errant. 95*b*
"Samble u leu u lievre? Va il i[s]nelement?"[23]   765
"Ciertes," fait li hermites, "je ne sai son samblant.
Bien le counisteras, se li angeles ne ment.
Si con li cuers me dist, jel sai a entïent,

Tes peres est li rois qui a non Orïent
Et Beatris ta mere qui a le cors vallant.   770
Tu n'iés pas Crestiiens, jet di premierement
Te feras baptisier et mettre .I. non mout jent.
Elias aies non, car jou le te coumant.
Cele a non Matabrune ki t'a mis en torment
Et cil ki les caïnes osta cascun enfant   775
A a non Malquarés, nus ne set son samblant.
Et Matabrune a fait au roi a entendant
Que ta mere ot .VII. ciens a .I. acoucement,
Mais del tout ment la vielle, n'en est pas voir disant.
Tant a dit a ton pere et ariere et avant   780
Que ta mere est jugie isi vilainement
Que ele sera arse ains le solel coucant,
Se tu ne l'en delivres a l'espee trencant.
Tu as trop demoré. Va t'ent isnelement."
Et li enfes respont: "Jel lo bien et creant."   785
En la voie se met o l'iermite plorant.
Il le couvoie .I. poi par mi la forest grant.
De reube n'avoit il fors seulement itant:
Une cote de fuelles, corte ne mie grant,
Caperon i avoit et mances ensement.   790
Ensi s'en vont andoi vers la cité errant.
Ancui orés batalle, par le mien entiant,
De .II. houmes armés dolerouse et pesant
Ains n'oïstes si fort de jovenet enfant.

40 Or s'en va li bons enfes dolans et esgarés,   795
Souvent reclaime Dieu et ses sains ounorés.
De reube n'avoit plus que vous dire m'oés
Et si estoit pelus con ours encaienés,
Les ongles grans et lons et les ceviaus mellés.
La tieste hulepee n'ert pas souvent lavés.   800
Si tenoit .I. baston ki desous ert quarés,
Qui de loing le veoit bien sambloit forsenés.
A l'issue d'un bos, a l'entree d'uns prés,
A veü li hermites que c'estoit la cités.
"Biaus fius," fait li preudom, "des or mais en irés; 805
Pieca que deuise estre arriere retornés.
Biaus fius, je m'en retor et vous tos en alés.
Gardés que de bien faire ne soiés oubliés,
Mais souvent Dameldieu de bon cuer reclamés.
Ancui vous ert mestiers, que si con il fu nés,   810
Que il vous soit garans, sires et avoés."
"Ce soit mon," fait li enfes, "par ses saintes bontés."
Atant est li hermites arriere retornés
Et li enfes cemine, ne s'est aseürés,
Vers la cité son pere dolans et abosmés.   815

Mais se Dameldieu plest, le Roi de majestés,
Encore ancui sera li enfes bien armés,
Pour sa mere desfendre ricement adoubés.
De la cartre l'avoit jetee Malquarés
Par le voloir la vielle, car ses jors ert només   820
A soufrir le martire dont ses cors ert penés.
Hom en sera encore et vencus et matés
Et gira en son sanc con recreans clamés,
Se Dieu plest et l'enfant ki noier fu portés.   95c
Or coumence cancons, s'entendre le volés;   825
Apres bataille fiere, ja mais tele n'orés.

41 Or s'en va li bons enfes, ains n'i ot conpagnon
Ne conseil ne aïe, se le Damieldieu non.
De sa mere a ardoir s'aprestent li glouton,
Les espines atraient et l'estrain environ.   830
Matabrune la vielle qui a cuer de felon
Li a les mains loïes a guise de laron.
Et la dame s'escrie: "Aidiés, Dex, par vo non!
Qui aidastes Susane del mauvais faus tesmon,
Tu me souscors, biaus Sire, par ta sauvatïon!"   835
"Ciertes," fait Matabrune, "ce ne vaut .I. bouton.
Hui cest jor seras arse, ja n'aras raencon."
Li sire ert ja levés et li autre baron,
Il n'i avoit remés escuier ne garcon,
Dame ne damoisiele ne petit enfancon   840
Qui tuit n'allent veoir cele dampnatïon.
Pour la dame font doel, ja tel ne vera on.
Le jour i ot fendu maint hermin pelicon
Et maint ceviel detrait et jeté el sablon.
Ensi tel dol faisant vers le fu le maine on.   845

42 Malquarés a la dame de la cartre jetee.
Matabrune la vielle ki est mal cuivree
Li a les mains loïes d'une coroie lee.
[Et] la dame s'escrie: "Ahi! mal eüree![24]
Dame sainte Marie, Roïne couronee,   850
Souscor moi en cest jor, or est ma vie alee."
Li sierf l'ont erranment de la tor avalee.
Malquarés sone .I. cor a mout grant alenee,[25]
Tout li sierf a la vielle ont grant joie menee.
Pour la dame font dol tout cil de la contree;   855
Le jor i ot de dol mainte dame pasmee,
Deront maint pelicon, mainte crine tiree
Et mainte rice cote fendue et desciree.
As piés cïent le roi et il en a juree
Sa tieste qu'est cenue, sa couroune doree,   860
Que il nen prenderoit plain .I. val d'or rasee

Pour tant que ne fust arse et la pourre ventee.
Ensi tel dol faisant vers le fu l'ont menee.
Li sire va devant sa tieste envolepee
D'un mantiel d'escarlate, de dol est sa pensee.   865
Sour .I. grant palefroi l'ambleüre sieree
S'en va devant les autres, sa face est esploree.[26]
Atant es vous l'enfant par bone destinee
Que nori ot l'iermites en la selve ramee,
Cil dira ja tel cose qui ert bien escoutee.   870
Il entre par la porte de deviers mer salee
Et a oï la noise, le bruit et la crïee.
Il cuide que soit beste c'on ait prise et bersee.
Or cuide bien li enfes k'il ait cace trouvee,
Si con il soloit faire en l'arbroie ramee.   875
A l'entrer de le porte a la tieste levee
Et a coisi sen pere ki a cainte s'espee.
De la paour k'il ot a la coulour müee
Quant il vit le ceval a la siele doree;
Ne vosist iluec estre pour l'or d'une contree.   880

43 Li enfes s'esmervelle des que sen pere voit,
    Onques mais a ceval houme veü n'avoit.
    "Dex! aidiés!" fait li enfes qui nul mal n'i pensoit.
    "Quel beste voi jou la? Je ne sai que ce soit.   95*d*
    Espoir c'est li cevaus dont mes peres parloit."   885
    Pensant et souspirant vers sen pere vint droit.
    Il tenoit en son puing son baston bien estroit,
    Vestus estoit de fuelles, desous pelus estoit;
    Houme fol et sauvaje mervelles resambloit.
    Li angeles Dameldeu sor s'espaule seoit   890
    Et quan k'il devoit dire de bien li ensignoit;
    Le roi a apielé, ensi con il savoit.
    "Hom," fait il, "ki és tu ki si te voi adroit?
    Cou qu'est sor coi tu siés? Mout le voi fort et roit.
    Ce n'est ne cers ne dains. Sés tu or se il m'oit?   895
    Il a boines orelles. Je ne sai se il voit."
    Quant li rois le coisi et si parler l'ooit
    Volentiers euist ris mes trop grant dol avoit.[27]

44 Li rois s'esmervilla quant il coisi l'enfant
    Si faitement pelu et en tel vestiment,   900
    Bien voit n'a pas esté a vile lonjement.
    Son fil a respondu tos et isnelement.
    "Frere, c'est .I. cevaus," fait il en souspirant.
    "Coument as tu a non ki si le vas brocant?"
    "Sans faille sui li rois c'on apiele Oriant."   905
    "Biele beste est cevaus," fait li enfes riant.
    "Que c'est! Manjue il fier? Que si le va mascant!"

"Biaus frere, ains est uns frains que il va derongant.
Et tu, coument as non? Ne me celer niant."
"Jou ai a non Biaus Fius, mais des ore en avant   910
Nen ai jou point de non, pour voir le vous creant."
"Or te tais," fait li rois, "car j'ai le cuer dolant."
"Et de coi?" fait li enfes. "Pour Dieu le Raemant,
Se tu li puises t'arme rendre al jujement,
Di moi por c'as tu dol tos et isnelement."   915
"Je le te dirai ja," fait li rois Oriant.
"Dolans sui de ma fame qu'en cel fu la ardant
Le ferai ja jeter, s'en ai le cuer dolant."
"Ardoir! Dex!" fait li enfes. "Et por coi et coumant?"
"Je le te dirai ja," fait li rois, "vraiement.   920
Je cuidai avoir fame mout loial et vallant.
Bien a .XV. ans passés, par le mien entiant,
Que ele giut as ciens cors a cors carnelment
Et si en ot .VII. ciens, ce fait on entendant.
Pour c'est ele jugie a si felon tourment.   925
En cel fu que tu vois qui la art et esprent
Sera or en droit arse, mout grans pitiés m'en prent."
"E! Dex!" dist li enfes. "Con felon jugement.
Tu ne l'as pas jugie coume rois loiaument
Et se il estoit nus ki s'en traisist avant   930
Que la dame euist fait si vilain couvenent,
A l'aïde de Deu, le Pere tout poiscant,
Le ferai jou jehir hui cest jor k'il i ment."
Li rois ot si grant joie quant le vallet entent
Nel fesist on si liet por plain .I. val d'arjent.   935

45 "Amis," ce dist li rois, "que est cou ke tu dis?
Tu sambles trop bien fol et en fais et en dis.
Seulement de parler és tu forment hardis."
"Dex, aidiés!" fait li enfes. "Pour cou ke sui petis,
Dex est grans et poiscans, ce trovons és escris.   940
Mes drois me puet aidier, et li Sains Esperis.
Tu n'as en ta cort home, tant soit amanevis,
A l'aïe de Deu ne soit ancui hounis,
Se il viut tiemognier la dame peceris   96a
De si vilain pecié ke tu ici me dis."   945
Et Matabrune en maine a grans bruis et a cris,
Batant, la boine dame ki a non Beatris.
Li sires les esgarde, tous est de doel noircis.
"Dex, aidiés," fait li enfes, "ki est en paradis
Et ki fais l'aighe douce et le vin es lairis!   950
Soucorés ceste dame, droit a, j'en sui tous fis."

46 "Rois, sés tu," fait li enfes, "que jou te voel
                                   retraire?

Le mauvais traïtor ne doit nus hom atraire,
Mais ta mere te fait canter de tel gramaire
Dont tu ne veras ja Jhesu Cris el viaire　　　　　　　955
Au jour del jugement, se tu crois son afaire.
Tu n'as houme en ta cort, tant soit provos ne maire,
Qu'a l'aïe de Dieu ne li face ancui faire
Jehir que il se ment, cui qu'il doie desplaire."
Quant li sires l'entent tous li cuers l'en esclaire. 960
"Ciertes," cou dist li rois, "je volroie avoir haire
Portee .XIIII. ans, si peuises cou faire
Que jou t'oi ci iluec conter et avant traire."

47　Li rois s'esmervilla de cou k'il li ot dire,
Mout cremoit Jhesu Cris, ne l'ose contredire.　　　965
Matabrune la vielle ki ja ne soit sans ire
En amenoit la dame batant a son martire.
Aprés la dame vient de jent mout grant enpire
Qui por la dame sunt en dolor et en ire.
Matabrune la vielle ne se tient pas de rire,　　　970
Venue est a son fil, par le mantiel le tire,
Par mautalent del col li esrage et descire;
Par mout trés grant desroit s'escoumuet et aïre.
"Or pert," ce dist la vielle, "que fos en fol se mire.
Vous avés fol trouvet, n'estes pas sajes sire.　　975
Venés ent tos au fu, ke par le cors saint Sire,
Ja ert vostre fame arse, que ja nen aura mire."

48　"Mere," ce dist li rois, "vous n'estes mie saje.
Vés ici .I. enfant ki bien samble salvaje
Ki dist que peciet faites et anui et outraje,　　　980
Que vous avés la dame a tort sus mis la raje.
Et dist que il donra vers .I. home son gage
Que la dame n'a coupes de si vilain hontaje
Con sus li avés mis, n'i a point de putage."
Quant la vielle l'oï, voiant tout le barnaje,　　　985
Li couru as ceveus, plus de .C. l'en esrage.
"Dex, aidiés," fait li enfes, "ci a felon pasage.
La gloriouse Dame u Dex prist aombraje,
Ele me puist vengier de cest mal encombraje.
Ce ne me faisoit pas mes pere en l'iermitaje,　　　990
Ains me dounoit del bien k'il trouvoit el boscaje;
Mais vous m'avés douné mout pesant guiounaje.
Sire," cou dist li enfes, "coument k'il avant age,
Bataille ne fis onques, ne faire ne le sage;
Mais or le volrai faire, par le dit del barnage."　995
Cil ki l'oënt hucier, a haute vois con saje:
"Li enfes dist asés, par les sains de Cartaje.
Rois, faites l'enfant droit, il est de haut parage.

Nus hom ne puet mius dire, tant soit de fin lignaje."

49 Tout escrïent au roi: "Tenés l'enfant a droit!   1000
    Dex le puet consellier ancui, se il a droit.
    Se il estoit vestus, gentis samble et adroit."
    Et la vielle s'escrie: "Dehait ait ki cou croit!
    Que teus hom se combate, fos est ki cou kerroit. 96*b*
    Gietés la dame el fu, je n'i voi autre esploit."   1005
    "Mere," ce dist li rois, "par cel Dieu qui tout voit,
    La dame n'ert pas arse, ains saurons que ce soit.
    Se li enfes puet faire cou dont il se porvoit,
    Bien devra estre quite, drois est qu'ele le soit."
    Quant Matabrune l'ot a poi que n'esragoit;   1010
    Malquaré a hucié, .I. traïtor maloit.
    "Armés vous," fait la viele, "que ja Dex hui n'i soit!
    Si me colpés la tieste cest garcon or en droit,
    Maufé l'ont aporté que trop vescu avoit."
    "Dex, aidiés," fait li enfes ki nul mal n'i pensoit.1015
    Et la dame plorant devant le fu seoit.
    Ele ot les mains loïes d'un sein mout estroit,
    Dieu apiele et reclaime u ele se fioit.
    Malquarés vest les armes qui la bataille amoit,
    Bien cuide que la dame pour cou francir le doit   1020
    Et pour le camp conquerre cevalier le feroit.

50 "Dame," fait Malquarés, "il estuet tot premier
    Que je soie adoubés pour estre cevalier.
    A l'enfant renderai ains vespre son louier
    De cou que por la dame se fait et fort et fier.   1025
    Des armes sai jou trop, car jou ai escuier
    Esté plus de .VII. ans, puis deving forestier."
    "Ciertes," fait Matabrune, "amis, je t'ai mout cier.
    Cevaliers seras ja et auras bon destrier
    Et armeüre gente et escu de quartier.   1030
    Si avrés," dist la vielle, "quan que vous ert mestier."
    "Or tos," fait Malquarés, "mout savrai del mestier,
    Se j'estoie adoubés de gré et volentiers."
    L'armeüre aporterent a lor mal encombrier.

51 Malquarés fait les armes en la place aporter 1035
    Et dui serf li coururent maintenant aprester.
    Matabrune le fait a son voloir armer:
    Unes cauces li lacent qui mout fait a löer,
    .I. hauberc rice et fort li a fait endosser
    Que .II. fees avoient forgié ens en la mer,   1040
    Coife fort et turcoise c'on ne doit pas blasmer.
    .I. elme d'or luisant li fait el cief fremer,
    A pieres precïeuses l'ot bien fait aorner,

Ja ne fera si nuit que on ne voie cler
Con se Dex euist fait le jor enluminer.   1045
A son col li pendirent .I. escu d'or boucler[28]
A .II. lions ranpans c'on i ot fait fremer,
Puis a fait d'une cambre .XXX. espees jeter
La vielle cui diable firent si main lever.
A Malquaré les baille et il en va sevrer   1050
Les .II. millors k'il puet pour son cors agarder,
Quar campïons en doit .II. avoec lui porter.
.I. bon destrier d'Arabe li ont fait amener,
Tous fu couvers de fier, si l'ot fait ensieler.
.II. jougleors i fait la vielle vieler,   1055
Sounés et cancounettes li fait asés canter.
Malquarés s'esbaudi, si coumence a crier:
"Mar i vint li garcons, se jel puis encontrer."

52 Malquarés a tel joie que il ne set k'il face,
    Cras et gros ert li fel, bien li pert a la face.   1060
    La u il voit l'enfant durement le manace
    Que de son sanc fera anqui vilaine trace.
    "Ciertes," dist Matabrune, "bien averiés ma g[ra]se;[29]
    De sa mort que j'atent, tous li cuers me solace." 96c
    Malquarés cui ja Dex joie ne bien ne face   1065
    Est venus au destrier qui estoit en la place,
    La lance prent el puign et l'escu fort embrace.
    La vielle li a cainte l'espee de Galace,
    L'elme li met el cief qui clers est coume glace,
    Devant une escarboncle, deriere une topase.   1070
    Or est li sers armés qui Dex ma[l]die et hace.[30]

53 Or est li sers armés a male destinee,
    Ancui en puist il traire dolerouse jornee.
    Matabrune la vielle li a cainte l'espee,
    Il sali el destrier tout de plaine volee   1075
    Et prent l'escu au col par la guige doublee.
    Matabrune la vielle li douna la colee,
    Puis dist al cevalier: "Iceste voir m'agree,
    Garde ta force soit maintenant esprovee
    Et que li gars del branc ait la teste colpee.   1080
    Se jel savoie mort buer seroie onques nee."
    "Dame," fait Malquarés, "par ceste moie gree,
    Ceste cevalerie ert anqui conparee.
    Ceste lance trencans ki si est aceree
    Sera del sanc del gars ancui ensanglentee."   1085
    Mais, se Dieu plest, n'ert pas tout selonc sa pensee
    Qu'il en gira ancui envers, geule baee.
    Se Deu plest, le Poisant, et la Bone-Euree,
    La glorïouse Dame, qu'est el ciel courounee.

54 Cevaliers est li siers a sa maleïcon,   1090
    La bataille demande a force et a bandon.
    Et Matabrune apele le roi par son droit non:
    "Quar faites tos armer le vostre campïon,
    Quar li miens est tous prés a guise de baron.
    Ancui donra le vostre a boire tel pusson   1095
    C'on en pora veoir le fie et le pomon."
    "Je ne sai," fait li rois, "que dire ne que non,
    Mais cascun rende Dex son droit et sa raison."
    L'enfant a apielé belement sans tencon:
    "Frere, que feras tu? Car me di tout ton bon.   1100
    Ardera on la dame u ensi le lairon?
    Se tu te vius armer, mout bien t'armera on."
    "Sire," cou dist li enfes, "par cest mien caperon,
    La dame n'ert mais arse, se on li fait raison;
    Si avra Dex moustré Malquaré le felon,   1105
    Se la dame est coupable de ceste mesprison."
    Quant Matabrune l'ot si fu en grant fricon
    Pour poi ne li cort seure a tout .I. grant baston.
    Les sorcius abaisa et lieve le grenon
    De mautalent et d'ire rougi coume carbon.   1110

55 La vielle ot mout grant ire, bien pert a sa coulor,
    Le roi en apiela par mervillouse irour:
    "Armés vostre garcon. Ancui ara mal jour!"
    Et li enfes respont doucement par amour:
    "Vous parlés folement, c'oënt bien li plusor.   1115
    Rois jou vous pri pour Deu le nostre Creatour
    Que vous tenés a droit vostre dolante oisour.
    Ciertes, se Matabrune ert arse en .I. cau for,
    Bien li averoit Dex merité sa labour.
    A l'aïde de Dieu, le Pere creatour,   1120
    Li cuit ancui jeter .III. grans cols par irour
    Dont li tolrai tel membre dont avera paor.
    Il me couvient armer, ci n'a mais que .I. tor.
    Cil Dex qui le flor fait iscir fors de la flour 96d
    Rende cescun de nous son droit par sa doucor."   1125
    "Dous amis," fet li rois, "armes et bel atour
    Vous ballerai, si rices, onques ne vi millour."

56 Quant li enfes oï de ses armes plaidier
    Et que il les auroit pour lui esbanoier:
    "Sire," cou dist li enfes, "cou fait a merciier.   1130
    Dex le vous puist merir, mais jou vous voel priier
    Que vous primes me faites lever et baptisier.
    Se crestïens estoie, lors auroie mout cier
    Que jou fusce adoubés a loi de cevalier.
    On doit bien avant metre le Dameldeu mestier."   1135

Et li rois li respont: "Bien fait a otroier.
Raisons est c'on te face crestïener premier."
.I. abé fait venir c'on apiele Gautier
Et il i est venus sans point de delaier.
Une cuve font metre d[r]oit devant le moustier[31]   1140
Et trestout le batesme font iluec manoier.
Les clokes de la vile, cou oï tesmognier,
Sounerent de lor gré droit al mestre moustier.
Se senefie ja grant joie au coumencier.
Cil ki les cloces oënt se prendent a sainnier   1145
Et dïent que Dex fait pour la boine moullier
Miracles et vertus pour son pris essaucier
Et li abes meïsmes en va Dieu mercïer.
Des ore vont l'enfant lever et baptisier.

57 Li abes fait grant joie de cou que il entent,   1150
    L'enfant a apelé et bel et doucement:
    "Frere que dites vous, car me dit ton talent."
    Et li enfes respont: "Crestïenté demanc
    El non del Saint Espir et par le sien coumant."
    "Et jou le te donrai el non d'amendement.   1155
    Frere," cou dist li abes, "tout premerainement
    Te frai rere cel poil, trop l'as pelu et grant;
    Et rouegnier tes oncles, bien seroit avenant.
    Mius en ert et plus bel, jel sai a entïent.
    Puis seras batisiés par Dieu le Raemant."   1160
    Et li enfes respont: "Jel lo bien et creant,
    Jou ferai de par Dieu vostre coumandement."
    Et li abes meïsmes unes grans forces prent
    Et .I. pigne d'ivore que il avoit mout gent.
    L'enfant ret et röegne biel et apertement.   1165
    Au col coisist l'enfant la caïne d'arjent,
    Ne li viut demander que c'est, sel laise atant.
    .I. mantel li afuble l'abes mout lïement,
    Au moustier l'en amaine prendre baptisement.
    "Hasteés," fait li rois a l'abé en plorant,   1170
    "Quar la bataille tarje Malquaré ki l'atent.
    Or tos del baptisier pour Dieu le vous coumant,
    Ciertes jou desir mout l'eure et l'aprocement
    Qu'il face la batalle pour la dame vallant."
    "Sire," cou dist li enfes, "grans mercis vous en
                                            rent   1175
    Se li gardés son droit onor ferés mout grant."
    "Ciertes," cou dist li rois, "bien ert d'or en avant."
    "Or oi," fait Matabrune, "parler mout folement.
    Cuidiés vous que cis gars aït cuer ne hardement
    De faire la batalle vers .I. home poisant?"   1180
    Et l'abes toute voies le cresme et l'ole prent,

L'enfant baptisera, ne tarjera nïent.

58 "Enfes," ce dist li abes, "ne me celer tu pas;
Di moi tout ton pensé en oiant non en bas."   97*a*
Et li enfes respont: "Dans abes, ja l'oras.   1185
Crestïenté demanc, el non saint Nicolas.
Se crestïen me fais, sés quel non me metras?"
Et li abes respont: "Or en droit le saras."
Le mantiel li desfuble, desous fu biaus et cras.
L'abes en est parins et li dus de Monbas   1190
Et une rice dame ki ot non Solomas.
Li abes le baptise, sel met non Elias.
Quant il fu batisiés et vestus de ses dras
N'ot plus bel baceler enfresi qu'a Baudas.
"E! Dex," cou dist li enfes, "qui le mont estoras   1195
Qui a ton saint mestier or en droit atrait m'as,
Soucor hui ceste dame, si con pooir en as."

59 Li enfes fu mout liés de la crestïenté
Et l'abé et le roi en a mout mercïé.
Et li dus ses parins li promet ireté,   1200
Se il plus de lui vit, de trestout son regné.
Li abes li promet avoir a grant plenté
Et sa bone marine, cele li a douné
.I. mantiel d'escarlate et d'ermine fouré
Et .I. fustane rice, bien fait et bien ouvré,   1205
Et braies et cemise et .I. braioel doré,
Sollers et rices cauces. Tout li a apresté.
Et li enfes l'an a par grant humilité,
Doucement l'en mercie, que Dex l'en sace gré.
"E! Dex!" dist Elyas. "Or ai jou bien ouvré,   1210
Mais de cou ai jou mout le cuer gros et enflé
Que je voi cele dame mener a tel viuté.
Rois, je vous pri por Dieu et pour sa pieté
Que cevalier me faites, car trop ai demoré.
Si ferai la bataille encontre Malquaré."   1215
"Biaus amis," fait li rois, "tout a ta volenté,
Cevaliers seras ja; joie et force et bonté
Te preste li haus Rois qui maint en Trinité."

60 "Dans rois," fait Elias; pour Dieu, car vous hastés."[32]
Et li rois li respont: "Volentiers et de grés."   1220
Il voit .II. siens cousins, ses en a apielés.
"Or tos!" fait il. "Signor, alés! Si m'aportés
Le millor armeüre que vous i trouverés."
Li escuier respondent: "Si con vous coumandés!"
A la tour vienent droit, si ont aubers trovés.   1225
Elmes, cauces de fier i trouverent assés.

Les millors armeüres prendent tout de lor grés.
A l'entrer de la sale pent .I. escus listés
Que Dex i envoia par ses saintes bontés.
Il estoit trestous blans n'ert autrement dorés,   1230
D'une grant crois vermelle est bien enluminés.
Li blans de cel escu sambloit humilités.
La crois qui est vermelle, ce saciés de vretés,
Senefie justice, hardement et bontés.
Par desour fu escrit qu'Elias fu dounés.   1235
Li .I. des escuiers estoit mout bien letrés,
De la lettre en l'escrit fu mout espoëntés:
Ja nus hom ki le porte nen ert en camp montés.
S'ore l'a Elias, mais qu'il en soit armés
Pour cou que ne li tolle li cuvers Malquarés,   1240
Ancui fera tel cose dont Dex ert aorés.

61   Les armes aporterent li [vallet] natural[33]
     Et l'escu a la crois le Pere esperital,
     Onques nus hom de car a son col nen ot tal.   97*b*
     Puis li ont amené .I. mout rice cheval   1245
     O caingles et sorcaingles et lacié le poitral.
     Devant le roi le maine [ki] n'i ent[ent] nul mal.[34]
     A l'escuier a dit: "Car me dites, vasal!
     U fu pris teus escus? Onques mais ne vi tal."
     Et li vallés respont: "Au piler de crestal   1250
     Le trouvames pendant, bien resamble roial."
     "Par foi," fait Orians, "la crois en est coral.
     Bien sai c'est de par Dieu, le Pere esperital."
     "A! rois," fait Matabruńe, "ci a mout lonc jornal,
     Malquarés vous atent armés sor son ceval.   1255
     Vostre garcon donra ancui son batistal.
     Ja sa crestïentés, par icest mien mantal,
     Ne li aura mestier vallant .I. grain de sal,
     Ne li espande ancui le cerviel contreval."

62   "Dame," dist Elias, "laisiés vostre plaidier,   1260
     Mout par est cil couars ki n'ose manecier.
     Je quic par vos paroles, m'en quidiés vous cacier,
     Mais toutes vos paroles ne pris jou .I. denier.
     Ja ne verés le vespre ne le solel coucier
     Que Jhesus en rendra Malquarés son loiier   1265
     Et vous ausi le vostre, ke poi doutés pecier.
     Rois, jou vous pri por Dieu me faites cevalier,
     Ceste fame me haste de son grant encombrier."
     Li rois li respondi: "Jou le voel otriier."
     Et .II. vallet li vont unes cauces lacier,   1270
     Doi sarrasin i misent .XIIII. ans au forgier.
     .I. auberc li vestirent ainc hom ne vit plus cier.

Coife ot fort et turcoise qui mout fist a prisier,
A Elias le baillent ki s'en fait fort et fier.
Mout l'ont bien acesmé et devant et derier.   1275
Elias sent les armes, si coumence a hucier:
"Sire, Pere poiscans, con ci a dur mestier."

63 Li enfes s'esmervelle del auberc durement:
"Ainc mes," cou dist, "ne vit cotiele si pesant."
Et doi vallet li lacent l'elme cler et luisant,   1280
Pour le mius recounoistre i ot bendes d'arjent,
En Inde le Maior le forgierent Parsant;
D'outre mer la porterent doi vallet bien sacant,
Cil estoient parent le bon roi Orïent.
.I. esporons mout rices li vont lacier atant.   1285
.I. ceval li amainent c'on apele Ferrant
Ensielé d'une siele mout rice et avenant:
Li arcon en estoient d'ivore reluisant,
Les alves, li estrier a fin or flanboiant
Et les .II. estrivieres d'un orfroi bien seant   1290
Par deseure couvertes d'un rice escarimant.
Tous fu couvers de fier et deriere et devant.
Et quant li bons cevaus la couverture sent,
Si se fait orgillous et mout fier par samblant.
Elias i monterent, trestous va cancelant;   1295
Se Dex ne le tenist, ceüs fust maintenant.
L'escu li ont baillié a la crois reluisant
Et li rois li a cainte l'espee flamboiant.
La colee li doune el non d'amendement.
Puis dist: "Cevaliers soies, Dex te prest hardement 1300
De ton droit de tenir, Elias, eranment."
Il respont: "Dex l'otroit par son coumandement."

64 Elias est montés el bon destier d'Espagne,
Trestous va cancelant, de la paour se saine.   97c
De la paour k'il a li couvient k'il se pregne   1305
A l'arcon de sa siele ki fu fais en Brecegne.
Le destrier ont saisi .II. vallet de Bretagne
Grant paor ont eü jus nel giet et mehagne.
Matabrune la vielle a Mauquaré l'ensegne:
"Biaus amis," fait la viele, "se Dex me prest
                                        gaaigne, 1310
Cis gars n'a point de cuer nient plus c'oë qui sagne,
Se jou le tenoie ore la sus en la montagne,
Jou l'avroie ja mort sans point de demoragne."
"Dame," fait Malquarés qui forment le desdegne,
"Ja li ferai ma lance passer par mi l'entragne."   1315
Quant la vielle l'entent, el bon pensé se bagne:
"Ne li aura mestier vallant une castegne

Ne elmes ne aubers n'escus ne autre ensegne."
Ele esgarde Elias, dist que maus li avegne.
"Amis," fait Matabrune cele vielle brehagne,   1320
"Je vous donroie Roies, n'a tel vile en Sarcagne."
"Ciertes," fait Malquarés, "ci a fole bargagne."
Or gart Dex Elias et la soie conpagne,
La bataille sera felenesque et estragne;
Or en soit Dex au droit, coument que aprés pregne.   1325
Li sers de son ceval la couverture acesme,
Ja ne cuide tant vivre que la batalle vegne.

65 Elias est montés, trestous branle et cancele.
    Trestous va cancalant en l'arcon de la sele;
    Li couvient qu'il se pregne, qu'il tranble con
                                    brancele.   1330
    .II. vallet li ballierent une lance nouviele
    A .I. lonc fier trencant ki fu fais a Tudiele.
    Et une bone espee dont trence l'alemiele
    Baillierent Elias ki Dieu prie et apiele.
    "Dame," fait Elias, "gloriöuse Puciele   1335
    Qui le nostre Signor noris a ta mamele,
    Secor moi hui cest jor." Devant une capiele
    A faite s'orison mout gloriöuse et biele.
    Matabrune la vielle Malquaré en apiele:
    "Amis, que ferés vous? Car me dites caiele!"   1340
    "Dame," fait Malquarés cui tous li cuers reviele,
    "Et lui et le destrier meterai a la tiere.
    Ne li vaura escus nes c'une viés assciele."
    Lors jure Malquarés le fie et le bouiele
    Qu'il li espandera contreval la cierviele.   1345
    Matabrune l'entent, de joie se sautiele.
    Or sunt andui monté, cou est cose nouviele.
    La sera la batalle par desous la torriele.

66 Or ne puet la batalle atargier n'arester;
    Ensamble les couvient aprocier et meller.   1350
    "Bons rois," fait Elias, "vous m'avés fait douner
    Une reube de fier qui mout me fait peser.
    Rois, je vous pri, por Dieu ki tout a a sauver,
    Qu'en ces rues de la [vous] me faites mener.[35]
    Cel vostre cousin faites ensamble o moi mener   1355
    Et si sera, por Dieu, por moi adoctriner,
    Quar jou ne sai coument jou me doie mener."
    Et li rois li respont: "Bien le voel creanter."
    .I. sien cousin li balle qui mout est fors et ber,[36]
    D'autre part une rue l'en a fait trespasser.   1360
    "Dites," fait il, "amis qui me devés garder."
    "Je le vous dirai voir se g'i puis assener."

"Mestre," fait Elias, "le vous voel demander:
Qu'est cou sour coi je siec? Coument me puet
                                porter?"   97*d*
"Sire, c'est .I. cevaus, ja nel vous quier celer,   1365
Vous le cevaucerés pour vous aseürer."
"Mestre," fait Elias, "couvient le mi douter?"
"Nenil," fet li vallés, "soiés en bon penser."
"Coument," fait Elias, "saverai jou noumer
Cel pot que on m'a fait sor ma teste fremer?"   1370
Li vallés de pitié coumence a plorer:
"Sire, cou est .I. heaumes pour vostre cief garder."

67 "Mestre," fait Elias, "pour Dieu et por son non,
Ceste cose de fier coument a ele a non?
Pour coi i a on fait tant petit pietruison?"   1375
"Sire," fait li vallés, "auberc l'apiele on.
Li pietruis a non malle, se n'i fait se bien non."
"Et que m'a on caucié? Mout sunt agu en son."
"Sire," fait li vallés, "ce sunt doi esporon
Et ces cauces de fier, ensi les apiele on."   1380
"Mestre," fait Elias, "de cel fiere baston
Vous voel jou mout priier que m'en dites raison."
"Sire," fait li vallés, "foi que doi mon menton,
Lance l'apielent tuit, escuier et garcon."
"Mestre," fait Elias, "se Dex me doinst pardon,   1385
Onques mais de tel cose n'oï nule raison.
Mius amasce une cote close et sans gieron
Et .I. sourcot de fuelles atout le caperon
Que trestout ces harnas que ci est environ.
Et cou qu'al col me pent, pour Dieu coument a non?   1390
A ceste crois luisant ki est de vermillon!"
"Par Deu, escut l'apielent Angevin et Breton."
"Mestre, de ces coutiaus, pour Dieu, qu'en fera on?"
"Sire, cou sunt espees, cou dïent li baron."
"Mestre," fait Elias, "por le cors saint Symon,   1395
Or sai bien tout nomer. Et plus en fera on?"
"Oïl," dist li vallés, "mout bien le vous diron.
Il vous couvient combatre a .I. malvais glouton,
Il a non Malquarés, nus ne set plus felon.
En vostre lance n'a baniere ne pignon,   1400
Mais ele est fors et roide, s'ouvrés coume preudom
Devant vous le portés el fuerre de l'arcon.
Del fier en mi le pis le ferés a bandon,
Si qu'il past le hauberc, le fie et le poumon."
Et Elias respont: "A Dieu beneïcon!   1405
Se Dex me viut aidier, ne ferai se bien non."

68 "Mestre," fait Elias, "bien consillié m'avés.

En l'escu le ferrai, bien m'en sui apensés,
Et il me referra, cou sai jou de vretés.
Se il m'abat a tiere quel conseil me donrés?"   1410
"Sire," fait li vallés, "se vous estes versés
Isnelement et tos en piés vous relevés,
De ceste espee bone mout grans cos li dounés
Et l'escu et le hiaume tout li esquartelés.
Et s'une espee brise a l'autre vous prendés   1415
Et se l'autre pecoie bras a bras vous prendés.
Se desous a la tiere par force le metés,
Se venés au deseure, la tieste li colpés.
Ne vous sai plus que dire, a Dieu vous en alés."
"Maistre," fait Elias, "cis grans bastons quarés   1420
Sera bien or en droit, se jou puis, esprouvés."
Il broce le destrier des esporons dorés;
Par la vertu de Dieu, si est aseürés
Et par bone aventure dont il est enlumrés   98*a*
Vers le mur d'une tor en est le cours alés.   1425
Si fiert de tel vertu que li fiers est quasés;
Li troncons de la lance est contremont volés.
"E! Dex!" dist Elias, "s'or i fust Malquarés
Jou quic que ja fust mors et a sa fin alés."
Et li vallés li dist en riant: "N'atendés.   1430
Ancui ara mal jor li cuvers parjurés."
"Mestre," fait Elias, "por Dieu car m'aportés
Une lance nouviele et bon fier i boutés."
"Sire," fait li vallés, "si con vous coumandés."
Une lance li baille dont li fiers est quarés.   1435
"Sire," fait li vallés, "soiés preus et senés."
Vers Mauquaré s'en va, es galos est entrés.
Or ert grans la bataille, des que Jhesus fu nés
Ne fu si grans veüe de .II. houmes armés.

69 "Mestre," fait Elias, "ne lairai ne vous die,   1440
Se vous le me loés, el non sainte Marie,
Irai ferir le serf en l'escu ki flanbie."
"Sire," fait li vallés, "jou nel vous deslo mie.
Dex qui est tous poissans soit hui en vostre aïe
Et le serf doinst sen droit qui mout est plains
                                   d'envie,   1445
Mais je vous casti bien, si ne l'oubliés mie
Que vous li desfendés de par Dieu ki tout crie
Qu'il ne fiere en la crois qu'en vo escu flambie."
"Mestre," fait Elias, "qui qu'en plort ne qu'en rie,
J'irai ja asaier quele est cevalerie."   1450
Il hurte le destrier ki ne ciet ne ne plie,
Si aslonje la lance u durement se fie.
Vers Malquaré s'en vait ki fierement li crie:

"Cou qu'est! Nen as tu pas laisié ta folie!"
"Oïl," fait Elias, "mais mon sens ne lais mie."   1455
"Ciertes," fait Malquarés, "li miens cors te desfie."
Et Elias respont ki a cou n'entent mie:
"Ne sai qu'est desfiers, se Dex me beneïe;
Mais jou te ferrai ja, se ma lance ne plie."
Matabrune la vielle a haute vois s'escrie: 1460
"Biaus amis, Malquarés, faites vostre envaïe!"
Quant Malquarés l'entent tous li cors li formie,
Il hurte le destrier ne s'aseüre mie.
En mi liu de la rue ert faite l'envaïe,
De gens i ot tel prese ains tant n'en fu coisie.   1465
Par tel aïr se vienent, si con l'estore crie,
Que la tiere sous aus en est toute bondie.

70   Or iert grans la batalle, ki k'en plort ne ki cant.[37]
Il metent lor escus en mi lor pis devant,
Ambedoi s'entrevienent par tel esforcement   1470
Que la tiere sous aus en va retentissant.
Il aslongent lor lances dont li fier sunt trencant   98*b*
Mervillous cols se fierent ens es dens de devant.
Les lances furent fortes et li hauberc tenant.
Ambedoi s'entrefierent par tel aïrement   1475
Que li arcon des sieles en vont tout debrisant,
Des cevaus sunt cheü par derier maintenant
Et li destrier s'en vont par la rue fuiant.
Or oiés grant miracle et mervillouse et grant.
Li destriers Elias vint l'autre consiuant,   1480
Des darrains piés le fiert en la teste devant,
Les ious li fait voler, toute la jens voiant.
Et Mauquarés saut sus, n'i va plus atendant;
Elias, d'autre part, saut sus en son estant.[38]
Et Malquarés li passe tout porpenseement,   1485
Elias vait ferir en l'elme ki resplent,
Si k'il en a copé .II. des bendes d'argent.
Le fu en fait voler ke le virent auquant.
Se Dex ne le gardast, ocis l'eüst atant.
Et la vielle s'escrie: "Malquaré, or avant!   1490
Mar i vint li garcons, il en erent dolant."
Et Elias se taist et si fait bel samblant,
Malquaré vait ferir a loi d'oume sacant,
Tout souavet le pas, Dameldeu reclamant.
Le serf feri sor l'elme si qu'il li trence et fant, 1495
Diables l'a tenu que de mort le desfent;
Au resacier l'espee va trestous cancelant.
Or est grans la bataille, par le mien entiant,
Ainc n'oïstes tant fiere en cest siecle vivant.

71   Or sunt icil andoi au combatre venu,   1500
     Malquarés fiert l'enfant desor son elme agu,
     Si que demi l'a tout et colpé et fendu.
     Se Dex ne le gardast, tout l'euist confondu.
     "Fel gars!" fait Malquarés, "mal vous est avenu;
     Or sera la dame arse, se t'avoie vencu."   1505
     "E! glous!" fait Elias, "et pour coi i mens tu?
     Ancui t'en rende Dex ton droit par sa vertu!"
     Lors fiert le traïtour amont sor son escu,
     Si que trestout li a et colpé et fendu.
     "Outre!" fait Elias, "or te sens tu feru!"   1510
     Et ses mestres en rist quant il l'a entendu.
     Ambedoi se requierent dolant et israscu,
     Malquarés ne le prise le monté d'un festu
     Ne l'enfes Malquaré nient plus c'un home nu.
     Lors revienent ensamble et si se sunt feru,   1515
     Fierement se requierent, si c'andoi sunt caü.[39]

72   Malquarés fait grant dol quant voit mort son destrier
     Et dist: "Petit me prise, se ne me puis vengier."
     Elias vait ferir et de son elme .I. quartier
     Li a fait contreval a tiere trebucier;   1520
     Se Dex ne le gardast ki tout a a jugier,
     Fendu l'euist li sers desi que el braier.
     Et Elias fiert lui sans point de manecier,
     De son elme partie li a fait trebucier;
     Le fu en fait salir del fier et de l'acier.   1525
     Malquarés refiert lui de l'espee d'acier,
     Mais li haubers fu fors, si ne pot damagier.
     "E! Dex!" fait Elias doucement sans hucier,
     "Ja me deviés vous et souscoure et aidier.
     Sire, secourés moi, or en ai je mestier."   1530
     A .II. mains tint l'espee et l'escu de quartier,
     Malquaré vait ferir sor l'escu k'il ot cier;   98c
     Jusqu'en la boucle fait couler le branc d'acier.
     Il a estort son cop pour l'escu pecoier,
     Mais diable d'infier ki le viut engignier   1535
     Li a fait son bon branc trés par mi pecoier.
     Matabrune le voit si coumence a hucier:
     "Mar i vint li garcons la dame derainier."
     Et Malquarés meïsme le prent a manecier
     Et dist k'il le fera dedens son sanc bagnier.   1540

73   Elyas entent bien del glouton la fierté,
     Grant dol a en son cuer quant son branc voit quasé.
     Maint en ont en la place de pïeté ploré.
     Elias maintenant a le bon branc combré,
     Quar ensi li avoit ses mestres enorté.   1545

Grant aleüre va requerre le maufé.
Plus fierement se vienent que lion enpené.
Elias a le serf fierement regardé:
"Jou te desfent," fait il, "pour Sainte Trinité
Que tu vers la crois n'aies force ne poësté.   1550
Se tu fiers en la crois de mon escu listé,
Ancui t'en renra maus, cou saces de vreté."
Et Malquarés respont: "Ne pour crois ne pour Dé
Ne lairai ne te fiere de mon branc aceré."
"E! Dex!" fait Elias, "ci a cuer de maufé   1555
Qu'encontre Dameldeu as tant fort meserré."
Lors fiert le traïtor sor son elme doré,
A l'aïe de Deu li a esquartelé
Et la coife entamee et la tieste delé.
Diable l'ont tenu que ne l'a mort rüé,   1560
Mais li sers reprent cuer a sa maleürté.
"Or i para," fait il, "que Dex a em pensé.
Jou ferrai en la crois qu'il m'en sace mal gré."
Sour le crois de l'escu li a tel cop douné
Si k'Elias cancele a poi k'il n'est versé,   1565
Mais Dex ki pooir a sour la crestïenté
Fait de la crois salir .I. fu tout alumé.
En mi le vis consiut le cuvert Malquaré
Si qu'il en ot le cuer et le foie escaufé,[40]
De desous son escu le giete tout pasmé.   1570
Quant Elias le voit grant joie en a mené;
Il le quide avoir mort, si ne l'a adesé.
Matabrune le voit, s'a de paour tramblé.
Et toute la gens prie: "Sire Dex, la vreté
En amenés deseure par le vostre bonté."   1575
Le serf de pasmison ont maufé ramené.
Il est salis en piés, bien samble forsené;
Vers Elias en vient, si l'a fort escrié.
Del grant brait que il giete l'a trestout estoné.

74 Malquaré fait grant dol qui de pasmer repaire,   1580
    Il röelle les ious con felon de put aire.
    Elias vait ferir en l'elme qui resclaire
    Si que des mestres las li a colpé .II. paire.
    Or coumence li sers a l'enfant a retraire:
    "Ja li crois del escu ki si m'a fait mal traire   1585
    Ne ci aura mestier nes c'une fuelle d'aire
    Que le cuer de ton ventre ne te face ancui traire."
    "E! glous!" fait Elias, "con tu iés de put aire!
    Encontre Dameldeu ne pués tu nul mal faire."
    Matabrune l'oï, si coumenca a braire;   1590
    Malquaré escria qui n'ert pas de boin aire.

"Mere," cou dist li rois, "vous faites grant
                                contraire.   98*d*
La u on se combat ne doit on noise faire."
Et Matabrune jure le cuer et le viaire
Qu'ele ne se taira pour provost ne pour maire.   1595
Li rois en a grant dol, mais il n'en set que faire.
Lors revienent ensamble, qui que doie desplaire.

75 Or revienent ensamble ambedui pié a pié.
Elias fiert le serf el fort escu cuirié,
C'un quartier en a jus a tiere trebucié.   1600
Li siers le referi sor son elme vregié
Si que trestout li a sor le cief esmiié;
Quant Elias le sent, s'a le cuer courecié.
Li sers ot tout le sien et frait et depecié.
Les coifes sunt fausees tant ont andoi maliié.   1605
A grant mervelle en sunt ambedoi afoiblié;
Bien plus de .IIII. lances se sunt entr'eslongié.
A .I. muret de piere sunt andui apoié;˙
Tant sunt andoi mené del sanc qu'il ont laisié
Qu'il ne pueent ester, ains se sunt apoié.   1610
Tout ont pour Elias et dolour et pitié.
Et la roïne crie: "E! lasse! quel pecié!
Or ne tenrai jou mais tiere ne iretié.
Lasse! or serai jou arse, c'on a men cors jugié;
Mais cou sera a tort. Mais petit ai priié: 1615
Mon petit campïon voi ja ajenellié."

76 La dame fait grant dol pour Elias l'enfant.
Ele ot les mains loïes mout angousousement,
Si doute mout le fu ki flame durement.
Dieu apiele et reclaime et si plore forment.   1620
"Sire Dex," fait la dame, "issi veraiement
Con tu fesis le ciel par ton coumandement,
La tiere et le solel et le mer et le vent;
Et mesis les estoiles, biaus Sire, el firmament;
A t'imaje formas le premier houme, Adam,   1625
Et moullier li fesis par ton devisement;
Puis furent en infier par lor trespassement
Qu'il f[i]rent del fruit par ton deveement;[41]
En infier furent puis il et tout lor parent
Qui t'avoient servi mout bien et lonjement;   1630
Sire, pour nous jeter de cel vilain torment
Presistes en la Vergene le rice aombrement
Dont encor sunt assés li plusior mescreant,
Et passïon soufris au venredi le grant;
Et au tierc jor, biaus Sire, presis susitement;   1635
En infier en alas, si en gietas ta jent

Qui tous jors te servirent et bien et loiaument;
El ciel vous en montastes puis le delivrement;
En paradis alastes, ce dïent li auquant,
U li angeles tenoit l'espee torniant;   1640
Marie Magdelaine fesis pardonement
Et saint Piere meïsme de son renoiement;
Les enfans garesis ens el grant fu ardant
Qui une nuit i furent jusqu'a l'ajornement;
Quant la gens i alerent au matin en plorant   1645
Ses troverent tous .III. en la flame juant;
Dex, isi con c'est voirs et que jou bien l'entent,
Me desfendés, biaus Sire, de cest jor hui issant.
Et si con a tort sui menee laidement
Soucorés hui, biaus Sire, cel cevalier enfant   1650
Qui pour moi se combat a cel serf malfaisant."
Lors ciet la dame a tiere, de paor va tramblant;   99*a*
Quant .I. dus le conforte c'on apiele Elinant.
Se li dist doucement: "Ne vous esmaiés tant.
Vés encor Elias, la merci Dieu, vivant;   1655
Ansi est tout en Dieu con au coumencement."
Et la dame se test qui ot le cuer dolant;
Ses mains jointes, esgarde tot droit vers Oriant.

77 La dame se dolouse, pour Elias s'esmaie;
    Deu apiele et reclaime que de peril le traie.   1660
    Et Elias saut sus que plus ne si delaie.
    Il a traite l'espee c'on noume Murgalaie,
    Vers Mauquaré s'en va ki li sane sa plaie
    Que il ne garde l'eure que a la tiere caie.
    Il est venus au serf, sa bone espee asaie   1665
    Et Mauquarés saut sus, que plus ne si delaie,
    L'escu devant le pis. Dex doinst qu'il en braie!
    De sa grant traïson li doinst Dex sa manaie!
    "Ciertes," fait Matabrune, "ne garc l'eure que j'aie
    Grant dol car tous le cuers de la paour m'esmaie;   1670
    Ci ne me puet aidier ne carmes ne caraie.
    Cis garcons est plus fiers que .I. gains ki abaie."

78 Quant Matabrune voit maté son campïon
    De mautalent et d'ire a levé le grenon.
    "Li diable," fait ele, "enportent cel garcon   1675
    Que jou nel vi hui mais si fort ne si felon."
    Elias a estors va ferir le glouton,
    L'escu li a perciẽ ki estoit a lion
    Et le hauberc del dos plus d'un piẽ environ.
    La coife fu si fort ains tele ne vit on   1680
    Et Elias enpoint le fier de tel randon
    Que la trẽs bone espee n'i pot avoir fuison:

Trés par mi le pecoie. E! Dex! quel mesprison!
Matabrune s'escrie, cui qu'en poist ne qui non:
"Or sera la dame arse, dalés li son garcon."   1685
"Ciertes," fait Malquarés, "gars de pute saison
Ne vous ne vostre crois ne pris jou .I. bouton.
Jou ferrai en la crois si que tout li baron
Le poront bien veoir ki ci sunt environ."
Et Elias respont: "Jou oi parler bricon.   1690
Se Dieu plest ki soufri et mort et pasïon,
Vous en arés ancui le vostre gueredon."
Malquarés n'avoit cure de conter tel sermon,
Sor la crois de l'escu va ferir a bandon.
Par la force de Dieu et par le sien saint non   1695
Descendi une nue ki fist mal al gloton,
La veüe li torble par tel devisïon
Ne veïst une goute por le tresor Othon.
Or oiés le miracle, le grant demostrison.

79   Malquarés fiert la crois, qui que en ait pesance.   1700
     Par la force de Dieu ki par tout a poissance
     Descendi une nue par grant senefiance.
     Malquaré le felon a mis en tel balance
     Ne veïst une goute pour trestout l'or de France.
     Or ara la roïne procainement venjance   1705
     Del traïtor felon qui Dex doinst mesestance,
     Par cui ses fius perdi et sa fille la france.
     Li sers pert la veüe, qui qu'en plort ne ki cante.
     Or ne fait Matabrune ne bal ne ju ne danse
     Et la gens prïent Dieu qu'Elias face aidance.   1710
     Or li sers est ceüs qui n'a point de creance
     Et Elias li saut de plain cours sor la pance,   99*b*
     La teste li debat a .I. troncon de lance.

80   Or oiés grant mervelle k'il avint al enfant.
     La tieste li debat del troncon maintenant.   1715
     Del copon de l'espee qu'encor el pug li pent
     Li decolpe les las de son elme luisant.
     Malquarés ot paor et angouse mout grant,
     A haute vois escrie: "Jou me rent recreant!"
     Et Elias respont: "De cou ne sai nïent.   1720
     Mes mestres me dist bien que nul acordement
     N'en prenge, mais la teste te colpe maintenant."
     Matabrune la vielle quant Elias entent
     S'en va grant aleüre par mi la gent fuiant;
     Nus ne le vot tenir, car mere ert Oriant.   1725
     Sor .I. ronci sans sele est montee erranment,
     Ains ne fina de poindre; si vint a Malbruiant,
     .I. castel fort et rice et del tout bien seant.

Mout le fait bien garnir de vin et de forment,
De quariaus d'arbalestre, qu'ele doute forment   1730
Qu'Elias ne li face .I. anui mout pesant.
Et a mandé ses sers et trestoute sa jent
Que il viegnent a li a lor esforcement,
Et il i sunt venu sans nul delaiement.
Cil ki sunt en la place prïent tot pour l'enfant.   1735
Del relever se paine Malquarés durement.
Elias a l'espee li colpe maintenant
La teste atout le haume, toute la jent voiant.
Puis est salis en piés, le roi en fait present.

81 Quant Elias li enfes ot Malquaré ocis   1740
La teste atout le heaume rent le roi tous joïs.
"Rois," cou dist Elias, "ai jou noient mespris?"
"Nenil," cou dist li rois, "Elyas biaus amis."
Lors corent jentil houme or .IIII. or .V. or .VI.
La dame desloier, joie font et grans cris;   1745
Et ele s'ajenoulle desor .I. marbre bis,
Dameldeu en rent grases et les soies mercis.
Lors cort a Elias, se li baise le vis.
"Fuiés!" fait Elias que ele tenoit pris,
"Mais s'il a ci nul houme qui ait non Markes vis,   1750
Jou vous pri durement que tos me soit tramis.
Il a les ious crevés, li mesfais m'en fu dis
Par .I. angele Jhesu ki vint de paradis.
Ensi le me conta mes pere ens el lairis.
Et cou fu por la dame et pour ses oirs petis   1755
Que Matabrune tient tant fort a peceris,
Mais ancois qu'il soit vespres ne li jors aconplis
Sarés la verité bien en soiés tous fis."
Markes est en la place dolerous et pensis,
A lui en est venus, ne fait ne ju ne ris.   1760
"Sire, veés me ci qui a tort fui malmis;
Ce fu por bien afaire que ensi fui hounis."
"Pieca que jou le sai et tu le me jehis."
Elias le regarde, si l'a par le puig pris:
"E! Dex!" dist Elias, "bons Rois de paradis,   1765
Esgardés cest preudoume qu'est a tort entrepris.
S'il ne fust, bien le sai, ne fuse or pas vis."
Puis li alaine es ious si con hom bien apris,
Par la force de Dieu le Roi de paradis
Est Marques ralumés. De joie s'est asis;   1770
N'i a cel ki de joie ne soit forment pensis.
"Dex, aidiés!" fait li rois, "icis est de haut pris. 99c
Dex l'a ci envoié, ne sai de quel païs;
Je voel savoir son estre, par la loi dont sui vis."

82 Marques ot mout grant joie, Dieu aore et son non;   1775
    Et maint des autres font grant joie pour Marcon.
    Li rois prent Elias par son jentil menton,
    Se li baise les ious et la clere facon.
    "Elias," fait li rois, "di moi en gueredon
    De quel tiere vous estes et de quel region.   1780
    Nel me seler, pour Dieu ki soufri passion."
    "Sire," fait Elias, "foi que doi saint Simon
    Mout m'avés conjuré, s'en orés la raison."

83 "Bons rois," fait Elias, "quant volés vous savoir
    Ki jou sui, volentiers vous en dirai le voir.   1785
    Sire, vostre fius sui. Icou saciés pour voir.
    Souvienroit il vous ore," fait Elias, "d'un soir
    Que ma mere vous dist que ne poroit avoir
    Fame plus d'un enfant? Ne dist mie savoir.
    Celui ki me nori el bos a son manoir   1790
    Manda Dex par .I. angele, par son digne voloir,
    Que cele nuit geüstes a li par bon espoir;
    .VII. enfans engenrastes par Dameldeu voloir:
    .VI. fius et une fille. Or ne sai lor manoir.
    Et jou en sui li .I. ki puis encor valoir."   1795
    "E! Dex!" fait Orians, "u sunt dont li autre oir?"

84 "Oiés," fait Elias, "u il sunt et coument;
    Mout ont esté tout .VII. malmené li enfant.
    La nuit quant fumes né a Dieu coumandement
    Ot cescuns a son col sa caïne d'argent.   1800
    Par le consel ta mere qu'est alee fuiant
    Fumes porté noier en une aighe corant.
    Marques ke vous veés ci ilueques devant
    Nous enporta noier, jou l'en trai a garant.
    Sor une aighe nos mist, si nos laisa atant.   1805
    Par le plaisir de Dieu, le Pere tout poissant,
    Nous trova .I. hermites de mout bon entient,
    Au mius k'il onques pot nous nori doucement
    Et une cirge ausi nous alaitoit sovent.
    Matabrune la vielle par son encantement   1810
    Nous envoia tolir nos caïnes d'arjent.
    Et les caïnes erent de tel afaitement
    Quant nous les avïons, si somes biel et jent.
    Vés encor ci la moie a mon col u il pent!
    Cil ki perdent les lor cisne sunt lor vivant.   1815
    Vés encore mes freres et ma serour vallant
    La jus en vo vivier u sunt cisne noant."
    Quant li rois l'entendi, si plora tenremant;
    La roïne se pasme sans point d'arestement.
    Atant es vous venu le loremier vallant   1820

Qui n'ot forgié mais une des caïnes d'arjent.
Quant il ot entendu la mervelle si grant,
Dont se retorne arriere a l'ostel lïement
Et a pris les caïnes, si s'en torna atant;
Et vint a Elias sans point d'arestement.   1825
"Sire," fait li orfevres, "de cou vous fac present.
Ore tenés ces .V., tant ai de remanant.
La siste n'arés mie, jou vous en fac creant.
Matabrune en fist faire une coupe d'arjent,
Plus fuisona li une que .VI. mons d'autre arjent   1830
Et jou les ai gardees des ici jusqu'a tant."
Elias l'en mercie, sel francist maintenant   99*d*
Et li rois li otroie mout deboinairemant.
Or lor a li preudom conté tout l'airemant.
Elias en apiele la roïne en riant: 1835
"Mere, encor arés joie, jou quic, procainemant.
Venés [ent] aprés moi trestout petit et grant[42]
Ja verés grant mervelle, par le Jhesu coumant."
Desi sor le vivier n'i ot arestement.
Elias lor coumande a seïr maintenant   1840
Et il s'asïent tout mainte coumunalment.
Lors apiele les cines et il vienent courant,
Tres par mi le vivier vienent joie faisant
Si con soloient faire pour lor pasturement.
Entor lor frere vienent de lor biés betelant[43]   1845
Et de lor blances eles revienent aletant.

85 Trestout assis se sunt duc et prince et demaine,
    Dames et cevalier tout contreval l'araine.
    Li cisne sunt venu, cescuns grant joie maine;
    Cescuns estoit plus blans que ne soit nois ne laine.1850
    Elyas a cascun redouné sa caïne:
    Li .IIII. en sunt vallet el non de bone estraine
    Et li cuinkime fille plus bele que sieraine.
    Li .I. i a fali et cil seus est en paine;
    Par .III. fois est pasmés, puis brait a grant
                                       alaine.   1855
    A son bec se demaine, toute la cars li saine.
    Tuit plorent de pitié pour le dol que il maine.

86 Li cisnes s'en retorne arriere tous dolans
    Et li rois fait grant joie de ses autres enfans.
    La dame s'esjoïst et s'est ses cuers dolans.   1860
    Pour celui qui est cisnes fait dol, car c'est piés
                                       grans.[44]

    Les enfans ont donés mout rices garnimens.
    Forment sunt esbahi, car petis est lor sens,
    Pres d'Elias se tienent ki ert lor counissans.

Atant s'en retornerent en la vile les jens,   1865
Li rois et la roïne en mainent lor enfans.
La bone Beatris et li rois Orians,
Par amours est entr'aus fais li açordemens.
Et Elias s'afice con de grans entiens
Que s'il puet esploitier et Dex li soit aidans   1870
Il volra Matabrune courecier ainc lonc tans.
Par la place s'en torne ki est et bele et grans
U Malquarés gisoit sans teste, tous sanglens.
En .I. fossé le gietent ki ert ors et puans;
Diable enportent l'arme, teus fu ses paiemens.   1875
Il ont mandé .I. prestre ki avoit non Jehans;
Aighe font avoir en .I. fons lés et grans,
Des or batisera li prestres les enfans.

87 Li prestres fait tous nus les enfans desvestir;
Dames et cevaliers ot assés a tenir,   1880
Li prestres les baptise el non del Saint Espir.
Les nons vous en dirai, se les volés oïr:
L'uns ot non Orians, ne vous en quier mentir;
Li autres Orïens et Dex le puist tehir;
Et li tiers Zacarie, Dex le puist beneïr;   1885
Li quars ot non Jehans, cou fu a Dieu plaisir;
Et la fille Rosette, on le puet bien tenir
A la plus bele dame ki fust dusqu'a Montir.
Quant furent baptisié, si les font revestir.
Or les amende Dex cascun a son plaisir.   1890
Or coumence tele oevre, bien le vous puis jehir,
Dont encor couvenra maint cevalier morir.   100a
Matabrune la vielle en puist a mal venir;
Si fra ele par tans, n'i puet mie falir.

88 Or aproce li termes et par tans avenra,   1895
Se Dieu plest, le Signour ki tout le mont forma,
De cou que a ouvré et de cou ke fait a.
"Segnour," cou dist le rois, "vescu ai grant piece a;
Bien a passé .C. ans et ma vie s'en va,
La couroune voel rendre Elias que voi la."   1900
Tout li ont respondu: "Dehait ki le laira!"
Et l'oumage des princes trestout li otria.
La li otrient tout et il les merchia.
Au moustier l'ont mené, li rois le corouna;
Rice fu li ofrande que sour l'autel posa.   1905
"Signour," fait Elias, "ne vous celerai ja.
Des or verrai jou bien ki mes amis sera.
Matabrune la vielle grant anui fait nous a,
Ma mere a fait grant honte, mon frere tolu m'a;
Mais par la foi ke doi celui ki me fourma,   1910

Ja ancois la semaine toute ne passera
Que li ferai jehir coument esploitié a."

89 "Signour," fait Elias, "fait m'avés feauté.
Or voús pri et coumanc que cescuns ait mené
Ses os a Malbruiant ains le quart jor passé;   1915
Qui plus en amenra, icil aura mon gré."
Et il respondent tout: "A vostre volenté!"
Cescuns prie, la vielle, k'ele ait male santé.
Et .I. garcons s'en tourne, cousins ert Malquaré,
Matabrune va dire cou k'il a escouté.   1920
Quant la vielle l'entent si a le sanc müé.
Ele entent qu'Elias a li rois courouné.
Ele tint .I. coutiel trencant et afilé,
Celui ki le mesage li avoit aporté
En fiert en mi le pis, si l'a jus mort rüé.   1925
"Dame," font li baron, "vous avés a mal ouvré
Quant le garcon avés pour nïent afolé."
"Signour," cou dist la vielle, "j'ai tout le sens müé;
Mout m'en poise forment, mais ce m'ont fait malfé.
Dont n'avés vous oï k'Elias a pensé   1930
Qui me cuide asegier ains le quart jor passé?
Mais, se jel puis tenir, le mal cuvert enflé,
Je li tolrai la teste par desous le costé."
Lors mande Matabrune ceus ki sunt si casé.
Mout a de gent la vielle en poi d'eure asamblé,   1935
Son castiel fait garnir et de vin et de blé,
Li mur sunt redrecié, li fosé reparé
Et ars et arbalestres ont mout bien encordé.
Mout demostre la vielle grant ire et grant fierté.

90 Or sera grans la guerre, que ne puet demorer.   1940
Mout a bien fait la vielle ses fossés reparer,
Lices et barbacanes fait assés atorner.
Et Elias, li enfes, est assis au souper
Et li autre baron pour lor joie mener.
Aprés mangier ont fait les grans tables oster.   1945
"Signor," fait Elias, "or des gens asambler
N'i a nul ne se paint de soi bien enorter."
Li baron as osteus s'alerent deliter
Et la gens Elias, si s'en veut reposer;
Si se coucent dormir desi a l'ajorner.   1950
Li baron en lor tieres s'en voloient raler,   100*b*
Cescun faire ses os et sa jent atorner.
Et Elias a fait toute sa jens armer,
Toutes ses armeüres a fait mout bien torser,
Mangouniaus et perieres a fait asés porter.   1955
Or ne puet mais la vielle sans ire demorer.

91 Or s'en va li grans os que conduist Elyas.
    "Biaus fius," cou dist li rois, "sés tu u tu iras?"
    "Peres," cou dist li enfes, "asés tos le saras.
    Remanés, sire. Pere, ma mere garderas.   1960
    Vostre tiere et l'ounor, sire, tout maintenras."
    Et li rois li respont: "El non saint Nicolas!"
    Lors s'en va Elias. Ce nen est mie a gas.
    Ses os maine et conduist, ne s'aseüra pas;
    Vers Malbruiant s'en va assés plus que le pas.   1965
    Iluec se sunt logié sor l'aighe de Torcas,
    S'i cort une riviere ki vient de vers Baudas,
    Malbruiant avirone tout entour a conpas.

92 Elyas est venus al castiel sans faintise.
    Bien se loge et atire trestout a sa devise,   1970
    La ot maint pavillon et mainte cube bise.
    Es vous le castelain ki estoit [nés de Fri]se[45]
    Qui amaine une gent de gu[ere bien] aprise,[46]
    Bien en a .IIII.M., l'estore le devise;
    Le castiel asegierent par de la devers bise.   1975
    Et d'autre part revient une gens toute grise,
    Il n'ont fors que les braies, n'ont cote ne cemise;
    Plus ont noires les cars que ne soit pois demise,
    Il ne doutent gielee ne froit ne noif ne bise.
    Cescuns a a sen col une grant hace mise,   1980
    Matabrune manacent qu'il en feront justise.
    Et la vielle estoit ja desour la tour assise
    Qui avoit cuer felon et sans point de francise.
    "Signor," ce dist la vielle, "par le cors saint Denise;
    De ces jens ai paour, li cors tous m'en desbrise." 1985

93 D'autre part le castiel revienent autre gent,
    Cil ki mains a de lonc a .XI. piés de grant,
    Si les conduist .I. rois c'on apiele Jonant.
    D'autre part vient .I. dus sor .I. ceval ferrant
    Qu'en amaine .X.M., par le mien entïent.   1990
    Cil feront Matabrune .I. damaje mout grant,
    Pour Elias aidier se traient tout avant,
    Mangouniaus et perieres amainent plus de .C.
    Et Elias lor crie: "Bien vigniés! Boine gent."
    Les princes et les dus va trestous merciant.   1995
    Une periere ont prise mout lonc et mout vallant,
    Pres del castiel le mainent tos et isnelement.

94 La perriere ont drecie et maint bon mangouniel,
    Lors s'aparellent tout pour jeter au castiel.
    Cil de laiens les virent, ne lor fu mie biel.   2000
    Une piere ont gietee si que tout li pumiel

Caïrent de la tour et li mestre cretiel,
.III. cevaliers ont mors par dedens le castiel.
Quant le voit Matabrune, si jure saint Marcel,
S'ele ataint Elias, tous li ors de [B]abiel[47]   2005
Ne li ara mestier le point d'un fusiel
Ne le face escorcier ausi con .I. caiel.

95 Ne puet mais demorer que il n'i ait mellee.
Lors ont une autre piere droit a la tour ruee
Si que demie l'ont a tiere craventee,   2010
Grant damaje ront fait a cele randounee.   100*c*
Matabrune le voit, s'a sa jent apielee:
"Or, cevalier! As armes! K'il n'i ait demoree,
S'issiés la fors a aus en cele biele pree.
Jou prenderai bien armes, se j'ai la teste armee.   2015
Qui prendra Elias, m'amor li ai dounee;
Trestoute ma grans tiere li ert abandounee."
Et il li respondirent: "Si soit con vous agree!"
Maintenant i ot mise mainte sele doree,
Armé sunt de lor armes sans lonje demoree,   2020
Si montent es cevaus la jens male eüree.
Cescuns a pris sa tarje et sa lance planee
Et li portiers lor a la porte desfremee
Et il s'en iscent fors cescuns lance levee.
Cil de l'ost Elias s'en sunt garde dounee,   2025
Tel .V.C. sunt o lui n'i a cel n'ait espee,
Vers ceus del castel vont a grant esporounee.
Par devant le castiel ara tele asamblee
Dont ancui i aura mainte teste colpee.
Estes vous Elias la ventalle fremee!   2030
Il a l'escut au col a crois enluminee,
Si aslonje la lance que il ot enfeutree
Et vait ferir .I. dus sor la tarje doree.
Par desore la boucle li a fraite et tröee,
La maille del oberc deronte et desafree,   2035
Par mi le gros del cuer li a outre passee
Que del destrier l'abat envers geule baee.
Au resacier sa lance a la crois escrïee.
La peuissiés veoir dolerouse ajornee
Et tant pié et tant puig, tante teste colpee;   2040
De la jent a la vielle fu la place pavee.
Il tornerent en fuies con gent desbaretee,
Matabrune s'escrie a mout grant alenee:
"Signour, ja sui jou ci, si ai la teste armee!
N'en fuiés mie ensi a tele esporonee!   2045
Retornés vous arriere, jou coumanc la mellee."
Ele quiert Elyas a mout grant randonee
U k'ele l'a veü batalle a demandee.

Et Elias respont: "Tout si con vous agree!"
Al retorner k'il fist l'a mout tos avisee,   2050
Il li escrie en haut a mout grant alenee:
"Este vous ci venue male vielle barbee?
Mout m'avés travillié, s'en arés vo soldee.
Maudite soiés vous quant onques fustes nee,
Diable vous ont or durement alevee   2055
Qui vous ont dusc'a or et conduite et guïe[e].[48]
Tout li mestre diable vous ont ore montee
Qui vous ont el ceval si bien encevalee."
"A!" fait ele, "maus gars, con avés grant posnee.
Je te ferrai el cors de ma lance quaree!   2060
Tu vius men cors destruire, s'en averas soldee."
Vers Elias s'en va sa lance amont levee
Et Elias vers li sans nule demoree,
Durement se requierent et de grant aïree.
La vielle vers l'enfant ne pot avoir duree,   2065
Ains est jus de la siele par la crupe volee
La tieste contreval en .I. mont reversee.
Mais si houme salirent qui l'en ont relevee,
Par force li tolirent, laiens l'en ont menee.
La a laisié la vielle la jens de sa contree,   2070
Li remanans s'en fuit coume gens esfraee;   100*d*
Dedens le bos entrerent desconfite et matee.
Elias et si houme ont la porte passee,
Mais se Jhesus n'en pense tart ert li retournee,
Quar li portier deseure ont la porte coulee.   2075
Matabrune le vit, s'a sa jent escriee:
"Or, cevalier! As armes! K'il n'i ait demoree!
S'or m'escape Elias, dont serai afolee."

96   Or coumence la noise el castiel contreval,
     Laiens fu Elias o lui maint bon vasal   2080
     Qui sunt pour Elias en grant peril mortal.
     Et la gens Matabrune lor livrent fort estal.
     Cil de l'ost Elias oënt le batistal,
     Il guerpirent les tentes ki erent de cendal.
     Cascuns a grant paor de son ami carnal,   ·   2085
     Vers le castiel s'en vont a pié et a ceval.
     Bien furent .IIII.M. tout a pié contreval
     Qui feront Matabrune et ses jens ancui mal.

97   As murs en sunt monté serjant et cevalier;
     A ceus defors coumencent a crier, a hucier: 2090
     "Or, signour, del bien faire nos en avons mestier!"
     Lors vienent a la porte plus de .C. arcoier
     Et li autre raportent picois et pius d'acier
     Et les haces danoises pour la porte brisier

Et s'aportent escieles c'al mur voelent drecier.　2095
Lors coumencent la porte mout fort a depecier,
Se fuscent a l'abatre .CCCC. carpentier
Ne fesisent tel noise, tant seüssent mallier.
La porte ont depecie, les veraus font froisier,
El fossé contreval ont gieté le portier.　2100
Quant Elias regarde sa jent si aprocier,
Il escrie la crois pour sa jent raliier.
La peuissiés veoir fort estor coumencier:
Tante lance brisier, tant escu pecoier,
Tant blanc auberc safré deronpre et desmallier;　2105
De la jent a la vielle font la place vidier.
Il tornent tout en fuies par dalés .I. moustier
Et la gens Elias, le nobile guerrier,
Les encaucent forment et font grant destorbier,
Plus de .CCC. en font en l'aighe trebucier.　2110
Le mestre porte passent, si le font vierillier.
Elias et si houme retornerent arier.
Matabrune le voit, le sens cuide cangier.
Ele ot fait ses ceveus tout entor rouëgnier,
Maintenant a vestu le coste .I. escier.　2115
La u voit Elias, si coumence a hucier:
"Ca te trai, gars enflés, jou te voel aresnier!
Oseras tu jouster a .I. seul cevalier
Par couvent s'envers lui ne te pués derainier
Qu'en ma merci seras d'ardoir u a noier,　2120
Tu et toute ta gens sans traire et sans lancier?
Et se tu le conquiers au fier et a l'achier
Si er[t] en la merci de vous tous a jugier.⁴⁹
Et Elyas respont: "Ja ciertes mius ne quier.
Selonc mon droit m'en puist hui Dex aidier."　2125
"Or dont," fait Matabrune, "jou ne voel plus targier;
Jou vois mon campïon armer et afaitier."

98　Matabrune s'en vient a sa jent, si lor crie:
"Savés vous que j'ai fait, bone jens signourie?
J'ai pris vers Elias mervillouse envaïe.　2130
Par .I. seul cevalier ai batalle arramie.　101*a*
S'Elias est vencus, il perdera la vie;
Il et toute sa jens sera en ma ballie.
Se li miens est vencus devers nostre partie,
Si seroumes trestout devers sa signorie."　2135
Quant li baron l'entendent, si font ciere marie;
N'i a .I. tout seul d'aus qui ne jurt bien et die
Ja nen prenderont arme de si fole envaïe.
Quant la vielle l'entent si est de dol noircie:
"A! biau signor!" fait ele, "ne me falés ja mie.　2140
Pourtant se jou sui fame, se Dex me beneïe,

Qui fera la bataille, jou li ferai aïe;
De toute ma grant tiere li otroi signorie."
Onques n'i ot .I. seul qui envers li mot die.
Quant voit la male vielle que nes atraira mie,   2145
Onques n'i ot .I. seul ki envers lui mot die,[50]
Ne par son grant promettre ne par bele baillie;
Ele s'en est entree en une cambre antie,
.I. tresor en a trait de grant ancisserie,
Nel poroient raiembre tout cil de Normandie.   2150
.XX. serjans apiela u ele mout se fie,
Del tresor sunt cargié si que li plus fors plie.
Lors apiele la vielle sa grande baronie:
"Qui or viut gaegnier mar ira en Hungrie!
Qui fera la batalle, se Dex me beneïe,   2155
Trestout cest grant tresor metrai en sa ballie."
Onques n'i ot .I. seul ki nes un mot li die
Ne mais c'uns cevaliers cui male mors ocie.
Hondrés avoit a non, l'estore le nous crie.
Quant il vit le tresor, si en ot grant envie.   2160
Oiant tous les barons a haute vois s'escrie:
"Dame, tout le tresor metés en ma ballie.
Jou m'en irai combatre, qui qu'en plort ne ki rie."
Quant Matabrune l'ot, envers lui s'umelie;
Ses bras li met au col, son tresor li otrie.   2165
Or sera la batalle qu'il ne remanra mie.

99   "Dame," ce dist Hongrés li cuviers malfaisans,
"Vostre cevaliers sui bien a passé .VII. ans.
Jou ferai la batalle pour voir le vous creans,
Mais j'avrai le tresor, teus est mes couvenans."   2170
"Voire," ce dist la vielle, "mes cuers en est joians."
Hondrés en prist l'avoir, toute la jent voians.
Puis dist a Matabrune: "Armeüres demans!
Elias sera ja rendus tous recreans!"
Quant la vielle l'entent clers en fu ses talens.   2175
En .I. celier s'en entre la vielle mal pensans,
Une armeüre en trait qui n'ert pas trop pesans.
Hondré arma la vielle et .I. vallés Jehans:
Unes cauces li lace ki mout erent vaillans,
.I. oberc li vestirent ki ert fors et tenans,   2180
.I. elme li lacierent ki ert clers et luisans,
Il ot cainte l'espee ki bien vaut .C. besans;
.I. ceval li amainent ki ot a non Ferrans,
Rice en est mout la siele et li afeutremens.
"Tenés or cest ceval, mout est bons et courans."   2185
Hondrés i est montés, nus ne l'en est aidans.
Hondrés est bien armés trestous a ses talens[51]
Et pendi a son col .I. escu qu'est luisans

Et a pris en sa main espiel qui est trencans
A .I. lonc fier quaré ki est agus et grans.   2190
.I. des houmes la vielle a desfremé errans   101*b*
La porte et il s'en ist a esporons brocans.
La lance porte droite, ses confanons pendans,
Dalés une forest qu'est bele et verdoians
S'est Hondrés arestés u Elias atant.   2195
Matabrune est remesse, si apele ses jens:
"Signor," [ce] dist [la vielle], "par le cors saint
                                                     Vincant,52
Forment douc Elias et ses fiers hardemens.
Alés vous adouber tos et isnelement
Vous .XII. u vous .XIIII., car jel voel et coumant. 2200
Si ferons en cel bos .I. agait coiement,
Se il mesciet Hondré d'armes ne tant ne quant,
Si salés fors del bos tout apresteement
Et jou donrai cascun tant fin or et argent
Que jamais n'ierent povre en trestout vo vivant."   2205
Et cil li respondirent: "Tout ferons vo coumant!"
.X. cevalier s'armerent de l'avoir couvoitant:
Li .I. avoit non Miles en droit baptisement,
Li secons Amaugins et li tiers Malpensant,
Eulans .I. siens frere, Malduis et Tornians,   2210
Aloris de Palerne et .I. fius Malfaisant;
Et .I. dus le conduist c'on apele Elinant.
Il vestent les aubers, lacent elmes luisans
Et caignent les espees as puns d'or flamboians,
Et montent es cevaus sors et bruns et baucans,   2215
Et pendent a lor cols les fors escus tenans,
Et ont prises les lances as confanons pendans.
Et li portiers lor oevre la porte maintenant
Et il s'en iscent fors a esporons brocant.
Par .I. guicet derriere u solaus est levans   2220
Ensus de l'ost se traient, si le vont costoiant.
En la foriest s'en entrent trestout celeement,
Li .I. fiance l'aut[r]e et si li fait creant53
Que s'Elias conquiert Hardré en combatant
Qu'il l'en amenront pris et loié tout sanglent.   2225
L'agait ont enbuscié dolerous et pesant,
Or gart Dex Elias par son digne coumans
Qu'il en perdra la teste se Dex n'est ses aidans.

100 Mout ont bien enbuscié et repus lor agait
    Et Elias li enfes ne set mie lor plait.   2230
    Quant voit armé Hondré el camp u il estait:
    "Signor, ne faites noise qu'il i ait, cri ne brait.
    Jou m'en vois vers celui a cui tout entresait
    Jou doi faire le camp, la bataille et le fait."

Et cil li respondirent tout ensamble a .I. brait: 2235
"Dex vous en soit aidans et de vous merci ait!"
Et Elias respont belement tout a trait:
"Dameldex le vous mire qui tout voit et tout fait!"
Ses armes demanda, on aporter li vait.

101 Elias fait ses armes aporter en la place   2240
Et doi bon cevalier l'armerent par sa grase.
Il a vestu l'auberc, cascuns cauce li lace;
.I. dansiaus biaus de cors et de vis et de face
Li a mis el cief l'elme qui clers est coume glace,
Si a cainte l'espee ki vint devers Galace.   2245
Armés est de ses armes, n'i a celui ne place.

102 Mout ont bien Elias li haut baron armé.
Elias maintenant a .I. prestre apielé,
Les sains fait aporter de Sainte Trinité;
Dedens .I. pavillon en sunt andui entré.   2250
Li prestres de par Dieu li a conseil douné   101c
Et Elias se drece, s'a les s[ai]ns encliné.⁵⁴
Atant es vous .I. angele qui giete grant clarté
En guise de coulon, cou dïent li lettré;
Son biec a Elias en l'orele bouté.   2255
"Elias," fait li angeles, "Dex t'a par moi mandé:
La u tu dois aler combatre vers Hondré
Matabrune a agait mis el bos a celé;
.X. cevalier armé se sunt el bos entré,
Il te cuident ocire ains que soit avespré.   2260
L'agais est devers destre desous .I. fau ramé.
Prent de tes cevaliers ki t'ont fait feauté
.XV. des mius vallans qui sunt en ton regné
Et refait .I. agait de par saint Ounoré.
Au besoing t'aideront, cou saces de vreté.   2265
Or pense del bien faire, j'ai ci assés esté.
A Jhesu te coumanc ki t'a fait et formé."

103 Elias fait grant joie de cou k'il a oï,
De la vois au saint angele a le cuer esjoï.
Il vient a ses barons, si lor a dit ensi   2270
Con li angeles li ot et conté et jehi.
Et si li respondierent tout ensamble a .I. cri:
"Aourés en soit Dex ki nous en a garni!
Nous sons petit et grant ensamble vostre ami.
Or eslisiés de nous, bien le saciés de f[i].⁵⁵   2275
Par ceus que eslirés sera l'agais basti."

104 "Signor," fait Elias, "bien dites s'il vous plest."
Li prince jurent Dieu k'il feront cel agait

Et li petit s'aficent que ja n'ert ensi fait,
Ancois le feront il, cou dïent entresait.   2280
"Signour," fait Elias, "ci ne doit avoir plait!
Je vous pri de par Dieu qui tout set et tout fait
Que il .VII. des petis et des grans .VIII. i ait.
Si cou vient au besoig et que mestier nous ait,
Adont verons nous bien li quel l'aront mius fait."   2285
Ensi l'ont otroïé li baron tout a fait.
Lors ont maint bon ceval fors de l'estable trait,
Si monterent ensamble qui qu'il soit bel ne lait.
Par ces avront li autre et paour et dehait
Qui sunt ens en l'arbroie entré par malvais plait.   2290

105 Trestout ont otroïé cou qu'Elias a dit.
Li .VIII. millor des grans sunt d'une part eslit,
D'autre part en ot .VII. de ceus qui sunt petit.
Des .VIII. grans vous dirai les nons sans contredit:
Li .I. ot non Guillaume si con l'estore dit,   2295
Et li autres Jehans par son droit non escrit,
Li tiers a non Henris cil qui onques ne rist,
Et li quars a non Hue et li quins Marlevit
Et li sistes Nicoles qui maint bel sens aprist,
Et li siemes Gautiers, ainc outraje ne fist;   2300
Li wimes Galïens, le nombre parfurnist.
Armé sunt de lor armes li cevalier eslit,
Si montent es cevaus et sans noise et sans crit.

106 Or sunt li .VIII. monté sor les cevaus errans.
Des petis se ralïent .VII. des mius vallisans: 2305
L'un apiele on Jefroit et le secont Morant
Et le tierc Felippon et le quart Engherant
Et li cuinkismes Pieres et li sisime Adont.
Armé sunt li petit, ainc ne furent tel jent;
Et montent es cevaus qui estoient courant.   2310
Cescuns pent a son col son fort escu pesant   101*d*
Et si prent en son puig fort espiel et tenscant.
Enbusciê se sunt tuit, or lor soit Dex aidant!
Elias est armés ki mout ot hardement,
Il sali en la siele del bon destrier courant,   2315
L'escu pent a sen col ki ne pesoit niant,
En son puig destre a pris .I. fort espiel seant.
Vers Hardrê s'en va droit qui l'atent tout pensant,
Quant il voit Elias s'a huciê: "Mal venant!
N'en irés sans bataille, se Dex m'en est aidant.   2320
Ancui averés jour dolerous et pesant."
Ambedui se desfïent sans plus de parlement.

107 Ambedui se desfïent li vasal aduré,

Cescuns point son destrier del esporon doré,
Si aslonjent les lances dont li fier sunt quaré.   2325
Sor les escus luisans se sunt grans cols douné
Que par desous les boucles sunt frait et estroé
Et li blanc auberc sunt deront et desafré,
Par dalés les escines en sunt li fier passé.
Les lances pecoierent, as brans sunt acordé;   2330
Amont par mi les elmes se sunt grans cos douné.
Elias a feru par mi l'escu Hondré,
Tres par devant le pis li a le branc coulé,
Si que par les espaules a son ceval colpé.
Hondrés caï a tiere del ceval afolé,   2335
Il est salis em piés si con hom foursené;
Elias vait ferir sor son escu listé,
Par de desous la crois li a frait et fausé.
"Jou quic," fait Elias, "mar i feris Hondré."
Il tint traite l'espee au pug d'or noëlé,   2340
Hondré feri sor l'elme, tout l'a esquartelé;[56]
Diable l'ont tenu que mort ne l'a rüé.
Quant Hondrés sent le cop grant et desmesuré,
La u voit Elias, si l'en a apielé.
"Elias, pour le cors," dist il, "saint Ounoré   2345
Par tans vous volrai rendre del ceval la bonté.
Or vous ont li diable si bien encevalé!"
Atant en va ferir le ceval abrievé,
La couverture est fors, ne l'a pas entamé.
Elias fait son tour, si a feru Hardré;   2350
Le puig atout le branc li a del brac sevré.
Hondrés se sent maumis, si a .I. brait jeté.
Cil de l'agait l'entendent, si sunt del bos sevré;
Elias courent seu[r]e de batalle abrievé.[57]
Or gart Dex Elias par la soie bonté!   2355
Li glouton de l'agait l'orent mout apresé.

108 Elyas a Hondré afolé et maumis,
Li glouton de l'agait salent tout a .I. cri.
A Elias crïerent: "Cuvert, vous estes pris!
Se vous ne vos rendés, vous n'escaperés vis."   2360
Elias a feru le premerain el vis,
Mort le rue a ses piés; puis, si est a aus pris
Et li autre se sunt entour Elias mis.
Se Dex ne le gardast, ja l'eüssent ocis.
Quant [sa gent le] saceurent qui el bos s'erent
                                        mis,[58]   2365
Il montent es cevaus k'il avoient de pris,
Brocent a esporon se sunt fors del bos mis.
Guillaume a hurté le bai u s'ert assis,
Jehans broce Morel qui ne vaut mie pis,

Gaufrois sist sor Ferrant si est es galos mis, 2370
Hues broce Moriel et Nicoles le gris 102*a*
Et Gautiers point le bai, si est au devant mis.
Les lances sor les feutres se sunt es galos mis,
Ainc ne vit si fort caple nus hom qui or soit vis.
Amaugin et son frere ont maintenant ocis; 2375
Le mal ont enpensé, drois est qu'il lor soit pis.

109 Mout par est fors li caples et dure la mellee.
Matabrune la vielle est en la tor montee,
Bien cuide k'Elias ait la teste colpee;
Ele esgarde ses homes qui sunt en la valee, 2380
Il s'en faut mout petit la vielle n'est dervee.
Lors fist souner .I. graile, s'a sa jent rasamblee;
En petit d'ore i ot maint brogne endossee.
Monté sunt es cevaus a lor maleüree,
Cescuns a pris sa lance et sa tarje doree 2385
Et li portiers lor a la porte desfremee
Et il s'en iscent fors, cescuns la teste armee.
Encontre le solel ont grant clarté jetee
Cil elme et cil escu a cele matinee.
Quant Elias les voit s'a la coulor müee, 2390
La mere Dameldeu a souvent reclamee.
Atant es vous venant la pute jens dervee.
Et la gens Elias ki est preus et senee
Laissent core vers aus par mout grant aïree.
Cescuns abat le sien de la siele doree 2395
As fiers trencans lor percent le pis et la coree.
A l'abatre et au braire ont tel noise menee
Que la gens Elias ont oï la crïee.
Li os est estormie tout contreval la pree,
Onques n'i ot mantel ne cape regardee; 2400
Vers ceus del castel vont a grant esporonee.
A la jent Matabrune est l'os toute mellee.
La peuisiés veoir dolerouse asamblee,
La ot tant pié, tant pug, tante teste colpee;
Et d'une part et d'autre fu mout grans la crïee. 2405
De la jent a la vielle fu la place pavee.

110 Mout est grans la bataille et li estors pesans,
D'ambes .II. pars se fierent sor les escus luisans.
Elias vit morir ses jens, s'en fu dolans.
Il hurte le ceval des esporons trencans, 2410
Son bon branc a sacié ki ert reflamboians;
Si se fiert en la prese con cevaliers vaillans.
Tout decolpe entor lui, car mout est bons ses brans,
Entor lui fait la voie des mors et des sanglens.

111 Elias voit ses houmes ricement maintenir,   2415
   A .II. mains tint l'espee, l'estor va departir.
   Cui il consiut a colp, bien le vous puis jehir,
   Ja mar mandera mire pour sa plaie garir.
   Le senescal la vielle vait en l'elme ferir,
   Desi en la coree li fait le branc sentir;   2420
   Mort le rue par tiere, cui quel doie haïr.[59]
   Quant la jens a la vielle se virent malballir[60]
   Il livrerent les dos, si pensent a fuïr.
   Onques jusc'al castiel ne se volrent soufrir.[61]

112 Les gens la vielle fuient, nus n'i est arestés;   2425
   El castiel se rentrerent ensamble de tous lés.
   Elias et si houme sunt tout outre passés,
   Ceus de laiens ont mors et trestous afolés;
   Plus en ont de .XL. ocis et decolpés.
   Il escrïent le fu ki ja soit alumés,   2430
   Quant Elias l'entent cele part est alés;   102*b*
   Ne viut que li castiaus soit ars ne alumés.
   Il descent del ceval au perron d'uns degrés,
   Amont en la grant sale est Elias montés.
   Matabrune a trouvee, avant li est passés.   2435
   Quant la vielle le voit, s'a les sorcius levés:
   "Cou que est?" fait la vielle. "Mal soiés vous trovés!
   Ne sai ki vous aïe, se n'est li vis maufés."
   "Ciertes," fait Elias, "avoec moi en venrés.
   Je vous ferai jehir coument avés errés,   2440
   Ancui arés mal jor, se Dex me doinst santés!"

113 Matabrune a grant dol quant Elias entant
   Et Elias s'escrie a haute vois sa jent
   Qui par le castiel vont ces cevaliers prendant.
   A la vois Elias s'en vienent tout errant   2445
   Et Matabrune saut en piés isnelemant,
   .I. espiel a saisi a .I. lonc fier trencant,
   Elias en feri par derier maintenant.
   L'armeüre li parte et l'auberc jaserant,
   Le sanc en fait caïr jus as piés del enfant.   2450
   Se Dex ne le gardast, ocis l'eüst atant.
   Et Elias s'en torne quant si feru se sent,
   Matabrune a saisie, par les cevaus le prent,
   Contremont l'a levee par si fier mautalent,
   Jus des degrés le giete contreval roëlant.   2455
   Sor une piere ciet et [mer]villouse et grant,[62]
   Le coste li pecoie et la teste li fent.
   Matabrune ont saisie doi serjant maintenant,
   Sor .I. ceval le lievent tos et isnelement,
   Les mains li ont loïes et les piés ensement.   2460

Et la gens a la vielle ont rendu erranment
Elias le castiel, k'il ne pueent avant.
Elias fu cortois, sel prent sans maltalent;
Feauté li font tout li petit et li grant.
Puis si ont pris congié cil ki sunt li sacant,   2465
Li baron en lor tieres se revont liemant,
Elias les mercie trestous mout doucement.
Matabrune la vielle en mainent mout batant,
Elias envoia .XX. cevaliers avant
Pour enfremer sen pere el mestre mandement   2470
Qu'il ne voie sa mere a dolerous torment.

114 Li cevalier s'en tornent qui n'ont soing d'arester,
Le roi font maintenant en la tor enserer.
Elias fait sa mere en la place amener
Pour cou que ele voie la vielle el fu jeter   2475
Et ele i est venue, ne si vot arester.
S'ele maine grant joie, nen fait mie a blasmer.
Et Elias s'en va, la vielle en fait mener.
Devant a envoié pour le fu alumer
Et dist que il fera Matabrune ens gieter.   2480
Lors sunt venu al fu qu'il ont fait embraser.
Elias fait la vielle devant lui amener,
Ele voit mout trés bien que n'en puet escaper.
"E!" fait ele, "Elias, laisse moi confiesser.
Ja iés tu fius men fil, car me laises aler!   2485
Et s'encor me voloies .I. seul respit douner
Tel cose [t]'aprendroie que mout porois amer."63
Et Elias respont: "N'ai cure de border.
Vostre mal vous ferai ancui guerredouner.
Counissiés vostre mordre, trop poés demorer."   2490
"Bien voi," ce dist la vielle, "que nen puis
                                   escaper.   102*c*
Or oiés grant mervelle, sel volés escouter."

115 "Or oiés," fait la vielle, "cevalier et baron.
Ja orés grant mervelle en ma confiessíon.
A .I. mot vous puis dire! Ainc ne fis se mal non!   2495
Jou n'amai onques Dieu ne son saintisme non,
Onques riens tant n'amai con mordre et traïson.
Se peuise encor vivre, foi que doi saint Simon,
Jou copase Elias le cief sor le menton
Et mon fil ocesise ancois l'Asentíon.   2500
Puis mesise la tiere a fu et a carbon,
Si fesise ses houme[s] traire male saison64
Et raensise tous et mesise en prison.
Et de la bone dame fis jou la traïson
Que je voi la ester a l'ermin pelicon.   2505

Les enfans envoiai tous noier par Marcon
Et puis fis men fil croire par malvaise raison
Que tout .VII. li enfant estoient .VII. kiencon.
Par mon gré fust ele arse et livree a carbon.
Se peuise escaper fors de ceste prison,   2510
Nus hom ne fist tant mal des le tans Salemon
Con jou seule fesise. Ains ne fis se mal non!
Jou n'oseroie dire que j'aie vrai pardom
Damedex nostre Sire desous qui nos manon.
Se jou vois en infier j'arai maint conpagnon   2515
Et des haus et des bas, en l'infernal maison.
Or aviegne qu'aviegne! Tout ert en abandon!"

116 Matabrune la vielle s'est mout mal confiessee,[65]
Tout cil en ont paour ki l'orent escoutee.
"Ciertes," fait Elyas, "vielle desesperee,   2520
L'uevre que fait avés vous ert guerredounee.
Tolu m'avés mon frere, s'en serés vergondee
Et jou vous en rendrai dolerouse jornee."
Lors prendent Matabrune, si l'ont el fu jetee.
Et la vielle s'est mout hautement escriee: 2525
"As diables d'infier soit m'arme coumandee
Et tout cil ki ci sunt dedens ceste contree!"
Lors s'estendi la vielle, toute est arse et brulee;
L'arme enportent diable, a aus estoit vöee.
Arriere s'en retornent quant ele fu finee,   2530
En la sale repairent ki est bele et pavee.
Li rois sot la nouviele, torblee ot sa pensee;
Mais ne vot noise faire car trop estoit faee.
Li jors est trespassés jusques a l'avespree,
Au mangier sunt assis la boine jent senee.   2535
Quant il orent mangié la table fu ostee,
Maint lit et mainte kiute ont el palais portee;
Si se coucent dormir desi a l'ajournee.
Elias ne dort pas, en Dieu ot sa pensee.   *102d*
Ains que la mïenuis fust toute trespasee   2540
Oï li ber tel cose dont fu grant renomee
Par France et par Auvergne et par mainte contree,
Sainte crestïentés en fu puis ounoree.

117 Tout dorment par la sale; Elias ne dort pas,
Deu apiele et reclaime et le ber Nicolas.   2545
Atant es vous .I. angele revestu de blans dras,
A Elias conselle tout belement en bas:
"Elias, biaus amis, sés tu ke tu feras?
Par moi te mande Dex, ne l'oublie tu pas,
Le matinet au jor bien matin leveras   2550
Et ton pere et ta mere a Dieu coumanderas

Et toute t'armeüre avoec toi porteras
Et l'escu a la crois mie n'oublieras.
Tel cose t'avenra dont tu ounor aras.
Tout droit sor la riviere ten pere t'en iras   2555
Et ilueques le cisne, ton frere, trouveras.
.I. batiel t'amenra bien fait tout a conpas.
Sa volenté, amis, outreement feras."
"Sire, mout volentiers!" cou respont Elias.

118 Li angeles s'en reva et Elias remaint.   2560
Au matin est levés, n'i a plus nul delaint,
Ains font grant joie tout, n'i a cel ki se faint.
Au moustier sunt alé quant souné sunt li saint,
.I. abes lor dist mese d'un beneoit cors saint,
Lors ofrandes ont faites, l'abes pas ne s'en plaint.2565
Del moustier sunt iscu, n'i a cel ne se saint.

119 En la sale repairent serjant et cevalier
Et li rois Orians et sa bone moullier.
Ne font ne cri ne noise, n'ont cure de tencier.
"Signor," fait Elias, "savés dont vous requier?   2570
Escoutés moi petit sans cri et sans noisier!
Peres," fait Elias, "por Dieu vous voel proier
Que pensés de ma mere, vostre france moullier.
Gardés que n'atraiés entor vous losengier.
Se haus hom prent ma suer a per et a moullier,   2575
La tiere li dounés c'on ne puet exillier;
Bien vaut par an .M. mars et d'argent et d'or mier.
Et se je ne revieng, tenés a iretier
L'ainné de tous mes freres, ne l'en faites plaidier.
Par couvent sera rois, con vous m'orés jugier: 2580
Que se Dex me ramaine en boine pais arier,
Quite rarai ma tiere sans traire et sans lancier.
Oriun dounés tiere ki fu au roi Hungier,
Rices hom en sera, s'il le set justicier.
Sacariés avera l'Ille de Valrahier.   2585
Jehans aura Monbel, bien s'en pora aidier.
Et si vous voel a tous coumander et proier
Que ne me demandés aler ne repairier,
Quar ne vous en diroie le monté d'un denier."
Li baron de pitié se prendent a sainier.   2590

120 "Signour," fait Elias, "ne puis plus demorer.
A Dieu vous coumanc tous qu'il m'en couvient aler."
Li baron de pitié coumencent a plorer.
"Biaus fius," fait la roïne, "venés a moi parler."
"Dame," fait Elias, "cou ne puis refuser."   2595
En une cambre a vote a fait son fil entrer,

.I. cor li a baillié d'ivore bel et cler.
"Biaus fius," ce dist la dame, "cest vous couvient
                                              porter
Quar il est mout vallans, si fait mout a löer. 103*a*
Encor venra .I. jors, nel vous quier a celer,   2600
Que vous ara mestier, se le poés garder.
La raison vous dirai pour coi fait a amer:
Le jor, jel vous creant, quel porés esgarder
Ne vous estevra ja de vostre droit douter."
A caaines d'arjent k'ele i ot fait fremer   2605
Li pendi a son col pour le mius conforter.
Et Elias s'en torne, n'i vot plus demorer.
Il a fait s'armeüre de devant lui porter
Et l'escu a la crois n'i vot pas oublier;
Espee ot bele et bone ki bien fait a löer,   2610
Armeüre mout rice c'on ne doit pas blasmer.
.II. escuiers les fait par devant lui porter.
Sor la rive s'en va u Dex le fait aler
Et li baron avoec n'ont cure de canter.

121 Tresque sor la riviere en vait toute la jent,   2615
    Li rois et la roïne en vont aprés plorant.
    Bon vin i font porter et bon pain de forment
    Et boins froumages durs i portent plus de .C.
    Sour le rivier s'arestent. Atant es vous venant
    Le cisne ki amaine le batiel trainant   2620
    A une grant caïne ki ert toute d'arjent
    Que Dex i envoia par son coumandement.
    Dedens le batiel metent l'armeüre vallant
    Et le pain et le vin et l'autre estoremant.
    Li rois et la roïne, cevalier et serjant   2625
    Le coumandent a Dieu doucement en plorant.
    Elias el batiel entra tout maintenant;
    Li rois demaine dol, la roïne ensemant.
    Il lor a dit: "A Dieu!" Puis s'en depart atant.
    Or le conduise Dex par son digne coumant!   2630
    El repairier sunt mis del vivier mout dolant,
    Tout ensamble a .I. bruit entrent el casement.
    Li batiaus s'en va droit la u Dex li consant,
    Del vivier est iscus tant qu'a la mer se prant,
    En haute mer entra, ne si vont delaiant.   2635
    Toute jor vont ensi et la nuit ensement
    Tant que vint el demain viers miedi sonant,
    Une cité coisisent de sarrasine jant.
    As murs erent monté et viellart et enfant,
    Il coisirent le cisne le batiel trainant.   2640
    Bien quident qu'el batiel ait mout or et argant,
    U cou soit une espie de crestïene gant.

Lors corent as galies li mauvais souduiant,
Armé sunt de lor armes tos et isnielement.
As galies s'en vont bien plus de .CCCC.,   2645
Dïent k'il asauront le batiel maintenant.
Del port sunt escipé, si s'en tornent atant;
Vers Elias s'en vont mout durement nagant.
Quant Elias les voit, si se va esmaiant;
Bien set k'il n'en ira sans batalle mout grant.   2650
Il souspire del cuer, si se va dolousant;
A sen frere le cisne se va mout conplagnant.
Ansi coume li cisnes euist entendemant,
Grant dol fait por sen frere, le ciel vait pourgardant;
A son bec se descire et deront et defait,   2655
Il brait et crie en haut, ne plore autrement.
Elias s'ajenelle tout droit vers oriant:
"Ahi! biaus Sire, Dex! par ton coumandemant
Aiés merci de m'arme. Biaus Sire, a vous me rent! 103*b*
A toi me rent confiés, biaus Sire, et nonporquant   2660
Jou me desfenderai vers la jent mescreant.
Jou ne voel qu'il me prengent sans ne sauf ne parlant,
Ja ne me troveront lanier ne recreant."

122 Li cisnes fait grant dol, durement brait et crie;
Son bec tent vers le ciel, doucement s'umelie.   2665
Elias Dameldieu durement merci crie.
Armés est de ses armes, ne s'aseüre mie;
Il a cainte l'espee dont li puns reflambie.
Tout droit de son batiel coisist le grant galie,
Devant toutes les autres [li sire qui les guie.]⁶⁶ 2670
Et dist que le batiel ara en sa baillie
Et tout l'or et l'arjent n'i aront partie
Cil ki arriere vienent, ce dist cil ki les guie;
Et celui del batiel ne laira ne l'ocie.
Au batiel vint errant, Elias fort escrie: 2675
"Ca lairés le batiel et la marceandie!"
Et Elias respont: "Signor, ne parlés mie
Que le batiel aiés en la vostre baillie.
Encor ne m'avés vous tolu membre ne vie."
Son pain prent et sen vin de coi a grant partie,   2680
En la mer le jeta ne viut que l'aient mie.
"Mar l'i avés gieté!" font cil de la galie.
"Vous le comperés ja ains eure de conplie.
Cel cisne arons nous ja en la nostre ballie,
S'en mangerons la car mais qu'ele soit rostie."   2685
La parole a li cisnes entendue et oïe,
Autresi con .I. hom de paour brait et crie.

123 Or voit bien Elias ke ne puet demorer,

Envers le galiot ne puet merci trouver.
Armés est de ses armes, ne viut plus demorer.   2690
Et li galios lance a lui pour afoler,
.I. quariel d'abalestre laise li .I. aler.
Quant li enfes le voit, Deu prist a reclamer.
Elias en consiut sor son escu boucler
Si que de sous la crois li fait outre voler;   2695
Par mi le brac senestre li fait outre passer,
Le sanc trestout vermel li fait au pié couler.
Quant li cisnes le voit, si coumence a crier;
A son bec se coumence trestous a descirer.
Lors regarde Elias tout contreval la mer,   2700
Si voit .XXX. galies les ondes sormonter
D'unes voiles mout blances, nus nel poroit conter,
Cescuns ot crois vermelle pour le mius aviser.
Vers Elias en vienent tant con pueent sigler
Quar Dex les i envoie ki tout a a sauver.   2705
Li cisne fait grant joie car bien set sans douter
Qu'il vienent pour sen frere grant aïe douner.

124 Les galies aprocent pour Elias aidier
Que Dex li envoia qui tout a a jugier.
Sains Jores les conduist devant el cief premier,   2710
Entre angeles et arcangeles i a plus d'un millier,
Tout sunt blanc revestu con prestre de moustier,
Vers Elias s'en vienent tant con porent nagier.
Li cisnes fait grant joie quant les vit aprocier.
Lors s'entrevienent tout sans traire et sans
                                      lancier.   2715
La mesnie saint Jore vont iceus essaier
Et li cisnes lor vait lor galies percier,
A son biec les descoupe por le mius empirier
Qu'il ne set autrement parler ne losengier.   103c

125 Les galies aprocent pour souscorre l'enfant   2720
Que Dex lor envoia par son digne coumant.
Durement les asalent et cascuns se desfent.
Une galie afondrent de la jent Tervagant,
En l'aighe sunt ceü et noié plus de .C.;
Toute est enplie d'aighe, au fons va tournant.   2725
Li autre se desfendent mout angousousemant,
La mesnie saint Jorge les grieve duremant.
Este vous .I. orage qui la mer va torblant
Et li galiot tornent par mi la mer fuiant.
Il n'ont gaires alé quant tounoiles les prent   2730
Qui se fiert es galies, tous les va craventant;
Au fons de mer les ploie et la galie fant.
Or ont assés alé li cuvert mescreant

Et les blances galies s'en retornent atant
Que Dex i envoia par son digne coumant.   2735
Et Elias lor huce: "Entendés, boine jant,
Dites moi qui vous estes, aumosne ferés grant."
Sains Jorges respondi: "N'en demande pas tant!
Dameldeu en rent grases, le Pere tout poisant,
De cou k'il t'envoia souscors procainement.   2740
S'il ne fust, nous fusciens tout livré a torment."
"E! Dex!" dist Elias, ".C. mercis vous en rent.
M'arme coumanc a vous et le cors ensement."

126 Or s'en sunt tuit alé, n'i a remés galie;
Dameldex les conduist et sains Jores les guie.   2745
Elias prent tel fains, tele ne fu oïe;
Il a bendé sa plaie ki n'estoit pas garie,
Mais pis li fist li fains ki durement l'aigrie.
"E! Dex!" fait Elias, "Dame sainte Marie!
Or morrai jou de fain, si n'en garirai mie."   2750
Li cisnes ot son frere, de dolor brait et crie.
Ensi s'en vont noant del jor une partie,
D'autre part une roce mervillouse et antie
Ont coisi .I. castiel de mout grant signorie.
Cele part vont tout droit, ne s'aseürent mie.   2755
A! Dex! con mal il vont se Dex ne lor aïe!

127 Elyas a grant fain ki durement souspire,
Il reclaime Jhesu k'il le gart de martire.
Il se conplaint au cisne qui mot ne li puet dire:
"Frere," fait Elias, "jou me metrai a rive.   2760
S'en irai el castiel car fains me fait deslire.
Le batiel gardés bien et a tous contredire.
Dex nos doinst a mangier qui de tous biens est Sire.
Mon escu et mes armes u mes cuers se remire
Lairai en cest batiel de par Dieu et saint Gire."   2765

128 Li batiaus est venus al castiel al riwage,
Cel castiel apiele on par son droit non Salvage.
Li sire qui ens maint est el grignor estaje,
Avoit non Agoulans, mout par a fier visaje.
Plus a de jent ocise qu'il n'en ait en Cartaje.   2770
"Frere," fait Elias au cisne qui le nage,
"Le batiel gardés bien, si vous tenrai a saje.
G'irai en cest castiel, li cors de fain m'esrage.
Si porterai mon cor, sel meterai en gage,
Se jou ne puis mius faire car tel sont li usajè."   2775
Li cisnes ne dist mot car ne set le langage
Et Elyas saut fors del batiel al rivage.
El castiel en monta, mais mout cier guiounaje

Li couvenra paier, si ert a son damage.   103*d*
Se cil Sires n'en pense, onques n'ot tel outraje.   2780

129 Elias en monta el castiel volentiers,
    Agoulant i trouva avoec ses cevaliers;
    Devant la porte sïent, mout i a losengiers.
    Elias les salue cui en estoit mestiers
    Et Agoulans respont: "Qui es tu, amis ciers?   2785
    Vius tu vendre cel cor? En prenderas deniers?"
    "Sire," dist Elias, "si m'aït sains Riciers,
    Ancois le vous donrai trestout pour .II. mangiers,
    Quar jou ne manjai gaires bien a .III. jors entiers."
    "Amis," dist Agoulans, "s'en aras volentiers;   2790
    Or gardés vostre cor k'il vous ara mestier."
    En la sale s'en entrent tout maintenant arier,
    Li serjant misent tables tout par mi ces soliers.
    Li baron ont lavé, s'asïent sans dangiers.
    Au mangier ont eü .X. més trestous pleniers,   2795
    Si ont assés beü de fors vins et de ciers.
    Elias ot mangié, s'est .I. poi trais arrier.
    Li damoisiaus fu mout et orgillous et fiers,
    Et Agoulans l'esgarde, li cuvers pautouniers.
    "Amis," dist Agoulans, "estes vous saudoiers?   2800
    U gaite de castiel? U doisiaus arcoiers?
    Vostre estre voel savoir, ja n'en serés mains ciers."
    Et Elias respont ki n'est ne fel ne fiers:
    "Sire, jel vous dirai de gré et volentiers."
    E! las! or li aproce dolerous encombriers,   2805
    Se cil Sire n'en pense ki est vrais justiciers.

130 "Sire," fait Elias sans ire et sans celee,
    "Quant vous volés savoir dont sui, de quel contree,
    Ma vie vous dirai, ja ne vous ert celee.
    Li bons rois Orians fist de moi engenree,   2810
    La roïne est ma mere ki est saje et senee."
    "Amis," dist Agoulans a la ciere dervee,
    "Je vous pri que me dites la verité prouvee.
    Que est de Matabrune? Est de cest siecle alee?"
    "Sire," dist Elias, "or saciés sans celee   2815
    Que par son mesfait fu ens en .I. fu jetee."
    "Amis, qui a cou fait? Si soit t'arme sauvee!"
    Lors li a Elias l'aventure contee
    Ensi con Matabrune a sa vie menee
    Et coument il l'a arse et en fu enbrasee.   2820
    Quant l'entent Agoulans, s'a la coulor müee;
    Quar Matabrune estoit sa suer la plus ainnee,
    Onques n'avoit tant rien coume la vielle amee.
    "Cuvers," dist Agoulans, "vostre vie est alee!

Quant je vous tieng as mains vous en arés saudee.   2825
Vous le conperés cier, c'est verités prouvee.
Mar avés ma seror Matabrune tüee!"

131 Agoulans fait tel dol, onques ne vi si grant.
Pour sa seror la vielle maine .I. dol si tres grant:
"Ciertes," fait il; "vasaus, je vous pendrai au
                                 vent.   2830
Se n'euisciés mangié a ma table seant,
La teste vous colpasse a m'espee trencant.
.VIII. jors n'avés vous garde de nul afolement,
Mais je vous jeterai en ma cartre puant.
Al cief d'uit jors tout droit, par mon dieu
                             Tervagant,   2835
Vous ferai jou gieter en .I. fu tout ardant."
Lors saut sus Agoulans par mout fier mautalent,
Vers Elias s'en va, par les ceviaus le prent.
Quant Elias le voit tous tainst de mautalant,   104*a*
Il a traite l'espee ki au gieron li pant,   2840
Ja ferist Agoulant sans nul arestemant
Quant .I. maus cevaliers si est mis au devant
Et Elias le fiert mout aïreemant
Que les moitiés en cïent de sor le pavement.
Quant Agoulans le vit mout ot le cuer dolant.   2845
Elias fu tous seus, si vit asés de jant;
Bien voit que sa desfense ne li valroit nïent
Et Agoulans l'ahiert mout aïreement,
Ses serjans apiela tost et isnelement.
Quant il l'ont entendu, si sunt venu corant.   2850
Elias ont saisi .X. vallet maintenant,
Les mains li ont loïes mout angousosement,
En la cartre le gietent sans nul arestement.
En cele cartre avoit maint anious serpent,
Laisardes et crapaus plains d'envenimement;   2855
Iluec a Elias pris son herbe[r]jement.[67]
Agoulans s'en retorne tos et isnelement,
Celui qui mors estoit entierent maintenant,
Pour sa suer Matabrune pleure mout tenrement;
Si baron, si casé se vont reconfortant.   2860
Iluec ot .I. garcon de mout bon entiant
Que li pere Elias ot nori lonjement,
Del castiel est iscus la nuit mout coïement,
Tant va par ses jornees c'al roi vint, Oriant.
La nouviele li conte que on a son enfant   2865
Gieté ens en la cartre le felon Agoulant
Et dist qu'il en prendra la venjance mout grant
Tel con de Matabrune qui mere ert Oriant;
Quar ardoir le fera, ja n'en ara garant,

Ains les .VIII. jors passés en .I. fu tot ardant.   2870
Quant li rois la nouviele oï et le couvent
A poi qu'il ne se pasme, et il et si enfant.
La roïne fait duel et orible et pesant:
"Lase!" ce dist la dame, "perdu ai mon enfant.
A! cuers pour coi vis tu tous jors en tel tormant?   2875
A! Elias, biaus fius, par le mien entiant
Ja mais ne vous verai, mon cuer en ai dolant."

132 "Sire," dist .I. des freres qui tint la roiauté,
Elias li avoit laisiet en ireté,
"Ne vous esmaiés mie pour Sainte Trinité   2880
Ne ne menés tel dol, car trestout est en Dé.
Nostre Sire nos done tout a sa volenté.
Oriant, sire, pere; vostre oncle, ce savés,
Qui mon frere Elias a si enprisoné,
Il a non Agoulans et si ne croit en Dé;   2885
Pour cou s'il m'apartient, par le cors saint Vïé,
Irai par tans sor lui a trestout mon aé.
Mes freres, Elias, m'a pour lui coroné,
Souscorre le m'estuet et moustrer ma fierté.
Se Dex me viut aidier, bien en sera ouvré."   2890
Le garcon ki li ot le mesaje aporté
Douna et argent et or et reubes a plenté,
Puis mande ses barons qui de lui sunt fievé
Que cescuns le sousceure, s'il viut avoir son gré.
Li baron se sunt tout a lor pooir hasté,   2895
Dedens les .II. jors ont asés jent amasé.
A grans paines entrerent trestout en la cité,
Des grans et des petis i avoit a plenté.
Li petit sunt venu de bataille abrievé   104*b*
Et cil as noires piaus ne sunt mie oublié,   2900
Ses conduist .I. Turcois del regne Giboé,
Nicolas avoit non par sa crestïenté.
Desi qu'a l'Illefort ne sunt pas aresté.
Orians et si fil sunt es cevaus monté;
La roïne, la dame, ont coumandé a Dé,   2905
De la cité iscirent de bone volenté.
Li garcons les conduist ki bien sot le regné,
Dedens l'uitime jor que il fu ajorné
Sont venu al castiel, [i]tant se sunt pené.⁶⁸
En .I. bos petitet bien follu et ramé   2910
Se sunt tenu tout coi ains n'i ot mot souné.
Cel castiel avoit on pres del boscet fondé,
Iluec se sunt logié tant qu'il fu ajorné.
Au matinet se sunt cil del castiel levé,
Agoulans et si houme sunt el palais listé,   2915
Il jure sa creance que por .I. mui rasé

De fin or et d'arjent et pour sa grant cité
Ne lairoit escaper Elias le sené
Qu'il ne l'arde en .I. fu ains m̃edi souné.
Isnelement et tos ont le fu demandé   2920
Et c'on atraie espines as aniaus a plenté
Et estrain tout entour voiant tout le barné.
Tout droit en mi la place ont le fu alumé.
Elias ont le serf de la cartre gieté,
Son cor a doucement a sen col regardé,   2925
Maint en ot en la place de pitié ont ploré,
Mais n'osent pas blasmer Agoulant le dervé.
Iluec ot .I. haut houme, plains fu de grant bonté,
Mais povretés l'avoit durement agrevé,
Si est tous deceüs par la grant povreté   2930
Que il et si enfant ont .X. ans enduré.
Simons avoit a non, ce d̃ent li letré.
Il a bien oï dire, sel set de verité,
Quant se deciet li hom d'avoir qu'a conquesté,
Ja n'en iert ascoutés entre rice barné.   2935
La u voit Agoulant, si l'a araisouné:
"Sire," cou dist Simons, "tu as le sens dervé
Qui l'enfant vius ocire. S'est de ton parenté!
S'il a Matabrune arse, c'est pour sa mauvesté;
Mais cis est cevaliers et si croit bien en Dé."   2940
Lors regarde [Agolans] celui ki a parlé:[69]
"Ahi!" fait il, "Symon, c'avés vous sermoné!
Par le vostre conseil ne seroit adesé,
Mais ne le ferai mie, pour Mahomet mon dé.
Ains serés ars o lui, si l'avons en pensé."   2945

133 Mout manace Simon li cuvers Agoulans.
"Sire," cou dist Simons, "mout par est Deu poiscans.
Il aïe les siens car teus est ses coumans.
Tu n'as en ta cort houme, tant soit fors ne vallans,
Se il voloit blasmer moi ne mes jugemens   2950
Qu'il ne fust hui cest jor par mon cors recreans.
Encor vous di jou bien et si en sui creans
Que s'Elyas est ars, peciés sera mout grans.
S'il a Matabrune arse, ele estoit mal pensans;
Mais cis est cevaliers et si est tes parens."   2955
Quant Agoulans l'entent ses cuers en fu dolans.
Il fait prendre Simon, s'en fait ses sairemens
Que o lui sera ars. Teus est ses paiemens.
Ans .II. les fait loier, qui que en soit dolans.   104*c*
Et li garcons estoit ens el castiel laians   2960
Qui l'ost a amenee que conduist Orians,
Del castiel est iscus sans nul delaiemans.
"Or tost!" fait il. "Signor, si.m'aït sains Jehans,

Elias est loiés et li fus est mout grans.
Se vous nel souscorés, c'ert .I. dels mout pesans." 2965
Quant li baron l'entendent n'i a cel qui soit lans,
Il monterent es seles des bons destriers corans,
Si pendent a lor cols les escus flamboians,
Si ont prises les lances as confanons pendans;
Vers le castiel s'en vont a esporons brocans.   2970
Et cil a pié le sivent qui mout sunt boines jens;
Il sounent ces buisines et ces cors flamboians.
De la noise s'esmaie li cuvers Agoulans;
Il demande que c'est a ses proimes serjans.
Cil dïent qu'al castiel vienent asalir jens;   2975
Ainc ne furent si fier, bien part a lor samblans.

134 Quant Agoulans entent des gens le huceïs
    A hautes vois escrie: "Signor, jou sui traïs!"
    Il monterent as murs et as grans rouleïs,
    As armes cort cascuns qui ert amanevis.   2980
    Elias ont laisié u de gré u envis,
    Il sunt andoi loié, tant est a lor oés pis.
    Et Agoulans s'en torne, li cuvers maleïs,
    Armé corent as portes, as murs et as postis.
    Et cil de fors les ont durement asalis,   2985
    Bien en ont .XXX. mors des cevaliers eslis.
    "Ciertes," fait Agoulans, "or sui jou bien hounis.
    Issons la fors a aus devant ces plaseïs,
    Or i parra ki ert bons cevaliers hardis."
    Et il respondent tuit: "Volontiers, non envis!"   2990
    La porte font ouvrir par devers le lairis,
    Sor les cevaus s'en iscent, Gascons et Arrabis;
    Les escus ont al cos; indes, vermaus et bis;
    Et lor oberc sunt fort bien cloé et treslis.
    Qui lor veïst cevaus brocier par ces lairis   2995
    Dire peuist pour voir: grans est li poigneïs!
    A l'asambler des lances fu grans li [foleïs].70
    Et al joindre des cols fu grans la bateïs.
    Les lances sont brisïes, fors fu li capleïs;
    Les espees ont traites et fors des fueres mis,   3000
    La place en est pavee de ceus qui sunt ocis
    Et la desconfiture est aparans des vis.
    Ainc si grande ne fu des le tans Anseïs.

135 Mout fu grans la batalle par devers le vregier.
    Li garcons ki ala le mesage noncier   3005
    Est courus Elias et Symon desloier,
    Quant il sentent lor mains n'i ot qu'esleecier.
    A l'ostel Symon corent par devers .I. sentier;
    Laiens se sunt armé sans noise et sans tencier,

Mais il n'i ont trouvé palefroi ne soumier. 3010
A pié ceurent andui pour lor honte vengier,
A l'iscir de la porte truevent .I. cevalier
Qui venoit de l'estour en la cité arier.
Navrés ert durement, ne se pot mais aidier.
Il le prendent andui et devant et derier, 3015
Jus del ceval le font voler et trebucier.
La le laisent gisant, s'en prendent le destrier.
Elias i monta par le senestre estrier,
Il met lance sor feutre, s'encontre .I. soudoier. 104*d*
Mervillous cop li doune, l'escu li fait percier, 3020
Le hauberc de son dos decouper et desmallier,
Par mi le gros del cuer li conduist son espiel,
Tant con anste li dure l'abat mort en l'erbier.
Puis saisi le ceval, Symon le va baillier[71]
Et li ber i monta, onques n'i quist estrier. 3025
Lors se fierent andui el grant estor plenier;
Lor lances pecoierent, s'ont trais les brans d'acier.
Elias a l'espee fait les rens claroier,
De la jent Agoulans fait la tiere joncier.[72]

136 Mout fu grans la batalle et li estors pesans, 3030
D'ambes .II. pars s'en vienent a l'estor qui est grans;
Ne d'une part ne d'autre ne furent recreans,
Ains s'en vienent ansi coume dervee jens.
Quant Elias le voit, s'en fu au cuer dolans.
Des mors et des navrés font tous couvrir les cans. 3035
Si fiert .I. soudoier en l'escu qui fu grans,
La boucle de la targe ne li fu pas garans,
Ne la cote armeoire, ne li bons jaserans;
Que par le pis ne soit deceüs li fiers coulans.
Ens el camp l'abat mort, liés en fu et joians. 3040
Puis escria: "La crois! Dex, aidiés vos serjans!"
La peuisiés veoir .I. estor ki fu grans.
Agoulans voit morir ses jens, en fu dolans.
Il broce le ceval des esporons trencans,
Vers Elias s'en vait qui n'estoit pas fuians, 3045
En l'escu le feri, mais l'aubers fu tenans.
Del destrier ne se mut li cevaliers vallans,
Ains a traite l'espee dont li puns est luisans.
Vers Agoulans s'en va tos et isnelement,
Durement le requiert al fier qui est trencans 3050
Et Agoulans vers lui ki ne l'est espargnans.
Mout par est grans li caples des .II. homes puisans,
Ainc nel fust plus orible Oliviers ne Rollans.

137 Elyas voit sa jent ricement maintenir.
A .II. mains tint l'espee, Agoulant vait ferir 3055

Et Agoulans ausi ses cols li va partir.
Tant se sunt conbatu par force et par aïr
Que la caurre del fier les a fais departir.
Lor lasse est isi grande qu'il ne s'osent ferir;
.I. entredeus li giete Elias sans falir   3060
Que li bons cercles d'or ne le puet garandir.[73]
Desi en la coree li fait le branc sentir,
Mort le rue a ses piés. Cou li vient a plaisir.
Et li frere Elias font tout l'estor fremir,
Que tous les plus hardis ont fais acouardir.   3065
Quant la gens Agoulant nel porent mais soufrir
Il tornerent les dos si prisent a fuïr
Et la gens crestïene qui Dex puist beneïr
Les prendent a ocire et font vilment morir.

138 Ocis a Elias le cuviert Agoulant,   3070
    Ses gens sunt desconfites, si s'en tornent atant.
    Et nostre barounie les vont au dos sivant
    Tout si con les ategnent, si les vont detrencant.
    Quant li haut houme voient le martire si grant
    A no barnaje crïent la merci tout avant: 3075
    "Signour, nos nous rendons trestout a vo coumant.
    Feauté vous ferons cescuns coumunalment."
    Et li nostre respondent: "Cou seroit avenant." 105a
    Lors est remés li caples, cescuns rendi son branc.
    Orians et si fil vont Elias querrant.   3080
    Lui et Simon encontrent, si le vont acolant.
    Puis entrent en la vile dont il erent devant,
    El palais descendirent qu'est de marbre luisant.
    Ancois k'il se desarment, lor font lor sairement
    Et foi et loiauté li petit et li grant.   3085
    Lors montent el dognon li frere maintenant,
    Cescuns a desvestu le hauberc jaserant;
    D'escarlate et de vert sunt vestu li auquant,
    Li autre de cendal et de vert bougerant.
    Les mors ont entierés li plus procain parent.   3090
    Au mangier sunt assis li nostre lïement.
    Elias en apiele Symon en souriant,
    Celui ki fu loiés pour lui estroitement
    Ne onques ne vot faire desloial sairement.
    "Symon," dist Elias, "cest bon castiel vous rent.   3095
    Jou voel que il soit vostres des ici en avant."
    "Sire," cou dist Simons, "deniers, mercis vous rent."
    A son pié s'abaissa, se li baisa atant;
    Grant joie fait sa fame et si petit enfant.
    "Simon," fait Elias, "entendés mon samblant.   3100
    Jou proi que cest garcon dounés tout sen vivant
    Reubes, cevaus et armes trestout a son talant.

Par lui soumes osté de dolerous tourmant."

139 Grant joie ont demené li baron cevalier,
Les tables ont ostees serjant et escuer.   3105
"Signor," fait Elias, "jou vous voel merciier;
Bien m'avés souscoru a men grignor mestier.
A tous coumunalment vous voel dire et proier
Que tout ens en vos tieres vous retornés arrier.
Dex garise men pere et sa france moullier."   3110
"Sire, mout volentiers!" dïent li cevalier.
Elias va ses freres acoler et baisier,
La ot .I. plorement et .I. dol si plenier.
Li baron en lor tieres prisent a repairier;
Elias est remés tous seus ens el gravier.   3115
A la rive repaire, ainc n'i ot escuier,
Et voit venir le cisne ki le dut convoier
La u Dex le voloit a Nimaie envoier.

140 Elias est venus au port sor la marine,
Il garde contreval, si a veü le cisne   3120
Qui s'en estoit fuïs pour la gent sarrasine.
Quant Elias le voit, lait sa gent entierine;
Cele part est courus sans noise et sans hustine,
Salis est el batiel que ses frere traïne.
Des or s'en vait noant. Dex a cui tot acline   3125
Les conduise ambes .II. et la Vergene Roïne.
Li cisnes en son biec portoit une racine,
Onques herbe grignor n'ot nient millor mecine;
A Elias le baille et met en sa saisine.
A sa plaie le touce, cou saciés sans devine,   3130
Lors fu et saine et blance coume flors d'aubespine.
Quant Elias le sent, si ot joie entierine.

141 Elias est mout liés, si maine grant baudor
De cou qu'il est garis; ne sent mal ne dolor.
De la mer est iscus sans noise et sans crior,   3135
Si se met ens el Rin par Dieu le Creatour.
Elias a veü et les murs et la tour
D'une rice cité et le palais au cour   105*b*
Et l'escarboncle cler ki rent grande luour.
Laiens en la cité avoit grande freor.   3140
Elias ot la noise et la fiere criour,
De l'escrois qu'il demainent a eü grant freour.
Ne va gaires avant, s'encontre .I. pesceor
En .I. petit batiel u conquiert sa labour.
Quant Elias le voit, se li dist par amor: 3145
"Frere, quel noise est cou dont j'oi si grant tabor?"
"Sire," fait li pescieres, "foi que doi vostre amor;

Cou est une mervelle, ainc n'oïstes grignor."

142 "Amis," dist Elias, "or me di verité
Se cou sunt sarrasin u sunt crestïené?"   3150
"Sire," fait li pesciere, "ja'n orés verité.
Il a en ceste vile .I. traïtor prouvé,
Li dus Reniers a non par sa crestïenté.
La dame de Buillon vot tolir s'ireté,
Li baron de la tiere i sunt tout ajorné;   3155
Ancui ert forjugie, jel sai de verité,
Se Jhesu Cris n'en pense par la soie bonté."

143 "Sire," fait li pesciere, "entendés ma raison.
Li Sesne est mout crüeus, nus ne set sa facon.
Tolu a a la dame la tiere de Buillon,   3160
N'est ki por li enprenge escu ne le baston."
"Non!" cou dist Elias, "que font dont si baron?"
"Sire, tout sunt torné envers le mal gloton;
Mout poi en a li dame qui ost jugier raison."
"A! Dex!" fait Elias, "par ta beneïcon,   3165
Quar i fusse jou ore au plait de cel gloton;
A l'aïe de Dieu et son saintisme non
I meteroie jou mon cors en abandon."

144 "Sire," fait li pesciere, "n'i soiés arestans.
Hastés vous ent, frans hom, que Dex vous soit
                                              aidans.   3170
Mout dout c'ancois ne soit courus li jugemans
Et la dame ait perdu cou dont ele est tenans."
Lors s'en va Elias, d'iluec est departans;
Au port est arivés maintenant ses calans.
Elias saut en piés con cevaliers vaillans,   3175
Son cor pent a sen col, qu'est d'ivore luisans;
Par tel aïr le soune que .II. liuees grans
En est l'oïe alee. Et tous li jugemens
En est remés a dire. Cescuns i est courans.
De la cort en sunt toutes esfraees les jens.   3180

145 Signor, or ascoutés pour Dieu de paradis.
Elias fu el Rin ki mout estoit pensis.
Ci le lairai, de lui bien serai revertis;
Dirai de la ducoise cui Jhesus soit aidis
Qu'a Nimaie ert venue a .X.M. fierviestis   3185
Et avoec li sa fille, la bele Beatris.
Venue estoit clamer de Rainier le marcis,
Sire estoit de Saisogne, .I. traïtres maudis.
Il li toloit sa tiere et trestout le païs
Pour cou que ses barons estoit mors et finis,   3190

Josiaumes de Buillon qui mout fu signoris.
El palais a Buillon avoit ses gardes mis,
Quatre cens chevaliers a vers hiaumes brunis.[74]
La ducoise se claime a ses barons jentis,
Mais tant doutent le Sesne, le cuviert maleïs,   3195
Qu'il ne s'osent drecier tant ert grans et furnis.[75]

NOTES

1. *B* is the only manuscript to provide a title rubric.
2. (*1*. 1) d. silenche *B*. Context suggests emendation on the authority of *E* in agreement with *C*.
3. (*1*. 21) *C* begins the epic twice. (See p. xxxiv-v.) The initial three laisses as contained in *BE* are found on *fol.* 5*c* and *d*. Here they are immediately preceded by an illumination similar to those found in *BE* at the opening of the poem. All show a tower from which Oriant and Beatrix are looking down at the young woman with two infants. The main body of the epic then begins on *fol.* 11*a* with two laisses found in *B* (*fol.* 105*c*) and *E* (*fol.* 20*d*) as a part of the transition to the second branch of the cycle. These are given below:

> Signeur, oiếs canchon ki mout fait a löer,   11*a*
> Par iteil couvent le vos puis je conter
> Que la viertus dou ciel le vous laisse escouter
> Et la pais Damediu puist en vous demorer.
> Je ne vous vorai mie mencougnes raconter   5
> Ne fables ne paroles pour vos deniers embler
> Ains vos dirai canchon u il n'a k'amender
> Del barnage de Franche ki tant fait a löer
> Qui proumerain alerent le sepuchre aourer.
> Chil prisent Anthyoche, nel vos quier a celer,   10
> Mais ancois lor couvint grans painnes endurer
> Fors estors et batailles, veillier et jeuner.
> Seigneur a thel termine que vous m'öếs conter
> Ains c'on seuwist en Franche la voie d'outremer
> Ne nus s'aparcheuwist de l'ost acheminer   15
> Avint une merveille que jou vos weil monstrer
> Car jamais nus jougleres ne vous dira sa per.
>
> La merveile fu grans et dire le doit on,
> Bien le doivent oïr tout chevalier baron.
> Ains c'on seuwist la voie par nule anuntïon   20
> Et que s'aparceuwissent Franche ne Bourgignon,
> Ert li dus Godefrois chevaliers a Buillon,
> Meschins et bacelers, n'ot barbe ne grenon,
> Et Bauduins ses freres que Dius fache pardon.
> Dius! Com lie la mere qui fist teil nourecon.   25

> De gentil dame issirent et de gentil baron,
> Puis furent roy li frere par electĩon,
> Si conquisent par forche le temple Salemon
> Et la grans tours David a coite d'espouron.
> Or coumenche ci droit la tres boine canchon   30
> Ki mais porés entendre se jou di voir ou non.

4. (*1.* 26) o. est est f. *B.*

5. (*1.* 33) *C* preserves this laisse in two forms. One is found on *fol.* 11*a* and *b* and is collated against *B.* The other is found on *fol.* 5*d* and is given in full below:

> Signor, or escoutés, bonne gent absolue;
> S'orrés bonne chancon qui n'est mie abseüe.
> L'estoire en a esté longement reponeu [sic],
> Ensi con li solaus qui cuevre sor la nue,
> Dedens une abeïe, mais or est fors issue
> Et que par les predomes soit oïe et seüe.
> Del chevalier au cisne avés chancon oüe,
> Il n'a el siecle homme ne femme si chenue
> Qui onques en oïst la premiere venue,
> De quel terre il fu nés, mais or est sor est
> entendue [sic].
> Jel vous dirai tres bien, se Dieus m'en prest
> aiue.

6. (*1.* 39) O. ensi l'oi noumer *B.* The reading of the base is a typical *cheville* and fails to introduce the following verse logically. Emended on the authority of *E* in agreement with *C.*

7. (*1.* 90) Li sire a la parole laisie en somiant *BE.* The reading of the base contradicts the context which is clearly established in lines 81, 82, and 91. It can be interpreted, then, as a common error of considerable importance linking *B* and *E.* Although there is no stemmatic evidence that the one available variant from *C* is more authentic, it does at least restore the logic of the passage.

8. (*1.* 106) E. que ke l. *B.*

9. (*1.* 209) s. fille a. *B.* Emended on the authority of *E* in agreement with *CGI H.*

10. (*1.* 266) *puis* < *pugnos.* Cf. *pug* 1716, 2340, 2404; *puig* 1764, 2040, 2312, 2317, 2351; *puign* 1067; *puing* 887. Also *besoig* 2284, *besoing* 2265, and *soing* 2472.

11. (*1.* 302) .II. liuess g. *B.* The emended letter was first written as an elongated *s* which appears to have been modified in an attempt to form an *e.* Cf. *liuees* 3177.

12. (*1.* 397) The last eleven lines of *fol.* 93*c* have been subjected to considerable wear so that a number of words are legible only with the aid of comparison with

a variant text. The reading in brackets is the text of
E in agreement with *G*, the text of *B* being entirely
obliterated at this point.

13. (*1*. 400) Quar l. *B*. The rejected reading is not con-
sistent with the context established by *1*. 399. It may
be a simple scribal error repeating the initial word of
the next line. Emended on the authority of *E*.

14. (*1*. 415) .VI. s. *B*. The immediate context, especially
1. 411 implies that all seven children have been left
alone. Also, Malquarés states explicitly in his report
to Matabrune, *1*. 428, that he has found that many.
Thus, the rejected reading is either a simple error in
transcription or an erroneous anticipation of the fol-
lowing episode in which Malquarés returns for the sil-
ver pendants and finds only the ill-fated six. Emended
on the authority of *E* in agreement with *CG H*.

15. (*1*. 426) q. novele d. *B*. Emended on the authority of
E. Cf. variant in *G*.

16. (*1*. 443) This treatment of the object pronouns is at-
tested elsewhere in the manuscript tradition. Cf. va-
riants for *11*. 442 and 443. Also *Elioxe 1*. 1935.

17. (*1*. 527) *G* adapts the content of laisse 29 as a conti-
nuation of laisse 28 beginning at this point. The re-
sultant lines are given in full with the variants for
1. 527 and *G* is indicated as wanting in the variants
for laisse 29. See note 26.

18. (*1*. 557) *E G* amplify the content of *11*. 557-561 and
treat the entire passage as a separate laisse. This
laisse, 30 *bis* with respect to *B*, is set off clearly in
E G from the preceding one by a space and by a large
initial capital. If rhyme is the essential unifying
factor in the laisse, then *B* is correct in treating
laisse 30 and 30 *bis* as one. The orthographic adjust-
ment (ie. frere > fraire) is noteworthy as it indicates
the importance of a visual aspect to rhyme here. In-
deed, this must have motivated the separation of 30
bis, although a reverse orthographic adjustment is ne-
cessary (ie. affaire > affere) in order for the separa-
tion to be consistent. The added lines are provided
among the variants for *1*. 561.

19. (*1*. 605) B. sunt d. *B*. The rejected reading contra-
dicts the sense of this passage. Line 606 clearly in-
dicates that Matabrune is referring to her own situa-
tion and it is obvious that she, not the children,
would be relieved by the permanent destruction of the
pendants. Emended on the authority of *E*.

20. (*1*. 659) s. et de grant region *B*. It is possible that
the rejected reading had its origin in an erroneous

transcription which omitted the second syllable of *relegion*. This error left the hemistich short by one syllable. Later the addition of *et* during a subsequent transcription restored the normal rhythm but separated the two elements of the verse so that it no longer expressed a single idea. Significantly, all available variant texts attest the authenticity of the proposed emendation. Although the rejected reading makes sense, it is emended on the authority of *E* in agreement with *CG H* because there is reasonable evidence that it arose through error rather than through conscious revision.

21. (*1.* 683) d. demain a. *B*. The reading of the base obscures the sense of the passage by depriving *desfendre* of its object. Emended on the authority of *E* in agreement with *CG H*.

22. (*1.* 724) The first hemistich is short by one syllable. The expected rhythm is restored on the authority of *E*.

23. (*1.* 765) Va il il nelement *B*. Emended on the authority of *E* in agreement with *CG*.

24. (*1.* 849) The first hemistich is short by one syllable. The expected rhythm is restored on the authority of *E* in agreement with *CG H*.

25. (*1.* 853) *C* abbreviates the following passage and attributes Oriant's desires to Matabrune.

26. (*1.* 867) At this point *G* (*fol.* 15*a*) introduces two laisses which are found in no other manuscript. These laisses represent an amplification of the passage narrating the arrival of Elias in his father's city and emphasize the boy's ignorance of worldly matters. It is possible that the development of the narrative at this point conditioned its abbreviation in laisse 29. (See note 17.) The latter passage describes the boy's visits within his father's city and the seneschal's distribution of bread, a passage which decidedly contradicts the implied background at this point. It is significant that *C H* avoid this inconsistency by deleting laisses 27 - 31. The text of the two laisses found in *G*:

> Signor, ici endroit lairons ester del roi,
> Si dirons del enfant ki vient a grant esploit.
> Li hermites retorne ki li a fait convoi.
> "He! Dex!" dist li hermites ki fu de boune loi,
> "U ira or cis enfes ki nului ne connoist?
> Comment se conbatra ne entenra en loi,
> Car onques il ne vit bataille ne tornoi."
> Et li enfes cemine tres par mi le caumois,
> Le cité vit son pere et le mestre bierfroi.

"He! Dex!" cou dist li enfes, "qu'est cou que
                                        jou voi?"
Quant l'enfes a veü les murs de la cité,
Les maissons et les sales de viel antiquité
Il ne set que cou est, forment i a pensé,
Car ains fors de boscage n'avoit jor conversé.
Atant es .II. gloutons issus de la cité,
Malfaisans et Turfiers issi furent noumé.
Et li enfes les voit, si lor a demandé:
"Li queus de vous," fait il, "gardés ne me celés,
Est Beatris ma mere qu'en ses flans m'a porté,
Que la viele maudite a a tort encoupé?
Se jou ataing la viele mar li est encontré
Car mes peres me dist quant de lui fui tornés
Que a li me presise s'eüsse poesté."
Quant cil l'ont entendu s'en ont ris et jabé
Bien sevent que fols est, si l'ont avirouné.
A tastons le queroient k'il ierent aullé
Por le pecié k'il fissent et le desloiauté
                                        fol. 15*b*
De celle boune dame dont je vous ai conté.
L'uns le tire vers lui, li autres l'a bouté
Et li enfes ausi Malfaissant a douné
Del grant baston k'il tient c'ot del bos aporté,
Qu'al premerain cop l'a mort et craventé.
A l'autre cop apriés a Turfier asené,
En mi le front devant l'a en boutant hurté
Si felenescement par droite cruauté;
Li cierviaus de la tieste li est aval coulés.
"Par mon cief," dist li enfes, "jou n'ai pas oublié
Cou que me dist mes peres quant de lui fui tornés.
Caus ki mal me feroient, n'eüsse deporté".
A iceste parolle entra en la cité
Mout peurousement, ce vous di par vereté,
C'onques maïs en sa vie n'ot en tel liu esté.
"He! Dex," cou dist li enfes, "par vostre poesté,
Sont ore cil hermite ki ci sont ostelé?
Jou ne quidoie mie, foi que doi saint Amé,
K'il en i eüst tant en la crestienté.
Maïs jou sai ore bien par fine verité
Que cist hermite ca ont plus grant ireté
Que mes peres nen ait el parfont gaut ramé."
As parolles k'il dist sanble bien forsenés.

27. (1. 898) At this point *E* (*fol.* 6*c*) adds the following
    laisse (43 *bis* with respect to *B*) which is found in no
    other manuscript:
        L'enfes voit le ceval que il mout redouta,
        Les .IIII. piés reons mervelles regarda.

> "Sire," dist il au roi, "entendés a moi cha.
> Pour l'amour Diu vous pri, qui le mont estora,
> Tenés le si estroit que il ne viegne cha."
> Quant li rois Orians l'oï et escouta
> Par mi son mautalent li rois grant joie en a.
> Volentiers eüst ris mais grant dolor mena.

28. (*1*. 1046) Cf. lines added in *CG* after *1*. 1054.
29. (*1*. 1063) m. garse *B*. The immediate context suggests an error in the transcription of *grase < gratia*. Emended on the authority of *E*. The orthography of the emendation is attested in *11*. 1747, 2241, and 2739.
30. (*1*. 1071) D. madie e. *B*. Emended on the authority of *E* in agreement with *G*.
31. (*1*. 1140) m. doit d. *B*. Emended on the authority of *E*.
32. (*1*. 1219) *B* does not indicate a new laisse at this point by means of the expected space and large initial capital. Separation is made in the edited text as required by the shift in rhyme and on the authority of *E* in agreement with *C H*.
33. (*1*. 1242) l. cuvers n. *B*. The reading of the base appears to be an error since reference is being made to the two noble youths sent to bring arms for Elyas. Emended on the authority of *E* in agreement with *G H*.
34. (*1*. 1247) m. kil nient nul m. *B*. Emended on the authority of *E* in agreement with *G H*.
35. (*1*. 1354) The second hemistich is short by one syllable. Emended on the authority of *G H*. *E* and *C* differ.
36. (*1*. 1359) s. cousin cousin l. *B*.
37. (*1*. 1468) Laisses 69 and 70 are separated in *B* by the rubric: Ci dist si con Elias et Mauquarés se conbatirent ensanle. Laisse 70 then begins with an illuminated capital depicting two mounted knights in combat.
38. (*1*. 1484) s. en son en son e. *B*.
39. (*1*. 1516) *CG* agree in making this the initial verse of laisse 72.
40. (*1*. 1569) foie et escaufe *B*. Emended on the authority of *E* in agreement with *CG DH*.
41. (*1*. 1628) Qu'il furent d. *B*. The context suggests a form of *faire* rather than *estre*. Emended on the authority of *E* in agreement with *C*. Cf. *G D*.
42. (*1*. 1837) Venes apres *B*. The first hemistich is short by one syllable. Emended on the authority of *E* in agreement with *CG D*.
43. (*1*. 1845) l. freres v. *B*. The swans are gathering about their brother, Elyas. Emended on the authority of *E*.
44. (*1*. 1861) *Piés* appears to be a syncopated form of

pitiés. The manuscript is clear and the line is rhyth-
mically correct. The available variants *E D* agree gen-
erally in their difference from the base, but do not
suggest an error. Cf. *fra* 1894; also Brussels BR MS.
10391, *fol. 7v*: Ma dame che dist Marques james nen
veres piés/ Car je leur ay copet et membres et leur
phiés.

45. (*1.* 1972) *B* is illegible. The curved upper quarter of
a letter is visible above the rubbed area just to the
left of the final *-se*. Since the scribe capitalizes
place names only when they occur as the initial word of
a verse, this would indicate *frise*, the reading of *E*,
rather than *pise*, the reading of *G DH*. The general
agreement of *BE* supports this suggestion, although it
does not prove it. Emended on the authority of *E*.

46. (*1.* 1973) *B* is illegible. Emended on the authority of
E in agreement with *G D*.

47. (*1.* 2005) o. delabiel *B*. *E D* read *babiel*, *CG baudiel*.
These suggest an initial *b*. Reference to Babel is cer-
tainly a common means of expressing the idea of orien-
tal opulence and such an idea is intended in this pas-
sage. Emended on the authority of *E* in agreement with
D.

48. (*1.* 2056) e. quie *B*.

49. (*1.* 2123) s. ere e. *B*. It is clear from the context
that the future is intended. This is confirmed by the
agreement *E G D* (*iert / ert*) and by the present sub-
junctive forms of *C H*. Emended on the authority of *E*
in agreement with *G D*.

50. (*1.* 2146) *B* is repeating line 2144. The variants sug-
gest that this may be erroneous.

51. (*1.* 2187) *D* employs a large capital to indicate a
laisse division at this point. None of the other manu-
scripts makes such a separation, however, and there is
no change in rhyme.

52. (*1.* 2197) S. dist Elyas p. *B*. Matabrune, not Elyas,
is speaking. Emended on the authority of *E* in agree-
ment with *G D*.

53. (*1.* 2223) f. laute e. *B*. Emended on the authority of
E in agreement with *G D*.

54. (*1.* 2252) l. siens e. *BE*. Context and variants indi-
cate these are the *sains* mentioned in *1.* 2249. The oc-
currence of the rejected reading in both *B* and *E* sug-
gests a common error rather than a radical orthographic
variant. Emended on the authority of *DH*.

55. (*1.* 2275) s. def *B*.

56. (*1.* 2341) Hondres f. *B*. Elyas strikes Hondré, thus
the objective case should be used. *B* is consistently

correct in its usage for this name as well as for the noun generally. Emended on the authority of *D*. Cf. *Oendon* (*Oende*, nom. sing.) *E*.

57. (*1*. 2354) c. seule d. *B*. Context and variants suggest that *courent seure* is the correct reading. Cf. Pour poi ne li cort seure ... *1*. 1108.

58. (*1*. 2365) Q. sanglens s. *B*. There is enough damage to the manuscript at this point to render the reading difficult, however, the nasal bar above *a* is clear. The *l* is recognizable. The last three letters are undertain. Emended on the authority of *E* in agreement with *CG DH*.

59. (*1*. 2421) t. cui qui quel *B*.

60. (*1*. 2422) Q. a la *B*.

61. (*1*. 2424) At this point *H* (*fol*. 324*a*) adds the following unique laisse (111 *bis* with respect to *B*):
     Or commence la noyse a l'entrer du chastel,
     Elyas y abat telz trente jovencel
     Qui gueteront la porte, le pont et le carnel;
     Puis va ferir ung duc qui sist sur ung pontel,
     Tel coup lui a donné dessus son haterel
     Qui lui a abatu le sang et le cervel.
     "Damedieu, Sire, Pere," dist Elyas le bel,
     "Donne moy que je tienne la vielle du chastel."

62. (*1*. 2456) The first syllable of *mervillouse* is rubbed away in *B*. Emended on the authority of *E*.

63. (*1*. 2487) c. maprendroie q. *B*. Emended on the authority of *E* in agreement with *CG D*.

64. (*1*. 2502) s. houme t. *B*. Emended on the authority of *E* in agreement with *CGT H*.

65. (*1*. 2518) Laisse 115 is separated from laisse 116 in *B* by the rubric: Ci dist si con li cevaliers au cisne fist gieter Matabrune el fu ki estoit espris. Line 2518 then begins with an illuminated Capital depicting a woman being forced toward a fire.

66. (*1*. 2670) a. coisist le grant galie *B*. Erroneous repetition of the preceding second hemistich. Emended on the authority of *E*.

67. (*1*. 2856) s. herbejement *B*.

68. (*1*. 2909) c. et t. *B*. Context and the evidence of all variant readings argue against co-ordinate clauses. The reading of the base could be the result of an erroneous transcription of *itant*. Emended on the authority of *E*.

69. (*1*. 2941) r. Elias c. *B*. It is Agolans who is speaking. Emended on the authority of *E* in agreement with *GT D*.

70. (*1*. 2997) l. pogneis *B*. The reading of the base appears to be a scribal error repeating the final word in the preceding line. Either *foleis* (*E C*) or *froisseis*

(*GT D*) would be acceptable. Emended on the authority of *E* in agreement with *C*.

71. (*1*. 3024) P. saisist 1. *B*. Context requires an indicative tense. Emended on the authority of *E* in agreement with *CGT D*.

72. (*1*. 3029) At this point *H* (*fol*. 325*a*) adds a unique laisse (135 *bis* with respect to *B*):

> Or commence le chapple et dure la meslee.
> Elyas y a point la ventaille fermee.
> Elyas va ferir sur la targe doree,
> En my le pis devant la lui a effondree.
> Le haubert fut si fort, maille n'en est faulcee,
> La piece de la lance est contremont volee.

> *fol*. 325*b*

> Quant Elyas le vit, si a traicte l'espee.
> Par my eulx s'est feru, si a crié Monjoye!
> Quant ses gens le congneurent, grant joye ont
> menee,
> Dedens ce sont ferus telz cent en la meslee;
> Chascun abat le scien de la scelle meslee.
> La ont tant pié, tant poing, tant de teste coppee,
> De la gent Agolant fut la place pavee.
> Ne povaient mes souffrir la bataille aduree,
> En fuyte sont tournez comme gens esfree. [sic]

73. (*1*. 3061) *B* repeats this line.

74. (*1*. 3193) *B* makes use of two spaces for this line.

75. (*1*. 3196) This line occupies the final space at the bottom of *fol*. 105*b*. The text of *fol*. 105*c* is immediately preceded by a rubric: Ci dist si con no baron en alerent le Sepucre aourer et prisent Andioce en lor voie. The first line of text is initiated by an illuminated capital and reads: Signour oiés cancon ki mout fait a löer. These features may function to emphasize the separation of Branches I and II. Note that laisse 145 which is preserved only in *BE* serves to announce a general change in subject matter. *E*, however, does not repeat the rubric found in *B* and does not begin the following laisse with an illuminated capital. The other available variants likewise have no physical indications of division and tend on the whole to unify the Rhine voyage and the arrival at Nimwegen even more.

VARIANTS

1. *BE C*
  1. o. entendes K. *E*; d. sience *E C*.
  2. e. amer e. *C*; *E wants*.
  3. S'orres b. *C*; c. de m. grant sapience *E*; d. scienche *C*.
  4. Ainc n. *E C*; n'oron s. v. des puis le tans silence *E*.
  6. a. et pais e. reverence *E*; e. silence *C*.
  7. C. vous dirai le prouvence *E*.
  8. a. com furent en esrence *E*.
 10. Coument f., a grande pestilence *E*.
 11. Ancui orres *C*; m. or m'en doinst Dix consence *E*.
2. *BE C H*
 12. S. oiies p. D. le pere e. *E*.
 13. d. la main a. *E C H*.
 14. k. en c. *C*.
 15. De m. *C*; d. samin e. *H*.
 16. v. dirai n. *C H*.
 17. *H wants*.
 18. Q. il est en ystoire *H*; e. escrit c. *C*; l'estore ce est tout v. *E*.
 19. fist la *C*; *H wants*.
 20. *H wants*.
 21. c. durable *C*; *H wants*.
3. *BE C H*
 22. o. entendes b. *E*; a. franche g. *C*; *H wants*.
 23. e. mie s. *C*; *H wants*.
 24. La chancon a, l. repronue *H*.
 25. Aussi com l'oisellet qui est mis en mue *H*; *C wants*.
 26. Devers u. *C*; m. ele e. *E*; *H wants*.
 27. Mais o. *H*; e. fors issue *C*.
 28. Et par *H*; q. de tous p. *E*.
 29. c. eue *H*; *C adds*: Il n'i a si biel homme ne femme si crenue.
 30. Mais n. *H*; n'i a si v. *C*; a si v. houme feme kenue (sic) *E*.
 31. Qu'onques e. *C*; Q. gueres ait oy l., venue veue (sic) *H*.
 32. i. ert n. *C*; m. s'or e. *E*; o. sera seue *C*; *H wants*.

33. Je le v. *C*; Mais je la vous diray, m. donne a. *H*;
    d. mout b., D. m'est en a. *E*; D. plaist et s'aiue *C*.
4. *BE C H*
34.   *H wants.*
35.   b. a o. *E C*; *H wants.*
38.   i. manoit ung roy riches e. *H*.
39.   O. cites ot (s'ot cites *C*) a garder *E C*; *H wants.*
40.   c. deporter *C*; *H wants.*
41.   b. .C. m. *C*; *H wants.*
42.   Qui avoit o soy m. et femme a son p. *H which adds:*
      La dame n'avoit oncques eu mal d'enfanter/ Quer
      Dieu ne lui voulloit filz ne fille donner/ Ce n'est
      pas par hayne mais pour eulz esprouver/ Maint grant
      ennuy a l'en souvent pour mesparler/ Si com eust
      puis la dame come orres parler.
43.   *H wants.*
44.   Si o. *C*; *H wants.*
45.   Ainc d., n'oi n. *E*; *H wants.*
46.   *H wants.*
47.   Ele ot n. B. ensi l. *C*; *H wants.*
48.   d. si con j'oi conter *C*; *H wants.*
49.   *H wants.*
50.   v. toudis h. *C*; *H wants.*
51.   j. furent l. *H*; e. sa femme monteis *C*.
52.   p. son c. *C*.
53.   Iluec gardent a. *C*; I. regardent a. *E*; Regarderent
      a. s. y virent a. *H*.
55.   Li s. les regarde si prent a souspirer *C*; l. voit
      s., a plourer *E*.
56.   D. deux i. *H*; c. en va l'aige couler *E*; *C wants.*
57.   Dame cou dist li roys p. n. devons a. *C*.
58.   C'onques D. *C*.
59.   Ves la u. *C*; Or v., m. querant va s. *H*; s. disner
      C H.
60.   e. doit a. *E C H*.
61.   s. eulx deulx j. c. saiches sans doubter *H*; j. por
      cou poons pener *C*.
62.   Il resanlent l'un l'autre m. *C*; s. et par i. *E*; *H*
      wants.
5. *BE C H*
63.   Sire c. *E C H*.
64.   N. puis croire nul h. e. che s. *C*; h. de c. *E*; *H*
      wants.
65.   a. ja plus d'un seul e. *C*; e. deux e. *H*.
66.   n'en est l. *E*; ne soit l. *C*; ne s'est l. *H*.
67.   N'en p. *C*.
68.   Mais j. *C H*.
69.   Quant li rois l. *C H*; e. mout o. le cuer dolant *E*;

e. s'en eut g. *C*; s. en eust m. *H*; g. marrement
C H.

70. C. dist i. *E C*.
71. a de tout p. *E H*; p. faus e. *E*; k. ne l'e. *H*.
72. P. son parler a *E C*; a l'en maint g. *H*.
73. Si comme eust p., d. oncquez n. *H*; *E C want*.
74. Ainsi comme orres ains l. *H*; d. se l'estoire n'en ment *E*; *C wants*.
75. v. est venus l. *E*; v. aprocha la nuis vint erramment *C*; v. s'approucha l. *H*.
76. Chele n. li roys o sa d. au cors gent *C*; *H wants*.
77. P. tout puissant *H*.
78. E. le seigneur en la dame vaillant *H*; Conçut lues .VII. *E*; a chel e. *C*; *H adds*: VII enfans celle nuit en ung engendrement.
79. d. nul d. *H*; a essiant *E C H*.
80. O. verra bien l. *H*; s. faus dis de d. *E*; *C wants*.
81. Puis d. *C*.
82. l. mout deboinairement *C*; l. a tout b. *H*; b. essient *E H*.
83. s. a essient *E*; *C H want*.
84. *C H want*.
85. *C H want*.
86. d. se mervelle q. *E*; *C H want*.
87. s. dist e. *E*; *C H want*.
88. d. qui devant l. *E*; *C H want*.
89. Qu'il n., p. desi en orient *E*; *C H want*.
90. Et la dame et li autre trestout communalment *C*; *H wants*.
91. m. en a. *E C*; a. tost et isnielement *C*; a. tous deux joyeusement *H*.
92. La messe font canter a. *C*; Et oyrent la messe a l'ostel s. *H*.
94. m. oye s'en vindrent D. *H*; t. ens ou palais plus grant *C*; *H adds*: Mainte aumosne donnerent le jour a povre gent.
95. v. diron d. *H*; dame en avant *C H*.
96. p. les e. .IX. mois en .I. tenant *C*; a l'enfantement *H*.

6. *BE C H*
97. a les e. p. tant com el d. *H*; d. les e. porte tant que d. *C*; s. com d. *E*; o. devoit *E C*.
98. T. qu'elle v. *H*; q. jesir d. *C*.
99. Au naistre des enfans p. *H*; d. nule f. *C H*.
100. F. une vielle dame qui en Dieu pou creoit *H*; s. que n. *C*.
101. Mere estoit au fiz la royne fort hayoit *H*; e. Diu ne creoit *E C*; *H adds*: A amasser avoir tout son

penser estoit.
102. a paine e. *H.*
103. s. que D. *C.*
104. *H wants.*
105. e. destinent q. *E*; f. si con lor a. *C*; *H wants.*
106. Et quant l'uns e. *C*; Si com l'un e. *H.*
107. d. fin a. *E H*; d. blanc a. *C.*
108. *H wants.*
109. c. ce torneroit *E*; e. ne que senefioit *C*; *H wants.*
110. n. et b. *E*; e. grant e. *C.*
111. L'une fu une f. *E*; Les six en furent filz une fille i *H.*
112. p. que grant m. *C*; p. que meuldre en f. *H.*
113. Li dyaules l. *C*; L'ennemy l. s. qui ouvrer la f. *H.*
114. a pensee d. *H*; d. venir li devoit *E.*
115. Grant h. et grant anui que d. *E*; s. deviser e. *C*; s. destine e. *H.*
116. D. li r. *E C*; Jhesucript lui r. *H.*
117. El s. h. ains k'ele m. *E*; Car h. en s. *C*; *H wants.*
7. *BE C H*
118. n. comme vois devisant *H.*
119. a par Damediu commant *C.*
120. *E C H want.*
121. *H wants.*
122. furent al d. *C*; *H wants.*
123. c. kainete d. *E*; *H wants.*
124. *H wants.*
125. F. seulement li v. c. Damediu c. *C*; F. que la male v. *E*; *H wants.*
126. s. et D. *E*; s. si nel a. *C*; *H wants.*
127. c. s'avoit o. *C*; *H wants.*
128. La vielle a appellee la dame maintenant *H*; Beatris demanda c. *E*; a demandet c. *C.*
129. Beatris d. *E*; l. dame p. *C H*; v. pour l., s. Vinçant *E H*; s. Amant *C.*
130. *H wants.*
131. Or v. souvienne ore d. *H*; d. fort d. *E*; *C wants.*
132. Car v. *C*; Quant v. *H*; j. si l. *E.*
133. Que f. ne pooit a. plus d'un e. *C H.*
135. m. sire p. *E.*
136. Qu'avec sept hommes avez geu en ung tenant *H*; a. .II. a., p. le mien ensïant *C*; l. vostre commant *E.*
137. *C H want.*
138. a. le mal pourpensement *E*; *C H want.*
139. Car l. *E*; *C H want.*
140. E. si p. *E*; *C H want.*
141. Sainte M. dame c'a dit chele em plorant *C.*
142. a. Roi tout poissant *E*; *C H want.*

143. Dame ne me soffres a *C*; Ne me soffrez c. a tort a *H*; m. si vilment *C*.
144. Dame che f. *C*; m. dist l. *E C*; v. foi que doi s. *C which adds*: Demain seres vos arse se puis esploitier tant; *H wants*.
145. Rien ne v. vault dist la vielle maintenant *H*; *E C want*.
146. La viele en est alee s'apiela son s. *C*; t. si apiela .I. *E*; s'en va appella ung sergent *H*.
147. Et icil ot non *E*; Il avoit a *C*; S'il a *H*.
148. P. estoit sages si avoit avoir grant *C*; P. fu e. *E*; P. est et l. et en Dieu bien creant *H*.
149. Siers estoit Matabrune la viele souduians *C*; *H*. fut a la vielle q., v. losengant *H*.
150. Qu'il face *E*; Ja li descouverra son cuer et son talent *C*; *H wants*.

8. *BE C H*
152. v. ai fait e. *C H*.
154. *H wants*.
155. Et b., faire me v. *E*.
156. Et Marques le respont j. *C*; D. fait il pour Dieu ja ne soit destourne *H*; j. ne m'ert *E*; e. trestourne *E C*.
157. f. toute vo volentet *C*; q. vendra a *H*; v. vient a *E*.
158. c. dist l. *E*; *C wants*.
159. Dusque v. le m'ares f. *E*; Devant que le m. *H*; *C wants*.
160. Et Marques l. *H*; *C wants*.
161. M. s'il eust sceu de vray q. *H*; i. le seust k'ele eust e. *E*; *C wants*.
162. f. mie pour l. *H*; *C wants*.
163. li conte chou qu'ele a em penset *C*.
164. v. ja vos sera contet *C*; v. par S. *H*.
165. m. homme sont or .VII. *H*.
166. Alez l. *H*; l. ent n. *C*; n. si n. *E*; nem iert t. *C*.
167. Moi n'en c. *E C*; *H wants*.
168. a arret *C*; *H wants*.
169. v. bons a. *E*; v. amis Marques t. *H*; t. poes demorer *C*.
170. Et g. vos iex q. *C*; Or g. *E*; *H wants*.
171. v. n'estoient tapit et bien celet *C*; *H wants*.
172. v. poroie faire et pendre et trainer *C which adds*: Et si feroie jou si me puist Dieus sauver; *H wants*.
173. *E C H want*.
174. e. de paour a tranlle *E H*; *C wants*.
175. *C wants*.
176. *C H want*.

177. Et sachies se bien faites chou que j'ai deviset *C*;
l. dame que bon fuissies vous n. *E*; c. dit la v.
bon f. *H*.

178. a. auroys tout a voz voulentes *H*; r. et deniers
averes *C*.

179. a. .XV. jours p. *C*; *H wants*.

180. v. les enffans querre e. *H*; c. remanres *C*.

181. D. cou a dit Markes si fu espaventes *C*; D. fait lui
proudons tout a voz volentes *H*.

182-83. *H wants*.

184. e. tel desloiaute *E*; t. cose e. car me secoures *C*;
H wants.

185. *C H want*.

186. Et l. *C H*; L. vielle s. *E C H*; e. tourne s. *C H*.

187. Car la mere les lui les avoit acostes *C*; l. mere a.
E H; m. deles li (m. en pres le *H*) les a les *E H*.

188. s'est e. que s. c. ot l. *E*; *C H want*.

189. *E C H want*.

190. Ele les prent tous .VII. si les en a portes *C H*; v.
et ses en a porte *E*.

191. U M. *E C*; M. l'atendoit d. *E*; M. les a. *C*.

192. T. ce dist l. *C*; T. dist Matabrune cist sont maleu-
re *E*.

193. n. ja n'en soit trestournes *H*; n. or tos si vos
hastes *C*; s. en f. mon g. *E*.

194. q. seres retourne *E*; *H wants*.

195. *C H want*.

196. D. dist l. *E C*; tout a *E*; p. a vostre v. *C*; v. vo-
lente *E C*; p. qui fu moult espoventes *H which adds*:
Vostre vouloir feray et ce que commandes.

197. p. atout s'en est ales *C*; .VII. d'illec s'en est
tournes *H*.

198. l. vanra n. *E*; *H wants*.

199. Se Dieus n'em pense li rois de majestet *C*; p. le
soie b. *E*; *H wants*.

9. *BE CGI H*

200. Desore s'en va Markes i. *E*; *C H want*.

201. Sa mere s. *G*; Et l. *E*; v. se r. *C*; v. va encontre
q. *I*; v. vint encontre q. *G*; e. tourne q. *E*.

202. c. en p. *E*; e. va trestout p. *I*; e. passoit t. *H*;
e. passe t. *CG*; p. isnelement *C*; p. maintenant *G*.

203. Sy a *H*; a trouve u. *I*; u. lisse k. *E CGI H*; k. tout
n. *G*.

204. Caaloit .VII. *G*; c. tout a .I. nascement *C*; c. ses
met en son devant *G*; .I. restonsement *H*.

205. p. tantost t. *E*; l. prist t. *C*; .VII. sel met e. *I*;
.VII. et mist e. *C*; .VII. les mist e. *H*; en son de-
vant *E CI H*; *G wants*.

206. l. tua a *C*.
207. Puis le giete en .I. trues (pus *G*) t. *CG*; p. la je-
      ta t. *I*; a ruee t. *E*.
208. f. en venue q. joie mainne g. *C*; v. maintenant es-
      raument *H*; ọ. joie menoit g. *E*.
209. s. feme a. *E CGI H*.
210. U qu'il v. *C*; Quant voit v. *I H*; v. sa mere s. *CI
      H*; l. vient a. *H*.
211. *E CGI H want.*
212. v. viele m. d. il en sospirant *C*; m. fait il en
      souriant *I H*.
213. *E CGI H want.*
214. B. f. ce dist la vielle t. *E GI*; B. f. ce dist la
      mere t. *H*; B. f. dist ele t. *C*; f. je a. *I*; f. mout
      a. *CG*; a. le c. *CGI H*.
215. l. rois p. *E G*; *CI H want.*
216. l. te d. *E*; n. ariestement *G*; *CI H want.*
218. .VII. c., e. a chest acoukement *C*; Elle a eu .VII.
      chiens il n'y a aultre e. *H*; n'en a *G*.
219. Vees l. *C H*; Voi l. *G*; l. cist t. *I*; l. ja t. *H*; c.
      tos .VII. *C H*; .VII. eulx s. *H*; .VII. en mon gieron
      d. *GI*; .VII. en mon escourc d. *C which adds*: Fem-
      me doit on amer ki porte teil prousent; *H adds*: A
      .VII. chiens soit livree vez ci le provement.
220. Contre Dieu a ouvre e. *H*; E. fet c. *I*; *C placed af-
      ter* l. 222.
221. Et si n'est pas l. sus Dieu l. *I*; *C H want.*
222. f. faites l. *E I H*; l. ardre e. *H*; a. tos et isnie-
      lement *G*.
223. a si d. *E I*; d. en cest siecle vivant *I*; d. ens el
      siecle vivant *G*; *C H want.*
224. Li rois a. *G H*; s. ot si grant dueil q. *H*; t. do-
      lour q. *E*; a paour q. *C*; l. noviele e. *C H*.
225. Qu'il ne s. q. die t. *E*; Il ne s. qu'il die t. *C*;
      Q. ne le sot q. *I*; n. sot q. d. moult fut son c. *H*;
      t. ot l. *I*.
226. M. dist l. *C*; f. li sire en present *E*; f. il en
      souspirant *CI H*; r. ensement *G*.
227. p. de ci en oriant *I*; pas en *E*; q. mie q. *C H*; e.
      ce s. *E G*.
228. f. or ne le cuit noiant *I*; f. en nostre Diu creant
      C; m. n'en c. mes tant *H*; o. nel c. *E*.
229. *G adds*: Voir cou dist Mautabrune bien sai son aire-
      ment/ Se jou l'osoie dire mais jou n'en ai talent;
      CI H want.
230. d. sa mere k. a fait sairement *C*; li a convenant
      I; k. fist son serment *H*.
231. i. ardera sa feme v. *C*; i. le fera ardoir sans nul

respitement *GI*.

232. l. mere t. alez atargant *I*; t. ales ariestant *G*; *C wants*.

233. *GI add*: De si desloial fenme com je vous vois contant; *I adds further*: Qui est la vostre fame lasse com sui dolant/ Lors fet samblant que pleure li cor Dieu la cravant.

10. *BE CGI H*

234. M. a n. *E*.

235. q. n'est faite ne vaut pas .I. *C*; n. donroie .I. *I which adds*: Qu'ele vous a forfait par fole entention/ Vous li oistez dire le mot et la reson/ Qu'ele avoit .VII. enfans d'une conception/ Or les poez veoir dedenz le mien giron/ Ces .VII. chiens a eu par fole mesprison/ Puis qu'ele a fet tel mordre essillier la doit on; *H wants*.

236. l. cors a. a fu et a c. *C*; e. ung f. de c. *H*; *C adds*: Il n'a si desloial jusc'a Carphanaron.

237. c. l'esprouvement et la d. *I*; *H wants*.

238. Ces .VII. ciens a eut q. *C*; j'ai en *CG*; *I H want*.

239. f. faites l'a. *E*; qu'il n. *C*; q. ja n. *GI*; *H wants*.

240. Bien garde qu'ele n'ait point de c. *I*; *C wants*.

241. Mere c. *CI H*; l. rois q. *CGI H*.

242. Quant j. *E CGI H*.

243. l. plevi j. *I*; p. je droit v. a maint baron *E*; *C wants*.

244. Par m. ne sera a. *C*; Elle n'iert ja par moy a. *H*; m. ne sera a. *I*; a. je vous di en pardon *E*; j. li d. *G*; d. le d. *I*.

245. Mais j. *E*; Q. mettre la feray e. *H*; l. ferai jeter e. *I*; c. parfont *E C*.

246. Et si n. *E*; Jamais n. *C*; Donc elle n'ystra m. *H*; Si n. *G*; istera ciertes *E C*; i. jamais c. *G H*; *I wants*.

11. *BE CGI H*

247. c. dit l. *H*; l. dame q. *E*; v. cuer aves de lanier *CI H*.

248. Quant v. *CI H*; Q. ne voules a. *H*; a. cheste vostre m. *C*; v. france m. *GI*.

249. Il n. *E GI*; a tant d. *G*; c. durent li ciel *E*; *C H want*.

250. n. l'oses ne vir (?) n. *C*; *H wants*.

251. f. ardoir a, s. a .II. siers et l. *G H*; s. par l. *E*; .II. sains l. *C*.

252. Ou j. *E*; e. la c. *I H*; e. ma c. *C*; c. errant sans atargier *H*; *C adds*: Ele i deuist ore iestre avalee tres ier; *I adds*: Ele deust bien estre arse sanz

delaier.

253. Dame c. *C*; l. rois k. *CGI H*; s. je r. *I*; r. pecie
      E GI.
254. Vo volentet feres car nel ose l. *C*; F. vostre p.
      H; v. voloir q. *G*.
255. e. va s. *C*; s. comme a *H*.
256. s. c'avoit noris M. *C*; s. qu'elle ot nourris M. *GI*
      H; o. qui pau font a prisier *C*; o. Malefant e. *H*;
      e. Turfier *GI H*.
257. C'erent d. *I*; Cist s. venut a li n'i vorent
      atargier *C*; t. ce o. *I*; t. que Dex doinst encon-
      brier *G*; *H wants*.
258. M. en v. *G*; v. ne l'osent delaiier *E*; q. il l'oent
      h. *GI H*; o. noisier *I H*; *I adds*: Que durement re-
      doutent et li et son dangier; *C wants*.
12. *BE CGI H*
259. D. dient li sierf v. nos ci en present *C*; d. Brui-
      ans v. *E*; d. Turfier v. *GI H*; v. moy et M. *H*.
260. Qui prestz s. de faire toust a v. *H*; v. commant *E*
      GI.
261. t. le v. *G*; v. talent *E G*; *CI H want*.
262. V. dist Matabrune puis s. *C*; v. et lors en va d.
      E.
263. Desi a. *G*; v. atargant *E*; *CI H want*.
264. La dame s. as siers (au ser *I*) par maltalent (s.
      de put semblant *I H*) *CI H*.
265. Torfiers l. *G*; *CI H want*.
266. d. ferant *G*; *CI H want*.
267. E. ele si s'escrie q. *I*; *H wants*.
268. C. mal d. *C*; d. relievement *GI*; *H wants*.
269. M. dist la dame en plorant *H*.
270. Roine couronee s. moi dignement *C*; *H wants*.
271. L. caitive U *GI*; *C H want*.
272. p. a poi le cuer m. *I*; *E C H want*.
273. Ahi set ore n. *E*; Ha Diex set or me sire i. *GI*;
      Pour quoy me fait mi sires i. *H*; n. ce m. *I*; n. ce
      dolerous torment *G*; n. cest m. *H*; i. martire si
      grant *I H*; *C wants*.
274. Se n. *H*; n. li f. *GI*; f. onques D. *GI H*; t. nul
      jour en mon vivant *E which adds*: Mes enfans ai
      perdus mout ai le cuer dolant; *H adds*: Lasse dist
      la royne et ou sont my enfans/ Trop les ay tost
      perdus le cuer en ay dolent; *C wants*.
275. *E CGI H want*.
276. Cou qui sont f. *G*; Qu'est ce f. *C H*; Or tost f. *I*;
      T. dist M. *E CI*; v. preschant *CH I*.
277. v. ara m. nus juises faisant *E*; Jou ne vos prise
      plus .I. denier v. *C*; m. une aguile v. *GI*; *H*

        wants.

278. v. seront g. *G*; v. iert g. *I*; *C H want.*

279. 1. durement *E*; s. prendele (sic) maintenant *C* *which adds*: En la cartre le jetent n'i font demorement/ Et ele crie Dieu reclame forment.

280. *E CGI H want.*

281. Et li ser 1. *GI H*; *C wants.*

282. En la c. la traient moult angoisseusement *I*; m. andoi si laidement *E*; m. moult felonneusement *H*; m. a angosos torment *G*; *C wants.*

13. *BE CGI H*

283. Mi sers en ont la dame portee t. *H*; s. emportent 1. *C.*

284. Fors d'une p., e. fut v. *C.*

285. A l. *E*; 1. jetent s. *CI H*; n. aresteue *E C*; s. plus de r. *H*; *G wants.*

286. Coussin ne kieute n'a avec lui eue *C*; a entor l. *E*; *H wants.*

287. 1. ruent c. *C*; c. bieste qu'est m. *G*; *C adds*: Et ele pleure et crie Dieu ausssse (sic); *G adds*: Ele pleure et si crie Sainte Marie aieue/ Si voir com dessendistes sire Dex de la lune/ Si souscoures vous hui iceste dur feue/ Ki çaiens est jetee u n'a point de veue/ Mar dis cele parole dont si vieus sui tenue.

288. Li s. *C H*; e. retournerent c. *G H*; e. tornerent c. *I*; r. a leur descouvenue *H*; c. li maufes argue *C.*

289. 1. force de D. perdirent leur veue *C.*

290. j. an ler (sic) des jors r. *C*; e. ce s. *G*; *H wants.*

291. Et cele qu'assi a *I*; f. esmeue *GI*; *C H want.*

292. Ne a n. *I*; a ent nul mal diable, o. veue *E*; *C H want.*

293. La d. *I*; *C H want.*

294. .XIII. a. *G*; .XI. a *H placed after* 1. 295; *C wants.*

295. d. qui'st a *E*; qui est a *G*; d. Dius li soit en aiue *C*; d. qui a tort est en mue *H.*

297. *C wants.*

14. *BE GI H*

298. *C wants.*

299. e. sot m. qui ot non O. *E I H*; m. ki a non O. *G*; *C wants.*

300. e. porta a. *H*; p. corrousceuz e. *I H*; p. a envis e. *E*; *C wants.*

301. t. tristes e. *E*; *C wants.*

302. E. passa la f. mout b. *I*; f. plus de .II. *E*; b. .IIII. l. *H*; *CG want.*

303. En u. *E*; Et vint a *H*; f. en vint *GI*; v. u l. *E G*
H; a. ert c. *I*; eve estoit grant *H*; *GI add*: Et li
marrais desous parfons et soudoians; *C wants*.

304. Markes prent les enfans d. *GI H*; p. qui les vot
jeter ens *E I*; p. si les vout getter ens *G H*; *C*
wants.

305. Et o. *I*; I. uevre s. *G*; m. d'euz noier fu hastans
I; m. de noiier fu hastans *E*; m. de naier est has-
tant *H*; m. del noier est hastans *G*; *C wants*.

306. He Dex a tel m. *G*; m. croist d. *E*; *CI H want*.

307. Or en pense Jhesus l. *H*; l. aide li P. omnipotens
E; *CI want*.

15. *BE CGI H*

308. M. prent (prist *C*) les enfans p. *CGI H*; l. avoit
pris p. *E*; *I adds*: Par le plesir de Dieu qui de
nous est tout Sire.

309. Commencent li enfant v. *I*.

310. Quant il les a veus forment dou cuer s. *C*; Et q.
Markes le vit d. *H*; p. les v. *G*.

311. E. dist li preudons caitis ke p. *C*; E. dist il
caitis E. *E*; He las fait li dolans E. *G*; E. ce a
dit Marques chetif q. *H*.

312. S. j'ocis *E CGI H*; a. s'en sera pire *E*; s. plus p.
C.

313. Car il s. g. home e. *GI*; *C H want*.

314. p. l'onour d. *E*; p. apierdre la vie *C*; o. de Pavie
G.

315. Qui les gart Damrediex q. *C*; q. lor s. *E C H*;
qu'il lor s. *G*; *I wants*.

316. La penne dou m. a une part d. *C*; Le pan de s. m.
de l'une part d. *EG*; La moitie de la panne de son
mantel d. *H*; La pane du m. d'une part en d. *I*.

317. Si met les enfans ens a une part adire *C*; m. et
l'un a l'autre tire *I*; a ariere *H*.

318. Si l. *C*; s. Sire *CI H*; s. Gille *E G*.

16. *BE CGI H*

319. e. sor l. *C*; e. sus l. *I*; e. les l. *G H*; l. rivie-
re m. *GI H*.

320. A Diu les commanda l. *C*; D. qui en la crois fu mis
G.

321. Qui l. *E C*; Que il l. *I*; s. bon pere bons aideur
b. *I*; s. en aie b. *E*; b. amis b. p. por nourir *C*;
H wants.

322. M. en r. li preudome pensich *C*; e. pensis *H*.

323. a. et p. *C*; a de (sic) p. *G*; p. Jhesu-Crist *CG*; p.
touz diz *I*; *H wants*.

324. Que il gart l. *I*; d. mort et de peril *C which*
adds: Tant a Marques alet par puis et par lairis/

Qu'il est revenus dont il se fu partis; *H wants.*
325. Matabrune le voit si l. *C*; Et M. en v. *G*; M. vint k. *I*.
326. v. vous dist ele s. *E*; v. dist e. *C*; f. la vielle s. *CGI H*; s. lui (sic) e. *H*.
327. Oil dist li preudons n. *C*; D. dist l. *E*.
328. C. dist M. *E CI*; M. vous e. *E I*; *H wants.*
329. Dont d. *C*.
330. *E CGI H want.*
331. Or sont li enfancon d. *C*; Et li e. s. la d. et malmis *E*.
332. v. desous l. *G*; p. sous l. *E I*; .I. d'encoste l'autre n'i a ne jeu ne ris *C*; *H wants.*
333. Or ascoutes merveilles por Diu de Paradis *C which adds:* Tele ne fu oïe tres le tans Anseis; *G adds:* Com iceste sera s'uns en escape vis; *H wants.*

17. *BE CGI H*
334. r. l'uns b. et l. *E C H*.
335. m. n'en o. *E*; i. point d'a. *E G*; m. n'o. secours ne a. *C which adds:* Or lor soit Jhesu-Crist peres li fius saint Marie; *H wants.*
336. v. desur l. *E*; v. desous l. *G*; p. sus l. *I*; b. esmarie *E*; *C H want.*
337. C. a son col a s. *CG*; c. la cainne s. *CI H*; c. une caine atacie *G*; s. kaine s. *E*; c. lacie *H*.
338. d. ne vous c. *E GI*; d. si ne c. *C H*; v. mentirai m. *E H*; v. le lairai m. *C*.
339. col a c. *CI E*.
340. Tant que ont les chaaines ne pevent m. *I*; T. k'aront les c. *E*; T. qu'il l'ara au col chaskuns ne morra m. *C*; c. il les aront n. *G*; c. eulx l'auront n. *H*; n. puent perir m. *G H*; n. moront m. *E*.
341. Et s. *CG*; i. l'a pierdue c. *C*; p. ice conte l. *E*; r. la v. *C*.
342. C. devient volans l'estoyre ne ment mie *C*; C. seront volant si com l'estore crie *G*; C. seront noant t. *I*; tout de ce ne doutes mie *E*; *H wants.*
343. Se il pert sa caine n'est homs q. *C*; S'il perdent l. *E*; *GI H want.*
344. C. l'estuet puis iestre tous les jours de sa vie *C*; e. si le c. *E*; *GI want.*

18. *BE CGI H*
346. Il ne pueent m. *C*; d. peril t. *H*.
347. Or soient tout s. *C*; M. soient a seur s. *I*; *H wants.*
348. s. noans p. *I*; *C H want.*
349. Li uns va par sus l'autre si li ceuvre le front *I*; *H wants.*

350. t. par la riviere iront *C*; l. fosse s. *E GI*; f. en
v. *E*; *H wants.*

351. Estes v. *E C H*; Atant es .I. *I.*

352. d. le m. *E*; *H wants.*

353. .III. a. *G*; a. et plus d. *GI*; *E adds*: Il aloit par
le bois et aval et amont; *C H want.*

354. Venus est aus enfans q. en p. *I*; e. est venus q.
C.

355. *E CGI H want.*

19. *BE CGI H*

356. e. sont demoret a t. *C*; e. sont a duel et a t. *E*
I; e. peine e. *H.*

357. Est venus li h. *C*; Estes v. *E H*; Atant es .I. *I*;
h. venu tout esranment *H*; o. tant l. *I.*

358. Demoret ens el bos par son entendement *C*; E. de-
dens le bois que î. *E*; b. que veu n'avoit j. *GI*; *H*
wants.

359. r. n'ot vestu .I. *I*; a. mie .I. *E*; .I. denier *CI*;
H wants.

360. Car li bos li avoit atournet a noient *C*; v. mau-
vaisement v. *E*; v. a tillete tenant *I*; v. et a
tille v. *G*; a. tenant *E G*; *H wants.*

361. Q. les enfans percut merveille soi forment *C*; i.
vit l. *H*; s. ploura t. *E H*; *C adds*: Damedieu en
appiele par son entendement.

362. D. dist l. *C*; D. dit l. *H*; f. il h. *E CGI H*; l.
pere p. *GI H*; l. sire p. *E*; t. disne coument *GI.*

364. S. ta volentes e. *C*; S. ton p., e. sire qui v. *H.*

365. Envoie moi s. *C H*; s. auques p. *I*; s. ici p. *H*
which adds: Dont les enfans nourisse que ci voy en
present.

366. Empres c. *G H*; A. cele p. *I*; p. n'atarga de n. *C*;
t. longement *E G H.*

367. Vit venir une biche par le bois erraument *H*; u.
ciere v. *E*; u. cievre v. *GI*; v. a Dieu commande-
ment *C which adds*: Plus plante comme nois par mi
le bos corant; *GI add*: Que Dex î envoia par son
disne coumant; *H adds*: Les enfans nourrira qu'a
Dieu vient a talent.

20. *BE CGI*

368. La u li boins h. *C*; Quant l. *GI*; li hermites ot *I*;
p. ainsi f. *I*; p. si f. *G*; *H wants.*

369. L'est venue un cierge k. *C*; Estes v. une ciere k.
E; u. kievre k. *GI*; *H wants.*

370. b. dehaitte *C*; b. rehaite *E I*; *H wants.*

371. k. du bien se dehaite *E*; t. adez les gaite *I*; les
agaite *G*; *H wants.*

372. e. santent l. *I*; e. oîrent l. *G*; s. la cierge k.

C; b. si entaite *CI*; b. ki a. *E*; b. kis a. *G*; *H wants.*

373. m. sucitie e. *C*; m. le suce et bien alaite *G*; m. sucie et avant t. *I*; e. vers l. *E*; *H wants.*
374. B. en s. *E C*; B. se s. *GI*; *H wants.*

21. *BE CGI H*

375. *C wants.*
376. Li hermites se saïnne des enfans a g. *C*; c. se mervelle e. *E H*; e. a g. *GI H*.
377. les loie *I*; *C wants.*
378. Vers se maison s. *C*; t. droite la v. *E*.
379. Et li cierge a pries apres iaus droitement l. *C*; l. biche le suit qui de pres l. *H*; b. des p. *G*; a. les c. *E CGI*.
380. Jusques a *I*; D. que chies l. *H*; D. au mes l. *C*; l'ermitte l. *C H*; l. envoie *GI H*.
381. L. cierge l. *C*; L. biche l. *H*.
382. Que Dius gar les enfans et m. *C*; Jhesu-Crist c. *I*; j. les m. *I*; j. que m. en b. *H*; a droite v. *E CGI H*.
383. e. a n. *E G H*; n'est n. *G H*; n. suit (sic) n. *E*; s. qui m'en c. *I*; k. cou ne c. *G*; k. le c. *H*; n. mescroie *I H*.
384. E. li e. *I*; *C H want.*
385. m. de nul pain fait a *G*; *CI H want.*
386. k. ombroie *E*; *C H want.*
387. r. de meures d. *G*; *C H want.*
388. Ainsi vecu .X. *I*; a. pour riens m'en mentiroie *G*; o. me c. *E*; *C H want.*
389. Que mangaissent fors lait on le treve en l'estoire *E*; C'on l. *I*; e. raisons est c'on me croie *G*; *C H want.*

22. *BE CGI H*

390. e. a n. *E H*; *E adds*: Li bons preudom hermites qui mout fu droitouriers.
391. Et le ciere aveuc lui p. *E*; L. cierge e. *C*; L. biche e. *H*; d. .XII. a. *C*.
392. *CGI H want.*
393. *CGI H want.*
394. Et li cierge remaint qui les enfans ot chiers *C*; L. biche s'en reva e. *H*; *GI want.*
395. L'ermite demoura qui les ayme et tient c. *H*; L'ermite les ama et si les ot mout chiers *I which adds*: Dirai vous com l'ermite si les ot aesies; *I adds further with G*: De racines vivoient iteus ert (est *I*) lor mangiers; *C wants.*
396. Et mangoient cenieles e. *GI*; m. pommettes d. *H*; e. fueilles d. *C*; *C adds*: Ne sevent que vins est ne

nus autres dainties; *GI add*: Li enfant furent
biel et fu cascuns legiers (Bien les norri
Jhesu le Pere droituriers *I*)/ Plus tost erent mon-
te contremont les rociers (le rochier *I*)/ K'esqui-
rius (Que chievre *I*) ne mostoile tant ert cascuns
manriers (legier *I*)/ N'avoient pas cotieles de ces
dras de Louviers (N'avoit pas cotele ne nul drap
ne chancier *I*)/ Mais des corces de faus de fuelles
de fighiers (*I wants*)/ En este n'en ivier n'aront
il ja caucier (a. es piez soler *I*); *G adds fur-
ther*: Les ongles on[t] plus durs que n'est fiers
ne aciers/ Il ne manguent onques ne cines ne pleu-
viers/ Ne il ne boivent onques ne clare ne vin
vies/ Mes l'aige del fosse çou estoit lor tain-
ties/ Se il ne sont ensanble ja .I. seus n'en ert
lies/ Quant li hermites va en bos et en ramiers/
Ausi vont devant lui si les a ensegnies/ Coume les
vaces vont par devant le vacier.

397. A merveille amenderent e. *C*; *H wants*.
398. f. robes d. *H*; c. de f. *G H*; *C wants*.
399. Li livres nos r. en l'estore a *C*; e. le r. *G H*; r.
qui est dedens P. *H*.
400. Qu'il l. *C*; C'or l. *E*; Cou l. *G*; l. crut g. *E*; g.
travaus e. *C*; m. grans e. *E C H*; f. destorbiers *H*.
401. Par la f. alloit .I. *H*; .I. mauvais f. *G H*; .I.
mais (sic) hons pautoniers *C*.
402. H. fut M. *H*; M. ses siers et s. *C H*; M. ses drus
et s. *E*; s. archers *H*; s. conselliers *G*; *C adds*: Il
ot non Mauquarres mout fu et fel et fiers.
403. En li e. *C*; c. renoiies *E C*; c. logengiers *G*.
404. p. son segnour d. *E*; p. ses s. *G*; p. as enfans d.
C; *H wants*.
405. g. honte et m. grant e. *E*; p. et destourbier *C*; *H
wants*.

23. *BE CG H*
406. Or entendes *E C H*; *G adds*: Li rois de sainte glore
ki onques ne menti.
407. v. aidier n. *G*; v. garder n. *H*.
408. f. avoit e. *H*; e. ce b. *E H*; *G wants*.
409. M. ot le sierf a. *G*; a. esleve et chieri *H*; *C
adds*: Mauquarres avoit non maint hom avoit mor[i].
410. En l. *C*; v. issi c. *G*.
411. L'ermite estoit ou bois vert et floury *H*; p. n'i
estoit mie e. *C*.
412. l. voient si se sont e. *C*; l. sorent t. *E*; v.
moult f. *H*.
413. f. forment s'en esjoi *C*; f. se mervella a. *E*; f.
s'en esmervela si *G*; f. fut aussi esbay *H*.

414. Quit dist l. *C*; Ainc fait li siers mavais p. *G*; Et
f. *H*; f. li forestiers p. *C H*; m. ce dist li gleus
p. *E*; g. pour Dieu qui ne menti *H*.
415. .VII. issi b. *G*; e. ensanle jou n. *C*; e. ensanble
mes n. *G*; e. oncques mais n. *H*.
416. *H wants*.
417. Le diray a M. *H*; a. qu'il soit aviespri *C*.
418. d. me croit *H*; s. Denis *C*.
419. c. des cos n. *CG*; c. qu'il ont n. *E H*; n'i reman-
ront e. *C*; l. demourront cy *H*; l. issi *G*.

24. *BE CG H*

420. t. si ne vot ariester *C*; t. n'y est plus a. *H*.
421. e. en maintenant t. *C*; e. est m. *E*; e. s'en est
tantost alez *H*.
422. e. racompte qu'il eust n. *H*; n. a conte q. *G*.
423. Et si e. *H*; c. k'estoit *E*; i. estoit t. *E C H*; i.
est t. *G*; e. fel e. *C*.
424. D. que a *H*; M. ne si e. *E C H*; e. pas a. *G*; e.
ariestes *E CG*; s. arresterez *H*.
425. *H wants*.
426. v. dist l. *E*; v. biaus amis a bien soies trouves
C; viele quel noviele savez *G*; q. noveles d. *E*; *H*
wants.
427. D. fait li maus hom james t. *G*; d. li mesages j.
tele n. *C*; D. fait le mauvais ung petit m'entendez
H.
428. Quer j'ay huy en cest bois .VII. *H*; bos .VII. *C*.
429. Tout .VII. sont d'un s. et d'un meisme a. *C*; u.
grant e. *G H*.
430. Onques n. *C*; v. mais s. *E G*; *H wants*.
431. *E CG H want*.
432. A. cou d. la viele f. *E G H*; d. Matabrune f. *C*.
433. O. ilz nulles chaennetes a. *H*; c. al col N. *E H*;
c. nel m. *C*; N. le c. *H*.
434. Chertes ma dame oil cou respont Mauquarres *C*; Amis
f. *H*; D. dist l. *E H*; l. traistre s. *H*; *G adds*
l. 428 in repetition.
435. Chascuns d'iaus en a une ja mar le mesquerres *C*;
Cascuns si en a une c'est fine verites *G*; A cascun
en a une ja mar le mesherres *E*; A chascun en pent
une au col c'est veritez *H*.
436. *E CG H want*.
437. N'i a celi ne vaut .X. mars d. *C*; Et les c. valent
.C. m. *E*; Et si valent mout bien .VII. *G*; m. et
plus assez *E CG*; *H wants*.
438. l. remanra m. *C*; *H wants*.
439. v. foi que vous me deves *E*; s. m'aportes *G*; a. les
m'aportez *H*; *C wants*.

440.   q. revenus seres *G H*; *C wants*.
441.   Et Mauquarre respont tantost vous les ares *H*; D. dist l. *E*; m. siers s. *G*; *C wants*.
442.   t. cou dist la viele a. *G*; M. si le mes (sic) aportes *C*; *H wants*.
443.   Et si le c. *C*; s. les mes (sic) o. *E*; c. trestous les o. *CG*; *H wants*.
444.   D. dist li traitres si com vos comandes *C*; d. tous c. d. je sui n. *E*; *H wants*.
445.   S'il nel velent laissier a m'espee doules *C*; *H wants*.
446.   Aront tous *C*; i. ja l. *G*; l. cies d. *E C*; t. du haterel caupes *E*; t. just des bus desevres *G*; t. des espaules sevres *C*; *H wants*.
447.   D. seront mi voloir fait d. *G*; d. la viele a. *E G*; *C H want*.

25.   *BE CG H*

448.   Matabrune l. *C*; v. a l. *E*; q. cius li ot juree *G*; c. li a dounee *E*; v. a sa raison finee *C*; Q. Matabrune oy durement lui agree *H*.
449.   Malquarres li traitres qui ait maise (sic) journee *C*; *H wants*.
450.   a. que n'i ait d. *E*; a. gardes n'et d. *G*; e. qu'il n'y ait demouree *H*; *C wants*.
451.   G. bien qu'a chascun s. *H*; q. a cascun s. *E*; c. soit le caine o. *E H*; q. les caines s. *CG*; c. soient chi apportees *C*.
452.   Qui l. *C H*; k. les c. *C*; k. la c. *H*; E. s'il l. *E*; l. contradira l. *C H*; l. contredient l. *E*; c. s'ait l. *CG*; c. ait l. *H*; t. aient c. *E*; a. la tieste copee *CG H*.
453.   m. je seroie buer n. *E*; m. de bonne heure fu n. *H*; *C wants*.
454.   D. dist l. *C*; l. traitres s. *C H*; l. tirans s. *E*; m. siers s. *G*; h. n'en soyes effree *H*.
455.   Adont a Malquarres sa voie aceminee *C*; l. serf s. *H*; l. fel s. v. arier tornee *G*.
456.   M. remaint qui est toute diervee *C*; M. retourne qui en fut esmaee *H*.
457.   Marke fait a. *E*; M. a fait mander s. *G*; Marques fait appellez il vint sans d. *H*.
458.   Ele li demanda l. *E C*; l. a dit l. *H*.
459.   La vie d. *C*; Qu'il d. *E*; Comme va des e. que n. *H*.
460.   l. raconte la v. prouvee *C*; M. si lui a l. *H*.
461.   Ensi com les laissa e. *G*; *E H want*.
462.   *E G H want*.
463.   m. si f. *C*; *E G H want*.
464.   Q. l'entent Matabrune si e. *C*; e. si fu si a. *E G*;

e. toute en est a. *H*; f. forsenee *E G H*.

465.   l. a creves sans nule d. *C*; c. illec sans d. *H*; v.
        demoree *C H*; v. mausenee *G*.
466.   L. dist l. *C*; L. ce a dit Marques si m. *H*; C. dure
        d. *G*; *C adds*: Sainte Marie Dame Roïne couronnee.
467.   d. que j'ai t. *CG*; qu'en sse (sic) t. *E*; a. tele
        s. *C*; *H wants*.
468.   *C wants*.
469.   Sa femme y a courut d. *E H*; A l'ostel l. *G*; r.
        qu'il avoit espousee *H*; *C wants*.
470.   Ariere l'ont boutee le pute gent dervee *E*; Ariere
        en meïne Marques dolante et esgaree *H*; *C wants*.
471.   *C H want*.
472.   Mauquarres a le f. traviersee *C*; Li traitres a *G*;
        E. Mauquarre si a la f. passee *H*.
473.   As enfans est venus s. *C*; i. vient a *G*; l'i. si
        a cainte (traicte *H*) l'espee *C H*.
474.   a. toute nue l. *E*; a. et a *G*; *C H want*.
475.   b. sus l. *E*; *C H want*.
476.   Or gard Dieu les enfans et v. *H*; e. la Vergene ou-
        noree *E G*; g. Jhesu-Cris par s. *C*.
477.   l. vie s. *G*; p. alee *E G*; j. ne soit a court tier-
        me f. *C*; a pou moult muee *H*.

26.   *BE CG H*

478.   Or s'en va li traitres k. *C*; Le serf a l'ermitaige
        est maintenant tournez *H*.
479.   v. hideus et h. *G*; v. s'ot le poil h. *E*; v. coure-
        chous et ires *C*; *H wants*.
480.   Oiies q. *E*; *C H want*.
481.   h. estoit en l'iermitaige a. *C*; h. estoit adonc ou
        b. *H*; p. iert ens el b. *G*; *C adds*: Par Dieu ens
        la foriest s'en est ales li ber.
482.   Avech lui ert un des e. remes *C*; Et a. *G H*; l.
        l'uns d. *G*.
483.   Et v. *G*; s. ert v. *E*; *C H want*.
484.   e. d'une feme e. *E*; *C H want*.
485.   e. ainmon l'un mius que les autres a. *G*; c. l'un
        des autres a. *E*; *C H want*.
486.   S. avoit l. *E*; *C H want*.
487.   l. traitres f. *C H*; m. hom plus q. *G*; s. mais q. *C*.
488.   l. pums f. *C H*; p. ert d. *C*; p. est quarres *E*.
489.   Si en a les enfans forment e. *C*.
490.   n'oserent m. *G*; a esfraes *E*; o. no Diu de nul
        grain reclamer *C which adds*: Tant les ot li trai-
        tres de peur espaventes; *H wants*.
491.   l. oste li cuvers Mauquarres *C*; l. rant (sic) l.
        E; l. osta les cuvers desfaez *H*; *C adds*: Tout .VI.
        devinrent cisne cou est la verites/ Nostre Sires

le vot ensi l'a destinet.

492. Il esbatent l. *CG*; E. ilz b. *H*; e. et si s'en e.
C; e. et si en e. *G*; e. trestous s'en e. *H*; e. en
e. *E*; en sont v. *CG H*.

493. O. est chascuns o. *C placed after 1.* 494; s. li
.VI. *G*; s. tous .VI. *H*; o. ensi c. vous o. *E*; m'o-
res *G*.

494. *C placed after 1.* 495.

495. p. ne se sont ariestet *C placed after 1.* 492; p.
en e. *E*; e. sont tous ui v. *H which adds:* Le fo-
restier s'en est arriere retournez.

496. c. parjures *C*; c. Mauquares *G*.

497. A la vielle les baille si l'en a merciez *H*; l.
porte qui l'en sara b. *C*; e. set m. *G*; *C adds:*
Teus novieles porta si com oir pores/ Dont fu
deshoneree ains que l'ans fust pases; *G adds:* Dame
dist li traitres certes vous ne saves/ J'ai veu
tel mervelle james tele n'ores/ Si tos com je lor
oc les caines ostes/ Cascuns devint oisaus volans
tous enpenes/ Onques de nule rien ne fui si es-
fraes/ La viele l'entendi si a .I. ris jetes/ Bien
set que senefie cou qu'erent faes; *H adds:* Or lai-
rons de la vielle et du serf Mauquarrez/ Et diron
de l'ermite qui est ou bois alez.

498. Et li hermites est a. *CG*; A sa maison s'en vint
moult fu espoventez *H*.

499. l. iert li enfes q. *G*; *C H want*.

500. Quant i. *CG H*; i. n'en a *G*; a ses a. *C*; l. enfans
e. *C H*; e. son hostel t. *H*; e. le m. *E*.

501. Tel dolour a au cuer a poi qu'il n'est dierves *C*;
d. a poi *E G*; *H wants*.

502. E Diex c. *C*; He c. *G*; e. c'avec lui fu asses (sic)
C; k. est o *H*.

503. f. de mal heure fut n. *H*; caitis mal eures *E*; cai-
tis mal eureus *C*.

504. Saincte Marie Dame comme souffert avez *H*; M. pour
coi s. *E*.

505. C'on m'a ore ma suer e. *C*; Que l'en m'a mes se-
rours e. *H*.

27. *BE G*

506. v. a l. *G* *C H want*.

507. q. si d. *E*; *C H want*.

508. *C H want*.

509. q. trouver ne poit *G*; *C H want*.

510. Lues quiert c. *E*; u nul n'en avoit *G*; u mix l. *E*;
C H want.

511. Par mi le bos rame *E*; r. issi c. *G*; *C H want*.

512. l. poit *E G*; *C H want*.

513. U une aloit dela l'autre c. *G*; a. de ça et l'autre
     retournoit *E*; *C H want.*
514. e. se rasit une autre se levoit *G*; *E C H want.*
515. e. le (sic) q. *E*; *C H want.*
516. h. bien l. *G   C H want.*
517. *C H want.*
518. p. remanoir m. *G*; m. tousjors a. *E G*; *C H want.*
519. *C H want.*
520. *C H want.*
521. h. prouvende l. *G*; h. a m. *E*; *C H want.*
522. c. cueloit *G*; c. avoit *E*; *C H want.*
523. Ensi c., c. que m. *G*; *C H want.*

28. *BE G*

524. e. iert m. *G*; *C H want.*
525. Et de membres bien f. *E*; c. avenans *E G*; *C H want.*
526. p. ventelans *G*; *C H want.*
527. De c. n'avoit .II. *G*; *C H want*; *G adds*: Par le bos
     kiert ses freres tous tristres et dolans/ Tant ala
     li boins enfes par le Jhesu coumans/ C'a l'isue
     dou bos vint les .I. desreubans/ La a trouve .VI.
     cines en .I. viviers noans/ Cou estoient si frere
     et sa suer li valans/ Cil viviers fu lor pere ki
     ot non Orians/ Tous droit sor le rivage fu l'enfes
     ariestans/ Quant a veu les cines forment fu tres
     pensans/ Car li cuers li dist bien c'est lor api-
     ertenans.
528. *CG H want.*
529. Pres a l. *E*; *CG H want.*
530. p. en t. *E*; *CG H want.*
531. r. si p. *E*; *CG H want.*
532. E. mout faisoit de bien as povres gens *E*;   *CG H
     want.*
533. c. ert e. *E*; *CG H want.*
534. l. povres genz *E*; *CG H want.*
535. *CG H want.*

29. *BE*

536. a. le roi va l'e. *E*; *CG H want.*
537. r. i l. *E*; *CG H want.*
538. .II. pains p. Diu et par a. *E*; *CG H want.*
539. *CG H want.*
540. m. le sien a. *E*; *CG H want.*
541. M. il g. le sien plus n'i f. sejor *E*; *CG H want.*
542. Ains r. *E*; *CG H want.*
543. *CG H want.*
544. *CG H want.*
545. *E adds*: Li cisne qui ja furent si frere et sa se-
     rour; *CG H want.*
546. d. tel p. *E*; *CG H want.*

547.   a. qu'il demenast d. *E*; *CG H want.*

30. *BE G*

548.   Alueques arestoit *E*; s'arestut l. *G*; *C H want.*

549.   La c. ne veoit q. *E*; Onques mais ne vit rien ki tant li p. *G which adds:* Com faisoient li cine k'il voit ens el rivaire; *C H want.*

550.   De joie va plorant car il n. *G*; *C H want.*

551.   l. couroient t. *E G*; d. contreval l. *E*; *C H want.*

552.   Quant il les reconnut mout en fist lie [c]hai[re] *G*; *C H want.*

553.   Car c'estoient s. *G which adds:* Maintenant a l'ostel ariere s'en repaire/ De pain lor aporta k'il prist en .I. aumere; *C H want.*

554.   Si lor en a doune c'a aus vilt il a. *G*; *E adds:* Li cuers li disoit bien k'ensi le devoit faire; *G adds:* Car li cuers li disoit que c'estoient si fraire; *C H want.*

555.   Et cil l'ont reconnu s. *G*; f. bien e. *E G*; *C H want.*

556.   Vers lui vinrent siflant joie li vorent faire *G*; *C H want.*

557.   *C H want.*

558.   *C H want.*

559.   a eu en lor c. *G*; *C H want.*

560.   Q. estoit l. et noire et h. et amere *G*; p. et h. et si f. *E*; *C H want.*

561.   e. atourt v. *E*; *C H want*; *E adds:* De le mauvaise vielle de Malquare le lere/ Qui par les cainetes avoit basti l'affere/ Dont li .V. fil estoient et le fille en misere/ N'il ne connurent onques lor pere ne lor mere/ Fors que l'ermite seul que tenoient a pere/ Et li enfes lor donne du pain a ciere amere; *G adds:* Cil esmie del pain et si lor en jeteue (?)/ Par mout tres grant amor qui li plaisoit a fere/ Cascuns venoit a lui de son col l'acoleuee (?)/ Del biec siflent vers lui des eles haleterent.

31. *BE G*

562.   *C H want.*

563.   t. entiers k. *G*; p. que n'i t. *E*; *C H want.*

564.   f. isi acoustumeement *G*; a. ensi f. *E*; *C H want.*

565.   a. endroit l'a. *G*; *C H want.*

566.   d. en l. *G*; *C H want*; *E adds:* Ensi revint souvent o le cuer mout dolent/ Quant il veoit les cisnes si faisoit doler grant/ Ne sot pour quel raison ains en avoit talent.

567.   i. n'en d. *E*; *C H want.*

568.   S. vorai r. a mon c. *G*; *C .H want.*

569. Et d. *E*; *C H want.*
570. Tant c'aie p. *G C H want.*
32. *BE CG H*
571. Li enfes est remes n'i a que courechier *C*; L'en-
fant est demoure ou n'a que courroucer *H*; f. ce m.
E G; *C adds:* Et li hermites pleure en lui n'a
c'airier.
572. Et Matabrune fait venir .I. *C*; Matabrune la vielle
fist venir .I. *H*; I. a fait mander .I. *G*; t. a
mande son l. *E*.
573. E. il i *CG*; E. l'orfevre y vint n. *H*; v. que ne si
v. targier *E*.
574. *E CG H want.*
575. A. cou dist la viele j. vos v. *E CG H*; t. vorai c.
C; ci bailler *H*.
576. a. dont jou vorai f. *C*; a. qui v. *H*.
577. c. me f. mout bien sans atargier *C*; f. ce vous vel
jou p. *G*.
579. D. ce f. *E H*; D. dist l. *E C H*; f. l'orfevres p. *E*
H; o. si m'ait Richiers *C*.
580. *E CG place entire verse after 1. 581; H wants.*
581. Jou n'en a. ja v. *C*; v. ne maille ne d. *H*; *E CG H*
place entire verse before 1. 580.
582. Dame f. *H*; C. dist M. *E*; a creaanter *H*.
583. e. retourne li orfevriers arier *CG H*; t. aveuc li
l. *E*.
584. c. li doune q. *E*; p. qui les v. *H*; p. qui mout
font a prisier *C*.
585. A se maison en vint sans plus de delaiier *E*; *CG H*
want.
586. Il e. *H*; p. ciere q. *G*; b. qu'il v. *E*; b. qui la
v. *H*; v. assaier *E H*.
587. f. ne q. *H*; c. tallier *G H*; *C wants.*
588. Et cele fu si biele c'on i ose t. *C*; Ele f. *G*; b.
ce o. *E H*; b. c'ai o. *G*.
589. .II. copes car s. *C*; c. Diex li vot aidier *C H*; c.
a celer nel vous quier *G*.
590. Onques mais se m'aist D. *H*; D. dist i. *CG*.
591. v. de t. foison ne a. *H*; n. d'argent ne d'or m. *C*.
592. De par Diu sont venues ce ne puis jou n. *C*; D. a
celer nel vous quier *G*; D. ne vous quier a n. *E*;
j. ne le q. *H*; *C adds:* Jou ne les renderoie por
l'ounour de Poitiers.
593. Par Diu c., d. je les metrai arier *C*; d. ces i. *E*;
d. je i. *H*.
594. E. pourront a autres et a nous proufiter *H*; n. pu-
et bien Damedieux conseillier *C*; D. mout b. *G*.
595. Par foi f. *C*; l. dist l. *E C*; l. orfevres et si

vous en requier *G*; p. bien f. *C*; *H wants*.

33.   *BE CG H*

596.   c. emporte 1. *C*; c. estiue 1. *G*; c. osta 1. *E*; c. estuya 1. *H*.

597.   E. son e. *C*; m. et b. *E C*; m. biel et avenant *C*; *H wants*.

598.   Li orfevriers s'en tourne d. *C*; E. l'orfevre les coppes qui sont de bon argent *H*; 1. preudom 1. *E*; 1. gentius orfevres d. *G*; 1. les bones coupes p. *E*.

599.   Une e. *C H*; une porte *E H*; e. porte a. *E CG H*; a. a s. *G H*.

600.   A la vielle est venu tost et isnellement *H*; e. vint ki le vit 1. *E C*.

601.   Et li lormiers 1. *E*; Maintenant 1. *H*; L. orfevres 1. *G*; d. sa c. *H*; *C wants*.

602.   C. dist M. *E C H*; a riche prousent *C*.

603.   Moult ont bien foisonne les chaennetes d. *H*.

604.   d. trestout coviertement *C*; d. assez bassetement *H*; *G wants*.

605.   De ches n'ai mais jou garde a. *C*; B. sui d. *E*; s. de ceulz d. alez s. voirement *H*; *G wants*.

606.   Se leur m. *H*; e. sa m. *G*; me chauldroit n. *H*.

607.   a. certes prouchainement *H*.

608.   P. est m. *H*; *C wants*.

609.   Tant feray a mon filz par mon enchantement *H which adds*: Que jamais n'aura femme ne vivra longuement/ Trestout mettray le royaume en douloureux tourment; *C wants*.

610.   Son fil en apiela si li dist erramment *C*; A son fil est v. *E G H*; v. la viele isnielement *G*; v. tost et isnelement *E*; v. tost et ligierement *H*.

611.   *E CG H want*.

612.   s. faite a biel p. *G*; *C H want*.

613.   Il par estoit si tristres et en son cuer dolent *G*; e. mout grant torment *E*; *C H want*.

614.   f. la gente qui'st en tel marement *E*; *C H want*.

615.   1. vint d. *E G*; v. par d. *G*; v. au d. *E*; *C H want*.

616.   f. ce d. la viele c. *C H*.

617.   t. pour mauvais et pour lent *H*.

618.   *G places this verse after 1.* 619; *C H want*.

619.   Que v. n'osez de celle p. le v. *H*; v. n'en v. *CG*; n. aves pris de celi v. *C*; p. justice maintenant *G*; d. li nul v. *E*.

620.   Qui si vos a hounit et menet f. *C H*; Si vous en a houni e. *G*; a. a tourment *C*; a. vilement *H*.

621.   a. tost et isnielement *G*; a. n'i ait delaiement *E*; n'y a tel vengement *H*; *C wants*.

622.   p. autre f. *E G H*; a. gre d. *H*; *C wants*.
623.   d. sa mere q. *C*; v. qui fist son siement (sic) *H*.
624.   i. ardera sa femme sans nul ariestement *C*; f. son
       barnage v. *G*; f. voiant toute sa gent *E H*; *G adds*:
       Or oiies del diable com fait enortement/ Il n'a
       sousiel abe ne mone de convent/ Que fenme n'engi-
       nast par son encantement.
625.   e. letres e. *C H*; r. .I. garcon p. *C*.
626.   Et m. *C H*; e. legierement *H*.
627.   Qu'il vignent a cort veir le jugement *C*; c. l'a.
       G; c. le douloureux tourment *H*.
628.   i. prendra d. *H*; f. merveileux   et   pesant *C*; f.
       devant toute sa gent *H*; n. delaiement *E G*.
629.   Or sera le dame arse a. *E*;   a. ne se vont delaiant
       C;   a. tost et legierement *H*; *C adds*:   Se Damediex
       n'en pense par son commandement.
630.   a. s'il n'est qui le d. *C*;   n. l'en d. *H*;   *G adds*:
       Au roi en poise mout mais il ne set comment/ Il le
       puisse laisier s'en jure durement/ K'il en prendra
       venjance en .I. fu tout ardant; *E wants*.
34. *BE CG H*
631.   c. fu a. et mout fu e. *G*; *C H want*.
632.   e. desmente l. *G*; e. gemist l. *E*; *C H want*.
633.   P. le vallant roine q. e. martiriie *E*;   Or sera la
       dame arse se Diex li (D. ne l'en *G*; D. ne luy *H*)
       aie *CG H*.
634.   *CG H want*; *C adds*: Or a estet .XII. ans en la car-
       tre perine/ Mout angousseusement n'est bons que le
       vos die/ Mout a fait dure fin et maine male vie; *G*
       adds: Que .XIII. ans a este en la cartre en her-
       mie/ De son cors a soufiert dolerouse hasie/ De
       fain et de mesaise iert forment afaiblie/ Il n'a
       home soussiel se il le voit ne die/ C'onques ne fu
       soole a nul jor de sa vie/ La dame ki n'estoit pi-
       nie ne trecie/ Povre estoit et desfaite et magre
       et enpalie/ Toute sa viesteure est de mine povrie/
       En mi le cartre siet dolante et esmarie/ Souvent
       reclainme Dieu le fil sainte Marie/ *Laisse 34 bis*:
       Mout par fu grans la cors quant la gens fu venue/
       Or ait Dieus la dame que sa fins est venue/ Ele
       estoit en la cartre dolante et irascue/ .XIII. ans
       l'avoit se sire en la prison tenue/ Por la viele
       sa mere ki si souvent l'argue/ La dame sist laiens
       ausi con bieste mue/ Tant l'a fait mal garder la
       viele malostrue/ Qu'en .II. jors c'une fois la da-
       me ne mangue/ Tant est laide et desfaite et dole-
       rouse et nue/ Qu'il n'a home el siecle se il l'a-
       voit veue/ Ne deist cou fust arme qui de cors fust

issue/ Dex com ele se plaint com ele se derue/
Souvent reclainme Dieu k'il li soit en aiue/ *Con-
tinuation of laisse* 34: La dame est en la cartre
ki souvent brait et crie/ Souvent reclainme Dieu
le fil sainte Marie/ Mout li poise k'il est si
longement en vie/ Quant ses drois sires l'a si
forment enhaie; *H adds*: Qui a este .VI. ans en la
chartre armye.

635. d. la vie *G*; *C H want*.
636. Li boins hermites est en la foriest antie *C*; Et
l'ermite si fut en une tour antie *H*; h. de la fo-
riest antie *G*.
637. Li enfes est o. *G*; E. l'enfant avec l. *H*; k. so-
vent brait et crie *C H*; s. gramie *E G*.
638. Por sa s. por s. *G*; f. que il ne set en vie *E*; c.
que n. *CG*; c. ne les voit m. *H*; *C adds*: Or ascou-
tes signeur que Diex fist por s'amie.
639. Endroit la m. *C*; Q. ce vient v. *H*; v. a m. *G*; g.
est e. *E G H*.
640. Et donques vint un a. de la Dieu c. *H*; a. de mout
grant signerie *C*.
641. *C H want*.
642. A l'ermite vint droit durement l. *C*; e. mout h. *G*;
l. escrie *C H*.
643. t. boins hon de sainte v. *G*; t. et h. *E*.
644. Nennil f. *H*; N. dist l. *E CG H*; p. Dieu le fil Ma-
rie *G*.
646. *C H want*.
647. c. si ne me tentes m. *G*; *C H want*.
648. Et li angles l. *CG H*; l. respont j. *E CG H*.
649. D. nostre P. ki nous a e. *G*; tout en *H*.
650. D. nel te celerai m. *C*; D. ne te celerai m. *G*; D.
ne le celerai m. *E*; D. le filz sainte Marie *H*.
651. Qu'avec toy a. *H*.
652. e. drois e. *C H*; e. c'on tel d. *E*; k. le te d. *C*;
k. je te d. *H*.
653. g. sens e. *C*; g. baronnie *E*; *H wants*; *CG add*: Et
si est fius au roi et de gentil lignie (*C wants*)/
Preudom iert par ses armes et par cevalerie (*C
wants*)/ Et fera mout plus d'armes que je ne vous
en die (*C wants*)/ Amis de cel enfant nestera tel
linie (Del e. n. mout grans chevalerie *C*)/ Ki con-
queront par force la tiere de Surie (Q. conquerra
p. *C*)/ Juskes en Antioce la fort cite garnie (Et
Nike et A. *C*)/ Et de Jherusalem aront la signorie/
Et prendront le sepucre u Dex ot mort et vie/ De
le grant tor Davit aront la signorie (Et l. g. t.
D. qui viele est et anthie *C*)/ Icil seront .III.

frere qui Jhesu beneie (Si s. li .III. f. de mout
grant signourie *C*)/ L'un en iert Godefrois a la
ciere hardie (Li .I. e. *C*)/ Bauduins et Ustases
cou raconte lor vie (U. corra toute l. *C which
adds*: Li .II. en seront roy de la citet garnie/ Et
li tres sera quans s'ara grant signourie)/ Toute
Chrestientes iert par aus essaucie (C. en sera e.
C).

654.   o. envers Diu s. *C*; o. envers lui s. *G*.
655.   Pou qu'il contoit de cel enfant l. *G*; Et li ange
lui compte d. *H*; d. .III. e. *C*.

35.   *BE CG H*

656.   L'ie. *C*; I. dist l. *E CG H*.
657.   p. les e. *C*; a. .VII. e. *G H*; e. Orians a a n. *G*;
O. ot n. *C*.
658.   B. lor m. *E CG H*.
659.   s. de grant relegion *E CG H*.
660.   e. en cartre .XIII. ans bien le savon *G*; *C H want*.
661.   Maitre li fist la viele q. *G*; T. c'a fait M. *E*; *C
H want*.
662.   E. eust .VII. *H*; *C adds*: Cil que tu as o toi sera
de grant renon.
663.   m. Oriant q. *H*; c. a f. *E C*; c. eust f. *H*.
664.   e. veoir (sic) p. ung scien serf b. *H*; h. Marcon
CG H.
666.   Les ieux li fist crever l. *C*; La vielle lui en
fist qui eust cuer de lyon *H*.
667.   Crever les yeulx du chief et mettre **en** prison *H*;
f. sacier a, m. glouton *G*; *C wants*.
668.   k. vint a p. *E*; *C H want*.
669.   e. dolereus g. *E*; *C H want*.
670.   Et cil ki les caines a cascun enfancon *G*; *E C H
want*.
671.   Toli c'est .I. traitres Malquares a a non *G*; *E C H
want*.
672-674.   *E CG H want*.
675.   Matabrune a fait m. *C*; La viele si fist m. *G*; fist
metre *E*; m. la roine em prison *CG*; l. grande p. *E*;
C adds: .XI. ans i a estet n'en faut se petit non;
H wants.
676.   Et s. *C*; s. demain a. *C H*; a. sans nule r. *C*; a.
ja n'ara r. *G*; a. sans point d'arrestoison *H*.
677.   S. Damedix n. *E*; p. qui Longis fist pardon *H*.

36.   *BE CG H*

678.   Or ai *G*; e. comme en est avenu *H*.
679.   e. sa m. *C*; e. lor m. *G*; e. la dame a. *E*; *H wants*.
680.   S. Damediex n. *C*; *H wants*.
681.   D. com a son s. *C H*; D. qui te tient a s. *E*; s.

         boin d. *C*; s. chrestien d. *H*.

682.   a. o toy .VI. ans tenu *H*.
683.   Estuet d. *CG*; Convient d. *H*; V. demain d. *CG H*; V. le m. *E*; d. sa mere a. *E CG H*; b. molu *E C H*.
684.   A la lance e. *C*; A escu *H*; a. et au destrier c. *C*; a. sor .I. c. *G*; a. et al c. *E*; a. et a c. *H*; c. grainu *CG*; c. charnu *H*.
685.   D. dist l. *E CG H*.
686.   o. armes n. *G H*; n. ceval n. *E G*.
687.   a. homme en chest siecle veu *C*; e. mont h. *E*; *H wants*; *G adds*: Car onques nen vit nul ne caus ne kievelus/ N'il ne set se il sont bistorne ne cornu/ Il counoist mius .I. arbre bien rame et follu/ U li miudres fruis croist k'il souvent l'a veu/ Bien counoist une espine .I. hous et .I. sehu/ Si counoist bien .I. cierf souvent i a couru/ Et .I. grant proc salvage et .I. grant leu velu/ Biestes de bos counoist n'a a el entendu/ Mais del siecle la fors la le veries si nu/ K'il s'en fuiroit mout tost quant il aroit veu/ Celui ki li voroit faire point de malhu/ Je ne quic pas qu'en canp l'eust on ja tenu/ Se cis sire n'en pense ki nous douna salu/ Ne quic qu'il ja valle a le dame .I. festu/ Se Dex n'i fait miracles par la soie viertu/ K'il ne set qu'est cevaus n'a chevalier veu.
688.   c. le cuide avoir p. *H*; b. l'avera p. *CG*; *C adds*: Ne set ques chevaliers de cheval abatus/ Quant il l'a gaigniet ne pris ne retenu.
689.   Car i. *E G*; *C H want*.
690.   N'i a *E*; Cou n. *C H*; m. dist l. *E C H*; a. trop ai atendu *C*; a. que ci ai trop estu *E*; *G wants*.
691.   C. lui fauldra ou nom du R. *H*; e. en l'ounour de J. *C*.

37.   *BE CG H*
692.   L'iermites *C*; I. dist l. *E CG H*; p. demorer *E C*.
693.   e. le m. *E H*; *C wants*.
694.   De matinet matin faites l'enfant l. *C*; f. bien matinet l. *G H*.
695.   Ains que soit miedis l. *C*; A. le miedi l'en estevra a. *E*; s. prinme li convient il a. *G*; c. aler *E G*.
696.   d. le convient presenter *G*; *C H want*.
697.   On l. *E G*; cose onques *E*; o. n'osa p. *G*; *C H want*.
698.   v. il ne puet d. *E*; n. puet pas d. *C*; n. puet plus d. *G*; *H wants*.
699.   *E CG H want*.
700.   n. nel porra g. *E*; *H wants*.
701.   C. dist l. *E C*; *H wants*.

702. v. cui qu'en doive peser *C*;   n. le doi   refuser *E*;
       v. nel doi p. *G*; *H wants*.
703. f. jou nel doi refuser *C*; c. qu'en doie peser *E G*;
       H wants.
704. A Jhesus te comment pres est de l'a. *H*;   O. tos c.
       CG.
705. Je te commant a Diu k. *E*; c. il m. *E G*.
706. e. tournent l. *C*; e. ala l. *H*;   *G adds*: Te Deon
       laudamus cou com doit Dieu loer.
707. k. fu e. *E CG H*.
708. Desi au matins n. *C*; Tant que vint el demain n. *G*;
       Toute le nuit ne pot dormir ne reposer *E*; n. qu'il
       vit le jour cler *CG*; *H wants*.
709. Pense comment   li   enfes se porra delivrer *E*; *CG H*
       want.
710. s. faura a., a. monter *E*; *CG H want*.
711. k. le mont dois s. *E*; *CG H want*.
712. *CG H want*.
713. *E CG H want*.
714. f. de r. *E*; *CG H want*.
715. g. parage c'on a fait assambler *E*; *CG H want*.
716. v. et e. *E*; *CG H want*.
717. v. al main n'al avesprer *E*; *CG H want*.
718. Jou f. v. que il *E*; *CG H want*.
719. b. le s. *E*; *CG H want*.
720. *CG H want*.
721. s. prist a *E*; *CG H want*.
722. f. vous c. aler *E*; *CG H want*.
723. s. de c. *E*; *CG H want*.
724. i. nous b. *E*; p. ne m. *E*; *CG H want*.
725. *E CG H want*.
726. *CG H want*.
727. p. pour mangier au disner *E*; *CG H want*.
728. *CG H want*.
729. *CG H want*.
38.   *BE CG H*
730. L'ermite demoura et l'ange s'en ala *H*; r. li a.
       s'en torna *G*.
731. p. de penser l'ermites n. *E*; l. preudons d. *CG H*.
732. Mout par s. *G*; d. et mout s. *EG*; f. se mervella *E*;
       C H want.
733. C. ses j. *C*; j. enfes b. souferra *CG*.
734. *C H want*.
735. Mout bien cuide et si pense james ne le vera *G*; g.
       penser d. *C*; *H wants*.
736. q. il voit le jors *C*; q. il vint le jor *G*;   q. il
       vit le jour son enfant esveilla *H*.
737. s. dist i. *E G*; f. li hermites et l'enfes s. *C*; e.

s'esveilla *H*.
738. i. demanda *E G H*.
739. Biaus peres u irons E. *C H*; k. voles v. *G*; d. nous
     je scay ou boys dela *H adds*: De trop bonnes pru-
     nelles qui meures sont pieca.
740. Em plorant li a dit biaus fius tout el i a *C*; Beau
     filz dist li hermite en plourant dit li a *H*.
741. D. ne te celerai ja *C*; D. plus c. *E*; *G H want*.
742. En ce j., c. te fauldra *H*.
743. C'on l., c. qu'ele onques ne p. *C*; c. onques ne le
     p. *E*; c. c'onques el ne p. *H*; o. ne p. *G*.
744. e. se mervelle d. *E*; e. quant il entendut l'a *C*;
     c. qu'oi a *G*.
745. K'il ne set ki e. *G H*; s. que ch'est arme ne cou
     qu'el siecle a *C*; m. ne semblance el a *H*.
746. Ne seit il n. *C*; Ne n. *G*; Il n'en s. *E*; c. que v.
     G; c. ne v. *E*; *H wants*.
747. m. ne s. *C*; m. ne le me celez ja *H*.
748. Sont ce o. *E*; S. il o. *CG*; b. ne le me c. *G*; b. ne
     me c. *E*; m. celer v. *E CG*; c. tu j. *C*; c. ja *G*
     which adds: Sauvage fruit ne bisse ki par le fo-
     riest va/ Se si faite est ma mere ja ne m'apertenra/ Fius cou dist li hermites tout autre cose i a;
     H wants.
749. Frere a. *C*; Ancois e. *G*; Beau f. c'e. *H*.
750. p. c'est le roy qui en ce jour l. *H*.
751. e. legierement c. *H*; i. que j. *G*; i. ja li eure s.
     E; c. grant jour sera ja *H*; j. grans jors s. *CG*.
752. *C places this verse after l.* 754.
753. Et la c. est pres b. *H*; e. ci p. *CG*.
754. Com vos l. *E CG*; Comme vous le feres c. *H*; b. et
     D. *E*; *G adds*: Pour lui vous conbates et ja ne vous
     faura/ Biaus pere dist li enfes batalle coument
     va/ Keurt on par le foriest u on repaire ca/ Est
     cou a .I. oissiel qu'on se conbatra/ U a bieste
     sauvage qu'on encontera/ Il n'i a nule seule ja si
     tos ne coura/ Que ne l'ataigne bien ja si tos n'en
     ira/ Et se couvient a arbres monte ne ca ne la/ Se
     ne sui li premiers dehait qui m'engenra/ Onques
     Dex ne fist bieste je quic ne n'estora/ Que bien
     ne me conbace que me mere droit a/ Et qu'a grant
     tort fu mise la u ele est pieca/ Quant li hermites
     l'ot grant mautalent en a/ Car bien voit et entent
     ja ne si conbatra/ Il ne set mie tant mais que Dex
     li manda/ Portant sui a seur k'il en escapera.
755. s. dist l. *E C*; e. que li c. *C*; c. en a. *E CG*; c.
     il a. *H*.
756. v. ne le r. *G*; v. je nel refusrai j. *E*; *H wants*.

757. En le garde Diu Jhesu-Cris que l. *C*;   Que D. *G*; k.
      le monde fourma *H*.

758. a. tout si c. *G*.

39. *BE CG H*

759. Biaus peres d. *C H*; e. or m. *E CG H*.

760. Comme pourray combatre en s. vous neant *H*.

761. C. dist l. *CG H*;   l. enfant hermite je scay bien
      mon enfant *H*.

762. Combatre t'estevra d. *C*;   c. ce s. *E*;   c. je le s.
      H; j. vraiement *E H*.

763. s. chevaliers p. *G*; c. sur ung destrier courant *H*;
      m. ensiant *E CG*.

764. Et q. b. est cheval *H*; e. chevaliers f. *G*; c. dist
      l'enfes erramment *C*;   c. ce respont pie estant *E*;
      c. ne le celez neant *H*; f. l'enfes en riant *G*.

765. S. il ne cien ne cat V. *C*;   S. il ne leu ne kievre
      V. *G*; S. leu ou lion V. *E*; *H wants*.

766. C. dist l. *C H*; h. c'est belle beste et grant *H*.

767. s. nature n. *CG*; *H wants*.

768. Tan tos com le veras par le mien e. *C*;   Si tos con
      le veres par le mien e. *G*; a ensiant *E CG*; *H wants*.

769. r. c'on appiele O. *C*; r. k'a a *E*; *H wants*.

770. m. a non au cuer v. *C*;   m. la dame al c. *G*;   m. le
      bele al c. *E*; *H wants*.

771. c. trestout p. *C*; c. jel d. *E G*; c. tout p. *H*.

772. T'estuet b. *C*; Fai toi b. *G*; f. crestiiener e. *CG*;
      b. a .I. non mout tres j. *E*; metre non *C*; nom gent
      H; m. grant *CG*.

773. E. aras n. *C H*; n. ainsi l. *H*.

774. k. te met e. *C*.

775. Ele vos envoia noiier tout vraiement *C*; E. cellui
      k. *H*; c. toli c. *G H*.

776. Par .I. homme Marcon mais il n'en fist noiant *C*;
      Si a *G H*; M. ung felon souldoyant *H*; n. vit s. *G*;
      C adds: Les iox en a perdus dont a le cuer dolant.

777. La viele fait entendre au roy a ensiant *C*; f. le
      r. *E*; f. de ce le roy creant *H*.

778. c. ele n'en fist noiant *C*;   c. mais le vielle si
      ment *E*;   c. mais pour vray el ment *H*; .I. delivre-
      ment *G*.

779. *E CG H want*.

780. *E CG H want*.

781. Pour cou l'a on j. *C*; Pour cou si e. *G*; Pour c'est
      ele j. *E*; Pour ce el livree i. *H*; j. a si felon
      (vilain *G H*) tourment *CG H*.

782. Hui l'ont fors de la cartre jete par jugement *G*;
      Qu'en cest jour sera arse par le mien escient *H*; *E*
      C want.

783. Ancui ert arse en feu se Diex ne l'en desfent *C*;
S'ele n'a chevalier ki de cou le desfent *G*; Se
Dieu ne lui aide le Pere omnipotant *H*; *E wants*; *G
adds*: Ele en mora a Dex par dolerous torment/ N'e-
le n'a en la cort ne ami ne parent/ Ki desfendre
l'en ost ne lui metre en present/ Pour la viele
maudite ki ait enconbrement/ Et tu ies li siens
enfes vai delivrement; *H adds*: Beau filz dist li
hermite dit te ay vrayement/ Du roy et de tes fre-
res tout le commancement.

784. La cite est ci pres V. *H*; T. pues t. demorer haste
toi biel enfant *G*; e. legierement *H*.

785. r. je l'octroy e. *H*; j. veil b. *C*; *G wants*.

786. Jou ferai de par Diu tout vo commande[me]nt *C*; A.
l. *E H*; met li hermite en p. *H*; m. et l. *E*; *G
wants*.

787. Sel c. *C*; Le c. *H*; .I. piece p. *C*; .I. pose p. *H*;
G wants.

788. Mais ains que de moi parte te donrai viestement *G*;
De nulle robe n'eust f. *H*; r. n'en ot i. *C*.

789. c. li fist li hermites errant *G*; f. courtes n. *C*;
c. menue et g. *E*; c. non m. *H*; *G adds*: De fuelles
et de rains et d'escorce de glant.

790. Se li fist .I. capiel par tel devisement *G*; a.
atakiet e. *C which adds*: Sollers ot de pisson non
pas de cor devant/ N'ot cemise ne braies ne autre
garnement/ Ceviaus n'ot onques res en jour de son
vivant; *G adds*: Des clices et de fuelles lacie
soutivement/ Atille li laca el cief estroitement/
.I. baston li douna de caisne mout pesant/ Car li
varle est fors se il seust nient/ Que ferai jou de
cou fait il pour saint Climent/ Tu en feras biaus
fius fait il ireement/ Se on te viut maufaire si
fiert premierement/ Et se tu vois la viele ceurt
li sus erraument/ Tu le veras ases laiens al par-
lement/ Par mon cief dist li enfes si iert il voi-
rement/ Or s'en ira li enfes por voir delivrement/
Sa cote fu de fuelles caperon i ot gent/ Solers ot
d'un tason plus noirs qu'airement/ Se li sanble
k'il soit viestus mout ricement/ Peres ce dist li
enfes a ce departement/ M'aves vous bien viestu
.C. mercis vous en rent/ Onques n'ot fius de roi
je quic tel viestement/ De la joie k'il a de son
cier garniment/ Illueques errannment par mi .I. pre
dessent.

791. Andui s. *G*; E. en va li enfes v. *C*; v. issi v. *G*;
v. a court v. *E*; v. eulx deux v. *H*; l. cite'rran-
ment *G*; *CG add*: Or le (les *G*) conduise Diex li Pe-

res tous poissans (D. par son digne commant *G*); *H*
adds: Mais se Dieu plaist le Pere qui tout fist de
neant.

792. Que ja o. *C*; Encor o. *H*; b. merveilleuse (doulou-
reuse *H*) et pesans *C H*; b. perellouse forment
G.

793. *CG H want*.

794. N'oistes onc plus fiere se Dieu garist l'enfant *H*;
o. millor por voir le vous creant *G*; s. fiere par
le mien ensiant *C*; f. et de si jovene e. *E*.

40. *BE CG H*

795. Desor s. *CG*; l. enfes ki n'est pas bien senes *G*;
l. enfant qui fut moult e. *H*; e. aïres *C*.

796. Damedieu reclama e. *G*; s. saintes bontes *E G*; *C H*
want; *G adds*: Sire conduisies moi ki pooir en
aves/ Ainc n'issi fors de bos en trestous mes aes/
Quant il vint as plains cans dont fu mout esfraes/
Il escria l'ermite biaus pere or m'entendes/
Qu'est li bos devenus quant nous fu il enbles/
Biaus fius dist li hermites ains a este copes/ A
dont s'en va avant ni a plus demore.

797. n'ot il p. *C*; n'eust il p. *H*; a. il plus que dire
m. *G*.

798. Pelus estoit com ours et com leus e. *C*; Velus es-
toit com leus et c'ours e. *G*; Velus estoit com
leus ou ours e. *E*; Velus fut tout ainsi comme ung
ours e. *H*; o. esfraes *C H*.

799. S'avoit les o. grans et les c. *E*; longs les c.
tous m. *H*.

800. n'est p. *E*; *H wants*.

801. k. devant e. *C*; k. deseure q. *G*; k. de tout fu q.
E; *H wants*.

802. l. voit b. *C*; l. veist b. *H*; *G adds*: Ne sanbloit
mie sages ains sanbloit *blank space*.

803. i. dou b., u. gues *CG*.

804. Avisa l. *H*; q. cou est l. *C H*.

805. f. dist l. *E C H*; l. hermites d. *CG H*; o. en poes
aler *C*; o. vous e. *E G H*; e. ales *G*.

806. *CG H want*.

807. *CG H want*.

809. Et D. *C*; M. Dameldieu de cuer mout souvent r. *G*;
M. Dame de gloire doulcement r. *H*; D. sovent par
son non apieles *C*.

810. Si vraiement qu'il fu en la Virgens esconses *C*; s.
comme f. *E*; *H wants*.

811. Vos soit en cest jour garans e. *C*; s. aide garant
e. *H*; g. li s. *G*; *H adds*: Mes or me dictes pere ou
est le bois alez/ Beau filz dist li hermite lais-

sez voz foleitez/ Il est ou il soulloit a Dieu
vous en alez/ Et l'ermite le laisse a Dieu l'a
commandez.

812. m. dist l. *E CG*; p. la soie pitet *C*; *H wants*.
813. Li hermites en est a. *C*; Plourant s'en est l'ermi-
te a. *H*.
814. E. l'enfant s'en entra ou grant chemin ferrez *H*;
e. en va ou cemin est entres *C*; e. cevauce n. *G*;
c. si est a. *E G*.
815. c. en va tous seus e. *C*; e. esgares *E C*; e. aires
G; *C adds*: Ne sanble mie sages ains sanle fourse-
nes.
816. S'il plaist a Jhesu-Crist l. *C*; s. Dieu p. *G H*; l.
Pere qui en croix fut penez *H*; R. qu'en Beliant fu
nes *CG*.
817. E. nuit s. *H*; e. fierviestis et a. *C*; e. tout a.
H; b. ames *G*.
818. d. qui tant a eut grieces *C*; d. sera bien a. *H*; r.
atornes *G*; *C adds*: Por li ardoir ert ja li grans
feus alumes.
819. c. l'a traicte le cuvert M. *H which adds*: Qui en-
cor sera mort et recreant gettez.
820. *E C H want.*
821. c. fu jetes *G which adds*: Dex l'en acat vengance
par la soie bonte; *E C H want*.
822. Il en iert vers le viespre recreans e. *G*; *E C H
want*.
823. c. traitres prouves *G*; *E C H want*.
824. *E C H want.*
825. *E C want.*
826. Aspre b. et f. *G*; *E C H want*.
41. *BE CG H*
827. v. l'enfant onc n. *H*; e. tous seus sa[n]s c. *C*; e.
c'ainc n. *G*; e. que n'i a c. *E*; n'y eust c. *H*.
828. De nului n'a consel s. *C*; s. de D. *E CG*; *H wants*.
829. Por femme a a. ont ja .IIII. garchon *C*; Pour veoir
sa mere ardre eurent ja l. *H*.
830. e. a traites e. *C H*; a. tout entor le dongnon *C*;
e. le feurre environ *H*.
831. Mauquarre a la dame gette de prison *H*; q. cuer a
de lion *C*; q. ot la cuer f. *G*; q. le cuer ot f. *E*.
832. l. ausi comme .I. l. *E*; l. en g. *H*.
833. e. a mout haute raison *C*; e. vray Dieu par ton
saint non *H*; *C adds*: Biaus peres Jhesu-Cris qui
formas Lazaron.
834. Q. sainte S. garis dou f. *C H*; S. de la mort au
lion *G*.
835. Ca m., b. Peres p. *C*; Aidies me b. dous S. *E*; Huy

m. *H*; p. ton s. *C*; p. vo s. *E*; t. saintime non *E*
C; t. beneicon *H*.

836. C. dist M. *E G*; M. ne vous v. *G*; M. or n. *E*; *C*
wants.

837. En c. *H*; j. seres a. *E G H*; a. sans autre r. *G*; a.
n'en ares r. *E*; a. qui qu'en poise ne qui non *H*; *C*
wants.

838. L. rois e. *CG H*; s. se fu l. *C*; s. en iert l. *G*;
s. est ja venu e. *H*.

839. Ne demeure en la ville e. *H*; I. n'en i a r. *C*.

840. p. valeton *G*; *C H want*.

841. Qu'il n'en aile v. *C*; Que t. *H*; c. destruction *C*
H.

842. d. ainc t. *C*; j. mais t. *H*; n. vora (sic) o. *G*; n.
fera o. *E*.

843. o. romput tant h. *C which adds*: Les dames dou pais
et li autre baron/ Por la dame se pasment entour
et environ; *H wants*.

844. c. rompu e. *E*; *G adds*: Des dames ki estoient del
pais environ; *H wants*.

845. E. grant d. f. au f. la mena o. *C*; f. les m. *G*; f.
l'en m. *E*; *G adds*: Il estoit ja espris si ardoit a
bandon/ Ja sera la dame arse s'elle n'a canpion; *H*
wants.

42. *BE CG H*

846. l. prison j. *C*; l. cite j. *H*.

847. v. c'a male eure fu nee *C*; v. de mal heure fut nee
H; k. ert m. *E*; m. euree *E G*.

848. L. eut l. *C*.

849. Et la d. *E CG H*; e. a mout haute alenee *C*; e. Vi-
erge ben euree *H*; e. lasse mal euree *G*.

850. *C adds*: Qui portastes celi qui vos avoit formee/
.VII. ans devant cele eure dame que fussies nee; *H*
wants.

851. Secourez moy cest j. *H*; m. hui c. *E CG*; j. car m.
C; j. que m. *G*; j. ou m. *H*; v. outree *E C*.

852. Toutes voies l. *CG H*; Tout li serf ont le dame de
le cartre jetee *E*; o. il d. *CG*; o. jus d. *H*.

853. *CG H add*: Et Matabrune i a une thymbre (M. a une
trompe *H*) (Matabrune si a une cloce *G*) sounee; *C*
adds further: Sa tieste en a juret qui d'or est
courounee/ Or ne remanroit mies por sa tor d'or
rasee/ Qu'ele ne fust arse a le pourre ventee.

854. s. de l. *G*; s. et l. *E*; *C H want*.

855. d. icil d. *E*; *C H want*.

856. *C H want*.

857. *C H want*.

858. c. desronte et despanee *E*; *C H want*.

859. Au pie c. *E*; Elle vit son signor al pie li est alee *G*; *C H want*; *G adds*: Sire por Dieu merchi ki fist ciel et rousee/ U ai jou desiervi ceste dure jornee/ Ains ne forfis vers vous icou dont sui retee/ N'ainc ne fui ne nul home fors de vous adesee/ Certes cou dist la viele trop i estes en parlee/ Bien est votre putages et votre uevre provee/ Tant a parle la viele que mar fust onques nee/ Et li rois s'aira sa couroune a juree.

860. *CG H want.*

861. K'il n. *E G*; p. mie p. *G*; p. pas p. mesure d. *E*; *C H want.*

862. a. a l. *E*; e. a p. *G*; *C H want.*

863. Entre lor dueil en sont au feu alee *C*; *H wants.*

864. Et l. *H*; L. rois v. *G H*; s. s'en v. *G*; s. en v. *E*; *C wants.*

865. e. dolans en s. *G*; *C H want.*

866. Desor .I. g. ceval bien une abalestree *G*; p. se face est esploree *E*; *C H want.*

867. a. mainte larme a e. *E G*; e. ploree *G*; e. jetee *E*; *C H want.*

868. Quant li enfes entra en la cite loee *G*; Adonques vint l. *H*.

869. *E CG H want.*

870. Il d. *E*; d. teil nouviele qui b. fu e. *C*; *G H want.*

871. I. entra p. *CG*; e. en l. *C*; p. devers la m. *E CG*; *H wants.*

872. Quant il entent l. *C*; Il a *H*.

873. Si c. *C*; c. cou s. *G H*; s. bisse u dain c'on ait b. *C*; b. qui soit leans b. *H*.

874. e. avoir c. *G*; *C H want.*

875. S. comme s. *E*; e. la bruelle r. *E G*; *C H want.*

876. l. chiere l. *H*; *C wants.*

877. c. le roy k. *C*; c. l'espee que ses pere avoit clere *G*; *H wants.*

878. i. a a *C*; *H wants.*

879. i. voit l. *C*; c. et l. *H*.

880. illec por *H*.

43. *BE CG H*

881. e. se mervelle d. *E H*; e. de cou que le roy v. *C H*; e. de son pere que v. *G*.

882. *H adds*: Il cuidoit qu'il mengast pour son frain qui (sic) mengoit; *C wants.*

883. D. aiwe dist il q. *C*; D. ai Dix dist l. *E*; D. aide dist l'enfant q. *H which adds*: Et la dame en plourant devant le feu estoit/ Elle eust les mains lies d'une couroye estroit/ Dieu appelle et recla-

me en qui el se fioit/ He Dieu ce dist l'enfant
qui pou de sens avoit.

884. b. est cela ne sce pas q. *H*; l. ne sai mais q. *C*;
H adds: Durement me roulle ne say se il me voit.

885. Je croy c'est le c. que mon p. disoit *H*; e. .I. c.
C.

886. Parlant et s. a s. *G*; s. vint vers le roy tout
droit *H*; v. le fieste en va d. *C*.

887. Et t. *C*; Et il tint e. *E*; En son col son baston
car en pense avoit *H*; e. sa main .I. b. *G*; b. a
.II. mains b. *C*; *H adds*: Qu'il ferroit a deux
poings s'assaillir le voulloit.

888. d. plus n'i avoit *C*; d. velus e. *E*; *G H want*.

889. H. sot e. *C*; s. a mervelle r. *E G*; s. a merveilles
r. *H*; m. bien r. *C*; m. sanloit *E CG H*.

890. L'ange a Dieu le Pere sur l'espaule s. *H*; s. sen
e. estoit *C*.

891. Que q. *G*; Que ce qu'il d. dire trop b. *H*; d. l'an-
gles l. *C*.

892. r. en apiela e. *E C*; r. en enseigna e. *H*; a. issi
c. *G*; e. comme s. *E*.

893. Dy f., t. que je voy ci a. *H*.

894. Ce qui est dessoulx toy tien lay ferme et adroit *H*
which adds: Que nul mal ne me face quer grant pe-
che seroit/ Durement me roille comme s'il me
hayoit.

895. S. i tu se il mort *E*; i. voit *G*; *C H want*.

896. o. mais jou ne sai s'il v. *C*; i. oit *E G*; *H wants*.

897. r. l'entendi e. *C*; r. l'a veu et issi p. *G*; r. a
choisi et qu'il ainsi parloit *H*; e. ensi p. *E C*;
p. l'oit *CG*; p. l'ot *E*.

898. V. en e. *H*; m. grant dolour a. *C*; m. si g. *E*; t.
dolent estoit *H*; *E adds*: Car li deus de se feme
mervelle li grevoit/ Pour cose que veist joie
avoir ne pooit.

44. *BE CG H*

899. r. mout s'esmervelle q. *G*; r. se mervella q. *E*; i.
oi l. *C*.

900. Pour coi estoit velus e. *G*; S. fierement p. *C*; S.
durement p. *H*; f. viestu e. *E C*; e. si diviers
samblant *C*.

901. B. voi n., e. en v. *C which adds*: Vos dites voir
dist il se Diex me soit aidans; *E H want*.

902. *CG H want*.

903. f. le roy voirement *H*.

904. *CG H want*.

905. Je sui li rois sans falle c. *E*; *CG H want*.

906. c. dist l. *E*; f. l'enfes en r. *E G*; f. il e. *C*; f.

cil e. *H*; 1. se Deus manant *C H*.

907. Mangu il dongues f. *C*; Et mengue le f. qui ainsi v. *H*; v. rongant *E*.

908. f. c'est son f. fait le roy maintenant *H*; f. qui le va destragnant *E*; *CG want*.

909. N. nel m. *C*; N. le c. *H*.

910. F. et d. *E*; *CG H want*.

911. Jou ne sai p. *C*; Jou n'ai p. *G*; Je n'ay or p. *H*; n. par Dieu omnipotent *C*; n. sire v. *G*; n. fait il se Dex mainent *G H*; *C adds*: J'avoie a non biaus fius quant iere ou bos manans/ Or n'en ai jou pas non d'ore mais en avant; *G adds*: Quant jou estoie el bos o l'ermite vallant/ S'avoie a non biaus enfes mes de ci en avant/ Nen ai je point de non fait il se Dex mainent; *H adds*: J'avoye nom beau filz sur l'ermite vaillant/ Ou j'ay este nourris des ores en avant/ N'ay sire point de nom pour vray le vous greant.

912. t. dist l. *C*; r. trop ai l. *CG H*; r. je ai mon c. *E*; *CG place this verse after l. 907.*

913. Dont as tu dit orendroit P. *C*; Pour c'as tu fait li enfes P. *G*; e. isi le cuer dolant *CG*; e. ne me celer neant *H*; D. omnipotent *E*.

914. *CG H want.*

915. Foit que tu dois a Dieu le Pere raemant (P. onipotent *G*) *CG*; p. quoy tu as en ton cuer duel si grant *H*.

916. Et j. *CG*; Et le roy respondi a l'enfant maintenant *H*; dirai fait *CG*; d. dist l. *C*; r. em plorant *CG which add*: Mout m'en as conjuret Diex te croisse en avant (c. et ament *G*).

917. e. ce f. *E*; *CG H want.*

918. j. ardoir s. *E*; *CG H want.*

919. *CG H want.*

920. *CG H want.*

921. J. cuidoie a. *CG H*; f. et l. *G*; e. mout gent *E*.

922. a .X. a. *C H*; p. et plus m. *C*; p. je cuid m. *H*; m. ensiant *E CG H*.

923. Qu'ele vint a .X. c. *C*; Qu'elle geust a sept c. *H*.

924. Si e. *CG H*; e. eust .VII. *H*; .VII. caiaus c. *CG*; o. creant *G H*.

925. Et por cou est j. *C*; e. livree a *H*; s. vilain t. *E H*.

926. f. sera arse orendroit en present *H*; v. c'on a. *E C*; l. alume e. *E CG*.

927. Ert encor ancui a. *C*; a. mais g. *CG*; *H wants.*

928. Arse Dieu dist l'enfant fait as fol jugement *H*; e.

si f. *G.*

929. N'a (sic) pas a droit j. *H;* T. n'as mie j. *CG.*
930. E. s'il e. n. hom k. *CG H;* k. n'en desist itant *C;* k. se mesist a. *E;* e. tirast a. *H.*
931. f. nul si v. convent *E; CG H want.*
932. P. raement *G;* P. omnipotent *E; H wants.*
933. L. feroie jehir *G;* j. ains la nuit k. *H;* j. que il m. *E C H;* j. s'en m. *G.*
934. r. eust s., q. la parole e. *H;* l. va entendant *C;* l. varlet e. *G.*
935. Ne fust pas si joyeux pour tout l'or d'Abilent *H;* p. or ne pour a. *CG.*

45. *BE CG H*

936. Enfant c. *H;* q. c'est que tu me d. *C.*
937. T. me sambles bien *C;* f. a tes f. a tes d. *CG.*
938. Quant de ce fais tu que fol h. *H; E G want.*
939. D. aiue dist l'enfes P. *E C;* D. m'aidera dist l'enfant com je truis *H.*
940. c. conte li e. *E C; G H want.*
941. Dex me p. bien a. *G;* m. puist a. *H.*
942. T. n'en as chevalier t. *G;* a. nul chevalier t. *C;* s. fier ne hardis *H.*
943. C'a l. *CG;* Ne l'en rende cest jour par mon seul corps h. *H.*
944. S'il v. *H;* d. a p. *C H which place this verse after 1. 942.*
945. p. con tu ci me descris *G; C H want.*
946. Atant est M. qui amaine a grant c. *H;* M. amainne a. *CG;* M. maine et g. b. et grans c. *E;* m. et a plours e. *C;* g. cris a grans huis *G.*
947. Ardoir l. *G;* l. biele d. *E G;* k. ot n. *C;* k. eust n. *H; CG add:* Oi (or *G*) sera la dame arse Diex (a. se D. *G*) n'en a miercis.
948. Oriant la regarde si est d. *H;* d. maris *E; CG want.*
949. E Diex ce dist la dame vrais rois de p. *C;* Ha Dex cou dist li enfes ki si ies poestis *G;* Dieu aide dist l'enfant qui regnes et qui vis *H which adds as the initial line of the following laisse:* L'enfant en a appella le bon roy de Baviere.
950. Ki fesis l. *G;* f. aige *E G;* e. les vins e. *E;* v. el l. *C;* v. et l'anis *G; C adds:* Si voirement dous sires com vos fustes laidis/ Et mis ens en la crois au jour dou venredi; *H wants.*
951. Si puissies vos secourre iceste pecceris *C;* Tu souscours c. *E G;* a et j. *E; H wants.*

46. *BE CG H*

952. Ses tu rois dist l. *CG H.*

953. Ja m. *CG H*; L. nul mal t. *G*; m. losengiers n. *C H*;
d. preudom a *E H*.
954. Ta mere Matabrune t. *CG H*; M. tu cantes et lis ore
d. *E*; m. t'ament t. *C*; m. te cace t. *G*; m. t'a
leu t. *H*; t. laituaire *C*.
955. j. Damrediu ou v. *C*; J. ens e. *E*; *H wants*.
956. c. tel a. *E*; *CG H want*.
957. a. si hardit home t. *CG*; c. qui soit p. et m. *E*;
CG add: Chevalier ne sergant s'il s'en ose (viut
G) avant traire; *G adds further*: Que la dame ne
soit loiaus et de boin aire; *H wants*.
958. O l. *G*; *H wants*.
959. i. i m. *G*; *H wants*.
960. l. rois l'entendi t. *CG*; *H wants*.
961. Par tous sains d. *CG*; *H wants*.
962. p. .XVII. ans se le p. *G*; *H wants*.
963. Con j. *G*; j. t'ai oi conter et voiant tous t. *E*;
o. avant aconter et t. *C*; o. orendroit c. *G*; a.
retraire *C E*; *H wants*.

47. *BE CG H*
964. r. fort s'esmervelle d. *G*; r. se mervella d. *E H*;
c. que il o. *CG*; c. que l. *E*.
965. Mais tant croit Diu que ainc n. *C*; Mais tant
crient et anuie que ne l'ose desdire *G*; *H wants*.
966. v. qui Jesus doist (sic) martire *E*; v. de venin
plain et de i. *H*; k. onques n'est s. *G*.
967. E. amainne l. *CG H*; d. Beatris por l'ardire *C*; *E
wants*.
968. Et des grans va apres .I. merveileus e. *C*; Et de
gent apries va une grant barounie *G*; Et de gens
vient apres merveilles g. *H*; *E wants*.
969. Por la dame font duel forment ja grant i. *C*; Por
la dame sont tout e. *G*; Qui tous sont pour la dame
e. *H*; *E wants*.
970. Et Matabrune cante n. *CG H*; v. et si commence a r.
G; *E wants*.
971. f. et l. *E*; p. mautalent l. *C*.
972. Son mantiel de son dos li desront e. *C*; *H wants*.
973. g. irour si escume s'aire *E*; *CG H want*.
974. Pieca c. *E G*; f. s'afie *C*; *H wants*.
975. t. vous n'iestes pas bons s. *G*; *H wants*.
976. Or en venes a. *C*; f. par le cors saint Lehire *G*.
977. Or e. *G*; a. ja n'i ara m. *C*; a. jamais n'en ares
mie *G*; a. et livree a martire *E*; a. sans avoir nul
m. *H*; aura remire *C H*.

48. *BE CG H*
979. Es ja .I. *C*.
980. Et d. *E*; K. dit q. *H*; e. envie e. *C*; e. hontaige

              H.

981. a. a tort la dame sus mis r. *G*; v. la dame a tort vous mettez sur putaige *H.*

982. d. k'il en d. *E G*; *C H want.*

983. a garde d. *G*; s. felon h. *CG*; *H wants.*

984. Que s. *E*; *CG H want.*

985. Q. Matabrune l'ot a poi de dueil n'enrage *C*; l. dame l. *G*; l'entent v. *G H*; o. a pou qu'elle n'enrage *H.*

986. L'enfant ceurt as ceviaus p. *C*; Aux chevaulx prent l'enfant p. *H*; de .M. l. *G.*

987. Ha Dex cou f. *G*; A. dist l. *CG H*; c. a mal a comtaige *H which adds*: Cest vielle hideuse a ens ou corps la raige/ Plus fait a redoubter que nul lyon sauvaige.

988. D. la u D. *G*; D. en qui D. *H*; D. prist onbrage *G H*; *C wants.*

989. M'envoye encor vengence de ce villain hontaige *H*; p. mout bien aidier de si fel acointage *G*; *C wants.*

990. f. mie m. *G H.*

991. *CG H want.*

992. m. felon g. *E*; *CG H want.*

993. *CG H want.*

994. *CG H want.*

995. *CG H want.*

996. Tout c. *CG H*; k. l'ont oi hucent a *C H*; k. l'oent crient a. *G*; k. l'orent oi li haute homme et li s. *E*; h. a haute visage *C*; h. en leur langaige *H*; v. a s. *G*; *E adds*: S'escrierent en haute voiant tout le parage; *H adds*: Ha roy de orient ne souffrez tel hontaige.

997. *G wants.*

998. R. tien l'enfant a droit i. *CG*; R. tien a l'enfant droit bien pert d. *H*; l'enfant il *E*; d. qui e. *C*; d. k'il e. *G*; h. linage *E.*

999. d. que tant soit de sens sage *E*; d. boin l. *C*; d. haute l. *G*; d. grant langaige *H which adds*: Dieu le t'a envoye pour dire cest messaige.

49. *BE CG H*

1000. e. le r. *G*; e. en haut T. *E*; T. a l'enfant d. *H.*

1001. D. les puist c. *C*; D. li p. bien aidier a. *E*; *H wants.*

1002. S'il estoit bien v. *C H*; v. beau seroit e. *H*; g. homs samleroit *C*; g. hom sanlle a droit *E*; *G wants.*

1003. dehait ki *E.*

1004. c. car de rien n'y a droit *H*; e. que cou ne croit

C; k. ice croit *E*; *C places this verse after 1.*
1001.

1005. d. ou f. *C H*; f. il n. *C*; f. car n. *E*; f. ja n'i
atendes ploit *G*; n'i a teil e. *E C*.

1006. p. Diu qui tous nos v. *CG*; p. le D. *E H*.

1007. Ne sera huy la dame arse qui est mise en destroit
H; e. mes a. *G*; a. si sarai q. *CG*.

1009. B. pora e. *G*; q. et drois est qu'elle soit *H*; e.
qui le laisoit *C*.

1010. Q. la viele l'entent a. *CG H*; o. por p. *G*; q. ne
marvoit *C*.

1011. M. appella le t. regnoioyt *H*; h. son t. destroit
C; t. renoit *E G*.

1012. v. dist l. *E C*; v. ja Dameldex n. *G H*; j. Dieus
nen i s. *C*; j. ci Dix ne s. *E*.

1013. Et si copes cest garcon orendroit la tieste *C*; Et
si c. *G*; t. ce g. *E G*; t. a ce gars ci endroit *H*.

1014. *H wants.*

1015. Dius dist l. *C*; e. que nul mal ne savoit *G*; *H*
wants.

1016. d. eplorant avant l. *C*; d. en p. *G*; f. estoit *C*;
f. s'estoit *G*; *CG add:* Em plorant son marthire la
aluec (illueques *G*) atendoit; *H wants.*

1017. o. ses m. *E*; *CG H want.*

1018. r. qu'ele bien creoit *G*; *H wants.*

1019. M. voit l. *C*; M. prent l. *G*; M. s'esbaudist que
la b. *H*; a. que l. *G*; b. avoit *E H*; *H adds:* Ja ne
cuide tant vivre que la bataille soit.

1020. *CG H want.*

1021. *CG H want.*

50. *BE CG H*

1022. D. dist M. *E G*; f. il il e. *C*; il couvient t. *H*.

1023. a. et puis fais c. *C*; a. se iere c. *G*; a. et soye
c. *H*.

1024. L'enfes sera rendus a. *C*; L'enfes sera ancui mout
pres de s. *G*; e. trencheray la teste ains l'anui-
ter *H which adds:* Et deux serfs lui coureurent
sans y point sejourner/ Armeures lui aportent
sans y contralier.

1025. Quant por iceste (Q. il por ceste *G*) dame se fait
ore si lies (fiers *G*) *CG*; *H wants.*

1026. j. mout c. je sui e. *G*; c. j'avoie e. *E*; j. fui
e. *C*; *H wants.*

1027. Plus de .VII. *C*; Plus a de .XVII. ans que d. *G*; *H*
wants.

1028. C. dist M. frere j. *E*; M. mes amis iestes c. *CG*;
H wants.

1029. C. seres j. boins iert vostre d. *G*; j. boins sera

tes d. *C*; e. s'aras b. *E*; *H wants*.
1030. Li a. iert riche et li e. boucliers *C*; Et l'a. boine et l'e. *G*; a. entire e. *E*; *H wants*.
1031. v. ce qui v. *E*; *CG H want*.
1032. Et respont M. foi que doi saint Ricier *E*; *CG H want*.
1033. a. a loi de chevalier *E*; *CG H want*.
1034. a. aporter ert a lor e. *E*; *CG H want*.
51. *BE CG H*
1035. M. si a fait les armes a. *G*; a. devant lui a. *C*.
1036. .VII. s. *C*; c. esranment aporter *E*; m. delivrer *C*; *G H want*.
1037. M. la viele li aiue (aida *G*) a a. *CG H*; a bon v. *E*.
1038. Puis li cauce unes cauces q. *E*; l. caucent mout fissent a *G*; q. bien f. *E*; m. font a *E C H*; a priser *H*; *C adds*: .I. espourons a or li fist es pies frumer.
1039. .I. blanc hauberc safre li ont el dos jete *G*; .I. b[l]anc auberc a safre l. *C*; l. ont f. *E C*; l. firent e. *H*.
1040. f. forgierent en .I. ille de m. *C*; f. en sus l. *E*; f. dedens l. *G*; *H wants*.
1041. La coiffe c'ot el cief ne fait mie a b. (cief fist forment a loer *G*) *CG*; e. tenant c. *E*; *H wants*.
1042. Puis li lacent .I. hiaume qui mout fait (fist *G*) a loer *CG*; e. mout dur lui font ou cher (sic) f. *H*; l. fist cief f. *E*.
1043. De p. *E CG*; o. on f. *CG*; f. tout ovrer *C*; f. a-torner *G*; *CG add*: El nasal par devant eut un carboncle cler; *H wants*.
1044. n. sera tant noir c'on nen puist veir c. *C*; n. c'on n'i voie si c. *E*; o. n'i v. *G*; *H wants*.
1045. l. soleil biel et cler (s. cler lever *G*) *CG*; *H wants*.
1046. *H wants*.
1047. l. d'argent c., f. ouvrer *E*; *G H want*.
1048. .XXX. espees a (ont *G*) fait d'une cambre aporter *CG*; *H wants*.
1049. v. Matabrune cui Dex puis mal doner *C*; v. que d. *G*; *H wants*.
1050. b. si en fait .II. s. *G*; en a sevret *C*; *H wants*.
1051. m. s'il p. pour cors convier *G*; il pot p. *C*; c. adober *C*; c. deporter *E*; *H wants*.
1052. *CG add*: La viele li a cainte cui que doie peser (v. l'encaint une voiant tout le barne *G*)/ Chevalier en a fait qui qu'en doie peser (*C wants*)/ La

colee li a dounee par verite (l. doune maus l'en
puist amonter *G*)/ Si fera il par Dieu cui que
doive peser (p. foit ains le viespre souner *G*)/
Se Diu plaist et ses sains cui (e. tous saint que
G) on doit aourer; *H wants*.

1053. .I. grant d. *CG*; d. d'espagne l. *G*; *H wants*.
1054. coviers si *C*; l'ont f. *E CG*; *C adds*: Le frain me-
tre ens el cief et le poitral; *CG add*: Mauquarres
i monta qui (que *G*) Dius puist craventer/ La vi-
elle (Et la v. *G*) li baille un fort escut boucler
(liste *G*); *C adds further*: A. .II. lions d'argent
qu'ele ot fait puinturer/ La lance ot roide dont
il vora jouster/ A .IIII. claus d'argent le con-
fanon fremer; *H wants*.
1055. La viele Matabrune li amainne .I. gougler *C*; j.
lui fait la dame amener *H*; *G wants*.
1056. Notes et c. li a faites c. *C*; *G H want*.
1057. M. s'esjoi s. *C*; a jurer *G H*.
1058. Que mors est l. *CG*; Mal i *H*; g. s'il le puet e.
CG H; *CG add*: Or le garisse Dieus qui tout a a
sauver.

52. *BE CG*
1059. j. qu'il ne set que il f. *C*; q. ne set que il f.
E G; *H wants*.
1060. a sa f. *E*; *CG want*.
1061. Il esgarde l. *CG*; e. mout forment l. *C*; *H wants*.
1062. Et dist que d. *CG*; s. vera a. *G*; a. la t. *CG*; *H
wants*.
1063. C. fait M. *G*; M. dont a. *E*; m. grasse *E CG*; *H
wants*.
1064. m. k'il a. *G*; c. m'asouage *CG*; *H wants*.
1065. M. fu armes en mi liu de la place *C*; M. que j. *E
G*; *H wants*.
1066. Se sist sor .I. ceval le millor de l. *G*; a. ceval
q. *E*; *C H want*.
1067. En sa main tint la lance le fort escu e. *CG*; e.
al col une targe *E*; *H wants*; *C places this verse
after l. 1071*.
1068. l. ot c., de Cartaige *C*; *H wants*.
1069. Puis laca l'iaume qui clers fu c. *C*; *G H want*.
1070. .I. escarboncle i eut et .I. rice t. *C*; D. ot .I.
e. et .I. rice t. *G*; e. et deva[n]t u. *E*; *H
wants*.
1071. l. fel amers q. *G*; *H wants*.
53. *BE CG H*
1072. Mauquarres est (s'est *G*) a sa male heuree *CG*; e.
le glout a. en sa maleuree *H*.
1073. Encor en puent (sic) i. *H*; A. traira d. *C*; e. au-

ra i. *G*; *E wants*.
1074. M. li a sa vois (sa raison *G*) escriee *CG*.
1075-1076. *CG H want*.
1077. l. a donne c. *E*; *CG H want*.
1078. Et dist chevalier soyes car durement m. *H*; c. or voi ce qui m. *E*; *CG want*.
1079. *CG H want*.
1080. Gardes que li garcons a. *CG*; *H wants*.
1081. s. je n. *E*; *CG H want*.
1082. p. Diu qui fist rousee *E*; m. greve (sic) *C*; m. levre (sic) *G*; *H wants*.
1083. *H wants*.
1084. Iceste l. *C*; C. glaive t. *CG*; t. et affilee *C*; *H wants*.
1085. Iert de son sanc ancui e. *C*; Iert anqui de son sanc trestoute e. *G*; S. anqui du sanc le garson sanglantee *E*; *H wants*.
1086. *CG H want*.
1087. Ains en jesra anqui son vis g. *E*; *CG H want*.
1088. l. vierge honneree *E*; *CG H want*.
1089. *CG H want*.
54. *BE CG H*
1090. Mauquarres est armes a *C*; a Diu m. *CG*.
1092. Matabrune a. *C H*; M. en a. *H*.
1093. Que f. *H*; v. conpagnon *E*.
1094. Li miens est adoubes a *CG*; e. arme a *H*.
1095. d. al vostre itele pasion *G*; *H wants*.
1096. *H wants*.
1097. s. dist l. *E CG*; ne coi non *C*; *H wants*.
1098. Cascun doinst Jhesu-Cris s. *C*; *H wants*.
1099. Il apiela (apiele *G*) l'enfant b. *CG*; Le roy l'enfant appelle doulcement s. *H*.
1100. q. me dis t. *C*; t. or m. *E C H*; d. ta raison *E*; d. or ton non *G*; d. tost tout b. *H*.
1101. Aideras tu le dame u nous ci l'arderon *E*; *CG H want*.
1102. v. aidier m. tresbien t'armeron *E*; *CG H want*.
1103. Et li enfes respont p. *CG*; S. fait le vallet p. *H*.
1104. Ains que on cante vespres ne die le lechon *E*; d. n'est (sic) pas a *H*; e. mie a. *C*.
1105. Avera D. *E*; S'ara Dex nostre sires pris droit de ce f. *G*; S. a D. *C*; *H wants*.
1106. Qu'ele n'est pas c. *G*; d. cele traison *C*; *H wants*.
1107. Q. la viele l. *C*; Q. la dame l. *H*; l'entent s. *C H*; o. s'en f. *G*; o. en eust f. *H*; s. mue e. *E*; e. teil f. *E CG*.

1108. A p. *G H*; P. poine li c. *C*.
1109. s. a leves si baisse l. *G*; a. si leva l. *C*; l. menton *CG*; *H wants*.
1110. m. devint si noire c'uns carbon *C*; m. devint plus rouge de carbon *G*; i. noirci c. *E*; *H wants*.

55. *BE CG H*
1111. v. a m. *CG H*; g. duel b. *H*.
1112. Son filz e. *H*; r. a apiele p. *G*; a. si li dist par i. *CG*; a. fierement par i. *H*; m. fierour *C*.
1113. g. en nuit a. *H*; a. paour *C*.
1114. e. respondi d. *H*.
1115. f. cou dient l. *CG*; f. ce oyent l. *H*; oent li *E*.
1116. D. qui est vostre seigneur *H*; le Creatour *E*; n. cier signor *G*.
1117. t. bien d. *H*; v. gentil o. *E C*.
1118. s. vostre mere estoit a. *H*; M. est a. *G*; .I. four *H*.
1119. Dex li auroit mout bien devant mis son l. *G H*; Se li aroit Dix bien m. *E*.
1120. *H adds*: Mauquarre sera huy vaincu par grant vigour.
1121. a. iver de .II. cols le millor *G*; j. .IIII. cos del i. *C E*; p. menour *C*; p. mellour *E*; *H wants*.
1122. *E CG H want*.
1123. a. il n'i autre t. *C*; a. n'i a autre retour *E*; a. n'i a ci t. *G*; *H wants*.
1124. l. fruit f. *E G*; l. foit f. *C*; f. fist i. *G*; *H wants*.
1125. R. a cascun son droit de nous p. (d. par la soie d. *G*) *E G*; c. son droit p. *C*; *H wants*.
1126. Amis cou dist l. *G*; Beaulx a. *H*.
1127. V. donrai jou si boins o. *CG*; V. donneray si bonnes onc homs n'eust m. *H*; b. et r. *E*.

56. *BE CG H*
1128. *CG H want*.
1129. Li cuers dedens son ventre li prent a esclier *E*; *CG H want*.
1130. c. fait l. *H*; e. bien f. *CG*; e. bien vous vueil m. *H*.
1132. Q. me faciez avant l. *H*.
1133. S'estoie crestiens jou l. *E G*; S. j'estoie crestiens l. *C*; e. l'aroie m. *E*; e. m'aroie m. *G*; *H wants*.
1134. Et j. *E*; *G H want*.
1135. *CG H want*.
1136. r. cou ne doi pas laissier *C*; r. cou ne vel jou laisier *G*.
1137. f. crestien tout p. *E G*; *H wants*.

1138.   o. appieloit G. *C H*; a. Garnier *C*.
1139.   E. cil i *C*; s. plus delaiier *G*; *H wants*.
1140.   c. mist on d. *C*; c. ont fait m. *G*; m. par d. *CG*; *H wants*.
1141.   Trestout le baptestire f. *CG*;   Ce que fault   pour baptesme f. *H*; b. li font m. *C*; b. ont fait m. *G*; f. tost m. *H*; i. appareillier *CG H*.
1142.   Et les clokes (Et cloques *G*)   par eles sonent par ces mostiers (e. sounerent el moustier *G*) (e. commencent a sonner *H*) *CG H*; v. c'oi je t. *E*.
1143.   *CG H want*.
1144.   Se fut segnifiance de j. *H*;   S. senefia j. *E*;   s. bien g. *C*; g. cose a. *C*; g. pais a. *E*; *G wants*.
1145.   *G H want*.
1146.   dient Dix *E*; 1. france m. *C*; *G H want*.
1147.   e. merci p. son droit   desraisnier *E*;   s. cors e. *G*; *H wants*.
1148.   e. cuert D. grasiier *G*; *H wants*.
1149.   D. or vora 1. *G*; D. or vorai 1. *C*; e. poursegnier *E*; *H wants*.

57.   *BE CG H*
1150.   a. ot g. *C*; *H wants*.
1151.   a baptisiet e. *C*;   a. si li dist d. *CG*; e. bielement *C*; e. courtoisement *E*; *H wants*.
1152.   Enfant ce dist l'abbe c. *H*; q. feras tu c. *CG*; q. voles v. dites moi vo t. *E*; v. or m. *C*; v. di moi tout t. *G H*.
1153.   E. l'enfant respondi C. *H*.
1154.   n. de Jesu ensi le vous commant *E*; *CG H want*.
1155.   Je ferai   de   par Dieu vostre coumandement *G*; *C H want*.
1156.   De par Diu d. *CG H*; c. fait 1. *G H*;   a. trestout p. *E C*; a. mes tout p. *G H*; t. premierement *E CG H*.
1157.   T'estuet r. *CG*; Ferai r. *E*; r. ton p. *E*; r. cest p. *H*; p. mout 1. *H*; t. est velus e. *C*; a. espes e. *E G H*.
1158.   o. ce s. *H*; b. seras a. *G*.
1159.   a essiant *E*; *CG H want*.
1160.   b. ce sacies vraiement *E*; *CG H want*.
1161.   Li enfes li respont J. *G*;   r. je l'otroi bonement *E*; r. jou l'otroi et coumanc *G*;   r. tout a vostre commant *H*; j. loth bien et creanch *C*.
1162.   Lors f. *E*; *H wants*.
1163.   *H wants*.
1164.   i. qu'il a. biel et cler *G*; m. grant *E C*; *H wants*.
1165.   roegne bien e. *C*; e. cortoisement *E H*; *G wants*.

1166. c. l'e. coisi une c. *C*; l. chaennette d. *H*.

1167. d. ains li laissa a. *G*; q. c'est segnefiant *H*.

1168. a. biel et cortoisement *G*; a. qui bien fut avenant *H*; a. boinnement *C*; m. belement *E*.

1169. m. sont ale p. *C*; m. l'ont mene p. *G H*; e. menerent p. *E*; a. faire b. *H*.

1170. Hastes vous f. *E CG*; H. dist l. *CG*; r. a la bataile erant *C*; *H wants*.

1171. Que l. *CG*; *H wants*; *G places this verse after l.* 1169.

1172. D. le raiement *C*; *CG add*: Et jou (Et j'en s. *G*) serai parins se Diex le me consent/ Que s'il fait (Se il f. *G*) la bataille je le vos acreant (b. ce vous di et creanc *G*)/ Apres (Qu'apries *G*) moi sera rois s'ara le casement (r. se il vit longement *G*); *H wants*.

1173. *CG H want*.

1174. b. a l. *E*; *CG H want*.

1175. Et li enfes respont g. *G*; *H wants*.

1176. Mais se vos bien me faites aumosne feres g. *C*; Mes parins ne seres vous ja en mon vivant *G*; g. s'ounour grant bien feres durment *E*; *H wants*.

1177. *CG H want*.

1178. Oies f. *G*; oi dist M. *E CG*; M. roy parler f. *CG*; *H wants*.

1179. Ki quide q. *G*; q. teus enfes ait c. et h. *C*; a. el cuer h. *G*; *H wants*.

1180. *CG H want*.

1181. a. esranment l. *E*; *H wants*.

1182. b. des or mais en avant *CG*; *H wants*.

58. *BE CG H*

1183. d. li rois n. *E*; a. nel me celes tu ja *C*; a. or ne me cele p. *H*.

1184. Mais di moi t. *CG*; Ton pense me jehi e. *E*; p. et en haut et en bas *C H*; p. u en haut u en bas *G*.

1185. E. il r. *C*; r. boins a. tu l. *C H*; r. biau sire j. *E G*; *E adds*: Al abe et a tous le di ne mie en bas.

1186. Crestiener me faites e. *G*; d. en l'ounor saint Thumas *CG*.

1187. *CG H want*.

1188. E. l'abbe lui r. *H*; r. t'aras non Elyas *E*; O. l'averas *C*; l. seras *G H*.

1189. Li abbes le baptise sel met non Elyas *CG*; L'abbe le baptiza si eust nom Helyas *H*.

1190. Il mismes fu p. *C*; a. si fut p., d. Mandras *H which places this verse after l.* 1194.

1191. *H wants*.

1192.   b. el non saint E. *E*; *CG H want*.
1194.   Ne fu p. *CG H*; o. si b. *G*; o. veu si b. *H*; b.
         valles e. *CG*; b. homme e. *H*; b. tres (des *H*) le
         tans Cyphas (Ipocras *G H*) *CG H*; b. l'ounour de
         Baudas *E*.
1195.   q. tot le mont formas *C*; *G H want*.
1196.   m. ci avech a. *C*; m. ordene et mis m. *E*; *G H*
         want.
1197.   Secoures c. *C*; Tu secours c. *E*; p. i as *C which*
         adds: Jou ferai la bataille el non saint Nicho-
         las; *G H want*.
59. *BE CG H*
1198.   e. est m. *G*; m. joyeulx d. *H*.
1200.   p. le trait a i. *C*; p. le tint a i. *G*; p. lui a
         acreante *H*.
1201.   De trestout son avoir et de tout son barnet *C*; De
         trestoute sa tiere de tout son irete *G*; v. tres-
         tout son herite *H*.
1202.   Et l'abes *CG*; *H wants*.
1204.   e. d'esterin bien ouvret *C*; e. de sebelin f. *G*; *H*
         wants.
1205.   .I. rice fustane b. *C*; E. mout rice fustane de
         soie bien o. *G*; *H wants*.
1206.   Et cemises (cemisse *G*) et braies o le b. (b.
         blances et b. bien ouvre *G*) *CG*; .I. braiiet d. *E*;
         H wants.
1207.   a aportet *C*; *CG add*: Mout l'a (a bien s. *C*) sa
         marine viestu et atire (conrae *C*); *H wants*.
1208.   Li enfes l'en mercie par mout grant amiste *E*; *H*
         wants.
1209.   D. mierciet q. *C*; *E H want*.
1210.   Chertes d. *CG*; D. ce dist li enfes O. *E*; a. cres-
         tiente *H*.
1211.   l. corage tourblet *C*; e. ire *G*.
1213.   D. et sainte carite *E*; s. poestet *C H*.
1214.   Chevalier me facies c. *H*; f. que t. *E G*; a. ari-
         este *G*.
1215.   e. cel maufe *C H*.
1216.   Dous a. *C*; Et le roy lui respont t. *H*; a. dist l.
         E C; a vo v. *C*.
1217.   ja se j'ai f. *C*; e. vie et santet *CG*; *H wants*.
1218.   Or vos croisse li sires q. *C*; T. croisse li haus
         sires q. *G*; *H wants*.
60. *BE CG H*
1219.   Sire cou dist li enfes p. *C*; Bons r. *E G*; *H*
         wants.
1220.   r. ja seres adoubes *CG*; *H wants*.
1221.   Le roy voit deux sergens s. *H*; .II. de ses houmes

s. *E*; s. siergans s. *C*; c. si les a *CG H*.

1222. Ales f. *C*; t. dist i. *E H*; f. le roy les armes m.
H; S. si vous hastes *C which adds*: Faites isnie-
lement por Diu si m'aportes.

1223. Les mellours a. *E*; a. que en ma tor veres *C*; a.
qu'en ma tour t. *G*; *H wants*.

1224. Et cil li respondirent S. *C*; Et il ont respondu
S. *E*; Et les varles s'en vont plus n'y sont de-
mourez *H*; *G wants*.

1225. t. sont venut haubers i ont t. *C*; t. vinrent tost
s. *E*; d. ont les haubers t. *H*; *G wants*.

1226. E. et harnois y avoit il a. *H*; f. dont il i eut
a. *C*; *G wants*.

1227. p. trestout de g. *C H*; p. la a l. *E*; *G wants*.

1228. l. porte p. *C*; l. tour prent .I. *G*; *H wants*.

1229. p. la soie bontet *G*; *H wants*.

1230. b. n'i e. *G*; *H wants*.

1231. v. estoit e. *E CG*; *H wants*.

1232. e. estoit h. *E CG*; s. enargentes *E*; *H wants*.

1233. v. hardemens et bontes *C*; *H wants*.

1234. e. fiertes *E G*; *C H want*.

1235. Et d. *CG*; d. a e. *C*; d. est e. *G*; e. de par Diu
fu d. *E*; E. soit d. *CG*; *H wants*.

1236. .I. de ces valles e. *C*; d. varles e. *G*; e. si fu
b. *E*; *H wants*.

1237. Des letres e. *CG*; l. des escus est m. *G*; e. l'es-
cut f. *E C*; f. tous e. *C*; *CG add*: Tant fu (est *G*)
boins li escus de par Diu fu faes (e. et de par
Dieu faes *G*); *E adds*: Et si avoit escrit ce est
la verites; *H wants*.

1238. Que j. *CG*; Ja hom *G*; p. ne puet iestre m. *C*; c.
mates *E CG*; *H wants*.

1239. Se or l. *CG*; E. et il e. *E*; m. que il s. *CG*; *H
wants*.

1240. Peruec q. *E*; Portant q. *G*; c. desfaes *E*; *C H
want*.

1241. e. honeres *C*; *H wants*.

61. *BE CG H*

1242. l. .II. v. aval *CG H*; vassal *C*; vallet *E G H*.

1243. e. et la c. *H*; c. de par l'e. *CG*; c. de Dieu l'e.
H.

1244. n. peceors a *G*; h. pecieres a *C*; h. n'eust en son
col nul mes t. *H*.

1245. l. a a. *C*.

1246. Caingles i eut de soie e. *C*; Cengle et surcengle
e. *E*; Caingle li ont mout bien e. *G*; Sengle et
soubzsengle lasche fut l. *H*.

1247. r. l'amainnent qui n'i entent (pensent *C*) n. *E*

CG H.

1248. En souspirant a *C H*; As escuiiers a *E*; En plorant
      li demandent C. *G*; e. li dist C. *C*; d. or m. *C H*.
1249. Dont vient si fais e. *CG*; p. cis e. *E*; p. cel e.
      H; O. homs n. *C*.
1250. E. li vallet respondent A. *E H*; A. peron d. *E*; p.
      d'un c. *G*.
1251. t. pendut mout bien sanle r. *C*; b. samble oeuvre
      r. *H*.
1252. Certes ce dist le roy c'est oeuvre esperital *H*;
      P. ma f. *C*; f. dist li rois ci a oevre c. *CG*; f.
      dist de par Diu l. *E*.
1253. Que bien est d. *G*; D. qui tout voit a estal *CG*; *H*
      wants.
1254. Dans roys f. *C*; r. dist M. que vault cest demoral
      H; a felon j. *E C*; a mortal j. *G*.
1256. g. ara a. *C*; a. grant b. *E*; a. tel b. *H*; *G wants*.
1257. p. cest m. *C*; p. le m. mentouval *E*; p. ce m. *H*;
      m. capital *C H*; *G wants*.
1258. m. le vallant d'un cief d'ail *E*; *G wants*.
1259. Que ne li fenge tout l. *C*; *G H want*.
  62. *BE CG H*
1260. D. fait E. *G H*; d. le varlet l. *H*; E. or l. le p.
      E.
1261. Cil par (Cellui *H*) est trop c. *CG H*.
1262. M'en cuidies vos pour manaches c. *C*; v. manaces
      ne cuides esmayer *H*.
1263. M. ja por tos vos dis n'entrerai en mostier *C*; M.
      ne pris vos manaces vallisant .I. d. *E*; M. por
      cosse que dites ne fuirai a moustier *G*; *H wants*.
1264-66. *CG H want*.
1268. f. se h. *C*; d. mon mal e. *E*; *H wants*.
1269. l. respont J. *CG H*; j. n'i ai que targier *C*; r.
      cou ne vel jou laissier *G*; r. bien fait a o. *H*.
1270. .II. v. *G H*; .II. escuiers l. *H*; l. ceurent u. *E*
      C H; l. coururent u. *G*; *C adds*: .I. espourons a
      or font en es pies cauchier.
1271. D. sarrasines misent .XIIII. *C*; *E G H want*; *C*
      places this verse after l. 1272.
1272. Et .I. *CG*; l. viest qui mout fait a prisier *C*; l.
      viestent a. *G*; v. nus h. *G H*; v. si c. *E G H*; *CG*
      add: Onques nus hons ne vit plus fort ne plus le-
      gier.
1273. o. il e. *C*; o. bone t. *E*; o. nueve t. que on ne
      pot prisier *G*; t. c'on ne pot empirier *C*; *H*
      wants.
1274. Et Elyas s'en fait et orgellous e. *E*; b. plus nel
      vorent laissier *C*; b. puis ne le vot cangier *G*; *H*

wants.
1275. b. atourne et avant et arrier *E*; *CG H want.*
1276. *H wants.*
1277. S. Dieu dist l'enfant c. *H*; P. dou ciel c. *C*; a fort m. *CG H.*
63. *BE CG H*
1278. Elyas s. *CG H*; e. sent les armes et l'aubierc qu'est pesans *C*; e. se mervele d. *E H*; a. jozerant *H*.
1279. Oncques mais je ne vi c. *H*; m. ne vit cotiele qui si li fust p. *G*; v. cote si tres p. *C*.
1280. Apres ce lui lacerent l. *H*; li sacent l. *C*; l. .I. hiaume c. *CG H*; l. le vert elme l. *E*; e. mout pesant *C*; e mout vaillant *G*; heaume luysant *H*.
1281. *CG H want.*
1282. M. les f. *E*; *H wants.*
1283. p. cou trovons nos lisant *C*; p. itant bon marceant *G*; v. mout s. *E*; *H wants.*
1284. C. qui les (le *G*) presenterent au b. *CG*; l. fort r. *C which adds*: L'amerent de boin cuer saves chertainement.
1285. Uns rices esporons li ont caucie a. *G*; e. a or lui ont chaucez a. *H*; l. ont lacies a. *E*; *C wants*; *G places this verse after l. 1294.*
1286. On li traist en la place .I. destrier auferrant *C*; .I. destrier li a. pumele et baucent *G*; a. qui avoit nom F. *H*; a. Baucant *E*.
1287. La siele fu d'yvoire et li estrier d'argent *C*; e. mout vallant *G*; *H wants.*
1288. L. .II. a. en ierent d. *G which adds*: Et la bende desus d'un rice bougerant; *C H want.*
1289. Et li estrier si sont d'un rice cordovan *G*; a. les estriers a or resplendissant *E*; *C H want.*
1290. *E CG H want.*
1291. d. couvers d. *E*; d. couvert d'un pallie e. *G*; *C H want.*
1292. T. est c. *CG*.
1293. *H wants.*
1294. S. en est o. et cuintes p. *CG*; *H wants.*
1295. Sour le destrier le lievent (montent *G*) t. *CG*; m. qui moult v. *H*.
1296. l. aidast c. *C*; t. il kaist vraiement *E*; t. ja queist erranment *G*; *H wants*; *C places this verse after l. 1297.*
1297. *C adds*: Au col li ont pendut tos et isnielement/ Elyas sent les armes trestous can (sic) cancelant; *H wants.*
1298. Li rois li cainst l'espee tan tos en souspirant

C; e. maintenant *E*; e. en souspirant *G H*; *C pla-*
ces this and the following four verses (11. 1298-
1302) after 1. 1284.

1299.   n. d'acordement *E*; *H wants.*

1300.   Et d., D. t'envoye h. *H*; t. croist h. *C*; t.
doinst h. *E G.*

1301.   d. a t. Elyas en riant *C*; d. a t. et Elyas riant
G; *E H want.*

1302.   Li r. *CG*; s. disne coumant *G*; *H wants.*

64.   *BE CG H*

1303.   E. fu m. *C*; m. sor le d. *C*; m. sur se d. *E*; m.
Dieu le tienne et enseigne *H*; el grant d. *G.*

1304.   Il cancele trestous de se main s. *E*; Moult va
fort chancelant d. *H.*

1305.   il ot l., se tiegne *E*; *H wants.*

1306.   d. la s. *E CG*; f. faite e. *CG*; f. a ouvragne *E*;
f. a Cartagne *G*; en Bretagne *C*; *H wants.*

1307.   Deux varles ont tenu le destrier d. *H*; d. Grifai-
gne *CG.*

1308.   Peur ont c'a force li destriers nel emmainne *C*;
e. k'a force nel m. *E*; e. li cevaus ne l'en mai-
gne *G*; *H wants.*

1309.   M. le voit a *C H*; M. le vit a *G.*

1310.   Amis dist Matabrune s. *G*; a. Mauquarres s. *C*; v.
qui eust au cuer legne *H*; a. dist l. *E*; m. duinst
g. *CG.*

1311.   Cel garcon n'a de c. ne que une povre yraigne *H*;
Cis n'a de c. nes c'une povre aragne *C*; C. gar-
cons n'a de c. *G*; p. que une feme *E*; p. que .I.
aragne *G.*

1312.   Certes se le t. la *CG*; *H wants.*

1313.   Ja l'averoie m. *C*; a. tue s. *G*; m. u a fust u a
laingne *CG*; s. plus d. *E*; *H wants.*

1314.   D. dist M. *E*; M. que mout fort l. *G.*

1315.   Jou l. *E CG*; f. passer me lance par l. *E*; m. gla-
vie p. *G*; *H wants.*

1316.   e. en boin penser s. *CG*; e. en grant joie s. *E*; *H*
wants; *C places this verse after 1. 1317.*

1317.   l. vauroit haubers nes c'une vies ensengne *C*; m.
ne haubert ne enseigne *H.*

1318.   Ne escus ne haubers ne hiaumes n'autre e. *E*; Ne
haubers ne escus ne nule a. *G*; *C H want.*

1319.   E. garda en bas que maus li aviegne *E*; *CG H want.*

1320.   Biaus amis Mauquarres fait la v. *C*; A. dist M. *E*;
G H want.

1321.   v. donrai R. *E CG*; d. Rohais n. *C*; d. tel cose n.
E; d. Rains n. *G*; e. Capaigne *C*; e. Sartagne *E*;
e. Canpaigne *G*; *H wants.*

1322.   Dame f. *C*; Par foit f. *G*; C. dist M. *C E*; a boine b. *CG*; a fiere b. *E*; *H wants*.

1324.   b. iert f. *C*; b. fera f. *E*; *G H want*.

1325.   d. qui prendre si p. *G*; q. li plais p. *E*; *C H want*.

1326.   c. ataigne *C*; c. aplagne *G*; *H wants*.

1327.   v. c'a l'estour ja parvaigne *C*; v. c'a l. *G*; *H wants*.

65.   *BE CG H*

1328.   E. fu m. *C*; *H wants*.

1329.   Si que il se tient al a. *C*; c. a l. *E G*; *H wants*.

1330.   Qui mout ert rice et avenans et biele *C*; c. que se tiengne qu'il ne ciet a le tere *E*; p. que mout est rice et biele *G*; *H wants*.

1331.   Et .I. valles li done u. *C*; Et li varles li balle u. *G*; *H wants*.

1332.   .I. boin fer t. *C*; .I. fier mout t., a Niviele *G*; *H wants*.

1333.   .I. autre b. *G*; E. .II. boines espees d. *C*; *H wants*.

1334.   Ont dounet E. *C*; On le baille E. que D. *G*; *H wants*.

1335.   D. dist E. *G*; *H wants*.

1336.   Q. nostre Sauveor n. *CG*; *H wants*.

1337.   Secores me ui cest jour de vrai cuer vos apiele *C*; *H wants*.

1338.   *C H want*.

1339.   M. le voit M. *C*; *H wants*.

1340.   A. que dires vos C. *C*; C. dites nous c. *G*; *H wants*.

1341.   c. forment se r. *C*; c. de joie r. *E*; *H wants*.

1342.   e. le ceval menrai jou a *G*; m. en gavele *E G*; *H wants*.

1343.   v. cervele *C*; v. astiele *G*; *H wants*.

1344.   l. cuer et le cerviele *G*; *E H want*.

1345.   l. tora le fie le cuer et la bouiele *G*; e. trestoute l. *C*; *E H want*.

1346.   M. le voit d. *C*; M. a tel joie que li cuers li s. *G*; *E H want*.

1347.   *E H want*.

1348.   Or s. *C*; Ja s., p. devant l. *G*; l. tour biele *C which adds as the initial line of the next laisse*: Signor or ascoutes por Diu le droiturier; *E H want*.

66.   *BE CG H*

1349.   La bataille ne puet des or mais atargier *C*; Segnor or ne puet plus la batalle a. *G*; Or ne pevent ilz plus de combatre arrester *H*; *CG add*: La

place fu mout grans por tourniier (p. venir et a-
ler *G*).

1350.   c. pourvenir et jouster *C*; c. venir et pour jous-
ter *G*; e. jointer *E*;   *CG add*: Elyas voit (vit *G*)
le roi sel prent (prist *G*) a appieler; *H wants*.

1351.   r. dist E. *E*; f. armer *H*.

1352.   D'une r. *H*; f. pesans est a porter *CG*; f. mais
moult la sent p. *H*.

1353.   Or vous p. *H*.

1354.   e. la place d. *CG*; la me faites pourmener *E*; l.
vous m. *G H*; f. amener *C*.

1355.   Un cest v. *C*; Et cest v. *G*; Et v. escuier f.
avecques m. *H*; c. me faites apieler *C*; faites o
G; ensamble moi *E*; m. aler *E G H*.

1356.   Si en ferai (Car se sera *H*) mon maistre *CG H*; m.
endoctriner *G H*.

1357.   Que j. *G*; d. guier *C*; *H wants*.

1358.   r. respondi ce ne qui[t] jou veer *G*; r. chou ne
vos doi veer *C H*.

1359.   Or y fait le vallet roy Orient aler *H*; s. sier-
gant l. *CG*; l. preste q. m. fait a loer *C*; m. fu
preus et b. *G*; e. frans e. *E*; *G adds*: Ne quic
qu'il ait si boin dusqu'en la rouge mer.

1360.   p. en la place l. *CG*; p. d'une r. *H*; r. les en a
fait aler *E*; r. le fait outrepasser *G*; r. l'avoit
f. *H*; f. amener *C*; *CG H add*: Sire fait li sier-
gans (varles *G*) que (Puis dist a Elyas q. *H*) vo-
les demander.

1361.   *E adds*: Coument me maintesrai ne me deves celer;
CG H want.

1362.   De (Del *G*) tout v. *CG*; Demandes je dirai s. *E*; *H
wants*.

1363.   M. dist E. *G*; E. ne me deves celer *CG*; E. je v. *E
H*.

1364.   j. suis C. *H*.

1365.   c. qui mout fait a loer *C*; c. je ne v. *E*; c. qui
est gentius et bers *G*; nel le q. *H*.

1366.   Ne cuic qu'il ait si boin dusc'a la rouge mer *CG*;
H wants.

1367.   Mais f. *H*; *CG want*.

1368.   N. dist l. *E*; v. ne vous fault esmayer *H*; *CG want*.

1369.   E. saurai le j. *E*; E. dictes fault il n. *H*; *G
wants*.

1370.   Cest p. *C*; Cou qu'est c'on me f. *G*; f. en m. *C*;
f. sus m. *H*; s. le t. *E*.

1371.   *CG H want*.

1372.   S. c'est .I. *H*; h. nel (ne *G*) vos quier a celer
CG which add: Certes fait Elyas mervelles oï con-

ter (*C wants*)/ Quant li siergans l'entent (l'oi
G) si commence a penser/ De la pitet de lui com-
mencha a plorer/ Durement s'esmerveille comment
pora durer (e. s'il en puet vis aler *G*)/ Et (Que
G) Mauquarres le haste qui vet (h. que viegne *G*)
a lui jouster.

67. *BE CG H*

1373. M. dist E. *E C G*; *C adds*: Parles encor a moi si
me dites raison.

1374. C. cote d. *G H*; c. l'apiele on *CG H*; *E wants*.

1375. Et pour quoy ilz sont fais tant menue p. *H*; p.
cravechon *C*; *E adds*: En ceste grant cotele que
nous vestu avon.

1376. S. dist l. *E*; l. siergans a. *C*; v. pour voir hau-
bert a nom *H which adds*: Qu'est ce que j'ay es
jambes comment l'appelle on/ Ce sont chauces de
fer ainsi ont elle a nom.

1377. m. ensi les apielon *C*; m. ne n'i f. *G*; n'i font
s. *E G*; *H wants*.

1378. E. qu'est ce en mes piedz M. *H*.

1379. S. dist l. *E G*; l. siergans c. *C*.

1380. l. apielon *C*; *CG add*: Par foit dist Elyas n'oi se
merveille (Certes fait E. n'oc se mervelles *G*)
non; *H wants*.

1381. Or me dites biaus sires de cest f. *C*; Ha maistres
dist Elyas de ce f. *E*; Et or me dites frere por
Dieu de ce f. *G*; E. de cest f. *H*; f. bordon *CG H*.

1382. V. velle m. *G*; V. vouldroye p. que j'en saiche le
nom *H*; q. me d. *E G*; d. le nom *G*.

1383. S. c'est une lance si ait m'arme pardon *C*; S.
dist l. *E*; S. c'est une lance f. *G*; S. lance
l'appelle escuier et garcon *H*.

1384. t. chevalier e. *C*; *H wants*.

1385. Sire f. *C*; M. dist E. *E*; E. si ait m'arme pardon
C; E. por Dieu et por son non *G*; *H wants*.

1386. *CG H want*; *E CG add*: Ains ne vi mais tel robe
puis le tans Salemon (r. foi que doi saint Simon
G) (*E wants*)/ Dont (Qu'en *G*) averai je cote sur-
cot et caperon (*C wants*).

1387. c. cousue s. *C*; c. des clices s. *G*; close sans *E*;
H wants.

1388. *E CG H want*.

1389. Q. ne fesisse tout ce harnas e. *E*; t. le h. *C*; t.
ce h. *G*; q. voi ci e. *CG*; *H wants*.

1390. Ce qui me pent au col p. *H*; p. coument l'apele on
E G; *H places this verse after l.* 1379.

1391. A cele c. vermeille k. *C*; c. vermelle qui est
luisans en son *E*; *H wants*.

1392. Biaus sire e. *C*; Biaus sire de par Dieu escu l'a-
       pielle on *G*; A. et Normant e. *C H*; *H places this*
       verse after 1. 1390.
1393. Sire d. *C*; d. cel coutel p. *E*; c. comment les
       apielon *C*; que fera *E*.
1394. S. dist li valles espee le noumon *E*; S. fait le
       varlet par le corps saint Fagon *H*; *CG add*: Et se
       dounent (Si en don on *G*) grans cols entour et en-
       viron; *H adds*: Espees les appellent escuier et
       garcon.
1395. M. dist E. *E G*; E. foi que doi s. *C*; E. et plus
       en fera on *G*; *H wants*.
1396. n. foi que doi saint Symon *G*; E. puis qu'en f. *H*;
       p. qu'en f. *C*; p. que f. *E*.
1397. Certes d. *E*; Or en fera ainsi comme nous vous di-
       ron *H*; O. fait li siergans bien le vos dira on *C*;
       v. bien vous dirai le non *G*.
1398. Qu'il vos estuet c. au plus m. *C*; .I. maistre la-
       ron *CG*; *C adds*: Qui soit en ceste terre n'en cest
       region; *H wants*.
1399. Si a *E*; M. qui tant par est f. *C*; M. jou ne sai
       si f. *G*; *H wants*.
1400. n'a cainture n. *C H*; n'a cendal n. *G*.
1401. r. si faites con p. *E*; *CG H want*.
1402. p. au feutre et a l. *C*; p. enfeutree es arcons *G*;
       p. ou feustre sur l. *H*; e. feutre d. *E*.
1403. Devant en son escut en feres le gloton *C*; Le serf
       en mi le pis en f. *H*; *C adds*: Que l'escu li pier-
       cies et l'obierc a bandon; *G wants*.
1404. Et tout li detrencies l. *C*; Et l'escu li piercies
       l. *G*; Si que vous lui perces l. *H*; *G adds*: Et
       mort le me gieties en la place el sablon.
1405. D. nous commandon *H*.
1406. D. m'en v. *C*; n. ferons s. *E*; *H wants*.
68. *BE CG H*
1407. M. dist E. *E CG*; E. entendes que jou di *C*.
1408. f. mout l'ai bien a devis *C*; b. me s. *E*; b. en s.
       G; s. pourpenses *E G*.
1409. i. requerra c. *H*; r. li cuviers d. *CG H*; j. par
       v. *E*; j. parjuris *C*; j. Malquares *G*; j. losenger
       H.
1410. t. que m'en dires amis *C*; m. dounes *E*; m. donner
       H; *G places this verse after 1. 1407*.
1411. l. siergans s. *C*.
1412. En pies resales sus onques (que ja *G*) n'i aries-
       tes *CG*; Legierement e., p. me r. *H*; *C adds*: Et
       l'escut et le branc par devant vos metes.
1413. D. vostre b. *H*; e. des g. *G*; m. grant caup l. *E H*.

1414. Son e. et son h. *C*; *G H want.*
1415. E. se m'e. *E*; E. se l'e. *G*; E. se l'une vous rompt a *H*; b. a forche le jetes *C*; v. tenes *E G*; *C adds*: Ensus de vous a l'autre vos prendes.
1416. s. ele vous brisse b. *G*; s. les deux vous faillent a liter v. *H*; p. a lui vous acostes *E*; b. ahierdes *C*.
1417. Desous vos a *C*; t. a f. *C H*; t. esranment l'abates *E*; l. getes *CG*.
1418. S'au desous le metes l. *G*; S'en venez au dessus l. *H*; v. au desus l. *C*.
1419. Jou ne s., d. la tieste copes *C*; d. en Dieu vous enfies *G*; d. mais en Dieu vous fiez *H*; a Damediu a. *E*.
1420. M. dist E. *E CG*; E. as g. *C*; E. de ce bourdon ferrez *H*; g. bordons feres *CG*.
1421. Se sera o. *G*; S'aray comme il est bon ja sera e. *H*.
1422. Puis b. *C*; I. hurte l. *CG H*; l. ceval des *G*; d. par andoi les costes *CG*; *C adds*: Et il li saut de tiere .XXX. pies mesures.
1423. *CG H want.*
1424. e. alumes *E*; *CG H want.*
1425. Au pignon d. *CG*; t. est Elyas a. *C*; t. s'en est outrepasses *G*; t. s'en est ale hurtez *H*.
1426. Puis f. *C*; Il f. *G*; De tel vertu y fiert q. *H*; t. air q. *CG*; l. fus e. *E*; *G adds a repetition of l.* 1425.
1427. l. sont c. *G*.
1428. Maistre d. *CG*; D. fait E. *CG H*; Elyas or *H*.
1429. Mien ensiant a sa fin fust a. *C*.
1430. Et il respont en riant ne cremes *C*; v. respont e. *G H*; r. n'est ames *G*; r. vous tamez *H*.
1431. Ancui morra li traitres prouves *C*; Encor a. *H*; c. desfaes *E H*; c. Malquares *G*.
1432. Sire f. *C*; M. dist E. *E G*; E. un petit m'entendes *C*; D. me raportez *H*.
1433. n. si me feres bontes *E G H*; *C wants.*
1434. v. volentiers et de gres *G*; *E adds*: Vers le castel retourne et n'i es demoures; *C H want.*
1435. Et cil l'en bailla une d. *H*; f. fu q. *E G*; *G adds*: Et Elyas s'en torne ne s'est plus soujornes; *C wants.*
1436. *E CG H want.*
1437. Lors s'en va Galias (sic) e. *H*; M. en v. *E*; e. torne e. *G*; *C wants.*
1438. O. en ier l. *G*; b. puis que Rollans f. *E*; *C H want.*

1439. N'oistes mais si fiere d. *E*; N'oi nus hom si fie-
       re d. *G*; *C H want*.
69. *BE CG H*
1440. M. dist E. *E*; E. por Diu le fil Marie *C*; E. nel
       l. nel v. *G*; *CG add*: Jou n'arai de nului (d. nul
       home *G*) ne secours ne aie/ Fors que Damedieu (q.
       de D. *G*) le fil sainte Marie.
1441. l. a ma lanche burnie (fourbie *G*) *CG*; l. ou n. *H*.
1442. Jou ira (sic) assaier quesche (sic) chevalerie *C*;
       Je ferai ja l. *G*.
1443. S. dit l. *E C*; j. ne le d. *H*; v. desdi m. *G*.
1444. Jesus li t. *E*; p. vos en soit en a. *C*; p. vous
       soit hui en a. *E G*; *H wants*.
1445. Le serf d. se deserte q. *E*; E. al s. *G*; q. tos e.
       CG; q. est si p. *E*; *H wants*.
1446. De par Dieu li veez et ne m'o. *H*; M. de tant vos
       castoi s. *C*; M. de cou vous casti s. *G*.
1447. Et v., t. guie *E which adds*: Et ses cors et se
       cars en ert anqui percie; *H wants*.
1448. en l'escu u la crois reflanblie *G*; c. ou le cou-
       lors rougie *E*; c. qui en l'e. *H*; *E places this
       verse after* l. 1446; *CG H add*: S'il fiert en la
       crois il en aura haiscie (f. bien le sai anqui
       sera hounie *G*) (Se il y f. bien scay sera honnye
       H)/ Ancui en cest place que cou est (p. ki ci e.
       G) (p. qu'ainsi e. *H*) establie.
1449. M. dist E. *E G*; E. ou nom saincte Marie *H*; n. qui
       r. *E CG*.
1450. Irai jou saiier ja q. *C*; Iray j. *H*; Je vois or a.
       E; a. ques e. *E C*; a. que e. *G*.
1451. l. cheval k. *G*.
1452. Et mist l'escut avant s'a la lance brandie *C*; Et
       a leve la lance dont tout l'acie[r] brunie *H*; *G
       wants*.
1453. V. Matabrune s. *C*; M. en v. *E C*; v. ne s'aseura
       mie *C*; v. et li fel li escrie *G*; k. hautement l.
       E; k. durement l. *H*; *C adds*: Quant Mauquarres le
       voit durement li escrie.
1454. Hee meschant gars n'as t. *H*; C. que est n'as tu
       pas oublie t. *E*; e. que n'as tu ta folie laissie
       C; e. n'as tu mie l. *G*.
1455. Si ai f. *CG*; Ouion f. *E*; s. n'oubli m. *G*.
1456. Par foi f. *C*; C. dist M. *E*; M. et mes cuers t. *G*;
       M. et mon c. *H*.
1457. Par foi dist Elyas qui cou n'entendi m. *G*; Elyas
       lui r. de ce n'estend je m. *H*; *C wants*.
1458. Jou n. *CG H*; e. defit [sic] s. *G*; D. le me benye
       H.

1459. m. bordons n. *C*.

1460. *H wants*.

1461. f. vos e. *C*; *H wants*.

1462. Q. li siers l'entendi t. *C*; l. sans l. *E*; l. cuers l'enaigre *G*; l. argie *C*; *H wants*.

1463. I. broce le ceval n. *E*; n. s'aseura m. *C which adds*: En mi la place de la grant tour antie; *G adds*: Tout droit devant la tor ki ert viele et antie; *H wants*.

1464. Iert faite li bataille et li grant e. *CG*; r. fu f. *E*; f. arramie *C*; *H wants*.

1465. i a t. *CG*; o. grant p. ne le mescrees mie *E*; p. tele ne fu oie *CG which place this verse after l. 1467*; *H wants*.

1466. a. s'en v. *CG*; s. vinrent s. *C*; *H wants*.

1467. La t. desous a. *C*; t. sour a. *G*; e. tonbist et fourmie *E*; t. entombie *C*; t. estormie *G*; *C adds*: Diu prent pour l'enfant qu'il li gart sa vie/ Or oies bataille que n'en mentirai mie; *E adds*: Et li ceval braidissent et font grant arramie/ Or ert grans le batalle qui k'en plourt ne qui rie; *H wants*.

70. *BE CG DH*

1468. O. sera l. *C*; O. sont les chevaliers sur les destriers courant *H*; i. ja l. *G*.

1469. Mauquarres seut des armes et Diex ait l'anfant *CG*; Armez sont des heaumes et d'escus reluisant *H*; m. les e. contre l. *E*; *H adds*: Eulz ont prinses les lances et les vont brandissant.

1470. Le diestrier broche p. *C*; Il hurtent les destriers p. *G*; *H wants*.

1471. t. et la tors en va toute r. *CG*; v. tranblant *C*; v. croslant *G*; *H wants*.

1472. I. desfeutrent l. *G*; a. les l. *E G*; *C H want*.

1473. En mi le (les *G*) pis devant se fierent (p. se fierent andui *G*) communaument *CG*; s. dounent ens ens (sic) es pis d. *E*; *H wants*.

1474. Li hauberc furent fort et les lances trenchans *C*; f. roides e. *G*; *H wants*.

1475. Eulz deux s. *H*; A. se sont feru p. *C*; p. autel couvenant *H*; *G wants*.

1476. Sour les a. *G*; a. deriere e. *E*; sieles vont *C*; v. trestoutes d. *C H*; v. andui cancelant *G*; t. ploiant *C*; t. depecant *E*; *C adds*: Cascuns fist les talons voler contremont vent/ Poitraus ne caingle ne li valu .I. gant; *G adds*: Poitral ne contre tal ne lor valu nient; *H adds*: Et les lances de fresne vont toutes tronchonnant.

1477.   A terre s. *H*; D. archons s. *E*;   c. kairent p. *E*; c. cient jus p. *G*; c. part d. *C*; c. des destriers m. *H*.

1478.   l. ceval s. *G*; p. la place f. *C*; p. les rues f. *E G*; *H wants*.

1479.   Or ores la m. *C H*;   Or escoutes m. *G*;   o. fier m. *E*; m. mout m. *G H*.

1480.   E. vait l. *G H*;   a. aconsivant *C*;   a. poursuivant *H*.

1481.   Des pies deriere l. *CG*;   Du destre pie le f. en mie le front d. *E*;   Des piedz en my le front le feri par devant *H*.

1482.   i. en f. *E C*.

1483.   Quant Mauquaree le vit plain fut de Mautalent *H*; s. ne va p. ariestant *G*; n'i atarga noient *C*.

1484.   Et Elyas tantost se leva en e. *E*; *CG H want*.

1485.   t. apenseement *E*; *CG H want*.

1486.   f. sour l'elme maintenant *G*; *H wants*.

1487.   .II. cainnes d. *E C*; *H wants*; *D enters*.

1488.   e. fist v. *G*; v. ce voient li a. *C*; v. si quel v. *G D*; v. si que le v. *E*;   v. la jant *D*; v. cent *E*; *H wants*.

1489.   n. li aidast o. *D*; g. mort l'eust esrainnement *E*; *CG H want*.

1490.   Matabrune la vielle cui li cors Diu cravent *C*; Matabrune s'escrie ce n'est pas cor (ci n'a pas cop *G*) d'enfant *G D*; *C adds*: Escrie Mauquarres le traitour pullent/ Par Mahomz amis ce n'est pas cos d'enfant; *H wants*.

1491.   Mar vint *D*; Ne vera li garçons mais le solel coucant *G*; g. ains le soleil coucant *C*; g. sempres se va dolant *D*; *C adds*: Le ferai trainer u ardoir maintenant; *H wants*.

1492.   t. qui mout f. *G*; f. douc s. *C*; *H wants*.

1493.   v. requerre a *CG*; *H wants*.

1494.   Trestout s. le p. va il Diu r. *C*;   p. n'i va plus ariestant *G*; *H wants*.

1495.   Mauquarret fiert en l. *C*;   Le fiert desour li aume s. *G*; s. fiert s. le hiaume q. *D*; e. que .III. doie li f. *CG D*; *C adds*: Fors fu la coiffe de haubierc jaserant; *H wants*.

1496.   Diable l'ont t. *CG D*;   a gari q. *C E*; t. quant en car ne le (l'en *G*) prent *CG*; t. qui d. *E D*; *H wants*.

1497.   De l'acier de l. *G*;   A. sachier de l. *C*; r. le brant v. *D*; *CG add*: Et Mauquarres li paie a (passe o *G*) son acerin brant; *E H want*.

1498.   O. ores l. *C*; O. iert g. *D*; O. oies l. *G*; b. mi-

raveilouse (b. et mervellouse *G*) et grant *CG*; m.
esciant *D which adds*: Du cuivert Mauquarre et
d'Elyas l'enfant; *E H want*.

1499.   o. si f. *C D*; o. millor e. *G*; t. faite e. *D*; f.
par le mien ensiant *CG which add*: Or en soit Dius
au droit par son commandement (*G wants*)/ La dame
ne soit (n'iert pas *G*) arse ne l'enfes ensement.

71.   *BE CG D*
1500.   s. li chevalier a. *CG D*; *H wants*.
1501.   *H wants*.
1502.   Que les flours et les pieres en a jus abatut *CG*;
d. li a t. *E D*; a quartele e. *D*; a et trencie e.
E; *CG add*: Le chiercle d'or trancha dusc'au lac
l'a romput (t. juske es las l'a fendu *G*); *H
wants*.
1503.   D. nel garandist t. *D*; n. li aidast t. *CG*; e.
porfendut *CG D*; e. abatu *E*; *H wants*.
1504.   Cuvers f. *CG*; g. dist M. *E C D*; *H wants*.
1505.   La dame sera arse s. *C*; Ja s. *E D G*; *CG add*: Ele
est plus desloiaus c'onques femme ne fu; *H wants*.
1506.   Leres f. *C*; g. dist E. *E CG*; E. cou qu'est (que
c'est *G*) pour coi m. *CG D*; *H wants*.
1507.   A. te rendra D. *CG D*; p. ta v. *C*; *CG add*: Elyas
tent (tint *G*) l'espee et met avant l'escut (e.
devant soi son escut *G*); *H wants*.
1508.   Et f., t. desour s. *CG*; a. desor l'e. *D*; sor l'e.
E; son ielme agut *E CG*; *H wants*.
1509.   Son hiaume l. *C*; Le son elme l. *D*; Tout son iaume
l. *G*; a embaret e. *E C*; a quartele e. *D*; a es-
quartele e. *G*; *H wants*.
1510.   E Diex f. *CG*; Hure f. *D*; O. dist E. *E C*; E. cis
glous (cist pos *D*) a trop vescut *CG D*; *H wants*.
1511.   Se Diex m'en vet (me viut *G*) aider tos l'aurai
porfendut (t. l'aroie vencut *G*) *CG*; *H wants*.
1512.   r. pensiu e. *C*; r. par mout ruiste vretu *E*; *H
wants*.
1513.   p. vaillissant u *E G D*; *H wants*.
1514.   N. Elyas M. *CG D*; M. plus que .I. h. *D*; *H wants*.
1515.   L. [f]ieramment se s. *C*; L. si que venrent e. *G*;
e. chascuns tint le bran nu *D*; se sont entreferut
CG; *H wants*.
1516.   Durement s. *G*; r. andoi li chevalier *CG*; r. et
par ruiste vertu *D*; *H wants*.

72.   *BE CG DH*
1517.   M. ot g. *H*; q. vit m. *E H*; v. si s. *E*; s. cheval
(sic) *H*; *C adds*: De maltalent cuide vis enragier.
1518.   Petit se prise s'il ne s'en puet v. *C*; P. se p.
s'il ne (p. se ne *G*) le puet v. *G D*; *H wants*.

1519. f. sour s. *CG*; f. de l'elme .I. grant q. *D*; f. que del e. *E*; f. en l'escu de quartier *D*; e. vregier *C*; e. d'acier *G*.

1520. Que flors et pieres en a jus trebuchiet *C*; Que les flors et les pieres en fait jus t. *G*; *CG add*: Le ciercle d'or trancha ne li vaut un denier; *H wants*.

1521. D. nel garesist k. *C D*; D. ne le garist k. *G*.

1522. Tout l'eust porfendu d. *G*; s. enfresi qu'el b. *G D*; s. jusqu'au neu du baudrier *H*.

1523. Elyas le refiert .I. cop sans delaier *CG*; Elyas trait l'espee dont le pont fut d'or mier *H*; E. le vait ferir sans espargnier *D*; d. l'espargnier *E*.

1524. Que la moitiet de l'ielme l. *CG D*; Les pierres et les fleurs l. *H*; p. a f. *C*; p. en fait jus t. *G H*; li fait *D*; f. voler arier *C D*.

1525. f. voler d. *E C*; *H wants*.

1526. Et M. *CG D*; M. le fiert de plain pour ostoier *D*; M. fiert lui del branc pour estecier *G*; r. pour ostoier *C*; *H wants*.

1527. Fors fu l'aubers s. *C*; Et l. *D*; M. li iaumes est f. *G*; f. ne le p. *E CG*; f. ainc nel p. *D*; p. empirier *CG*; p. desmallier *E*; *H wants*.

1528. D. dist E. *E C*; E. que tout as a jugier *C*; E. adonques s. *D*; E. belement s. *E*; E. qui tout as a baillier *G*; *H wants*.

1529. Vous me deves biaus sire e. *G*; m. deves v. *C D*; v. sire e. *C*; v. hui e. *D*; *H wants*.

1530. m. car jou en ai m. *C*; m. car or en ai m. *D*; m. car j'en ai grant m. *G*; *H wants*.

1531. m. prent l. *CG*; e. met l'escut arier *C*; e. l'escu mist arrier *D*; e. si le mait arier *G*; *H wants*.

1532. Elyas v. *G*; Le coup est devale sur l. *H*; f. en l. *CG D*; f. de l'espee d'acier *E*; e. de quartier *CG DH*.

1533. Dusqu'en *E D*; Duske a l. *G*; Jusc'a l. *C*; b. d'or li fait le brant glacier *E*; f. entrer son b. *C*; *H wants*.

1534. Et cil e. *H*; e. depecier *CG D*.

1535. M. l'ennemy d. *H*; i. le volrent e. *D*; i. qu'il le vouldrent e. *H*; l. vot e. *G*.

1536. Qui li ont fait son b. *D*; Lui firent s. *H*; a faites l'espee t. *G*; s. espee tout p. *C*.

1537. M. la vielle s. *H*.

1538. Mal y venist garcon l. *H*; M. vint ca l., d. calengier *G*.

1539. l. prist a *C H*; a escrier *D*.

1540. i. li f. *C*; f. ens en s. *D*; s. cors b. *C which adds*: La soie espee qu'il aimme et tient chier.

73. *BE CG DH*

1541. d. laron l. *CG*; d. mal serf l. *D*.

1542. G. dolour fait q. ot son branc q. *C*; d. ot e. *D*; q. le b. *E*; b. vit froe *D*; b. a fause *G*; *H wants*.

1543. Mout e. *C*; e. ot e. *E C*; e. a e. *G D*; p. qui en eurent pitet *C*; p. c'ont de pite plore *G*; d. pitie ont p. *E D*.

1544. Tout maintenant avoit son autre b. *H*; a l'autre b. *E CG D*; b. recouvre *G*.

1545. Ensiment l. *C*; e. bien l'avoit fait son maistre doctriner *H*; m. rouvet *C*; m. coumande *G*.

1546. a. en v. *G D*; v. rescorre l. *C*; *H wants*.

1547. Puis s'entrevienent con .II. l. *C*; f. s'en v. *G*; q. doi serpent e. *D*; q. doi l. *G*; l. crestet *CG D*; l. abrieve *E*; *H wants*.

1548. *CG H want*.

1549. desfench de par la T. *C*; i. de par le T. *E G DH*; *H places verses* 1549-1555 *after the lines added following* 1. 1560.

1550. Que sur la croix ne fiere sur mon escu lisce *H*.

1551. f. sor l. *CG*; c. cou saces de verte *G*; *H wants*.

1552. e. venra m. *E CG D*; r. mar c. *D*; m. saces en (par *D*) verite *C D*; m. oiant tout le barne *G*; *H wants*.

1554. Ni lairoie n'i f. *G*; l. que n'i f. tot a ma volente *C*; l. que ne f. *H*.

1555. D. dist E. *E C DH*; E. cius a le sens dervet *C*; E. cist a *G D*; E. cil a *H*; a cors d. *E*.

1556. Encontre D. *C*; Qui contre D. *G D*; Quant contre D. *E*; D. a tante fois alet *C*; D. a tantes fois m. *G D*; D. veut ensi meserer *E*; f. esre *D*; f. ouvre *G*; *H wants*.

1557. Mauquarre va ferir ou heaume lisce *H*; e. gemet *CG*; e. gesine *E*.

1558. D. l'a tout e. *G*; *H wants*.

1559. La coyffe lui faulsa le test a entame *H*; c. fausee e., t. entame *D*; *H adds*: Le sang vermeil en est contreval devale; *CG want*.

1560. o. guery q. *H*; t. quant n. *D*; q. mort ne l'ot r. *C*; q. mort ne l'ont r. *DH*; q. mort ne l'a jete *G*; *H adds*: Quant le serf sent la playe a poy qui n'est deve/ Et Elyas lui dit quant son coup voit leve.

1561. M. il a repris c. *C*; l. fail r. *G*; *H wants*.

1562. Et dist or i parra q. *CG*; p. dist i. *E*; *H wants*.

1563. Il fera e. *C*; c. qui que en ait m. *D*; c. qui qu'en aie m. *G*; c. cui qu'en doive peser *C*; *H wants*.

1564. Lors feri s. *C*; En l'escut s. *G*; crois li *CG*; a grant c. *E CG DH*.
1565. Elyas cancela a. *C*; c. por p. *E CG D*; p. ne l'a v. *D*.
1566. *D illegible to* pooir; Mais qui *C*.
1567. *D illegible to* crois; Fist d. *H*; F. del escut s. *C*; c. yssir .I. *H*; .I. grant fu a. *D*; .I. sierpent embraset *C*.
1568. 1. pis c. *CG*; 1. cief c. *E*; v. parsiut 1. *H*; 1. maufes *C*; c. deffae *E D*; c. parjure *H*.
1569. il li o. *C H*; e. a l. *CG DH*; f. entame *E*.
1570. Par d. *C*; Desure s. *E*; Et desour s. *G*; Que d. *H*; 1. rue t. *E*; 1. getta t. *H*; *D wants*.
1571. v. si a Diu a *CG*; D. aouret *C*; D. reclame *G*.
1572. K'il 1. *G*; Il cuide qu'il soit m. *H*; m. mais n. *D*; a atouche *H*.
1573. v. de peor a t. *D*; v. si coumence a trambler *E*; *H wants*.
1574. g. huche S. *CG D*; g. crient S. *E*; *H wants*.
1575. a. desus p. *G*; *H wants*.
1576. d. pamisons o. *E CG*; o. diaule r. *CG*; o. le serf r. *H*; m. releve *E H*; m. aportet *G*.
1577. p. si coumence a crier *E*; *C H want*.
1578. e. vint s. *E CG*; e. va s. *H*; v. grant cop li a dounet *C H*; v. mout forment aire *E which places this verse after 1. 1579.*
1579. Qu'il ne set que dire de peor a tramble *D*; Que tout l'a esbahi sacies en verite (e. forment l'a estourne *G*) *CG*; Que l'enfant chancela si fort l'a e. *H*; *C adds*: Se Dius nel garandi il l'euist affole; *G adds*: Or oiies grant batalle ja nen iert trestourne.

74. *BE CG D*
1580. d. quant d. *G D*; d. de pasmisons r. *C*; *H wants*.
1581. Il a ouvers 1. *G*; i. fel fu et d. *D*; i. comme ciens d. *CG*; *H wants*.
1582. f. sor 1. *C D*; q. esclaire *E C D*; *G H want*.
1583. m. bendes en a *D*; m. cercles en a *C*; *G H want*.
1584. Lors c. *CG*; 1. fel a *G D*; s. vers 1. *C*; *CG D add*: Elyas dist (fait *G D*) li sers par le cors saint Elaire; *H wants*.
1585. La crois de ton e. *CG*; e. me fist ore m. *C*; e. m'ara hui fait m. *G*; k. ja m'a *D*; k. tant m'a *E*; f. contraire *CG D*; *H wants*.
1586. N. t'avera m. *E C*; N. t'aura ja m. *G*; m. ne c. *E D*; *H wants*.
1587. Q. ne te face le cuer dou ventre t. *C*; t. voille a. *D*; *H wants*.

1588. He c'a dit E. comperes d. *G*; g. dist E. con es de
put asfaire *E*; E. dolereuse semainne *C*; d. mal a.
D; *C adds*: Te sera ajornee par Diu et sainte
Elainne/ Ains que m'escapes te ferai je croich
traire/ A l'ame de Diu qui tant est de boin aire;
G adds: A l'aie de Dieu te ferai anqui braire; *H*
wants.

1589. t. rien mesfaire *E*; *CG H want*.

1590. M. le vielle s. *D*; M. l'entent s. *CG*; s. coumen-
ce a retraire *G*; *H wants*.

1591. M. cort li sus chevaliers d. *D*; M. passe avant
chevaliers d. *E G*; *D adds*: Ocis moi cel garchon
mout par has son affaire; *C H want*.

1592. r. ci a mout g. *C*; v. me faites c. *G*; *H wants*.

1593. d. nus n. *E*; *H wants*.

1594. j. les ex e. *E CG D*; *H wants*.

1595. n. targera p. *E*; *H wants*.

1596. g. ire m. il ne s. *E*; d. et si ne s. *C*; *H wants*.

1597. Dont r. *D*; q. qu'en d. *DE*; *CG H want*.

75. *BE CG DH*

1598. Lors r. *DH*; Li chevalier s'en vienent a. *G*; O.
s'en vienent e. *C H*.

1599. Mauquarre fiert l'enfant ou heaume geme *H*; Et f.
C; s. desor l'e. *D*; s. en l'escut de quartier *CG*.

1600. .I. q. *D*; Que trestout li a fait quarteler et
brissier *G*; Les pierres et les fleurs en a jus t.
H; t. envoie *D*; *H adds*: Se Dieu ne le gardast ja
l'eust engrie; *C wants*.

1601. Et li s. refiert lui s. *G D*; Et il fiert Elyas
s. *C*; r. en l'escut sans laier *G*; *H wants*.

1602. Qu'il t. *E*; a le chercle e. *D*; a en la tieste e.
C; *G H want*.

1603. l. voit s. *E*; s. le cuer en a c. *C*; s. s'en a *E*
G; s. ot l. *E*; c. iriet *E CG*; *DH want*.

1604. Et Elyas le son a trestot defroissie *D*; L'ielme
de Mauquarres a desrout par le cief *C*; Al sierf a
le sien ielme et frait et pecoiet *G*; s. a tout
son heaume d. *H*; et ront et *E*.

1605. Lor c. *G D*; c. en sont taintes t. *C*; s. fallies
t. *G*; t. sont entremalie *E*; a. sainnie *CG D*; *H*
wants.

1606. C'a *C D*; Par g. *H*; merveille sont *E CG DH*; m.
sont eulx deux a. *H*.

1607. d. quatre lieues ce sont tous appresie *H*; *E wants*.

1608. A .II. perrons sont (parois de piere s. *D*; perons
de piere s. *G*) andoi a. *CG D*; *H wants*.

1609. T. ont a. raie d. *D*; T. fort furent m. *C*; o. sai-
nie *G*; *H wants*.

1610. Ne porent sus e. *C*; Ne se p. *H*; a. sont agenoil-
lie *CG DH*.

1611. La gent pour E. ont ploret de p. *C*; e. plore et
proie *D*; e. paour e. *G*; *E adds a repetition of 1.*
1609.

1612. c. quel tort et Q. *D*.

1613. O. n'arai j. *E D*; terai jamais *G*; j. jamais t. *E*
D; m. chastiel n. *D*; m. vile terre ne fies *C*; m.
ne vile n'i. *E*; m. nule tiere ne fies *G*; *H wants*.

1614. Or s. *CG H*; j. ja a. *C H*; j. voir a. *G*; a. que a
C; a. com mon corps est j. *H*.

1615. t. lasse mal a. *G D*; t. lasse mar a. *C*; t. car
j'en ai poi p. *E*; *H wants*.

1616. v. jou ageneillier *C*; v. la a. *E G*; v. moult
afloibie *H*.

76. *BE CG DH*

1617. L. royne a g. *CG*.

1618. E. a 1. *G which places this verse after 1. 1619*;
C H want.

1619. Et si doute le f. que f. *C*; Que redoute le f. *G*;
f. et le flamme drument (sic) *E*; k. tot ades es-
prent *CG D*; *H wants*.

1620. Une oroison commence doucement en plourant *H*; D.
en a appielet s. *C*; a. de cuer et angouisseuse-
ment *E*; r. et pleure f. *G*; p. asprement *D*; p.
tenrement *CG*.

1621. Si[re] D. dist 1. *C*; Tout ensi dist le dame sire
Dix vraiement *E*; Hax Dieu pere du ciel par ton
saint comment *H*; i. tres vraiement *C*.

1622. Que t. *C*; c. et tot le firmamant *G D*; c. et le
coumenchement *C*; *H wants*.

1623. Et solel et estoiles et le lune ensement *D which*
adds: Et tot ce fesis tu sire al commencement; *CG*
H want.

1624. E. mesistes estoiles sire en el *C*; e. lassus el
E; *G DH want*.

1625. Adan fourmastes sire par vo devisement *E*; i. fe-
sis 1. *C D*; *H wants*.

1626. f. a ton comandement *C*; f. por coumandement *G*; t.
porveemant *D*; t. otroiement *E*; *H wants*.

1627. i. por 1. *G*; p. le t. *G D*; *H wants*.

1628. Quant i. *C*; i. orent fait d. *G D*; i. firent d. *E*
C; f. desor ton veement *D*; f. ton deveagement *C*;
f. sour ton d. *G*; *H wants*.

1629. Mout i furent grant tans et il et si enfant *D*; *CG*
H want.

1630. s. et b. *E*; *CG DH want*.

1631. n. garir d. *G*; d. l'infernal t. *D*; d. ce v. *E G*;

H wants.

1632. Presis tu e. *G D*; P. vos dous sire en la Virgene ombrement *C*; V. biax sire a. *G D*; 1. saint a. *E*; *H wants.*

1633. De coi e. en s. *D*; *CG H want.*

1634. Al venredi soufris le passion mout grant *E*; *H wants.*

1635. j. presis sire s. *E*; *CG DH want.*

1636. Droit a ynfer alas s. *D*; a. et s'en g. *G*; *H wants.*

1637. Q. t'avoient servi et ame (e. vescut *G*) 1. *E CG D*; e. longement *D*; *H wants.*

1638. Et el chies en montas por 1. *D*; Lor montastes es cius pour lor devenement *C*; Puis en montas es chius ce fu vostre coumans *G*; m. pour lor d. *E*; *H wants.*

1639. p. entras c. *D*; p. alas c. *CG*; c. sevent 1. *C D*; c. virent 1. *G*; *H wants.*

1640. a. tenoient l'e. tout criant *E*; e. flamboiant *G D*; *H wants.*

1641. Sire la M. *CG*; M. f[es]ys le pardon grant *H*.

1642. P. de Rome d. *D*; *G wants.*

1643. e. saint Vistasse (s. Laitasse *G*; e. Eustasse *G*) garis del (de *G*) f. *CG D*; *H wants.*

1644. f. dusc'a 1. *E CG D*; *H wants.*

1645. Que 1. *D*; Q. les grans iluec vinrent a. *C*; Q. les g. *E*; g. les oirent a. *G*; al matinet p. *D*; *H wants.*

1646. S. trovent ans .II. e. *D*; *E adds*: Dont en orent grant joie li petit et li grant; *H wants.*

1647. Sire son ce est v. *C D*; Sire si c. *G*; Ainsi comme c. *H*; e. jol croi vraiemant *D*; e. jou ensi creanch *C*; e. je le suis creant *E*; e. bien en suis creans *G*; e. je pour b. *H*; *G adds*: Et issi con tu ses que jou sui en torment.

1648. M. garissies d. *C*; M. jetes vous b. *G*; M. gardez huy b. *H*; d. vous Dex d. *D*; d. hui S. *E*; d. cel vilain tourment *E*; d. ce fu ci ardant *G*; d. mal et de tourment *H*; c. fu ci devant *C D*.

1649. E. ansi con tu ses c'a tort ai cest tormant *D*; m. villement *E*; *CG H want.*

1650. Biax Sire deffendes c. *D*; Et gardez beau doulx pere c. *H*; *CG want.*

1651. a ce s. *H*; s. mescreant *E H*; *CG want.*

1652. d. arriere d. *E G D*; ciet a tiere *C*; *H wants.*

1653. Q. uns d'aus le relieve c. *G*; d. l'en relieve c. *C D*; c. qui ot non E. *E*; c'on apeloit E. *D*; a. Climant *G D*; *H wants.*

1654.   Ki 1. *G*; d. dolce dame N. *CG D*; N. te va esmaiant *C*; N. t'esmaier nient *G*; *H wants*.

1655.   E. Diu merci en estant *E*; *H wants*.

1656.   e. ore e. *G D*; e. orendroit c. *E*; *H wants*.

1657.   d. s'asist q. *G*; q. a 1. *CG*; *H wants*.

1658.   De ses biaus iox garde contre Euriant *C*; Cele te-noit adies ses mains v. *G*; S. iex tent et e. *D*; *H wants*.

77.   *BE CG DH*

1659.   L. royne a gran duel p. *CG*; d. fait grant dol p. *DH*.

1660.   D. deproie e. *D*; D. reclama de lui siervir s'es-saie *C*; d. pecie 1. *E*; d. torment 1. *G*.

1661.   Elyas s. *CG*; E. sali s. *C*; s. en pies q. *G*.

1662.   Et tint t. *D*; L'espee tint estrainte fu et biele et vraie *C*; L'espee estraint forment que il pas ne s'esmaie *G*; e. qui ot non M. *DH*; o. claimme M. *E*.

1663.   Mauquarres va requerre k. *CG*; v. et s. *C*; v. que s. *G*; v. sa bonne espee ploye *H*; k. si s. *CG D*; k. se plaint et esmaie *E which adds*: De se plaie se plaint et mout se contralaie.

1664.   Ne g. *C*; q. il a t. *E C D*; *GH want*.

1665.   Au sierf en vient sen espee i a. *C*; Elyas vint a. *E*; e. a traite *G*; *H wants*.

1666.   s. qui Dex doinst sa manaie *D*; s. qui malement s'essmaie *C*; s. qu'il n'a pooir qu'il traie *G*; *H wants*.

1667.   e. contre son p. *C*; q. li meskaie *E*; q. se b. *D*; *H wants*.

1668.   Et de sa t. *C*; 1. face Dex sa paie *D*; *H wants*.

1669.   C. dist M. *E C*; f. Mauquares n. *E G*; e. qu'il caie *D which adds*: Por le plente del sanc qui fors del cors li raie.

1670.   Paor que t. *E*; d. ai t. *D*; d. au cuer car tos li cors m. *C*; d. que t. *G*; c. m'afebloie et e. *G DH*; c. durement m'en e. *E*.

1671.   n. mires n. *G which places this verse after 1. 1672. C wants*.

1672.   q. n'est chiens k. *E C D*; q. uns ciens k. *G*; *H wants*.

78.   *BE CG DH*

1673.   *CG DH want*.

1674.   Matabrune de dol a *D*; Matabrune la viele a *C H*; La malle viele a *G*.

1675.   Le vil dyable emport fait il ce g. *H*; d. empor-tent fait el cest g. *C*; d. d'infier enport hui cest g. *G*; e. enporte c. *E*.

1676.   Car j. *C*; Je ne vi oncques mais tant fier ne s.
        H; j. ne v. ainc m. *CG D*; m. isi felon campion *C*;
        s. fail n. *G*.
1677.   Et Elyas empeint le serf ed tel rendom *H*; E. fu a
        (en *G*) piet qui (bien *G*) resanble baron *CG*; E.
        par fierte v. *E*; a estet v. *D*; *CG add*: Va ferir
        en l'estour (a estaie *G*) Mauquarres le felon.
1678.   Tel cop lui a donne sur l'escu a *H*; l. pierche k.
        C; k. est pains a *D*; k. fu boins a *C*; k. fu poins
        a *G*.
1679.   E. l'auberc c'ot viestu p. *G*; E. de l'auberc *D*;
        E. du h. *E*; *C H want*.
1680.   f. c'ainc t. n'ot nus hon *G*; *C H want*.
1681.   Elias a empaint l. *D*; E. refiert l. *E*; l. brant
        d. *D*; l. serf d. *E G*; f. par t. *E D*; *C H want*.
1682.   A l'estordre qu'il fist de traitre gloton *D*; La
        boinne e. *C*; Q. se t. *E G*; bonne n'y *H*; e. ne p.
        G; n. peut a. *C*.
1683.   Est p. *D*; Par m. *E C*; mi pechoie E *D*; l. brise E
        C; l. pecoia E *E*; p. oes q. *D*; pecoie Dex quele
        m. *G*.
1684.   Certes dist Matabrune c. *C*.
1685.   Estera l. *D*; a. par deles s. *E CG*; d. lui s. *D*;
        d. le g. *E C*; d. le scien g. *H*; *C adds*: Et Diex
        fait Elyas par ton saintime non/ Or sai jou bien
        mal me fera cil gloutons/ Or ai jou bien mestier
        de ta beneichon.
1686.   C. dist M. *CG*; p. facon *G*.
1687.   n. prisson .I. *G*; n. prise .I. *H*.
1688.   Or f. *G*; c. voiant t. *CG*; q. maint conpagnon *C*; *H*
        wants.
1689.   b. oir k. *D*; v. tot (ci *E*) entor e. *E D*; *C H*
        want.
1690.   r. j'oi p. .I. b. *G D*; r. or oi p. glouton *E*; r.
        vous parler (sic) com b. *H*; *C wants*.
1691.   k. por nous fu mis a (qui souffri *H*) passion *G*
        DH; *C wants*.
1692.   La crois de mon escu ne tochera nus hom *D*; Il
        vous en puet bien rendre anqui le g. *G*; Ja pour
        toy ne sera la dame mise a destrucion *H*; V. ave-
        res anuit l. *E*; *C wants*.
1693.   Chiertes fait (dist *G*) Malquarres par tans (tan-
        tost *H*) le vera on *G DH*; d. trestout ce s. *E*; *C*
        wants.
1694.   S. l'escut va ferir en (a *G*) la crois a *CG*.
1695.   Et Dex par sa vertu ki n'aimme se bien non *G*; D.
        qui ainc n'ama felon *D*; D. ainc n'ama se bien non
        C; D. qui n'ayme se bien non *H*; *C adds*: Et que le

> gloutonie vet rendre le glouton.

1696. Fait de la crois salir sans plus (nule a. *C*) (point *G H*) d'arestoison *CG DH*.

1697. .I. serpent a .II. testes ja (onques *C H*) tel ne vera (vit *C H*) on *CG DH*.

1698. A une ague coe longue et graisle en son (u. longe queue qui fu ague e. *G*) *G D*; *C H want*.

1699. Ories grant m. et g. *G*; O. orres le m. et tel destruction *H*; o. grant merveille ainc tele ne vit on *C*; m. et g. *D*; m. et le d. *E*; *H adds*: Que Damedieu y fist qui incarnacion/ Print a la saincte Vierge pour noz redempcion.

79. *BE CG DH*

1700. qui au cuer a. *C*; e. a p. *E*; *H wants*.

1701. Et l. *G*; l. vertu d. *H*; k. de t. *D*; k. sur t. *H*.

1702. Fait (Si saillit *H*) de la crois sans autre demorance (c. .I. serpent sans doutance *G H*) *G DH*; *D adds*: .I. grant serpent hisdeus or sachies sans dotance; *C wants*.

1703. Tot (Trestot *C*) droit a Malquarre a (en *G*) la (sa *H*) veue (d. Mauquarres a levee la *C*) lance (v. se lance *H*) *CG DH*; *CG H add*: En l'elme se toelle (s'entoreille *C*) (s'entortaille *G*) par grant senefiance; *G DH add further*: Les .II. testes li crieve (cuevrent *G*) (crevent *H*) les iex (les deux yeulx *H*) sans demorance (doutance *H*).

1704. u. cosse p. *G*; *H wants*.

1705. *CG DH want*.

1706. *CG DH want*.

1707. P. lui p., f. le gante *E*; *CG DH want*.

1708. p. le veoir q. *E*; v. illecques sans arrestance *H*; q. en Dieu n'a fiance *G*; *C wants*.

1709. Matabrune ne fait n. *G*; n. joie ne beubance *D*; *C H want*.

1710. Les gens prioient D. sans orguel sans beubance *G*; g. proie D. qu'il garisse l'enfance *D*; Diu Elyas *E*; *G adds*: Que il gart le varlet et la roine france; *C H want*.

1711. Et l. *G D*; Mauquarres e. *C*; e. tumes q. *C D*; e. verses q. *G*; *E H want*.

1712. s. tout erant s. *C*; p. vol s. *G*; p. coup s. *H*; *E wants*.

1713. l. defroisse a *C*; l. martelle a *H*; d. del t. *D*; d. al t. *E G*; d. d'un t. *H*; t. d'une l. *E*; d. la l. *G D*; d. sa l. *H*.

80. *BE CG DH*

1714. *CG DH want*.

1715. Elias li debat la teste duremant *CG DH*.

1716. Al tronchon d. *G D*; A .I. pumiel d'espee *C*; Du pommel d. *H*; e. qui al coste l. *D*; e. qui a son col l. *H*; encor au p. *C*; encor al col l. *G*.
1717. Les las copa del ielme durement *C*; L. desfroise les bras a l'ielme verdoient *G*; l. du heaume *H*.
1718. M. a p. *CG DH*; o. dolour e. *G*; p. mout angoissosement *E G DH*; p. car grant anguisse sent *C*.
1719. Lui crie a haulte voix que recreant se rent *H*; A vois *C*; v. s'escrie *D*.
1720. E. a dit D. *C*.
1722. Ne p. *D*; e. presisse vers toi fors la tieste eramment *G*; p. plus fors le cief m. *C*; p. fors la teste te coupasse ensement *H*; t. decolpe m. *D*; t. que j'arai m. *E*.
1723. Et Matabrune q. *C*.
1724. Parmi la presse voiant toute la gant *C*; e. ala g. *H*; v. par mi ses gens maintenant defuiant *E*; a. fuiant par mi (entre *H*) la jant *DH*; a. entre la gent mucant *G*.
1725. *CG DH want.*
1726. Si est montee sour .I. ronchi errant *C*; s. en monta maintenant *E*; m. plorant *G D*; *H wants*.
1727. Onc n. *H*; fina si *C*; d. corre s. *G DH*; p. desi a *D*.
1728. castiel riche *C*; c. bel e. *E*; e. de t. *E DH*; e. mout tres b. *G*.
1729. Bien le garnist de vins et de formens *C*; M. l'ot f. *E*; d. pain e. *D*.
1730. Et d'arbalestiers q. *C*; Et d'ars et d'arbalaistres car mout estoit doutans *G*; *DH want*.
1731. f. encor a. mout grant *CG D*; *H wants*.
1732. *CG DH want.*
1733. *CG DH want.*
1734. *CG DH want.*
1735. *CG DH want.*
1736. Et Malquarres se paine de relever formant *CG DH*; De r. *E*; *CG add*: Mais li tors le honist (houni *G*) qu'il va (aloit *G*) porcacant.
1737. E. li copa a l'espee trencant *G*; E. de son espee lui trencha erramment *H*; l. trence m. *E*.
1738. Le cief a. *E*; t. jus del bus t. *G*; t. lui couppa t. *H*; h. voiant tote la jant *E G DH*; h. verdoiant *C*.
1739. Em pies sali l. *C*.
81. *BE CG DH*
1741. t. o l. *C*; rent al roi esjois *E*; rent al roi l'ocis (sic) *G*; r. mout j. *D*; t. pensis *C*; *H wants*.
1742. Biax r. *D*; Boins r. *CG H*; R. fait E. *C DH*; j. de

rien m. *E CG DH*.
1743.   Je vos c. *D*; E. dous a. *E*.
1744.   Leur courent gentilz dames o. *H*; c. chevalier o.
        C; h. ne sai ou .V. ou .VI. *C DH*; h. ca .III. ca
        .V. ca .VI. *E*; h. je ne sai .V. u .VI. *G*.
1745.   La roine deslient grant jeu font et grant ris *D*;
        La royne desloient li conte et li marcis *C*; d.
        delivree joie font et grant ris *E*; d. desloiie-
        rent en grant joie l'ont mis *G*; d. ont deliee
        grant geu et grant ris *H*.
1746.   a. desus .I. *DH*.
1747.   Dieu e. *C*; A Jhesus e. *H*; e. a cure e. *G*; r. gra-
        ce e. *H*; g. le roi de paradis *CG DH*.
1748.   Et quant vit E. *G*; L. ceurent Elyas et baisier et
        joir *C*; c. sus E. *E D*.
1749.   Laissies f. *C*; F. dist E. *E G*; f. li varles q. *G*;
        f. l'enfant q. *H*; E. qui tel jeu n'ot apris *D*; E.
        car jou n'ai pas apris *C*; E. france dame gentis
        E; E. que cou n'ot pas apris *G*; E. qui se n'eust
        mie apris *H*.
1750.   M. se ci a *H*; h. c'on ait non Marcon mis *D*; a. a
        non Marquis *G*.
1751.   S'il a (Et ait *G*) (Qui eust *H*) les iex creves
        tost me soit ci (c. si me soit tost *G*) tramis *CG
        DH*.
1752.   *CG DH want*.
1753.   J. le roi d. *E*; *CG DH want*.
1754.   e. es l. *E*; *CG DH want*.
1755.   Que c. *E*; *CG DH want*.
1756.   Qu'il dut porter noiier dedens le gaut follis *E*;
        CG DH want.
1757.   j. oscourcis *E*; *CG DH want*.
1758.   *CG DH want*.
1759.   M. vint e. *D*; M. ert e. *CG*; e. a l. *C*; p. devant
        lui e. *D*; p. a lui vint e. *C H*; p. a .I. les e.
        G; d. tos p. *CG DH*.
1760.   n. ju n'i fist n. *E*; *CG DH want*.
1761.   Biau sire ves m. *C*; Et dist ves me ci sire q. *G*;
        Veez moy a fait il sire q. *H*; q. ensi sui hounis
        E; t. sui m. *CG D*; t. fu m. *H*; *C adds*: Ses iox li
        a leves com hons de bien apris.
1762.   e. sui h. *E*; *CG DH want*.
1763.   q. si en sui si forment malbaillis *E*; *CG DH want*.
1764.   Et E. l'esgarde s. *C*; r. par la face l'a p. *H*; p.
        les iex p. *D*; l. cief p. *CG*.
1765.   D. fait E. *C D*; E. biax pere d. *G DH*; E. vrais r.
        C; E. dous r. *E*; r. dols amis *G D*; r. poestis *H*.
1766.   Regarde c. *D*; Ralumes ce p. *C*; Regardes c. *G H*;

          p. c'a tort est e. *D*; p. a tort fu il honis *C*; p. qui'st a *E G*; p. qui tant e. *H*; t. mesballis *G*.

1767. *C H want.*

1768. Il l. *G*; P. alaine en ses iex com hom de b. *D*; i. com .I. h. *E*; i. coume h. *G*; *C H want.*

1769. l. vertut d. *G H*; D. qui est de tout poestis *G*.

1770. E. tost enluminez si fut de joye espris *H*; M. alumes D. *E D*; r. si s'est de joie a. *D*; r. si est de joie fis *G*; j. est sus salis *C*.

1771. Nus ne le vit qui n'en soit trespensis *C*; Tous en eurent grant joye les grans et les petis *H*; k. le voit n. *G*.

1772. Par Dieu cou dist l. *G*; Diex dist l. *C*; D. aide dist l. *H*; A. moi dist Markes I. *E*; r. cist hom e. *CG DH*; d. grant p. *E CG DH*.

1773. *D places this verse after l.* 1774; *H wants.*

1774. e. si m'ait Jhesu-Cris *C*; e. grans talens m'en est pris *G*.

82. *BE G D*

1775. *C H want.*

1776. E. mout d'autre f. joie pour l'amour de M. *E*; *C H want.*

1777. p. desos le m. *D*; p. le destre giron *E*; p. desour l. *G*; *C H want.*

1778. i. le vis et la f. *D*; e. prie par amours et son nom *G*; *C H want.*

1779. E. dist l. *E G*; r. dites par g. *G*; *C H want.*

1780. t. es tu nes e. *D*; t. tu es e. *E*; *C H want.*

1781. Por l'amor del signor k. *G*; s. tu mie por Deu et por son non *D*; *C H want.*

1782. S. dist E. *E G D*; E. par le cors s. *G*; d. mon menton *D*; *C H want.*

1783. c. le voir vous en diron *D*; *E adds*: Pour nul homme vivant ja nel vous cleron/ Que ne die dont sui et de quel region; *C H want.*

83. *BE CG DH*

1784. Sire fait E. quant voulez s. *H*; E. se v. *C*.

1785. s. bien le sai si vos d. *C*.

1786. Jou sui vos fius che sacies vous de v. *C*; s. ce saches vos p. *D*; s. jel sui bien sans espoir *G*; s. ne le vueil pas celoir *H*; s. et vostre oir *E*.

1787. Vous souvient il point o. *H*; S. vous dist E. *C*; S. ore vous dist E. dou s. *G*; o. dist E. du s. *E*.

1788. d. c'on n. *G*; n. pooit a. *E G DH*.

1789. N. fist m. *E*; *G adds*: Se ele a plus d'un home ne faisoit son voloir.

1790. Icil qui m'a nouri ens en vostre pooir *E*; *CG DH want.*

1791. L'angle li tramist Dix p. *E*; *CG DH want*.
1792. La nuit jeustes vous a *CG DH*; Icelui n. *E*; l. sans remanoir *G*.
1793. e. Dex a de (del *G*) (sur *H*) tot pooir *CG DH*.
1794. l. povair *H*; *C wants*.
1795. Jou sui li .I. del fius cou sacies vous de voir *C*; *G DH want*.
1796. Elyas dist li dame u sont mi a. *C*; D. ce dist li rois U *G DH*; D. dist O., s. tout l. *E*; d. mi a. *DH*.

84. *BE CG DH*

1797. O. dist E. *E G*; E. et u s. *E C*.
1798. *CG DH want*.
1799. n. que f. *CG H*.
1800. c. en s. *H*; c. chaaine d'or luisant *D*; c. la c. *E C*; c. une c. *G H*; *C adds*: Encor ai jou la moie ves le chi en present.
1801. c. vo m. *E CG DH*; m. c'alee en est f. *D*; m. qui or en est f. *C*; m. qui s'en ala f. *E*; m. car ele en est f. *G*; m. qui alee est f. *H*.
1802. n. a u. *E*; e. l'aige c. *G*; u. gue soudoyant *H*; a. mout grant *D*; *C wants*.
1803. v. ici vostre oil voiant *D*; v. yci pour le present *H*; c. devant vous seant *G*; c. iluec en present *E*; *C wants*.
1804. Si nos porta n. *D*; N. i porta n. *DH*; N. porta pour n. *G*; n. si l. *D*; n. lui e. *G*.
1805. La nous laissa sur l'aige si s'en ala atant *E*; S. la rive n. *CG H*; m. puis n. *DH*; s. le l. *C*.
1806. l. force d. *C*; l. vertut d. *G*; *H wants*.
1807. Illec vint .I. *H*; b. esciant *E CG DH*.
1808. A. plus bel que il p. *CG D*; m. que il peust nous nourrist d. *H*; n. longement *G H*.
1809. u. quievre a. *G*; n. alaita s. *E*; n. ala alaitant *G*; *C DH want*.
1810. s. efforchement *C*.
1811. Les chaaines nous fist tolir d'or fin luisant *D*; t. les c. *G H*; n. chaennetes d. *H which adds*: Par son serf Mauquarre qu'ay ocis vous veant.
1812. c. estoient d. *H*; d. si (moult *H*) grant faement *CG H*; *D wants*.
1813. Tant con l. *D*; Tant que les euissiemes fussiemes biel et grant *C*; Que quant nous les aviesmes nous fumes bel enfant *E*; Que tant con les eumes fumes nous biel enfant *G*; a. s'estions b. *D*; a. estions b. *H*.
1814. e. le moie a mon col ci pendant *E*; *CG DH want*.
1815. Et chil qui le perdoit (perdroit *H*) chisnes ert

son vivant (c. seroit voyant *H*) *DH*; Et cil qui
les perdirent furent cisne volant *CG*; k. n'ont
pas l. *E*.

1816. Veoir povez m., m. seur nageant *H*; m. suer le v.
G; s. noant *C*; s. volant *E*.

1817. En cel vivier la jus que cisne vont sanlant *C*;
Laiens e. *E*; Laiens en cel v. qui sont cine vo-
lant *G*; Illec en ce v. dont j'ay le cuer dolant
H.

1818. r. l'a oit s. *C*; s. plore t. *E CG D*; p. fondam-
ment *E*; *H wants*.

1819. p. se pleure tenrement *E*; s. plus d. *D*; s. nul d.
G; *C H want*.

1820. Estes vos a itant le lormier venant *D*; Adonc vint
l'orfevre qui la parole entent *H*; v. illuec .I.
orfevre venant *G*; l. avant *C*; l. esranment *E*.

1821. Q. une des caaines ot forgie devant *D*; Q. ne for-
ga que l'une d. *C*; Q. forgie en ot u. *G*; f. que
u. *E*; *H wants*.

1822. *CG DH want*.

1823. Adont s'en retourna a *E*; Ala querir les chaennes
les rendi a l'enfant *H*; *CG D want*.

1824. e. retorne a. *E*; *CG DH want*.

1825. *E CG DH want*.

1826. S. ce dist l'o. *E*; l. preudom d. *G*; d. ces v. *D*;
G D place this verse after 1. 1827; *C H want*.

1827. Les .V. tint en ses mains (sa main *CG*) a Elyas
les tant (rent *CG*) (.V. lui a baillees voyant
ceulx maintenant *H*) *CG DH*; Or en t. *E*.

1828. s. n'aves m., v. di et c. *E*; *CG DH want*.

1829. M. la vielle je vous di vraiement *G which adds*:
Les mesballa biaus sire si vous dirai coument/
Pour faire une grant coupe mout rice et mout val-
lant; *C DH want*.

1830. P. en fuisonna l'une que .VII. sans d. *E*; P. en
fuisonna une que son .V. pois d'a. *G*; *C DH want*.

1831. g. dus k'a ci bonement *E*; *CG DH want*.

1832. Sire fait Elyas .C. miercis vos en rench *C*; m.
puis l'a franchi errant *H*; f. erranment *G*; *C*
adds: Erramment l'en francist n'i atarga nient.

1833. Li rois li otroia la francise ensement (o. de gre
et bounement *G*) *CG*; r. l'octroya m. *H*; o. bel et
courtoisement *E*.

1834. Li prodon li a ja c. *D*; *CG H want*.

1835. Et Elyas appiele la r. erranment *C*; *H wants*.

1836. M. ancui averes joie p. *E*; e. averes vous joie p.
D; j. jel sai a ensiant *G*; *H wants*.

1837. V. ent a. *E CG D*; V. tost a. *H*; m. le petit et li

grant *C H*; t. precainement *G*.

1838. g. miracle p. *E D*; m. lors s'en tornent atant (or s'en vienent a. *C*) (lors s'en torna a. *G*) *CG D*; *H wants*.

1839. Dus que s. *D*; Jusque s. *CG H*; l. riviere n. *E*; v. ne se vont atargant (ariestant *G*) *CG*; v. s'en vont tout maintenant *H*; *C adds*: Li roys et la royne et trestoute la gent/ Elyas les commande ses freres ensement/ Li cisne l'entendirent a lui vinrent courant/ Contreval la riviere en sont venut errant/ Il demainnent grant joie juskes as pies l'enfant.

1840. Et il lor commanda a *C*; E. les c. *G D*; *C adds as the initial verse of the next laisse*: Elyas fu a piet les la rive soutainne; *H wants*.

1841. s'asistrent t. *D*; s'asisent t. *E*; t. n'i vont plus ariestant *G*; *CH want*.

1842. v. noant *D*; v. avant *G*; *C H want*.

1843. Droit par mi la riviere v. *G*; *C H want*.

1844. *CG DH want*.

1845. l. frere v., l. besbe lietament *E*; *CG DH want*.

1846. e. en vienent a. *E*; *CG DH want*.

85.   *BE CG DH*

1847. Tuit se sont la assis prince conte demaine *D*; Li autre sont a. *C*; Or se se sont tout a. *G*; a. prince et conte e. *G*; a. prince conte e. *H*; e. conte e. *E C*; *C adds*: Li rois et la roine qui est de tout bien plainne.

1848. e. autres gens tout c. la rive *C*; *H wants*.

1849. Il appelle les cisnes c. *H*; j. demaine *G*.

1850. Il estoient p. *G*; q. n'estoit une l. *E*; s. lins n. *G*; *C DH want*.

1851. c. rendue a s. *G DH*; c. a chaskune (sic) s. *C*.

1852. .IIII. sont *C*; s. mescin e. *E*; b. ouvraignes *G*; *H wants*.

1853. E. la quinte fu f. *G*; l. autres fu cisnes p. *C*; f. qui'st bele com s. *E*; b. de s. *CG*; *H wants*.

1854. L'autres i *C*; L'uns n'ot pas se caine dont il fu en grant p. *E*; Li uns i *G*; Mais il en f. une cellui fut en grant p. *H*; f. celui est nee p. *C*; f. si li nestra teus p. *G*; c. a encontre p. *D*.

1855. .IIII. f. *D*; .IIIII. f. *C*; P. .V. f. *E*; Plus de .III. *G*; f. s'est p. *DH*; f. se pasma p. *C*; f. se pasme p. *G*; p. si b. *C*; p. et grant dolor demaine *E*; p. et b. *H*; puis crie a *G*; a longe a. *DH*; a haute a. *CG*.

1856. s. piet s. *C*; b. trait ses plumes t. *G*; s. depiece t. *E C D*; *H wants*.

1857. p. et demainent p. *H*; d. qu'il demaine *G D*; i. mainent *C*.

86. *BE CG DH*

1858. e. repaire a. *G*; r. el (au *C*) (ou *H*) vivier t. *CG DH*; a. moult d. *H*.

1859. Li rois fait joie por s. *C*; La royne fait joie d. *H*; *D wants*.

1860. Et la roine ausi mais le cuer ot pesant *G*; e. li cuers fu d. *E*; *C DH want*.

1861. c. refont grant dol les jans *D*; c. font grant duel li auquant *E*; *CG H want*.

1862. As e. *C DH*; e. a d. *C*; o. viestus de rices bouge- rans *G*; m. rice garnement *E*.

1863. s. esmari c. *E*; s. esmaie que p. *G*; *CH want*.

1864. s. traient k. *G*; k. est l. *E DH*; *C wants*.

1865. A. si r., v. lor gent *E*; *CG DH want*.

1866. *CG DH want*.

1867. *CG DH want*.

1868. a. rest e. *E*; *CG DH want*.

1869. a. coume (com *C*) hom (h. de *C*) bien sachans (h. bienvalans *G*) *CG D*; g. essiant *E*; *H wants*.

1870. Se il p. *G*; l. est a. *D*; *C H want*.

1871. Qu'il v. *C*; I. fera M. *CG D*; M. corechie a. *D*; c. as grans dans *CG D*; *C adds*: Pres d'Elyas se traient trestout li .V. enfant/ Car plus cier l'ont que nul home vivant; *H wants*.

1872. En l. *D*; A l. *G*; p. retorne k. *G D*; p. retornent k. *E*; t. Elyas li sacans *G*; k. ert e. *E*; e. lee e. *E D*; *C H want*.

1873. *C H want*.

1874. l. jete k. *G*; k. est o. *E D*; k. fu o. *G*; *C H want*.

1875. D. en orent l. *G*; a. ce f. *E*; t. est s. *E D*; f. lor p. *E*; f. li Dex coumans *G*; s. penitans *D*; *C H want*.

1876. Iluec droit vint .I. *D*; Laiens avoit .I. *G*; Illec vint .I. *H*; p. s'avoit a n. *G*; k. ot a n. *E*; k. eust nom Elimans *H*; n. Florans *D*.

1877. L'eve (aige *CG*) f. *CG D*; f. aporter e. *E CG D*; fons qui sont grant *C*; *H wants*.

1878. Maintenant b. *C*; Trestous b. cius p. *G*; l. peres l. *E*; *C adds*: Si lor a mis biaus nons et avenans; *H wants*.

87. *BE CG DH*

1879. p. si a fait l. *G*; *C wants*.

1880. a. au t. *G DH*; a. pour t. *E*; *C wants*.

1881. n. de S. *E D*; *C H want*.

1882. *C wants*.

1883. L'eust n. Orions ou nom du Saint Esperit *H*; e.
voil m. *D*; *C wants*.

1884. a. Orions e. *G D*; a. Orient e. *H*; 0. Dex li puis-
se cherir (benir *G*) *G DH*: 0. que D. *E*; *C wants*.

1885. t. Acaryes sans noise et sans aïr *D*; t. ot non
Jehans Dex le puisse tehir *G*; Z. sans neant en
mentir *H*; p. maintenir *E*; *C wants*.

1886. Jehan eust nom le quart qui moult fist a merir *H*;
n. Ivoins si vint de D. *G*; J. c'estoit a *E*; *C D
want*.

1887. R. sel puet on b. *G*; R. la deust b. *H*; l. pot b.
D; *C wants*.

1888. Pour l. *G*; b. feme k. *E*; b. nee k. *G*; k. soit d.
G D; k. oncques peust mourir *H*; f. juske en Atir
G.

1889. Q. il sont b. *C*; f. baptizer se firent r. *H*; l. a
fait viestir *C*; l. vont r. *G*; *C adds*: De rices
garnimens trestout a lor plaisir.

1890. *CG DH want*.

1891. Encor sera tel ore bien pora avenir *G*; c. can-
chons b. *C*; *H wants*.

1892. Dont tant maint chevalier en couvenra m. *G*; *H
wants*.

1893. v. cui p. *E*; e. puisse m. *G*; p. mal (maus *E D*) a-
venir *E C D*; *H wants*.

1894. Si fera il p. *E CG D*; p. foi n. *D*; p. Diu n. *C*;
t. e li n'i puet f. *E*; t. ja n'i pora f. *G*; *E
adds*: Je croi de mal mort le fera on morir; *H
wants*.

88. *BE CG DH*

1895. 0. comenche bataille e. *C*; l. tans et mout tost
a. *E*; t. que Matabrune aura *CG DH*; *E adds*: Hontes
et grans anuis Matabrune avera.

1896. Grant anui se Deu plaist k. *G DH*; Mout grans
anuis jou croi li avenra *C*; qui le *H*.

1897. c. qu'ele a *E G*; e. du mal k. *E*; *C DH want*.

1898. r. j'ai vescu g. *E G DH*; r. jou ai vescu pieca *C*;
a. long temps a *H*; g. piecha *E*; g. tans a *G*.

1899. Plus a *C*; B. ai p. *E C DH*; a de .CC. ans e. *C*; a.
nel vous (ne le c. *H*) celerai ja *C DH*; *G wants*.

1901. Et il respondent tuit si soit con vous plaira *D*;
Et il dient trestout que mout bien lor plaira *C*;
Et il o., D. quil veera *G*; *H wants*.

1902. o. de primes t. *E*; *CG DH want*.

1903. L. corone li rent (doune *DG*) e. *CG D*; t. li rois
bien l'enplora *G*; i. l'en m. *C D*; *CG D add*: Elias
prent l'onor et li rois l'otria (o. Damediu en
loa *C*) (e. si l'en mercia *G*)/ La roine en fait

(roine fait *G*) joie qui mout (j. car ele *G*) grant
droit en a (droit a *G*) (*C wants*).

1904. m. l'en menerent l. *E*; m. ont mene l'enfant qui
       rois sera *G which adds*: Adont fu courounes et
       puis ofrir ala.

1905. q. sus l. *D*; q. on li prousenta *C*; a. mis a *E*; *C*
       adds: Houmage li ont fait que plus n'i demora/ A
       l'issir dou moustier les hommes apiela; *H wants*.

1906. S. dist E. *G*; f. il nel v. *C*.

1907. Or verai jou qui *C*; Mais o. *G*; Tantost v. *H*.

1909. m. m'a fait honte m. *C*; fait honte *H*.

1910. Mais foit *C*; m. porta *G*.

1911. Ja la *C*; Jamais ceste s. *G*; Ja avant l. *H*; l.
       quinsaine t. *E*.

1912. c. ele esploita *DH*; *CG D add*: Se Diu plaist le
       poissant jamais n'amendera (p. son loier en aura
       D) (p. que ja n'en mentira *G*).

89. *BE CG D*

1913. S. ce dist li rois f. *C*; S. dist E. *E*; a. seurte
       G; *H wants*.

1914. O. proi jou a cascun tenpre m'ait amene *G*; p. jou
       chascuns ait amenet *C*; coumant cascuns m'ait ame-
       ne *E*; *H wants*.

1915. Son ost a *CG*; o. sor Valbruiant a. *D*; a mainbur-
       nir a. *E*; a. .III. j. *C*; *G adds*: Tant de gent
       k'il en aie a force et a plente; *H wants*.

1916. p. m'en a. cius avera m. *G*; a. plus avera m. *C*;
       a. si avera m. *D*; *H wants*.

1917. E. cil r. *G*; i. li respondirent t. *CG*; i. ont
       respondu A v. *E*; A vo v. *CG*; *H wants*.

1918. Il prient c'a la viele avoit Diex mal dehe *C*; C.
       dist que (a *G*) la v. doinst Dex m. *G D*; *H wants*.

1919. .I. garcons s'en torna neveus fu M. *C*; c. fu M. *E*
       G; *H wants*.

1920. d. quanqu'il a *E G D*; *H wants*.

1921. e. tout a *C*; e. pres a *D*; l. sens m. *E D*; l. cuer
       m. *G*; s. desve *E G D*; *H wants*.

1922. Quant ele ot q. *D*; Et ce k'Elyas est coume r. *E*;
       De cou que li rois a Elyas c. *G*; *H wants*.

1923. *H wants*.

1924. Le garchon qui li a la novele (cel mesage *E*) con-
       te (l. ot le message aportet *G*) *E G D*; *H wants*.

1925. f. par m. *C*; p. que m. *C D*; s. que m. *E G*; a cra-
       vente *C*; a jete *E*; *H wants*.

1926. He d. *G D*; D. dient l. *C*; D. dist uns dus v. *G*;
       f. si homme v. *C D*; b. mout a. mal esre *D*; *E H*
       want.

1927. Que l. *G D*; Q. ce g. aves a si grant tort tuet *G*;

n. mort jete *D*; *E H want*.

1928. d. Matabrune tout ai le sanc m. *C*; v. je ai le s.
E; v. car j'ai le s. *G*; s. desve *E D*; s. torblet
G; *H wants*.

1929. Or m. *E G D*; c. me font m. *D*; c. m'a fait malfes
G; *C H want*.

1930. En aves v. *CG*; a. entendut k. *C*; *H wants*.

1931. Qu'il m. *E G D*; m. violt a. *G*; a. .IIII. jors p.
C; *H wants*.

1932. s. jo p. *G D*; j. tieng sacies de veritet *C*; m.
glouton derve *E*; *H wants*.

1933. l. trairai l. *CG D*; l. cuer p. *E CG D*; p. an .II.
les costes *C*; *G adds*: Se li ferai jehir coument
il a ouvre; *H wants*.

1934. s. prive *E G*; *C H want*.

1935. M. grant gent a li v., e. mande *G*; *C H want*.

1936. c. a garnit e. *G*; f. drecier e. *E*; d. pain e. *D*;
d. lonc et de le *E*; *D adds*: De vin et de viandes
a grandisme plente; *E adds*: Et si l'a fait garnir
et de vin et de ble; *C H want*.

1937. Les murs fait redrecier les fosses reparer *G*; s.
amende li f. rejete *E*; *C H want*.

1938. E. arc et abalaistre furent tost e. *G*; a. a m. *D*;
C H want.

1939. Or d. *G*; M. demaine l. *E D*; g. bruit e. *E*; *C H
want*.

90. *BE CG D*

1940. La guerre sera grans q. *G*; g. ne puet mais (plus
E) d. *E G D*; *C H want*.

1941. M. bien fist Matabrune s. *C*; f. relever *G*; *H
wants*.

1942. b. ja faites frumer *C which adds*: Magouniaus et
perrieres pour les pieres jeter/ Ses barons fait
la viele tous mander/ Nus n'i remaigne qui puist
armes porter/ Et il i vinrent tout li cuvert par-
juret/ Damediex les confonde car ne l'osent veer/
Caskuns a fait sa gent venir et asanler/ Tres et
aucubes sour leur diestriers porter; *G adds*: Ses
barons et ses princes a fait trestous mander/ Ki
de lui tienent tieres villes et fermetes; *H
wants*.

1943. e. fu a. *D*; *C H want*.

1944. p. la j. *G*; *C H want*.

1945. f. ces blans napes o. *G*; *C H want*.

1946. S. dist E. *E G*; d. os a. *G D*; *C H want*.

1947. nul que ne penst de se gent armer *D*; nul qui ne
voist de bien faire aprester *G*; s. paine de bien
faire e. *E*; *C H want*.

1948. a. reposer *G D*; a. delivrer *E*; *C H want*.
1949. E. refont les (lor *G*) lis parer *G D*; E. s'alerent deporter *E*; *C H want*.
1950. d. qu'a l. *G*; *C H want*.
1951. t. se vellent retorner *G*; v. aler *E*; *C DH want*.
1952. C. a fait s. *D*; C. fait ses grans o. *G*; s. gens garnir et aprester *E*; e. ses gens a. *D*; j. asambler *G D*; *C H want*.
1954. Ses cameus et ses bugles a *D*; Ses cameus et ses mules et ses soumiers t. *G*; *C H want*.
1955. p. i fait asses mener *G D*; p. en f. *E*; *C H want*.
1956. O. nen p. *C*; p. Matabrune s. *CG D*; p. plus l. *E*; s. grant anui aler *C*; s. anui escaper *G D*; *H wants*.

91. *BE CG DH*

1957. Elyas lors s'en va qui ne tient mie a gas *H*; o. sel c. *G*.
1958. Elyas d. *C*; r. di moi ou tu vas *D*; s. or u *E*; t. que tu feras *C*.
1959. Ouyl c. *H*; l. rois ases le saveras *C*; l. varles a. *G*; e. apar main l. *E*; *D wants*.
1960. Remain si te conroie tes enfans g. *C*; Remain chi et sejorne tes freres gardans *D*; Remain si te deporte o les enfans que t'as *G*; Revien si te sejourne tes enfans g. *H*; *E wants*.
1961. Mes freres et ma mere et ma suer aideras *CG*; Et ta mere autresi et moi conforteras *D*; Ma mere et mes hounours s. *E*; *D adds*: Biau pere dist li enfes taisies ne dites pas/ Se ne veng (sic) ceste honte trop iere vius et mas; *H wants*.
1962. r. ou n. *C*; r. de par s. *E*; r. sire con tu voras *G*; *DH want*.
1963. Et Elyas s'en torne C. *C*; Or s. *D*; A ces mos de son pere se parti Elyas *H*; v. li varles nel tenes m. *G*; E. mais ce n'est m. *E D*.
1964. De la grant ost qu'il maine qui vient de totes pars *D*; c. mais ce n'est mie gas *E*; n. s'aseure p. *G*; *C H want*.
1965. Desi a Malbruiant onques n'i ariesta *C*; A Mabruiant vint que n'y demoura pas *H*; M. en vint a. *E*; e. tornent a. *D*.
1966. Iluekes sont l. *C*; s. assis s. *E*; d. Galas *CG*; d. Chieras *D*; d. Torgas *E*; *H wants*.
1967. Cou est u. *CG*; Che fu u. *D*; k. est d. *C*; *H wants*.
1968. M. sierre t. *C*; M. clot et serre (euvre *G*) t. *G D*; a. d'une (celle *G*) part a *E CG D*; *H wants*.

92. *BE CG DH*

1969. E. avironne le c. *E*; *CG DH. want*.

1970.   1. Elyas t. *CG DH*; e. atourne t. *E*; a. del tot a *D*; a. de tout a *G*.

1971.   m. tente b. *E*; *CG DH want*.

1972.   Lors vint 1. *H*; v. .I. c. *DH*; d. Pise *G DH*; *C wants*.

1973.   Il a. *G*; Une guerre amena de gent b. *H*; *C wants*.

1974.   .IIII.XX. en a bien 1. *G*; B. i furent .IIII. mois 1. *C which places this verse after* 1. 1975; *H wants*.

1975.   c. ont assis p. *CG*; a. onques n'i ot faintise *C*; p. devers le falisse *G D*; *H wants*.

1976.   p. revienent u. *E D*; p. revint u. *G*; *C H want*.

1977.   q. lor b. *G D*; 1. piaus n. *E*; o. cotes n. *G D*; n. cemises *G*; *C H want*.

1978.   p. remise *D*; p. bolie *E G*; *C H want*.

1979.   Ne n., gelee froidour ne n. *E*; ne vent ne n. *G*; *C DH want*.

1980.   u. machue m. *G DH*; *D places this verse after* 1. 1981; *C wants*.

1981.   m. que il f. *C*.

1982.   v. s'estoit j. *CG DH*; e. en une t. *C H*; e. a .I. cretel a. *D*; e. sour une t. *G*; *D adds*: Ses homes apela si lor dist sa devise.

1983.   *CG DH want*.

1984.   S. fait (dist *G*) Matabrune p. *CG*; v. foit que doi s. *E C*.

1985.   D. tex j. *D*; D. cais ai tel p. *G*; D. ce gars que je voy 1. *H*; t. me d. *E H*; e. troublie *G*; *C wants*.

93. *BE G D*

1986.   c. vienent une a. *D*; c. revint une a. *G*; *C H want*.

1987.   a bien .IX. p. *G D*; *C H want*.

1988.   c. li rois de l'isle de jouvent *G*; .I. dus de l'isle d'oriant *D*; r. qui sire est de Joument *E*; *D adds*: D'une part le castel vont ensamble loiant; *G D add further*: Lors regarde Elyas devers solel cochant; *C H want*.

1989.   Si vit (voit *G*) venir .I. *G D*; c. corant *D*; c. seant *G*; *C H want*.

1990.   S'en a. *E D*; Ki amaine .XM. et plus mon e. *G*; m. esciant *E G D*; *C H want*.

1991.   Cil qui plus (mains *D*) a de lonc n'a que .VII. (1. a bien .V. *D*) pies de grant *E D*; Tous li menres n'a que .VII. pies en estant *G*; *C H want*.

1992.   *C H want*.

1993.   *C H want*.

1994.   E. s'escrie bien soies vous venant *G*; 1. huce B.

E; *C DH want*.

1995. Elias vait encontre si les vait m. *D*; Par tres par pavellons les va tous m. *G*; *D adds*: Del secors qu'il li font et gent et avenant/ Et cele jent se logent terre vont porprenant; *C H want*.

1996. periere mout *G*; m. bone et bien jetant *D*; m. rice e. *E G*; *C H want*.

1997. Vers le c. le draicent t. *G*; *C H want*.

94. *BE CG DH*

1998. Une p. drechent e. *C H*; p. en amainent e. *D*; d. tres devant le castiel *C*.

1999. Dont s'apareillent escuier et dansiel *C*.

2000. l. voient n. *D*; l. sevent n. *E*; *C H want*.

2001. p. getterent qui trestout l. *H*; t. le p. *CG DH*.

2002. Abat jus d. *C*; Abatent d. *G D*; Abati d. *H*; e. le m. *CG DH*; m. chercel *D*; m. carnel *H*.

2003. c. ocist p. *H*; m. et .I. jovle (rice *G H*) dansel *G DH*; *C wants*.

2004. Matabrune le voit s. *CG DH*; Q. ce vit M. *E*; M. s'en j. *C*; M. ne lui mie fut bel *H*.

2005. e. tient E. *E CG D*; d. Baudiel *CG*; d. Babel *E D*; *H wants*.

2006. l. aroit m. *E*; m. c'a un trenchant f. *C*; m. nel poigne d. *D*; l. pointe d. *E G*; u. coutiel *CG D*; *H wants*.

2007. Trestout ne le pourfenge enfresi au cierviel *C*; Et nel f. *D*; Que nel face e. a .I. sien garconciel *G*; .I. aigniel *D*; *H wants*.

95. *BE G DH*

2008. p. plus d. *H*; m. remanoir q. *E G*; *C wants*.

2009. a cele t. *E*; t. jetee *E G H*; *C wants*.

2010. o. a la tiere jetee *G*; *C H want*.

2011. .XL. (Soixante *H*) en ont ocis a *G DH*; d. l'ont f. *E*; f. en une r. *H*; *C wants*.

2012. v. sa gent a. *H*; j. escriee *G H*; *C wants*.

2013. a. ja n. *G D*; a. que n. *E*; *C wants*.

2014. Si en issies aval la fors en mi le p. *G*; Ysson hors a eulx enmy celle p. *H*; f. as chans tres en mi cele estree *D*; *C wants*.

2015. J. porterai b. *E*; *CG DH want*.

2016. l. ert d. *E G*; *H adds*: En moult poy d'eure y eust moult belle gent armee; *C wants*.

2017. l. soit a. *E G*; *C H want*.

2018. E. respondent trestout ensi c. *G*; i. respondent tuit S. *E D*; S. ert c. *E*; *C H want*.

2019. *C H want*.

2020. s. plus de d. *D*; s. nule d. *E G*; *C H want*.

2021. c. a lor mal e. *E G D*; *C H want*.

2022. Si ont prises lor lances mainte targe doree *D*; p. sa lance et sa targe listee *G*; *C H want*.
2023. *C H want*.
2024. Lors s'en yssirent hors c. *H*; E. cil s. *D*; *C wants*.
2025. E. quant s. *D*; *C H want*.
2026. s. monte n. *E G D*; *C H want*.
2027. c. brocent a *D*; *C H want*.
2028. Tres d. le palis ert faite l'a. *D*; Droit d. le c. ont faite l'a. *G*; *C H want*.
2029. anqui avera m. *E which adds*: Et mainte vallans dame en ert veve clamee; *CG DH want*.
2030. Aves v. *G*; *C H want*.
2031. L'escu tint as enarmes a *D*; c. a la crois luminee *G*; *C H want*.
2032. Il deffeutre la lance qui fu bien acheree *D*; Mait la lance sour feutre trencant et afilee *G*; *C H want*.
2033. Si v. *G D*; t. roee *E D*; t. listee *G*; *C H want*.
2034. *C H want*.
2035. o. li a fraite et fausee *G*; e. despanee *E*; *C H want*.
2036. a l'anste p. *G D*; *C H want*.
2037. Del diestrier l'abat mort e. *G*; *C H want*.
2038. l. s'a l. *E*; *C H want*.
2039. Lors p. *D*; d. meslee *E G DH*; *C wants*.
2040. La ot tant pie (puing *G*) trencie t. *G D*; Tant pie tant p. *E*; La eust maint pie coupe et mainte tieste c. *H*; *C wants*.
2041. v. est l. *D*; l. tiere p. *G*; p. poplee *G D*; *C wants*.
2042. Et li tornent en fuies coume gent effree (sic) *D*; I. tornent tout e. *G*; *C H want*.
2043. *CG DH want*.
2044. S. je sui ici s. *E*; *CG DH want*.
2045. Ne fuiies mie e. a cele randounee *E*; *CG DH want*.
2046. *CG DH want*.
2047. a. grant esperonnee *E*; *CG DH want*.
2048. *CG DH want*.
2049. r. ensi c. *E*; *CG DH want*.
2050. t. asenee *E which adds*: Matabrune connut que mal fust ele nee; *CG DH want*.
2051. l. a escrie a *E*; *CG DH want*.
2052. v. bravee *E which places this verse after l.* 2050; *CG DH want*.
2053. *CG DH want*.
2054. v. coume mal euree *E*; *CG DH want*.
2055. *CG DH want*.

2056. e. amenee *E*; *CG DH want.*
2057. *E CG DH want.*
2058. *E CG DH want.*
2059. c. as male p. *E*; *CG DH want.*
2060. l. aceree *E*; *CG DH want.*
2061. d. s'avera le s. *E*; *CG DH want.*
2062. E. en va le l. *E*; *CG DH want.*
2063. *CG DH want.*
2064. r. sans nule demoree *E*; *CG DH want.*
2065. *CG DH want.*
2066. e. dusk'a le tere jus keue pasmee *E*; *CG DH want.*
2067. *E adds:* Et Elyas s'areste ja li eust caupee/ Le teste a tout le hiaume voiant le gent armee; *CG DH want.*
2068. h. i coururent si l'ont sus r. *E*; *CG DH want.*
2069. f. le t. puis si l. *E*; *CG DH want.*
2070. *CG DH want.*
2071. *CG DH want.*
2072. l. borc e. *E G D*; b. s'en (en *G*) entrent la pute gent desvee *G D*; *C H want.*
2073. e. li sien o. *G*; *C H want.*
2074. t. en ert r. *E*; *C H want.*
2075. Et l. *D*; Que l. *G*; l. portiers desore a l. *G D*; *C H want.*
2076. *C H want.*
2077. a. que n. *E*; *CG DH want.*
2078. o. s'en vait E. *G D*; E. je serai foursenee *E*; E. or s. *G*; d. sui jo malmenee *G D*; *C H want.*
96. *BE G D*
2079. *C H want.*
2080. E. si ot maint bon v. *E*; l. ot maint v. *G D*; *C H want.*
2081. Q. crent pour l'enfant e. *E*; Q. pour lui ierent mis en dolerous jornal *G*; s. coumunalment e. *D*; *C H want.*
2082. A la gent Matabrune livrent sovent (mout fier *G*) e. *G D*; *C H want.*
2083. E. orent l. *E*; *C H want.*
2084. I. guerpissent l. *G D*; g. lor t. *E*; *C H want.*
2085. p. por s. *E D*; d. l'anemi mortal *D*; *E adds:* Qu'il ne soient ocis et livre a grant mal; *C H want.*
2086. *C H want.*
2087. B. mainent .IIII. mil de petis c. *D*; f. .IIII. cent de la gent Elyas *G*; *C H want.*
2088. M. anqui mauvais jornal *G*; e. sa gent a. *E D*; *E adds:* Car ne les aiment pas de grant amour coral; *C H want.*
97. *BE CG DH*

2089. *C alters and abbreviates this laisse to 1.* 2116:
Matabrune la viele cui Diex duinst encombrier/ A
dit a ses barons ascoutes chevalier/ Se vous is-
sies la fors pour a iaus tournoier/ Par le mien
ensiant ne pores repairier/ Vos n'iestes pas
.DCC. et il son dis milier/ As feniestres en vint
dou grant palais plenier; *H alters this laisse to
1.* 2095: Les chevaliers s'en fuyent par deles ung
rocher/ Et les gens Elyas les chacent par der-
rier/ Et Elyas leur crie retournez chevalier/ Si
prenons le chastel pour Dieu le droittrier/ Tres
devant le chastel vindrent le chevalier/ Helyas
fait venir plus de trois cens archier/ Et avec
eulx y vindrent bien .III. cens charpentier; e.
escuier *E*; *G D want.*

2090. Or coumencent les gens Elias a *G D*; c. et c. et
h. *E*; *C H want.*

2091. O. del bien assalier serjant et cevalier *G D*; *C H
want.*

2092. d. .II.C. archier *D*; d. .XL. arcier *E*; d. .II.M.
arcier *G*; *C H want.*

2093. 1. petit aportent p. *D G*; a. aporterent et maus
e. *E*; e. pis d. *E D*; e. maus d. *G*; *C H want.*

2094. p. les peus detrenchier *D*; p. les pons pecoiier
G; *C H want.*

2095. Et aportent *E*; e. c'as (e. aux *H*) murs v. *G H*; m.
ont la drecier *E*; *C D want.*

2096. p. forment a pecoiier *G*; m. tost a *E*; a demail-
lier *D*; *C H want.*

2097. a le bare .CCCC. *E*; a le porte .CCCC. *G*; *C DH
want.*

2098. n. entrans pour nul denier *G*; *C DH want.*

2099. o. detrencie 1. *E H*; o. pecoie et 1. *G*; d. le ve-
rel f. *E G*; v. brissiet *G*; *C D want.*

2100. Contreval le fosse o. *H*; *C wants.*

2101. Q. la gent (les gens *G*) les vit si esploitier (1.
voient aprocier *G*) *E G*; *C H want.*

2102. Lors (Si *G*) escrient la c. por lor j. *G D*; j. re-
haitier *E*; *C H want.*

2103. Dont p., v. fier e. *D*; v. grant e. *E*; v. .I. e.
G; *C H want.*

2104. Tant chevalier abatre tante lance brisier *G*; 1.
brisie t. *D*; b. et tant escu p. *E*; t. fort e. *D*;
e. perchier *E D*; *C H want.*

2105. hauberc desromper e. *E*; hauberc deronpre e. *G*; s.
rompu e. *D*; *G adds*: Tant mort deseure l'autre
verser et trebucier; *C H want.*

2106. 1. tere v. *E*; p. joncier *E G*; *C H want.*

2107. Et il to[rn]ent en *D*; I. tournerent e. *E G*; .I.
rocier *E*; *C H want*.

2108. *C H want*.

2109. e. apres qui sont (forment coume *G*) bon chevalier
G D; *C H want*.

2110. *C H want*.

2111. p. puis l. *E G D*; *C H want*.

2112. h. se retraient a. *D*; h. s'en retornent a. *E*; h.
sont retorne a. *G*; *C H want*.

2113. M. les v. *G*; l. vit l. *G H*; v. du sens cuida des-
ver *H*; *C wants*.

2114. E. fait s. *G DH*; c. maintenant r. *D*; c. et tondre
et r. *G*; c. autour du chief r. *H*; *C wants*.

2115. Et puis si a *D*; M. afula le coife .I. *E*; viestue
cote a .I. *G*; *H adds*: Aux fenestres s'en va du
hault palais plainer; *C wants*.

2116. Lor comenche la viele Elyas a *C*; E. sel c. *E G*;
s. le prent a *H*.

2117. Or me di g. *C*; C. trait toy g. *H*; j. vel a toi
raisnier *G*; v. demander *H*.

2118. j. contre .I. *C which adds*: Par ton cors seul a
seul car jou plus nen i quier.

2119. P. ce point que vers lui ne te d. *H*; c. se vers
l. *E CG D*; p. justichier *C*.

2120. m. te mette d. *H*; d. pendre u *E*; a. et a *D*; u de
n. *E CG DH*.

2121. Toy et toutes tes gens sans traire ne lancer *H*;
e. ti compaignon s. *C*; e. toutes tes gens s. *G*.

2123. Tu ayes en ta merci povair de nous juger *H*; S.
soit e. *C*; e. ta m. de nous t. *CG D*; *CG add*: Qui
(Et *G*) trestous nos poras occire et detrenchier.

2124. Et li varles r. millor consail n. *G*; E. li dist
et jou mius ne vous q. *C*; r. chiertes mout m. *D*;
r. certes mieulx ne te q. *H*.

2125. S. le d. que j'ai m. *CG*; d. me p. *E CG*; e. puisse
D. *C*; p. li rois del ciel a. *D*; p. nostre segnour
a. *E*; p. Jhesus a. *G*; *H wants*.

2126. O. tos dist M. *CG*; M. si vous appareillies *C*; *H
wants*.

2127. c. d'armes apareillier *G*; e. haubregier *C D*; *E G
add*: Qui fera le batalle pour mon cors (Que vers
vous se conbate pour mon droit *G*) desraisnier; *H
wants*.

98. *BE CG DH*

2128. M. la viele cui Jhesu-Cris maleie *CG*; M. vient
droit a *D*; M. la viele va aux sciens s. *H*; e.
vint a se j. si les c. *E*; *CG add*: A sa gent vient
mout douchement lor prie (g. est venue a haute

vois s'escrie *G*).

2129. S. que jou ai f. *C D*; j. esbaudie *CG H*; j. res-
baudie *D*.

2130. p. a E. *H*; E. une rice e. *C*; E. une fiere e. *E*;
m. aatie *G D*.

2131. D'un chevalier vers lui a b. furnie *C*; c. a b. *E*;
c. de b. antye *H*; *C adds*: Cors a cors seul a seul
n'i ara compaignie.

2132. Se il i e. *G*; v. perdu aura l. *G DH*.

2133. Et si home seront dou tout e. *C*; j. seront e. *E*
H; *C adds*: Por faire mon voloir u de pierdre la
vie.

2134. Et se li miens estoit vaincus en la p. *C*; Et se
li max revient (1. pis en vient *H*) d. *G DH*; v. de
la n. *E D*; v. en la n. *H*.

2135. Nous s. *G*; S. reserons t. *G D*; S. demourrons t.
H; s. nos tout en la soie baillie *C*; s. ausi de-
dens s. *G*; t. desos s. *DH*.

2136. Q. si home l. *E D*; l'oirent s. *C*; e. n'i a celui
ne die (c. qui rie *H*) *C H*.

2137. N'en i a nul d'aus tous q. *E*; a cellui d'eulz
tous q. *H*; .I. sol d'ax (de *G*) tos q. *G D*; e. fie
E; *C wants*.

2138. Que j. *C H*; J. ne p. *D*; n. prendra a. *H*; p. armes
ne envaie *C*; p. armes vers s. *D*; p. a si faite e.
G; p. armes pour icelle e. *H*; f. aatie *G D*.

2139. Q. Matabrune l'ot dire est toute n. *C*; e. de duel
fu si n. *G*; e. a poy n'est enragye *H*.

2140. f. de car n. *G*; f. vous m. *D*; f. or m. *E*; fales
mie *G*; *C H want*.

2141. Pour quant s. *E*; *C H want*.

2142. b. tos jors serai s'amie *G D*; *C H want*.

2143. l. doins la s. *G D*; *C H want*.

2144. O. n'en i ot .I. qui mot ne son en die *G*; q. .I.
sol mot li d. *D*; q. vers li .I. m. *E*; *C H want*.

2145. *CG DH want*.

2146. *CG DH want*.

2147. N. pour son grant tresor ne pour se grant b. *E*;
CG DH want.

2148. En .I. cambre entra qui fu viele et a. *C*; Et la
vielle si (s'en *G*) entre e. *G D*; En ung celier
s'en va Damedieu la maudie *H*.

2149. t. i avoit d. *G*; e. jeta d. *C*; e. tira d. *H*.

2150. Ne le raemberroit li dus d. *C*; N. peussent r. *G*
D; p. nonbrer t. *G*; c. d'Esclobonie *E*; *H wants*.

2151. .III. s. *D*; a. de (en *G H*) qui ele s. *G DH*; s'en
f. *G*; *C wants*.

2152. t. les charga s. *H*; c. que li plus fors en plie

G; *C wants*.

2153. Adont revint l. *G*; L. escrie l. *C*; L. escria l. *D*; L. s'escrie l. *H*; v. a s. *CG H*; v. la g. *E D*; s. chevalerie *C*; s. grant b. *H*.

2154. Cil qui v. *C*; g. mal i. *H*; m. face contredie *E*; m. voist e. *G*; i. coroussie *C*.

2156. Cest tresor li donrai (metrai *G*) trestout (del tout *G*) e. *CG*; T. cis grans tresors si est e. *E*.

2157. O. n'en i ot .I. ki mot ne sun en d. *G*; o. celui qui .I. sol m. *D*; *C H want*.

2158. .I. chevaliers se drece cui Jhesu-Cris (Fors .I. seul chevalier que Jhesu *G*) maleie *CG*; Lors vint ung chevalier que m. *H*; m. .I. c., m. maudie *E*; *G adds*: Del tresor que il voit a eu grant envie.

2159. Il avoit non Hondres Damediex le maudie *C*; n. se Dex me beneie *G*; e. le crie *H*; *G adds*: Et si a-vons trouve qu'il iert nes de Hungrie.

2160. Dou grant avoir qu'il vit a eut g. *C*; s. ot mout g. *D*; *H wants*.

2161. O. tot le barnage a *DH*; *C wants*.

2162. D. se l. *CG DH*; t. me metes en b. *G*.

2163. Jou ne lairai or pas ne face l'arramie *C*; Jo fe-rai la bataille q. *G DH*; c. se Dex me (D. le m. *H*) beneie *DH*; c. ne vous en faurai mie *G*; e. poi-se n. *E*; *CG add*: Armes son mon destrier la fors en la berrie (A. fors m. d. caint l'espee fourbie *G*).

2164. Q. la viele l'entent e. *C DH*; Q. l'entent Mata-brune se li jure et afie *G*; o. vers le serf s. *D*; o. moult en fut resjoye *H*; *E adds*: De le joie qu'ele ot fu forment esbaudie; *G adds*: Que tres-tout le tresor ara en sa ballie.

2165. l. mist au col le t. *C which adds*: Que trestout li donra sa foit l'en a plevie; *G D want*.

2166. b. que n. *D*; b. si n. *E*; *CG H want*.

99. *BE CG DH*

2167. *C alters this laisse to 1*. 2198: S'Ondres se fist armer trestout couvertement/ D'auberc et d'ielme et d'escut a argent/ Ses cauces sont de fier n'en mentirai noient/ On li traist en la place .I. boin diestrier courant/ Et il i saut c'a archon ne si prent/ Et si ot lanche roide a gonfanon pendant/ La porte fist ovrir tos et isnielement/ Hondres en ist a espourons brochant/ Dela une foriest et biele et verdoiant/ Est Hondres aries-tes es Elyas atant/ Matabrune remaint si appiela sa gent/ Segnor dist ele entendes mon sanlant; c. a dit H. *E G*; H. armeures vous demant *H*.

2168.   Jo sui vos cevaliers b. *D*; p. .X. a. *G*; *H wants*.
2169.   b. bien en soies c. *G*; p. vos je le creant *D*; v. creant *E*; *H wants*.
2170.   t. iert m. *G*; e. li c. *E D*; *H wants*.
2171.   V. voir d. la v. ja n'en soies doutans *G*; *H wants*.
2172.   p. le fort s'en fu plus seurans *G*; *DH want*.
2173.   M. armer voel maintenant *G*; *DH want*.
2174.   E. vous rendrai u ferai recreant *G*; j. maintenant r. *E*; *DH want*.
2175.   e. ses cuers en fu (dont fu ses cuers *G*) joians *E G*; *DH want*.
2176.   c. se met l. *E*; e. entrer l. *H*; v. malfaisans *D*; v. maintenant *H*; *C wants*.
2177.   Unes (une *H*) armes e. *G H*; e. jete ki n'ierent pas p. *G*; t. moult riche et moult vaillant *H*; p. mout p. *D*; *E C want*.
2178.   H. arme l. *G D*; H. en ont arme tost et legierement *H*; v. Sorans *G*; *C wants*.
2179.   l. caucent k. *D*; l. lacent k. *E G*; m. furent v. *E*; *C H want*.
2180.   Li o. *D*; k. est f. *E D*; k. estoit jaserans *G*; *C H want*.
2181.   k. fu c. *E G*; *C DH want*.
2182.   Une espee lui ceignent qui fu roide et trenchant *H*; I. a c. *E D*; c. une espee qui valoit .C. *E*; *H adds*: Or est Hendris arme du tout a son talent; *CG want*.
2183.   k. avoit nom F. *H*; *CG want*.
2184.   Tout fut couvert de fer et derriere et devant *H*; l. atournemans *E*; *CG want*.
2185.   T. or fait (ce dist *E*) la vielle m. *E G D*; c. cest bon cheval vous rans *D*; c. cis e. *E*; c. ce boin ceval ferant *G*; *C H want*.
2186.   Et il est m. sus n. *E*; m. oncques n'y eust aidant *H*; n. li est a. *E G D*; *C wants*.
2187.   Hendres monte el cheval nus ne li est aidant *D*; Or est Hondres a. *G*; a son talent *E G*; *E G D add*: Et si est (Il sali *E*) (Et il est *G*) de plain vol salis desus Ferrant (v. sur le ceval courant *E*) (s. en l'auferant *G*); *C H want*.
2188.   Si p. *G D*; Puis p. *E*; A son col lui pendirent .I. *H*; c. son e. *D*; .I. fort escu pesant *G D*; e. reluisant *E H*; *C wants*.
2189.   Si a *E G*; e. son poing son (.I. *G*) fort espie t. *G D*; m. .I. e. qui'st t. *E*; *C H want*.
2190.   f. burni qui fu a. *D*; q. agus iert de g. *G*; k. ert a. *E*; a. devant *E G D*; *C H want*.

2191. Li portiers li defferme la porte maintenant *G DH*;
v. desfrema maintenant *E*; *C wants*.

2192. Et Hendres s. *D*; Et il s. *G H*; e. est yssu a *H*;
i. fors a *D*; i. defors a *G*; *C wants*.

2193. d. le (al *G*) gonfanon pendant *E G D*; *C H want*.

2194. u. riviere q. *D*; f. ki'st b. *G*; e. resplendissant
E D; *C H want*.

2195. En un pre d'un boys descendi a ytant *H*; a. et E.
G; *C wants*.

2196. M. avoit dit a ses gens maintenant *H*; r. sa jant
(sic) si apela s. *D*; a. sa jant *E G D*; *C wants*.

2197. S. ce d. li vielle p. *E G D*; *C H want*.

2198. e. son fier (le sien *G*) hardement (maltalant *D*)
E CG D; e. son contenement *H*.

2199. Dix de vous ou .XIIII. s'adoubent maintenant *H*;
A. si vos armes t. *C*.

2200. U vos .XII. *E CG*; V. .V. u *C*; V. .X. u *G D*; .XII.
u .XIII. que j. *E*; v. .X. c. *C*; v. .XII. c. *G*; c.
je le vos c. *E CG D*; *H wants*.

2201. S. feres c. *C*; S. faites e. *G H*; c. bruel .I. *G*;
a. ci devant *C*; a. maintenant *E*.

2202. S'il m. *G H*; m. Elyas d. *G*; m. Hondret t. *C*; m. a
Hendris d. *H*.

2203. Vous saures lues d. *D*; s. de l'agait t. *CG*; b.
aidies lui esromant *D*; b. tost et isnielement *C*;
b. tost et apertement *E*; b. hardit et conbatant
G; *CG H add*: Puis (Si *H*) copes Elyas (A Elyas co-
pes *G*) la tieste maintenant; *H adds further*:
Quant les barons l'entendent n'y a cil qui soit
lent/ Eulz vestent les haubers et heaumes lui-
sant/ Armes sont de leurs armes les chevaliers
vaillant; *H wants*.

2204. Tant vos donrai entre or fin e. *C which places
this verse after l.* 2200; c. et roge o. *D*; c.
ases o. *G*; t. d'or et tant d'argent *E*; *H wants*.

2205. Ne seres jamais p. *C places this verse with verse
2204 after l.* 2200; j. n'en iert p. *D*; p. en jor
de v. *C*; e. cest siecle v. *D*; t. lor v. *E G*; *H
wants*.

2206. E. il l. *CG*; c. ont respondu T. *E C D*; c. respon-
dent dame T. *G*; r. nous f. *E*; T. a vostre c. *CG
D*; *E adds*: Car cascuns ert forment d'argent desi-
rant; *H wants*.

2207. .XX. c. *E*; a. d'avoir sont c. *CG D*; a. ilueques
maintenant *E*; a. desirant *G*; *H wants*.

2208. L'uns avoit a n. *G*; .I. ot a n. *E*; *C H want*.

2209. t. Malquidant *E*; *C H want*.

2210. Et Fornis et Tieris M. et Corocans *G*; e. Corians

E; *C DH want*.
2211. Et Loros de Pavie et li f. *G*; e. li preus Maldui-
        sans *E*; f. Malparlant *G*; *C DH want*.
2212. Li .I. d'ax l. *D*; d. les c. *E G D*; a. Balant *G*;
        G D add: Arme sont de lor armes li cors Deu les
        cravant; *D adds further*: Quant tot .X. sont arme
        n'i ot arestement/ Il ont laichie lor elmes ou li
        fins ors resplant; *C H want*.
2213. Puis v. lor a. dont la maile est tenans *D*; *C H*
        want.
2214. Si c. *D*; p. reflamboians *E*; o. reluisans *D*; *C H*
        want.
2215. Es siele[s] sont monte et es chevaus courans *G*; *C*
        DH want.
2216. Cascuns pent a son col .I. fort escu pesant *G*; c.
        lor f. *D*; e. pesans *E D*; *C H want*.
2217. *C H want*.
2218. Li p. l. ovri l. *G D*; *C H want*.
2219. De la vile issent trestout communaument *C*; Puis
        s'en yssirent a *H*; E. cil s. *D*.
2220. P. le g., s. va levant *E*; *CG DH want*.
2221. *C H want*.
2222. f. s'ariestent maintenant *C*; f. se metent t. *E*;
        f. en entrent t. communaument *G*; *C adds*: Les .I.
        brueillet par dales .I. pendant; *H wants*.
2223. a. si li vait creantant *D*; *C H want*.
2224. Q. se Huondres conquiert Elyas c. *G*; *C H want*.
2225. Qu'il en a. *D*; Que il l'en menront p. *E*; p. ou il
        morront s. *D*; p. coureciet et dolant *G*; *C H want*.
2226. o. atourne orgillous e. *G*; *C H want*.
2227. s. coumandement *D*; *H adds*: Elyas fait ses armes
        aporter maintenant.
2228. Il e. *E*; D. ne li deffant *D*; *CG H want*.
100. *BE G D*
2229. b. li felon enbuissie l. *G*; *C H want*.
2230. n. fist mie lonc p. *G D*; m. le p. *E*; *C H want*.
2231. Q. vit Endon el camp vint iluec et e. *E*; *CG DH*
        want.
2232. S. fait Elias or sachies entresait *D*; S. cou dist
        li enfes tout bielement a tret *G*; n. dist il ne
        n'i ait plait *E*; *C H want*.
2233. Ves la .I. cevalier arme ou il s'estait *G D*; *C H*
        want.
2234. Envers lui doi jo faire la bataille sans plait *D*;
        Vers qui jou doi conbatre a batalle entresait *G*;
        l. plait *E*; *C H want*.
2235. E. il respondent sire t. *G*; .I. fait *D*; .I. trait
        E; .I. hait *G*; *C H want*.

2236. *C H want.*
2237. r. or soit com il li plaist *D*; r. doucement et a
E; b. et sans plait *G*; *C H want.*
2238. Or m'armerai je donques et puis armer s'en vait
G; t. et voit et f. *E*; *C DH want.*
2239. a. li aportent et il armer se fait *D*; d. aporter
li ont fait *E which adds*: Et Elyas s'arma ilue-
ques tout a trait; *CG H want.*
101. *BE G DH*
2240. Deux bons chevaliers l'ont arme e. *H*; *C wants.*
2241. .I. varlet biel de cors et de vis et de face *G*;
c. n'i font lonc arestage *D*; p. lor g. *E*; *C H
want.*
2242. .I. hauberc li vestirent et ses cauces l. *D*; Li a
v. l'auberc et les cauces l. *G*; c. cauces l. *E*; *C
H want.*
2243. d. de grant pris qui ert de son lignage *D*; c. de
viaire e. *E*; *CG H want.*
2244. Et puis li lacha l. *D*; Puis a laciet son ielme q.
G; *C H want.*
2245. Et a c. l'e. qui fu del tans d'Aage *D*; Il a trai-
te l'espee dont fera sans manace *G*; Une espee lui
ceignent de l'oeuvre de G. *H*; *G adds*: Ricement
est armers (sic) Dex doinst que bien li face/ Li
armure k'il a quant venra en la place; *E C want.*
2246. Arme l'ont d. *E*; Elyas est arme n. *H which places
this verse after l.* 2241; a. or li prest Dex sa
grace *DH*; *CG want.*
102. *BE CG DH*
2247. *C alters this laisse*: Cil de l'ost Elyas ne sont
mie arieste/ Mout ont bien lor signor garni et
conrae/ De toutes armes de ceval abrievet/ Et il
s'est maintenant a Jhesu-Cris commandes/ Sires
peres propisses par tes saintes bontes/ Me garis-
sies mon cors qui ne soie affoles/ Atant es .I.
preudoume fu de grant aet/ Del castiel est issus
coiement atelet/ Freres estoit Marcon que Diex ot
ralumet/ Mout ama Elyas si l'en a appielet/ Sire
fait il a lui or oies mon penser/ La devens en
cel bos a .I. agait frumet/ Il sont mien ensiant
.X. chevalier armet/ Qui vos welent occire ains
qu'il soit aviespret/ Prendes de vos barons si
les faites armer/ Si faites .I. agait de par
Saint Ouneret/ Au besoing vos aidront ja nen iert
trestourne/ Quant Elyas l'entent s'en a Diu aou-
ret/ Ensi con li preudons li ot dit et conte/ Se
sont .X. chevalier maintenant conreet/ D'armes et
de cevaus se sont bien atornet/ Et ont fait lor
agait si sont ou bos entret/ Or ores la bataille

et estour mortel; Elyas ont mout bien et ricement a. *G*; M. par ont bien l'enfant l. *D*; *C H want*.

2248.   .I. capelain en a maintenant a. *G*; *C wants*.

2249.   s. font a. *D*; *C wants*.

2250.   p. se sont eulz deulx e. *H*; *C wants*.

2251.   *C H want*.

2252.   Elyas s'agenoulla s. *H*;   d. les sains a e. *DH*;   *C wants*.

2253.   Adonc vint .I. *H*;   q. ert de g. *D*; q. getta g. *H*; *C wants*.

2254.   E. guison d. *H*; g. d'un c. *G H*; *C D want*.

2255.   e. son o. *H*; *C D want*.

2256.   E. dist l. *E G H*; *C wants*.

2257.   c. saces envers H. *G*; *C wants*.

2258.   A Matabrune mis son agait a *DH*; M. i a mis son agait a *G*; m. ens el bos rame *E*; *C wants*.

2259.   Il sont .X. chevalier tout d'armes conraet *G*; a. sont a l'agait ale *D*; *E C H want*.

2260.   Qui t. *G DH*; a. qu'il s. *D*; a. le viespre soune *G*; a. qui s. *H*; *C wants*.

2261.   Lor a. est a destre les .I. arbre r. *D*; destre desour .I. *E*; *CG H want*.

2262.   f. seurte *E*; *C wants*.

2263.   De .XV. chevaliers deu mex de ton barne *D which places this verse after l.* 2264; s. de t. *E*; *CG H want*.

2264.   Si r. *G DH*; E. en fait .I. *G*; E. fait tost .I. *H*; a. el non s. *E*; *C wants*.

2265.   a. ja n'en iert trestorne *G D*; *C H want*.

2266.   Si p. *E*; f. que j'ai ci trop e. *G*; *C H want*.

2267.   Va a Dieu te comment qui te croisse bonte *H*; c. qu'il te preste barne *D*; *E G H add*: Et li angles (Lors *G H*) s'en va (e. torne *G*) (e. reva *H*) n'i a plus demoure; *G adds further*: Elyas saut en pies si a Dieu reclamet; *CG want*.

103.   *BE G DH*

2268.   *C H want*.

2269.   Elyas les sains enclinez et joy *H*; v. le s. *G*; *C wants*.

2270.   Ses barons le conta tout en sont esbaudit *G*; A ses hommes s'en vient s. *H*; I. vint a *E*; *C wants*.

2271.   Comme l'ange l'a conseille e. *H*; l. a e. *D*; *CG want*.

2272.   Lors se sont escriet t. *G*; E. il l. *E D*; E. eulx l. *H*; *C wants*.

2273.   A. soiies Dex que nous aves garis *G*; k. si nous a *E*; *H adds*: Seigneurs fait Elyas pour amour je vous pri/ Que vous facez un guet emmy ce boys

yci/ Se j'ay mestier de vous que me soyez ami. *C wants.*
2274. Mout sont p. *G*; *C H want.*
2275. Eslissies de vostre homes b. *G which places this verse after 1. 2273*; n. car bien s. *D*; n. que bien s. *E G*; *C wants.*
2276. Cex qui coumanderes feront l'agait forni *D*; a. furni *E which adds:* Et Elyas l'otroie que il le veut ensi; *CG H want.*

104. *BE G D*
2277. S. dist E. *E G D*; E. or d. *G D*; d. se v. *E*; *C H want.*
2278. Et li grant j. *E D*; Li gent Elyas j. *G*; f. cest a. *G D*; *C H want.*
2279. p. ont dit q., e. isi f. *G*; *C H want.*
2280. l. ferons nous issi iert e. *G*; i. bien sacent e. *D*; *C H want.*
2281. S. dist E. *E G D*; E. or n. *D*; *C H want.*
2282. p. por Jhesu qui tot coumande et f. *D*; q. fait et biel et lait *G*; t. bien set et f. *E*; *C H want.*
2283. Q. des grans i ait .VII. (.X. *G*) des petis .VIII. *G D*; g. i ait siet *G*; *C H want.*
2284. e. il m. *E G*; m. i a. *E*; m. m'en est *G*; *C H want.*
2285. A. saurons n. *D*; l. qex l'aura m. *E D*; *CG H want.*
2286. Il respondent ensanble si soit t. *G*; l. petit t. *D*; b. entresait *G D*; *C H want.*
2287. f. de lor tentes t. *D*; *CG H want.*
2288. m. es seles q. que s. *D*; q. soit bel ne qui l. *E*; *CG H want.*
2289. Anqui auront peor cil qui sont en l'agait *D*; *CG H want.*
2290. e. el bruellet e. *E*; *CG DH want.*

105. *B G D*
2291. o. quanqu'E. *D*; *E C H want.*
2292. Les .X. millors des autres ont d. *G*; L. .VII. m. *D*; *E C H want.*
2293. e. sont .VIII. d. *D*; e. a .VII. *G*; *E C H want.*
2294. Mout par sont bien armet trestout s. *G*; D. .VII. g. *D*; *G adds:* D'armes et de cevaus ainc n'i ot nul respit/ Or en soit Dex al droit et li Sains Esperis; *E C H want.*
2295. e. dist *D*; *E CG H want.*
2296. L'autres ot non J. si com il est e. *D*; *E CG H want.*
2297. t. fu mout vaillans si ot a non Tierris *D*; *E CG H want.*
2298. Li quars ot a n., q. Bellevit *D*; *E CG H want.*
2299. N. et a clergie a. *D*; *E CG H want.*

2300. G. vilenie ne fist *D*; *E CG H want*.
2301. *E CG DH want*.
2302. *E CG H want*.
2303. c. sans noise et sans despit *D which adds*: Tuit cil .VII. sont cosin raisons est c'on li sist; *E CG H want*; *H adds as initial verse of the following laisse*: Or ont basti le guet les chevaliers vaillant.

106. *BE CG DH*

2304. Monterent es chevaulx sans targer tant ne grant *H*; Tuit .VII. en sont m. *D*; s. tout .XX. armet s. *CG*; c. corans *CG D*; *G adds*: Lances roides sour feutres et escus verdoians.
2305. s. relisent li .VIII. des meillors jans *D*; p. s'aparellent .VII. *E*; *CG H want*.
2306. Li .I. ot non Henris et li autres Morans *D*; *CG H want*.
2307. E. li autres Phelipes et li quars Engerrans *D*; *CG H want*.
2308. E. le cinquisme Piere et le s. *E*; l. sistes Adans *D which adds*: Et li semes Herbers .I. dus fors et poissans/ Li huitimes apres fu apeles Hermans; *E adds*: Et le seme Girart qui mout estoit vallant; *CG H want*.
2309. f. tex jans *D*; t. grant *E*; *CG H want*.
2310. c. qu'il avoient corans *D*; *CG H want*.
2311. Et pendent a lor cos les fors escus pesans *D*; c. .I. fort escu luisant *E*; *CG H want*.
2312. Et prenent en lor poins les fors espies trenchans *D*; p. .I. fort espil tenscant *E*; *D adds*: A .III. clox de fin or lor gonfanons pendans; *CG H want*.
2313. Bien se sont embusciet desous les desrubans *C*; Ou boys s'en sont venus sans targer tant ne quant *H which adds*: Dessoubz ung olivier descendent maintenant/ Or diray d'Elyas qui fut preux et vaillant.
2314. a. grans fu (est *G*) ses hardemans *G D*; *C H want*.
2315. Elyas est montes grans est ses hardemens *C*; Il sist sour .I. destrier qui avoit non Ferans *G*; Il monta en la scelle du bon destrier courant *H*; d. destrier qui est corans *D*; b. ceval c. *E*; *CG H add*: Il (Si *H*) hurte le destrier (Il le fiert durement *G*) des espourons trenchans (brochant *H*).
2316. Et pendi a *E*; e. prist a le crois qui n'estoit pas pesans *D*; c. l'escu qui fu vallant *E*; *CG H want*.
2317. Et prist e., d. l'espie qui fu trenchans *D*; .I. bon espil trenchant *E*; *CG H want*.

2318. H. en v. *C*; e. vient d. *G*; e. ala qui pres du bois l'atent *H*; v. tost q. *D*; q. l'aloit atendant *E*.

2319. A haute vois escrie mal vous est couvenant *E*; Q. Hendrys l'apparceust si cria M. *H*; E. si huce M. *CG D*.

2320. Sen bataille n'yres s. *H*; D. me soit a. *DH*; e. garans *D*; *CG want*.

2321. A. vos iert cis jours dolereus (perillox *D*) (oribles *G*) et pesans (nuisans *D*) *CG D*; *C adds*: Vos i mentes lecieres dist Elyas li frans/ A cest mot laisse corre le boin diestrier corant; *G D add*: Et Elyas respont vassal com ies vaillans (v. trop ies parlans *G*)/ Anqui verra on bien qui en iert (q. sera *G*) recreans; *H wants*.

2322. A ces mos s. *G*; Eulx deux se d. sans nul delayement *H which adds*: Grans coups s'entre donnerent es escus reluisant/ Que les lances de fresne vont toutes tronchonnant; *C wants*.

107. *BE CG DH*

2323. A ces mot s. *C*; Eulx deux s. *H*; d. n'i ont (sont *H*) plus ariestet *C DH*; d. sans plus de demore *E*; *G wants*.

2324. Il hurtent les destriers d. *D*; C. a s. *CG*; p. le d. *E CG*; s. ceval d. *E G*; d. des esperons d. *E CG D*; e. hurtet *CG*; e. dores *E*; *H wants*.

2325. Et deffeutrent l. *D*; a. lor l. *E*; *CG H want*.

2326. escus se *C*; e. devant s. *D*; e. des cols se vont g. *G*; *CG add*: Les hantes brisent s'en sont li fier voler (Et li troncon des lances sont contremont vole *G*)/ Que li .I. ne li autres n'est plaies ne navres/ Li ceval sont tirant si sont outre passet (Li chevalier se tienent outre s'en sont p. *G*) *H wants*.

2327. b. les ont frait et troe *E D*; *CG H want*.

2328. Li b. a. des dos s. rot e. *D*; s. et ront et desfausse *E*; *CG H want*.

2329. P. dejoste les costes e. *D*; l. aisseles e. *E*; *CG H want*.

2330. Il traient (sacent *G*) les espees dont li puing sont doret *CG*; p. li brant sont trait letre *D*; b. ont recoure *E*; *H wants*.

2331. Desour leur e. *C*; A. dessous l. *G*; *CG add*: Que flours et pieres (Q. les flours et les pieres *G*) en ont jus craventet; *H wants*.

2332. E. va ferir .I. caup desmesure *E*; f. sor son e. *C*; *CG add*: Si que trestout li a fraint et esquartelet (a fendut et enbare *G*); *D adds*: Que il li a

fendu et l'auberc entame; *E adds:* Amont par mi
son elme qu'il ot a or geme; *H wants.*

2333. Et p. *D*; p. est li brans jus coules *G*; *E C H
wants.*

2334. Que le ceval Oendon a par mi troncoune *E*; a le c.
D G; *C H wants.*

2335. H. ciet a *CG*; c. est vierses *C*; c. abrieve *G*; *H
wants.*

2336. p. a guise de maufes *C*; p. bien samble f. *D*; p.
bien resanble maufe *G*; h. desmesure *E*; *H wants.*

2337. Va ferir Elyas s. *CG*; E. a feru s. *D*; f. de son
branc acere *G*; s. ielme jemet *E C*; *G adds:* Sour
la crois de l'escut li a grant cop doune; *H
wants.*

2338. .I. petit sos l. *D*; Desur le boucle d'or l. *E*;
.I. poi desour l. *G*; e. quasse *D*; e. caupe *E*; e.
troe *G*; *C H want.*

2339. Chiertes f. *D*; m. m'i feri H. *G*; i seres H. *E*; *C
H want.*

2340. Helyas trait l'espee dont le pom fut dore *H*; I. a
t., a. pont d. *D*; *CG want.*

2341. Sour son hiaume le fiert de si tres grant fierte
G; Et broche le cheval et va feri[r] Hendrye *H*;
Hendre fiert sus l. *D which adds:* Et la coiffe
desos et le bachin froe; *G adds:* Que trestout
l'esquartielle pour poi ne l'a tue/ Elyas fait
Huondres or m'as tu engane; *C wants.*

2342. t. quant m. *D*; q. il n. *E*; a jete *D*; a tue *E*; *CG
H want.*

2343. H. voit l. *E*; c. pres va le sens desve *D*; *CG H
want.*

2344. v. le vassal si l'a araisoune *E*; *CG H want.*

2345. *CG DH want.*

2346. Jo vous rennerai par tans ceste b. *D*; *CG H want.*

2347. *C H want.*

2348. A estoc v. *D G*; *C H want.*

2349. c. ert f. *D*; a mie passe *G*; p. empiret *C*; *H
wants.*

2350. De l'espee d'acier s. *H*; s. tout s. *C*; t. .I.
(tel *G H*) cop li a dounet *CG H*; t. ala ferir H. *E*.

2351. Que le p. et l'espaule lui a dessevre *H*; a. l'es-
pee l. *CG*; l. bras li a del cors s. *E D*.

2352. s. navret s. *CG H*; .I. poing j. *H*.

2353. Et ceulx d. *H*; a. l'oirent si se sont destraiiet
C; a. se sont tous s. *H*; e. del bois sont s. *G D*;
b. desrote *G DH*; *H adds:* Quant Elyas les vit si a
Hendris tue.

2354. Vers Elyas en viennent (s'en tornent *G*) d. *CG*; c.

sus de b. apreste *E*; b. atourne *G which adds*:
Quant Elyas les voit si a Dieu reclame/ Le cief
de son ceval a devers eus tourne; *DH want*.

2355. 0. le consaut li Sires qui en crois fu penes *G*;
s. pitie *D*; *C H want*.

2356. Que cil de l'a. l'ont mout forment a. *D*; o. si a.
E; *CG H want*.

108. *BE CG DH*

2357. *C wants*.

2358. Cil d. *CG*; Et cil d. *DH*; a. salirent t. *E C*; a.
issent t. *G*; s. trestout .X. *C*; s. ensamble tres-
tot (tous *H*) dis *G DH*; s. a .I. cris *E*.

2359. Elyas escrierent C. *C*; Si crient Elyas C. *G*; E.
escrient C. *DH*.

2360. r. n'en e. *E G D*; *CG add*: Quant Elyas l'entent ne
fu mie esbahis (entrepris *G*)/ Il hurte le dies-
trier trait le brant coulorich (1. ceval des es-
porons masis *G*); *G adds further*: En sa main tint
l'espee dont li puins fu brunis; *C H want*.

2361. Va ferir le premier sour son ielme burnit (p. de-
sour son escut bis *G*) *CG*; Et Elias en fiert l.
DH; l. premier ens e. *E*; *CG add*: Tout li trencha
et le coiffe (Trestout li a trenchiet et le bouce
G) et le vis.

2362. Li bers estort son cop cil ciet mort el lairis *G*;
M. l'avoit enverse or vait as lor en p. *D*; M.
l'abbat a ses p. or est aux autres p. *H*; a. pis
DH; *C wants*.

2363. Et .IX. (Et li .IX. *G*) laissent courre les cevaus
ademis (destriers arabis *G*) *CG which add*: Elyas
ont ferut devant en (vont ferir sour *G*) l'escut
bis (ademis *G*); *G adds further*: Se Dex ne li ai-
dast et li Sains Esperis; *H wants*.

2364. Ja l'euissent enki Elyas mort u pris (e. illuec
detrenciet et ocis *G*) *CG*; *H wants*.

2365. Et s. *H*; Q. sa gent (ses gens *D G*) l. *E CG D*; Q.
la g. Elyas se sont du bois hors mis *H*; b. furent
m. *CG*; b. se sont m. *D*; b. erent m. *E*; *H adds*:
Vers les gens a la vielle s'en vont tous estour-
dis.

2366. *CG H want*.

2367. B. as esperons s. *D*; *CG H want*.

2368. u ert *D*; *CG H want*.

2369. n. vait m. *D*; *CG H want*.

2370. Et Gautiers point le vair et Arondel Henris *D*; *CG
H want*.

2371. Et Phelipes Bauchant et Pierres l'arabis *D*; b.
Vairon e. *E*; *CG H want*.

2372. Et Herbers Passeavant qui a le col tot bis *D*; e.
       bien ademis *E*; *CG H want.*
2373. Lances s. *C*; l. enfeutrees s. *D*; f. vinrent (vie-
       nent *G*) tout ademis *CG*; f. vont vers (sur *E*) lor
       anemis *E D*; *H wants.*
2374. Ne vit si grant estour n. *G*; h. de mere v. *D*; *C H*
       want.
2375. *D adds*: Li .I. viennent as autres bien se sont
       envais; *CG want.*
2376. m. orent pense d. est qui aient p. *E*; *CG DH want.*
109. *BE CG DH*
2377. Or commence la noyse ou pre et l. *H*; p. fu f. *D*;
       e. durs l. *C*; e. fiers l. *G D*; e. fiere l. *E C*;
       CG add: Li .X. contre les .X. (.XX. *G*) n'orent
       onques duree/ Tout furent mort et pris en miliu
       de la pree (*C wants*)/ Hondres i fu ocis s'ot la
       tieste (o. et la tieste ot *G*) copee/ Et fu tos
       detrenchies en miliu de la pree (*G wants*)/ De
       l'avoir que il ot a pris maises denrees (qu'il ot
       pris a eut sa sodee *G*).
2378. v. fu e. *CG*; e. sa t. *C DH*; *CG add*: Si a oit la
       jus la noise et la criee (o. la noisse tout con-
       treval la pree *G*).
2379. Or c. *G*; B. cuida k. *C*; B. velt que E. *D*.
2380. Sa gent regarde q. *C*; e. sa gent q. *G*; h. mout
       (si *G*) le voit malmenee *CG*; l. meslee *D*; *H wants.*
2381. Por .I. sol petitet n. *D*; *CG H want.*
2382. Chiaus dedens crie a mout grant alenee *C*; Ele a
       .I. cor sounet s. *G*; Elle sonna ung cor sa gent a
       r. *H*; g. assamblee *E DH*; g. escriee *G*; *C adds*:
       Issies la fors signor a bataille noumee/ Et il si
       fisent caskuns lanche levee; *H adds*: Or aux armes
       fait elle ja n'y ait demouree/ Ysson la hors a
       eulx en my celle pree/ Qui Elyas prendra m'amour
       lui ay donnee/ Bien .VII. cens sont montez chas-
       cun d'eulz a espee/ Vers Elyas s'en vont chascun
       lance levee.
2383. o. mout bele gent armee *G D*; *G adds*: .X.M. en
       sont arme ains n'i ot ariestee; *C H want.*
2384. Et montent e. *D*; *CG H want.*
2385. Il ont prise lor lanches et lor t. *D*; *CG H want.*
2386. *CG H want.*
2387. De la ville s'en issent a batalle ordenee *G which*
       places this verse after l. 2388; c. lance levee
       D; *C H want.*
2388. Contre le s. ont mout g. *G which places this ver-*
       se after l. 2389; *C H want.*
2389. Li e. et li e. *G D*; *C H want.*

2390. Q. les vit a la c. *H*; E. le v. *E G*; *C wants*.
2391. m. Dieu apielle souvent l'a r. *G*; *C H want*.
2392. v. devant l. *E*; v. venue l. *G*; *C H want*.
2393. E. leur est encontre alee *C*; k. france est e. *D*;
       H wants.
2394. a. a mout grant alenee *D*; a. coume gens houneree
       E; a. une grant randounee *G*; *C H want*.
2395. l. son d. *D*; *CG H want*.
2396. l. fendent les pis et l'eskinee *E*; *CG H want*.
2397. A l'abaissier des lances oissies grant criee *CG*;
       a. brait o. *E D*; b. a t. *D*; b. ot t. *E*; *H wants*.
2398. C'on les peust oir plus d'une grant liuee *G*; Et
       quant ces chevaliers oyrent l. *H*; ont le noise
       escoutee *E*; *H adds*: Es chevaulx sont montez chas-
       cun teste armee/ Quant les vit grant joye en a
       menee; *C wants*.
2399. c. l'estree *D*; *E adds*: Adont se fu li os mainte-
       nant armee; *CG add*: Ki ains ains qui mius mius
       ont lor gent ordenee (*C wants*)/ Or en iert la ba-
       talle toute renouvelee (*C wants*)/ A cel poindre
       ont (La ot tante anste fraite *G*) tante targe tra-
       wee/ Tant clavain rout tante enseigne doree (c.
       desronput tante malle fausee *G*)/ Vers la gent Ma-
       tabrune est la pierde (dolours *G*) tournee/ Que
       del sanc de lor cors est vermelle la pree (*C
       wants*)/ Trestout communaument ont la porte passee
       (*G wants*)/ Contreval le castiel vinrent a la mel-
       lee (*G wants*).
2400. c. demandee *E*; *CG H want*.
2401. a mout g. *D*; *CG H want*.
2402. e. li os assamblee *D*; *CG H want*.
2403. d. meslee *D*; *CG H want*.
2404. L. eust maint poing coupe et mainte t. *H*; t.
       poing trenchie t. *D*; *CG want*.
2405. *CG H want*.
2406. j. Matabrune f. *D*; v. est l. *DH*; l. terre p. *D*; *H
       adds*: Ne peuvent mais souffrir la bataille adu-
       ree/ En fuite sont tourne comme gens esfree; *CG
       want*.

110. *BE D*
2407. M. fu g. *E D*; *CG H want*.
2408. f. en l'estor qui est grans *D*; *CG H want*.
2409. m. se gent s. *E*; j. mout f. *D*; *CG H want*.
2410. l. destrier d. *D*; *CG H want*.
2411. Si tint traite l'espee dont li pons fu luisans *D*;
       b. avoit trait k. *E*; *CG H want*.
2412. *CG H want*.
2413. T. detrenche e. *D*; b. li b. *E*; *CG H want*.

2414. v. de mors et de s. *E which adds*: Et le gent Ma-
tabrune vont entour lui fuiant; *CG H want.*

111. *BE G DH*

2415. E. vit s. *D*; v. se gent fierement m. *E G*; v. ses
gens r. *H*; *G adds*: De lances et d'espees mout
ruistement ferir/ Il escrie segnor pour sa gent
esbaudir; *C wants.*

2416. *C H want.*

2417. Ce qu'il attaint a c. tantost couvient mourir *H*;
v. os j. *D*; *H adds*: Et les gens a la vielle ne
pevent plus souffrir/ Au chastel sont venus et
font la porte ouvrir; *C wants.*

2418. m. vienra mires p. *D*; p. les (ses *G*) plaies g. *G
D*; *C H want.*

2419. *G D add*: Trestot li esquartielle coisfe nel pot
garir (Que li chercles a or ne le p. garandir *D*);
C H want.

2420. D. qu'en l. *D*; l. cervielle l. *G*; *C H want.*

2421. M. l'abat p. *G D*; r. contre t. *D*; r. a ses pies
coi q. *G*; c. qu'en d. *E G D*; d. marir *D*; d. ave-
nir *G*; *G adds*: Cil cols k'il ont veut les fait
tous esmarir; *C H want.*

2422. Q. les gens a *E*; *CG H want.*

2423. I. tornerent l. *D*; I. lor livrent l. *E*; I. ont
tourne l. *G which adds*: Matabrune les voit dou
sens quida issir/ La porte lor a fait isnielement
ouvrir/ Tuit ensanble i entrerent nel porent re-
tenir/ Per les caces coumencent lor cors a depar-
tir; *C H want.*

2424. Enfresi c'al c. *D*; O. dus k'al c. *E*; c. nes pot
on retenir *D*; v. tenir *E*; *CG H want.*

112. *BE CG DH*

2425. La gent l. *CG D*; Des gens le male v. *E*; *H wants.*

2426. Ens el c. *E*; c. s'en r. *D*; s. entrerent e. *E D*;
CG H want.

2427. Et la gen Elyas ont les portaus (le postie *G*) p.
CG; Or sont les chevaliers ens ou chastel entrez
H; h. ont les pons trespasses *D*; s. el tourel en-
tres *E*; o. passe *G*.

2428. Tous les o. *C*; l. occient et gietent es fosses *CG
D*; *H wants.*

2429. d. .VC. o. *C*; d. .II.M. o. *G*; .XL. et mors e. *E*;
e. affoles *CG D*; *H wants.*

2430. Puis crierent au feu ja tout fut embrassez *H*; f.
environ de tous les *C*; f. que il s. *E*; f. es mas-
sons l'ont boute *G*.

2431. Mais E. l'enfant c. *H*; E. lor est isnelement (a-
vant *H*) passes *E DH*; p. s'est a. *G*.

2432. l. cevax soit mors ne affoles *E*; s. ne ars ne brules *C*; n. embrases *G D*.
2433. p. des d. *E*; *CG DH want*.
2434. Ou palais monte les marberins *C*; Il monta en la salle contremont les degres *G*; Il est monte a-mont par les maistres degrez *H*; A. une g. s. en montent les degres *D*.
2435. M. trouva sus ou palais licez *H*; a. en (li *G*) est ales *CG*.
2436. l. vit a l. *H*; les grenons l. *CG*; les cex (sic) l. *D*.
2437. Qu'est cou f. *C H*; Ce qu'est f. *D*; Que c'est f. *G*; e. dist l. *E C*; f. Matabrune M. *CG DH*; s. ar-rivez *H*.
2438. Que es cou que t'aiue s. *C*; a. est cou (se c'est *DG*) Diex u m. *CG D*; *H wants*.
2439. C. dist E. *E CG*; E. mal fustes arrivez *H*; *G pla-ces this verse after* l. 2441.
2440. Diex vos face j. *CG D*; Mourir vous couvendra c. *H*; c. ouvre aves *E CG DH*; *H adds*: Elle print Elyas en feri au senestre costez/ Quant Elyas le vit a poy n'est forcenez.
2441. Encor a. *C*; j. car desiervi l'aves *CG*; *D adds*: Car de vilaine mort iert vos cors tormentes; *H wants*.
113. *BE CG DH*
2442. M. fait d. *CG*; *H wants*.
2443. E. escrie a *D*; E. en apielle a *G*; *C H want*.
2444. Et par le castiel veront si chevalier plorant *C*; v. les c. *G*; *DH want*.
2445. Et cil i sont venu qui mex mex a e. *D*; E. en v. *C*; E. se sont venu e. *E*; E. aceurent maintenant *G*; t. corant *E C D*; *H wants*.
2446. s. tantos i. *C*; *H wants*.
2447. Et saisi un espiel (une espee *G*) a *CG*; .I. cou-tiel t. *C*; *H wants*.
2448. Va ferir Elyas p. *CG*; f. deriere m. *D*; *H wants*.
2449. Qu'ele li passe le haubierc j. *C*; Le hauberc li pecoie et le coste c'ot grant *E*; l. perce et le hauberc li fent *D*; l. trence et li elme verdoi-ant *G*; *H wants*.
2450. f. raier j. *E D*; f. voler j. *G*; c. desi as pies l'e. *D*; c. dus qu'al pie d. *E*; p. eramment *G*.
2451. D. nel garandist o. *D*; *CG H want*.
2452. Elyas se regarde q. *G*; Quant Elyas le vit si en fut mout dolent *H*; E. il garda ariere q. *C*; q. il f. *CG D*.
2453. M. saisi p. *E C*.

2454. Amont le lieve p. *C*; Contreval (sic) l. *D*; p. mout f. *E*; s. grant m. *D*; *G H want*.

2455. Contreval les d. *C*; Que .VI. d. *D*; Par les d. *E*; Contreval l'a jetee les degres r. *G*; Trois degrez l'a gettee contreval va r. *H*; g. maintenant *C*.

2456. p. jut mout dure et mout g. *D*; c. mervileuse et g. *CG*; e. pesant *CG D*; *H wants*.

2457. .II. (.II. des *G*) costes li brisa (brisse *G*) e. *CG*; Li costes l. *D*; Le col l. *H*.

2458. Deux sergens appella tost et legierement *H*; M. saisirent d. *G*; s. escuier et siergant *CG*; s. maintenant .X. serjant *D*; d. vallet m. *E*.

2459. .I. ronchi l. *DH*; l. ruent t. *E*; l. troussent moult felonneusement *H*; *CG want*.

2460. *CG H want*.

2461. E. les gens a *E*; g. Matabrune o. *E CG*; v. se sont r. errant *C*; v. n'y font delayement *H*; r. maintenant *E G D*; *C adds*: Li castiaus une liue ot d'entreprendrement; *H adds*: A haulte vois s'escrient trestous communement/ Merci font il pour Dieu le pere omnipotent/ Le chastel vous rendron moult debonnairement.

2462. c. qui n. *E D*; c. si ens iert d'ore envant *G*; n. pot en a. *E*; *C H want*.

2463. Et Elyas fu dols sans maltalent les prant *D*; f. moult doulz sans contredit le prent *H*; c. si le prent liement *E*; *CG want*.

2464. Seurtet l. *G*; l. ont fait l. *E CG DH*.

2465. Lors s'en tournerent trestout coumunaument *C*; D'illueques s'en tourna Elyas et sa gent *G*; s. plus s. *E*; *DH want*.

2466. En lor pais en vont li chevalier vaillant (l. teres ariere s'en revont liement *E*) (p. s'en vont chevalier et siergant *G*) *E CG*; e. vont seuremant *D*; *C adds*: Et Elyas avech en va devant; *G adds*: Et ensanble Elyas en a mout nonporquant.

2467. E. en mercient t. *D*; m. cascun mout liemant *E*; *D adds*: Et la gent Elyas ne si vait atarjant; *E adds*: Adont ont pris congie si s'en vont maintenant; *CG H want*.

2468. S'en mainne Matabrune la viele m. *C*; e. amainent b. *G*; m. tout b. *E C D*; *H wants*.

2469. Et Elyas envoie .XX. *C*; E. en envoie .XX. *E G*; e. .X. c. *CG H*; c. devant *H*.

2470. P. son pere garder et metre en mandement (g. d'air et de torment *G*) *CG*; *C adds*: En la plus haute tour qui fu faite a ciment/ Metera Matabrune qui Diex duinst mal torment/ Por cou fait

Elyas qui n'en ait mautalent/ Quant il vera sa
mere mener si tres viument; *G adds*: Et lor mande
par eus qu'il ne laist nient/ K'il ne voist en sa
tour el plus haute mandement/ Car il ne voroit
mie qu'il eust mariment/ Quant il veroit sa mere
morir a tel torment.

2471. Ne veult que de sa mere voye le jugement *H*; m. en
d. *E*; *H adds*: Et les chevaliers firent tout son
commandement; *D CG want*.

114. *BE CG DH*

2472. Les messaigers chevauchent sans y sejourner *H*; c.
en t. *C*; e. vont q. *CG*.

2473. En une chambre firent le viel roy entrer *H*; r.
ont fait en sa grant tour monter *C*; t. enfremer *E*
G D; *C adds*: Qu'il ne voie sa mere si vieument
demener; *H adds*: Et Elyas a fait ses grans gens
ordonner.

2474. Et sa m[er]e meismes qu'il eut fait aler *C*; m.
devant lui a. *G*; *CG place verses* 2474, 2475, 2476
and 2477 *after* 1. 2480; *E DH want*.

2475. Si que vera la v. ardoir et tormenter *G*; Pour que
e. *C*; *E DH want*.

2476. v. ains n'i v. *C*; v. n'i est pas a. *G*; *E DH want*.

2477. Se el mainne joie ne fait a demander *C*; Se demai-
ne g. j. nus ne l'en doit b. *G*; *E DH want*.

2478. Elyas devant lui fait la viele guier *CG*; Matabru-
ne la vielle fait devant luy m. *H*; E. en v. *E*; *CG
add*: Pour cou ne li escape (Que ne li estorsist
G) pour sa vie sauver.

2479. Il envoi (envoia *G H*) avant p. *CG H*; *H adds*: A la
voye se mettent plus de cent bacheler/ De fagos
et d'espines font le feu alumer/ Matabrune la vi-
elle y firent amener/ Pute vielle mauvaise dist
Elyas le ber.

2480. d. qu'il i f. *CG D*; d. qu'il fera ens M. *E*; Mata-
brune jeter *CG*; M. ruer *E D*; *H wants*.

2481. Il s. *CG*; f. c'on ot f. *C D*; f. si l'ont f. *E*; *H
wants*.

2482. *CG H want*.

2483. Et ele voit mout b. *D*; Matabrune a (ot *G*) paour
si commence a tranler *CG*; *H wants*.

2484. E dist e. *E*; E. laissies me c. *G*; *H wants*.

2485. c. m'en laisies a. *E*; *CG DH want*.

2486. E. se vous me volies encor r. *G*; v. .II. jors r.
C; v. .XV. jors respiter *D*; *H wants*.

2487. c. t'a. *C D*; c. t'aprendrai q. *E G*; q. porroies
a. *D*; m. porras a. *E G*; *H wants*.

2488. Elyas li r. *CG*; *H wants*.

2489.   V. max vos fera hui grant 'honte   endurer *D*;   *CG H*
        want.
2490.   Se tos n'iestes confiesse tart venres   au   parler
        CG; Tant c., m. ca ne povez demourer *H*.
2491.   v. fait Matabrune jou (que *G H*) ne p. *CG H*; v. ne
        le puis mais celer *D*; v. ne porrai e. *E*.
2492.   O. ores g. *C*;   oies ja merveiles s. *CG*; m. ses v.
        C; m. se v. *G D*; *CG add*:   Onques n'oi nus hons de
        se fiere parler; *E adds*: Que Damedix. de gloire si
        vous puist bien douner; *H wants*.
115. *BE CGT DH*
2493.   Oiies f. *CG D*;   Geisiez f. *H*;   o. dist l. *E C*; f.
        Matabrune c. *CG DH*;   v. franc chevalier b. *CG*; v.
        damoisel et b. *D*; *CG add*:   Dames pucieles escuier
        et garcon (Et d. et p. qui ci sont environ *G*)/
        Clerc et provoire et siergant et baron (Li c. et
        li p. escuier et garcon *G*).
2494.   m. et m. *H*.
2495.   p. que onc ne f. *H*.
2496.   n. ses sains ne son n. *E H*.
2497.   *C wants*.
2498.   S. jo peusse vivre si ait m'arme pardon *D*;   v. si
        aie je pardon *E*; *CG H want*.
2499.   J. trencaisse E. *E*; c. sos l. *D*; *CG H want*.
2500.   Je tuasse mon filz se Dieu me doint pardon *H*;   o.
        encore en sa maison *CG*; o. d'un fust ou d'un
        planchon *D*; *CGT D add*: Trencasse lui le cuer le
        fie et le (Ou d'un cotel trenchant le ferisse el
        D) poumon.
2501.   Puis eusse la terre en ma possession *H*; t. en fu
        et en c. *E D*; *CGT want*.
2502.   Et f. *CG DH*; f. la gent t. *D*; f. les h. *E H*; s.
        hommes t. *E CGT H*; t. a male achoison *H*.
2503.   Retenisse le tour e. *G*; E. maumesisse t. *C*; *H*
        wants.
2504.   la dame *C*; l. mesprison *H*.
2505.   j. la voi la a chel hiermin p. *C*; *E DH want*.
2506.   Ses e. *E CGT*; e. enperir p. *G*.
2507.   Puis fis mon fil a c. *CGT D*;   Et fis a m. *H*; p.
        mout male r. *CGT*; p. mortel traison *D*; m. ocoison
        E.
2508.   Et t. *T*; enfant erent petit k. *C*; e. chaellon *T*
        DH; e. caaignon *G*; .VII. gagon *E which adds*: Fors
        que une lissete pour vrete le dison.
2509.   Mon voil fust ele ore a. et tornee a *D*; Le mien
        g. *G*; A m. *T*; m. vouloir l'eust arse sans avoir
        garison *H*; f. ore a. *C*; l. en c. *T D*.
2510.   Certes se je peuisse (s. g'escapasse *G*) bien dire

le puet on *CG*; Se je peusse vivre jusque a l'as-
cension *H*; e. dire le peust on *D*; e. pour vrete
le dison *E*; *T wants*.

2511. n. vit t. *G*; m. puis l. *CD*; m. tres l. *G*; *H*
wants.

2512. Que j. *E CGT D*; f. onques n'amai raison *CGT D*; *H*
wants.

2513. Ja ne (nen *D*) prierai Diu qu'il me (que m'en *D*)
face p. *CGT DH*; q. j'eusse p. *E*.

2514. D. li nos S. *E which adds*: Me consaut et ait mout
sui en grant fricon; *CGT DH want*.

2515. *G places this verse after 1.* 2517.

2516. E. de h. et de b., i. prison *E*; *CGT DH want*.

2517. a. que puet T. *C*; a. tos soie a abandon *D*; T.
soit e. *CGT H*; T. est e. *E*; e. mis a bandon *H*.

116. *BE CGT DH*

2518. Matabrune c'est mal c. *H*; v. est m. *C*; v. fu m.
G.

2519. c. orent p. *G*; p. qui oent le desvee *DH*; *GT add*:
Ainc Dieu ne reclama ne la vergene honoree.

2520. C. dist E. *E CGT D*; *CGT add*: Mainte mauvaise ˙sau-
se (s. est pour v. *T*) aves vous destempree (Main-
tes mauvaises oevres sont par vous alevees *G*).

2521. Li euvre k'aves faite v. *E*; *CGT H want*.

2522. f. ma mere a tort blasmee *DH*; f. si s. *E*; *CGT*
want.

2523. Or endroit en ares d. *H*; e. donrai d. *E D*; d.
soldee *DH*; *CGT want*.

2524. Il p. *CG*; M. ens el (ou *C*) feu l'ont j. *E C*; o.
ou f. *T*; f. ruee *C*.

2525. Matabrune la viele est en haute e. *CG*; v. s'es-
toit h. *H*; s'est hautement *D*; m. durement e. *E*.

2526. Ha dyable fait elle trop m'avez oubliee *H*; Au dy-
able d. *T*; As .C. d. *C*; d. coumant tos cex de ma
contree *E D*.

2527. k. sont ci de toute ma (sa *T*) *E DH*; *CGT want*.

2528. L. se taist (traist *T*) Matabrune t. *CGT*; L. re-
chigna l. *D*; L. descendi l. *H*; v. tos fu a. *C H*;
t. iert a. *G*.

2529. Diaule emportent s'arme a *D*; a. en prisent dya-
bles a *T*; d. tex est (ce fut *H*) sa destinee *GT*
DH; a. cui ele est v. *E*; *T adds*: En infer le hi-
deus illuec est ostelee; *C wants*.

2530. Et quant ele fu morte et a sa fin alee *C*; Lors
s'en tournent trestout q. *G*; r. et (quant *G*) la
vielle est f. *GT D*; f. alee *T*; *H wants*.

2531. El chastel sont venus la grant gent honnouree *H*;
s. monterent k. *CGT*; s. s'en vienent k. *D*; s.

        s'en entrent k. *E*; k. fu b. et paree *C*; k. estoit
        bien p. *E*; e. biele pavee *G*.

2532.   r. ot 1. *E C*;   r. set 1. *G*;   s. ces noveles t. *D*;
        n. que sa mere ert (est *G*) alee (finee *T*) *CGT*; n.
        sa pensee est troblee *D*; t. est s. *E*; *H wants*.

2533.   Il n. *CG*;   Ainc n. *E*; M. n'en v. *G D*; f. trop par
        e. *D*; f. que t. *E G*; e. dervee *CGT D*; *CGT add*: La
        roine est mout (en est *G*) lie   car   trop   l'avoit
        (qu'ele l'ot mout *G*) penee (grevee *T*)/ Grant joie
        mainnent desi c'a la viespree (Or demainent grant
        joie quant ele fu finee *G*); *H wants*.

2534.   Li nuis est trespassee desi a l'ajornee *E*;   t. si
        revient l'a. *D*; *CGT H want*.

2535.   m. est assise 1. *E*; a. quant l'eave fut donnee *H*;
        CGT want.

2536.   Apres menger si ont chascune table o. *H*;   o. sou-
        pet 1. *C*;   m. et la table est o. *CT D*; m. les ta-
        bles ont ostees *G*.

2537.   k. ot e. *D*; k. eust e. *H*; o. il (par *G DH*) laiens
        paree *CGT DH*.

2538.   Et s. *E*;   Ou trestout le bernaige   se   coucha   la
        vespree *H*; d. jusques a la viespree *C*; d. dus k'a
        la matinee *E*; desi qu'a 1. *G*.

2539.   p. a D. *C D*; p. allours est s. *E*; D. a s. *CG DH*.
2540.   Apres   1. *CG*;   m. deviers la matinee *C*;   m. quant
        ele fu passee *G*; f. venue ne passee *H*.

2541.   Ot oi t. *E*; d. puis f. *E H*; f. en pensee *E*; g. la
        r. *D*; g. parlee *DH*.

2542.   *E CG DH want*.
2543.   p. amontee *E*; *CG want*.

117.   *BE CGT DH*

2544.   d. ou (el *G*) palais E. *CG*;   d. en 1. *E H*;   E. n'i
        d. *D*; s. excepte Elyas *H*.

2545.   a. sovent le ber saint N. *C*; a. forment et le ber
        saint Thomas *GT*; e. deproie e. *D*; 1. bon N. *E*
        DH.

2546.   Es v. *C*; Adonc vint ung ange r. *H*; a. viestus de
        mout biaus d. *C*; a. afule d. *E*; d. bons d. *G H*.

2547.   E. respont tot soavet e. *D*; E. a dit et conseille
        moult b. *H*; c. coyement tout e. *T*.

2548.   *H wants*.
2549.   D. si   ne   l'oublie p. *GT*;   l'oublier t. *C*;   *E DH*
        want.

2550.   Que le matin bien (Q. demain par matin *G*) au jour
        te 1. *CGT*;   j. esramment 1. *D*;   j. matin te 1. *E*;
        j. bien main te 1. *T*.

2551.   Tom (sic) p. *D*.
2552.   Puis si   prent t'armeure ne l'oublier (oublie *G*)

tu (Et pren tes armeures ne les oublie *T*) pas *CGT*; Trestote t. *D*; Toutes (Trestoutes *H*) tes armeures a. *E H*; a. mes amis p. *D*; a. o toy en p. *H*.

2553. e. et l. *H*; c. amis n. *G*; *E C want*.

2554. d. grant o. *DH*; *CGT want*.

2555. Sour le vivier tantos amis (ton pere *G H*) (trestout droit en *G*; tout droit tu t'en *H*) i. (Sur le v. tout droit biau frere t'en i. *T*) *CGT H*; s. le vivier biax amis t. *D*; s. le rivage t. *E*.

2557. b. a conpas a. *D*; b. en menrra trestout fait a *H*; a. mout bien fait a *E G*; a. illuec t. *T*.

2558. La v. *G*; v. ton (biau *T*) frere o. *GT*; v. isnielement f. *C*.

2559. Volentiers sire c. *C*; Et jo m. *D*; Volentiers biaus dous sires c. *GT*.

118. *BE CGT DH*

2560. Lors (Or *G*) s'en va (revait *G*; torne *T*) l'angeles (li angeles *GT*) e. *CGT*; L'ange s'en retourna e. *H*.

2561. m. sont l. *E DH*; l. conte duc chastelain *D*; a nul plus lonc plaint *E*; a cil qui doel maint *H*; *T wants*.

2562. Tot font ensamble joie dont sonnent li saint *D*; s. plaint *E*; *CGT H want*.

2563. A. matin s. *H*; m. s'en vont tuit q. sonnerent l. *T*; a. car s. *CG*; q. sounent l. *E*; q. sonner ont l. *H*; *D wants*.

2564. Messe leur ont cantee .I. capelains *C*; Messe lor cante .I. abes d'un glorious (u. lorier des sains *T*) c. *GT*; u. presios c. *E DH*.

2565. L'offrande fisent mout tres courtoisement *C*; Lor o. *E G DH*; L. ofrande i o. *G*; f. n'i a cel qui se faint *E*; f. grans dons y donne maint *H*; n. se faint *D*.

2566. Arier retornent (A. s'en r. *GT*) n'i a cel (nul *T*) qui duel maint (que Dex n'aint *GT*) *CGT which add*: Pour l'onor (amour *G*) Elyas s'en esbaudissent (esjoissent *GT*) maint.

119. *BE CGT DH*

2567. Apres messe retorne (s'en tornent *G*) ensamble dou moustier *CG*; s. s'en entrent s. *E*; s. retournent s. *H*; r. n'ont cure de tenchier *DH*.

2568. O. o s. *E*; *CGT DH want*.

2569. Venut sont ou palais n. *C*; Mout demaine[n]t grant joie n. *GT*; f. nule novele n. *E*; d. noisier *C which adds*: Elyas vit son pere sel prent a araisnier; *DH want*.

2570. Taisez f. *H*; S. dist E. *E*; E. por amor Deu vous
quier *D*; E. veul que veullez prier *H*; s. que v.
E; *CGT want*.

2571. Que tuit facent silence et laissent le n. *D*; En-
tendes moi .I. poi s. noise et s. tencier *E*; *D*
adds: Puis regarda son pere si coumence a hu-
chier; *CGT H want*.

2572. P. ce dist li enfes p. *C*; P. dist E. *E GT*; E. je
vous pri et requier *H*.

2573. d. mes freres et de vostre m. *D*; *C adds*: De ma
suer de mes freres qui mout font a prisier/ Car
jou m'en veil aler a celer nel vos quier.

2574. Et g. qu'entour vous ne traies (v. n'atrayez l.
T) l. *GT*; q. ne traiies e. *E*; a. en vous nul l.
H; *C wants*.

2575. *C wants*.

2576. t. Matabrune li voil jo otroier *D*; d. que n. *G*;
d. qui ne p. esliger *H*; *C wants*.

2577. v. mil mars d'argent et .M. bb (?) d'or mier *D*;
v. .CM. m. *E H*; m. que d'a. que d. *GT*; m. de fin
or monnoyer *H*; *C wants*.

2578. j. revieng en serai i. *E*; r. j'otroi a *GT D*; *H*
wants.

2579. Mon ainsnet frere n. *C*; Nourissies bien mes fre-
res n. *E*; f. n'en ferai nul p. *E D*; f. trestout
le miler fief *G*; *H wants*.

2580. P. teil couvent c. *C*; c. seront tel c. *E*; c. ert
r. *T*; o. nonchier *C D*.

2581. Se Diex me ramenoit e. *C*; *H wants*.

2582. Rarai cuite ma t. sans ire et sans tencier *C*; Au-
rai quite m. *D*; J'arai quite m. *G*; Q. tesrai ma
t. et tout m'iretier *E*; t. sans noise et sans
dangier *G*; *H wants*.

2583. Donne a Orrons la t. *H*; O. ait (doins *E*) le t. *E*
D; r. Hugier *E D*; r. Oger *H*; *CGT want*.

2584. Si rices hom s. *E*; R. iert asases s. *D*; R. en se-
ra moult si la puet j. *H*; l. veut j. *E*; *CGT want*.

2585. S. aura l. *E DH*; I. dela le V. *E*; d. Monrahier *D*;
d. Valregnier *H*; *CGT want*.

2586. Et Jehans Moncible b. *E*; *CGT want*.

2587. t. demander e. *E*.

2588. Quer n. *H*; d. n'aler n. *D*; d. ou je vueil r. *H*.

2589. Que n. *E G*; d. vallissant .I. d. *G*; l. montant d.
D; *C adds*: Quant ses peres l'entent le sens cuide
cangier.

2590. Et toute l'autre gent se prisent a *C*; Et trestout
se coumencent de paour a *G*; d. peor s. *D*; pite
prendent a larmoiier *E*; *H wants*.

120. *BE CGT DH*

2591.   S. dist E. *E G*; p. arester *D*; *H wants*.
2592.   A Jhesu v. *CG*; comanch il *C*; tous il *E*; m'en es-
         tuet a. *G*; *H wants*.
2593.   b. commencerent de pitie a *H*; *CG want*.
2594.   f. dist l. *E H*; *G wants*.
2595.   D. dist E. *E*; *CG DH want*.
2596.   A u. *H*; c. l'en fait la dame aler *CG*; v. le fait
         sa mere e. *DH*.
2597.   Son c. *C*.
2598.   l. mere c. *C DH*; d. il v. *C*; d. ce v. *E G H*.
2599.   Che d'or d'yvoire que tant fait a *C*; *E G DH want*.
2600.   *E CG DH want*.
2601.   *E CG DH want*.
2602.   *E CG DH want*.
2603.   j. que le pores veir ne e. *C*; j. ce v. *G DH*; j.
         quel vous pores icel cor e. *E*.
2604.   v. couvenra j. *E CG H*; v. estovera a v. *D*; e.
         mies d. *C*; e. il d. *G*.
2605.   A .I. grant caaine d. *C D*; A une caine d. *G H*; c.
         pent d'ivore k. *G*; a. luisant (grant *G*) (ki fu
         luisant *H*) et cler *CG DH*.
2606.   Li a au col pendut pour lui reconforter *C*; Il le
         mist a *G*; m. remembrer *H*.
2607.   Elyas va avech n. *C*; E. iluec ne v. plus arester
         G D; E. n'y voult illec plus sejourner *H*.
2608.   a. devant lui aporter *E C D*; *C adds*: Sen espee et
         sa lance et son escut boucler/ Li roys et la roi-
         ne li demainne et li per/ Pour la pitet de lui
         pleurent au desevrer/ Li rois et la roine et tou-
         te l'autre gent; *G H want*.
2609.   Ne l., c. ne v. *G*; *C H want*.
2610.   k. mout f. *E D*; a. douter *E*; *CG H want*.
2611.   A. a m. *D*; *CG H want*.
2612.   *E CG H want*.
2613.   Juske al vivier son pere ne vot il demorer *G*;
         Tout droit sur le vivier s'en commence a a. *H*; l.
         fist a. *D*.
2614.   Et cil s'en vont apries n'ont cure d'ariester *G*;
         b. apres n. *D*; *E adds*: Or le conduie Dix qui tout
         a a sauver; *C H want*.

121. *BE CGT DH*

2615.   Jusques s. *C H*; s. le vivier e. *E CG DH*; r. n'i
         (ne *G*) font ariestement *CG*; r. s'en (en *E*) vont
         t. *E DH*; v. trestout esrant *E*.
2616.   r. et tot coumunalmant *D*; r. s'en vont arier p.
         G; r. rembrace doulcement *H*; *CG add*: Grant dueil
         demainnent pour amor al enfant (Mout demainent

grant duel et toute l'autre gent *G*)/ Qui si s'en
vet aler par son cors seulement (*G wants*); *C
wants*.

2617. Boins vins i *C*; Assez y font porter pain et vin
et fourment *H*; i fait p. *E*; e. clare et piument
G; p. ensement *C*; *H adds*: Le cisne baiserent en
plourant tendrement.

2618. d. pour durer longement *E*; i maine p. *G*; *C H
want*.

2619. S. la rive s. *G*; l. vivier s. *E C D*; v. noant *E
C*; *H wants*.

2620. k. amainent (sic) l. *C*; *H wants*.

2621. c. qu'est de fin or luisant *D*; k. est de boin a.
C; e. de fin a. *G*; *H wants*.

2622. D. li e. *C*; s. disne coumant *E G D*; *H wants*.

2623. Devers l. *C*; b. mait s'a. *G*; a. erranment *H*.

2624. a. atornement *E CG D*.

2625. r. et toute l'autre gent *CG*; r. embracent tot
plorant *D*; *CG add*: Li clerc et li provoire ki la
sont en present/ Tot demainnent grant duel pour
amor al enfant (p. Elyas l'e. *G*)/ Qui si s'en vet
(doit *G*) aler par son cors seulement; *D adds*: Le
chisne si l'embracent mout amiablemant; *H wants*.

2626. *CG DH want*.

2627. E. ou b. *C*; E. en sailli ou batel erranment *H*; b.
est salis (entres *G*) m. *CG D*.

2628. Tos les commande a Diu li enfes en plorant *CG*; Le
roi et la roine et tote l'autre jant *DH*.

2629. Et son pere et sa mere et toute l'autre gent *CG*;
A coumande a Deu d'iluec se part atant (D. si
s'en part erranment *H*) *DH*.

2630. D. le pere omnipotent *H*; *CG want*.

2631. Li rois et la roine s'en retorne plorant *D*; *E CG
H want*.

2632. Ariere s'en repairent sans nul delaiement *D*; *E CG
H want*.

2633. Et li cisnes s. *CG*; Or s'en va Elyas comme D. *H*;
v. si con D. *CG D*; D. le c. *E DH*.

2634. i. et a l. *E G*; t. qu'en la m. s'espant *D*; *C
adds*: Li rois et la roine se pasment erran-
ment/ Et li conte et li duc cevalier et sier-
gant/ Et dames et pucieles qui la sont en pre-
sent.

2635. m. s'en vait n. *D*; m. se met n. *E*; e. n'i vait
plus d. *E D*; *CG H want*.

2636. Tout le j. *H*; T. nuit ont courut jusc'a l'ajorne-
ment *CG*; T. nuit v., l. jour e. *E*.

2637. Lendemain par matin (au jor cler *G*) endroit prime

s. *CG*; v. al d. vers m. *E*; v. lendemain endroit m. *H*.

2638. Virent une cite d. *CG*; *G adds*: Et li cisnes s'en vait si con Dex li consent.

2639. m. estoient e. *C*; m. se monterent vel et cil de jovent *H*; m. li turc et li piersant *CG*; m. tot v. *D*.

2640. Et le cisne parciurent et le batiel courant *C*; Et c. *D*; Et virent au blanc c. *H*; I. virent le batiel et le cine noant *G*; c. son b. *D*.

2641. Il q. *D*; q. el b. *G*; *H wants*.

2642. U que ce soit e. *E*; *CG DH want*.

2643. Il c., l. sarrasin puant *D*; l. cuivert s. *E*; *CG H want*.

2644. *CG H want*.

2645. En lor g. *CG*; Es g. *E D*; g. entrent b. *CG*; g. s'en entrent b. *D*; g. en v. *E*.

2646. *CG H want*.

2647. *E CG H want*.

2648. E. en v. *E*; e. vienent d. escriant *D*; v. si l'escrient atant *G*; v. tost et appartement *H*; m. esbaudiement *C*.

2649. l. vit s. *C H*; v. si eut (s'en a *G*) paour mout grant *CG*; s. plore durement *D*; s. en eust marrement *H which adds*: Il a vestu l'aubert le heaume luisant/ Et les galios l'ont escrie haultement.

2650. B. voit k. *E*; *CG DH want*.

2651. *CG DH want*.

2652. c. les (le *G D*) moustre en souspirant (tot esrant *D*) *CG D*; m. dementant *E*; *H wants*.

2653. *CG DH want*.

2654. Li cisnes crie et brait son biec vers le ciel tent *C*; Li chisnes fait grant dol vers le chiel son bec tant *D*; v. regardant *E*; *G H want*.

2655. e. depece e. *E*; e. defant *E D*; *CG H want*.

2656. Et b. *E*; crie haut *E D*; h. et pleure tenrement *E*; n. parole a. *D*; *CG H want*.

2657. a. el batel maintenant *G D*; *G adds*: Dameldieu reclama le pere tout poissant; *C H want*.

2658. A. Dex fait il pere P. *D*; A. fait Elyas sire a toi hui me coumanc *G*; S. peres P. *E*; *C H want*.

2659. d. moi m'arme et mon cors terant *D*; a. dous pere a. *E*; *CG H want*.

2660. c. dous pere e. *E*; Sire neporquant *D*; *CG H want*.

2661. m. conbatrai v. *G*; d. ja vers ceste male jant *G D*; *C H want*.

2662. v. que m. *E*; n. vif n. *D*; n. vivant *E*; *CG H want*.

2663. Il ne me trouvront ja l. *G*; *GT add*: Que bien ne

me desfende a mon acerin branc; *C H want*.

122.   *BE CGT DH*

2664.   c. de (a *G*) paour d. *CG*; *H wants*.

2665.   c. et vers Deu s. *D*; c. durement s. *E*; *CG H want*.

2666.   Et Elyas li enfes vers Damrediu en prie (e. Dieu reclaimme et deprie *G*) *CGT*; d. en mercie *E*; *CGT add*: Qu'il (Que son cor *G*) li garisse ses membres et sa vie/ Et le cisne son frere n'a (n'ont *G*) plus de conpaignie; *H wants*.

2667.   A. s'est d. *D*; s'aseura m. *E*; *CGT H want*.

2668.   *CGT H want*.

2669.   Les galios approuchent Jhesu-Cript les maudie *H*; b. a coisi le navie *E*; *CGT D want*.

2670.   Li ung des sarrazins a haulte voix s'escrie *H*; Devant les *C*; D. trestos l. *E D*; a. en vient (autres vient *D*) (a. s'en v. *G*) .I. galie (v. le maistre g. *D*) *CGT D*; a. li sire qui les guie *E*.

2671.   Dient qu'il averont (que il aront *G*) le batiel en lor baillie (b. en b. *G*) *CG*; Qui d. *D*; *H wants*.

2672.   L'or et l'a. qui au batiel acline (sic) *C*; a. aura en sa baillie *D*; a. nus n'i aura p. *G*; *E H want*.

2673.   Et cil deriere c. *C*; Et cex qui sont ariere dist il tos les engigne *D*; v. ne s'aseurent mie *CG*; *H wants*.

2674   *CG H want*.

2675.   Vers Elyas escrient n'emporteres la vie *C*; Rimant vient al batel E. *D*; Ains escrient en haut bien est lor vois oie *G*; e. et Elyas e. *E*.

2676.   e. l'autre m. *CG*; e. vostre m. *H*; l. marcandise *C D*.

2677.   Elyas lor r. *CG*; r. de ce ne p. *H*; S. nem p. *C*; S. n'en p. *E G D*.

2678.   l. nostre batel a. en vo b. *E*; *CG want*.

2679.   Ancois m'averes mort et tolue la vie *G*; *C adds*: Del mien ne vos lairai vailissant .I. aillie; *E DH want*.

2680.   Prent son pain e. *CG*; v. dont il avoit (ot grant *G*) (eust grant *H*) p. *CG H*; c. ot g. *E*.

2681.   m. l'a jete n. *DH*; v. qu'en a. *H*.

2682.   Mal lui a. *H*; g. fait c. *D*; l. navie *C*.

2683.   c. cier cou ne remanra (c. il ne demora *G*) mie *CG which add*: Ca laires vos les (c. nous laires l. *G*) armes et le (armes le *G*) cor qui flambie (reflambie *G*); *E DH want*.

2684.   Le c. *CG D*; c. averons n. *E CG D*; a. nos en l. *C*; a. ja en l. *G D*; a. nous en l. *E*; a. huy en nostre b. *H*.

2685. Si m. *G H*; c. quant el sera r. *H*.

2686. Quant li cisnes l'entent de paour (e. durement *G H*) brait et crie *CG H*; Quant Elyas l'entent mout forment s'en gramie *D*.

2687. *E adds*: Si a paour de mort con se fust hon de vie; *CG DH want*.

123. *BE CGT DH*

2688. k. trop p. *E G D*; *C H want*.

2689. E. les galios n. *E G D*; *C H want*.

2690. A. s'est d. *D*; a. n'i v. *E D*; a. mout est et frans et bers *G*; *C H want*.

2691. Li galiot escrient ne pores escaper *C*; Les galies approuchent Dieu les puist gueter *H*; g. traient pour le mius a. *G*.

2692. a. laissa 1. *C H*; a. li a laissie a. *E*; a. laissent vers lui a. *G*; *E adds*: Il brandist et descoce si le laist desteler.

2693. *E CG DH want*.

2694. e. feri s. *C H*; c. devant al encontrer *C*; c. par dessoubz le bouclier *H*; *G D want*.

2695. o. passer *E*; *CG DH want*.

2696. Si que p. *D*; Tres par devant son pis le f. *G*; m. l'escu 1. *D*; s. le sanc en fist voler *C*; *E D add*: Le hauberc li desmaille outre li fait (d. du cors li fist *E*) voler; *E H want*.

2697. v. fait a ses pies c. *D*; v. et chault en fist jus devaler *H*; 1. fist a. *E*; f. aval c. *E G*; *C wants*.

2698. 1. vit s. *H*; a plourer *E*.

2699. *C adds*: Il ne set autrement losengier ne crier; *DH want*.

2700. E. contreval vers 1. *C*.

2701. S. vit .XXX. *E DH*; g. isnielement s. *CG D*; g. de l'onde s. *E*; g. legierement s. *H*; o. aler *CG*; o. noer *D*; o. nager *H*.

2702. Voiles on[t] blances pour le plus tos aler *C*; Toutes ont blans les voiles pour le mius conforter *G*; Et eurent blanches voilles n. *H*; n. hom ne vit sa (les *H*) per *DH*; n. ne les puet celer *E*; *C H add*: Saint Georges les conduist qui fu gentius et ber (c. ung leger bacheler *H*); *C adds further*: Quant Elyas le voit Diu prent a mierchier/ Bien set que de par Diu le vienent visiter.

2703. A unes crois vermeilles p. *D*; A une c. *G*; p. mex encolorer *D*; p. bien enluminer *G*; m. en conter *E*; *C H want*.

2704. E. tornent t. *G*; v. quanques p. *E*; p. aler *G*; *C H want*.

2705. Que D. *DE*; *CG H want*.
2706. j. quant il les voit esrer *D*; *CG H want*.
2707. *E adds*: Et qu'il vienent pour lui garandir et tenser; *CG DH want*.

124. *BE GT DH*

2708. Leais g. *G*; *GT add*: Quant Elyas les voit n'i ot ques l'aie cier/ Bien sevent de par Dieu les vienent consellier/ Les galies vienent n'ont cure de targier; *C wants*.
2709. D. i e. *E D*; *CGT H want*.
2710. c. qui (dont *GT*) Dex fist (fu bons *E H*) cevalier *E GT DH*; *E adds*: Et li ber sains Morisses qui mout fist a prisier; *H adds*: A haulte voix leur crie mal l'ossastes toucher; *C wants*.
2711. Et d'a. et d'a. *T D*; Que d'a. que d'a. *G*; i ot p. *GT D*; *C H want*.
2712. *CT H want*.
2713. E. en v., c. puent n. *E which adds*: Car Dix les i envoie qui tout puet justicier; *CGT H want*.
2714. l. voit a. *D*; l. sent a. *E*; *D adds*: Les galies a-procent por Elias aidier; *CGT H want*.
2715. t. por t. et por l. *D*; t. al t. al l. *E*; *CGT H want*.
2716. Les galies s. *G*; La galie s. *T*; La peust on veoir grant estour commencier *H*; J. fait l'estor cou-menchier *D*; v. les tours e. *GT*; *C wants*.
2717. v. les g. *E G*; g. procier *T*; *C D want*.
2718. De son b. leur d. *H*; l. depaice p. *GT*; p. eus m. *GT H*; *C D want*.
2719. Il n. *GT*; n. plaidoiier *E*; n. ensegnier *GT*; *C D want*.

125. *BE CGT DH*

2720. Li galiot saint George a. *C*; Saint George s'a-proucha p. *H*; g. saint Jore asalent l. *GT*; s. du-rement *CGT which add*: As (Les *G*) galies les (as *G*) turs assalent firement (t. que mout sont mes-disant *G*) (*T wants*)/ Et li turc se desfendent mout orgeileusement (aireement *G*; efforciement *T*)/ Et li cisnes a fait un pietruis fort (le *G*; lait *T*) et grant/ A .I. des galies mist son piet (g. a son biec *GT*) maintenant.
2721. D. i e. *E D*; *CGT H want*.
2722. D. assalirent et cil sont deffendant *D*; *CGT H want*.
2723. g. tume d. *D*; a. a la jent mescreant *E D*; *CGT H want*.
2724. *CGT H want*.
2725. Emplie est d. *C*; f. en va rollant *E*; f. s'en vont

atant *G*; f. en va plunjant *T*; v. affondant *C*; *DH want*.

2726.   *GT H want*.
2727.   J. acroissent d. *CGT*; J. rime mout d. *D*; *H wants*.
2728.   Es .I. o. *C*; Adonc vint .I. *H*; .I. ore q. *T*; v. crollant *E*; v. tremblant *H which adds*: Les .IIII. vens venterent le ciel va rougeant.
2729.   Les galies as turs en (s'en *GT*) tournent f. (e. tournerent atant *G*) *CG*; Li g. s'en fuient p. *E*; Et les sarrazins fuyent p. *H*; g. tochent p. *D*; m. nagant *E H*.
2730.   Mais n. *CGT*; n'alerent g. que la fouldre l. *H*; g. foi q. *T*; q. li tempies l. *CG*; q. .I. ores l. *D*; q. .I. tempeste l. *T*; t. descent *CG DH*.
2731.   Es galies se f. tost l. *H*; f. as g. se l. *C*; g. et toutes les pourfent *E*; g. si l. *T*; l. vont c. *G*; v. effondrant *C*; v. deronpant *D*.
2732.   El f. *D*; f. les plonce l'aige e. *G*; d. le mer va et le gent mescreant *E*; l. ploncent maintenant *C*; l. plonge e. *T DH*; p. tost et legierement *H*; e. les galies f. *GT D*.
2733.   a. a boire l. *C D*; a. beut l. *GT*; l. glouton m. *C*; c. souduiant *E C D*; *CGT add*: Quant (Onques *T*) Elyas le (les *G*) voit a Dieu grasces en rent; *H wants*.
2734.   Les galies saint George sans (sic) r. *H*; g. en (s'en *G*) vont arier (g. vont ariere *T*) sivant (siglant *GT*) *CGT*; e. tornerent a. *E*.
2735.   s. coumandemant *D*; *CGT H want*.
2736.   Elyas lor a dit E. *C*; Elyas leur demande qui estes b. (d. entendez mon semblant *T*) *T H*; l. crie E. *D*; l. dist E. *G*; h. attendes b. *C D*; h. escoutes b. *E*.
2737.   e. onor f. *CGT*; a. m'aves (aves *D*) fait g. *CGT D*; *H wants*.
2738.   Et s. *CG*; J. li r. *E*; J. respont N. *E CGT*; r. ne d. *D*; r. or ne d. *GT*; r. laisse ester a ytant *H*.
2739.   Dieu en aoure l. *C*; Jesu Crist en aeure le Pere omnipotent *T*; e. grassie l. *E*; e. a cure l. *G*; *CGT DH add*: Et Elyas respont a ton (son *GT D*) commandement (r. beau sire a son commant *H*)/ Soit mes sierviches (s. de moi si iert [est *H*] il *DH*) (s. Jhesus de moi garde *G*) d'ore (des or *G D*) mais (des ce jour *H*) en avant (...nt Diex garde de moi par son bon escient *T*).
2740.   *CGT DH want*.
2741.   f. vous fuissies t. *E*; *CGT DH want*.
2742.   E. .VC. m. t'en r. *E*; *CGT DH want*.

2743.   e. mon c. *E*; *CGT DH want.*

126.   *BE CGT DH*

2744.   Sains Jorges en (s'en *GT*) reva (r. o li s. *T*) il
et sa compaignie *CGT*; Ariere s'en retornent n. *D*;
a. ainc n'i remest g. *E*; *CG add*: Et Elyas remaint
tous seus sans compaignie (s. en sa gallie *GT*)/
Et li cisnes apres ne s'aseura mies (Ses frere
aoure Dieu et deprie et mercie *G*; ...e avec li
qui Diex apele et prie *T*); *H wants.*

2745.   *E CGT H want.*

2746.   Tes fains prist Elyas t. *E*; E. a t. *G*; f. a poi
que ne marvie *C*; f. ainc tex n. *GT D*; *H wants.*

2747.   Sa plaie bende qui n'est encor g. *C*; p. qu'il n.
D; *H wants.*

2748.   Et p. *C*; M. li fains et li sois k. *D*; d. le mais-
trie *C*; *H wants.*

2749.   D. dist E. *E*; *CGT want.*

2750.   f. et si ne garrai m. *E*; f. que je n'y gary m. *H*;
CGT want.

2751.   Quant li chisnes l'entent durement b. *D*; d. paour
b. *E*; *CGT H want.*

2752.   Issi s. *G*; Toute nuit vont ainsi jusque l'aube
esclarcie *H*; n. de jor mout grant p. *GT.*

2753.   r. qui fu (iert *G*) viele e. *CGT*; *H wants.*

2754.   Coisirent .I. *C*; d. grant ancesorie *H*.

2755.   p. vint t. *C*; s'aseura m. *E C*; *CGT add*: Li sires
de la vile fu (iert *G*) plains de dierverie (fe-
lounie *G*, *T unavailable*)/ N'a (N'ot *G*) plus mal
traitour en toute Romenie/ Plus a ocis (trais *G*)
de gens qu'il nen ait d'en (g. que nen n'ait en
G) Pavie (... d'argent qu'il n'a en payennie *T*)/
Freres est Matabrune la grant viele sorchie (F.
estoit M., v. haye *T*) (Frere fait Elyas a son
conpaing al cine *G*)/ Agoulans avoit non li cors
Diu le maudie (Que Elyas fist ardoir devant la
baronnie *T*; *G wants*); *H wants.*

2756.   E las C. *E CG*; D. pour coi i. *E*; C. mar i. *CG D*;
m. i vint s. *C*; m. i v. *E G D*; n. li a. *C*; *H
wants.*

127.   *BE T DH*

2757.   *CG DH want.*

2758.   Damediu reclama k. *E*; A Dix fait Elyas gettez moy
d. *H*; *CG D want.*

2759.   Frere fait il a. *DH*; *CG want.*

2760.   *CG DH want.*

2761.   G'irai a (en *H*) cel castel li cors de moi empire
(d. fain m'enpire *H*) *DH*; S'enterai el c. que
grans fains me martire *E*; *CG want.*

2762. b. a ce vous voil eslire *DH which place this ver-*
se after 1. 2759; e. bien le contredites *E*; *CG*
want.

2763. D. me d. *D which adds*: Mes cuers m'en avenist que
li fains trop m'aigrie; *CG H want.*

2764. a. en qui jo mout me r. *D*; c. si se r. *E*; s. fie
E D; *CG H want.*

2765. L. tot el b. *D*; e. ce b. *E*; D. qui tot crie *D*; *CG*
H want.

128. *BE CGT DH*

2766. Le cisne e. *H*; L. castians e. *E*; Vers le chastel
tout droit va li cisne a. *T*; b. en (s'en *G DH*) va
droit a. *CG DH*; c. ou r. *C.*

2767. Li catiaus avoit non p. *C H*; Le c. *E*; c. apeloy-
ent p. *T*; *G wants.*

2768. q. en ot (a *G DH*) l'onour (l'avoir *G*) et l'eri-
taige (e. tot l'usage *G DH*) (Et cil qui du chas-
tel tient l'avoir et l'usage *T*) *CGT DH*; e. plus
haut e. *E.*

2769. Si ot non A. *E*; A. et p. *G*; A. s'avoit f. *T*; m.
ot (s'ot *G*) fier le v. *E CG H*; *D wants.*

2770. a ocis de gent q. *CG*; o. que n'ait en Alemaigne
C; o. qu'il n'ait en une marche *D*; o. que ne va
e. *E*; *H wants.*

2771. F. dist E. *E CT*; *H wants.*

2772. Ce b. *GT*; b. et v. *T*; *H wants.*

2773. Et g'irai au (el *G*) c. *CG*; Je irai ou c. *T*; e.
cel c. *E D*; c. mes c. *CG*; f. esrage *E CG*; *H*
wants.

2774. c. si (et *T D*) le metrai e. *E CGT D*; *H wants.*

2775. Jou le puis voir bien f. *G*; *E H want.*

2776. m. et s'entent l. *D*; m. qui ne sot nul l. *E*; *CGT*
H want.

2777. Elyas est salis d. *CGT*; s. sus d. *D*; b. el r. *E*
CG; b. ou r. *H*; a. passage *C D.*

2778. Ou c. *CT H*; c. entre m. *C*; c. s'en m. *DH*; c. est
entres par (molt *T*) m. *GT*; e. entra *E D*; mais en
eust cher truaige *H*; mout fier g. *CG*; mout fort
g. *D.*

2779. p. et s'iert a *D*; p. ou il aura d. *H*; e. en s. *G*;
e. molt grant d. *T.*

2780. S. Damredieus n. (s. Jhesu Crist n. *T*), p. et sa
saintime ymage *CGT*; p. ou onques n'ot o. *E DH.*

129. *BE CGT DH*

2781. E. monte ou castiel a premiers *C*; E. est montes
e. *GT*; E. s'en m. *H*; m. ou c. *T H*; e. palais v. *T.*

2782. A. a trovet a. *E CGT*; t. entre s. *CGT*; t. et tos
s. *D*; t. o lui s. *H.*

2783. A sa porte ert entre ses l. *C*; En mi le salle fu
m. *GT*; p. siet trop i *E*; i ot l. *E GT D*; *H wants*.

2784. E. le s. *E C*; s. car chou li fu m. *C*; s. li enfes
droituriers *GT*; e. fu li m. *DH*; *H adds*: Le vray
Dieu vostre pere qui est sur tous le pere/ Soit
avec ses seigneurs et ses bons chevaliers/ Amis
fait Agolant estes vous chevaliers/ Ou guette de
chastel ou sergent ou archers.

2785. r. dont e. *C*; Q. estes a. *T*; t. chevaliers *E C*;
t. messagiers *G*; *H wants*.

2786. Vendras tu ce cor a mes d. *C*; v. ce c. *G H*; c.
prendras en tu d. *D*; c. prenderas tu d. *E*; c.
prendras tu d. *G*; c. prendras tu les d. *H*.

2787. Elyas dist foi que doi saint Richier *C*; S. dist
E. *E*.

2788. Ains le donroie par Diu le droiturier *C*; v. don-
roie t. *E H*; d. por iseul .II. *D*; d. pour .IIII.
(tant *T*) bons m. *GT*; d. seul pour .II. bons m. *H*.

2789. Pour mi conrer par vrete le sacies *C*; m. puis a
H; g. il a *E*; a .II. j. *D*.

2790. Agolans dist s. *C*; A. fait A. *G D*; A. les a. *H*; *T*
wants.

2791. Jou vos retieng avec mes chevaliers *C*; c. il v. *E*
G; c. car v. *H*; i. me samble mout chiers *D*; *T*
wants.

2792. Vers la sale s'en vont isnielement a. *C*; s. re-
montent t. *D*; *GT H want*.

2793. Les nappes misent par deseur les tabliers *C*;
Maintenant mettent tables varles et escuiers *H*;
s. metent t. *GT D*; t. tres par mi .II. s. *D*; t.
pour seoir al mangier *E*; t. par mi .II. grans s.
G; t. ou dessus l... *T*.

2794. Quant il orent l. *C*; Et cil qui o. *D*; S'assirent
au menger qui fut riche et planiers *H*; l. s'asis-
trent s. *D*; l. s'asisent s. *E*; a. volentiers *E*
CT; a. au mangier *G*.

2795. A m. *E*; Et Elyas menga qui eust fain voulentiers
H; m. eurent plus de .X. mes entiers *C*; e. de .X.
(e. .XII. *T*) mes tous p. *GT*; t. entiers *E*.

2796. Et ont beut des fors vins et dentiers *C*; o. eu
a boire de bons v. *T*; a. eut d. *G*; d. vies *E*; *H*
wants.

2797. E. a m. *T D*; E. nen pot mais sil asist al mangier
E; E. al mangier s'est .I. poi rehaities *G*; *H*
wants.

2798. L. enfes est m. *GT*; m. prox corajox et legiers *D*;
m. preus et coragous e. *GT*; e. coragous e. *E*; *C H*
want.

2799. Agolans le regarde l. *CGT H*; e. si come p. *C*; c. losengiers *G H*.
2800. v. chevaliers *C H*; v. mesagiers *D*.
2801. U garde d. *C*; U siergans u archiers *CG DH*.
2802. Savoir le weil j. *C*; V. nom v. *H*; s. menconniers *E*; *G wants*.
2803. Elyas respondi qui ne fu mies f. *C*; r. bielement sans irier *G*; *H wants*.
2804. Jel v. d. ja nen serai laniers *C*; S. fait Elyas or diray voulentiers *H*.
2805. a. s'ire et ses destorbiers *D*; a. ses morteus e. *G*; *C H want*.
2806. S. Dameldex n'en p. li peres droitouriers *G*; *C H want*.

130. *BE CGT DH*
2807. Dist Elyas or oies ma pensee *C*; E. le diray sans c. *H*; s. noise e. *D*; s. posnee *G H*.
2808. s. qui s. *D*; s. en le c. *E*; *C H want*.
2809. Mon iestre v. donrai sans nule demoree *C*; *H wants*.
2810. O. a la chiere membree *CG*; O. cil me fist e. *H*; *GT add*: Certes il m'engenra c'est verites prouvee.
2811. e. preus e. *G H*; *E C want*.
2812. A. o la male journee *H*; c. menbree *E G*; *C wants*.
2813. Dites moi veritet n'i a mestier celee *C*; q. vos d. *D*; *H wants*.
2814. Se Matabrune est morte (arse *D*) (vive *G H*) E. *CGT DH*; M. u vive demoree *C*; M. et d. *D*; M. u d. *G H*; E. a sa fin a. *E*.
2815. S. fait E. *D*; E. sacies sans redoutee (demoree *G*) *CG*; s. dotee *E DH*.
2816. Que Matabrune est morte (arse *G DH*) en un fu (et en feu *H*) embrasee (a. et la porre ventee *D*) (a. et a sa fin alee *G*) *CG DH*; *H adds*: Oncques puis que nostre sire fist la resucitee/ Ne fut si male vielle ne veue ne trouvee.
2817. Qui a cou fait si ait t. *C*; *E G DH want*; *C adds*: Sire jel vos dirai ja n'i ara celee.
2818. E. la nouviele c. *C*; *E G DH want*.
2819. M. eut s. *C*; *E G DH want*.
2820. E. con fu a. *C*; *E G DH want*.
2821. Agolans l'ot s. *C*; e. si a c. *H*.
2822. Que M. *E C*; M. fu s. *E*; e. morte et a fin alee *C*; s. et est l'aisnee *H*; *G wants*.
2823. Riens tant n'amoit con Matabrune *C*; C'onques *D*; Car il n. *G*; r. con Matabrune a. *G D*; *H wants*.
2824. C. fait A. *G D*.

2825.   v. ares vo s. *E*; *CG DH want*.
2826.   De vostre euvre me fu le v. *E*; *CG DH want*.
2827.   Matabrune ma suer m'aves arse et t. *D*;   M. mi a. ma suer ensi (s. Matabrune *G*) t. *CG*;   s. et ocise et t. *E*; *H wants*; *C adds*:   Mais n'arai jo cou est cose   prouvee/ Vo car aurai a le pourre ventee; *E adds*: Li arme vous en ert fors du cors desevree.

131.   *BE CGT DH*
2828.   A. a t. *C*;   f. grant d. quant Elyas (d. de ce que il *G DH*) entent *CG DH*; d. ainc nus ne vit s. *E*.
2829.   s. suer Matabrune m. *G DH*;   s. l'ainnee m. *E*;   v. se pasme isnelement *D*;   v. fait .I. *G*;   v. ploure moult tendrement *H*; si pesant *E*; *C wants*.
2830.   Dist Agolans jou venterai a. *C*;   C. dist i. *E*;   v. metrai a. *DH*;   v. pendisse a. *E*; *C adds*: La vostre car se Jhesu-Cris m'ament.
2831.   m. o moy communement *H*;   t. en s. *G D*; *C wants*; *CG D add*: Se n'euisses (Et n. *D*) (Et e. *G*) beut a mon hanap (me colpe *G D*) d'argent.
2832.   v. trencasse a m'espe da (sic) *C*; e. erranment *H*; *C adds*: Mais vos aves mengiet a ma table enseant.
2833.   Devers .IIII. jour n'as   garde   de torment *C*; De huit j. n'avez   garde *H*;   j. n'ares   vous (j. n'i ares g. *G*) g. *E G*.
2834.   M. vous seres gette en ma c. erranment *H*;   v. ferai maitre e. *G*; *C wants*.
2835.   jours par *E*;   p. le cors saint Vinchant *G D*;   *C H want*.
2836.   Auquant seras ars mout vilainnement *C*; V. referai ardoir e. *D*; j. ardoir en .I. fu le et grant *G*; *H wants*.
2837.   Agolans saut p. *C*; p. les ceviaus le prent *CG DH*.
2838.   E. en vint p. *E*; *CG DH want*.
2839.   v. si t. *C*; *E G DH want*.
2840.   I. traist l'espee as bruns coutiaus luisans *C*; *E G DH want*; *C adds*:   Agolans saut a tiere quant il piercut le bran.
2841.   J. l'euist Elyas ferut   de   maintenant *C*;   *E G DH want*.
2842.   .I. chevaliers est tos m. *C*; *E G DH want*.
2843.   f. de l'espee trencant *C*; *E G DH want*.
2844.   m. caient ou p. *C*;   *E G DH want*; *C adds*:   Estorst son cop mort l'abat maintenant.
2845.   *E CG DH want*.
2846.   s. trop i avoit d. *C*; *E G DH want*.
2847.   Li siens desfendres n. *C*; *E G DH want*.
2848.   *E CG DH want*.
2849.   Deux sergens s'approucha t. *H*;   *C wants*;   *H adds*:

Vers la chartre le mennent moult fellonneusement.

2850. Lors i sont tout courut chevalier et siergant *C*;
Et il i vienent tost sans nul delaiement *D*; *G H
want*; *C adds*: De toutes pars vienent li soudui-
ant.

2851. .X. glotons m. *D*; *C H want*.

2852. L. poin l. *D*; l. tost et isnielement *G*; m. dole-
rosemant *D*; *C H want*.

2853. Ens e. *C*; Et le mettent dedens s. *H*; l. rue s. *E*;
g. maintenant *C*; n. delaiemant *G D*; *C adds*: Mout
fu a malaise ce vus di vraiement.

2854. Avec lui en la c. ot tortues siflans *G*; c. es-
toient tortues et s. *D*; *C H want*.

2855. *CG DH want*.

2856. *CG DH want*.

2857. Et Agoulans s'en torne arierement criant (t. ari-
ere maintenant *G*) *G D*; A. retorna ou palais main-
tenant *C*; *H wants*.

2858. q. fu ocis e. *C which places this verse after l.
2859*; *E G DH want*.

2859. P. Matabrune va grant dueil demenant *C*; M. fait
.I. dol mout pesant *D*; *H wants*.

2860. Li b. et li prince le v. *E*; *CG DH want*.

2861. Laiens o. *C*; I. eust .I. g. qui eust bon e. *H*; b.
ensiant *E CG DH*.

2862. Li p. E. l'ot n. douchement *C*; Qui l. *D*; l. preus
E. *E*; E. eust n. *H*.

2863. c. ist l. *C*; i. par n. *E*; n. tout c. *E C*; *H
wants*.

2864. T. a alet li gars et ariere et avant *C*; j. qu'il
vit roy O. *H*; *C adds*: Qu'il a trouvet le boin roy
Euriant.

2865. Trestout li c. c'on fist a *C*; D'Elyas lui compta
comme il est en tourment *H*; L. nuit li a conte
con sist a *E*; c. de Elyas s. *G*.

2866. Com Agoulans li cuivers souduians *C*; En la char-
tre jete al f. *D*; Et com est en le cartre le cui-
vert A. *E*; K'il est ens e[n] la cartre le fort
roi A. *G*; En la chartre Agolant qui ne l'ayme ne-
ant *H*; *C adds*: A mout juret et fait son saire-
ment.

2867. Qu'il e. *C*; i. l'ardera ains le quint (quart *D*)
jour passant *CG D*; *H wants*.

2868. Et tout pour Matabrune la viele souduians *C*; d.
serour qui m. est O. *E*; *G DH want*.

2869. *E CG DH want*.

2870. A. .XV. j. *E*; *CG DH want*.

2871. Li rois ot la nouvielle poi ot d'esleaicement *G*;

Q. Orians oi icel coumandement *E*; r. l'entendi
parler si faitement *C*; r. l'entendi a poy d'ire
ne fent *H*; n. si felenesse entant *D*; *C adds*: Dont
mainne un dueil onques ne vi si grant.

2872. p. que ne s. *E G*; *C H want*.
2873. Et la royne se pasma tout ierrant *C*; r. en f. *D*;
r. par fait .I. duel isi tres grant *G*; *H wants*; *E*
adds: Pour Elyas son fil se va mout dolousant.
2874. l. royne oy ay le cuer dolent *H*; *C wants*.
2875. A cors p. *G*; C. com es viex tos jors es en tor-
ment *D*; vis tous *E*; v. tous jors ies enpirans *G*;
C H want.
2876. Elyas biax dols f. *G D*; m. esciant *E G D*; *C H*
want.
2877. v. li cuers de dol me fant *D*; v. s'en ai mon cuer
d. *E*; v. or vous soit Dex aidans *G*; *C H want*.

132. *BE CGT DH*
2878. Peres d. *CG*; Mere d. *DH*; S. fait .I. *G*; d. l'en-
fes q. *C*; d. Orians q. *G DH*; q. eut l. *C*; q.
tient l. *G D*.
2879. *CG DH want*.
2880. N. t'esmaier tout est en Damerede *C*; m. qu'il est
del tot (m. car il est tout *G*) (m. quer trestout
H) en De *G DH*.
2881. *CG DH want*.
2882. Diex done et si retot (s. tost *H*) t. *CG DH*.
2883. Cil est oncles mon pere Oriant le sene *E*; *CG DH*
want.
2884. E. tient s. *E*; *CG DH want*; *E adds*: Ensi ont tout
ensamble li frere devise.
2885. *CG DH want*.
2886. Cil qui le tient ensi pris et enprisoune *E*; *CG DH*
want.
2887. m. barne *E*; *CG DH want*.
2888. Elyas li miens freres m. *C*; M. bon f. *H*; m'ot p.
E.
2889. e. se Diex m'a destinet *C*; e. mon chier frere
l'ainsne *D*; e. o mes freres senes *G*; e. tout en
sui en preste *H*.
2890. a. li rois de majestet (pite *G*) *CG D*; *H wants*.
2891. Al g. *G H*; k. leur eust le messaige compte *H*; l.
a l. *D*; *C wants*.
2892. Done e. *E G D*; Donnent or et argent tout a sa
voulente *H*; D. argent et bon o. *G D*; D. argent et
o. *E*; *C wants*.
2893. Et l'a mandet ses freres q. *C*; P. manda les b.
E; s. prive *G D*; s. chace *H*.
2894. Qu'il le seceurent se il leur vient en g. *C*; s.

qui avoir veut s. *E G*; *H wants*.

2895. Et l. *CG DH*; b. s'en s. *E G*; sont a *CG DH*; t. en
leur pais alet *C*.

2896. Au (d. le *G DH*) secont jour o. tant (grant *D*) j.
CG DH; D. .II. jours ont il mout de j. *E*.

2897. C'a p. *C D*; Que a paines entrassent (pourent *H*)
en une grant c. *G H*; p. entrent en la boine c. *C*;
p. en a tant en une raiaute *D*.

2898. De g. et de p. i a. assanlle *E*; De gent i a mer-
velle a mout tres grant p. *G*; *C DH want*; *E adds*:
Bone cevalerie a mout grande plente.

2899. Et li petit i vienent d. *G D*; v. a b. *E*; *C H
want*.

2900. n. armes n. *E*; p. n'i s. pas o. *G D*; *C H want*.

2901. .I. hons les conduisi d. *C*; L'ost c. .I. haus hom
d. *G D*; t. de l'Ille G. *CG D*; *H wants*.

2902. n. en s. *D*; p. la c. *G*; *H wants*.

2903. Entres q. *D*; Desi a *E*; n. se sont a. *G D*; *C H
want*.

2904. Orions e. *D*; e. li sien s. *E*; s. frere s. *G D*; *C
H want*.

2905. Le roi et la royne o. *C*; Le viel roi et la dame
o. *G D*; r. lor d. *E*; *H wants*.

2906. c. s'en issent par b. *G*; *C H want*.

2907. Li gars les mainne k. *C*; k. savoit l. *D*; *H wants*.

2908. Quant ce vint au quart j. *C*; j. quant i. *D*; j. si
qu'il f. *G*; j. ains qu'il f. *H*.

2909. c. qu'il ont tant desiret *C*; c. itant s. *E*; c.
dont tant s. *G D*; c. quer moult s. *H*; *C adds*:
Laiens entrerent trestout outre lor gret.

2910. A un brueillet b. *C*; Ains se sont en .I. bos pe-
titet esconse *E*; .I. petit bosquet b. *G DH*; p.
qui fut dru et r. *H*; *C adds*: La s'enbuscierent
tant qu'il furent armet.

2911. Et s. *E*; c. que n. *E G H*; a. mot n'y ont s. *H*; *C
wants*; *H adds*: Et le varlet estoit lors ou chas-
tel ale/ De la chartre ont Helyas tire.

2912. Et cel bois a. *D*; Ce boskel a. *E*; Icel bos a. *G*;
d. castel f. *E G D*; b. plante *D*; b. freme *E*; b.
cope *G*; *C H want*.

2913. La s'esturent tot coi t. *D*; s. le nuit et logie
et sere *E*; l. desi c'a l'a. *G*; *C H want*.

2914. Et cil (Cil *G*) del castel sont (se sont *G*) coumu-
nement (coumunalment *G*) l. *G D*; *C H want*.

2915. A. li traitres a desour (a sor tos *G D*) sains ju-
ret *CG D*; *H wants*; *C places this verse followed
by 2919 after l. 2923.*

2916. j. Dameldiu le roi de maiste *E*; *CG DH want*.

2917. Que pour .I. mui d'argent et d'or tout esmere *E*; *CG DH want*.
2918. *CG DH want*.
2919. C'Elyas ardera a. *C*; Que n. *E*; i. ardra Elyas a. *G D*; a. le midîe s. *G*; m. passet *CG*; *H wants*; *C see 1*. 2915.
2920. t. a l. *E*; *CG DH want*.
2921. Et (Ens *D*) en mi (Par devant *G*) le castiel eut (a *G D*) on ja trainet (o. atraine *D*) (j. aporte *G*) *CG D*; e. et ansuiaus [sic] a *E*; *H wants*.
2922. e. que n'i ait demoure *E*; *CG DH want*; *E adds*: Voiant tous les barons ont il tout assanlle.
2923. Les grans espines pour le feu alumer *C*; Espines et fagos et l. *D*; Et buisses et espines et l. *GT*; D'espines et de ronces ont ung f. *H*.
2924. Fors de la cartre ont Elyas g. *C*; Lors (Fors *T*) ont trait de la chartre Elyas l'adure (E. le sene *G*) *GT D*; Et devant le feu ont Elyas amene *H*.
2925. c. ont d. *G*; *T H want*; *C adds*: Quatre siergant l'en ont au feu menet/ Li baron dou pais i furent assanblet.
2926. e. a e. *D*; e. ont en la p. pour Elyas p. *GT*; *C H want*.
2927. M. il n'osent b. *C*; M. ne l'ossent b. *G*; *H wants*.
2928. .I. haut baron i eut p. *C*; I. eust .I. *H*; h. mais en (de *D*) grant povretet *CGT DH*.
2929. *CGT DH want*.
2930. p. sa g. *E*; *CGT DH want*.
2931. Avoit plus de .X. (.XV. *T*) ans et sa maisnie (A. et si enfant plus de .X. ans *G DH*) estet *CGT DH*; Et i., o. grant pîece e. *E*; *C adds*: Preudons estoit et de grant parenteil.
2932. n. ainsi fut appelle *H*; *C wants*.
2933. s. sent d. *E*; *CGT DH want*.
2934. *CGT DH want*.
2935. Il n'ert ja a. *E*; *CGT DH want*.
2936. Agolant apiela a loy d'ome senet *C*; Ou qu'il v. *D*; s. l'en (lui *H*) a apele *GT DH*.
2937. S. dist li preudons ki Simons ert clames *C*; Agolant d. *H*; d. il a lui t. *E*; t. es fol et d. *H*; *C adds*: Foit que jou doi a Damredieu porter/ Tu fais pecciet et grande cruaute.
2938. Quant celui ves ardoir S. *C*; o. qu'est d. *C DH*.
2939. Se Matabrune est a. *C*; a. qui caut c'est un maufes (e. tout ale *T*) *CT D*; a. qui tant s'est mesale *G*; a. ne te chault c'est passe *H*; *C adds*: Qui traitor espargne ja n'ait il jour santet/ Dist Agolans Simon par saint Omer.

2940. Et c. *G*; M. il e. *T H*; c. si croit molt e. *T*; c. en Damelde *G*; *C wants*.
2941. Quant Agolant l'entent si a le chief croullet *H*; A. Symon qui ot p. *T*; *C wants*.
2942. Symon mar le (en *GT*) pensastes (parlastes *G H*; parlas *T*) par ma (la *H*) crestiente *GT DH*; *C wants*.
2943. *CGT DH want*.
2944. m. par M. *E*; *CGT DH want*.
2945. Avec lui s. *CGT DH*; s. ja n'en iert trestornet *C*; a. ensi l'ai e. *GT D*; a. par lui seres brule *H*.

133. *BE CGT DH*

2946. Dont m. *T*.
2947. p. iestes vailans *C*; *H wants*.
2948. Qui a leuwet celui qu'est vos apiertenans *C*; Qui aide le son qu'est a lui apendans *D*; s. homes c'a lui sont pendans *G*; *T H want*; *C adds*: Mais Diex est encor plus si con jou sui creans.
2949. t. si face v. *GT D*; t. i soit v. *E*; *C H want*.
2950. Sil me v. b. ensi (b. trestout s. *T*) sans jugement *GT*; m. gaiemans *D*; *C H want*.
2951. Que n. *T*; Nel fesisse h. *G*; *C H want*.
2952. E. le d. *C*; d. a droit e. *G D*; j. par Dieu le raemant *C*; e. ensi s. *E*; *T H want*.
2953. Q. se Elyas argies p. feres m. *G*; e. mors p. *D*; a. cou s. pites g. *C*; *H wants*.
2954. Se Matabrune est a. *C*; a. il e. *G*; e. ert molt m. *T*; m. faisans *E CT*.
2955. M. li chevaliers est e. *C*; c. mout bien (c. et b. *G D*) en Diu creans *CGT D*; *H wants*.
2956. e. si en fu mout d. *E*; *CGT D add*: Symon (S. mar en parlastes si m'ait sains Amans *G*; S. mar le pensastes si m'ait sains Clymans *D*) dist Agolans ja n'en soies doutans; *CGT DH want*.
2957. S. si a fais s. *E*; *CGT DH want*.
2958. Avec lui seres (seras *GT*) a. *CGT D*; Qu'il sera ars o lui c'est tes coumandemens *E*; a. ja n'en ares garant *C*; a. n'en soies ja dotans *D*; T. iert tes p. *GT*; *H wants*.
2959. A deux le fist lyer qui qu'en fust d. *H*; l. loient a .IIII. fors siergans *C*; *GT D add*: Al fu les amenerent (Pries del fu les menerent *G*) jeter les volrent ans.
2960. Li g. ert ens ou c. *CT*; l. valet e. ou c. entretant *H*.
2961. o. ot a. *E G D*; o. eust a. *H*; *C wants*.
2962. c. ist que n'i est atargans *C*; i. a l'ost vient (vint *G*) esmaians (maintenant *H*; courant *T*) *GT*

DH; i. al bruelet vint essrant *E*; *C adds*: A l'ost
vient si lor va escriant.

2963. Siegneurs fait le varlet se Dieu me soit aidant
H; tos signeur, s. Amans *C*; s. Vincans *G*; s. Cle-
ment *T*.

2964. e. menes al fu qui mout est g. *D*; e. ardans *E C*
H; *D places this verse after 1.* 2965.

2965. Se tost nel s. mais n'i venres a tans *D*; S. ne le
s. ars sera maintenant *H*; s. li damages iert
grans *GT*; d. î p. *E*; *C wants*.

2966. Q. cil l'ont entendut n. *C*; a cil qu'il s. *H*.

2967. Vers le castiel en vont sour les d. *C*; Eulz tous
monterent sur les d. *H*; b. cevaus c. *E CG D*.

2968. l. fors escus pesans *E G D*; *C H want*.

2969. Et o. *E DH*; l. qui les fers ont trenchant *H*; *C
wants*.

2970. l. cite s. *E*; *C wants*.

2971. p. s'en vont q. *E*; *H wants*.

2972. Teil noise mainnent que l'oi Agoulans *C*; Chil del
chastel s'escrient que les ot (e. rent l'enfant
G) Agolans *G D*; c. d'olifant *E*; ... gent l'entent
T; *H wants*.

2973. l. fors rois A. *E*; *CGT DH want*.

2974. I. demanda q. *C*; d. qui c. *E*; d. cou qu'est a .I.
de ses s. *G*; e. un paisant *C*; e. et .I. sous pai-
sans *D*; ... mande que c'est a .I. sien paisant *T*;
s. procains parens *E*; *H wants*.

2975. Li d. *E D*; Li dist a son c. *G*; C. li dist c'au c.
asaloient grant j. *C*; Il dist q., a. une g. *T*; *H
wants*; *C adds*: Tos seres pris si estes..ois te-
nans/ Tos sera pris li castiaus a teil gent.

2976. Onques si freres ne vit en mon vivant *C*; Ne vit
onques s. *GT*; n. virent si f. coume sont par san-
lans *E*; s. bele bien ont l. *T*; *H wants*.

134. *BE CGT DH*

2977. A. oi d. *C*; l. hurteich *C D*; l. hueis *E H*; l.
husteis *G*; *C adds*: Et il entent le noise et les
plors et les cris.

2978. v. crie jou s. *C*; e. ha las j. *T*; *C H add*: Or tos
(Armez *H*) coures as murs (portes *H*) et as postis;
C adds further: Et si soit bien chaskuns d'armes
garnis/ Et il si fisent tout ains n'i eut contre-
dit.

2979. I. en montent a. *E*; *CGT DH want*.

2980. q. est a. *E*; *CGT DH want*.

2981. l. volentiers non (ou *T*) envis *CGT D*; l. mais ce
fut bien envis *H*; *G adds*: Et Simon le courtois
qui mout iert entrepris; *H adds*: Sur leurs che-

vaulx s'en yssent courans et arrabis.

2982. 1. mout fu chascuns pensis *D*; 1. a lors cors en
est p. *E*; 1. desour .I. arc votis *GT*; *C H want*.
2983. *CGT H want*.
2984. a. armes a. *D*; a. palis *E*; *CGT H want*.
2985. Mais la gent Elyas 1. *H*; d. la defors 1., o.
bien a. *C*; o. ruistement a. *D*; o. fort a. *H which
adds*: Eulz brochent les chevaulx de courre res-
joys/ Chascun abat le scien sur le pont tournoys;
GT want.
2986. c. de pris *C which adds*: Quant cou voit Agolans
tous est de duel noircis; *GT H want*.
2987. A hautes vois crie bien sui h. *C*; C. dist A. *E*;
GT H want.
2988. Il sont la f. arme en mi cel p. *D*; f. selonch
cest p. *C*; d. cel p. *E*; *GT H want*.
2989. c. de pris *D*; c. eslis *E*; *D adds*: Faites ovrir
les portes ja feront envais; *GT H want*.
2990. E. cil r. *E*; *GT H want*.
2991. Lors ouverent (L. font ouvrir *E*) la porte p. *E C*;
o. et le maistre postic *C*; p. dales 1. *E*; d. .I.
1. *E D*; *GT H want*.
2992. Puis issent fors sour les diestriers de pris *C*;
i. nus n'i est esbahis *D*; *GT H want*.
2993. c. fors quiries et jointis *D*; *CG H want*.
2994. E. li o. *G D*; E. li baron s'en viennent arme et
fervestis *T*; f. et c. *D*; b. tenant e. *E*; b. siere
e. *G*; *CGT D add*: Par (Tres de d. *D*; Tres p. *GT*)
devant le castiel (d. la porte *GT D*) vienent au
puineis (poingneis *GT D*); *C adds further*: Cil de-
fors se desfendent as boins espius forbis; *CH
want*.
2995. v. hurter cest destriers arrabis *D*; c. poindre p.
E; *CGT H want*.
2996. D. deust p. *D*; *CGT H want*.
2997. De ciaus de fors i a grant f. *C*; l'assanlles d.
E; 1. foleîs *E C*; 1. froisseis *GT D*; *C adds*: Des
mors et des navres est joncies li pais/ Quant
Agoulans l'entent forment en fu maris; *H wants*.
2998. *CGT DH want*.
2999. b. grant sont 1. *E*; *CGT DH want*.
3000. *CGT DH want*.
3001. *CGT DH want*.
3002. *CGT DH want*.
3003. f. tres 1. *E*; *CGT DH want*.
135. *BE CGT DH*
3004. Tres devant le chastel fut l'estour planier *H*; M.
est g. *T*; p. desous le gravier *C*; p. dales 1. *E*;

C adds: De toutes [p]ars dou traire et dou lancier; *GT D add*: D'ambes (De *G*) .II. (De toutes *T*) pars se fierent el grant (p. s'entrevienent *G*; s'en viennent *T*; al fort *GT*) estor plenier; *H adds*: Pour Agolant secourre font le baille viuder/ Qui crient qui n'y ait tant hardy combatant chevalier/ Qui ou chastel demeure sur la teste coupper/ Et tous s'en yssent hors pour Agolant aider/ La peusses veoir grant estour commencer.

3005. L. valet k. *H*.
3006. E. ales E. *E GT*; *H adds*: Du chastel s'en yssirent sans noise ne tencer.
3007. Quant il sont desloiiet n. *GT*; m. nus nes puet corechier *GT D*; *C H want*.
3008. En la maison S. les un moustier *C*; S. vienent p. *GT*; p. deles .I. *E GT DH*; .I. rocier *E H*; .I. vregier *GT*.
3009. Armet se sont s. *C*; Et puis s. *T*; a. ne volrent detriier *D*; a. sans nul point y targer *H*.
3010. M. n'i troverent p. *C*; t. ne cheval n. *D*; n. diestrier *E CGT DH*.
3011. p. s'en vont eulx deux p. *H*.
3012. Au passer outre encontre .I. *C which adds*: Nies estoit Agolans le cuviert pautounier/ Symons le feri si de l'espee d'achier; *C adds further with GT DH*: La tieste li copa (t. en font voler *DH*) (1. coperent *G*; coupent *T*) si (puis *H*) a pris (pregnent *GT DH*) le diestrier.
3013. *CGT DH want*.
3014. d. il ne se pot a. *E*; *CGT DH want*.
3015. *CGT DH want*.
3016. *CGT DH want*.
3017. g. si p. *E*; *CGT DH want*.
3018. Et E. y monte oncques n'y prist e. *H*; E. fait monter sans atargier *C*; m. manois (li ber *GT*) par son e. *GT D*.
3019. Prent une lanche s. *C*; Et met la lance ou feutre encontre .I. *H*; l. sus f. si fiert .I. *T*; .I. chevalier *CGT D*.
3020. Teil c. *C*; d. sour l'escut de quartier *E C*; l. fist p. *T*; *C adds*: Si que la boucle a faite peccoier.
3021. Et l. *C*; Que l. *E*; Son h. *GT*; haubierc desrompre e. *C*; h. li fait d. *E T*; h. li a fait d. *GT*; d. desrompre e. *E CGT D*; *H wants*.
3022. *CGT H want*.
3023. Toute plaine sa lance l. *GT*; c. tint l'anste l'abati e. *C*; m. dou diestrier *CG DH*.

3024. Par le frain le saisi S. *C*; Le destrier a saisi S. *GT*; P. saisi l. *DE*; c. si fait Symon monter *H*; l. cort b. *D*; *C adds*: Qui en sa main tenoit le brant d'achier/ Elyas tient le sien qui tant a fait pierchier/ Hiaumes escus et haubiers des-maillier/ Devant iaus fuient par mi l'estour ple-nier/ Con li aloe fuit devant l'esprivier.

3025. m. esrant par son e. *D*; m. que il n. *E*; m. par son seniestre e. *GT*; *C H want*.

3026. Puis s. *D*; s. mettent eulx deux dedens l'e. *H*; a. ens l'e. *E*; e. fort e. *G D*; *H adds*: Pour venger leur hontaige font leurs lances ployer/ Chascun abat le scien de dessus leur destrier.

3027. Les l. *E D*; p. traient l. *G D*; *C H want*.

3028. a s'e., r. esclairier *G*; *C H want*.

3029. Par l. *T*; *C H want*.

136. *BE G D*

3030. *C H want*.

3031. p. se fierent en l. *E G D*; q. fu g. *D*; *C H want*.

3032. a. n'en fu (n'i est *G*) nus r. *G D*; *C H want*.

3033. A. se fierent a. *G D*; *G adds*: Agoulans laisse coure li cuvers souduians/ Vait ferir Elyas en l'escut reluisans/ Que par deles la crois li pe-coie et pourfent/ Li haubers fu si fors que malle n'en desment; *C H want*.

3034. v. mout fu ses cuers d. *G D*; c. joians *E*; *E D add*: Il hurte le destrier (ceval *E*) des esperons trenchans; *C H want*.

3035. n. faisoit c. *E*; *CG DH want*.

3036. Et f. *D*; Il f. *G*; s. sor l. *D*; s. de son espiel trencant *G*; e. qu'est luisans *D*; f. blans *E*; *C H want*.

3037. Desos (Desour *G*) la bocle d'or li pechoie et por-fant (desment *G*) *G D*; b. ne le t. si ne li fu g. *E*; *C H want*.

3038. Et le (Le blanc *G*) hauberc del dos li desmaile et desmant (l. va tout desronpant *G*) *G D*; c. a armer n. *E*; *C H want*.

3039. Par mi le gros del cuer li mist l'espie (l. mait le fier *G*) trenchant *G D*; p. derier le p. ne soit la ens c. *E*; *C H want*.

3040. Tant com hanste li dure l'abati mort sanglant *G D*; *C H want*.

3041. P. escrie l. *E G D*; D. secores vo (no *G*) jant *G D*; D. aidier vrais amans *E*; *C H want*.

3042. Lors p. *G D*; e. si pesant *G*; *C H want*; *G D add*: La ot tant elme (hauberc *G*) frait tant hauberc jasarant (f. et tant escut d'argent *G*).

3043. A. vit m. *G D*; m. sa gent e. *E G D*; j. mout f. *G D*; j. s'en f. *E*; *C H want*.
3044. I. hurte le destrier d. *D*; *CG H want*.
3045. Vait ferir E. sor l'escu qu'est luisans *D*; E. en v. *E*; *D adds*: Que par desos le crois le pechoie et porfant; *CG H want*.
3046. Li haubers fu si fors que maile n'en desmant *D*; *CG H want*.
3047. Onques ne s'en crolla (n. s'en crollerent *G*) l. *G D*; m. no chevalier vaillant *G which adds*: Ne Elyas ausi li gentius et li frans; *C H want*.
3048. e. al pont (puing *G*) d'or reluisant *G D*; p. fu l. *E*; *C H want*.
3049. Ja avera (Or a mout grant *G*) peor li quivers Agolans *G D*; A. en v. *E*; *C H want*.
3050. *CG DH want*.
3051. l. ne l'est pas e. *E*; *CG DH want*.
3052. .II. barons p. *E*; *CG DH want*.
3053. n. fist p. *E*; *CG DH want*.
137. *BE CG DH*
3054. E. vit s. *G D*; v. ses gens r. *E DH*; j. fierement m. *E*; r. contenir *H*.
3055. t. s'espee par air *C*; e. mout fu de grant air *D*; *C adds*: Qui dont veist ces traiteurs fuir/ Li plus hardis est devant lui partis/ Tant en i a de mors par vrete le vous di/ Qui del sanc peuist on .IIII. touniaus emplir/ Elyas de s'espee va Agoulant ferir; *D adds*: Sor son elme luisant vait Agolant ferir.
3056. A. ses caus iluec l. *E*; *CG DH want*.
3057. *CG DH want*.
3058. *CG DH want*.
3059. e. si tres g. que n. *E*; *CG DH want*.
3060. .I. entreget l. *E*; *CG DH want*.
3061. Onques li c. *G DH*; l. pot g. *E G DH*; *C wants*.
3062. En la cierviele l. *C*; D. que a la gorge l. *G*; D. que e., l. fist l. *H*; l. fier s. *G*.
3063. Son cop estorst si l'a fait jus keir *C*; M. l'abat a *G H*; l. trebuce a terre qui qu'en doie marir *D*; a le tere par force et par air *E*; p. coi qu'en doie avenir *G*; p. quar moult le pot hair *H*; *C adds*: Outre fait il cuviers Dieu anemis/ Cou que m'as fait te ferai chier merir; *H adds*: Ce qu'il attaint a cop tost le couvient mourir.
3064. f. si l. *G D*; *C H want*.
3065. Q. tout le plus hardi o. fait a. *E G*; o. tos acoardis *D which adds*: Trestos li plus poissans se fus mis al fuir/ Se il seust coument de l'estor

departir; *C H want.*

3066. Q. les gens A. *E G*; p. plus s. *E G D*; *C H want.*
3067. Quant si home le voient s. *C*; s. prendent a *E C*;
C adds: U il velent u non l'estour covient salir/
Au plasir Elyas les couvint tous venir; *H wants.*
3068. E. les gens c. *E G*; g. Elyas q. *G D*; D. puisse
cherir *D*; p. maintenir *G*; *C H want.*
3069. L. ocient et tuent e. *E*; p. et ocient e. *G D*; *C H
want.*

138. *BE CG DH*
3070. Signour or ascoutes de la gent A. *C*; Fuiant s'en
vont la gent (les gens *G H*) al (le *G*) quivert A.
G DH; *C adds*: Quant voient que sont tout vaincut
et recreant/ Et Agoulans fu mors u erent aten-
dant/ Le castiel ont rendut Elyas maintenant.
3071. d. il s. *E*; *CG DH want.*
3072. E. la gent (les gens *G H*) Elyas l. *G DH*; b. en va
a. *G*; v. tos (mout *G*) detrenchant *G DH*; *H adds*:
Trois cens en trencherent delez ung derubant/ Et
les autres leur crie merci des maintenant/ Le
chastel vous rendron moult debonnairement/ Elyas
fut mout doulx sans mautalent le prent; *C wants.*
3073. l. consivent s., v. ociant *E*; *CG DH want.*
3074. Atant home vienent qui mout sont esmaiant *D*; l.
baron le v. si en furent dolant *G*; l. damage s.
E; *C H want.*
3075. Elyas (A E. *G*) escrient maint et (e. trestout *G*)
coumunalment *G D*; *C H want.*
3076. Sire por Deu merchi t. *G D*; r. tot soit a *E G D*;
C H want.
3077. F. li ont fait c. *C*; F. te f. *G*; F. lui font tous
c. *H*; v. feront c. *G D*; f. li petit et li grant
CG DH; f. trestout a vo talent *E*; *H adds*: Et de-
vindrent ses hommes tost et legierement/ Et Elyas
n'enquist conseil ne petit ne grant/ A Symon don-
na tout voyant tout maintenant/ Apres si lui pria
bel et courtoisement/ Qui donnast au valet assez
or et argent/ Qui porta le messaige au bon roy
Orient/ Ou chastel sont plus n'y vont attendant/
En la sale monterent plus n'y quiest (sic) belle
et grant/ A menger sont assis dont eurent bon ta-
lent.
3078. E. Elyas respont seignor et jel creant *G D*; *C H
want.*
3079. L. remaint li assaus sans plus d'arestement *D*; c.
et cascuns rent s. *E*; *CG H want.*
3080. *CG DH want.*
3081. s. les v. *E*; *CG DH want.*

3082. Au (El *G D*) castiel en (s'en *D*) tournerent (en-
trerent *G D*) maint et (trestout *G*) communaument
CG D; v. la u e. *E*; *CG D add:* Elyas et si frere
et Symons ensement (maintenant *G*); *H wants.*

3083. En (S'en *D*) (Si *G*) montent ou (el *G D*) palais
(castiel *G*) tout liet et tout joiant (p. et tote
l'autre jant *G D*) *CG D*: d. qui'st d. *E*; *H wants.*

3084. A. que s. *E*; d. sans plus (nul *G*) d'arestemant
G D; f. le s. *E*; *C H want.*

3085. Li fissent feute l. *G*; l. lor vont trestout ju-
rant *E*; *C DH want.*

3086. *CG DH want.*

3087. Lors se vont desarmer sans autre couvenant *G*; d.
son h. *E*; *C DH want.*

3088. d. vair s. *E*; *CG DH want.*

3089. *CG DH want.*

3090. l. ami li p. *D which adds:* Agolans fu jetes en
.I. putel puant; *D adds further with G:* Puis ont
mises les taules el palais qui fu grans (t. li
vallet maintenant *G*); *CG H want.*

3091. a. chevalier et serjant *D*; *CG H want.*

3092. E. apiela S. *C*; *H wants.*

3093. *D adds:* Chevaliers fu loiaus et de bon esciant; *C
H want.*

3094. d. jugemant *G D*; *C H want.*

3095. S. fait E. *D*; E. ce castiel boun v. *G*; *H wants.*

3096. d. or mais e. *CG D*; *C adds:* Feautet li fait faire
a trestoute sa gent; *H wants.*

3097. Et Simons l'en miercie mout deboinairement *C*; S.
.C. merchis vous en r. *E D*; *H wants.*

3098. Contreval s'a. as pies li vait caant (v. courant
G) *G D*; l. baise en plourant *E*; *C H want.*

3099. j. mainent li petit et li grant *C*; j. en demena
se f. et si e. *E*; *H wants.*

3100. Segnour f. *E*; S. dist E. *E C*; E. jou vos pri boi-
nement *C*; *H wants.*

3101. Que c. *C*; J. vous p. cel g. *D*; J. voel q. ce val-
let d. *G*; d. a s. *E C*; *H wants.*

3102. e. autres garnimens *C*; a. ades a *D*; *H wants.*

3103. l. sui je garis de cest t. *C*; s. gari d. *G D*; *C
adds:* Bien sai k'il iert preudons en son vivant/
Boins cuers ne puet mentir ciertainnement; *C
adds further with G D:* Symons respont (r. biaus
G) sire (Sire ce dist Simons *D*) jel vous creanch
(s. tot *D*) (s. trestot *G*) (a vostre talant *G D*)/
Ja n'averai (J. nen aurai *D*) (Jou n'aurai ja *G*)
sans lui .I. denier (.II. deniers *D*) valissant; *C
D add further:* Li garcons le miercie au piet

      (Quant li g. l'entent as pies *D*) li va ceant (v.
colant *D*)/ Le mangier ont li keu atornet ricement
(Li baron ont mangie ensamble liemant *D*)/ Si ont
mangiet ensanle douchement (Les tables ont ostees
chevalier et serjant *D*); *H wants*.

139. *BE CG DH*

3104. Li baron ont lavet s'aseent au mengier *C*; Au men-
ger sont assis le noble c. *H*; d. sergant et c. *E*;
b. al mengier *G D*.

3105. Quant eulx eurent menger les napes font oster *H*;
o. vallet e. *E*; *C D want*.

3106. S. dist E. *E CG*; E. mout vos doi m. *C*; E. or v.
G; *H wants*.

3107. Car secourut m'aves a mon m. *C*; a mout tres grant
m. *G*; m. meillor m. *D*; *C D add*: Jel merirai (Et
jo vous ferai bien *D*) se jou puis repairier; *H
wants*.

3108. En sour que tout vos veil jou or proier *C*; Or vos
voil a tos dire que repairies (retournes *G*) ar-
rier *G D*; Oez fait Elyas nobile chevalier *H*.

3109. Ainsi com vous venistes vous en yres a. *H*; *CG D
want*.

3110. Mon pere salues et ma mere au vis fier *C*; Salues
moi m. *G D*; Dix vous garisse peres et vo f. *E*; Et
me salueres mon p. tout premier *H*; *E adds*: Cor le
me salues pour Diu le droiturier; *H adds*: Et puis
ma doulce mere sa courtoise moullier/ A Dieu vous
comment tous cy ne puis plus targer/ Je m'en iray
au cisne qui est pres ce rocher/ Les barons font
grant doel quant leur couvient laisser/ En leur
pais s'en vont n'ont cure de targer.

3111. Et il respondent sel ferons volentiers *C*; *E H
want*.

3112. E. prent ses f. ses baisa sans dangier *C which
adds*: Ariere en vont n'ont cure de targier/ Et
Elyas tous seus ains n'i eut escuier/ S'en va sor
la marine Jhesus li puist aidier; *H wants*.

3113. *CG DH want*.

3114. t. s'en volent r. *D*; *CG H want*.

3115. s. sans esquiier *D*; *CG H want*.

3116. Al port s'en repaira Dex le puist conseillier *G
D*; *C H want*.

3117. k. devoit c. *E*; *CG DH want*.

3118. l. devoit a *E*; *CG DH want*.

140. *BE CG DH*

3119. v. tous seus s. *C*; p. sos l. *D*; *H wants*.

3120. Warda aval si vit venir l. *C*; *H wants*.

3121. Fuis en ert p. *C*; g. maleie *D*; *C adds*: Pour le

dueil de son frere a plumet sa poitrine; *H wants*.

3122. Elyas voit navre sa joie li desfine *G*; Q. il voit Elyas si ra sa joie fine *C*; Q. il le v. venir se joie est e. *E*; *DH want*.

3123. Elyas volentiers s. *CG D*; c. onques n'i eut h. *C*; s. corine *E CG D*; *H wants*.

3124. Est salis (entres *D*) el *CG D*; e. ou b. q. li cisnes t. *D*; *H wants*.

3125. Isi s. *D*; Ensi s. *G*; o. en v. *E*; e. vont najant D. *G D*; n. cil Dex qui t. *D*; *C H want*.

3126. l. vraie r. *G which adds*: Li vrais Sires del ciel qui est nostre devine/ A envoie le cisne une telle racine/ Ki li vint aflotant par devant le poitrine; *C H want*.

3127. c. a s. *C*; b. aporte u. *C D*; *G H want*.

3128. O. nule (n. bone *D*) h. n'en ot m. *C D*; h. a nul tans n'ot gregnour m. *E*; h. n'ot itele m. *G*; *H wants*.

3129. Il le b. Elyas e. *C*; b. sel m. *D*; *H wants*.

3130. t. or s. *D*; t. et s. *G*; sans devise *E*; sans dotrine *G*; *H wants*.

3131. Que tantost fu plus sains que nule flor d'espine *G D*; f. plus sains que une flors d'espine *C*; *H wants*.

3132. Q. le voit Elyas dont a j. *E*; E. cou voit Dieu aeure et mercie *G*; *C DH want*.

141. *BE CG DH*

3133. Or s'en va Elyas a la fiere vigour *H*; E. s'esmerveille s. *G D*; l. de cou qu'il voit le jor *CG D*; l. ainc n'ot joie gregnour *E*.

3134. Si e. *C*; Que sa plaie fu saine n. *G*; D. sa plaie e. *D*; g. mainne joie et baudor *E*; *H wants*.

3135. m. issent s. *C*; s. freour *C DH*; s. irour *G*.

3136. El Rin entrerent p. *C*; S. sont (est *H*) entre e. *CG DH*; R. de par l. *E G DH*; *DH add*: A Nimaie s'en vienent une cite auchor (e. vont par moult grande vigour *H*).

3137. Tant que il virent une mout rice t. *C*; Li enfes Elyas a veue une t. *G*; v. le palais e. *H*.

3138. Et la citet qui est de grant valour *C*; p. autour *E*; *C adds*: Par mi la mer voient les murs entour; *G DH want*.

3139. escarboncle qui r. grant resplendor *C*; *E G DH want*.

3140. Devens (sic) la vile oent si grant criour *C*; c. mainent si grant f. *G*; *DH want*.

3141. La noise (n. en *G*) ot on d'une grant liue (on bien de .III. liues *G*) entour *CG*; *DH want*.

3142. Elyas l'entendi si en a g. *C*; Elyas s'en esmaie
si c'il a g. *G*; g. paour *CG*; *E DH want*.
3143. Gaires n'ala s. *C*; N'ala gaires avant si vit (s.
trouva *H*) .I. *G H*; a. si trove .I. *D*.
3144. A un b. ki c. *C*; b. pour quere s. *E*; u pourcuert
s. *CG D*; c. son l. *E D*; *D adds*: Dont il se puist
garir et ses enfans le jor; *H wants*.
3145. Amis dist Elyas or me di p. *C*; Elyas lui demande
que c'est en celle tour *H*; Q. li vassaus l. *E*; l.
vit s. *G*.
3146. Quel noise est cou laiens u j. *C*; Preudom q. *E*;
d. jou oc le freor *G*; o. itel t. *E*; g. criour *E C*
D; *H wants*.
3147. Dist l. *C*; S. dist l. *G*; p. par Dieu le creatour
H; q. jou doi m'oisour *C D*; d. ma seror *G*.
3148. C'est une tel (grans *G*) (telle *H*) m. *G DH*; est
merveille *C*; m. oncq n. *H which adds*: Ung sesne
veult tollir une dame l'onneur/ Huy luy est fort
jugee sans avoir nul destour/ Car la dame n'a
homme ne prince ne contour/ Qui contre lui eust
ne force ne vigour/ Hee Dieu fait Elyas par vos-
tre grant doulceur/ Que my laisses venir que le
plait n'est greigneur/ J'en donneroye gaige de-
vant l'empereour/ La bataille feroye pour Dieu le
creatour.
142. *BE CG D*
3149. A. fait E. *D*; E. dites moi v. *CG D*; d. ton pense
E; *H wants*.
3150. Est cou or de paiiens u de c. *G*; s. crestien ou
sarrasin desve *D*; u gent c. *C*; *H wants*.
3151. S. dist l. *E*; p. dons j. *C*; p. ja en orres verte
D; p. ja o. *G*; *H wants*.
3152. En cest regne a .I. *C*; c. terre .I. *G D*; t. morte
E; *D adds*: A tort a amene par sa ruiste fierte/
.X. mile chevaliers qui tot sont fer arme; *H
wants*.
3153. n. s'est de s. *D*; p. son c. *C*; s. grant parentel
(g. parente *D*) (g. cruaute *E*) *E C D*; *C adds*: Si
desous lui a cest siecle acordet/ Que vers lui
n'osent muever estrangne ne privet; *H wants*.
3154. Une dame a tolue trestoute s. *C D*; B. a tolu s.
G; *C adds*: Pour cou qu'ele n'avoit signour ne
avoet; *C adds further with D*: Ducoise ert de
Buillon cou dient li lettret (fieve *D*); *D adds
further*: N'avoit mais c'une fille qui est de
grant biaute; *H wants*.
3155. Hui en sont li baron tot ensamble a. *G D*; *C H
want*.

3156.   *C H want.*
3157.   S. Dameldex n'en p. et 1. *G*; *C H want.*
143.   *BE CG DH*
3158.   S. dist 1. *E CG*; p. se Diex me duinst (fait *D*)
        (s. ja aie *G*) pardon *CG D*; p. par Dieu et par son
        nom *H*.
3159.   Mout est cruex cil (e. cuvers li *G*) saisnes n. *G*
        D; Horgueilleux est le sene n. *H*; L. sers est
        mout cremus n. *E*; est crueus ainc ne vi s. *C*; c.
        jo ne sai s. *D*; c. nul n'est s. *H*; s. si (plus *E*
        H) felon *E CG DH*.
3160.   Toute a toulut (Il veult tollir *H*) la (sa *G H*)
        tiere la dame d. *CG H*; Qui tolue a 1. *E*; *C adds*:
        Et sa file la gente a la clere fachon/ Pour cou
        qu'ele n'avoit signour ne conpaignon/ Encore ert
        forjugie se Diex n'en a raison; *D adds*: Hui en
        sont ajorne ensamble li baron/ Anqui iert forsju-
        gie jel sai a abandon/ Se Jhesu-Cris n'en pense
        qui soffri passion; *H adds*: La dame a une fille
        de moult gente facon/ Il n'a plus belle fille en
        ceste region/ Voulentiers la donroit a aucun gen-
        til hom/ Et trestoute la terre de l'onneur du
        Bullon/ Qui demain voulsist estre pour le son
        champion.
3161.   p. lui prenge escut ne b. *C*; e. ne escu ne b. *E*
        G; *DH want.*
3162.   E. et que font li b. *E*; *CG DH want.*
3163.   t. devers 1. *E*; *CG DH want.*
3164.   *CG DH want.*
3165.   D. dist E. *E C H*; P. ton saintime non *C D*; P. sa
        b. *E*; *H adds*: Que je puisse venir a la maistre
        maison/ Ains que la dame perde honnour sans a-
        choison.
3166.   Se j'estoie o. *C*; o. a p. *G*; d. cest g. *C*; d. ce
        g. *E*; *C adds*: Que volentiers oroie sa raison; *H*
        wants.
3167.   *C H want.*
3168.   Et meteroie mon *C*; En m. *D*; Li feroie ge maitre
        tout mon cors a bandon *G*; *D adds*: Que Dex i de-
        mostrast qui auroit droit ou non; *G adds*: Sire
        dist li pescieres mout feries que preudon/ Hastes
        vous biaus dous sire pour Dieu et pour son non/
        Mout douc c'ancois ne soit finee la raisons/ Et
        li jugemens dis de maint gentil baron/ Que la da-
        me ait pierdue tout sa region/ Lors s'en va Elyas
        s'est en grant soupecon/ Ki or vora entendre s'o-
        ra boune cancon/ Si com il desfendi le dame de
        Buillon; *H wants.*

144. *BE C D*

3169. Dist li p. *C*; S. dist l. *E*; p. mout par iestes (sanles *E*) vaillans *E C D*.

3170. Ales biaus sire ne soies atargans *C*; e. biax sire q. *D*; e. pour Diu vous est a. *E*.

3171. d. ne soit a. tornes l. *C*.

3172. Que l. *C D*.

3173. Quant Elyas entent n'i est plus atendans *C*; i. s'en part atant *D*; *C adds*: Ver le castiel en tourne sans nul ariestement/ Et li cisnes l'en maine qui bien set ses talens.

3174. Tant que desous la tour ariva li c. *C*; *E adds*: E Dix dist Elyas biaus Peres roi amans/ Coument porront savoir en le cite laians/ Que ci soie arives a tout ce mien calant/ Pour secoure le dame qui le cuer a vallant/ Et se gente de fille qui est mout avenans.

3175. *C wants*.

3176. Il a soune son cor q. *C*; c. qui est d'yvoire blanch *E C*; qui d'ivoire est l. *D*; *E adds*: Puis le met a son col et puis si l'est sonnans.

3177. P. isi grant viertut q. *C*; s. .II. liues en tout sens *E*; q. tos li jugemans *D*.

3178. Ot on la vois mout est li cors vaillans *C*; e. li vois a. a tous les j. *E*; *C adds*: Cil dou castiel l'oirent mout se vont merveilant/ Quant il ont entendut trestout le jugement; *D wants*.

3179. Tourna ariere C. *C*; Et cascuns des barons i est venus c. *E*; d. cele part vont c. *C D*; *C adds*: Vers le batiel li petis et li grant; *D adds*: Onques n'i atendi li peres son enfant.

3180. *C D want*; *E C D add*: Et l'empereres (L'empereres meismes *E D*) i est venus corant (poingnant *D*); *C adds further*: Il ont veut le cisne le batiel trainant/ Au col une caainne toute blance d'argent/ Et virent en la nef .I. chevalier gisant/ Deles lui sen escut sen espee trencant/ Et .I. mout boin espeil par le mien ensiant/ Jou cui que sen espee que le forjast Galans/ Nus hons de car ne vit plus rice brant/ Li cisnes ariva droit au port son calant/ Dou palais avalerent li petit et li grant/ Onques n'i atendi li peres son enfant/ Le chevalier truevent sain et vivant; *C adds further with D*: L'empereour salua douchement (e. salue dolcement en riant *D*)/ Et les autres barons car bien set lor romant (b. sot le romans *D*)/ Puis prent s'espee au puin d'or reluisant (Premiers a pris l'e. al pont d'o. flamboiant *D*)/

L'escut　la lanche (Et l'e. et la l. *D*) au confa-
non pendant/ Dou batiel est issus a lou de comba-
tant (a loi d'ome sachant *D*)/ Apres a dit au cis-
ne va a Diu te coumanch/ Et se jo ai mestier　ra-
maine mon chalant (*C wants*).

145.　*BE*
3181.　D. qui ne menti *E.*
3182.　e. petis *E.*
3185.　A N. est v. a .VC. f. *E.*
3186.　E. le fille le gente l. *E.*
3187.　V. s'est c. *E.*
3189.　t. son p. *E.*
3190.　s. sire est et mors et enfoiis *E.*
3193.　c. avoit a elmes bis *E.*
3194.　b. petis *E.*
3195.　d. des saisnes les cuivers maleis *E.*
3196.　e. fors e. *E.*

INDEX OF PROPER NAMES

Jehans (prestre), 1876.
Jehans, s., 2963.
Jehans (chevalier d'Elias), 2296, 2369.
Jehans (vallés), 2178.
Jhesus, 13, 101, 199, 297, 668, 677, 680, 691, 705, 955,
      965, 1265, 1438, 1753, 1838, 2074, 2267, 2758, 3157,
      3184.
Jonant, 1988.
Jores, s., 2710, 2716, 2727, 2738, 2745.
Josiaumes de Buillon, 3191.
Mahomet, 2944.
Malbruiant, 1727, 1915, 1965, 1968.
Malduis, 2210.
Malfaisant, 256, 259, 264.
Malfaisant (fius d'Aloris de Palerne), 2211.
Malpensant, 2209.
Marcel, s., 2004.
Marie Magdelaine, 1641.
Marie, s., 141, 226, 269, 504, 850, 1441, 2749; Dame, 988,
      1089, 1335; Puciele, 270, 1335; Vergene, s., 712,
      1632, 3126.
Markes, 147, 191, 300, 304, 308, 319, 457, 460, 1750, 1759,
      1770, 1775, 1776, 1803, 2506; Macres, 200.
Marlevit, 2298.
Matabrune, 44, 49, 101, 234, 258, 276, 325, 328, 402, 409,
      417, 424, 442, 456, 497, 571, 582, 600, 602, 616,
      661, 774, 777, 831, 836, 847, 946, 966, 970,
      1010, 1028, 1037, 1063, 1074, 1077, 1092, 1107,
      1118, 1178, 1254, 1309, 1320, 1339, 1346, 1460,
      1537, 1573, 1590, 1594, 1669, 1673, 1684, 1709,
      1723, 1756, 1810, 1829, 1871, 1893, 1908, 1920,
      1934, 1981, 1991, 2004, 2012, 2043, 2076, 2082,
      2088, 2113, 2126, 2128, 2164, 2173, 2196, 2258,
      2378, 2402, 2435, 2442, 2446, 2453, 2458, 2468,
      2480, 2518, 2524, 2814, 2819, 2822, 2827, 2859,
      2868, 2939, 2954.
Mauquarés, 422, 427, 478, 670, 776, 819, 846, 853, 1011,
      1019, 1022, 1032, 1035, 1050, 1057, 1059, 1065,
      1082, 1105, 1171, 1215, 1240, 1255, 1265, 1309,
      1314, 1322, 1339, 1341, 1344, 1399, 1428, 1437,
      1453, 1456, 1461, 1462, 1483, 1485, 1490, 1493,
      1501, 1504, 1513, 1514, 1517, 1526, 1532, 1539,
      1553, 1568, 1580, 1591, 1663, 1666, 1686, 1693,
      1700, 1703, 1718, 1736, 1740, 1873, 1919.
Miles, 2208.
Monbas (duc de), 1190.
Monbel, 2586.
Montir, 1888.

Vergene (See Marie, s.)
Vïé, s., 2886.
Vincant, s., 92, 144, 215, 2197.
Zacarie, 1885; Sacaries, 2585.

GLOSSARY

This glossary is selective. The English equivalents which it provides pertain to the indicated context.

The following abbreviations are used: *adj.*, adjective; *adv.*, adverb; *cond.*, conditional; *f.*, feminine; *fut.*, future; *ger.*, gerund; *imperf.*, imperfect; *impers.*, impersonal; *ind.*, indicative; *infin.*, infinitive; *intr.*, intransitive; *m.*, masculine; *n.*, noun; *pl.*, plural; *part.*, participle; *pers.*, person; *pr.*, present; *prep.*, preposition; *refl.*, reflexive; *s.*, singular; *subj.*, subjunctive; *tr.*, transitive; *v.*, verb.

abosmés, *adj.* dejected, overcome; 191.

acesmé, *past part.* of *tr. v.* acesmer to equip, to outfit; 1275.

adés, *adv.* continuously; 379.

adesé, *past part.* of *tr. v.* adeser to touch; 1572.

adouber, *infin.* of *tr. v.* to dub, to arm as a knight; 696.

agaite, *3rd pers. s. pr. ind.* of *tr. v.* agaitier to watch, to be on the alert for, to lie in wait for; 371.

agree, *3rd pers. s. pr. ind.* of *tr. v.* agreer to show favor, to please; 449.

ahiert, *3rd pers. s. pr. ind.* of *tr. v.* aherdre to seize, to lay hands on; 2848.

airement, *n. m. s.* affair; 1834.

aïree, *adj.* angry, furious; 464.

ajornement, *n. m. s.* daybreak, dawn; 81.

alemiele, *n. f. s.* blade, cutting edge; 1333.

aletant, *ger.* of *tr. v.* aleter to flap; 1846.

ambleüre, *n. f. s.* gait; 866.

amendement, *n. m. s.* pardon, correction, reparation; 1155.

ancui, *adv.* today; 11.

angles, *n. m. pl.* angles, corners; 474.

aombrage, *n. m. s.* incarnation; 988.

aombrer, *infin.* of *intr. v.* to become incarnate; 712.

araine, *n. f. s.* sand, shore, beach; 1848.

arisent, *3rd pers. pl. preterit* of *tr. v.* arire to smile at; 461.

arramie, *past part.* of *tr. v.* arramir to fix, to promise; 2131.

asauront, *3rd pers. pl. fut.* of *tr. v.* assaillir to assualt; 2646.

aslonje, *3rd pers. s. pr. ind.* of *tr. v.* aslonger to extend; 1452.

asolue, *adj.* absolved; 22.

atornoit, *3rd pers. s. imperf.* of *impers. refl. v.* s'ator- ner to be attributed to; 109.

atour, *n. m. s.* preparation, background, 539; equipment, 1126.

aversité, *n. f. s.* fiendish act; 184.

avoés, *n. m. s.* lord; 811.

ballerai, *1st pers. s. fut.* of *tr. v.* baller to give, to provide with; 1127.

bargagne, *n. f. s.* deal, affair; 1322.

batistal, *n. m. s.* noise, commotion; 2083.

baucans, *adj.* piebald; 2215.

bersee, *past part.* of *tr. v.* berser to shoot (arrows); 873.

betelant, *ger.* of *trans. v.* beteler to snap; 1845.

biés, *n. m. pl.* beaks; 1845.

border, *infin.* of *intr. v.* to lie; 2488.

bors, *n. m. pl.* village; 40.

bougerant, *n. m. s.* buckram; 3089.

bouiele, *n. f. s.* bowel, gut; 1344.

braire, *infin.* of *intr. v.* to shout, to cry out; 1590.

braioel, *n. m. s.* belt; 1206.

brait, *n. m. s.* cry; 349.

brancele, *n. f. s.* twig; 1330.

brehagne, *adj.* sterile; 1320.

broie, *n. f. s.* meal, flour; 385.

buer, *adv.* in a good hour; 177.

caellon, *n. m. pl.* puppies; 674.

caiaus, *n. m. pl.* puppies; 204.

caiele, *n. f. s.* bit, piece; 1340.

caingle, *n. m. s.* enclosure, limit; 543.

calans, *n. m. s.* boat; 3174.

caperon, *n. m. s.* hood; 790.

caraie, *n. f. s.* incantation; 1671.

carmes, *n. m. s.* charm; 1671.

castegne, *n. f. s.* chestnut; 1317.

cau, *adj.* hot; 1118.

caurre, *n. f. s.* heat; 3058.

cendal, *n. m. s.* silk, taffeta; 2084.

ciere, *n. f. s.* face; faire ciere marie to be sad faced; 2136.

cirge, *n. f. s.* doe, hind; 367.

coiement, *adv.* quietly, softly; 604.

combré, *past part.* of *tr. v.* combrer to seize; 1544.

consenche, *n. f. s.* knowledge, information; 7.

consiut, *3rd pers. s. pr. ind.* of *tr. v.* consiure to reach, to strike; 1568.

contor, *n. m. pl.* counts, nobles; 545.

coral, *adj.* hearty, pleasing; 1252.

coroie, *n. f. s.* strap, cord; 848.

corsable, *adj.* current, well-known; 17.

coulon, *n. m. s.* pidgeon, dove; 2254.

cravent, *3rd pers. s. pr. subj.* of *tr. v.* craventer to crush; 125.

cretiel, *n. m. pl.* crenels; 2002.

crues, *n. m. s.* hollow; 353.

cube, *n. f. s.* a type of tent; 1971.

cuivree, *adj.* furious, wrathful, irate; 847.

darrains, *adj.* rear, hind; 1481.

dejouste, *prep.* beside; 355.

delé, *past part.* of *tr. v.* dalier to cut, to hew; 1559.

deporter, *infin.* of *tr. v.* to amuse, to relax; 52.

depriant, *ger.* of *tr. v.* deprier to request, to beg; 150.

derainier, *infin.* of *tr. v.* to defend, to protect, to uphold; 1538.

deront, *past part.* of *tr. v.* derompre to tear; 857.

desafree, *past part.* of *tr. v.* desafrer to shatter the enamel trim (of the hauberk); 2035.

desbaretee, *past part.* of *tr. v.* desbareter to defeat; 2042.

desfaee, *adj.* infidel, perverse, awful; 465.

desfiers, *n. m. s.* defiance, challange; 1458.

desloier, *infin.* of *tr. v.* to untie; 1745.

destroit, *n. m. s.* distress; 102.

devisé, *past part.* of *tr. v.* deviser to tell, to relate; 115.

devisemant, *n. m. s.* statement, pronouncement; 131.

doisiaus, *n. m. s.* apprentice; 2801.

encombriers, *n. m. s.* difficulty, obstacle; 400.

enfeutree, *past part.* of *tr. v.* enfeutrer to brace in or against the felt; 2032.

engoulés, *past part.* of *tr. v.* engouler to edge, to line; 15.

enhaite, *3rd pers. s. pr. ind.* of *tr. v.* enhaitier to cheer, to encourage; 370.

enki, *adv.* there; 411.

enorté, *past part.* of *tr. v.* enorter to exhort, to urge; 1545.

entragne, *n. f. s.* gut, entrails; 1315.

entredeus, *n. m. s.* blow to the head; 3060.

envaïe, *n. f. s.* attack, assault; 2138.

escines, *n. f. pl.* spine, backbone; 2329.

escrin, *n. m. s.* box, chest, case; 597.

escoumuet, *3rd pers. s. pr. ind.* of *refl. v.* s'escoumovoir
        to become enraged, to be moved to anger; 973.

escrois, *n. m. s.* noise, cracking; 3142.

esmaiant, *ger.* of *tr. v.* esmaier to be troubled, to be
        afraid; 137.

esploree, *adj.* wet with tears; 867.

espoënté, *past part.* of *tr. v.* espoënter to terrify; 181.

esrage, *3rd pers. s. pr. ind.* of *tr. v.* esragier to tear
        away, to rip away; 972.

estal, *n. m. s.* position; livrer fort estal to attack; 2082.

estoier, *infin.* of *tr. v.* to store, to put in safekeeping;
        593.

estoné, *past part.* of *tr. v.* estoner to stun; 1579.

estoremant, *n. m. s.* supplies; 2624.

estrain, *n. m. s.* straw; 287.

estraine, *n. f. s.* origin, extraction; 1852.

estrivieres, *n. f. pl.* stirrups; 1290.

exillemence, *n. m. s.* distress, danger, destruction; 10.

faés, *past part.* of *tr. v.* faer to destine; 494.

faitierement, *adv.* in such manner; 200.

faoné, *past part.* of *tr. v.* faoner to bear, to bring forth;
        204.

festu, *n. m. s.* straw; 689.

fierviestis, *n. m. pl.* men equipped with protective armor;
        3185.

foleïs, *n. m. s.* slaughter; 2997.

for, *n. m. s.* oven; 1118.

forjugie, *past part.* of *tr. v.* forjugier to condemn; 3156.

formie, *3rd pers. s. pr. ind.* of *tr. v.* formier to crawl, to
        tingle; 1462.

forsenee, *past part.* of *tr. v.* forsener to drive made, to
        enrage; 456.

fraite, *past part.* of *tr. v.* fraindre to shatter, to break;
        2034.

francist, *3rd pers. s. pr. ind.* of *tr. v.* francir to free;
        1832.

fremer, *infin.* of *tr. v.* to lace on; 1042.

freor, *n. f. s.* noise, commotion; 3140.

fuerre, *n. m. s.* sheath; 1402.

fuison, *n. f. s.* profusion, abundance, quantity; 591.

fusiel, *n. m. s.* spindle; 2006.

fustane, *n. m. s.* fustian, 1205.

gains, *n. m. s.* watch dog, dog; 1672.

galos, *n. m. pl.* galop; 2373.

gastiel, *n. m. s.* cake; 385.
gieron, *n. m. s.* lap, apron; 205.
greant, *pr. part.* of *tr. v.* greer, to consent; 136.
gué, *n. m. s.* ford, water-filled ditch; 167.
guiounaje, *n. m. s.* leadership, protection, care; 992.

haire, *n. f. s.* hair shirt; 961.
hucier, *infin.* of *tr. v.* to shout; 255.
hulepés, *adj.* shaggy, unkempt; 479.
hustine, *n. f. s.* shouting, commotion, noise; 3123.

ingal, *adj.* equal; 62.

jaserant, *adj.* of oriental mail; 2449, 3087; jaserans, *n. m.
        s.* coat of oriental mail; 3038.
jehir, *infin.* of *tr. v.* to state, admit; 959.

kerroit, *3rd pers. s. imperf.* of *tr. v.* querre to seek, to
        want; 1004.
kiute, *n. f. s.* mattress; 286.

lasse, *n. f. s.* fatigue; 3059.
leus, *n. m. pl.* wolves; 324.
lices, *n. f. pl.* lists; 1942.
lïement, *adv.* happily; 600.
lisce, *n. f. s.* bitch; 206.
listés, *past part.* of *tr. v.* lister to stripe, to edge;
        1228.
louier, *n. m. s.* pay, reward; 1024.

mallier, *infin.* of *tr. v.* to hammer; 2098.
maloite, *adj.* cursed; 125.
manaie, *n. f. s.* right, power, just reward; 1668.
manecier, *infin.* of *tr. v.* to menace; 1261.
manoier, *infin.* of *tr. v.* to arrange, to prepare; 1141.
maris, *adj.* troubled, grieved; 322.
mautalant, *n. m. s.* anger; 69.
meller, *infin.* of *tr. v.* to join in combat; 1350.
mentes, *n. f. pl.* mint, an herb or edible plant; 387.
merir, *infin.* of *tr. v.* to recompense, to reward; 1131.
mesestance, *n. f. s.* misery, affliction; 1706.
molle, *adj.* soft, molten; 587.
müé, *past part.* of *tr. v.* müer to change; le sanc muer to
        pale; 174.

ocoison, *n. f. s.* accusation, motive; 673.
oirs, *n. m. pl.* heirs; 1755.
oisour, *n. f. s.* wife; 1117.

orine, *n. f. s.* origin; de pute orine of low birth; 256.

pance, *n. f. s.* stomach; 1712.
paresis, *n. m. pl.* coin of Paris; 416.
parfurnist, *3rd pers. s. preterit* of *tr. v.* parfurnir to complete; 2301.
pautouniers, *n. m. s.* coward, rogue; 403.
pelice, *n. f. s.* fur cloak; 284.
picois, *n. m. pl.* a type of shafted weapon; 2093.
pietris, *n. f. pl.* partridges; 330.
pietruis, *n. m. s.* hole, opening; 1377.
piler, *n. m. s.* column; 1250.
pis, *adj.* worse; 323.
pius, *n. m. pl.* a type of shafted weapon, pike; 2093.
pois, *n. f. s.* pitch; pois demise molten pitch; 1978.
posnee, *n. f. s.* pride; 2059.
puig, *n. m. s.* fist; 2040. See note 10.
pumiel, *n. m. s.* grip, stem (of a drinking vessel); 580.

raemberroit, *3rd pers. s. cond.* of *tr. v.* raembre to ransom, to redeem; 173.
randon, *n. m. s.* violence; 1681.
randounee, *n. f. s.* assault, attack, act of violence; 2011.
rasee, *past part.* of *tr. v.* raser to fill; 861.
rasacier, *infin.* of *tr. v.* to withdraw, to recover; 1497.
resclaire, *3rd pers. s. pr. ind.* of *intr. v.* resclairer to shine; 1582.
ret, *3rd pers. s. pr. ind.* of *tr. v.* rere to shave; 1165.
ronscoie, *n. f. s.* canebreak, break; 387.
rouegnier, *infin.* of *tr. v.* to pare, to trim; 1158.
rouleïs, *n. m. pl.* fortifications, palisades; 2979.

saier, *infin.* of *tr. v.* to attempt, to try; 586.
sainnier, *infin.* of *tr. v.* to ring; 1145.
sains, *n. m. pl.* signs, symbols, 2249; bells, 2563.
sautiele, *3rd pers. s. pr. ind.* of *refl. v.* se sautieler to dance, to jig; 1346.
sein, *n. m. s.* belt, bond; 1017.
selve, *n. f. s.* forest; 461.
sieraine, *n. f. s.* siren; 1853.
sieree, *adj.* close; ambleüre sierree slow-gaited, even-gaited; 866.
sorcaingles, *n. m. pl.* double girths; 1246.
susitement, *n. m. s.* resurrection; 1635.

tabor, *n. m. s.* noise; 3146.
tehir, *infin.* of *tr. v.* to increase, to favor; 1884.
tence, *n. f. s.* dispute; 5.

torriele, *n. f. s.* turret, small tower; 1348.

torser, *infin.* of *tr. v.* to load, to pack up; 1954.

tramis, *past part.* of *tr. v.* transmettre to send; 1751.

trestorné, *past part.* of *tr. v.* trestorner to refuse, to oppose; 166, 198.

tumant, *ger.* of *intr. v.* tomber to fall, 350; tume, *3rd pers. s. pr. ind.*, 349.

vergonder, *infin.* of *tr. v.* to shame; 50.

vierillier, *infin.* of *tr. v.* to bolt, to bar; 2111.

viuté, *n. f. s.* misery, low estate, baseness; 1212.

vivier, *n. m. s.* pond, fish pond; 463.

APPENDIX : The Turin Fragments

The following is a complete transcription of the *Beatrix* material surviving in Turin MS L-III-25. The text has been partially edited in order to facilitate its use. All abbreviations have been resolved and proper nouns have been capitalized. Spaces, either in place of a line or within a line, indicate that the text at that point is totally illegible and suspension points, the illegible portion of a word. A question mark within parentheses follows all words which were read only through comparison with related manuscripts. Each line has been identified when possible with the corresponding laisse and line of the edited text, BN MS 786. Folio and column are given with reference to Turin MS L-III-25 itself. Otherwise the text reads as it does in the manuscript.

All variation has been recorded in the critical apparatus, but, because of extensive damage to the text in these fragments, the record of agreements is based on incomplete evidence in some instances. This appendix is offered as the most practical means of clarifying the exact state of the textual tradition at such points.

The editor is especially grateful to Mr. Geoffrey M. Myers whose work with Turin MS L-III-25 resulted in the identification of these fragments and who willingly gave of his knowledge and precious time in their transcription.

(115)   (*fol.* 1*b*)

li le cuer	2500
se ses hommes tre...	2502
...isisse touz et mesisse	2503
...ame fis je la ...sson	2504
voi l... a l'erm... pelicon	2505
Ses enfanz envoyait tous ...er par Marcon	2506
Puis fis mon filz a croire par molt male raison	2507
Et tuit li .vii. enfant estoyent chaelon	2508
A mon gre fust elle arse et livree en charbon	2509
Nus hons ne fist tant mal des le tens Salemon	2511

```
      Que je seule faisse onques n'amai raison        2512
      Ja ne proyerai Dieu qu'il me face pardon        2513
      Se je vois en infer j'arai maint conpaingnon    2515
      Or aviaigne c'avieigne tout soit en abendon     2517
```

116 Matabrune (?) la vieille   mal
                                 confessee   2518
             en ont   escoutee   2519
      Ainc (?) Dieu   ...ma ne l...   *GT Add*
      Certes dist   vieille desesperee   2520
           ...sse est pour vous destrenpee   *CGT Add*
        Matabrune si (?) l...   ou feu jettee   2524
       la vieille s'est   escriee   2525
      Au dyable d'infer soit s'ame conmandee   2526
         tuit cil qui ci sont de toute sa contree   2527
      ...ors se traist Matabrune toute est arse et
                                          brulee   2528
          ame en prisent dyables telle est sa
                                     destinee   2529
      En infer le hideus illuec est ostelee   *T Add*
                             la vieille est
                                        alee   2530
            ...terent qui est bele et pavee   2531
            novele (?) que sa mere ert finee   2532
                 quar trop estoit dervee   2533
               molt quar molt l'avoit grevee   *CGT Add*
             grant joie deci a l'avespree   *CGT Add*
                     la table est ost...   2536
                        en laye...   2537
```

(117)                                           (*fol. 1c*)
```
               et le ber s...   2545
           ...ge revestu de   2546
         conseille (?) coyement tout   2547
        biaus amis ses tu que (?)   2548
      ...r moi te mande Dieu si ne l'oblie pas   2549
       le matin au   ...r bien main te leveras   2550
      Et ton pere et ta mere a Dieu conmanderas   2551
      Et pren tes armeures ne les oublie pas   2552
      Et l'escu a la   mie n'obieras (sic)   2553
      Sur le vivier (?) tout droit biau frere t'en
                                          iras   2555
      Et illeuques ton frere le cisne trouveras   2556
                   illuec tout a conpas   2557
      Sa volente biau frere outreement feras   2558
      Volentiers biau douz frere ce respont Elyas   2559
```

118  Lors s'en torne li anges et Elyas remaint         2560
```

Au moustier s'en vont tuit quant sonnerent
                  li saint   2563
Messe leur chante .i. abbes d'un lorier des
                  sains   2564
Leur offrandes ont faites l'abes pas nen
                s'en plaint   2565
Arriere s'en retornent n'i a nul qui Dieu
                n'aint   2566
Pour l'oneur Elyas s'en esjoissent maint   *CGT Add*

119   Apres messe s'en issent ensamble du
                mostie...   2567
Molt demainent grant joie n'ont cure de   2569
Pere dist Elyas pour Dieu vous voeil proyer   2572
Que penses de ma mere vostre franche
                moillier   2573
Et gardes qu'entour vous n'atrayez losengier   2574
Se haus hons prent ma suer a per et a
                moil...   2575
La terre li donnes qu'on (?) ne puet es ..   2576
Bien vaut par an mil mars que d'argent que   2577
Et se je ne reviaing j'otroi a i...   2578
L'aisne de tous mes freres ne l'en fa...   2579
      tel couvent ert rois con vous   2580
      me remainne en b...   2581
        aye cuite sanz   2582
        tous con   2587

(121)   *(fol. 2a)*
                           ...ecreant   2661
                              brant   *GT Add*
                                      at 2663

122   ...ait et crie   2664
                            et prie   2666
                                vie   *CGT Add*
                         ...gnie   *CGT Add*
                         ...lie   2670

(124)   *(fol. 2b)*
Bien set q...   *GT Add*
                                      at 2708
Et les galies vienent n'ont cur...   *GT Add*
                                      at 2708
Sainz Jeorges les conduist dont Diex fist
                chevalier   2710
Et d'anges et d'archanges y ot plus d'un
                millie   2711

La galie saint Jeorges vont les turs
                    essillier   2716
Et li cisnes leur va leur galie procier   2717
A son bec leur despiece pour eus plus
                    ...yer   2718
Il ne set autrement parler ne enseignier   2719

125 La galie saint ..   assaillent durement 2720
Et li turs se   ...dent molt efforciement   *CGT Add*
Et li cisnes a fait .i. pertuis lait et
                         grant   *CGT Add*
      des galies de son bec
                    maintenant   *CGT Add*
          amplie d'ya... au fons en va
                         plunjant   2725
          saint Jeorge acroissent durement   2727
          .i. ore qui la mer va troblant   2728
      galies as turs s'en tornoyent fuiant   2729
...ais (?) n'ont gaires foi quant tempeste
                    les prent   2730
      se fiert es galies si les va craventant   2731
Au fonz de mer les plunge et les galies fent   2732
Or ont assez beu li felon mescreant   2733
Onques (sic) Elyas le voit a Dieu graces en
                         rent   *CGT Add*
Et les blanches galies vont arriere siglant   2734
Elyas leur demande entendes mon semblant   2736
Dites moi qui vous estes honeur m'avez fait
                         grant   2737
Sainz Jeorges respont or ne demandes tant   2738
Jhesu Crist en aeure le Pere omnipotent   2739
      Elyas respont a son conmandement   *DH CGT*
                                                Add
...nt Diex garde de moi par son bon escient   *DH CGT*
                                                Add

126 ...ins Jeorges s'en ala o li sa conpaingnie 2744
      Elyas remaint tous seus en la galie   *CGT Add*
      ...e avec li qui Diex apele et prie   *CGT Add*
          tel fain ainc tel ne fu oye   2746
          sa playe qui n'estoit pas
                         garie   2747
          la fain qui durement l'aigrie   2748
          par molt grant partie   2752
          vieille et entie   2753

                                   (fol. 2c)
      Romanie   *CGT Add*
                                   at 2755

                    d'argent qu'il n'a en
                          payennie   *CGT Add*
                                         at 2755
        Frere estoit Matabrune la grant vieille haye *CGT Add*
                                         at 2755
        Que Elyas fist ardoir devant la baronnie   *T Adds*
                                         at 2755

128 Vers le chastel tout droit va li cisne au
                                    rivage   2766
     Ce chastel apeloyent par son droit non
                          Sauvage   2767
     Et cil qui du chastel tient l'avoir et
                          l'usage   2768
     Avoit non Agoulans s'avoit fier le visage 2769
     De gent a plus   a en Cartage   2770
     Frere dist Elyas   qui le nage   2771
     Gardez bien ce batel et vous tenrai a sage 2772
     Je irai ou chastel de fain mon cuer enrage 2773
     Si porterai mon cor et le metrai   2774
     Se je ne puis miex faire quar tiex   ...ge 2775
     Elyas est saillis du batel ou riv...   2777
     Ou chastel est entrez mais molt felon pa... 2778
     Li convendra payer si ert molt grant dam... 2779
     Se Jhesu Crist n'en pense et son saintisme
                          ymage   2780

129 Montez est Elyas ou palais volentiers   2781
     Trouve a Agoulant entre ses chevaliers   2782
     En mi la sale fu molt y ot losengiers   2783
     Elyas le salue li enfes droituriers   2784
     Et Agoulant respont qui estes amis chiers   2785
     Veus tu vendre ce cor prendras en tu deniers 2786
     Sire dist Elyas se m'aist sainz Richiers   2787
     Ancois le vous donrai pour tant bons mang... 2788
     Quar je ne manjai gaires bien a .iii. jo... 2789
     Li serjent metent tables ou dessus les   2793
     Li baron ont lave s'assieent vole...   2794
     Au mangier ont eu .xii. mes tous   2795
     Si ont eu a boire de bons vins   2796
     Elyas a mangie .i. pou s'est   2797
     Li enfes est molt preuz   2798
     Agoulans le   2799
     Amis dist Ag...   2800
     Ou gar...   2801

(130)   (*fol.* 2d)
     Li b...   2810

```
        Cer...                                     GT Add
        La                                         2811
        Amis                                       2812
        Se M...                                    2814
        Sire                                       2815
```

(131)   (*fol.* 3*a*)

```
                                          ...ant   (?)
                                          ...ant   (?)
                                          ...ment  (?)
                                          ...ant   (?)
```

132   ...aute 2878

                                                   (*fol.* 3*b*)

```
        Et busches et         par                  2923
        Fors ont trait de la chartre Elyas le      2924
        Maint en ont en la place pour Elyas pleure 2926
        Mais n'osent pas blasmer Agoulant le derve 2927
        Illuec ot .i. vieil homme qui en grant
                                      poverte      2928
        Avoit et si enfant plus de .xv. anz este   2931
        Symon avoit a non ce dient li lettre       2932
        La ou voit Agoulant si l'en a apele        2936
        Sire ce dist Symons tu as le sens derve    2937
        Qui l'enfant veus ardoir s'est de ton
                                      parente      2938
        S'il a ars Matabrune cui chaut c'est tout
                                          ale      2939
        Mais il est chevaliers si croit molt en De 2940
        Lors regarde Agoulanz Symon qui ot parle   2941
        Symon mal en parlas par ma Crestiente      2942
        Avec li seras ars ainsi l'ai en pense      2945

133     Dont menace Symon le cuvert Agoulant       2946
        Sire ce dist Symon molt par est Dieu
                                      puissant     2947
        Tu n'as homme en ta court tant se face
                                      vaillant     2949
        S'il me vouloit blasmer trestout sanz
                                      jugement     2950
        Que ne fust hui cest jour par mon cors
                                      recreant     2951
        Que se Elyas est ars pechie sera molt grant 2953
        S'il a Matabrune arse elle ert molt mal
                                      faisant      2954
        Mais cis est chevalier et en Dieu bien
                                      creant       2955
```

Symon mal le penses si m'aist Saint Vincent   *D CGT Add*
Avec li seras ars tiex ert ton payment   2958
Andoi les fait loyer qui que en soit dolent   2959
...res du feu les menerent jetter les
                voelent enz   *D GT Add*
...arcons estoit enz ou chal (sic) layenz   2960
...t am...   que conduist Oriant   2961
   ...issus a l'ost   vient
             courant   2962
  ...ist il se m'aist saint Clement   2963
        fu est molt grant   2964
      ...mag... ert   2965
          qui soit   2966

               (*fol.* 3*c*)
       gent l'entent   2972
  ...mande que c'est a .i. sien paisant   2974
Il dist qu'au chastel viennent assaillir une
                gent   2975
Ni vi onques si bele bien ont le semblant   2976

134 Quant Agoulanz entent des genz le hu...ais   2977
A haute voiz s'escrie ha las je sui trais   2978
Elyas on (sic) laissie volentiers ou e...   2981
Il sont andoi loye dessous .i. arc vostis   2982
Et li baron s'en viennent arme et fervestis   2994
Tres par devant la porte viennent au
              poingneis   *D CGT Add*
A l'assembler des lances fu granz li
              froisseis   2997

135 Molt est grant la bataille par devers le
              vergier   3004
De toutes pars s'en viennent au fort escus
              plenier   *DH CGT*
                Add
Li garcons qui ala le message noncier   3005
Est ales Elyas et Symon deslier   3006
Quant il sont deslie nus nes puet corrocier   3007
A l'ostel Symon viennent par delez .i.
              vergier   3008
Et puis se sont arme sanz noise et sanz
              tancier   3009
Mais il n'i ont trove palefroi ne destrier   3010
A pie queurent andoi pour leur honte vengier   3011
A l'issir de la porte truevent .i. chevalier   3012
La teste li coupent si prennent le destrier   *DH CGT*
                Add

Elyas monta li bers par son estrier   3018
Il met lance sus feutre si fiert .i.
                              chevalier   3019
Merveillous coup li donne l'escu li fist
                              ...er   3020
Son haubert li a fait desronpre et   3021
Toute plainne sa lance l'abat   3023
Le destrier a saisi Symon   3024
Et li bers monta par son   3025
Lors se fierent andui   3026
Les lances   ...yer...   3027
Elyas   fait les   3028
Par la gent Agoulant   3029

(136)   (*fol.* 3*d*)
       D...   (?)

       P... (?)   (?)

       L...   (?)
       Ag...   3048 (?)
       Lors   3049 (?)

137 Elyas (?)   3054 (?)